Better
than
an
draft

Social Control

JOSEPH S. ROUCEK, Ph.D.

*Chairman, Departments of Sociology and Political Science
University of Bridgeport*

AND ASSOCIATES

SECOND EDITION

D. VAN NOSTRAND COMPANY, Inc.

PRINCETON, NEW JERSEY

TORONTO   NEW YORK   LONDON

D. VAN NOSTRAND COMPANY, INC.

120 Alexander St., Princeton, New Jersey
257 Fourth Avenue, New York 10, New York
25 Hollinger Rd., Toronto 16, Canada
Macmillan & Co., Ltd., St. Martin's St., London, W.C. 2, England

*All correspondence should be addressed to the
principal office of the company at Princeton, N. J.*

First Edition, June 1947
Four Reprintings
Second Edition, January 1956

Dedicated to
Dr. Henry W. Littlefield
Vice-President, University of Bridgeport
a scholar and a good friend

Associates

ELIAS T. ARNESEN　　　[CHAP. 14]
Professor of English
San Francisco State College

RAYMOND F. BELLAMY　[CHAP. 15]
Professor of Sociology
Florida State University

H. C. BREARLEY　　　　[CHAP. 1]
Professor of Sociology
George Peabody College for Teachers

FLOYD A. CAVE　　　[CHAP. 6, 31]
Professor, Division of Social Sciences
San Francisco State College

CHARLES W. COULTER　[CHAP. 3]
Professor of Sociology
University of Rochester

JOHN F. CUBER　　　　[CHAP. 8]
Professor of Sociology
Ohio State University

NEAL B. DeNOOD　　　[CHAP. 13]
Professor of Sociology
Smith College

ALVIN GOOD　　　　　[CHAP. 7]
Professor of Sociology
Northwestern State College
(Natchitoches, La.)

E. W. GREGORY, JR.　　[CHAP. 2]
Professor, Chairman of the Department
　of Sociology
University of Richmond

J. O. HERTZLER　　　　[CHAP. 29]
Professor, Chairman of the Department
　of Sociology
University of Nebraska

GLENN E. HOOVER　　[CHAP. 22]
Professor, Chairman of the Department
　of Economics and Sociology
Mills College

H. B. KIRSHEN　　　　[CHAP. 21]
Professor, Chairman of the Department
　of Economics and Sociology
University of Maine

JOHN M. MACLACHLAN　[CHAP. 24]
Head Professor of Sociology, Professor
　of the Social Sciences
University of Florida

ERNEST MANHEIM　　　[CHAP. 30]
Associate Professor of Sociology
University of Kansas City

CHARLES F. MARDEN　[CHAP. 18]
Assistant Professor of Sociology
Rutgers University

HAROLD D. MEYER　　[CHAP. 16]
Professor of Sociology, Director, North
　Carolina Recreation Commission
University of North Carolina

C. C. NORTH　　　　　[CHAP. 10]
Professor of Sociology
Ohio State University

GEORGE E. OUTLAND　[CHAP. 26]
Former member, U. S. Congress; Profes-
　sor of Social Sciences
San Francisco State College

VERNON J. PARENTON　[CHAP. 5]
Assistant Professor of Sociology
Louisiana State University

JOSEPH S. ROUCEK　[CHAP. 12, 20]
Professor, Chairman of the Departments
　of Political Science and Sociology
University of Bridgeport

T. LYNN SMITH　　　　[CHAP. 5]
Professor, Chairman of the Department
　of Sociology
University of Florida

EDWARD A. SUCHMAN [CHAP. 27, 28]
Executive Officer
Department of Sociology and Anthro-
　pology
Cornell University

HUGH H. SMYTHE　　[CHAP. 23]
Department of Sociology and Anthro-
　pology
Brooklyn College

P. F. VALENTINE　　　[CHAP. 9]
Dean of the College
San Francisco State College

PAUL WALTER, JR. [CHAP. 4, 19, 25]
Professor, Chairman of the Department
　of Sociology
University of New Mexico

M. J. WEBSTER　　　　[CHAP. 11]
Professor of Sociology
University of Nevada

LESLIE D. ZELENY　　[CHAP. 17]
Professor of Sociology and Chairman,
　Department of Social Science Studies
Colorado State College of Education

Preface to the Second Edition

The popularity of the first edition of the present work, originally published in January, 1947, has certified the need for systematizing the area of Social Control for the growing number of courses in this field. Yet, the rapid advancement in the technological means of Social Control has already surpassed one aspect not treated in the original edition, namely, the field of Television. This revision contains a chapter on this ever-more-important means of public communication and control. The chapters on Public Opinion, Propaganda, and Motion Pictures have been rewritten. Most of the others have been revised in their conclusions, and all have additional bibliographical references to the latest literature.

Special appreciation is given for technical and typing assistance to Miss Dianne McDougall and Emilio F. Riccio, both of the Political Science Department, University of Bridgeport.

JOSEPH S. ROUCEK

University of Bridgeport
Bridgeport, Conn.
November, 1955

Preface to the First Edition

This book is designed to serve as an introductory text for the growing number of courses in Social Control in our higher institutions of learning. The subject encompasses the whole field of sociological thought, especially as it seeks more concretely to answer specific problems growing out of the present characteristics of our civilization. In this respect, the volume will also be useful in the introductory courses to Sociology and Social Psychology. The organization and treatment are such that it can be used in advanced courses as well.

From the time that the American Sociological Society devoted its *Proceedings* in 1917 to this topic, Social Control has become one of the main centers of American sociological interest and has produced considerable literature exploring the various ramifications of this vast field. Yet, there are very few volumes that summarize and synthesize the widely available studies, possibly because there is little agreement about the definition of the term, the field concerned, or the boundaries of this branch of Sociology.

This book aims to fill the definite need of bringing to the student and layman a wealth of knowledge that has been accumulating through the work of many scattered experts, but all bearing upon the central theme —Social Control. A notable eccentricity of our age of specialization is for one author to attempt to be panoramic, for the flood of materials in every field is so great that even specialists find it difficult to keep abreast of their own specialties. In the plan of this book, experts and teachers in the varied phases of Social Control have contributed those chapters for which they are best qualified by virtue of close and continuous study. It is believed that this method is well adapted to bringing to readers a comprehensive, thorough, and well digested presentation of contemporary factual knowledge and thought. The reader will find the volume well integrated; furthermore, the questions, suggestions for term papers, and bibliographies at the end of each chapter will be useful tools for instructors as well as students.

Societies have always regulated their members by means of social control described here. But modern knowledge raises new and pressing issues, by making possible the deliberate and scientific exploitation of the avenues through which meanings are communicated and experiences shared. Especially is this true with the rise of large masses of more or less politically conscious people, nearly all of whom are accessible to the propagandist at any time and regardless of the factor of distance. No government has been able to ignore these recent trends. But in our democracy, which depends upon the informed, the educated, and the responsible citizen for its very survival, the need for an understanding of the basis of social control is immediate and vital.

The task of being an editor of a volume so conceived is difficult. The job could not have been done without the effective cooperation of the co-authors, to whom my thanks are extended. Special credit is due to my friend, Professor Paul Walter, Jr., University of New Mexico, who brought the plan to realization.

JOSEPH S. ROUCEK

Hempstead, Long Island
January, 1947

Contents

Contents

PART I

The Foundations of Social Control

FOREWORD

Group life is a phenomenon common to all living things, but at the human level it is distinguished by balance between stability and flexibility. Among many animal species group activity is transient and unstable; among others, notably ants, termites and bees, it is stable and lasting but rigid and inflexible. The significance is that man alone enjoys the benefits of continuous organized cooperation and at the same time the ability collectively to modify his relationships and ways of life. But he also, alone of living things, stands constantly on the brink of disasters which may at any time result from his own collective follies.

Social control makes possible this distinctively human balance between stability and flexibility in organized group life. The foundations of social control are in the psycho-biological equipment of the individual and in the social framework within which he moves. Until these twin-rooted foundations are clearly understood the vast and intricate superstructure which ages of cumulative social heritage have built upon them remains essentially meaningless.

The first five chapters of this book treat in turn the Nature of Social Control, Socio-Psychic Processes in Social Control, Social Control and the Conditioning of Personality, the Fields of Behavior, and Social Cohesion and Social Control. They are designed to give the reader a graduated portal by which to enter into the complexities which lie beyond.

CHAPTER I

The Nature of Social Control[1]

The increase of crime and chaos in the postwar world and the develop‌ment of weapons of war far more destructive than those of the past are only two of the reasons for being concerned with problems of the control of human conduct. Are peoples and cultures to disintegrate under the disruptive forces of contemporary discord and frustration? Is some ruthless nation to use atomic energy to slaughter half the world and then to enslave the survivors? Such questions reveal the disparity between man's increasing control of natural phenomena and his failure to progress in the control of the behavior of human beings. While the techniques for managing the forces of nature have become increasingly dependable and predictable, methods of social control are little, if any, more effective than they were in the dawn of history, even with the recent development of such agencies for mass propaganda as the press, the motion picture, and the radio. Yet if mankind is ever to be free from fear of aggression, individual or collective, the wise control of human conduct is far more significant than any degree of mastery of the world of nature.

As used in this volume, *social control is a collective term for those processes, planned or unplanned, by which individuals are taught, persuaded, or compelled to conform to the usages and life-values of groups.* Social control occurs when one group determines the behavior of another group, when the group controls the conduct of its own members, or when individuals influence the responses of others. Social control, consequently, operates on three levels—group over group, the group over its members, and individuals over their fellows. In other words, social control takes place when a person is induced or forced to act according to the wishes of others, whether or not in accordance with his own individual interests.[2]

Social control should be distinguished from self-control, although the two are closely akin. At the individual level social control refers to the attempt to influence others, while self-control refers to the individual's

---

[1] Much of this chapter has been published in *Sociology and Social Research*, XXVIII (November-December, 1943), pp. 95-102. It is reprinted with permission of the editors.

[2] For a similar definition see Kimball Young, *Sociology* (Cincinnati: American Book Co., 1942), p. 894.

attempt to guide his own behavior in accord with some previously developed ideal, goal, or purpose. The goal is, of course, usually determined by the values and folkways of the group to which the individual belongs. In a sense, then, self-control is derived from, and originates in, social control. For example, a boy may exhibit self-control in a doctor's office, but his effort to avoid crying out from pain probably comes from his ideal of the proper conduct of a teen age boy, and, as every school nurse knows, his self-control will be strengthened by the presence of one of his comrades. For convenience, consequently, social control and self-control are to be separated, but their close relationship needs to be recognized.

Social control should not be confused with personal leadership. When one person tries to control the behavior of others, he is usually thought of as exercising leadership rather than social control. But when he gathers a group of followers who join with him in endeavoring to influence the conduct of a larger group, he is acting as an agent of social control. In addition, it should be noted that leadership is sometimes used as a term of approbation for those whose attempts at social control are in harmony with one's own wishes or life-values. Somewhat similarly, propaganda may be a term to indicate the speaker's disapproval of some effort at social control.[3]

The Development of the Concept of Social Control

As a generalization about human behavior social control is both old and new. In the earliest and most primitive forms of human life, social control existed as a potent force in organizing socio-cultural behavior. Just as the individual is enveloped in the atmosphere, he is also surrounded from birth to death by social control of which he may be unaware unless insight or unusual experience leads him to its recognition. Accordingly any formal statement of the concept is comparatively recent, although it is foreshadowed in Plato's *Republic*, 369 B.C., and, much later, in Comte's *Positive Philosophy*, 1830-1842, and it is greatly clarified in Lester F. Ward's *Dynamic Sociology*, 1883.

In 1894 Small and Vincent, in discussing the effect of authority upon social behavior, observe that even leaders are greatly influenced and limited by the will of their followers. These authors then conclude, "The reaction of public opinion upon authority makes social control a most delicate and difficult task."[4] This somewhat incidental reference seems to have been the first use of the term in scholarly writing.[5] In the same

---

[3] The subject of leadership is treated in detail in chapter XVII of this book, and propaganda in Chapter XXIV.

[4] Albion W. Small and George E. Vincent, *Introduction to the Study of Society* (New York: American Book Co., 1894), p. 328.

[5] A. B. Hollingshead, "The Concept of Social Control," *American Sociological Review*, VI (April, 1941), pp. 217-224.

year Ross "developed the germs" of the first book in this field.[6] This volume finally appeared in 1901.[7] In it Ross acknowledges his debt to Lester F. Ward, his friend and counselor.

In his treatment of social control Ross excludes the influence of the individual upon the group and minimizes the importance of crowd behavior. Consequently his conception now seems somewhat narrow. He emphasized what were once called "social instincts"—sympathy, sociability, and a sense of justice—and the means by which the group brings pressure upon the individual, especially in crises, to induce him to act in accordance with the folkways and mores. The so-called social instincts are now neglected, but the means of social control have continued to receive the attention of scholars, even though the tendency is now to emphasize the pervasiveness of social control in everyday life as well as its power in times of crisis.

In the year following the appearance of Ross' pioneer volume, Cooley presented a conception of social control that admirably supplements that of Ross.[8] Cooley's emphasis is on the effect of group pressure upon the personality of the individual and the necessity for studying a person's life history in order to understand his behavior. In particular, his discussion of "the looking-glass self" and the social origins of the conscience have been far-reaching in leading others to study the process of socialization and the interaction between the individual and his group.[9]

A third aspect of social control is emphasized by William Graham Sumner.[10] According to this author, social behavior cannot be understood without a study of the folkways, mores, institutions, and value-judgments which underlie the rules of conduct of the group. These socio-cultural forms which organize the responses of individuals are of primary importance in deciding the direction in which social control operates. In other words, the life-values and social organization of the group largely determine whether the agents of social control will encourage or inhibit any specific item of behavior. Sumner's volume, which has been called "the Old Testament of the sociologists," treats of social control only incidentally but is of great significance in showing, largely by a profusion of illustrations, how folkways and institutions limit the behavior of individuals—"the mores can make anything right and prevent condemnation of anything." [11]

---

[6] Edward A. Ross, "Recollections of a Pioneer in Sociology," *Social Forces*, XX (October, 1941), p. 32.

[7] Edward A. Ross, *Social Control* (New York: The Macmillan Co., 1901).

[8] Charles H. Cooley, *Human Nature and the Social Order* (New York: Charles Scribner's Sons, 1902).

[9] *Ibid.*, chapters V and X.

[10] *Folkways* (New York: Ginn and Co., 1906).

[11] *Ibid.*, especially chapter XV.

Thus three of the "founding fathers of sociology" made important contributions toward developing an understanding of the nature and effects of social control. From these early writings to the present day the concept has been little altered in its essentials, although there have been significant variations in emphasis. These variations seem to fall into three groups somewhat representing the approaches of the pioneers described above: those who, like Ross, discuss the number and complexity of the means by which the agents of social control attain uniformity of behavior; those who, like Cooley, devote their efforts to explaining the effects of social control upon the development of personality; and those who, like Sumner, are concerned with the rules and agencies that organize human behavior into patterns. These emphases are, of course, mutually supplementary, and leaders in each group have made important contributions to the topics presented in this volume.

Social Control and the Academic Disciplines

Social control is to be studied as an approach to the understanding of group behavior rather than as an established department of teaching and research. For example one phase of social control is education which, in its broadest meaning, is a collective term for the agencies which transmit the social heritage, either unchanged or altered in form or function. In its restricted sense education is used to indicate collectively the organization and activities of schools and other institutions for training individuals in accordance with the cultural patterns and life-values of the group. Generally, however, education is used to refer chiefly to the intellectual or indirect means of influencing conduct; in the study of social control, the more overt or immediate means of altering behavior, especially through the emotions, are emphasized.[12]

The study of social control is an important aspect of sociology and of social psychology, but it is not co-extensive with these branches of learning. Sociology is the discipline which emphasizes group patterns of conduct and the interaction of individuals and groups. Social psychology deals with the intellectual and emotional aspects of the individual's response to the behavior of others. Social control is, accordingly, intimately connected with both sociology and social psychology as an important topic of both disciplines.

Other academic disciplines have also contributed to the understanding of social control. Cultural anthropology has provided data on the rules and life-values of diverse primitive societies and has aided in increasing the objectivity of studies of contemporary civilization. From psycho-

---

[12] Education and social control is treated more fully in chapter IX of this book.

logical research has come understanding of the learning processes by which individuals are conditioned by the practices and precepts of their fellows. Many of the contributions of the social sciences to social control will be indicated in subsequent chapters.

Without further discussion, it should be evident that social control is a concept that is significant for many fields of knowledge and that cuts across the boundaries of the traditional academic disciplines. It is, therefore, a unifying factor in the study of human behavior. This partial integration of several fields of investigation is one of the more significant aspects of the study of social control. The great success of such natural science integration as is illustrated by engineering or architecture lends encouragement to the development of similar concepts and practices in the field of the social sciences. This volume, consequently, makes one of its most important contributions in stimulating further study and research in a synthesizing approach to social science.

Purposes of Social Control

The aims of social control, according to Kimball Young, are "to bring about conformity, solidarity, and continuity of a particular group or society." [13] These purposes may possibly guide far-seeing statesmen or social scientists, but most individuals who endeavor to control their fellow men show little perspective in their efforts. Often they merely struggle to increase the acceptance of the modes of conduct that they themselves prefer. This preference may be based upon childhood training, insight derived from life experience, or the desire to exploit others in order to gain power—economic, personal, or political. Social control, it is true, often perpetuates the accumulated wisdom of men long gone, but only rarely are living men and women cognizant of the significance of the cultural patterns they transmit or modify. Some reformers and exploiters do seem aware of their purposes and aims, but most of them either lack insight or conceal their true motives by "good reasons" in the form of altruistic rationalizations. Examples of such rationalizations may easily be observed in radio or newspaper advertising.

In long-time perspective the social scientist can note that the efforts of men to obtain greater acceptance of their own values and patterns of living do result in a greater regularity and predictability of social behavior. The assumption, however, that men in general are concerned with the advantages of regularity or predictability of conduct is difficult to accept without also assuming that the average man possesses a high degree of insight and social understanding.

---

[13] Young, *op. cit.*, p. 898.

The student may well attempt for himself an analysis of the purposes of social control by observing a number of examples and then attempting to discover the motives involved, especially those that are concealed or unconscious. Advertising and propaganda in their varied forms can readily be classified as more or less exploitative. But it is more difficult to understand the motivation of parents who endeavor to train their children in outmoded patterns of conduct. Such parents may be unconsciously identifying themselves with their own parents, they may be assuming that what proved satisfactory to them will also be good for their children, or they may be acting primarily from habit and distrust of the unfamiliar. Self-appointed guardians of respectability and morals may be honestly trying to prevent others from making costly errors or they may be covertly struggling for recognition in the community.

The motivation of teachers illustrates the complexity of the purposes behind efforts to control the conduct of others. All teachers are active agents of social control, but their motives are not easy to catalog. A few obviously enjoy the prestige of exercising control over the behavior of others. Some cautiously adhere to the preferences of the powerful, while others, warped or embittered by their own experiences, use their classrooms as vantage points for attacks upon the prevailing folkways and life-values. Many carry on the traditions without much attempt at revaluation or realistic alteration to meet contemporary needs. Some, at least, have identified themselves with the attempt to improve human conditions by training others. Such an analysis of the motives of teachers and of other agents of social control can easily be continued to great length but perhaps sufficient indication has been given of the complexity and of the obscurity of the purposes of those who endeavor to influence the behavior of others.

If a simple classification is desired, however, the general purposes of the agents of social control can be designated roughly as (1) *exploitative*, motivated by some form of self-interest, direct or indirect; (2) *regulatory*, based upon habit, and the desire for behavior of the customary types; and (3) *creative* or constructive, directed toward social change believed to be beneficial. But again it should be remembered that motivation is often too complex or too obscure for easy analysis or classification.

Means of Social Control

The means by which individuals or groups induce or compel conformity to their preferences in conduct are so numerous and varied that a large portion of this volume is devoted to their treatment. In considering these means the student should bear in mind that the significance of institutions and agencies of control depends largely upon the cultural or social setting. For example, in a homogeneous rural community, gossip may be a potent means of enforcing conformity but would be of little importance in the impersonal life of an American metropolis. Similarly, in West Africa the threat of employing magic or witchcraft may intimidate the boldest but would be of small influence in Denmark or Switzerland. Adolescent boys and girls may be quite fearful of ridicule by their age-mates but almost oblivious to criticisms by teachers or parents.

The overt techniques, such as ostracism or infliction of pain, should not, moreover, be overemphasized. Perhaps even more effective are those means of control that gradually build up in children social attitudes and values that are approved by the group. These in turn aid in developing the personality patterns, "persistent behavior traits," that facilitate the desired types of conduct and inhibit others. As W. I. Thomas has aptly said, "The condition of morality, as well as of mental life, in a community depends on the prevailing copies." [14] The social models persistently brought to the attention of the young and impressionable have a profound influence in determining the development of ideals, habits, and other personality traits.

The strength and pervasiveness of social control is well illustrated by the fact that an individual may be alone and yet be clearly under its influence. The unhappy drunk, stumbling homeward, is overwhelmed by the recollection of his mother, "What would she say if she saw me now?" On his tropical island, Robinson Crusoe was so conditioned by his childhood in England that he was distressed over his lack of garments even though he had no companions and the climate was suitable for a minimum of clothing. Similarly, the conscience, a resultant of social training, pricks the secret violator of the mores of his group.

The relative efficacy of the means of social control varies with changes in the social organization and life-values of the group. For example, in a static society, custom is a powerful means of influencing the responses of individuals. "This is the way our fathers always did" carries prestige and conviction. In contemporary American life, however, the influence of tradition has been weakened, except perhaps in law, politics, and religion. Similarly, during the Middle Ages the tenets of feudalism exercised vast control over social behavior, from the serf's hut to the nobleman's castle, but today they have only historical significance.

Attempts to classify the diverse means of obtaining social control are many and varied. In this volume the institutional and the non-institutional agencies are treated separately, partly as a matter of convenience. The verbal and gestural or symbolic means may be contrasted with those involving force. Punishment typifies the negative or repressive means of

[14] W. I. Thomas, "The Psychology of Yellow Journalism," *American Magazine,* LXV (March, 1908), p. 496.

eliminating undesired behavior, while rewards and praise are often used positively to induce socially approved activities. Informal means of social control are very powerful in primary social groups where interaction is on a personal basis. Formal sanctions, typified by law and its administration, are usually associated with the larger secondary social groups where impersonal relationships predominate. The weakening of informal social control in the larger and more mobile communities has been noted by many observers, some of whom attribute to this source a recent deterioration of American character in urban areas.[15]

Social Control and Maladjustment

When the agencies of social control lose their power, the behavior of the group becomes unstable and unpredictable. If the society is a changing one, the lack of standards of conduct may be the result of conflict between the old and the newly developing rules of conduct. This conflict of standards leads to social disorganization. Social disorganization is often only a temporary disturbance while old rules are being replaced by new ones. Sometimes, however, a clash of cultural values may weaken all codes of conduct and result in an amoral society, where even previous incentives for action become insignificant. Under such circumstances a people may be so overcome by apathy that they lose the desire to work, to rear children, or even to live.[16] This destruction of the zest for living, especially for living according to the established norms, frequently occurs when a pre-literate culture is overwhelmed by the introduction of a complex civilization. Often members of such a group may be properly described as "de-tribalized"—emancipated from social restraints and freed from adherence to the values and mores of the tribe. A somewhat similar deterioration may accompany a change in environment that makes the former codes of conduct inapplicable or inadequate.[17]

The dramatic consequences of social disorganization or of cultural deterioration should not, however, obscure the obvious fact that social norms are perhaps never completely realized in the behavior of every member of a group. Even though the child is surrounded from birth by adults with relatively unvarying standards of conduct, he may develop

---

[15] Fuller treatment of this subject will be found in Chapter XIX.

[16] G. H. Lane-Fox Pitt-Rivers, *The Clash of Culture and the Contact of Races* (London: George Routledge and Sons, 1927), pp. 197-206 and 217-233. See also W. H. R. Rivers, *Essays on the Depopulation of Melanesia* (Cambridge: Cambridge University Press, 1922).

[17] Pauline V. Young, *The Pilgrims of Russian Town* (Chicago: University of Chicago Press, 1932).

traits in conflict with the norms—perhaps by chance, through inability to learn, or individual variation in response, or even because of an abnormality. At any time, therefore, even in the most stable societies, some deviation from the idealized cultural norms may be found, as illustrated by psychopaths, eccentrics, and criminals.[18]

In any culture, moreover, social control rarely operates uniformly upon all groups. Minority peoples, for example, frequently differ from the dominant group both in social norms and in control of conduct. The private courts of immigrant groups or so-called "gangster trials" illustrate how such minorities may develop in-group ethical codes and may even organize their own legalistic agencies for the settlement of intragroup conflicts. On one of the islands off the Carolina coast Negroes often have trials before the congregation of the church, partly to escape appearance before the legally constituted courts, which are often referred to as administering "the unjust law" or "the white folks' law." Similarly, in each socio-economic class, variations in social control may direct behavior into different channels or result in attitudes easily separable from those of other groups in the same culture area.[19] Members of any group, accordingly, are likely to be subjected to rather different social pressures and may develop diverse and conflicting attitudes and life-values.

In most societies, consequently, there are conflicting patterns of conduct. The individual may then have to choose his own standards. His choices will vary with his own personality trends and with his responses to the social control exerted by his differing associates. Such cultural conflict, of course, increases greatly any tendencies toward personal deterioration or social disorganization.

The results of social control are, therefore, not always beneficial to society or to the individual. Exploitation is obviously often injurious to many. Even attempts at constructive reform may merely confuse the public and end in inactivity. Efforts to regulate behavior in accordance with the established norms may have such harmful consequences as blind adherence to custom, cultural lag, mental conflict, emotional instability, neurosis, and even psychosis. These untoward consequences vary with the individual and with the culture. An aggressive individual may suffer from social control in a peace-loving group, although he might be honored in a warlike society. The outcast squaw-man who could not pass the initiation tortures of the plains Indians might have been a leader among the more artistic pueblo dwellers.

[18] Bronislaw Malinowski, *Crime and Custom in Savage Society* (New York: Harcourt, Brace and Co., 1926). See also W. I. Thomas and Florian Znaniecki, *The Polish Peasant in Europe and America* (New York: Alfred A. Knopf, 1927).

[19] For examples, see Alfred Winslow Jones, *Life, Liberty, and Property* (Philadelphia: J. B. Lippincott Co., 1941).

Special codes also often run counter to the justifiable interests of individuals or of minority groups. For example, established norms may be too restrictive for the creative or too conservative for the adventurous individual. Moreover, the regulations are often formulated by a dominant group and may be openly or secretly opposed by others. This results in a constant struggle between opposing wishes. These wishes may not be demonstrably harmful—they may merely happen to be in conflict with the rules prevailing in a particular culture. Yet such conflicts often result in social and emotional maladjustment.[20]

Social Control and the Future

One reason for the increasing importance of social control is that an individual acting alone has become almost powerless to cope with social problems. Consequently he must endeavor to influence others to join him in working for the goal that he desires. For example, individual initiative can hardly solve unemployment in the United States when millions are hunting for work. This impotence of the individual has led, especially in the democracies, to a significant multiplication of the voluntary agencies of social control—committees, conferences, clubs, associations, leagues, institutes, bureaus, corporations, and foundations. Proposals, counter-proposals, demands and protests compete for public attention. Only the discerning can hear the voice of wisdom in the babel of discord.

The effectiveness of social control, whether democratic or authoritarian in nature, also largely decides the success or failure of social planning. One source, in fact, of the interest in social control is the reaction against evolutionary determinism, a doctrine that represented society as the resultant of forces, often mechanistic, that operate almost automatically, regardless of man's efforts. In opposition to such a fatalistic view of society, Lester F. Ward proposed his conception of "social telesis," the possibility and efficacy of intelligent collective planning and superiority of the human mind over the blind forces of nature.[21] Ward's position has been strengthened by the recent collapse of *laissez-faire* economic individualism and the general recourse to governmental aid and control of business.

The disintegrating forces which frequently develop in complex modern cultures are likely to be accompanied by strenuous efforts to secure uni-

---

[20] Karen Horney, *The Neurotic Personality of Our Time* (New York: Norton and Co., 1937). See also Sigmund Freud, *Civilization and Its Discontents* (London: The Hogarth Press, 1930).

[21] Lester F. Ward, *Dynamic Sociology* (New York: Appleton and Co., 1883), vol. I, pp. 74-75. See also Samuel Chugerman, *Lester F. Ward, the American Aristotle* (Durham: Duke University Press, 1939).

formity of conduct. This tendency is increased by greater familiarity with effective methods of influencing behavior. "Having the knowledge we may set hopefully at work upon a ccurse of social invention and experiment." [22] In the totalitarian states, emphasis upon social control already has reached near the maximum in state direction and regulation. The increasing complexity of culture is, however, likely to increase rather than to diminish the need for effective social control, either voluntary or authoritarian, especially of those who may unleash upon mankind the destructive forces of atomic energy.

Summary

The term social control, as used in this book, refers to the processes, planned or unplanned, by which individuals are taught, persuaded, or compelled to conform to the usages of groups. It is distinct from self-control, although the latter, in so far as it reflects group norms, is derived from social control.

Social control is as old as human society, but its deliberate study as a discipline which cuts across all social science fields, is quite recent in origin. Ward, Sumner, Cooley, and Ross, in the pioneering days of American sociology, made significant contributions to the concept and its study. They provided varying emphases on the means, the sources, and the personality phases, which have been followed in later studies and writings.

The motivations behind deliberate exercise of social control are many and complex, often not fully realized by the person who exercises control. Only for convenience may they be classified as exploitative, regulatory, and creative. The means employed vary with the cultural settings of various groups. They may be institutional or non-institutional, symbolic or coercive.

All groups show some lack of uniformity both in the standards and effectiveness of social control. Always there are some maladjustments and conflicts, as illustrated by the psychopaths, the eccentrics, and criminals. In times of rapid social change deviations may be so numerous and widespread as to be characterized as social disorganization. When preliterate peoples come under the domination of complex civilizations the old norms and controls may become so weakened as to destroy all incentive for ordinary life activities, and even the zest for living.

Significant for the present and future is the decline in individual adequacy to cope with social forces, and the resultant need for group action. This has led to multiplication of voluntary agencies of social

---

[22] John Dewey, *Human Nature and Conduct* (New York: Henry Holt and Co., 1922), p. 148.

control in democracies, with varying proposals and counter-proposals among them, and to the rise of almost complete state regulation in totalitarian states. Even more complex cultures of the future will further increase pressures for social control, either voluntary or authoritarian.

QUESTIONS

1. In what ways is social control to be distinguished from control of nature?
2. How is self-control to be separated from social control?
3. When is leadership an aspect of social control?
4. Are persons who are alone still subject to social control?
5. What means of social control are more effective in small intimate groups?
6. In what ways may social control be modified among minority groups?
7. What are some of the injurious consequences of social control?
8. How has social planning increased the importance of social control?
9. Do you think "human nature" will rebel against an increase of social control?
10. Is military or school morale or "spirit" a form of social control?

SUGGESTED TOPICS FOR TERM PAPERS AND FURTHER RESEARCH

1. The place of social control in the study of the social sciences.
2. An analysis of the methods of social control among students.
3. An analysis of the methods of ten observed overt social control situations.
4. The weakness of informal means of social control in American city life.
5. Newer means of social control.
6. Unfavorable consequences of excessive social control.
7. Social control in totalitarian states.
8. The future of social control in the United States.
9. Wartime rationing as a form of social control.
10. Social control of the atomic bomb and similar weapons of war.

BIBLIOGRAPHY

Books

Morroe Berger, Theodore Abel, and Charles H. Page, eds., *Social Control and Individual Freedom in Modern Society* (New York: D. Van Nostrand Co., 1954). Essays by the students of Robert M. MacIver.

L. L. Bernard, *Social Control in Its Sociological Aspects* (New York: The Macmillan Co., 1939). A keen analysis of social control.

John Maurice Clar, *Social Control of Business* (New York: McGraw-Hill Book Co., 1939). The relation of social control to economic life.

Charles H. Cooley, *Human Nature and the Social Order* (New York: Charles Scribner's Sons, 1902). A classic study of the influence of social pressures upon the personality of the individual.

Leonard W. Doob, *The Plans of Men* (New Haven: Yale University Press, 1940). How the hopes and plans affect social control.

Georges Gurvitch, "Social Control," Chapter X, pp. 267-296, in G. Gurvitch and A. E. Moore, eds., *Twentieth Century Sociology* (New York: Philosophical Library, 1945). An excellent survey of the theoretical aspects of this field.

Rudolf Heberle, *Social Movements* (New York: Appleton-Century-Crofts, 1951).
A valuable evaluation of the attractiveness and means used by social movements
of the modern times.

Paul H. Landis, *Social Control: Social Organization and Disorganization in Process*
(Philadelphia: J. B. Lippincott Co., 1939). A textbook dealing with the working
of the social institutions and other regulatory patterns.

R. T. LaPiere, *A Theory of Social Control* (New York: McGraw-Hill Book Co.,
1954). An effort to combine the theoretical and practical aspects.

Halford E. Luccok, *Communicating The Gospel* (New Haven: Yale University
Press, 1954). The theological aspects of religious social control.

F. E. Lumley, *Means of Social Control* (New York: The Century Co., 1925). Still
valuable as a description of many of the means of enforcing norms of conduct.

Karl Mannheim, *Essays on the Sociology of Knowledge* (New York: Oxford University
Press, 1952). Noteworthy essays on the field known as the sociology of
knowledge.

Margaret Mead, *Sex and Temperament in Three Primitive Societies* (New York:
William Morrow and Co., 1935). A dramatic account of the organization of personality
under diverse social pressures.

James R. Newman and Byron S. Miller, *The Control of Atomic Energy* (New York:
Whittlesey House, 1948). Problems of the legal and social control of atomic
fission.

Roscoe Pounds, *Social Control Through Law* (New Haven: Yale University Press,
1942). The law and the courts as means of social control.

Edward A. Ross, *Social Control: A Survey of the Foundations of Order* (New York:
American Book Co., 1901). A pioneer work with an excellent description of the
means of social control.

William G. Sumner, *Folkways* (New York: Ginn and Co., 1906). The classic treatment
of the folkways and mores as bases of social control.

John Van Sickle, *Planning for the South* (Nashville, Tenn.: Vanderbilt University
Press, 1943). An inquiry into the economic social controls.

Periodicals

Read Bain, "Verbal Stereotypes and Social Control," *Sociology and Social Research*,
XXIII (May, 1939), pp. 431-446.

Harold Benjamin, ed., "Education for Social Control," *Annals of The American
Academy of Political and Social Science*, CLXXXII (November, 1935), pp. 1-242.

L. L. Bernard, "Methods of Generalization for Social Control," *American Sociological
Review*, V (June, 1940), pp. 340-350.

E. S. Bogardus, "Rationing and Social Control," *Sociology and Social Research*,
XXVII (July, 1943), pp. 472-479.

Lee M. Brooks, "Fifty Years Quest for Social Control," *Social Forces*, XXIX
(October, 1950), pp. 1-8.

Robert Alan Dahl, ed., "The Impact of Atomic Energy," *The Annals of the American
Academy of Political and Social Science*, CCLXXXX (November, 1953).

John Dewey, "Social Science and Social Control," *New Republic*, LXVII (July 29,
1931), pp. 276-277; "Education and Our Present Social Problems," *School and
Society*, XXXVII (April 15, 1933), pp. 473-76.

A. B. Hollingshead, "Concept of Social Control," *American Sociological Review*, VI
(April, 1941), pp. 217-224.

C. L. Hunt, "Religious Ideology as a Means of Social Control," *Sociology and Social
Research*, XXXIII (January, 1949), pp. 180-187.

Harold Lasswell, "The Garrison State and Specialists in Violence," *The American
Journal of Sociology*, XCV (January, 1941), pp. 455-467.

E. M. Lemert, "The Folkways and Social Control," *American Sociological Review*,
VII (June, 1942), pp. 394-399.

Simon Marcson, "The Control of Ethnic Conflict," *Social Forces*, XXIV (December, 1945), pp. 162-164.

E. C. McDonagh, "Military Social Controls," *Sociology and Social Research*, XXIX (January, 1945), pp. 197-205.

F. B. Parker, "Social Control and the Technicways," *Social Forces*, XXII (December, 1943), pp. 163-168.

E. George Payne, "Personal versus Social Control," *Journal of Educational Sociology*, XIII (November, 1939), pp. 132-139.

A. J. Reiss, Jr., "Delinquency as the Failure of Personal and Social Controls," *American Sociological Review*, XVI (April, 1951), pp. 196-208.

A. D. Ross, "Social Control of Philanthropy," *American Journal of Sociology*, LVIII (March, 1953), pp. 451-60.

E. A. Ross, "Social Control," *American Journal of Sociology*, I, 513, 753; II, 96-433, 547, 823; III, 64, 236, 328, 649; V, 475, 604; VI, 29-550.

E. A. Schuler, "V for Victory: A Study in Symbolic Social Control," *Journal of Social Psychology*, XIX (May, 1944), pp. 283-299.

CHAPTER II

Socio-Psychic Processes in Social Control

The study of the processes of social control gives rise to a very significant question: How does it happen that man is able to develop intricate social relationships with his fellows and a complicated social orderliness? The answer lies in an understanding of the nature of the human being and his capacity for responding to the objects, the ideas, and the other human beings that make up the social environment in which he lives. In other words, men learn in social experience how to maintain an orderly system of life. There are, then, two essential elements in the explanation: man's capacity for an orderly social life and the social experience which furnishes the matrix or mold in which that orderliness finds expression. These are not distinct elements but interweaving factors, each dependent upon the other.

Socio-Psychic Process Defined

The psychic nature of man cannot be viewed, except theoretically, apart from the social experience in which it functions. The human being does not simply respond but rather he responds to situations that confront him, and the responses he makes are greatly influenced by his previous response-experiences. Endowed with the most complex nervous structure of all animals, man is capable of an enormous variety of responses. Human social behavior cannot be described adequately in terms of either psychic processes alone or in terms of social experience alone but in term of the two functioning together more or less inseparably. The analysis of social relationships and social orderliness may be approached in terms of what are called socio-psychic processes, which are *those characteristics of thought and feeling which arise in interactions among persons in organized group life, and which are basic to all human social behavior*. Every social act of an individual involves his capacity to respond, conditioned by previous experiences.

Although it is possible to distinguish a number of socio-psychic processes that are involved in social control, the treatment that follows is concerned primarily with perception, symbolism, conceptual learning, the influence of social control on personality development, and the emergence of social consciousness. Since all social control is dependent upon communication, these processes are discussed with particular reference to the communicative process.

Communication. The basic essential of social control and of all processes involving human social relationships is communication. Communication is the transmission of meaningful stimuli between individuals and provides the technique for sharing experiences and developing understandings. In its absence social life cannot exist since relationships among human beings and social orderliness cannot be achieved. Communication is fundamental to all social processes and is necessarily involved in every single act of social behavior.[1]

The Methods of Communication. The many and varied methods of communication include all the ways by which meaning is transferred from individual to individual. It is possible to distinguish two classes of techniques in the communicative process. The primary techniques are universal and embrace principally language and gesture; the secondary techniques facilitate and extend the process of communication, and include writing, printing, the means of transportation, telegraph, telephone, radio and motion pictures.[2] These media of communication have the effect of vastly extending in space and of speeding up the transfer of meanings, thus enlarging the possible areas of contact for the individual.

The place of communication in social control may be demonstrated in several ways. In the first place, the human individual must become aware of the group objectives and values that serve as guides to social behavior. The nature and significance of the folkways, mores, and institutions must be learned. The established modes of behavior to which he must conform and the importance of conforming are made known to him by language and gesture and by various of the mediated methods of communication. In the second place, the means and techniques of social control are dependent upon communication. Social inducement to conformity, either in the form of sympathetic guidance or of group pressure, obviously involves the communicative process. The possibility of penalties inflicted for departures from the group code is communicated to the individual and the knowledge of these penalties is often sufficient to bring about conformity. Punishment involves suffering, either physical or mental, loss of prestige, or inconvenience, and an awareness of this as a possible consequence of non-conformity is in itself a deterrent. This awareness depends upon communication.

---

[1] Edward Sapir, "Communication," *Encyclopaedia of the Social Sciences*, IV, p. 78.
[2] *Ibid.*, pp. 78-80. For a more extended treatment, see William Albig, *Public Opinion* (New York: McGraw-Hill Book Co., 1939), chapter III

Perception

In the course of his normal experience the individual becomes aware daily of hundreds of objects distinct from himself. He sees trees, houses, people, and automobiles; he reads the newspaper, a letter from a friend, or a magazine; he hears people talking and engages in conversation with some of them; he listens to music over the radio or at a concert; and he handles numerous objects—pencils, clothes, books, and apples. The process of becoming aware of and responding to them is called perception. This awareness is achieved through the senses with which the individual is endowed. But the sensory equipment alone does not explain the process of perceiving; the sense organs are merely the physical apparatus that receives impressions of the objects which we encounter.

Our interest is in seeking to understand what happens when perceiving takes place. When any one of the objects mentioned in the preceding paragraph—pencil, tree, apple—is encountered, the person reacts to it as a unit [3] and not to the particular items or related individual stimuli that are involved. The perception "pencil" or "tree" or "apple" is in each instance a total experience. In the case of the apple, it is possible to distinguish certain particular items in the perception such as its color, shape, odor, and the like. But in the perceptual experience "apple" these items are not reacted to as such. It is true, to be sure, that any one of these single qualities or characteristics may be focused upon, but in that case a very different perceptual experience takes place. The reaction is then to color or shape and not to the apple. This is, of course, not the same as the perception "apple." The essential point to understand is that in perceiving the reaction is not to the individual stimuli but to the relationships among them.

In perception we react to "patterns" or "configurations," that is, to totalities of individual items.[4] If a chord is struck on the piano, it is heard as a chord and not as the individual tones that compose it. The tones compose the chord, to be sure, but the reaction is to the whole pattern and not to the particular items in it. When a series of notes are played in succession, we hear them not as individual notes but as music, that is, as a pattern. Writing is reacted to not as so many individual black marks on paper but as words. These may be arranged in innumerable patterns and convey many different meanings.

The perceptual pattern is independent of its constituent parts. This fact may be illustrated by referring to what is known in music as "trans-

---

[3] This approach has been developed and elaborated in Gestalt Psychology. See William Stern, *General Psychology From the Personalistic Standpoint*, translated by Howard D. Spoerl (New York: The Macmillan Co., 1938), chapter V.

[4] Stern, *op. cit.*, p. 112.

posability." This means simply that the pattern may be transposed from one set of individual items to another without disturbing the pattern. In music the same melody may be played in any one of several different keys, each involving different tones. But the melody remains the same. When the tune of the "Star Spangled Banner" has been learned, it can be recognized easily regardless of the key or the instrument on which it is played. In the same manner, the same words, once they are learned, are recognized whether they are written with a black pencil on white paper or written with white chalk on a blackboard.

Several pertinent questions relating to perception naturally arise at this point. Do different persons react in the same manner to the same perceptual patterns? Does a person necessarily react in the same manner at different times to the same or similar patterns? Consideration of some of the factors that enter into perceptual experience will throw some light on these questions. Obviously reactions to similar patterns vary with different persons and with the same person at different times. Whether a given stimulus will be reacted to in one or another way depends upon the past experience of the person and the habits of perceiving he has formed, the preoccupation or mental set at the time he has the perceptual experience, and the setting or context in which the stimulus occurs. We may note, then, three significant influences on perceptual experiences: habit, mental set, and context.[5] Obviously, these influences are developed in social experience.

Habit. The way a person perceives depends on his previous experience and the habits of perception he has formed. Persons tend to react in the manner to which they have become accustomed. The experienced driver of an automobile sees before him at an intersection a red traffic light. He responds by bringing his car to a stop and refrains from starting again until the red light goes off and a green one comes on. There is nothing about the color red that necessarily denotes danger and there is nothing in the nature of the individual or in his visual sense that makes him respond to a red light in a particular manner. Why, then, does he respond in this manner? The answer lies in his previous experience; he has formed the habit of reacting in this way. Another person, unfamiliar with traffic signals, would most probably not respond in this fashion at all.

The trained scientist in a laboratory reacts to an experiment in a manner very different from the layman who has no knowledge of laboratory techniques and the subject matter of the science. An expert telegrapher's response to the clicking of the telegraph instrument is very

---

[5] Each of these has been tested experimentally. For reports of some of these experiments and for a more extended treatment of these factors, see John F. Dashiell, *Fundamentals of General Psychology* (Boston: Houghton Mifflin Co., 1937), pp. 448-462.

different from that of the casual bystander who has had no experience with telegraphy. Examples of habits in perceptual response are numerous. We are all familiar with the many different reactions that are made to words, musical notes, signs, and signals to which we have learned to respond in certain ways.

Mental Set. A person's mind plays an important part in the way one responds to objects, sounds, and persons. The manner in which people react depends to a considerable extent on the way they are prepared to react at a particular moment. A simple remark that might be passed as a mere pleasantry at one time is reacted to as an insult at another time. A person reading a very exciting mystery story late at night is likely to be disturbed by sounds in and around his house that would ordinarily not disturb him in the least.

Context. The context in which a stimulus-pattern occurs influences the response that is made to the pattern. The driver of an automobile does not stop his car at any red light. He distinguishes a red traffic light from a red light in a residence window at Christmas time or a red light in a store sign. The difference is not in the light but in the setting in which it appears. We are aware of how words and phrases differ greatly in terms of their contexts. They can convey totally different meanings when used in different relations to other words or under different circumstances.

Symbolism

Communication among human beings is carried on by means of symbols. Words, gestures, signs, and objects of various kinds are employed by human beings to convey meanings to each other. A symbol is something that is associated with or stands for something else; it is a substitute for another object, response or situation.[6] Reaction to symbols depends upon a recognition of their relationship to or association with the thing for which they stand. Symbols may be and usually are quite unlike the things for which they stand. Words as symbols are usually very different from the objects and situations they designate. The word "apple," whether written or spoken, bears no resemblance to the fruit. At the same time the word can arouse certain responses similar to those elicited by the sight of an apple.

Every culture includes a great variety of symbols by means of which thoughts, ideas, and images are transmitted to the persons sharing that culture. Symbols as cultural elements have to be learned. They are not inborn but are acquired only in social experience. They have evolved in

---

[6] Dashiell, *op. cit.,* p. 461.

culture essentially because of their economy and convenience in human group living. Their use increases enormously the number of environmental influences which can elicit a given response; it would be very inconvenient if the idea of an apple or a factory could be conveyed only by displaying these objects. Symbols also are a simple means of representing complex and sometimes abstract reality [7] that could not otherwise be communicated without a much greater expenditure of time and effort. Symbols are a valuable means of preserving the experiences of the past. They afford us contacts with the men and events of years gone by.

There are many group symbols that play an important part in the life of every society. Flags, mottoes, songs, statues and slogans are symbols of this sort. Many such symbols are associated with experiences through which the group as a whole has passed. They are held in reverence and defended emotionally. These symbols serve to arouse group spirit and loyalty and to remind the group members of their obligations.

The significance of symbolism in social control is obvious. Much of the control in human society is achieved symbolically. The modes of behavior to which conformity is expected are made known to the individual by means of symbols, principally by language. Group symbols are employed constantly to inspire conformity by serving to recall group sacrifices and achievements in the past as well as to present group ideals and standards. There is nothing inherent in the symbol itself that induces conformity; the symbol is employed in social control only as a device for transmitting meaning.

Conceptual Learning

A significant part of every culture is a body of concepts or generalizations. A concept designates certain common properties of objects and situations that have a meaning independent of their immediate setting.[8] Fruit, for instance, is a concept that indicates certain properties or characteristics common to a great number of very different kinds of objects. The concept covers properties possessed by apples, oranges, bananas and grapes. These common properties have a meaning quite apart from the specific objects or kinds of objects with which they are connected. Each of the specific kinds of fruit falls into this category because of the elements common to all of them.

Origins of Concepts. All concepts originate empirically. Repeated experiences with various objects and situations may lead to the recognition of common characteristics possessed by certain of them. The process

---

[7] Albig, *op. cit.*, p. 72.

[8] Norman L. Munn, *Psychological Development* (Boston: Houghton Mifflin Co., 1938), pp. 348 ff.

whereby these characteristics are differentiated from objects and situations is known as *abstracting.*[9] A concept is, of course, an abstraction and has a meaning of its own. Concept formation is illustrated by Hull in an interesting account of how a child may arrive at the concept "dog." A young child finds himself in a number of somewhat different situations, to which he reacts by approach, and hears each situation called "Dog." The specific situations are separated from each other in time by an indeterminate period during which other absorbing situations are confronted. In this way the child is not able to anticipate the "dog" experiences. With each situation called "dog" he is faced with the problem of how to react. In time the child has a "meaning" for the word dog. This meaning is found to involve the characteristics more or less common to all dogs but which are not common to other animals or objects in his experiences. He has abstracted from the situations involving dogs those properties that are common to all of the situations but not to the other situations to which he has reacted.[10]

In a well-controlled experiment with adults, Hull used a number of complicated Chinese characters which were shown one at a time to each subject participating in the experiment. The characters were arranged in twelve separate series. Each of the characters in a series, although very different from the others, contained an element common to all in that series. As each character was displayed, a word corresponding to the series to which the character belonged was pronounced and the subject repeated the word. The problem confronting the subject in the experiment was to learn that all of the characters having a common element are designated by a given term.[11] The problem was obviously one of abstracting the common element in the different situations presented. Other experiments with the process have been made.

Verbal Symbols. Concepts are usually expressed in verbal symbols, but they are not always or necessarily verbalized. We are so accustomed to expressing concepts in words that we find it difficult to realize that responses on a conceptual basis can be made without being able to report the generalization underlying the response. Experiments have indicated that certain animals below man may learn to respond on a conceptual basis although they are incapable of verbalization. Other experiments with both children and adults have demonstrated the same possibility in

---

[9] Munn, *op. cit.,* p. 349. Arnold L. Gesell, *How a Baby Grows* (New York: Harper and Brothers, 1945) is a valuable collection of stills from the Yale films of child development, a seven years' research project on the growing baby.

[10] C. L. Hull, "Quantitative Aspects of the Evolution of Concepts," *Psychological Monographs* XXVIII (1920), pp. 5-6. Quoted in Munn, *op. cit.,* pp. 349-350.

[11] Hull, *op. cit.* For a concise description of this experiment, see Dashiell, *op. cit.,* pp. 556-558.

human beings. In these experiments, responses were made to the common elements or properties in situations that were different in all other respects, but no reports could be given of the basis for the responses.[12]

Vicarious Acquisition of Concepts. Although all concepts originate in experience, it is not necessary that all persons develop concepts out of *direct* experience with objects and situations. Concepts may be acquired vicariously, that is, from indirect experience. Once developed and verbalized, a concept may be explained or pointed out to other persons and transmitted to large groups. In the case of Hull's experiment using the Chinese characters, it would be a simple matter to point out in advance of experience with the characters the common elements in each of the series. As a matter of fact, a large part of our formal instruction in various subjects in schools and colleges is explaining concepts. Objects and situations are placed in classes or categories in terms of the common attributes that characterize the particular things included in those classes or categories.

In everyday life we communicate to one another the general nature and principal characteristics of an object or situation by designating the class into which it falls. We are thus employing concepts in the transfer of knowledge from person to person and in the development of understanding of objects and situations. The dictionary is consulted frequently for the meaning indicated by this or that concept. The use of the dictionary is, of course, a form of vicarious experience that affords a relatively easy access to the meaning of concepts already formed.

The Usefulness of Conceptual Learning. Conceptual learning is highly significant in the adjustments that persons must necessarily make in social life. It provides a generalized way of recognizing the structure and characteristics of objects and the principal elements in situations. Adjustments to things are usually easier if the general properties of those things and the uses to which they may be put can be learned in advance of direct experiences with them. The ability of human beings to convey meaning by use of concepts greatly facilitates the development of social orderliness and the process of social control. Social values such as justice, honor, truth, and liberty, which we are expected to uphold, are concepts. Modes of behavior such as monogamy, marital fidelity, and loyalty to our country, which we are expected to follow, are concepts. These designate meanings apart from the actual situations to which they are common.[13]

---

[12] Munn, *op. cit.*, pp. 148, 348-349.
[13] Chapter XIII develops fully social control uses of conceptual means.

Personality and Social Control

Personality represents the sum-total of adjustments of the individual to the social and cultural order in which he lives and of which he is a part. It is not inborn but is achieved in social experience. Its development depends quite obviously upon communication whereby the cultural attainments of the group are transmitted to the individual who comes at birth into a cultural setting that is already existent. Through contacts with his fellows he learns the patterns of social life, acquires the culture of the group, and achieves an adjustment to the requirements of the social order.

Culture provides the framework of personality development. The totality of social traits displayed by the individual personality reflects the previous social and cultural experiences of the person. The various elements of culture are reacted to by the individual and these reactions influence the course of his development. In every culture there may be distinguished two general classes of elements: material and non-material. Material culture includes inventions, machines, tools, weapons, clothing, and all the other material objects. Non-material culture includes language, beliefs, codes of conduct and the like. Personality development involves reactions and adjustments to both aspects.

Personality Adjustment. For the most part personality adjustment is made to the culture of a particular society. Outside of this general cultural order the individual may find himself more or less bewildered and confused, that is, when he is confronted with a strange culture to which he has not made adjustment. A person reared in America, if suddenly transported to the society of a primitive African tribe, would not know how to act or what to expect of others. The development and widespread use of mediated methods of communication, however, have vastly extended the range of contact so that cultural barriers, while still very important, are becoming less significant socially than they have been.

Social control does make for social stability in human society, but it also serves the functions of orienting the individual to the social order and of guiding him in the development of meaningful social relationships with his fellows. In this way social control is of great significance to the human individual in the "development of an integrated socially effective personality." [14]

---

[14] Paul H. Landis, *Social Control: Social Organization and Disorganization in Process* (Philadelphia: J. B. Lippincott Co., 1939), p. 32. Ralph Linton, *The Cultural Background of Personality* (New York: D. Appleton-Century, 1945), is a valuable analysis of the interrelations of culture, society and the individual.

Social Consciousness

The emergence of social consciousness is a significant aspect of the process of social control as well as of personality development. Social consciousness is an awareness on the part of the person of the attitudes of others toward him and toward various kinds of behavior. It involves a recognition of the fact that others are reacting to the same objects and situations and that there are certain similarities or differences between their reactions and his own. Social consciousness includes not only an awareness of the reactions of others toward one's actions but also imagery of the probable reactions of others toward certain forms of behavior.[15]

The Process of Interstimulation. The development of social consciousness results from the reactions on the part of the individual to the responses made by other persons to his actions. His actions operate as a stimulus to responses from other individuals, and their responses in turn stimulate further action on his part.[16] The process is one of interstimulation in which the mutual responses of individuals take on social meaning.

As a result of the emergence of social consciousness, the individual becomes aware of his relative position in the social group. He feels that he has a certain prestige, honor, or place of dignity. In short, he regards himself as having *status*. This consciousness of status operates as a powerful element in social control. The individual tends to conform to the established modes of behavior and to avoid those actions which incur group displeasure or disapproval. This does not mean that he does not subscribe in thought and sentiment to the codes prevailing in the group. He may believe wholeheartedly in the code, but this belief is a product of social experience and participation in group life. There are usually in every group, however, individuals who because of limitations of hereditary capacity or faulty socialization do not understand the code or do not respect it and violate it.

Consciousness of Kind. Another aspect or phase of social consciousness that influences the process of social control is what Giddings designated as the "consciousness of kind." This refers to "a state of consciousness in which any being, whether low or high in the scale of life, recognizes another conscious being as of like kind with itself." [17] Within the larger

---

[15] Floyd H. Allport, *Social Psychology* (Boston: Houghton Mifflin Co., 1924), p. 329. See also: Helen F. Dunbar, *Emotions and Bodily Changes* (New York: Columbia University Press, 1946).

[16] George H. Mead, "Social Consciousness and the Consciousness of Meaning," *Psychological Bulletin* VII (1910), p. 397. Cf. F. B. Karpf, *American Social Psychology* (New York: McGraw-Hill Book Co., 1932), pp. 321 ff.

[17] Franklin H. Giddings, *Principles of Sociology* (New York: The Macmillan Co., 1896), p. 17.

groups to which the individual belongs are usually a number of smaller groupings of persons. The individual is identified with some of these groups and not with the others. Membership in these smaller groups is based on certain similarities of the members within the group which distinguish them from others on the outside. These similarities and differences may be on the basis of kinship, beliefs, interests, skills, knowledge, training or previous experience, or other factors that indicate similarities and differences in society.

Classes of groups characterized by a consciousness of kind include family, occupational, economic, religious, intellectual, and others. Members of specific groups in each of these classes recognize their similarities to each other and their differences from the members of other groups. Each of the specific groups subscribes to certain modes of behavior and exerts pressure upon its members to conform. The consciousness of kind obviously serves not only as a factor in group formation and integration but also as an element in social control and personality development.

Summary

The development of relations within groups and of social orderliness is explained in the processes of perception which involves habit formation, mental set, and the context within which experiences occur for the individual; symbolism and the communicative process; and conceptual learning. The development of personality, a product of social experience, is involved, and of particular importance from the standpoint of social control is the emergence of social consciousness, with its concomitant "consciousness of kind." These are the principal psycho-social factors which make possible the control of the individual member by his group and by others, and his development into mature social membership.

QUESTIONS

1. What do human beings respond to?
2. How can human social behavior best be explained?
3. Define communication.
4. What are the media of communication and what are their effects on social relationships?
5. How is the place of communication in social control demonstrated?
6. What happens when perceiving takes place?
7. What do we react to in perception?
8. Do different persons react in the same manner to the same perceptual patterns?
9. Will an individual react in the same manner at different times to the same or similar patterns?
10. What are the significant influences on perceptual experiences?
11. What is habit and what are some examples of perceptual habits?
12. By what means are ideas transmitted to the people of a particular culture?

13. How are symbols acquired?
14. How do concepts originate?
15. Explain the vicarious acquisition of concepts.
16. Define the process of interstimulation.
17. What is consciousness of kind?

SUGGESTED TOPICS FOR TERM PAPERS AND FURTHER RESEARCH

1. The philosophy of individualism and social control.
2. The primary techniques of communication.
3. The role of mental set in perceiving.
4. Acquisition of symbols.
5. The empirical basis of conceptual learning.
6. Consciousness of kind in occupational groups.
7. The process of interstimulation.

BIBLIOGRAPHY

Books

Alfred Adler, *Practice and Theory of Individual Psychology* (New York: Harcourt, Brace and Co., 1924). An introduction to Adler's theories of psychology.

William Albig, *Public Opinion* (New York: McGraw-Hill Book Co., 1939), chapters III-IV. An interesting and well illustrated treatment of communication and the psychological processes involved in public opinion.

James H. S. Bossard, *The Sociology of Child Development* (New York: Harper and Brothers, rev. ed. 1954). A pioneer work in this field.

Norman Cameron, *The Psychology of Behavior Disorders, A Biosocial Interpretation* (Boston: Houghton Mifflin Co., 1947). A study of psychological disorders from the biosocial viewpoint.

Charles Horton Cooley, *Social Organization* (New York: Charles Scribner's Sons, 1909), chapters I-III, VI-X. Social consciousness and its relation to primary group experience; communication and its relation to human nature and individuality.

Albert Deutch, *The Mentally Ill in America* (New York: Columbia University Press, 1949). A good introduction to the "abnormal area" of personality.

Arnold L. Gessel, *How a Baby Grows* (New York: Harper and Brothers, 1945). An authoritative study of the growth of the individual.

John Dollard and Neal E. Miller, *Personality and Psychotherapy* (New York: McGraw-Hill Book Co., 1950). An analysis in terms of learning, thinking, and culture.

Robert E. L. Faris and H. W. Dunham, *Mental Disorders in Urban Areas* (Chicago: Chicago University Press, 1939). An ecological study of schizophrenia and other psychoses.

R. J. Havighurst and Taba Hilda, *Adolescent Character and Personality* (New York: John Wiley and Sons, 1949). An able introduction to this field.

A. B. Hollingshead, *Elmtown's Youth* (New York: John Wiley and Sons, 1949). On the influence of the urban environment on the formation of the personality.

Clyde Kluckholn and H. A. Murray, eds., *Personality* (New York: Alfred A. Knopf, 1948). Offers a wealth of material on personality in nature, society, and culture.

Ralph Linton, ed., *The Science of Man in the World Crisis* (New York: Columbia University Press, 1945). Articles by specialists in the various branches of anthropology, offering their conclusions about man and his present problems in an effort to synthesize the knowledge of sciences that deal with human beings. See also

Linton's *The Cultural Background of Personality* (New York: Appleton-Century-Crofts, 1945).

Fred McKinney, *The Psychology of Personal Adjustment* (New York: John Wiley and Sons, 1949). An enjoyable combination of scholarship and popularization.

Gardiner Murphy, *Personality* (New York: Harper and Brothers, 1947). An excellent biosocial study of the personality.

W. H. Mikesell, ed., *Modern Abnormal Psychology* (New York: Philosophical Library, 1950). A useful symposium.

Edward Sapir, "Communication," *Encyclopaedia of the Social Sciences,* VI. IV, pp. 78-80. A concise statement of the nature of communication and its social significance.

Periodicals

Franz Alexander, "Psychoanalysis and Social Disorganization," *American Journal of Sociology,* XLII (May, 1937), pp. 781-813.

Read Bain, "The Concept of Social Process," *Publication of the American Sociological Society,* XXVI (August, 1932), pp. 10-18.

B. Baxter and B. Shirzaher, "Language Contributions to Democratic Social Behavior," *Elementary English Review,* XXI (April, 1944), pp. 121-125.

K. D. Benne and W. Stanley, "Reactions Against Antomism: Sumner's Folkways," *Educational Forum,* VII (November, 1942), pp. 51-56.

Herbert Blumer, "Social Disorganization and Individual Disorganization," *American Journal of Sociology,* XLII (May, 1937), pp. 871-877.

Claud C. Bowman, "American Culture and the Problem of Personal Organization," *Social Forces,* XIX (May, 1941), pp. 483-491.

H. C. Canady, "Contributions of Cultural Anthropology to the Study of Human Behavior," *School and Society,* LXVIII (October 16, 1948).

F. Stuart Chapin, "Definition of Definitions of Concepts," *Social Forces,* XVIII (December, 1939), pp. 153-160.

R. H. Danhof, "The Accommodation and Integration of Conflicting Cultures in a Newly Established Communist," *American Journal of Sociology.* XLVIIII (July, 1943), pp. 14-23.

Kingsley Davis, "Extreme Social Isolation of a Child," *Ibid.,* XLV (January, 1940), pp. 554-565.

Joseph H. Fichter, "Marginal Catholic," *Social Forces,* XXXII (December, 1953), pp. 167-173.

John Gillin, "Personality in Preliterate Societies," *American Sociological Review,* IV (October, 1939), pp. 681-702.

H. G. Gough, "Sociological Theory of Psychopathy," *American Journal of Sociology,* LIII (March, 1948).

F. N. House, "Social Relations and Social Interaction," *Ibid.,* XXXI (March, 1926), pp. 617-633.

Ruby J. R. Kennedy, "Single or Triple Melting Pot," *Ibid.,* XLVIIII (January, 1944), pp. 331-339.

R. E. Lane, "Businessmen and Bureaucrats," *Social Forces,* XXXII, 2 (December, 1953), pp. 145-152.

Ronald Lippitt, "Field Theory and Experiment in Social Psychology: Autocratic and Democratic Group Atmospheres," *American Journal of Sociology,* XLV (July, 1939), pp. 26-49.

Bronislaw Malinowski, "The Group and the Individual in Functional Analysis," *American Journal of Sociology,* XLIV (May, 1939), pp. 938-964.

A. R. Mangus, "Personality Adjustment of Rural and Urban Children," *American Sociological Review,* XIII (October, 1948), pp. 566-575.

J. W. Polley, "Teacher Community Approach to Educational Problems of Great Cities," *Teachers College Record,* LV (December, 1953), pp. 153-159.

W. Riley and S. H. Flowerman, "Group Relations as a Variable in Communications Research," *American Sociological Review,* XVI (April, 1951), pp. 174-180.

A. M. Rose, "The Popular Meaning of Class Designation," *Sociology and Social Research*, XXXVIII, 1 (September–October, 1953), pp. 14-21.

S. A. Stouffer and Jackson Toby, "Role Conflict and Personality," *American Journal of Sociology*, XVL (March, 1951), pp. 395-405.

Howard Woolston, "The Process of Assimilation," *Social Forces*, XXXIII (May, 1945), pp. 416-424.

CHAPTER III

Social Control and the Conditioning
of Personality

Against the background of the chapters dealing with the nature of social control and the nature of the human unit over whom the control is exercised, this chapter will be limited to the point at which social control impinges upon personality. Mention should be made at the outset of two fallacies underlying popular thinking about control: that social control may be entirely impersonal, and that it can be automatic. Like some other seductive thinking, the fallacies lurk in the vagueness of the terms used and may only be avoided by keeping in mind: first, that control is a relationship between persons. In the last analysis, it is the impingement of one personality upon another personality. Customs, processes, institutions of themselves effect no control. They do not exist apart from persons. Rather those who observe customs, those who participate in social processes, those who belong to institutions, exercise the control. Persons with customs, ideas and ideals undertake to enforce conformity to them on the part of other persons. In this sense, the person, in the measure of his capacity, experience and activity, is the society, and control is but a function of personality conditioning. Thus, when it is said that individuals are controlled by certain customs and institutions it will be understood that that control is exercised through persons.

A second consideration is no less important—namely, that social control is never entirely automatic. It may sometimes seem so in its operation, especially as the individual becomes more habituated to conforming socially, more eager for the approvals which flow from submission to the conventions than for the satisfactions which come from the exercise of personal desires when these are in violation of social codes. In some cases the wish for approval may become so highly developed that a person will deliberately seek to discover an unfamiliar code or group pattern with the purpose of moulding both his thought and his behavior to it. But even here the process is conscious and deliberate rather than automatic. If personality conditioning by the physical environment may properly be said to exist, it would be more nearly automatic. In any case, it would not be on the level of social control and so may be omitted from consideration here.

Personality is Acquired

It is now generally conceded by psychologists that the human infant is born without any fixed patterns of life. Earlier writers reasoning by analogy from animal behavior attributed to the human infant inborn mechanisms of social adaptation which were called instincts—love, fear, hate, acquisitiveness, pugnacity, religion, etc. As a result of the work of Freud, Jung, Watson, Allport, Bernard and others, these so-called instincts are now generally thought of as chaotic, undefined reflexes, visceral changes, appetites, and physical sensations. When they are defined as clear-cut wants and satisfactions by the experience of the individual, they may function much like animal behavior patterns.

The manner in which the experience of the developing child satisfies these explosive tendencies will determine the measure of his social conformity. There is no known limit to the patterns which the human personality can acquire although they are built up within the framework of his interaction with the various persons and groups contacted. Normally the child first takes over the patterns of his family. From his play group he acquires other patterns somewhat dissimilar. These may be added to, substituted for, or blended with those characterizing his family. In his later, wider relationships, in order to avoid conspicuousness or censure, he finds it expedient to acquire community patterns which may differ from those of either family or play group. Every succeeding grouping throughout life adds new or slightly different patterns to his facilities for group adjustment. The series must be measurably integrated in his personality. The acquisition of attitudes, patterns, emotional sets, and ideational systems once started, however, is not an entirely haphazard affair, nor is it mechanically determined. The personality tends to organize and systematize its experience at every stage of its development and thus to determine the meaning and value of influences later brought to bear upon it. This organized experience also determines what will be selected for inclusion or what can be integrated if included.

Personality is Orderly and Consistent

Why it is that personality ever tends to harmonize the elements of new experience into the constellation of factors it already possesses is not definitely known, nor is it known why experiences which fit the constellation bring satisfaction while inconsistent ones produce fear, distress, and irksomeness. While this tendency makes for integration of personality, it also makes for conservatism and retards the speed of personality development. This conservatism is somewhat neutralized by human suggestibility. The human animal early discovers that by acting upon the suggestions and following the action patterns of his fellow beings, he can increase his satisfactions and reduce the risks and pains of living. This discovery makes him both suggestible and imitative. It is through society's better understanding and use of these mechanisms that both social control and social progress have been facilitated. No evidence exists that there has been an upturn in the curve of fundamental mentality or that any improvement in the I.Q. of the average human animal has taken place within the past five millenniums. In the absence of practical eugenics, hereditary nature has changed little. The upswing of civilization seems to be due to the growth of vast social resources for redirecting the expansion of human nature and substituting preferred activities for those condemned by experience. Thus, although man is not equipped by nature with patterns for pursuing existence in human society, he inherits an equipment capable of acquiring an unlimited variety of them through experience and contact with many different groups.

Progressive Conditioning

Studies in conditioning of response in animals and human infants have demonstrated that it is an essential step in the learning process. Theoretically, conditioning can be distinguished from learning of which it is usually the accompaniment. When contrasting the processes, conditioning is usually spoken of as extra-organic and learning as mainly intra-organic. As the two are never found operating entirely independently of each other, we use learning as the broader and more generic of the two terms. At a very early age, through the association of taste and vision, the sight of the milk bottle will produce the same salivary reaction as actual ingestion; a further association of the sound of a ringing bell with the sight of the bottle may produce an identical reaction. How completely the substituted stimulus produces the original response depends upon a number of factors including the nervous reaction of the organism, the vividness of the substituted stimulus which identifies it with the original in the mind of the child, and the number of times the procedure is repeated. A part of the conditioning of no small importance is the subtle change which takes place in the nerve routes, emotions and thought patterns accompanying it.

The Process of Learning. This complex process, while not as yet completely understood, is of sufficient practical value to be used in the transmission of culture through the teaching-learning techniques. From the viewpoint of the individual, learning is the only process through which social control can be exercised. This process of learning, operating through the child's long infancy upon his delicate nervous system, makes it possible for him to acquire the culture of the groups with which he is brought into contact. He becomes accustomed to having each group expect certain things of him and of expecting certain things of it. Comparing his activities with those of others, he gets meanings from the responses his actions produce in other members of the group.

Transmission of Culture

Culture. Culture is a general term covering a group's ways, techniques, concepts, interpretations, notions, paraphernalia and material possessions. It is not the society but the society's function as represented in its arrangements, material and non-material. Culture transmission, which is a distinctly human trait, is immensely speeded up by the use of symbols. The speech symbol greatly facilitates conditioning by the group and learning by the child. The use of symbols is not uniquely human. Animals react to symbols as when the bark of a dog attracts other dogs, or the crude vocalization of the anthropoid communicates the emotion of pain, fear or love. These stereotyped symbols, however, seldom pass beyond the communication of emotional states. Animals are unable symbolically to describe objects or situations. They lack the linguistic facilities which make for cumulative culture transmission.

Symbolic Learning. Symbolic learning is the medium through which society exercises control over the individual. Conceptions of size, shape, substance, texture, taste, smell, sound, to mention only a few of the less complex, can be conveyed from one person to another by language with a vividness and reality almost equal to that of experiencing them through the various senses represented. Emotional states and the infinitely more complex, abstract ideas, are likewise conveyed by word symbols.

Learning normally begins in the home through the intimate contact of parent and child. The patterns there acquired are later modified and embellished by contacts with playmates, neighborhood, school, church, and with other local groups. Each group, through its relations with the individual, undertakes to mould his habit patterns so as to fit him for participation in an orderly manner. As he passes to each new group with slightly different requirements he may at first experience a sense of bewilderment. As new group contacts multiply, bewilderment tends to give place to a mild anticipatory pleasure. He may even seek new contacts for the sheer joy of discovering and adjusting to the patterns involved.

Acquiring Social Patterns

We may say that the human animal possesses the appetites, passions, and organic drives of his animal ancestors, but that he is without the instinctive controls which they possess. He has certain broad, general, social capacities but no social patterns, so that above all other creatures, he needs and must have direction. That direction is provided in the many patterns available to him and forced upon him by his society. These group patterns are present due to the fact that his ancestors have built an orderly and measurably consistent system of living. The group habits are the result of the balancing of trial and error over a long period. They are neither innate, instinctive, absolute, nor the result of revelation. The individual is capable of embracing this orderly life but his only guide to it is his experience. His experience comes primarily from his own limited range of action, but he is theoretically capable of taking over all the acquired patterns of the race. Race experience is passed down from one generation to another in the form of culture. Society has acquired considerable skill in initiating each new member into the complexity of its culture. If society can be said to have any object in controlling the individual, it is to help him to assimilate the greatest possible amount of the group's culture in the shortest possible time.

Society is a never-ending, ever-changing stream of tested individual and group experiences. The individual, being what he is, fits into this stream, becomes part of it, conforms to it, and may slightly modify it. For this reason social control is comparatively easy of realization.

Learning the Rules for Living in Society. Orderliness is a primary requisite of human society. There can be no game unless the players observe the rules. It cannot be said that the individual is orderly but that he has the capacity for the acquisition of orderliness. He must learn every rule. He is born with no pattern for effective social functioning. He must not only take over the content of his group's culture, but he must also discover ways to acquire it. The group's culture is orderly but it is not entirely consistent, for its rules and practices often conflict. Not infrequently the precepts it places before its young are quite inconsistent with its own behavior. No educator teaches his students to smoke but many indulge in the practice; students may listen to what the teacher says, but imitate what he does. No child appropriates the Simon-pure culture which his group desires him to have and entirely eschews its undesirable phases. The child cannot or does not follow all the rules. Even when he has reached adulthood, the group still finds it necessary to have a set of elaborate devices and restraints designed to curb his appetites, desires, perversities, his unwillingness to observe the rules and to stay in line. This procedure, however, is subordinate in its effectiveness to the imposition of control through the early learning process. In view of this, it is obvious that the emphasis should be placed on the problem of building personality out of raw and unformed human material through early discipline and guidance, that the individual may be fitted for living as harmoniously as possible with his fellow men.

To take for granted that the child, because of some inherent powers, will naturally acquire the necessary orderliness to fit him into his society, is to fail to understand both the nature of man and of his society. The system of rules, conventions, and requirements which make up the orderliness of human society is artificial, arbitrary, sometimes not altogether defensible. In all societies, it has been, and in ours can only be, maintained by the vigilant and insistent exercise of control.

Resistance to Social Pressures. It is necessary, therefore, to consider the stimuli at the point of their impingement on the individual, and, at the same time, to consider what resistance is set up within the individual as a result of the conditioning of his responses. These seem to be exercised on three levels, depending upon his age and development. The most primary of them operate on the organic, automatic, and reflexive levels and form the earliest behavior patterns. Here the resistance is negligible. The behavior of the child with respect to his parents, the habits of eating, sleeping, excretion, and cuddling fall into this category. As personality develops, the emphasis shifts to an intermediary social level on which suggestion, imitation, inhibition and other forces function and the personality of the individual is more deliberately shaped by the group. The method of the control largely dictates the resistance on this stage. A growing child's acceptance is no longer organic but socio-organic. He may dislike the taste of spinach but, for the sake of the social reward, recognition, or escape from censure (real or imagined) for nonconformity, he acquires the spinach-eating pattern and may come to like it. Later, the control is on the higher and more complex culture level on which the group-accepted patterns, ideations, regulative and restrictive devices and other symbolic techniques are brought to bear upon him. Here the resistance may be stubborn. Persons of maturity are spoken of as being conservative in comparison with youth. When confronted with new patterns, the mature person examines and analyzes them, and questions their fitness for inclusion in the constellation of measurably integrated patterns already a part of his personality. If the new way is not easily assimilated or threatens the consistency of the pattern system already present, he may stubbornly resist the social pressure to accept it.

If both environmental stimuli and original nature were uniform, the problem of fitting the individual into human society would be simple and the reactions of the individual would be predictable. But the environments and heredities, even of identical twins, differ and the differences become marked with the unconscious development of individual likes, dislikes, sentiments, impulses and other by-products of the child's cumulative experience.[1] Nor is the acquisition of the group's culture patterns uniform. There is infinite opportunity for the play of finely shaded choices so that, while the resulting constellation of factors in one individual's experience, theoretically, might be identical with that of another, for practical purposes, it never is.

There is no intention to imply that all choices are mechanically determined to the degree that they can be predicted. Some experiences are forced upon the individual and brook no exercise of choice. Even here, their effect upon one may differ markedly from that upon another. This depends not only on the fund of experience already present, but upon those long recognized, deep-seated hereditary or acquired biological factors like the shape, size and proportions of the features of the head and parts of the body; the functioning of the endocrines or glands of internal secretion; sickness or disease; body chemistry; rapidity and quality of nerve reaction; and a host of other physical qualities which are sometimes lumped together under the term "constitutional factors." Not only does this imponderably complex "constitution" determine the personality effect of experience that has been forced upon one, but it also colors likes and dislikes and thus sets limits to choice of the elements which an individual will deliberately select for inclusion in his personality.

Identification of Individual and Group

The choices of the individual are limited by the group's culture. He can neither choose what is not present, nor is he allowed to elaborate patterns which lie too far beyond the limits of the culture of which he is a part. To do so may jeopardize not only his freedom, but his life, a fact which Galileo discovered when he insisted that the sun stood still and the earth moved. Particularly is this true on the first and second developmental levels. On the third level, the individual has been so accustomed to the group's patterns that his excursions beyond them are seldom more than a projection of certain phases of the existing culture. Inventions of mechanical devices and the many discoveries in the field of science, law and government are found to be projections based upon group culture already accumulated. Even the person who "goes insane" does so in terms of his own culture. For the most part, the individual, in the measure of his knowledge, activity and experience, becomes but the carrier of his group's culture. In this sense, the group is but another part of himself and culturally he has no identity apart from it. As Cooley has pointed out "self and other do not exist as mutually exclusive social facts." [2] The

---

[1] See James Reinhardt, *Social Psychology* (Chicago: J. B. Lippincott Co., 1938), pp. 128-177, for a complete discussion of this point.

[2] Charles H. Cooley, *Human Nature and the Social Order* (New York: Charles Scribner's Sons, 1902), p. 126.

person and the society are part of one complex social whole. When personality is stressed, the individual aspect of society is emphasized. When society is spoken of, we are emphasizing the social aspect. Self and society are twin born and independent ego is an illusion.[3]

In this fact we have a clue to the explanation of the individual's conception of himself, to his standards, conscience, stereotypes, and other attitudes, why it becomes necessary for him to rationalize, why mental conflicts arise, as well as to his feelings of satisfaction and well-being. All of the elements he appropriates from the culture of his group must be resolved into the organized and consistent whole of his personality.

This is not the way the growing child thinks of himself. He has been at pains to distinguish his body from the physical environment. He probably suffered a series of shocks as he discovered that the toes on his feet belonged to him, were movable at his will and were apart from the rest of the world; that he was quite separate from the crib which confined him or the mother who fed him. This early egocentric conception of himself is gradually reversed with the realization that he is a part of the group and that his mind is never fully divorced from the minds of others. It would appear, however, that such a realization is never complete or absolute. Even down to old age, he clings to the shreds of his separateness and gets a thrill out of boasting that he is "not as other men are."

Self As a Reflection of Group Definition. Actually, one's conception of himself is the reflection in his consciousness of how others regard him, how they have defined him, what they conceive his role to be, as these facts are evidenced in the words and actions of all he contacts. Out of his multiple observations comes his general definition of his place, his role and worth in society. The combinations in self-definition arising from interaction with others are infinite, so that probably no two persons have ever had identical conceptions in this particular. Always the individual has his eye upon his group to catch the infinitesimal changes in the attitudes of others toward him and to modify his self-definition accordingly. This consciousness of the reaction of others in his *milieu* seems to increase rather than diminish with age and the attainment of social prominence. Failing complete approval of the living, he may even look for it from the great dead or the unborn of the future. But no one can escape the process as long as he is human. Thus we speak of man as highly suggestible and generally amenable to social control.

Men boast of individual codes, standards of conduct, and moral principles. Properly understood, these are not separate from the group but

---

[3] Charles H. Cooley, *Social Organization* (New York: Charles Scribner's Sons, 1909), p. 267; Ralph Linton, *The Cultural Background of Personality* (New York: D. Appleton-Century, 1945).

rather combinations of elements taken over from the culture and organized into fairly consistent systems. They are usually defended as better than other systems, similarly elaborated, from which they differ. Incidentally, they satisfy the ego and bid for a change of social attitudes which will further individualize the mirrored self.

Diversity of Codes and Standards. Anomalously enough, the more complex and dynamic the civilization, the greater the diversity of codes and personal standards. In isolated societies restrictions and taboos are more imperative than in advanced societies. There is less opportunity for selection, for balancing fine lines of personal discrimination, and thus for individual variation. It is this lack of variation in arrested society that makes it conservative and gives it the appearance of drabness to a highly civilized traveler. The Babemba in northern Rhodesia has one approved way in which to hunt, to fish, to cook, to plant his crop, and indeed to order his life. There is a simple set of tribal laws applying to the murderer, the thief, as well as to the inheritor of rank, cattle, or wives. I have seen Chitamakulu, a Babemba chief, when visiting one of his outlying villages, adjudicate a score of disputes to the complete satisfaction of his subjects within a period of two hours. It was not an arbitrary performance but the application of recognized regulations. Had similar cases been tried in one of our courts, the procedure, because of the many laws and precedents, would have taken many days. A less extreme comparison is to be found if one compares a simple rural with a complex urban society. The rural child is seldom forbidden to play on the road in front of his house. The urban child is restricted in such activities by city ordinances. In cosmopolitan society, there are a larger number of elements from which to draw and the controls, while no less insistent, make allowance for greater variation. When aroused to avenge its standards against one of its members, the punishments its metes out to the recalcitrants are frequently harsher than those in primitive society.

Conscience

Individual codes, standards of conduct and moral principles are unified into a pattern which becomes the criterion of one's behavior, commonly referred to as conscience. Conscience is so compulsive and insistent that it has long been thought of as a God-given standard for the ordering of one's personal relations—a trustworthy, innate, categorical and authoritative guide or criterion of individual conduct. In the light of the newer conception of the self, however, it turns out to be the voice of one's group. It comes, not from the soul of man, but from the selected judgments of his society as voiced by the mirrored self. There is and can be no more uniformity of conscience than of the self. As there are a vast variety of gradations of standards in the group from which to choose and the choices are conditioned by thousands of factors in constitution and experience, the identity of two or more consciences would be highly improbable. Conscience is the organization of selected social taboos rationalized as appropriate for determining one's conduct. The judge has a conscience, but it may be no more logical, defensible or appropriate to his way of life, in view of his experience, than is the conscience of the hardened criminal. The selections of standards for years have been made with differing purposes. Habits of thought and action have become stabilized. They have flowed along divergent grooves. The law-abiding group from which the judge sought recognition and approval differed from the gang which applauded the criminal's behavior. When the judge breaks over his code, i.e. his expectation of himself mirroring the group's expectation of him, he suffers pangs of conscience. In no essential particular do they differ from those which the criminal experiences when he "squeals" on his accomplice or forsakes his confederate in a "tight squeeze." Each is afraid of the real or fancied disfavor of the group to which he belongs.

It is possible for one to develop a conscience which will justify any kind of conduct which better fits him to his group. Indeed, he may have as many consciences as necessary to cover the standards, beliefs or practices of the various groups to which he belongs or to which he desires to belong. When these standards conflict it creates an unhappy state of mind for the individual, so that in straining to maintain the consistency of his mental organization his consciences tend to coalesce, or he may solve his problem by deliberately adopting standards of the group which has greatest appeal to him. The group ordering his conscience may be as small as a family or as large as a nation. One family has a conscience about going to church, another definitely not. Germans under Nazi rule were anti-Semitic, Americans were not. Each group profoundly justifies the conscience which determines its conduct. Conscience then, like the self, is made, not inherited or God-given. It is the result of a process of social molding. Nothing is more highly significant in the exercise of social control as it results from social interaction and is intimately tied up with social values.

By similar devices even the thinking of the individual, which he usually conceives of as essentially his own, is indirectly controlled by the group's culture and activity. The only way in which the individual can know what his society thinks is by what the individuals in it say, write, or do. His awareness that the thinking of others differs from his own causes him to re-examine his thinking in the light of it lest he be rated as ignorant or aberrant and thus not quite belonging. Above all else, he must belong. Nothing can be a greater affront to personality than to be criticized, despised or ridiculed by those whom he respects. Non-conformity is always painful. Sometimes the fear of a ridicule which does not exist, but which he imagines, is enough to modify his thinking. To forestall it, he exchanges his thought with others, always with an eye to its modification in general accordance with the group's standards. Much conviviality and gregariousness are traceable to the fear of ridicule. General but not specific conformity in thinking becomes a habit which carries with it the amenability to control.[4]

Attitudes

Attitude is one of the most distinctive and indispensable concepts in social psychology. An individual's attitudes are so significant in determining the effects of controls brought to bear upon him and so modified by these controls that no treatment would be complete without a brief discussion of them. That they are tempered by the deep bodily sets as well as the hereditary temperamental make-up of the individual is generally conceded. But they are much more than this. Allport defines attitude as a "mental and neural state of readiness, organized through experience, exerting a directive or dynamic influence upon the individual's response to all objects and situations to which it is related."[5] It will be noticed that the state of readiness which determines one's response is shaped by experience. It may result from deliberate thought, participation, recollection, observation, something which has been heard or read, or an incident which seemed at the time of its occurrence to have been trivial and unimportant. Any one or all of these elements, and in any degree or combination, may contribute to the mental or neural state which will determine the individual's response to the new stimulus presented. For this reason it is difficult or impossible for one completely to explain the origins of his attitude on law, race, government, a belief, a personality, or any other situation or object by which he is confronted.

Attitudes Factored. The most which can be said is that any one or combination of four factors may enter into the attitude forming process. First, there may be an accretion of experience from responses of a similar type. The individual may meet with many people who have similar ideas about government, in which case the responses tend to become integrated. Second, the attitude may be set by the observation that it differs from the attitudes of others, or by overt opposition. This gives conciseness and

---

[4] The use of ridicule and similar devices in social control is further discussed in Chapter XIX of this book.

[5] See G. W. Allport, "Attitudes," in *Handbook of Social Psychology*, edited by C. Murchison.

distinction to it. It may, in his eyes, place an individual in a pro or anti class. Third, a vivid or dramatic experience may precipitate an attitude in much the same way that a habit results from a single striking experience rather than from repetition. Some particular act of government may leave its mark upon a person and create the attitude. An attitude created in this way, because of its emotional accompaniment, may appear arbitrary or unreasonable but it is no less difficult to change. Fourth, the attitude may be taken over from parents, playmates, or others, consciously or unconsciously, by imitation. The latter process accounts for children of a Republican parent being Republican or those of a Democratic parent being Democrats. Whatever the composition of attitudes, they show a high degree of similarity, whether they are positive or negative, general or specific, individual or characteristic of a group.

Like muscular habits, attitudes become automatic to such a degree that in the past they have been confused with instincts. The effectiveness of any attempt to control the individual at any stage of his development depends upon how a proposal fits into this mental and neural state of readiness.

The Significance of Stereotypes. Many attitudes carry with them mental images which are more or less vivid mind-pictures of persons, situations, and things with which the individual has had experience. They may even be word images. These are referred to as stereotypes. An object would be only a jumble of visual, auditory, or other uncorrelated sensations to a person if there did not exist in his mind a framework of concepts or stereotypes on the basis of which these sense impressions could be interpreted. These pictures may be clear or vague, reasonable or unreasonable, real or imaginary, tentative or stubbornly entrenched. Any control, to be successful, must, in some measure, take these stereotypes into consideration. They are a part of the individual's attitude combination. Before the control can be mentally acceptable to him it must synchronize with or replace the stereotype. If the stereotype can be utilized without modification the control is easier to affect. The individual's social conformity depends upon the method and nature of the modification. Stereotypes of the propagandist, the atheist, the capitalist, the criminal, or the politician may be stupid and indefensible, but they must, none the less, be reckoned with when the group attempts to change the individual's thinking about them, his attitude toward them, or his behavior in relation to them. Generally recognized methods of accomplishing this purpose and the social means used to this end will be treated later. Our purpose here is to emphasize that they offer resistance to any kind of control. Accumulated experience gives to the mature person stereotypes which can be justified and defended and, for that reason, less easily changed. On the other hand, we speak of the young as plastic and formative because the stereotypes and attitudes are less deeply entrenched.[6]

The Rationalization of Attitudes. The strain toward orderliness in both society and the individual above referred to gives to man a definite urge, reasonably to justify both his attitudes and behavior. The process is designed to demonstrate to others and himself his consistency. His justifications may not be the real reasons; but they are the reasons he uses even though more realistic ones have to be disregarded. This we call rationalization. Only occasionally will one admit that he has resorted to rationalization, as when he says: "My country may she always be right, but right or wrong, my country." Usually he is trapped by the logic of the facts which he is willing to accept after the reasons that do not appeal to him have been excluded. Thus, on the basis of the accepted facts before the bar of his own judgment he is both logical and consistent. Rationalization takes place to a lesser or greater degree in the formation of all attitudes. The criminal, the war-monger, the member of the mob engaged in lynching, the subversive and revolutionary, although condemned by society, find logical reasons for what they contemplate or do.

Elements in experience which cannot be rationalized produce mental conflicts which destroy the illusion of consistency and produce unhappiness. The social controls which are most successful in their operation are exercised with the fullest knowledge of these elements of experience which have their place among the many difficult factors in the complex make-up of the man's personality. The failure of many of the past controls which have carried the fullest social approval has been due, not to their impropriety, but to an unclear understanding of the personality factors of those over whom the control was to be exercised. Hence, there is need of care that control techniques be sufficiently flexible in their application to avoid creating mental conflict and thus defeat the essential purpose of the control. In the last analysis, this is a matter of personal knowledge, judgment and skill, as the control is exercised not by an institution, a group or a society, but by one individual upon another. The effectiveness of the control frequently rests not upon the reasonableness or the expediency of conforming, but upon the personal relationship.

Summary

Social control, whatever its source, is ultimately the action of one personality upon another, and an understanding of social control neces-

---

[6] For further treatment of stereotypes in social control see Chapters XXIII and XXIV.

sitates knowledge of the processes and elements which enter into personality formation. Human capacities for acquiring personality are practically unlimited, but only in social experience do these capacities develop into specific adjustment patterns. The strain toward orderliness, both in society and the individual, tends to bring about a high degree of consistency in reactions to stimuli. The culture of the group sets limits to what attitudes and habits may be acquired by members, although within any culture there is a wide variety of possible combinations of elements that may enter into personality, and therefore variety in the resulting personalities.

Important in the consideration of social control is the fact that individuals define their status and roles in the light of the judgment of others. The universal desire for approval of one's fellows is powerful in bringing about conformity to generally accepted standards.

In mature social members, tendencies to cling to stereotypes and to justify or rationalize conduct must be considered in efforts to control them, or these may prove insuperable obstacles.

QUESTIONS

1. What fallacies underlie popular thinking about control?
2. What is the relationship between institutions and the individual?
3. What factor will determine the extent of one's social conformity?
4. From where does man draw his patterns for pursuing existence in human society?
5. Distinguish between learning and conditioning.
6. What is the only process through which social control can be exercised from the individual viewpoint?
7. What is culture?
8. Distinguish between culture and society.
9. Where and in what manner does the learning process begin?
10. What is society's object in controlling the individual?
11. What is a primary requisite of human society?
12. Why is it wrong to assume that the child will naturally acquire the necessary orderliness to fit into his society?
13. What are the three developmental levels?
14. Define conscience.
15. What is the ultimate source of social control?

SUGGESTED TOPICS FOR TERM PAPERS AND FURTHER RESEARCH

1. Symbolic learning.
2. Desire for approval and social control.
3. Rationalization in effective social control.
4. The strain toward orderliness.
5. Stereotyping and social control.
6. Conscience in relation to social control.

7. Basis of the progressive learning.
8. Conditioning of personality.
9. Groups characterized by a consciousness of kind.

BIBLIOGRAPHY
Books

Franz Alexander, *Our Age of Unreason* (New York: J. B. Lippincott Co., 1942). A study of irrational forces in social life.

John E. Anderson, *The Psychology of Development and Personal Adjustment* (New York: Henry Holt and Co., 1949).

Julian M. Blackburn, *Psychology and the Social Pattern* (New York: Oxford University Press, 1945). A good general analysis.

Herbert Bloch, *Disorganization, Personal and Social* (New York: Alfred A. Knopf, 1952). One of the best recent studies in the problems of social psychology.

James H. S. Bossard, *The Sociology of Child Development* (New York: Harper and Brothers, 1954). A pioneer work in this field.

Conference of Educational Problems of Special Culture Groups (New York: Columbia University Press, 1949). A survey of some of the special areas which are problematic.

Lloyd A. Cook and Elaine Cook, *A Sociological Approach to Education* (New York: McGraw-Hill Book Co., 1950). One of the best introductions to the field of educational sociology.

Walter Coutu, *Emergent Human Nature* (New York: Alfred A. Knopf, 1949). A rather technical but a good study.

Ruth Cunningham and associates, *Understanding Group Behavior of Boys* (New York: Bureau of Publications, Teachers College, Columbia University, 1951). A good survey of conditioning of children studies from all significant angles.

Richard Dewey, *Human Nature and Conduct* (New York: The Macmillan Co., 1951). Studies cultural factors in determining societal organization.

Seba Eldridge and associates, *Fundamentals of Sociology* (New York: Thomas Y. Crowell Co., 1950), Chapter 25. A specialized study of the family as a unit.

Anna Freud and Dorothy G. Burlingham, *War and Children* (London: Medical War Books, 1943). Describes in detail, with some thoroughgoing case histories, the institutional experience of bombed-out children; this experience of British children in the war affords many insights into the child's concepton of the adult world.

Anna Freud and Dorothy G. Burlingham, *Infants Without Families* (New York: International University Press, 1944). "The case for and against residential nurseries." The general conclusion is that a "normal" home life is indisputably superior in preparing children for later-life adjustment than the best institution.

Arnold L. Gesell and C. S. Amatruda, *The Embryology of Behavior* (New York: Harper and Brothers, 1945). An analysis of behavior patterns as they originate in the fetus and as they become more distinct and definite depending on their stage of growth at the time of birth in later infancy.

Marshall Greco, *Group Life* (New York: Philosophical Library, 1950). The causes of harmony and disunity in human associations.

Joyce Hertzler, *Social Institutions* (Lincoln, Neb.: University of Nebraska Press, 1946). One of the best systematized studies of the rise and operation of the social institutions.

Eric Hoffer, *The True Believer* (New York: Harper and Brothers, 1951). Concerning the nature of mass movements.

George Caspar Homans, *The Human Group* (New York: Harcourt, Brace and Co., 1950). A good study of the factors affecting human group behavior.

Abram Kardiner and others, *Psychological Frontiers of Society* (New York: Columbia University Press, 1945). Central thesis: because of a common core of child-hood experience all persons in a given culture will share a "basic character structure." An ambitious undertaking, involving a consideration of several socie-ties, attempting to explain the "projective systems" (religious and other ideologies and structures) as a reflection of the "basic character structure." The rub, as Kar-diner admits, is exactly what is to be included within the key-concept.

David Krech, *Theory and Problems of Social Psychology* (New York: McGraw-Hill Book Co., 1948). A serious analysis of the field.

Harold D. Lasswell, Daniel Lerner, and Ithiel de Sola Pool, *The Comparative Study of Symbols* (Stanford, Calif.: Stanford University Press, 1952). The best recent systematized study of the power of differing means of social control on society.

David M. Levy, *Maternal Overprotection* (New York: Columbia University Press, 1943). An intensive analysis of case-history material depicting the effects on per-sonality of mother and child of complete absorption of the child. A valuable monograph which lacks any relevant sociological explanation of the phenomenon.

Alfred Lindesmith, *Social Psychology* (New York: Dryden Press, 1949). A good text on the study of this new field.

Periodicals

George H. Armbruster, "An Analysis of Ideologies in the Contest of Discussion," *American Journal of Sociology*, L (1944), pp. 123-133.

D. Barclay, "Independent Members of the Group," *New York Times Magazine* (March 29, 1953), p. 50.

Gregory Bateson, "The Frustration-Aggression Hypothesis and Culture," *Psycholog-ical Review*, XL (1941), pp. 350-355.

Ernest Beaglehole, "Character Structure," *Psychiatry*, VII (1944), pp. 145-162.

Ruth Benedict, "Continuities and Discontinuities in Cultural Conditioning," *Psy-chiatry*, I (1938), pp. 161-167.

J. Bernard, "Normative Collective Behavior: A Classification of Societal Norms," *American Journal of Sociology*, XXVII (1941), pp. 24-38.

Luther S. Cressman, "Ritual the Conserver," *American Journal of Sociology*, XXXV (1930), pp. 564-572.

Kingsley Davis, "Sociology of Parent-Youth Conflict," *American Sociological Review*, V (1940), pp. 523-535.

Robert M. Dinkel, "Attitudes of Children Toward Supporting Aged Parents," *American Sociology Review*, IX (1944), pp. 370-379.

Arnold W. Green, "The Social Situation in Personality Theory," *ibid.*, VII (1942), pp. 388-393.

Everett C. Hughes, "Institutional Office and the Person," *American Journal of Sociology* XLIII (1937), pp. 404-413.

Gustav Icheiser, "Real, Pseudo, and Sham Qualities of Personality: An Attempt at a New Classification," *Character and Personality*, IX (1941), pp. 218-226.

C. Kluckholn and O. H. Mower, "Culture and Personality: A Conceptual Scheme," *American Anthropology*, XLVI (1945), pp. 1-29.

Harold D. Lasswell, "Psychological Policy Research and Total Strategy," *Public Opinion Quarterly*, IV (Winter, 1952-53), pp. 491-500.

Ernest G. Lion, *et al.*, "Strabismus and Children's Personality Reactions," *American Journal of Orthopsychiatry*, XIII (1942), pp. 121-124.

Robert K. Merton, "Role of the Intellectual in Public Bureaucracy," *Social Forces*, XXIII (1945), pp. 405-415; "Bureaucratic Structure and Personality," *ibid.*, XVIII (1940), pp. 560-568.

M. Sanai, "Relation Between Social Attitudes and Characteristics of Personality," *Journal of Social Psychology*, XXXVI (August, 1952), pp. 3-13.

Mapheus Smith, "Group Centered Behavior," *Journal of Social Psychology*, XXXVIII (May, 1953), pp. 237-248.

M. L. Story, "Decline of Social Consciousness," *School and Society*, Vol. 77 (April, 1953), pp. 259-261.

Clara Thompson, "The Role of Women in this Culture," *Psychiatry*, IV (1941), pp. 1-8.

Jacob Tuckman and Irving Lorge, "Attitudes Toward Old People," *Journal of Social Psychology*, XXXVII (May, 1953), pp. 249-260.

Louis Wirth, "Ideological Aspects of Social Disorganization," *American Sociological Review*, V (1940), pp. 472-482.

CHAPTER IV

The Fields of Behavior

Most of the preceding chapters have had to do with the individual equipment of man as a behaving and thinking animal, and the kinds of social stimuli to which he reacts. For the study of social control it is necessary, as well, to understand that human behavior is never simply a matter of a reacting mechanism and a given set of stimuli. Behavior always takes place in situations, and a function of society is to give meaning to whole sets of circumstances so that behavior may be interpreted as good or bad, expedient or inexpedient, normal or eccentric.[1] Precisely the same reaction to apparently the same stimuli may be considered, under one set of circumstances, good and fitting, and under other circumstances, bad or out of place. A pleasing bit of oratory may stimulate a crowd to wild cheering in a political convention hall, but loud applause of the same words spoken in the same manner would be quite inappropriate during church services. A policeman who went down the street under normal circumstances, and shot every frolicking dog he saw would be considered cruel and even vicious; but during a serious epidemic of rabies the same behavior on the same street might be considered necessary and wise.

Variability of Cultural Situations. The study of various culture groups shows that each has its own ways of defining situations and assigning to them appropriate ways of acting. For an American to offer to kiss the feet of a woman he had just met would seem ridiculous, but for a Spanish gentleman to make the same offer under the same circumstances is considered quite appropriate. In many primitive cultures an injury to one's relatives must be personally avenged, while in our custom the proper appeal is to the courts for legal redress. In fact a large part of the training of every child in any culture group consists of teaching him to make fine distinctions between social situations and to alter his behavior patterns

[1] The term situation, as used in this chapter follows E. B. Reuter: "A concept incorporating the totality of inner and outer worlds in which behavior occurs. The configuration of roles of the persons in and attitudes toward the conditions, and the cultural definitions that influence the manner in which experience is received." *Handbook of Sociology* (New York: The Dryden Press, 1941), p. 154. See also "Definition of the Situation," *ibid.*, p. 110.

accordingly. It is wrong to lie to the teacher about one's unprepared lessons; but it is only a "white lie," and therefore quite appropriate, to tell a hostess you have had a "nice time" even though that is not the case. Those who have witnessed criminal trials realize the importance of what are called "mitigating circumstances" when persons are accused of misdeeds, and most of the evidence in such trials describes, not what the accused did, but under what social circumstances the deed was performed.

Very slight alterations in situations may be quite important in the judgment of conduct. A difference of a few hours in the time of day, a few feet in distance, a few years in the age of persons, a few words in a conversation may be sufficient greatly to alter social significance, and therefore the type of behavior most appropriate. To wear formal dress to a supper beginning at six is quite different from the same attire for dinner beginning at eight. The weary worker home at the end of the day may remove his shoes in his own parlor and relax to read his newspaper; but in most communities to do so in another person's home would be looked upon with disapproval. A group of friends may banter each other mercilessly as long as the tone is uniformly one of good fun, but let one member become serious and utter an insulting remark, and the whole situation becomes tense.

These considerations are important for social control and enter into every practical problem in the field. One cannot change the whole habit equipment and thinking process of a group overnight so that any controls by the group over its members must be largely in terms of existing schemes of situational analysis.[2] It was relatively easy to convince the natives of the tropical islands of the South Pacific that they should wear clothes, but to get them to wear them on the right places at the appropriate times took a full generation of education. Civilians in military training can readily be taught to salute army officers, but the whole etiquette involving just what respect to show toward whom and under what circumstances in military life calls for long training and practice.

Classification of Behavior Situations

The conduct of members of any group may be classified according to the influences and preconditioning which usually enter into situations in which it takes place. Such a classification can help considerably in clarifying problems of social control and in preventing errors in analysis and practice.

Habits. Much behavior is a matter of unthinking habit when the situa-

---

[2] For discussion of the obstacles to change in habits of action and thought, see William F. Ogburn and Meyer F. Nimkoff, *Sociology* (Boston: Houghton Mifflin Co., 1940), pp. 833-840.

tions which induce it are frequently recurring experiences. Three meals a day, every day, over many years bring about certain eating habits which are fairly uniform for our culture. Unless one is among strangers or the situation is a very unfamiliar one, we go about the business of eating with our minds on other things than the mechanics of lifting food to our mouths, chewing, and swallowing. All these have to be learned to be done in a socially acceptable manner but, in time, they become so thoroughly a matter of habit that we can perform them quite satisfactorily while reading a newspaper, carrying on a conversation, or otherwise having our attention focused on matters other than our routine acts.

Alternative Choices. A large part of our behavior, on the other hand, calls for some attention from us, involving alternatives among various possible ways of reacting. If a man enters a store to purchase a necktie he must think about various patterns, the scale of prices, whether to charge the article or pay cash for it, and whether to heed the salesman's appeal that he also buy a pair of socks. A number of choices are involved in this simple transaction, and blind habit is not, for most of us, sufficient to carry it through to a satisfactory conclusion. Thus there are clearly two types of human behavior with situational implications. One may be called "automatic" since it takes place without any specific thought process to direct it. The other involves necessary choice and therefore a degree of awareness of what one is doing.

Conscious behavior may be subdivided into that in which there is a clear-cut guide in social morality as to the decisions which are most fitting, and that in which no such guides exist or apply. Whenever, under the necessity of making a decision, one realizes that one course is clearly "right" while alternatives are clearly "wrong"; whenever what is "good" and what is "bad" are obvious, behavior problems are relatively simple. But there are also many situations in which there are no morals to guide one's decision. All depends upon the individual's notion of expediency and his weighing of probable alternative results from his act. The man choosing a necktie finds himself in such a position, for usually it is no more "right," in a moral sense, to select a Scotch plaid than it is to choose a gunpowder blue. Yet the choice must be made.

Institutional Behavior. For purposes of arriving at a simple classificatory scheme, the conduct which requires conscious choice, but where there are clear-cut guides as to what the choice should be, may be called "institutional" behavior. This name is appropriate, from a sociological point of view, because the appraisal of right and wrong is a function of institutions, each type of institution having its own scale of values and its own rules of appropriate conduct and thought. Many moral guides come from religious institutions and apply within activities and situations which have religious significance. Others come from educational institutions and apply within activities and situations which have educational significance. There is no moral guide, in the religious sense, to govern where a comma should be placed or omitted in a literary theme, but there is, nevertheless, a "right" and a "wrong" way to place commas. Business and trade institutions have their standards of right and wrong, appropriate to purely business and trade situations, and often unsuited for other kinds of situations. It is perfectly right, in the business code, to sell a customer a little more than he can afford to buy, and usually wrong not to attempt to do so. But the same rule, except by the loosest of analogies, could not apply in other fields of activity. Thus, where clear standards are set up to guide decisions, choice is institutionally determined in so far as it conforms to those standards; and it invokes institutional disapprovals and penalties when it diverges from prevailing standards.[3]

"Doubtful" Behavior. Activity in situations where there are no guides in terms of good and bad or right and wrong may well be called "doubtful" behavior. It is the least predictable, and judgment passed upon it is always a "matter of opinion" on which members of the same group may disagree. There are endless arguments among automobile fanciers about the wisdom of choosing one make of car or another, a sport model or a conservative sedan, etc., but one does not condemn a neighbor or an associate as immoral or unethical if he chooses to disagree on such matters.[4]

The Fields of Behavior

Activities with consideration of the types of situation in which they occur are probably most conveniently classified as different fields of behavior. Three concentric circles, as in the diagram, are a handy device for presenting the scheme, with the area inside the innermost circle, the core of mature human activities, representing automatic behavior; the area within the second circle, the field of institutional behavior, and that within the outer circle as the field of doubtful behavior. Much of the normal conduct of those whom we observe can be quite readily ascribed to one of these three fields and problems of control become clearer when this has been done.

Habit Breaking and Substitution. If actions are so clearly a matter of unthinking habit as to fall in the field of automatic behavior, then to

---

[3] For a realistic analysis of American morality, pertinent to this problem, see J. H. Tufts, *America's Social Morality* (New York: Henry Holt and Co., 1933).

[4] Ellsworth Faris makes a somewhat similar classification of behavior situations, recognizing that some behavior is "automatic" and some "reflective," but he does not break his reflective behavior down into "institutional" and "doubtful" behavior. *The Nature of Human Nature* (New York: McGraw-Hill Book Co., 1937), pp. 146 ff.

alter them requires "breaking" habits, and, perhaps, establishing new habits to take their place. The habitual smoker would be an example. A little observation will show that, without stopping to think, he reaches into his pocket for a cigarette, places it in his mouth, and lights it. Only if his attention is called to what he is doing does he seem to be aware of it. Many smokers have tried to break the smoking habit and find they must go through a period when they "catch" themselves in the preliminary movements to which they have been habituated before they realize what they are doing. While the habit itself may call for no mental effort, the breaking of it may be extremely difficult and call for the utmost concentration and "will power."

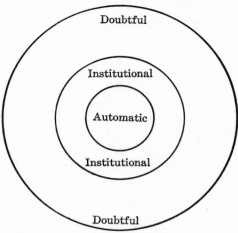

The Fields of Human Behavior

Habit breaking and habit substitution devices will not serve, however, as direct approaches in the field of moral judgments. If a person is convinced, in terms of some institutional values, that what he is doing is clearly "right," then his behavior can only be controlled by convincing him that his judgment of right and wrong is erroneous; either that he has misinterpreted the factors in the situation, or that he has applied inappropriate institutional guides. A prisoner may feel that it is right, in terms of standards of loyalty, to refuse to give information that would involve his associates. This is not unthinking habit. It involves a conscious choice and the application of standards. Unless he can be convinced that his standard is inapplicable he may be a very difficult problem of social control, as any police officer can testify.

Multiplicity of Social Control Agencies. It is in the field of doubtful behavior that the problems of social control are most varied, but where most social control agencies operate. Salesmanship, advertising, journalism, most law, and a large part of education which is not chiefly "character-building" come into play here.[5] We, in our culture, are bombarded day and night, on the street, in the office or home, in every store and streetcar we enter, with appeals in this field. The approaches are multitudinous and bewildering. We are swept this way and that, pleaded with, lorded over, argued with "man-to-man," as the group or some segment of it urges us to buy the soap which flatters the complexion, refrain from using public drinking cups, or to support a particular candidate. Where the course of action is doubtful to begin with the chance of channelizing it in desired directions is most inviting. It is easier to control the man without contrary convictions and habits than it is one who already is "set" against our proposition.

To further clarify the meaning of fields of behavior let us follow an imaginary John Doe through a few simple and characteristic situations. Situation 1: he emerges from an office building at noon reading a newspaper and, without appearing to observe where he is going, he enters his acustomed lunch room. Inside, without hesitation, still reading his paper, he seats himself at his usual booth to await service. Thus far his conduct may be classed as automatic. He has simply not been aware of what he was doing beyond reading his newspaper, and he has made no conscious decisions relating to his immediate actions. Every day at noon, for years, he has done the same thing.

He puts down his newspaper and finds, lying on the table, a few coins. Thus we come to situation No. 2. He is now aware of surrounding circumstances. He is equipped with no unthinking habit for dealing with coins on one's table in a restaurant. Being a business man he is accustomed to picking up coins from a counter and putting them in a cash register. There may be a slight muscular movement as he makes the barely perceptible beginning toward reaching for the coins. But he is also making a decision based upon a clear-cut guide in morality. *It is wrong to take the money*. It is a tip from a previous customer meant for the waitress. It must be left untouched where it is. The decision is made with reference to obvious institutional values.

The waitress arrives, picks up the coins, smiles, and places a menu before our John Doe. Again the circumstances have changed. A new choice must be made, but this time without clear-cut moral guides. One cannot say, in a moral sense, it is right to choose roast beef with mashed potatoes and wrong to select a plate of cold meats. This is situation No. 3, and clearly it is one in the field of doubtful behavior. A well-placed and carefully illustrated sign on the wall saying, "Try our roast

---

[5] See L. L. Bernard, *Social Control in Its Sociological Aspects* (New York: The Macmillan Co., 1939), chapters XIX-XXII.

beef—special today," may decide the issue as Mr. Doe rests his eyes from the menu and permits them to roam about the room while he ponders his problem.

How We Get That Way

In the illustration just given it would be folly to say that Mr. Doe was born with all the equipment needed for walking "absent mindedly" from his office to his usual table in the lunch room, for deciding not to take the waitress's tip, or to choose between roast beef and the other tempting offerings of the menu. Yet little had been left to chance. He had been trained since early childhood to distinguish between fields of behavior by their situational elements, and to govern himself in terms of such distinctions. He had formed habits of muscular control which enabled him to walk and read, a feeling for direction and distance, and other habits, all as a result of careful training and long practice. Most of these habits are quite similar to those of others of his group, and they are used to much the same purposes.[6] Their appropriateness can hardly be questioned by one familiar with his culture group and its ways.

The Problem of Choices. From earliest childhood, one has been taught certain rules about honesty, and especially in regard to the money of others. One is not born knowing that money taken in over the counter for goods is quite properly one's own, while that found on a restaurant table is not. This calls for an ability to analyze situations and to apply to them notions of good and bad, as socially prescribed. Such abilities are just as important to Mr. Doe's welfare, or yours and mine, as the basic habits of muscular control. One cannot stop to consider all the possible consequences of activities which involve moral values. To consider that the waitress might buy gin with the coins she received for a tip, and therefore would be better off, as would society, if she were deprived of them has no bearing whatever on the problem which confronted Mr. Doe. Things are simply right or wrong in the field of institutional behavior, and that is all there is to it.

Mr. Doe also had to be equipped to wrestle with the problem of the menu, but neither habit nor moral guidance would do in this case. Here he had to consider the probabilities—the taste of the food, the effect on his digestion, the length of time until his next meal, what he had had for luncheon the day before, and other things. In a highly complex civilization such decisions in the field of doubtful behavior call for a large fund of many types of information, and all of our lives we are being educated to choose among alternatives where expediency and probable consequences are our principal guides.

---

[6] See Richard T. LaPiere and Paul Farnsworth, *Social Psychology* (New York: McGraw-Hill Book Co., 1936), p. 58.

Complicating Factors

Predictions of Behavior. From the point of view of social control the scheme of types of behavior, as presented so far, is simple and offers few difficulties. The value of the classification lies in the extent to which it permits prediction of individual and group behavior in given situations, according to whether such situations are likely to induce habit reactions, institutionally controlled decisions, or choices based upon the weighing of probable concrete consequences. Thus it can be predicted quite accurately for any large group that the noon hour is most likely to be given over to luncheon, and even what the foods most called for and consumed will be, knowing that time and food habits are quite general and uniform and operate with great regularity under ordinary circumstances. It can also be predicted that in time of national crisis the great majority of people will make decisions with reference to the values of patriotism. All such predictions depend mainly upon a knowledge of institutional controls; but in the field of doubtful behavior one must know the facts or supposed facts available to a people and their bearing upon their immediate futures in order to predict, even approximately, what course large numbers of people will choose.

Complicating Factors. Actually, however, there are complicating factors which often enter and make the classification of behavior into fields more difficult. These complicating factors are mainly of three kinds: lack of entire unity in any culture, so that there is an overlapping of the three fields;[7] differences in the training of individuals and groups to analyze and respond to various type situations;[8] and changes which take place through time in the ways in which groups and their members define situations.[9]

Much of the conduct characteristic of our group is never strictly in the field of habit, conscious moral choice, or doubtful behavior. Even the individual analyzing his own behavior may not be sure whether a choice was actually involved, and if so, whether it was a moral choice, principally, or one of expediency.[10] Many sequences of acts involve all three of the fields of behavior, so that the utmost care is necessary in

---

[7] The concept of "rationalization" as used by the social psychologists emphasizes the extreme complexity of the problem. What is purely habitual may be justified to oneself and others as of "moral" import, or expedient. What is purely expedient may be justified as moral, etc.

[8] See E. T. Hiller, *Principles of Sociology* (New York: Harper and Bros., 1933), chapter XXIX.

[9] William F. Ogburn and Meyer F. Nimkoff, *Sociology* (Boston: Houghton Mifflin Co., 1940), chapters XXIV-XXVI.

[10] Here, again, rationalization enters in to confuse the issue.

attempting to break down such sequences into component parts and to classify the parts.

A simple problem may illustrate such complexities. A woman enters a familiar grocery and from force of habit, and quite "absent-mindedly" goes from shelf to shelf in various parts of the store. If one were to stop her in this routine and ask her where to find the salt she would hesistate for a moment to consider, even though she had just walked to the shelf which contained the salt and selected a package. She is aware that her grocery budget for the month is running low, and institutional guides come to bear on her in her buying. She must select less expensive items because that is right under the circumstances. She is, at the same time, planning a menu for the next few meals, calculating in terms of recent meals, of the likes and dislikes of her family, and of left-overs now in her refrigerator, calculations which require considerations of expediency and probable consequences of one kind or another. In the simple acts involved in buying her groceries she is behaving in all three fields, and their precise separation would call for very close scrutiny and analysis. Yet, presumably, with enough care and patience, her behavior could be broken down into its component parts to permit of the exercise of fairly effective controls, as experts in marketing and advertising know.

In such a case it would be a valuable aid to analysis to know whether the shopper was a woman of a particular socio-economic class, whether she was shopping in a rather exclusive grocery catering to "high class" clientele; whether the woman was a Chinese in a Chinese shop; whether she was a middle-aged housewife, rather "set in her ways," a young bride, or a girl in her teens casting wistful glances at the candy counter. Each component group in our population has its own bases for acting in given situations, and gives somewhat different weight to the habitual, moral, and other factors. Different culture groups, socio-economic or occupational levels, the sexes, and various age-groups, all have different degrees and kinds of preparation for recurring sets of circumstances.[11] Even within each sub-group there are individual differences, since the training for maturity is never precisely the same for any two individuals and the circumstances governing any two cases necessarily differ somewhat.[12]

The third type of complexity arises from the changes which are always taking place through time in the tastes, moral codes and habitual equipment of peoples. Today the woman shopping for groceries would probably arrive in an automobile, select her own groceries from open shelves, and have "modern" ideas of dietary and budgetary limits, in contrast with the shopper of a few generations ago who would arrive at

---

[11] See E. T. Hiller, *op. cit.*, chapters XXXI-XXXIII.
[12] *Ibid.*, chapters XXXV-XXXVI.

the store in a carriage, simply tell the grocer what she desired, and have the ideas appropriate to her time. It was once right to persecute witches, and to have slaves to operate one's household. It was expedient for the entire family to wear long woolen underwear and bathe only on Saturday nights. Such notions, whether right and wrong, or in consideration of probable concrete consequences, change; and often, as in the case of styles in women's hats, they may change rapidly.

When these complexities are brought to mind the task of analyzing and classifying behavior according to fields appears an almost impossible undertaking; yet, except for the perfectionist, it is quite practicable and commonplace, even though a practice of which we are not usually aware. All of us in attempting to exercise control over the activities of others act in reference to such a scheme. Think of a parent attempting to control the behavior of a child. There is the necessity for breaking habits, say, of thumb sucking or speaking at the table when the mouth is filled. These are readily and easily classified as habits and are so treated. Appeals to morals and expediency may be made but they are ineffective. The only solution is to break the habits. Other behavior, such as occasionally telling lies or taking food from the refrigerator without permission may clearly fall in the field of right and wrong behavior, and may best be controlled by appeals to conscience. Still other alternatives in behavior, as wearing rubbers when it is damp, or brushing teeth, may call for appeals in terms of probable concrete consequences.

If one analyzes social controls in the worlds of economic and political activities one will find that those who have the responsibility of controlling others use the system suggested in this chapter constantly, whether they use it well or poorly. Those who are the best leaders and disciplinarians are those who most shrewdly classify behavior, and are most adept in using controls consistent with such classification. The bungling leader is the one who makes moral appeals when dealing with activities in the fields of doubtful or habitual behavior, or who makes practical appeals in the matters of right and wrong.[13]

The question, then, is not whether such a scheme of classification and analysis *can* be useful, for it is in use all around us every day. It is, rather, a question, for the student of social control, of systematic rather than unsystematic application of the scheme, and of knowing what one is about rather then trusting to intuitive processes.

Applications in Social Control

The classification of human behavior by fields is of value to the understanding and exercise of social controls to the extent that it can be related

---

[13] See LaPiere and Farnsworth, *op. cit.*, pp. 307-481.

directly to the problems of social control. In general it might be said that where there is an apparent need for exercising controls, what must be done is to transfer the conduct in question from one field to another. Where it is desirable to control the habits of the individual or a group of individuals, the aim must be to transfer them to the fields of awareness and conscious choice, where appeals to standards of right and wrong, or to expediency, may operate. The process, however, involves two fundamental steps, not one. The first step is to make the subject aware of what he is doing. In the case of the child who habitually sucks his thumb a rag wrapped about the thumb may serve to do this. Only then will the child stop to think about what he is doing. In the case of the housewife who habitually goes to a particular shelf at the grocery for salt, some alteration must be made in the arrangement of things to call her attention to the fact that she is now purchasing salt. Then an appeal may be made to change her buying habits.

Institutional Morality. If the behavior to be controlled lies in the field of institutional morality, the objective must be to remove it to the field of unthinking habit, or to the doubtful field. As long as the person to be controlled knows that what he is doing is right, there is little chance that he will change. The man who has always attended church on Sunday morning because it is right may be told by someone of sufficient prestige, say his family physician, that his health requires him to spend his Sundays in the open, at the golf course or taking long drives into the country. If he can be so persuaded, the method of employing his Sunday morning becomes, not a moral issue, primarily, but one of expediency and probable concrete consequences. If the woman who has never smoked because it is not right for women to smoke, can be induced, in an unguarded moment now and then, to smoke a cigarette despite her conscience, it is possible that smoking may become an unthinking habit. Cigarette manufacturers more than doubled their market by applying this principle.

In the case of behavior lying in the doubtful field, the first problem of those desiring to control it is to remove it to the institutionally controlled field, or to that of unthinking habit. Most producers of highly competitive commodities have as their goal the removal of the purchase of their commodities from the doubtful field to the automatic field. Their appeal is to "get the habit of calling for so-and-so flour," instead of stopping each time a flour purchase is to be made to decide which brand to buy. Such a change from the doubtful field can often be achieved, with sufficient effort, because stopping to think through every little problem of behavior is an irksome task, and often involves embarrassment due to hesitation at inconvenient times. There are few things so annoying as having to decide, in a crowded and busy drug store, among twenty brands of shaving cream on the basis of known or probable actual merits. How much simpler and more comfortable to call for the same old brand through force of habit!

Religious and political leaders, in their exhortations, usually try to transfer decisions from the doubtful field to that of "good" and "bad" considerations. Voters who go to the polls to decide between two candidates on the basis of all the knowable facts about them, and all the probable consequences of their election, are unpredictable voters, and politicians like to count their votes in advance. How much less complicated it is both for the voter and the politician if the voter is simply deciding between the fellow who is right and the fellow who is wrong. Undoubtedly most elections are decided on moral issues rather than on the basis of a myriad of complicated facts and probable consequences which enter into them. The minister, in preaching to his congregation, attempts usually to reduce complicated and doubtful issues to clear-cut statements of good and bad. The notion that it is good to give generously to the church and bad not to will bring fuller collection plates than the reading of long and involved financial statements, and the listing of possible alternatives in terms of consequences of putting one's money elsewhere.

Summary

The application of the classification of human behavior here suggested to specific problems of social control is seldom simple. Just as given sequences of activities involve habits, moral considerations, and decisions based upon expediency, effective control in fairly complicated situations must recognize the need for several types of devices in a given situation. The politician must recognize the element of habit and pre-existing moral notions in the group to which he appeals, as well as the doubtful elements. The appeals and techniques used must anticipate the various elements involved. Devices of control can never be fitted exactly and precisely to a given situation; at best they are approximations and contain elements, in every case, of trial and error. Yet leaders who most effectively control the conduct of others are those who most shrewdly fit their appeals and methods to well-analyzed situations, and in order to do this they are best equipped if they know what they are about. To maintain leadership they must make allowances for differences among subgroups and individuals to whom they address their appeals. They must be keenly aware of time changes taking place in the habits, institutional values, and notions of expediency in the group. It is because of the very complexity of their problems, whether as parents guiding the training of a child, or as national leaders attempting to win the support of millions of voters, that a realistic and yet workable scheme of classifying fields of behavior is important.

QUESTIONS

1. Define situation according to Reuter.
2. In what terms may control be exerted over a group?
3. How may the conduct of the members of a group be classified?
4. What types of human behavior exist with situational implications?
5. Explain institutional behavior from a sociological point of view.
6. What are the fields of behavior?
7. Why is it difficult to break habits?
8. Will habit breaking or substitution methods serve in the field of moral judgments? Why?
9. How can one be convinced that his moral convictions are erroneous?
10. In the field of doubtful behavior, what facts must one have access to in order to predict the actions of large numbers of people?
11. How is the value of a classification of behavior determined?
12. Explain the concept of rationalization according to the social psychologist.
13. What factors serve to complicate the classification of fields of behavior?
14. What is the basic question involved in considering a scheme of classification?
15. How may the habits of an individual be controlled?
16. In transferring habits to the field of awareness, what steps must be taken?
17. How may behavior in the field of institutional morality be controlled?
18. How may behavior in the doubtful field be controlled?
19. Would there be more doubtful behavior in a highly civilized group or a primitive group? Explain.
20. Distinguish between expediency and morality.

SUGGESTED TOPICS FOR TERM PAPERS AND FURTHER RESEARCH

1. Social control and the variability of cultural situations.
2. The role of habit in social control.
3. Institutional behavior in social control.
4. Proper methods of classification of behavior.
5. Methods of habit breaking and substitution.
6. Prediction of behavior.
7. Morality and social control.
8. The problem of mental conflicts in social control.
9. The use of moral issues in political campaigns.
10. The control of behavior by a religious appeal.

BIBLIOGRAPHY

Books

Harry E. Barnes, *Society in Transition* (New York: Prentice-Hall, 1936 and 1952). How "culture lag" influences American life.
Jessie Bernard, *American Community Behavior* (New York: The Dryden Press,

1949). A most suggestive analysis of the American areas of behavior in terms of conflicts.

Herbert Bloch, *Disorganization, Personality and Social* (New York: Alfred A. Knopf, 1952). Establishes a theory of personal and social disorganization and indicates how such a theory may be applied to the range of social problems confronting us.

C. Buehler, *The First Year of Life* (New York: John Day, 1930). The process of socialization from the genetic approach.

Lenoas Burlingame, *Heredity and Social Problems* (New York: McGraw-Hill Book Co., 1951). How much a part the actual factors of heredity do play in social action.

Stuart Chase, *The Proper Study of Mankind* (New York: Harper and Brothers, 1948). A systematized survey of man based on association of all factors of social importance.

Amos M. Hawley, *Human Ecology* (New York: The Ronald Press, 1950). A theory of community structure.

Rudolf Heberle, *Social Movements* (New York: Appleton-Century-Crofts, 1951). An analysis of the current trends in the field of mass movements.

John A. Kinneman, *The Community in American Society* (New York: Appleton-Century-Crofts, 1947). A dependable introduction.

B. Malinowski, *Crime and Custom in Savage Society* (New York: Harcourt, Brace and Co., 1926). Illustrations of definitions of situations by primitive peoples, and effects upon individual behavior.

Margaret Mead, *Coming of Age in Samoa* (New York: W. W. Morrow and Co., 1928). Excellent analysis of the effects of situational factors on primitive thought and behavior.

A. E. Morgan, *The Small Community* (New York: Harper and Brothers, 1942). Stresses the democratic processes.

William F. Ogburn, *The Social Effects of Aviation* (Boston: Houghton Mifflin Co., 1946). Probably the only sociological systematic book on this growing important area.

•T. B. Veblen, *The Theory of the Leisure Class* (New York: Buebsch, 1919). A classic in the field of analysis of situational influences on individual conduct.

Edward Westermarck, *The Origin and Development of Moral Ideas* (London: The Macmillan Co., 1912). An exhaustive treatment of the nature of morality from the historical viewpoint.

C. C. Zimmerman, *The Changing Community* (New York: Harper and Brothers, 1938).

Periodicals

E. H. Bell, "Age-Group Conflict in Our Changing Culture," *Social Forces*, XII (1933), pp. 237-243.

H. A. Block, "Towards the Development of a Sociology of Literary and Art Forms," *American Sociological Review*, VIII (June, 1943), pp. 310-320.

Kingsley Davis, "Final Note on a Case of Extreme Isolation," *American Journal of Sociology*, LII (March, 1947), pp. 432-437.

William LaBarre, "Wanted: A Pattern for Modern Man," *Mental Hygiene*, XXXIII (April 1949), pp. 2-8.

Kurt Lewin, Ronald Lippitt, and R. K. White, "Patterns of Aggressive Behavior in Experimentally Created Social Climates," *Journal of Social Psychology*, X (1939), pp. 271-301.

Ronald Lippit, "An Experimental Study of the Effect of Democratic and Authoritarian Group Atmospheres," *University of Iowa Studies in Child Welfare*, XVI (1940), pp. 43-198.

Joseph S. Roucek, "The European and American Professor: A Study in Contrasts," *American Association of University Professors Bulletin*, XXX (Autumn, 1944), pp. 393-399.

Chapter V

Social Cohesion and Social Control

The systems of social control prevailing in human societies are extremely varied. As is indicated in other chapters of this volume, complex factors determine the particular system existing in a given society. Occupying an important place among these factors determining the pattern of social control in any particular society or group is the nature of the social solidarity or cohesion. The object of this chapter is to analyze the manner in which the type of social cohesion uniting the group is related to the processes of social control within the society.

Attention is first directed to the nature of group cohesion and to a consideration of the various influences that contribute to solidarity within the group. Following this the major problem of the discussion is approached, an analysis is made of the manner in which the type and strength of social cohesion are reflected in the nature of social control in the group. Since social solidarity varies in kind from that found among the most isolated and undifferentiated of the primitive communities to that found in the most highly differentiated urban or hyper-urban portions of society, it is necessary to select type situations for analysis and description. In the pages that follow the material will relate chiefly to three phases of social life: social solidarity and social control in the more primitive cumulative communities, in the present-day rural community, and in the more highly urbanized parts of the contemporary city.

Social Solidarity

Social groups are the cells out of which the great society is constructed. A person detached from his group relationship is almost inconceivable. As is the case for the human infant, so for the adult; survival is dependent upon participation to some extent in group life or at least in making use of the products of human association. It now seems probable that the child who is separated from his parents at birth and reared by non-human foster parents will lack all the essential elements of human personality. For these reasons it is valid to refer to the social group as a primary element in human society. This is why groups are basic units into which a society may be reduced. This being the case, the question arises: What is the nature of the social cohesion or solidarity within the group?

Social solidarity is a term denoting the cohesion that exists among the members of an association, a social group, a social class or caste, and among the various persons, groups, and classes that go to make up a society or any of its subdivisions. This cohesion seems to have its roots in such essential structures and processes as kinship, possession of a common language or religion, territorial proximity; in the interdependence of man and woman, or the participants in a highly differentiated and complex economic organization; and in common participation in and sharing of painful and pleasurable experiences. This social solidarity that is produced by similarities, mutual interdependence of parts, and common experiencing is the cement that binds into a collective unity such readily distinguishable wholes as the family, the neighborhood, the community, and the state. Although less obvious it will also be found in all of the other of society's innumerable groupings. The potency of this variable, its type and strength, determine the extent to which a society and its subdivisions are weakly knit together or closely integrated.

Types of Social Solidarity. Of social solidarity there are two principal types, both of which are present in greater or lesser degree in practically every social grouping. This is evidenced by an examination of the analyses of the principal sociological theorists. Herbert Spencer early called attention to the fact that the ingredients in social solidarity have changed as culture has accumulated and civilization has increased in complexity. His famous definition of evolution as the transition "from an indefinite incoherent homogeneity to a definite coherent heterogeneity," [1] indicates clearly the nature of the change. Obvious is the fact that Spencer considered the change from a unity based on similarities to a cohesiveness brought about by specialization, division of labor, and the resulting mutual interdependence of parts as a primary factor in evolution.

Despite numerous minor differences, essentially similar analyses have been made by other well-known sociologists. Probably the most ably developed exposition is that of the noted French sociologist, Émile Durkheim. According to him there are two principal types of social solidarity—one based upon similarities and one founded upon differences and the resulting lack of self-sufficiency among the parts. The cohesion that arises because the members of a group are of the same race, are kin to one another, speak the same language, owe allegiance to the same flag, live in the same neighborhood, have similar political or religious beliefs, share the same experiences, and possess other common traits may be thought of as arising more or less spontaneously. Durkheim referred to

[1] Herbert Spencer, *First Principles* (New York: A. L. Burt Co. n.d.), p. 343.

this type of unity as *mechanical solidarity*,[2] a term that at first may be slightly confusing to English-speaking persons. Essentially this concept is the same as that of Giddings who identified all of the similarities contributing to cohesion under his classic expression, "consciousness of kind."[3] That it had an earlier existence in the collective expressions of our society is evidenced by the proverbs: "blood is thicker than water," and "birds of a feather flock together." These basic similarities are also the sources of what Töennies has called *gemeinschaft*,[4] "a creation of natural group will." Solidarity of this type is all-important where the social group is small, isolated, homogeneous, static, and immobile. It is weak where the population is large, heterogeneous, mobile, and where contacts are numerous and culture is in a rapid state of flux. As society passes from its small, simple, elementary, segmented, stable forms to its large, interdependent, complex, and mobile types, the importance of this type of solidarity is greatly reduced. Social solidarity of this type is usually strong where division of labor is slight. For example, in the economic field similarities may make for competition and conflict rather than cohesion.

To the second variety of social cohesion Durkheim gave the name *organic solidarity*. Unlike the mechanical type, this kind of unity is one that is founded on differences. But it is important to note that not all social or bio-social differences make for cohesion, some of them being divisive in their effects. The particular kinds of differences that contribute to social cohesiveness are those that complement one another. Thus the differences between the sexes make man and woman mutually interdependent; a similar lack of self-sufficiency and mutual interdependence arises in the economic sphere when division of labor and specialization have progressed. In both of these and in numerous other social ways there develops in society a solidarity that in analagous with that found in the individual organism in higher types of animal life. It is for this reason that Durkheim chose to call the unity based on differences "organic solidarity."[5]

It should be emphasized that both of these types of social solidarity are present in almost every social grouping. However, in certain cases one of them will be of greater importance, whereas at other times and places the second type will be primary. In general, small isolated popu-

---

[2] Cf. George Simpson, *Emile Durkheim on the Division of Labor in Society* (New York: The Macmillan Co., 1933), p. 86.

[3] Franklin H. Giddings, *The Principles of Sociology* (New York: The Macmillan Co., 1913), pp. 17-19.

[4] Charles P. Loomis, *Fundamental Concepts of Sociology* (New York: American Book Co., 1940). Cf. Rudolf Heberle, "The Application of Fundamental Concepts in Rural Community Studies," *Rural Sociology*, VI (1941), pp. 205-209.

[5] Simpson, *op. cit.*, p. 131.

lations will be the ones in which solidarity of the mechanical type will be of overwhelming importance. At the other end of the scale are the extreme cases of urbanization in which there will be few evidences of mechanical solidarity and society will be almost entirely dependent upon organic solidarity for its cohesiveness. In the modern world one must go to primitive peoples who have been little affected by civilization to find the best examples of the communities in which mechanical solidarity plays a dominant role. However, the influence of this type of cohesion is still considerable in rural parts of our nation, particularly those parts in which the high development of a commercialized agriculture has not been introduced to bring about a fundamental transition in local mores. In general, Spencer's formula might be revised to read that as social evolution has progressed there has been a fundamental weakening of the solidarity based upon homogeneity in social traits and characteristics and an increased complexity brought about by the growing division of labor, specialization, and consequent lack of self-sufficiency on the part of the individual members of the social group.

Social Solidarity and Social Control in Primitive Communities

When an aggregate of individuals has adjusted and organized individual behavior, either consciously or by trial and error, toward group consciousness and a feeling of *esprit de corps*, it has transformed itself into a society with some degree of social solidarity.[6] To insure its continued existence the society must have some agency or agencies of control to regulate adult behavior and inculcate in the young the mores and folkways of the group. In most rural societies the kinship unit or the family (real or assumed) has been largely responsible for the development of social solidarity and the regulation of social behavior. Thus individuals were united into family groups and these in turn formed communities.

Sorokin, Zimmerman, and Galpin in their analyses of group solidarity stress the point that "the real social group . . . exists only when it *lives and functions as a unity*." This unity comes into being when the individual members are bound by certain *ties or bonds* which "make their lives and behavior closely interdependent, and infuse into their minds . . . feelings of oneness, solidarity, and community of interests."[7] In their opinion, the following are "group-creating bonds": (1) Kinship and community of blood (real or assumed [totemic]); (2) marriage; (3) sim-

---

[6] R. Linton, *The Study of Man* (New York: D. Appleton-Century Co., 1936), pp. 92-96.

[7] P. A. Sorokin, C. C. Zimmerman, and C. J. Galpin, *A Systematic Source Book in Rural Sociology* (Minneapolis: The University of Minnesota Press, I, 1930), p. 307.

ilarity in religious and magical beliefs and rites; (4) similarity in native language and mores; (5) common possession and utilization of land; (6) territorial proximity; (7) common responsibility for the maintenance of order; (8) community of occupational interests; (9) community of economic interests; (10) subjection to the same lord; (11) attachment to the same social institutions or agency of social service and control; (12) common defense; (13) mutual aid; (14) general living, experiencing, and acting together.[8]

According to these authors, there must be at least one of these bonds in operation before individuals are united into a real social group. A group held together by only one of these ties or bonds, in their terminology, is *elementary*, whereas a group bound by two or more ties is termed *cumulative*. Groups vary in their degree of solidarity according to the nature and number of bonds. In general these authorities show that primitive communities were characterized by many of these unifying bonds, and that European communities organized on a village pattern of settlement have retained, up to a relatively recent time, a majority of the bonds, thus providing a high degree of social unity. They further point out that the members of the cumulative community are like-minded, have a well-developed community consciousness, and exhibit a feeling of oneness and solidarity that is deeply rooted. As they express it, "the community engulfs the individual and makes him an integral part of itself."[9]

Durkheim, in his analysis of the undifferentiated type of society, as opposed to the differentiated one, clearly shows how a lack or slight division of labor in primitive society develops a type of solidarity based on likeness which, as has been shown, he terms *mechanical solidarity*. To Durkheim, social solidarity is a moral phenomenon which can be studied best through an analysis of the very factor which brings about the principal forms of social solidarity, and that is law. A classification of the different types of law, then, reveals the different types of solidarity corresponding to it.[10]

In an undifferentiated society "an act is criminal when it offends strong and defined states of collective conscience."[11] The term *collective conscience* is descriptive of that type of society. The type of law established in such a society he shows to be an index of the strength of the collective conscience, i.e., of the common beliefs and sentiments. This is repressive law. His analyses of numerous law codes of ancient civilizations reveal

[8] *Ibid.*, pp. 307-308.
[9] *Ibid.*, pp. 308-326.
[10] Simpson, *op. cit.*, p. 68.
[11] *Ibid.*, p. 80. Durkheim defined this most famous and much discussed concept as follows: "the totality of beliefs and sentiments common to average citizens of the same society forms a determinate system which has its own life; one may call it the *collective or common conscience*," p. 79.

that repressive law (criminal law) is predominant over civil law. The social homogeneity and moral consensus of individuals is so strong in such a society that even relatively minor offenses (from our viewpoint) bring about severe repressive punishment which is administered, not in a "rational" manner but with a "passionate" or emotional reaction, from the members as a whole. Therefore, the greater the degree of social cohesion, the stricter are the regulative methods of social control.[12]

The findings of Sorokin, Zimmerman, and Galpin, in their analysis of rural social control and comparative rural-urban criminality, corroborates in many respects the study of Durkheim. The fact that there is less criminality among the rural population in general as opposed to the urban is associated with a more efficient rural social control; a greater stability of the family; a lower degree of heterogeneity, density, and mobility of the population; and a "less complex, less intensive, and less broad system of social interaction of the population as compared with the urban." [13]

These authors further contend that the greater degree of social solidarity existing in cumulative rural communities is associated with the following social characteristics:

(1) The population of the cumulative rural community is more strongly atached to the community and less strongly attached to the world outside itself. (2) The solidarity of the population of a cumulative rural community is concentrated and localized within it. The community embraces all the members but it does not extend much beyond the local group. (3) "Neighbor" in the cumulative rural community means all the members of the community. The "neighbor" . . . is "like-minded" in his religion, occupation, and language, is often a kinsman, and is a co-partner in land possession and the totality of rights and privileges. (4) The fault of a member is the fault of the community; the achievements of a member are the achievements of the community; the community rather than the individual is the social unit that bears the responsibility.[14]

Here again their summary of the fundamental factors which bring about strong social cohesion in rural cumulative communities studied on a world-wide basis is in close agreement with Durkheim's analysis of mechanical solidarity based on likeness and similitude.

A classic sociological analysis of social cohesion and social control as it functioned in an old, traditional peasant society is presented in the introduction of Thomas and Znaniecki's monumental work, *The Polish Peasant in Europe and America*.[15] The fundamental element or core of

---

[12] *Ibid.*, pp. 70-110.
[13] Sorokin, Zimmerman and Galpin, *op. cit.*, II, pp. 265-287.
[14] *Ibid.*, I, pp. 321-326.
[15] W. I. Thomas and F. Znaniecki, *The Polish Peasant in Europe and America*, (New York: Alfred A. Knopf, 1927), I.

the society is the family which "is a social group including all the blood and law relatives up to a certain variable limit—usually the fourth degree." [16] On the other hand the married couple plus their children is known as the "marriage group," and simply represents one nucleus in a "plurality of nuclei" forming the family group. The relations which ensue among the various interconnected nuclei of this complex group are called by these authors *familial solidarity*, and "it manifests itself . . . in assistance rendered to, and in control exerted over, any member of the group by any other member representing the group as a whole." [17] Familial solidarity is itself greatly reinforced by the social opinion of the local community. In fact it is pointed out that the social environment of the peasant extends as far as the social opinion regarding himself and his family diffuses. Indeed, social opinion is so strong a means of social control that "the negative influence of public blame in criminal matters goes so far that suspicion of crime, just or unjust, is one of the most important causes of suicide." [18] The homogeneous religious attitudes of the peasant in turn strongly reinforce the familial and community attitudes which develop social solidarity and control.

Social Solidarity and Social Control in the Present-Day Rural Community

The social factors which effect solidarity and the methods of social control employed in the present-day rural community are in a large measure determined by the relative degrees of "ruralization" or "urbanization" of its population. Environment, occupation, forms of human association, mobility, the degree of social change, the ethnic composition and cultural background of the population, and many other factors help to determine the nature of social solidarity and control in the contemporary American rural community. Furthermore, such factors as forms of settlement, size of land holdings, and land tenure have a decided effect on the rural social structure which is in turn reflected in the types of solidarity and control.[19]

It is no doubt true, as Landis points out, that the modern neighborhood group has lost much of its effectiveness "as a unit of control in the

---

[16] *Ibid.*, p. 87,

[17] *Ibid.*, p. 89. This type of familial organization is quite similar to Frederic Le-Play's patriarchal familial organization, which is treated at length in C. C. Zimmerman and M. E. Frampton, *Family and Society* (New York: D. Van Nostrand Co., 1935).

[18] Thomas and Znaniecki, *op. cit.*, p. 150.

[19] Cf. T. Lynn Smith, *The Sociology of Rural Life* (New York: Harper and Brothers, 1940), pp. 201-309; C. M. Arensberg and S. T. Kimball, *Family and Community in Ireland* (Cambridge: Harvard University Press, 1940), *passim.*

nation." [20] With increased mobility and improved means of communication, ideas of innovation and change gradually diffuse within the various rural groups and bring about a weakening of the cumulative unifying bonds basic to mechanical solidarity and control. Nevertheless, there are regions in this country where these bonds of similarity fostering cohesion and control of the mechanical type still persist in varying degrees. For instance, a large number of the rural neighborhoods in the mountainous and hilly sections of the eleven southern states included in Odum's classification of the Southeast [21] cling to many of the old mores and regulative principles associated with mechanical solidarity. The like-mindedness of these people in politics, religion, racial attitudes, and general experience and cultural background help to sustain a respect for the "old ways"—frontier patterns—and serve as a restraining influence on many innovations and social changes. Furthermore, the bi-racial organization of society characterized by occasional inter-group racial conflicts bring about a certain degree of intra-group solidarity among these native-born white people of early American stock.

It appears, however, that as this region gradually evolves from the neighborhood stage to a more complex type of social organization the forms of social cohesion are also being modified, and they take on certain aspects of solidarity based on a greater division of labor, specialization, and contractual relationships associated with Durkheim's organic type of solidarity. At the same time, the informal means of social control functioning within the primary group lose effectiveness and are gradually replaced by more formal devices. Thus as the forces of urbanization impinge on the present-day rural community, the type of solidarity and forms of control must of necessity become more impersonal and formalized.

An illustration of how the forces of urbanization and change are operating in rural America, even among closely-knitted religious groups is shown by a recent study of a Mormon village in the Utah Valley:

". . . Salem in its early history represented a type of social relationship in which . . . 'gemein-schaftliche' elements largely predominated. It was based on common bonds, like interests, and similarity of experience. These 'community' elements became strong and were developed after the settlement of Salem. Though some members of the village were related by blood and marriage these connections were not the principal

---

[20] Paul H. Landis, *Rural Life in Process* (New York: McGraw-Hill Book Co., 1940), p. 319; his *Adolescence and Youth* (New York: McGraw-Hill Book Co., 1945) describes the social adjustments of growing up in urban, town and rural environments.

[21] Howard W. Odum, *Southern Regions of the United States* (Chapel Hill: The University of North Carolina Press, 1936), pp. 4-22. These states are Virginia, North Carolina, South Carolina, Kentucky, Tennessee, Georgia, Florida, Alabama, Mississippi, Louisiana, and Arkansas.

basis for the formation of the community. Rather it was the common acceptance of and belief in Mormonism. Since that time certain 'associational' elements have tended to weaken these common bonds. Relationships of a more contractual nature have arisen and expressed themselves. The church, in order to meet these new and challenging forces, has adopted various measures, some of which have been partially successful. In other respects it is finding it exceedingly difficult to maintain its authority and influence. This trend toward an increase of the 'associational' elements in the village can only be explained in the light of the great and rapid changes which have occurred in our present-day society. Urbanization and all its influences have made themselves felt in the most remote rural districts and as a result certain traits of an 'associational' nature have tended to rise. Salem as present is still in a period of transition. What the eventual adjustment will be will have to be left to the future." [22]

As early as 1929 John H. Kolb had observed and described how the neighborhood groups in less isolated areas were losing their importance as "organization units" to new types of groups "largely determined by the interests, the deliberate intent (and) the purposive action of the people." [23] Since that date numerous studies have pointed to the shifting nature of community solidarity from one of consciousness of kind to one based on interdependence of parts.[24] Generally speaking, many if not all of the various trends and changes taking place in the present-day rural community appear to be either directly or indirectly associated with the major force of urbanization, which is in turn reflected in a more formalized system of social solidarity and social control.

Social Solidarity and Social Control in the Present-Day Urban Community

One of the outstanding characteristics of the American nation has been the tremendous increase of its population, and in particular the phenomenal growth of American cities. In 1790 only about five per cent of the nation's population lived in urban centers; today the majority are urban dwellers. Heavy streams of migration from rural areas as well as from foreign countries were mainly responsible for the massing of the divergent ethnic and cultural strains found in the metropolitan cities.

[22] Reed H. Bradford, *A Mormon Village: A Study in Rural Social Organization,* a thesis submitted to the faculty of the Louisiana State University in partial fulfillment of the requirement for the master's degree, 1939, p. 64.

[23] J. H. Kolb and A. F. Wileden, "Special Interest Groups in Rural Society," *Wisconsin Agricultural Experiment Station, Bulletin 84,* Madison, 1929, p. 2.

[24] T. Lynn Smith, "Trends in Community Organization and Life," *American Sociological Review,* V (June, 1940), pp. 325-334; cf. Carle C. Zimmerman, *The Changing Community,* (New York: Harper and Brothers, 1938).

A group of social scientists have expressed the opinion that:

"Never before in the history of the world have groups of people so diverse in social backgrounds been thrown together into such close contacts as in the cities of America. The typical American city, therefore, does not consist of a homogeneous body of citizens, but of human beings with the most diverse cultural backgrounds, often speaking different languages, following a great variety of customs, habituated to different modes and standards of living, and sharing only in varying degrees the tastes, the beliefs, and the ideals of their native fellow city dwellers. In short, far from presenting a picture of a single unified body of human beings, the American city is a motley of peoples and cultures forming a mosaic of little worlds which in part blend with one another, but in part and for a time, remain segregated or come into conflict with one another." [25]

The highly urbanized city with its numerous and complex groups represents the polar extreme of the cumulative community which derives its social solidarity from like-mindedness and consciousness of kind. The social dynamics of modern cities, as opposed to the stable and relatively static condition of agricultural communities, is well expressed in the following statement:

"The city puts a premium upon innovation and progress and is able, through the collective power of great masses, to achieve fundamental changes in the existing order. Cities have traditionally been regarded as the home of inventions and revolutions. They secularize the sacred beliefs, practices, and institutions; they democratize knowledge, fashions, and tastes, and, consequently generate wants and stimulate unrest. The urban mode of life tends to create solitary souls, to uproot the individual from his customs, to confront him with a social void, and to weaken traditional restraints on personal conduct." [26]

It is precisely this power of the city to "achieve fundamental changes in the existing order" that endangers and weakens the measures of social control in urban society. The regulative means such as public opinion, custom, fear of gossip, group indignation, and moral sanctions, which are so effective in rural communities have little if any effects at all in a highly complex and depersonalized city life. Thus nonlegal measures of control are replaced by formal, organized legal agencies of control. This fundamental difference in the measures of social control between the city and the rural community is probably the basic factor for many of the social maladjustments experienced by rural migrants to urban cities.

Such social solidarity as there is in these metropolitan cities appears to

[25] National Resources Committee, *Our Cities, Their Role in the National Economy* (Washington: Government Printing Office, 1937), p. 10.
[26] *Ibid.*, p. 52.

be based largely, although not entirely, upon formal and contractual relationships arising out of a great division of labor, specialization, and a certain degree of mutual interdependence of the various social units. But at best it is an unstable type of solidarity subject to the varied processes and forces of social change. Unlike the solidarity arising out of similarities, its effect on social control is largely negative. The same phenomena which are responsible for this type of solidarity—namely, the processes of differentiation caused by an increase in the density of the population—are also factors which favor the increase of crime, suicide,[27] and amoral behavior in urban life. Between the two polar extremes— the cumulative community showing a high degree of positive relationship in its type of solidarity and social control, and the highly urbanized metropolitan city whose solidarity is only weakly or even negatively related to its system of control—stand the present-day rural and urban communities, with their varying degrees of relationship of types of solidarity to methods of control.

Implicit in any discussion of cohesion and social control is the problem of societal integration. To what extent are the various rural and urban groups of the nation held together by the sharing of common ends or values? The intense individual and group competition as well as class conflicts characteristic of our modern culture does not seem to be conducive to common orientation of purpose. A recent study on this subject concludes that the multiplication and emancipation of "free standing groups from the local community" are a step in the direction of disintegration rather than integration, because these groups "have disrupted an older type of moral community" which as yet has not been replaced by "an equally strong one of a new type." [28] It may be that from this crisis through which we are now passing there will emerge that "strong moral community" in the form of a new social order, but that is in the realm of speculation.

Summary

The types of social control in any society are relative to the kind of social cohesion which binds the community together. The principal

---

[27] Significantly enough, Durkheim in his classic study of suicide (*Le Suicide*, Paris, 1930 ed.) shifted his emphasis of attempting to derive organic solidarity solely through differentiation caused by density of population. Instead of contrasting the collective conscience of mechanical solidarity to the organic solidarity of "contractual" society as he had done in his *Division of Labor*, he stressed two types of influence of the collective conscience. What he terms the "non-contractual element of contract" is shown to be an essential factor underlying the basis of order in a "differentiated individualistic society." For a most thorough analysis of Durkheim's works, see Talcott Parsons' *The Structure of Social Action* (New York: McGraw-Hill Book Co., 1937), pp. 301-470.

[28] R. C. Angell, *The Integration of American Society* (New York: McGraw-Hill Book Co., 1941), pp. 204-220.

division in kinds of solidarity is that which is based upon similarities among the members of the group, called by Durkheim "mechanical" solidarity, and by Giddings "consciousness of kind," and that which comes from differentiation, specialization, and division of labor. As society becomes larger and more complex, the latter type gains predominance. In our own society, the difference is most clearly represented in the rural-urban social differentials, the social cohesion of rural groupings being more largely dependent upon similarities, and that of the urban of the kind which arises from specialization, division of labor, and the resulting interdependence of the parts.

Where cohesion based upon likeness is dominant, the informal controls are very strong. Where differences of function are the integrating factor, impersonal controls, such as those of law, are the main reliance.

QUESTIONS

1. What is the primary element in society?
2. Define social solidarity.
3. What factors contribute to social cohesion?
4. According to Spencer and Durkheim, what are the principal types of social solidarity?
5. Explain Töennies's term *Gemeinschaft.*
6. When is social solidarity of the type described by Durkheim as "mechanical solidarity" strong?
7. What type of social differences contribute to social cohesiveness?
8. In what types of societies will organic solidarity be prominent?
9. When does the real social group exist, according to Sorokin, Zimmerman, and Galpin?
10. Distinguish between elementary and cumulative groups according to the above authors.
11. According to Durkheim, what is collective conscience?
12. What characteristics are associated with social solidarity?
13. What is the effectiveness of the neighborhood as a unit of control, according to Paul H. Landis?
14. What is the relation between urbanization and the growth of formal means of control?
15. What does Angell say about social integration in the United States?
16. What basic institution has been largely responsible for the development of solidarity and the regulation of social control in rural societies?
17. What are the factors which foster the creation of a group?
18. What factors were responsible for the high degree of social solidarity among the Polish peasants?

SUGGESTED TOPICS FOR TERM PAPERS AND FURTHER RESEARCH

1. Compare control in primitive societies with that of civilized societies.
2. Methods used by religious groups to exert control.
3. The influence of urbanization on informal control.

4. The division of labor and social control.
5. The neighborhood and social control.

BIBLIOGRAPHY

Books

Jessie Bernard, *American Community Behavior* (New York: The Dryden Press, 1949). A penetrating study of social solidarity and cohesion in the modern city, with emphasis on the factors making for disintegration.

J. L. Gillin, *The Wisconsin Prisoner* (Madison, Wis.: University of Wisconsin Press, 1946). How restricted society operates.

A. I. Hallowell, "Sociopsychological Aspects of Acculturation," pp. 171-200, in Ralph Linton, ed., *The Science of Man in the World Crisis* (New York: Columbia University Press, 1945).

Alain Locke and J. Bernhard Stern, eds., *When Peoples Meet* (New York: Progressive Education Association, 1942). A collection of readings.

Charles P. Loomis, *Fundamental Concepts of Sociology* (New York: American Book Co., 1940). The English version of Töennis' analysis of rural and urban solidarity.

T. Lynn Smith, *Brazil: People and Institutions* (Baton Rouge: Louisiana State University Press, 1946), chapters 13-18. One of the first attempts to apply the methods of sociological analysis perfected in the United States to the study of social solidarity in a Latin American country.

—— *The Sociology of Rural Life* (New York: Harper and Brothers, 1953), chapters II and X-XVI. A detailed analysis of social cohesion in a rural society.

Pitirim A. Sorokin, *Society, Culture, and Personality* (New York: Harper and Brothers, 1947), especially chapters XXII-XXIV, XXXVIII. A mass of well-digested material on social cohesion.

William G. Sumner, *Folkways* (Boston: Ginn and Co., 1907). A sociological classic; shows the tremendous power of custom and the variability of social codes.

W. I. Thomas and Florian Znaniecki, *The Polish Peasant in Europe and America*, Vol. I (New York: Alfred A. Knopf, 1927), pp. 87-302. A landmark in the sociological study of a peasant society in Europe and its transformation in America.

Periodicals

Earl H. Bell, *Culture of a Contemporary Rural Community: Sublette, Kansas* (Washington, D.C.: U.S. Department of Agriculture, Rural Life Studies 2, 1942).

Neal Gross and William E. Martin, "On Group Cohesiveness," *American Journal of Sociology*, LVII (1952), pp. 546-554.

Donald P. Kent and Robert C. Burnight, "Group Centrism in Complex Societies," *American Journal of Sociology*, LVII (1951), pp. 256-259.

Olen E. Leonard, *Pichilingue: A Study of Rural Life in Coastal Ecuador* (Washington, D.C.: Office of Foreign Agricultural Relations, Foreign Agriculture Report No. 17, 1947).

—— *Canton Chullpas: A Socioeconomic Study in the Cochabamba Valley of Bolivia* (Washington, D.C.: Office of Foreign Agricultural Relations, Foreign Agriculture Report, No. 27, 1948).

—— and Charles P. Loomis, *Culture of a Contemporary Rural Community: El Cerrito, New Mexico* (Washington, D.C.: Department of Agriculture, Rural Life Studies 1, 1941).

Charles P. Loomis, "Rebuilding American Community Life," *American Sociological Review*, V (1940), pp. 311-324.

—— "Rebuilding American Community Life," *American Sociological Review*, V (1940), pp. 311-324.

Robert K. Merton, "Social Structure and Anomie," *ibid.*, III (1938), pp. 672-682.

Bryce Ryan, "Primary and Secondary Contacts in a Ceylonese Peasant Community," *Rural Sociology*, XVII (1952), pp. 311-321.

Robert L. Skrabanek, "Forms of Cooperation and Mutual Aid in a Czech-American Rural Community," *Southwestern Social Science Quarterly*, XXX (1950), pp. 183-187.

———— and Vernon J. Parenton, "Social Life in a Czech-American Rural Community," *Rural Sociology*, XV (1950), pp. 221-231.

T. Lynn Smith, "The Role of the Community in American Rural Life," *Journal of Educational Sociology*, XIV (1941), pp. 387-400.

Anselm Strauss, "Research in Collective Behavior: Neglect and Need," *American Sociological Review*, XII (June, 1947), pp. 352-354.

R. H. Turner, "Value-Conflict in Social Disorganization," *Sociology and Social Research*, XXXVIII, 5 (May–June, 1954), 301-308.

PART II

Institutions as Elements of Social Control

FOREWORD

The most obvious and uniform manifestations of social control are found in social institutions, which exist both to stabilize societies and to provide means for orderly and continuous adaptation and change. It is here that the most direct and systematic observations of social controls may be made. Precautions must be taken, however, against over-simple and superficial interpretation of institutions and their social control functions, especially in our own complex and dynamic age.

Part II sets up these safeguards with an opening chapter on "State, Law, and Government," and a closing chapter on "How Science Modifies Institutions." Between, separate treatment is given to the principal institutional patterns of modern life: Religion; Marriage, Home and Family; Education; and Social Classes. Together these provide the principal framework of social structure, the study of which is logically the preparation for further investigations of less obvious and more subtle aspects of control.

CHAPTER VI

State, Law, and Government

The Power Theory and the Role of Government

In conformity with the central theme of this volume, the point of view taken in this chapter assumes that power-holders seek to use political agencies to enable them to employ the measures necessary to assure to themselves the dominating positions in society. Since in recent generations, political institutions have become more and more important as a means of control, the struggle on the part of contending groups to win and hold power over the state has intensified to a feverish pitch. The paramount position of government and the monopoly of force which political agencies possess enable the groups who win command of political institutions to effectuate their purposes more completely than would be possible in any other way. These advantages become more apparent as a government extends its sway over areas of life dedicated in the past to private endeavor. Hence, the power struggle to possess and manipulate the massive authority of government knows no limits.

The Nature of the State. In order properly to envisage how power is secured and exercised by the political elite, it is necessary to devote a little time to certain definitions. Conceptions of the state in the past have been confused because of the tendency of political scientists to define the state in legalistic terms. Although most of them took pains to point out that the state as they defined it was only an abstract generalization of the characteristics of actual states, their attribution of absolute and unlimited power to the state (sovereignty) and doctrine of law as a "command of the state" seemed to give to the concept, state, a real being which it does not possess.[1] Bosanquet and other writers of the Idealistic school attributed to the state a mystical personality which they conceived of as more real and more valuable than the personalities of individual human beings. Thus, they strengthened the doctrines of the legalists regarding the state making of it a "spiritual organism" of the highest order whose authority must not be questioned and from whom commands issued, eventuating in the form of laws to which obedience must be

---

[1] Cf. R. G. Gettell, *Introduction to Political Science* (New York: Ginn, 1910), pp. 10-14; and W. F. Willoughby, *The Government of Modern States* (New York: D. Appleton-Century Co., 1936), chapter II.

rendered.[2] By this type of reasoning, the authority and majesty of the state were placed in what was thought to be an unassailable position. In this way, the power-holders in control of the organs of the state would be able to govern with a high degree of security and thus promote their objectives because they were supported by an ideology which surrounded them with an aura of quasi-divinity and which was impervious to the assaults of opposing logicians.

The Pluralists. Objection to this absolutistic conception of the state came principally from the pluralist school which flourished during the 1920's and was headed by H. J. Laski, Hobson, John Dewey, and others. These writers rejected *in toto* the authoritarian implications of the "metaphysical" state and attempted to remove the entire conception from the category of politics. Laski and Dewey both pointed out that political affairs are actually in the hands of certain officials who are placed there by various means but who always represent a combination of personal and group interest. Since all the powers of government are in the hands of individual persons and are exercised by them, the idea of the state has no reality apart from the institutions of government. Far from originating from on high, the powers of government are erected by men to serve human purposes and are valuable only as long as they do so. Authority is dangerous because any man or group of men in power is apt to use it for selfish ends. Consequently, all governmental power should be limited and subject to adequate checks.[3]

The Sociologists. The doctrines of pluralism have found a friendly reception from sociologists generally. Undeterred by the ponderous logic of the juristic school, sociologists set to work to discover the facts regarding the origins of political institutions and the exercise of political powers. These investigations disclosed that political institutions have not always been the main reliance of society for the exercise of social control. In the past, custom, the family, the tribe, and religion have played a weightier part. The notion that politically organized groups must be fixed upon a certain territory was exploded thus demonstrating that territory is not an infallible attribute of political organization. Studies of the origins of political power clearly showed that sovereign power does not come from some mystical or mysterious source beyond the ken of ordinary human beings but, on the contrary, is the product of leadership, war, prestige factors, and functional specialization and, therefore, is limited, fluctuating and dependent at all times upon support by the group.[4]

---

[2] F. W Coker, *Recent Political Thought* (New York: D. Appleton-Century Co., 1934), chapter XV.

[3] *Ibid.*, chapter XVIII.

[4] H. E. Barnes, et al., *Contemporary Social Theory* (New York: D. Appleton-Century Co., 1940), pp. 652 ff.

Sociological analysis of the concept of the state tended to relate it to the concept of society and other social institutions. Most sociologists took the view that government is merely one of the many institutions of control in society. Considered in relation to society as a whole, the state is an association of the people of a given society organized for political purposes. As an association it is a functionally specialized organ of society devoted to the performance of certain necessary social purposes and differentiated from other associations by its universality, i.e., the fact that its jurisdiction extends over all persons within its spatial extent; by its involuntary nature, since most of its members belong to it by the fact of birth and have little choice even if they wished to change; and by its exercise of physical power which is so preponderant that all other associations must yield to it. Nevertheless, sociologists insist that the mere fact of the preeminence of the state in physical force does not necessarily give it priority as regards the value of its services to society as compared with those of other associations.

If this view of the state is accepted, it follows that the state is an agent of society to promote the social welfare as regards the political phase of social activities. This raises the question of what is the social welfare and at this point the conflict begins. From a power theory standpoint, what constitutes the general welfare is determined by the ideas and policies of the power-holders which rest in turn upon the traditional bases of their thinking and upon their conceptions of what will most conduce to the satisfaction of their own interests and those they represent. Thus, it may happen that the conduct of government may come into conflict with the best interests of society as a whole considered objectively and apart from the purposes of the power-holders. Opposition to the government may arise, therefore, not only from intransigeant groups out of power but from scientists who see in governmental policies or acts tendencies harmful to society as a whole.

Some writers have preferred to distinguish between the concept of society as the sum total of all human relationships, and the community, or the politically organized group, which is differentiated from other groups by consciousness of its members of fellowship in a common life. Such groups are national communities. Each national community, these writers maintain, is organized as a political association ordinarily referred to as the state. Nevertheless, it is still necessary to distinguish between the state and the government. The position of the pluralists that the state is merely another term for the government proves untenable in the end because some political activities and relationships are not capable of being entirely included in the concept of government. Governments come and go and their procedures vary from time to time but the politically organized community remains. Its permanence and solidity pass beyond the transitory fluctuations of governmental activities. Hence, the concept of the state as the abiding form of political organization within the community is valuable and should be retained but emptied of all metaphysical content.

In attempting to achieve this result, certain theorists have defined the state as the totality of all political acts performed by human beings in a given society in so far as they relate to the struggle to secure control of political institutions and their effects upon society in general. Provided this theory takes time into account and includes tradition, usage, and continuity of behavior as factors in political behavior, it may be accepted as in conformity with the power theory and sufficiently comprehensive to satisfy the principal requirements. It obviates the idea of fixed territorial limitations, takes care of the size and complexity of governmental activities and relates political actions definitely to human agencies. Yet, it is clear from the definition that the concept of the state is purely an abstraction. The state, as defined, does not exist in actuality. It is a conscious attempt to see the field of political endeavor as a whole in all of its relationships both tangible and intangible.[5]

If the state is defined as the sum total of political activities in society, what then is the role of the government? Political legalists conceived of the government as the political organization of the state. Political pluralists considered the institutions of government to be the only political realities. The sociologist tends to see the government as merely a group of persons occupying certain offices which they have secured by appointment, inheritance, election or other means. Incumbency in the offices gives to such persons the powers attached to the offices by law, custom, or political mandate. Consequently, the term government is simply the generalized concept of the various political offices occupied by the "governors" who exercise control over the governed. Yet the latter are also included in the term "state" since they may engage in political activities of one kind or another. The state, therefore, includes both the governors and the governed in one political association.

The problem for those who aspire to exercise political power is first to win control of the offices of government and then to use the powers at their disposal to gain their ends. The interpretation of the state as a metaphysical entity, therefore, consciously or unconsciously obscured the actualities and promoted an idealized conception of the nature of political institutions which made easier compliance with the exercise of authority by the power-holders. Sociological interpretation, on the other hand, attempts by scientific analysis to reveal the actual origins, nature, and exercise of power so that the facts may be clear to all. The scientific,

---

[5] On this point see C. H. Titus and V. H. Harding, *Government and Society*, (New York: Crofts, 1929), pp. 48-53.

sociological view also leads to a more democratic attitude toward the exercise of political power since it is conceived as a responsible service to the community in terms of the common welfare rather than the welfare of a ruling elite.

Nevertheless, contemporary political practice reveals a definite tendency to revert to political mythology. In the face of rapid scientific and technological changes, the masses of mankind turn in their uncertainty and insecurity to the authority of the state. Confused by the puzzling evidences of scientific advance, they readily accept the mythological doctrines apotheosizing the state and its leaders. Eager to exercise unimpeded power, rulers, particularly the dictators, have taken advantage of this attitude to promote by propaganda and censorship a still more religious attitude toward the state. Even in the democracies these tendencies are being manifested, although accompanied by less crudity and violence. Hence, the efforts of social scientists to lighten the dark recesses of politics and restore to society as a whole the control over its government are being nullified.[6]

Law

Definition. Laws are a form of social rule emanating from political agencies differing somewhat from the rules of other social instrumentalities but essentially the same in character. All social rules, including political rules, or laws, originated first in custom or folkways of long standing and are based upon existing conceptions of justice and right in a given community. In time, custom is formulated into written statements which designate a certain type of desired behavior in order to secure more perfect conformity to it. What is desired as behavior depends upon the values placed upon various forms of conduct by a given society and the values, in turn, are produced under the sponsorship of the influential members of the group as accepted and supported by the rank and file. Each association within a given society develops rules, both written and unwritten, which pertain to the functions peculiar to the association. In the case of political associations their rules are differentiated from those of other associations, by several characteristic features: (1) they are formal, deliberately enacted or adjudged statements in the form of commands or orders; (2) they are not the result of voluntary consent of the persons against whom they are directed; and (3) they are ordinarily accompanied by punitive sanctions in case of their violation.

Law has been defined as something that organizes and systematizes power and makes power effective toward the maintaining and further-

---

[6] On this section see E. Cassirier, "The Myth of the State," *Fortune*, XXXIX (June, 1944), pp. 165-167.

ing of civilization. The definition is acceptable except for the last phrase which indicates an ideal end. Sociologically speaking, this is the end at which law ought to aim. More to the point is the statement that law is an authoritative canon of value laid down by the force of politically organized society.[7]

The Origins of Law. As regards the origin and source of law, opinions have varied according to the times and the school of thought. The original Greek idea of natural law, or law inherent in the order of nature itself, was brought down to modern times through the *Ius Naturae* and the *Ius Gentium* of the Middle Ages and during the age of seventeenth century rationalism was generally accepted as the source of all fundamental legal precepts. Man-made laws were unacceptable, unless they embodied these basic principles, and could be disregarded. Natural law was the product of right reason and the principles of law which could be made to apply to human affairs could only be discovered by rational means. This ideal conferred upon law the authority of nature and reason and purported to give it the precision of the laws of physics. During the heyday of natural law philosophy, legislatures were considered relatively unimportant and natural law was presumed to be correctly declared by the judges whose decisions were at work rounding out a system of common law. Case law, according to Pound, was an attempt on the part of courts and judges to determine just law on the basis of experience.[8] Nevertheless, in making their decisions, the judges were influenced not only by custom but by their own basic valuations of life and property. English law of the medieval and early modern period, for instance, reflected the dominant position of the feudal nobility and gave particular emphasis to safeguarding the land holding and property rights of the barons.[9]

Overthrow of the natural law philosophy was followed by Darwinian concepts of law as the most successful system of social rules surviving from the competitive struggle of social systems and later by biological analogies in which law was seen as the order or system in the social organism determining its modes of functioning according to the predetermined biological interaction of its various parts. When this analogy was shown to be untenable, sociologists turned to more pragmatic interpretations.[10]

With the advent of the twentieth century, legal theory was faced with the overthrow of all fundamental rationalizations justifying or idealizing

---

[7] Cf. Roscoe Pound, *Social Control Through Law* (New Haven: Yale University Press, 1942), pp. 49-53.

[8] *Ibid.*, pp. 2-3.

[9] Morris R. Cohen, *Law and the Social Order* (New York: Harcourt-Brace and Co., 1933), p. 42.

[10] W. E. Sandelius, "The Question of Sovereignty," *Twentieth Century Political Thought* (New York: Philosophical Library, 1946), pp. 165-167.

law as a system of power or, in other words, of social control. Natural law theory was gone in spite of the efforts of Stammler, Duguit, with his law of the social services, and Krabbe, with his "sense of right." [11] Gone also beyond recall were the doctrines of the analytical jurists that law was the command of the sovereign state, and of the philosophical idealists that law is the will of the absolutely perfect metaphysical state.

Into the vacuum that was left, Pound threw his sociological jurisprudence or theory of interests. According to his view, in order properly to understand the nature of law, it is necessary to go behind the machinery of law-making and comprehend the various social interests which the law represents and seeks to serve. The interests in question are claims or demands of individuals or groups upon the law-making and law-enforcing organs of the government. According to Pound, these interests are found by the government—not made by it. They grow out of the various needs and desires of individual persons and are reflected either through personal or group action in the form of demands for enactment of appropriate legislation by the law-making power or appropriate judicial decisions by the courts.[12] Those claims that are recognized by designated political agencies represent the values of a given legal order over a period of time and reflect the ethical values of the social order. In consequence, the legal system is a system of values declared and enforced by governmental authorities. Constant pressure is exerted upon government to recognize new claims and thus the legal system changes. However, there is a tendency for legal rules to lag behind social change so that the existing social order find itself discommoded by out-of-date laws, and friction between underprivileged groups and the legal system ensues.[13]

Pound fails to mention, however, the reason why some claims are recognized and implemented in law and administration and others are disregarded. The lag between law and social progress may be interpreted as the inability of the law-making organs to keep up to date but a more correct position is that these organs respond mainly to pressure and the recognition which they accord to various claims is roughly in proportion to the weight of the pressure which the proponents of the claims can bring to bear.

Law Making. The deliberate enactment of legal rules is a comparatively modern development. As pointed out before, law has its roots in custom, and in the early stages of man's development these rules were unwritten. Interestingly enough, convention and tradition still play a considerable part, particularly in public law. In ancient societies, there were law

---

[11] *Ibid.*
[12] Pound, *op. cit.*, p. 65 ff.
[13] *Ibid.*

givers and legislative bodies but their functions were supposed to consist mainly in discovering and declaring the laws of nature which were applicable to their situation. Modern legislative assemblies are a product of the late medieval and early modern periods and developed largely from the need of monarchs for money and the desirability of consulting the taxpayers before levying taxes upon them. Thus, the law-making organs had their origins definitely in the need for satisfying a basic interest. Modern legislatures have extended their sphere of action to an almost unlimited range of human activities and consequently the importance of their work has increased accordingly.

In the modern legislature the question of which interests will be recognized in law and which will not depends to a large degree upon the power of the groups which lay their claims before it. Practically all legislation is passed to satisfy the demands of certain groups presented to the legislature either directly or indirectly. Political parties which nominate candidates to the legislature are themselves a combination of pressure groups and the candidates which are chosen are definitely representative of the elements dominant in the party. After election to office, members of the legislature, if they are to stay in office, must give consideration to the requests of their supporters. In many cases, the plurality they were able to secure over their opponents is small and a comparatively slight shift to the other side might encompass their defeat. Hence, even small groups, if well organized, may be able to force recognition of their claims. To be sure, this is more true of state and local than national legislatures, but even in national legislatures the same principles are at work.

In the American House of Representatives, the short term of office and the district system of election makes the members extremely sensitive to the demands of small groups in their districts. On the other hand, they need pay less attention to necessities of large groups throughout the nation if such groups are not well represented in their particular districts or are inadequately organized. An excellent example of this was seen in the recent enactment of an OPA law which was demanded by an overwhelming majority of the people but because of the complaints of business and farmers' groups was emasculated almost to the point of absurdity. Many major pieces of legislation come from the president or the executive offices but these also reflect the desire of the chief executive and his principal officers to maintain the support of the major organized groups in the country by recommending legislation satisfactory to their interests. Under the conditions of today, the huge combinations of labor, capital, and agricultural elements with their national offices, expert lobbyists, and wealthy treasuries, are able to compel recognition and secure desired legislation. Only the fact that these groups are competing with each other, thus enabling the executive and the legislature to play off one group against another, prevents the government from becoming a helpless instrument in their hands. Even so, the grinding impact of competing pressures upon the government requires political astuteness of a high order to keep them satisfied and prevent the withdrawal of political support in the next elections. In Great Britain, where the executive which is able to command a majority in the House of Commons dominates all branches of the government, including the legislature, the possibility of small groups securing their ends by pressure upon the legislature is much less, but the great national combinations operate just as effectively upon the government as in the United States. The present Socialist majority, for instance, was placed in power by a popular vote much larger than the normal membership of the Socialist Party. Unless the policies of the party are such as to continue to hold the support of the non-Socialist groups, its popular majority will soon dwindle away.

The above analysis demonstrates that the legal system, in so far as enacted law is concerned, is the product of the pressures of the most powerful and effective interest groups in society. By powerful is meant effective power in terms of the number of votes at the group's disposal or the amount of money it can command, its prestige in the legislature, the effectiveness of its organization, the skill of its lobbyists, and the support it is able to secure from public opinion by means of its propaganda.[14]

Law Enforcement. Having secured the enactment of a statute satisfying one or more of its demands, the problem for the pressure group is to make sure that it is properly carried into effect by the administrative and judicial agencies of the government. The fact that a law is on the statute books means nothing unless it is enforced. Thousands of laws are added to the statute books yearly and very few of them are ever repealed. Hence, over the years an immense mass of legislation accumulates, much of which is forgotten in the course of time. The laws that are enforced are those selected by administrators and judges as worthy of enforcement. What they consider worthy of enforcement depends partly upon their own political, economic, or social preconceptions and partly upon the efforts of interested groups to influence their actions. Here, the task of the pressure group begins all over again. Administrative officials may have a point of view to the law in question different from that of the legislators. They may be in a more strongly entrenched position and hence be less subject to pressure, or they may have changed their attitude toward the measure as a result of a shift in the political situation.

The law placed before an administrative official represents merely a

---

[14] R. V. Peel and J. S. Roucek, *Introduction to Politics* (New York: T. Y. Crowell, 1941), pp. 3-13.

statement of policy. Even if couched in mandatory language, it is still subject to administrative interpretation. Usually, however, laws are stated in permissive language which gives the administrator an opportunity to decide to enforce it or not. Actually, therefore, the law is a dead letter unless the administrator decides to enforce it. If he does so, it is by means of executive orders, and rules and regulations. As E. S. Griffith points out, the operations of law enforcement consist of an interplay of leadership by government officials aided by expert research and advice and the activities of pressure groups seeking their special objectives. The impact of group pressures upon departments encounter little resistance, he points out, unless the groups in question are in conflict. Each agency has its own clientele of pressure groups in the national government. The wide scope afforded department heads and top executive officials in administering the laws entrusted to them enables them to free themselves from presidential control to a large degree. Backed by big business, agricultural or labor groups, they have established principalities of their own within their particular departments where they become virtual dependencies of such groups.[15] The impediments encountered by pressure groups in securing enforcement of the law are, consequently, not too great if they are large and powerful groups. In the case of small groups, their chances are less good but they may be able to produce some results by aligning themselves with larger groups and winning their support or by becoming very vocal about their needs.

The enforcement of a law may require action by the courts because of violation of the rights secured by the law in one way or another or because of failure to carry out its provisions. How the law will be adjudicated depends upon the attitude of the judges toward it and the pressures for or against it by its sponsors and opponents. As Judge Cardozo pointed out, much of the law is judge-made because judges, by their decisions, must fill in the gaps in constitutional and statute law. How they will decide will depend upon their outlook upon life and there can be no guarantee of justice in their decisions except the personality of the judge.[16]

The personality of the judge, however, depends upon his background and training. The majority of judges are selected from the most successful attorneys at the bar and this may mean having served the interests of large property-owners. The effect of this may be to produce in the minds of judges an extreme sensitivity to the claims of property owners.

[15] Cf. E. S. Griffith, "The Changing Pattern of Public-Policy Formation," *American Political Science Review*, XXXVIII (June, 1944), pp. 445-459; and Pendleton Herring, "Executive-Legislative Responsibilities," *American Political Science Review*, XXXVIII (December, 1944), pp. 1153-1156.
[16] B. J. Cardozo, *The Nature of the Judicial Process* (New Haven: Yale University Press, 1921), pp. 10-19.

This tendency is reinforced by the employment of able attorneys by large propertied interests so that their claims are more adequately presented to the courts than those of less wealthy individuals or groups. These influences brought to bear upon the judges may consciously or unconsciously influence their decisions. According to Cohen, most judges having unconsciously determined to decide one way or another look for and find reasons or precedents for their decisions. If their decision departs too far from precedent, they may create legal fictions to mask changes in the law.[17]

In the selection of judges, appointing officers frequently pay particular attention to their economic and social views. If they are elected by popular vote, they are apt to come under the influence of the party leaders or even, in the case of municipal courts, party bosses and racketeers. Substantially, in the case of the courts, the result is the same: members of groups which are politically powerful have too often been able to win recognition in the decision of the courts while those less powerful have had to take their chances.

The Limits of Effective Law Enforcement. The basic aim of government should be to act as an arbiter between conflicting interests, to compromise differences, and to endeavor so far as possible to achieve a maximum of satisfaction for the claims of all individuals and groups in society. Law as the expression of this function is supposed to regulate the behavior of individuals and groups and provide and maintain property and personal rights so that the fundamental purposes can be secured. To the extent that it achieves this purpose, a condition of peace, based upon an equilibrium of competing forces, will ensue. If, on the other hand, law fails to recognize substantial elements in the community or make what seems to them adequate provision for their needs, the resulting dissatisfaction may eventuate in agitation for new legislation ranging all the way from feeble protests to outright violence. In every society some disequilibrium prevails because it is never possible to satisfy the demands of every group in full no matter how fair and just the governors may be. A successful ruling elite will endeavor to preserve harmony and maintain justice because it is farsighted enough to see the probable results. For the governing clique and the groups supporting it to use the powers of government to the point of open exploitation is usually too expensive a process because the costs of suppressing opposition are too great. In democratic countries where the processes of popular elections and the free expression of opinion enables underprivileged groups to expose and defeat officials who misuse their powers, this is particularly true. In result, the governing class will endeavor to satisfy as many demands as possible if not too

---

[17] Cohen, *op. cit.*, pp. 123-126.

greatly in conflict with their own basic aims. Court machinery is established to apply existing laws to particular cases according to long established orderly procedures. The majesty of the law and the overshadowing force of traditions of equity and justice, particularly in the Anglo-Saxon communities, together with the independence of judges in terms of long tenure and satisfactory salaries, constrain the judges very often to apply the law in terms of abiding concepts of justice rather than to yield to the demands of the holders of political office. Nevertheless, judicial concepts of justice are prone to reflect the interests of dominant political groups and in this way the courts secure for the ruling combination its primary objectives.

Law enforcement, however, encounters many obstacles in its practical application. Pound lists these as (1) difficulties in ascertaining the facts; (2) the intangibleness of many kinds of duties and the ease with which they made be evaded; (3) the subtlety of modes of seriously infringing important interests; (4) the inapplicability of legal machinery to remedy many important human relations and wrongs; (5) the limited capacity of the means of punishment; and (6) ordinarily the law must be set in motion by some individual or group which has been injured.[18]

Ultimately, the law must carry with it the sanction of public approval. Although it may have behind it the force of the physical powers of the government and the majesty and prestige of the state, these will not be enough to secure passive obedience to the law if it infringes too far upon "the sense of right" of the individuals and groups to which it applies. It is true, as Austin pointed out, that in well-ordered states, the people have a "habit of obedience" to law and it is also true that the rapidity and intensity of the reaction against a law depends greatly upon the character of the population. A stupid or illiterate peasantry might accept the most extreme forms of legal exploitation with passivity while an alert, intelligent, and informed people is apt to resist unjust or exploitative laws much more quickly and effectively.

Government

Organization. Attempts of political scientists to classify the forms of government have not passed much beyond Aristotle on the one hand and Austin on the other. Some contemporary texts in political science still adhere to the Aristotelian trinity of the One, the Few, and the Many. Others attempt to classify states and governments in terms of Austinian legalism as Confederate, Federal, or Unitary forms in terms of the degree of territorial concentration or dispersion of legal power; or in terms of Parliamentary or Presidential forms, stressing the relationship of the

---

[18] Pound, *op. cit.*, pp. 54-60.

executive to the legislature. The chief criticism of the sociologists to these types of classification is that they are formal and superficial as regards understanding of the actual political processes at work, particularly in the origin, exercise, and dispersion of political power in the government and its ultimate result from the standpoint of the control function. Thus Bentley attacks the classification of state and government as incidental and confusing. In his view, it leads nowhere but to a "dead political science." Far preferable, he thinks, would be the classification of governments in terms of the differences of techniques employed by various societies to promote, adjust, and compromise group interests.[19] Giddings, Pareto, and Mosca have pointed out the fallacy of trying to classify governments in terms of the Aristotelian trinity because of the universal fact that all governments are ruled by a few. Michels, in agreement, has erected this idea into an "iron law of oligarchy" in which he contends that every association tends to be ruled by the few. The weight of authority among sociologists is behind the doctrine of control of government by an elite class or group. This does not mean a particular party but any group which is able to dominate in terms of wealth, age, military power, religion, or intelligence. If this is a true statement of the facts, then there could not be a government by the many except in a very broad use of the term where participation in the government is widely extended and the underlying population thus has a check on the government. Such a check, however, does not enable the people to rule but only to review the acts of the rulers.[20]

Rejecting the classification of governments in terms of forms, sociologists have attempted to classify them according to the character of their ruling classes. Thus, Ratzenhofer and Small projected two categories of "conquest state" and "culture state" depending upon whether the rule is based upon physical force or guided by liberalism and high cultural standards. Ward approved monarchy and aristocracy as satisfactory classifications for earlier governmental forms but divided democracy into three possible types: physiocracy or extreme individualism, plutocracy or domination of the government by an organized and exploiting wealthy class, and sociocracy or an ideal government by social scientists. E. A. Ross would characterize governments according to the essential nature of their ruling groups such as clericalism, militarism, officialdom, capitalism, liberalism, and individualism. Other writers, such as Stein, Cooley, Small, and Ellwood, have stressed particularly the fallacy in the use of the term democracy when the actual facts of exploitation, graft, and

[19] A. F. Bentley, *The Process of Government* (Chicago: University of Chicago Press, 1908), pp. 162, 320.
[20] F. H. Giddings, "Social Control in a Democracy," *Papers and Proceedings of the Twelfth Annual Meeting of the American Sociological Society*, XII (December, 1917), pp. 201-206.

economic inequalities indicate that the government is not functioning in the interests of the whole of society.[21]

Although it is important to show that existing classifications of governments are inadequate and misleading, it is also necessary from the point of view of social control to study the mechanisms of government in order to understand how the pressure groups, of which Bentley speaks, are able to make their purposes effective in the government. Consideration has already been given to the manner in which laws are enacted and enforced. It is now necessary to consider the purposes behind the constitutional forms of government so as to understand how, in the manner in which the public powers are adjusted, the aims of controlling groups are effectuated. This is what Bentley refers to as "differences in techniques." Perhaps the most trenchant illustration of the purposes of a ruling class to establish a constitution which would definitely retain and perpetuate their control is to be found in the "check and balance system" of the American federal government. The evidence on this is so well established as to be uncontrovertible. The movement for the constitution was promoted by the wealthy commercial aristocracy of the times, the constitutional convention was engineered by this group, and its membership was almost exclusively made up of its principal representatives. The *Federalist Papers* which rationalized and propagandized the interests of the mercantile group clearly indicates the purposes of the dominant class.

In view of the purposes of the Federalists, what kind of a constitution did they set up? It was definitely intended to place effective checks on the "propertyless majority" and to confer upon the propertied class a secure hold upon the major offices of the government. By means of indirect election and longer terms of office, the President, Senate, and Supreme Court were put beyond the control of the majority, and through a system of varied terms of office, a popular sweep could not gain control of all the offices at once. The powers of government were divided rather than separated in such a way that each department could interpose checks upon the others and thus prevent any action unless those branches controlled by the propertied groups were willing to acquiesce. The same technique was employed in the provision for ratification which called for a two-thirds vote of both houses of Congress and a favorable vote by legislatures in three-fourths of the states.[22]

With the extension of the suffrage, the removal of office-holding qualifications, and subjection of the President to popular vote (through election by the people of the electoral college) as well as the rise of political

[21] H. E. Barnes, "Sociological Contributions to Political Theory," *Twentieth Century Political Thought* (New York: Philosophical Library, 1946), pp. 52-55.

[22] C. A. Beard, *The Economic Interpretation of the Constitution* (New York: The Macmillan Co., 1913).

parties, the American constitution has been considerably democratized, yet the system of checks and balances created by the framers continues to function in such a way as to favor the property-holding classes. This results from the essentially negative character of the constitutional system in that the relations of the public powers are so constituted that it is easier to block action than to obtain cooperation of all agencies. Since change tends to favor the nonpropertied usually, the system favors the upper class elements. Moreover, the different terms of the various offices and the inability of the executive to exercise leadership over the legislative and judicial branches promotes independent action and friction among all branches. Lack of cooperation may be used as a means of deluding the majority and of hiding actual collusion behind the scenes by putting up the appearance of conflict with other branches while actually the leaders of each branch are cooperating in passing legislation desired by the groups they favor. On the other hand, if legislation proposed by groups to whom government leaders are hostile is actually opposed by them, they can put up an appearance of attempting to pass it while at the same time cooperating secretly to have one branch or another defeat it. In addition, the legalistic character of the written constitution and the tradition of the judicial veto by the Supreme Court enables powerful propertied interests to refuse to obey legislation enacted at the behest of the president and congress while litigating the matter in the courts and perhaps obtaining a favorable decision by a compliant court resulting in nullification of the law.

In the so-called parliamentary or "cabinet" form of government, the ability of the cabinet or executive to exercise control over all branches of the government, subject to an adverse vote by parliament or defeat at a popular election, enables it to enact into legislation the policies of the party and make sure that they are enforced in fact by administrative and judicial agencies. In this way, the promises of the party leaders can be made good and the groups which supported the party and placed it in power can be more assured that their interests will be satisfied. Hence, the constitutional system tends to assure the dominant groups unobstructed access to the means of securing their ends through government. This system is probably more satisfactory from a social standpoint because it makes government more responsive to underlying pressures and assures closer approximation between the actual power situation in society and the response of government to the power situation in its various phases. In dictatorships, the practice is to concentrate all governmental powers in the hands of the executive and remove all checks upon him. In result, the controlling position of the dominant group is publicly revealed and the people become more fully conscious of its measures. In order to prevent concerted opposition, all other organized social groups are disbanded and any attempts to reorganize are prevented by an all pervasive secret police. Although physical force is resorted to in larger measure than in representative systems, an extensive attempt is made to secure cooperation through monopolistic control by the government over the means of communication and to indoctrinate the people with the official ideology.

The Dynamics of Government

The two most basic factors in politics are the struggle for economic goods and the struggle for the means of power. Power may bring income through control over the organs of government or conversely income may yield, besides material gratifications, prestige and social status as well as ability to dominate others. Since the control of the state, more than any other form of control, opens the way to both power and wealth, the struggle to gain the mastery of political instruments reaches the highest pitch of intensity. Experience has taught that the attainment of such goals in a project as large as this can best be secured by group action, and the tendency in contemporary affairs is for individuals to rely more and more upon groups to secure their political objectives. Saenger shows in his study of voting trends in New York City that social status as determined by income and religion are the dominant factors in a person's vote in that area. Group membership, he found, was more important than party membership or exposure to propaganda in determining a voter's choice. More significant was the tendency of voters to follow their group leaders.[23]

People join groups to a large degree because they find it to their interest to do so. Hence, group actions relative to politics are based upon policies intended to further the basic economic or social interests of their members. Since individuals have many diverse interests, they join various groups according to the purposes they have in view. Hence, an examination of group organizations shows that they are of many types: employers, workers, and farmers groups, professional groups, religious and welfare groups, and many others. These are organized on local, regional, and national or even international levels and may be oriented toward particular branches of the government. Each group has its particular set of attitudes and these are projected in the form of ideological programs which are so stated as to win outside support and at least nullify or reduce the degree of opposition. Each group has its organization which tends to be dominated by leaders who have the controls in their hands yet are responsible to the group for results. Many groups of the "pressure type"

[23] G. H. Saenger, "Social Status and Political Behavior," *American Journal of Sociology*, LI (September, 1945), pp. 103-113.

require dues, build up large treasuries, employ expert lobbyists or political agents, and devote much time and effort to securing appropriate results through various governmental agencies.

More particularly, the major groups seek to control the government directly so that its agencies will fall into their hands and can be used to suit their purposes. This they are able to do by offering or withdrawing support to political parties and the candidates put forward by them. Political parties are largely combinations of pressure groups and their leaders gain and retain power through their ability to formulate programs satisfactory to the major economic, social and religious groups. Consequently every party which gains power represents a particular combination of groups depending upon the circumstances of the times, the astuteness of the leaders, and the stakes at issue. Since the power struggle is largely over the division of economic income between the various producing agents, the problem often resolves itself into a question of how labor, capital, and agriculture as organized into groups will combine. These combinations in turn are split up into regional groupings with their particular interests, large and small business, skilled and unskilled labor, etc. Cutting across these economic group lines are other factors of religion, tradition, family and neighborhood relationships, and personal tendencies.

Public opinion represents the summation of all of these individual and group interests and attitudes plus the ability of leaders to bring about a shift of attitudes through the use of education or propaganda. Their ability to do this depends upon many factors including the intensity of the propaganda, the emotionalism of the masses, the influence of custom and tradition, and the capacity of the masses to see their basic interests and not to be blinded by propaganda. The business of "engineering consent" has become a highly scientific and practical one and much time, effort, and money are employed by pressure groups and government leaders to secure the desired results.

Government Control Devices

Having obtained control of the government, how do the dominant groups use the government to secure their ends? Briefly, the following instruments of control are available to them:

1. The legal, traditional, and political powers belonging to the various departments of government. These powers are very great, ranging over almost all phases of society, and can be used to suit the purposes of the governors. This can be done by (1) the use of discretionary power, i.e., selecting from the great numbers of statutes those which they wish to enforce; (2) defining and interpreting the powers available to them in

ways most satisfactory to themselves and the groups they represent; (3) adding to already existing powers by enacting new legislation or securing desired constitutional amendments; (4) enforcing the laws which they have selected by appropriate measures such as physical punishment, fines, confiscation of property, withdrawal of privileges of various kinds, threats, intimidation, or even mass slaughter in extreme cases; (5) employing war or threats of war to compel concessions from other states or to divert the attention of the people at home from their domestic policies; (6) using the taxing power of the government in such a way as to favor the groups in power and impose heavier burdens on the others, or to obtain larger public funds which may be diverted either by legal or illegal means into their own pockets and those of their supporters; (7) using the contempt power of the courts to enforce respect for the courts and obtain conformity to their decisions; (8) administering the schools in such a way as to foster the ideology of the dominant groups; (9) promoting propaganda activities through government literature, broadcasts, newscasts, etc., intended to inculcate the ideology of the master class. (10) supporting and securing the cooperation of the church and religion so as to gain the allegiance of religious people for their program; (11) giving special favors to and promoting the activities of the major groups supporting the government such as business groups in a capitalist, or labor groups in a communist society.[24]

In "engineering consent" through the channels of communication, commonly used techniques are (1) appeals to patriotic sentiments and the spirit of nationalism; (2) the use of slogans and key words appealing to accepted customs and traditions or deep-seated prejudices; (3) linking the program with high-sounding ideals of the past or present; (4) use of lies and double-talk to delude the public into thinking that the program is better than it is. Leadership also plays an important part because of the tendency of people to glorify and follow a great national leader. Each contending group tries to popularize its leaders and use their prestige to win additional support.

Checks on the Government by Society

Since it is clear that the instrumentalities of government are used to promote the selfish ends of the groups which have obtained control of it, it is important in the interests not only of groups out of power but of society as a whole that adequate checks be placed upon the office-holders so that exercise of the powers at their disposal will not be carried beyond the canons of right conduct as determined by the traditions of a given society. Among the most important of such checks are the following:

[24] Titus and Harding, *op. cit.*, pp. 152-183.

(1) the force of *custom and tradition*. This is very powerful, and sustained violations might lead to revolt. (2) *Public opinion*. Resting upon tradition and the mores of a given society as well as the interests of individuals and groups who may not be represented in the government, public opinion may be marshalled at times with overwhelming force against wrongdoers in the government. (3) *Elections*. By means of elections in democratic states political combinations and their political agents may be removed from power and others representing different interests installed. This is an effective weapon at times but is often ineffective through lack of public interest and manipulation by political bosses. (4) *The opposition of political groups out of power*. By exposing the mistakes and corruption of the office holders, the opposition may be able to win support to their side. (5) *Legislative bodies and popular legislation*. Opponents of the dominant groups may use their positions to expose government officials and organize the opposition against them. In some countries and in some states of the United States, the people themselves may initiate and adopt legislation, and prevent laws passed by the legislature from going into effect. The recall of public officers is also used in some instances. (6) *The jury system* may act as a check on the courts. (7) If the governing groups carry their exploiting activities to excess, the opposition may resort to *armed violence* against them. The Russian Revolution and the Spanish Civil War are excellent examples.[25]

In addition, opposing groups may resort to many of the techniques also available to the government. They can appeal to tradition, try to arouse public opinion, use propaganda, employ their leaders to win support, seek to influence or control educational and religious institutions, organize resistance among their families and neighbors, and secure the support of reform or uplift groups. Nevertheless, the party in power is apt to be in the most advantageous position even in a democracy. This is particularly true if the principal parties are representative of upper class groups and the lower income groups are relatively unorganized. On the other hand, the impatience of certain ruling groups in European countries with the processes of democracy, which at least give the lower classes a chance at power, led them to support dictatorships under which all opportunity for opposing group action was eliminated.

Summary

The struggle for power of contending groups in society over the division of economic income and the resultant power and social prestige which such income confers is focussed primarily upon the agencies of

---

[25] *Ibid.*, pp. 76-142.

government because it has become the primary instrument of social control. This power struggle in the realm of politics is carried on by means of the marshalling of public opinion and of votes by the major pressure groups usually through the instrumentality of political parties which act as their brokers. In the interacting political struggle which ensues, a certain combination of pressure groups wins control of the government and proceeds to use the powers at its disposal in the form of constitutional grants and statutes and to enact new laws which are then administered and adjudicated in such a way as to secure the major purposes of the groups in power. Their ability to retain power and thus enjoy the fruits of their labors depends upon the degree to which they satisfy their supporters, keep the opposition under control, and persuade ignorant or doubtful voters of the righteousness of their acts.

QUESTIONS

1. Discuss the various theories of the state.
2. Define state, government, and law. Why the tendency to mythicize the nature of the state?
3. What forces within a state determine its legislation?
4. Describe the symbolism of the legal system.
5. How do interest groups secure their aims in the enforcement by law by administrators and courts?
6. Discuss the origin and nature of law.
7. How do judges perpetuate their own class existence?
8. What are the limits of effective law enforcement?
9. How does the American Constitution illustrate the efforts of a ruling class to retain its power?
10. Is the British system or the American system of government more satisfactory from a social standpoint?
11. How does the exercise of power in a dictatorship differ from that in representative governments?
12. What is the basis of the struggle for power?
13. How does the exercise of power in a dictatorship differ from that in representative governments?
14. How are government offices conducted so as to promote the purposes of the ruling classes?

SUGGESTED TOPICS FOR TERM PAPERS AND FURTHER RESEARCH

1. Trace the role of the theory of the separation of powers in history and show how it favored propertied interests.
2. Study the influence on interstate relations of the juridical concept of the state.
3. How does the state differ from other forms of human association?
4. Show how the taxing power has been used to favor groups in power.
5. Trace the history of national elections in the United States and relate it to popular checks on the governing classes.
6. Explain the relationship between the state and the other social institutions.

7. Make a study of the "metaphysical theory of the state."
8. Trace the role of ideals in jurisprudence.
9. Discuss the effectiveness of pressure group in deciding legislation.
10. Show how wealthy, upper-class groups may have the advantage in the courts.

BIBLIOGRAPHY

Books

T. W. Arnold, *The Symbols of Government* (New Haven. Yale University Press, 1946). Shows devastatingly the contrasts between political theories and facts.

E. Barker, *Principles of Sociology and Political Theory* (New York: Oxford University Press, 1951). Considers the relations of state and society from a historical and philosophical viewpoint.

B. J. Cardozo, *The Nature of the Judicial Process* (New Haven: Yale University Press, 1921). Valuable for its exposition of the nature of law.

W. Friedman, *Law and Social Change in Contemporary Britain* (London: Stevens and Son, 1951). An effective study of the interrelations of law and social change in Britain.

Rudolph von Ihering, *Law as a Means to an End*, Modern Legal Philosophical Series, V (Boston: Boston Book Co., 1913). Includes his famous doctrine of self-interest as the basis of law.

E. Jordan, *Theory of Legislation* (Chicago: University of Chicago Press, 1952). Shows the influence of culture in the formation of law.

Harold D. Lasswell, *The Political Writings of Harold D. Lasswell* (Glencoe, Ill.: The Free Press, 1951). Includes his well-known "Psychology and Politics," and "Politics: Who Gets What, How, When," which stress the Max Weber approach. See also: Lasswell and Ithiel de Sola Pool, *The Comparative Study of Symbols* (Stanford, Calif.: Stanford University Press, 1952).

—— and Daniel Lerner, eds., *The Policy Science: Recent Developments in Scope and Method* (Stanford, Calif.: Stanford University Press, 1951). A valuable approach to policy formation and the consequences of decision.

Niccolo Machiavelli, *The Discourses of Niccolo Machiavelli*, translated by Leslie J. Walker (New Haven: Yale University Press, 1950). A new translation of this classic.

Robert M. MacIver, *Democracy and the Economic Challenge* (New York: Alfred A. Knopf, 1952). The discussion is concerned with the "central conflict of the twentieth century . . . (which) rages over the question of the proper role of government in the economic area."

C. E. Merriam, *Political Power* (New York: McGraw-Hill Book Co., 1934). Demonstrates how political power affects social control.

Robert K. Merton and others, *Reader in Bureaucracy* (Glencoe, Ill.: Free Press, 1952). Fifty or more selections, dealing with American and West European political organizations, intended to emphasize the sociological study of bureaucracy.

Roger E. Money-Kyrle, *Psychoanalysis and Politics* (New York: W. W. Norton and Co., 1951). An attempt to explore the unconscious processes that influence political desires and beliefs.

Felix A. Nigro, *Public Administration Readings and Documents* (New York: Rinehart and Co., 1951). A source book of basic principles and problems of public administration.

Alexander H. Pekeles, *Law and Social Action* (Ithaca, N.Y.: Cornell University Press, 1950). Essays on the power of private individuals or groups to act in ways that would be unconstitutional if they were government officials.

Roscoe Pound, *Justice According to Law* (New Haven: Yale University Press, 1951); *New Paths Of the Law* (Lincoln, Neb.: University of Nebraska Press, 1950). The sociological approach to law by a famed jurist.

Joseph S. Roucek and Robert L. Chason, "Political Science," Chapter II, pp. 54-112, in Philip L. Harriman, Joseph S. Roucek, George B. de Huszar, eds., *Contemporary Social Science*, Vol. I, Western Hemisphere (Harrisburg, Pa.: The Stackpole Company, 1953). A documented survey of the various theories covering the concepts of state, government, law, etc.

D. B. Truman, *The Governmental Process* (New York: Alfred A. Knopf, 1951). An effort to formulate systematically the role of interest groups in the political process.

UNESCO, *Contemporary Political Science* (New York: Columbia University Press, 1951). An invaluable survey of methods, research, and teaching in various countries.

R. C. White, *Administration of Public Welfare* (New York: American Book Co., 1951). Covers recent changes in public welfare organization and administration.

F. G. Wilson, *Elements of Modern Politics* (New York: McGraw-Hill Book Co., 1936). Although a text, it is also a valuable introduction to the development of Western attitudes toward the state and to the major problems of democracy in principles and operation.

Periodicals

Paul H. Abbleby, "Political Science, The Next Twenty-Five Years," *American Political Science Review*, XLIV (December, 1950), pp. 924-932.

M. H. Bernstein, "The Scope of Public Administration," *Western Political Science Quarterly*, V (March, 1952), pp. 124-137.

P. E. Corbett, "The Casuistry of Dictatorship," *World Politics*, III (July, 1941), pp. 539-544.

North E. Long, "Bureaucracy and Constitutionalism," *American Political Science Review*, XLVI (September, 1952), pp. 808-818.

F. M. Marx, "Administrative Ethics and the Rule of Law," *ibid.*, XLIII (December, 1949), pp. 119-144.

B. L. Nathanson, "Central Issues of American Administrative Law," ibid., XLV (June, 1951), pp. 348-385.

Joseph S. Roucek, "Political Behavior as a Struggle for Power," *Journal of Social Philosophy*, VI (July, 1941), pp. 341-351.

G. P. Stone and W. H. Form, "Instabilities in Status: The Problem of Hierarchy in the Community Study of Status Arrangements," *American Sociological Review*, XVIII (April, 1953), pp. 25-34.

Edward A. Shils, "Types of Power and Status," *American Journal of Sociology*, XLV (September, 1939), pp. 171-181.

Erich Voegelin, "Extended Strategy," *Journal of Politics*, II (May, 1940), pp. 189-200.

F. G. Wilson, "Political Suppression in the Modern State," *Journal of Politics*, I (August, 1939), pp. 237-257.

CHAPTER VII

Religion

Ordinarily one's first reaction to the term "religion" is to think of the powers ascribed to gods or other supernatural beings and man's relations to such powers. It also includes any knowledge man has of a God, gods, or other supernatural powers and his actions in obtaining their favor or avoiding their hostility, and the influence of these recognized relations upon the control of man's behavior as an individual or as a member of a group. It will not be a part of this chapter to describe the various types of religion or of the gods or supernatural powers except as it will be necessary to analyze them in order to show the nature of the control the religious institutions have upon man's social behavior. If, for instance, the central power of a religion is a universal, omnipotent God, as most Christians assume, the influence upon man's behavior will be quite different from a religion based upon numerous animistic spirits, a tribal god, or a dictator of a deified super state.

Religion and Intellect of Man

Religion's Universal Function. The universal function of religion is the interpretation and control of man's relations to the forces of his physical and social environment. These in turn are thought to be under the control of some supernatural power.[1] It is evident that in order to interpret man's relations to these forces there must be some intellectual comprehension of their nature. Consequently, all religions are built upon the knowledge of the forces of the environment extant at the time of the development of the religion and upon whatever else the founders and leaders contribute to that knowledge.

Religion and Life Processes. From this point of view it is evident that religion results from the intellectual powers of man. Instincts apparently did not determine the relations of man to the environment any more effectively in the early stages of man's development than they do at

---

[1] For the development of this thought see Alvin Good, *Sociology and Education* (New York: Harper and Brothers, 1926), pp. 342-346; and John Clark Archer, *Faiths Men Live By* (New York: Thomas Nelson and Sons, 1934), p. 16.

present. Man's chief power of survival has always resided in intellect
and not instincts. Nor is it any more accurate to say that religion is based
upon instinctive feelings and emotions in order to explain the strong
emotional accompaniments of many religious experiences. The emotional
accompaniments of religion result from the vital life processes involving
food, protection, and sex which religious experiences attempt to make
successful by interpreting and controlling the relations of man's experiences to the forces of the environment. Naturally, as these life processes
are endangered or blocked by ineffective experiences, any religious expressions to overcome or remove these unsatisfactory conditions are
accompanied by strong emotions. When enemies threaten, the war dance
is used to arouse emotions, and to obtain the favor of the tribal god.
When drouth threatens prospective food supplies, strong emotions accompany ritualistic ceremonies honoring the rain god. Moreover, the
religious experiences and interpretations which have resulted in the past
in the more effective protective and agricultural activities permitted the
devotees to survive and maintain their religion while those of the devotees
of less effective religious, military, and agricultural activities did not.
The thrift and industry taught by Puritan religious groups were important factors in the welfare of individuals and groups through several
generations of New England stock. On the other hand, the rejection of
sex activities even for reproduction caused the religious group known as
Shakers to disappear, even though they considered the denial of sex effective in bringing to them future rewards in another life.

For effective functioning religion, as well as other forms of man's
experience, becomes institutionalized. Ritual, ceremony, prayer, sacrifices, and authority of priests and officers develop to control thought and
behavior.

Methods of Social Control Through Religion

The control of individual and social behavior through intellectual
powers depends upon habits, attitudes, and information. All these depend upon institutions in the social environment by which the mind of
each individual is trained for that uniformity of behavior which is the
objective of social control. The types of institutions, religious or otherwise, vary from time to time and from culture to culture. In like manner,
the methods of exerting social control which become a part of the institutions differ. All depend more or less upon the amount and accuracy
of the prevailing knowledge and information.

Among preliterate groups of people the limited amount of accurate
knowledge of the forces of nature and of social relations resulted in the
acceptance of explanations which now are considered superstition. The
priest (sometimes known as the medicine man) was usually consulted

before any activities were begun in connection with hunting, war, marriage, or other economic or political endeavors.[2]

Early religious leaders accepted the prevailing interpretations of the forces of the environment or else attempted themselves to improve upon these interpretations. Naturally those who by chance or through intellectual processes more accurately interpreted the forces of the physical and social environment could more effectively determine successful relations of man to those forces. As civilization evolved, other persons, scientists, philosophers, and political leaders, developed knowledge which in varying degrees religious leaders accepted or rejected. Consequently, religious institutions are organized to control man's relations to social and physical forces either as the forces were previously understood or as they are more or less accurately interpreted by modern students (see also Chapter IX).

In contrast with prescientific civilizations, peoples in modern civilizations are not apt to consult religious leaders and carry on religious rites in their efforts to control the physical and social environment, but consult scientists, artisans, economic leaders, or statesmen instead. Modern men and women consult radio and automobile technicians, choose among motion picture producers and exhibitors, and make use of bankers, merchants, lawyers, and physicians for direction and effective use of the forces in their environment. However, when they attempt to choose or to control the use of these special activities from the point of view of the injury or benefit to themselves and others, they enter into the field of religion.

Authority of Religion

The Extent of Religious Authority. The extent to which religion controls the behavior of men depends upon the degree to which its adherents accept its teachings as authoritative and valid explanations of desired behavior. When no other explanations of desirable behavior in relation to the forces of the environment, or of the forces themselves, are available except those of the religious institutions, behavior is apparently closely under the control of religion. For instance, before natural causes of diseases were known, a religious or a political leader could announce that a fever was caused by a hostile spirit or god who was displeased by a disobedience or violation of a religious requirement. There was seldom any reason for doubting the authoritative statement of the priest or medicine man.[3] To the extent to which persons in modern life believe

---

[2] For illustrations and further development see Robert H. Lowie, *Primitive Religion* (New York: Boni and Liveright, 1924), pp. 3-4; and Alfred Bertholet, *Encyclopedia of Social Sciences*, XII, pp. 389-390.

[3] For role of priesthood see A. Bertholet, *op. cit.*, pp. 388-395; and Paul Radin, *Social Anthropology* (New York: McGraw-Hill Book Co., 1932), pp. 329-333.

that religious teachings and practices are absolute truth and therefore authoritative, their individual and social behavior is controlled by religious institutions.

Religion and Political Authority. In many situations during the development of civilization, especially when political power became specialized in the state, religious institutions either shared with the state the control of social behavior, contended with it for certain fields of control, or attempted to use the state to enforce their own orders and regulations. Among many primitive peoples there is no sharp distinction between religious and political institutions.[4] In some more advanced groups, as among the Hebrews when they comprised an independent state,[5] the religious group and state were combined but did not lose their individual identities. During the latter part of the Middle Ages and still later in some states, the religious institutions assumed sovereign power over the state governments and used them, when necessary, to exert their authority.[6] In both of these situations the control through religious institutions added the punitive power of the state to their teachings and influence in order to control human behavior, and the state used religious sanctions to maintain its control.

In many times and places religious institutions have developed separately from the political. Under such conditions, when the two separate groups have attempted to control the same activities, each used its own method of control, as is illustrated by the control over divorces in the United States. Often there are many activities which each controls and the other ignores, as attendance at church and the payment of taxes. At times one of the groups may require an activity which is prohibited by the other thus bringing about a serious conflict. Illustrations of this situation in modern civilization are the prohibition of the salute to the flag of the United States by certain religious groups and the demand on the part of the Japanese government before World War II that children of the Christian mission schools give obeisance to the Shinto shrines as a political practice.

As civilizations develop, control through religious institutions tends to be weakened so far as authority is concerned, when other sources of information and authority develop. In order to prevent this weak-

---

[4] For illustrations of identity of religious and political institutions, see the Bible, the *Pentateuch;* Alfred Bertholet, *op. cit.,* pp. 391-392; Franz Boas, and others, *General Anthropology* (New York: D. C. Heath, 1938), pp. 650-652; J. Milton Yinger, *Religion in the Struggle for Power* (Durham, N. C.: Duke University Press, 1946).

[5] See Edmund Davison Soper, *The Religions of Mankind* (New York: The Abingdon Press, 1921), pp. 261-265; and the Bible, I and II Samuel, I and II Kings, I and II Chronicles.

[6] For a brief account of relation of church and state see Augustin Fliche, *Encyclopaedia of Social Sciences,* vol. XIII, pp. 253-262.

ening of influence, religious institutions develop ritual, ceremony, and various types of beliefs, propaganda, and training. For the most part these are the methods being used by religious groups in Western civilization.

Ritual and Ceremony. Ritual and ceremony, especially if they are elaborate, repeated, and associated with mysterious powers, are accompanied by strong emotions. These emotions of pleasure, awe, and admiration re-enforce the influence of religious teachings so that the adherents either do not question the authority and correctness of the religious controls or conform to the teachings through force of habit and custom even though logical reasoning may raise doubts as to the validity of the teachings. When faith in religion partakes of the nature of credulity, it usually is maintained chiefly by ritual and ceremony. More simple ritual and ceremony, of course, are used chiefly for economy of effort and are accompanied by less strong emotions. Blind acceptance of religious controls becomes less important and a more rational interpretation of religious beliefs and practices prevails as elaborate ritual and ceremony disappear.

Religious leaders often succeed in establishing the belief that rites and ceremonies have effects that are inherent neither in the emotional accompaniments nor in the habitual and customary ways of acting. Not only do many primitive religious devotees believe a sacrifice to a hostile god will persuade the god to turn aside the evil effects of disobedience, but many modern religious followers ascribe a literal effect of being cleansed from evil to a ritual involving the use of water, or of receiving a blessing in material goods from faithful attendance upon religious ceremonies.

Beliefs and Knowledge. All religious institutions depend upon beliefs, knowledge, and training to exert their influence upon their members. When there was little scientific knowledge to contradict the beliefs prevalent in religion, the beliefs readily controlled social behavior. It was necessary, however, for religious leaders to provide means by which their followers could obtain the knowledge or information inherent in the religious teachings and a training both in religious ceremonies and in the activities of other phases of life that the religious institutions attempted to control. Religious groups in all stages of development have used a program of education and propaganda of one sort or another to persuade their members to accept their doctrines and controls.

In varying degrees modern religious institutions have organized to make effective use of science and other sources of information for a better understanding of the forces of the environment. They have adapted their own doctrines and practices in interpreting and controlling the relations of man to these forces. Such institutions retain influence over their members and extend their control over nearly all aspects of life to the extent that their teachings harmonize with rational thinking and the followers participate effectively and intelligently in the religious activities.

When scientific knowledge radically changes the prevailing explanations of the environment, it frequently requires that the religious teachings of man's relations to the environment need also to be changed. When it was thought that a hostile spirit caused malaria, religious doctrines insisted upon sacrifices to the hostile spirits. When malaria is known to be the result of the bite of an infected mosquito, religious teachings insist upon measures for drainage, screening of houses, the use of quinine and D.D.T., and the instruction of their followers in the necessary health measures. The institutions also include cooperative measures to make it possible for the ignorant and poor to have the advantages of good health conditions.

At times, because new scientific explanations of the forces of nature require that vital changes be made in religious teachings dealing with man's relations to those forces, both the religious leaders and followers reject not only any change in their teachings but also the scientific knowledge itself. Since acceptance of Galileo's teaching would have required religious leaders to revise their concepts of the location of heaven and hell, they rejected the teaching and persecuted Galileo. But when ultimately they had to acknowledge the form of the earth, they sent missionaries around the world to preach their religion. In like manner, religious leaders accept the discoveries of scientific students in biology, chemistry, psychology, economics, and other fields. Since the acceptance of new scientific knowledge often requires changes in religious teachings, religious institutions on the whole serve as a conservative agency requiring scientific discoveries to be tested before they are generally accepted. Any form of religion which rejects all scientifically discovered truths and does not adjust itself to them will in the long run be weakened in controlling man's relations to the forces of the environment and will tend to disappear.

Aspects of Life Controlled Through Religion

Religion is involved in almost all phases of man's relations to the environment. But the aspects of life to be discussed here will be limited to conditions found now in Western civilization, and chiefly to those related to the teachings of Christianity. They will include man's relations to the religious concept of Divine Power, or God, to the religious institutions themselves, to the physical environment, to health and disease, to membership in the family, and to political and economic institutions.

Relation to God. The effectiveness of social control in other than religious activities is partially determined by the concept of the God or gods which the followers of the religion have. A religion based on the principle that gods are either ancestors of its living members or that the gods would injure or destroy persons who dishonorably vary from the customs and teachings of their ancestors tends to prevent change and development of culture. Ancestor worship then becomes an integral part of the religious institutions, and the culture of the people becomes static. It is probable that this aspect of Chinese religious institutions has been a factor in the stability of the Chinese culture and in the slowness with which the Chinese have made use of modern cultural accomplishments. Tribal gods tend to maintain tribal solidarities and prevent the consolidation of the tribes into larger political and religious groups. It apparently took a thousand years to eliminate the conflicting tribal gods of the early peoples from which the Hebrews developed. When they finally did develop their concept of Jehovah, which became a permanent part of their religious institutional life persisting through the last 2500 years, the thoroughly institutionalized concept of the God of the Jews became a chief factor in keeping the Jews a separate people although they have lived among many peoples and adopted other aspects of their cultures.

Built upon the broader concepts of a universal God as portrayed by the Hebrew prophets, Christianity has enormously expanded its concept of God to include many characteristics not found in any other concept of God. To the Hebrew all-powerful God of Justice and Law, Jesus added the concepts of Love, Truth, and of a Heavenly Father interested in the welfare of man. While certain forms of Christian institutions have at times reverted to formalized and static teachings and practices, their chief characteristic has been the search for truth and righteousness in interpreting the forces of the physical and social environment and man's relations to those forces.

This concept of God and man's relations to Divine Power apparently is the explanation of the close relationship of Christian institutions and the development of Western culture. Without a final and complete analysis of the causal relations of Christianity and modern civilization, it is still evident that they have been mutually interacting factors. Scientific discoveries have been encouraged or opposed by various aspects of religious teachings and practices. In like manner economic institutions have at times modified religious institutions and have been in turn modified by them.

Training for Religious Groups. In any institutional form of social relationships and activities, it is necessary to train a number of the participants for the special functions of leaders. In addition, all members and persons

in any way related to the institutional organization need to be trained
for effective participation. Religious institutions, therefore, have provisions for training for effective control of their leaders and their members.
If they do not have, the institutions themselves disintegrate. Thus, the
religious institutions of early Hebrew culture selected the Levites for
priests and other leaders.[7] Through them and their prophets the people
were instructed.[8] And the fathers of all the families were enjoined to
teach their children the religious principles and practices.[9]

In the earliest stages of culture, practically all formal education was
provided by religious leaders. In the development of many civilizations
only religious training remained under the control of the religious institutions. In the first several centuries of Christianity's control over
European culture formal education was provided chiefly by religious
institutions. Education of members was accomplished more or less effectively through religious rituals and ceremonies with some teaching by
priests and monks. In the Middle Ages schools and colleges developed
under the auspices of the religious institutions. Later, in the separation
of church and state, many religious groups attempted to retain the
control of formal education by continuing parochial schools and colleges in which both secular and religious education was offered. In some
places, especially among the Protestants in America, secular education
was left to the public and nonreligious private schools while religious
training was attempted in regular religious services and the special groups
of Sunday schools, Bible schools, and young people's societies. Nearly
all religious groups, however, had and still have colleges and seminaries
for the special training of their leaders.[10]

When practically the only formal education was under the control of
religious institutions, religion had a direct affect upon social control of
both religious and other activities. The administration and teaching were
in the hands of professional men and women who were more or less
trained to direct both secular and religious education. They selected
knowledge, habits, skills, and attitudes which served to train boys and
girls to be leaders as well as followers in the religious institutions. At the
same time the secular education offered was only that which developed
knowledge, habits, skills, and attitudes in other fields of social life which
were in harmony with the religious principles. Thus the religious institutions had a direct control over economic and political institutions.

Since at present public schools provide for most of the formal educa-

---

[7] Numbers, chapter 8.
[8] Deuteronomy, chapter 10, verses 9-13.
[9] Deuteronomy, chapter 11, verses 18-25.
[10] For a short history of the relation of control through formal education to religious institutions see George S. Counts, *Encyclopedia of Social Sciences*, V, pp. 403-
414; and H. Richard Niebuhr, *ibid.*, pp. 421-425.

tion of children, religious institutions can have only indirect control over economic and political institutions. In addition it is difficult for religious leaders to train the children of their members in religious activities. The time and efforts of their children are spent in the public schools and in family and recreational activities so that only a relatively small part of each week is available for religious instruction. It cannot be interwoven with secular education as in the past. In the little time available in Sunday schools, Bible classes, and other attempts at formal training, there is no challenge for the teachers and leaders to prepare themselves for religious teaching as a profession. Consequently, the religious training offered is generally poor and under the auspices of more or less untrained volunteer leaders. In so far, therefore, as individuals of each generation are less effectively trained than those of preceding ones to participate in the religious institutions and fail to become loyal followers of their teachings, the religious institutions are less effective in the indirect control of the social activities of their members in other phases of living as well.

Religious and Secular Education. In order to overcome this hiatus between religious and secular education plans of cooperation are being developed between religious institutions and public schools. One plan provides that children may be dismissed from certain hours of school work if the religious groups arrange for an effective program of religious training under the direction of trained teachers. Another plan provides that the public schools give credit for religious education taken out of school hours, as on Sunday, if an effective program is offered by the religious institutions. A third plan is to provide religious training in the public schools themselves. In the separation of church and state and among peoples of various religious sects, this plan is possible only to the extent that in any school community the religious sects can agree on what religious training can be offered to all alike in the schools.[11]

Control of Physical Forces. Before man had scientifically studied the physical forces of the environment and had discovered the laws of physics, chemistry, biology, and astronomy, many happenings in nature seemed entirely fortuitous. Such physical phenomena as the apparent movements of the sun and stars were regular and dependable. Since the physical welfare of man was so closely connected with these apparent movements and the seasons, apparently among many peoples the sun,

---

[11] For further description of these plans, see the statement for the provisions for released time for religious education in New York City, *Elementary School Journal,* XLI (February, 1941), p. 411; M. D. Davis, "Weekday Classes in Religious Education Conducted on Released Time for Public School Pupils," *U.S. Office of Education Bulletin,* III (1941), pp. 1-60. For opposition to the plans, see G. George Fox, "An Old Issue in a New Guise," *Christian Century,* VIII (August 20, 1941), pp. 1027-1030.

moon, and stars became associated or identified with a god or gods who had control over the physical forces. Consequently early religions included attempts to obtain control of the physical forces by appeals or sacrifices to the spirits or gods. Also the religious institutions incorporated into their practices true or false knowledge, customs, and habits and attitudes in man's behavior toward these forces. The hunt was organized or timed according to the knowledge of the religious leaders, so that it would be more successful. Early man obtained more corn if he planted a fish in each hill to appease the God of plants, although he did not know the facts of chemistry and plant growth.

After scientific explanations of the physical and social environment were discovered, religious institutions in Western civilization continued their chief function of evaluating the use of those forces for man's individual and social welfare. Religious teachings, therefore, include the requirement that the members become educated in the sciences and arts so that they may make use of the knowledge for their own welfare. But if religion is effective in this requirement, it becomes the task of religious leaders to discover just what uses man should make of chemistry, physics, biology, and the other sciences. To the extent that modern religious groups accept science, art, and all phases of modern knowledge and succeed in the interpretation of man's use of them for his individual and social welfare, religion may be effective in social control. Of course, religious institutions often include the teachings of relationships which are destructive. Ultimately, however, unless the teachings are changed or rejected, the religion itself will disappear with the destruction of its adherents.

Health and Disease. In no field of behavior did religion more quickly accept the discoveries of science than in that of disease and health. As mentioned earlier in this chapter, the medicine man and priest were often identical. Although some religious sects in Western civilization attempt to maintain that identity and reject medical practices, for the most part religious institutions are now established on the basis of a separation of functions. The leaders of the religious institutions, however, encourage effective use of modern knowledge to develop and maintain health. Not only do they encourage their members to use modern medical services but they determine the rightness or wrongness of such activities as drinking alcohol upon the basis of their effects upon the physical and mental welfare of man.

Religious institutions are also including as a part of their functions a number of activities for the curing of diseases and the maintenance of health. The use of medicine by missionaries as a means of entrance among backward peoples not only improves the health of those groups but raises their standards of living to include types of behavior which cause the development of personalities in harmony with the religious teachings. Also, in Western civilization activities of religious institutions have included the establishment and maintenance of hospitals and nursing service for more effective use of medical service. Many healthful recreational activities, in addition, have become a part of the function of religious institutions, as in the institutional churches, mission schools, and the work of the Young Men's and Young Women's Christian Associations.

Marriage and Family Life. The household gods of early Roman civilization and the family shrines of many oriental religious practices illustrate the close relationship of religious and marital institutions. The vital effects of sex and reproduction upon man's welfare and the mystery involved in these life processes resulted in their explanation and control becoming a part of the function of religious institutions. Unfortunately for Western civilization, when Christianity developed, sex was freely exploited in ways that were destructive to the welfare of men and women. Consequently, the religious interpretation of sex was that it was inherently evil and could be condoned in marriage only because of the resulting good, the reproduction of mankind. Upon this interpretation of sex, the religious leaders built their teachings and controls of family life. The result was that the religious institutions succeeded in making a part of Western civilization the contradictory attitudes and practices that sex, the physical and psychic basis of marriage, was evil and should be repressed as much as possible and that the birth and rearing of children was good. The physical needs and social status of parents and children were thus secured and sex was supposed to be limited to its only acceptable use. There was practically no attempt to obtain scientific knowledge in this field before the first part of the twentieth century.

Although religious leaders were slow in changing their principles and practices toward sex and the family, many of them now are not only accepting more scientific data in sex, marriage, and training of children, but there is being incorporated into the religious institutions plans to discover additional material and to educate their members and leaders to a more intelligent and satisfactory control of sex, marriage, and family life.[12]

Political and Economic Activities. In the earlier stages of man's development religious leaders were frequently consulted before economic and political activities were begun. When religious and political institutions

---

[12] For the development of attitude and practices of Christian institutions in connection with marriage and the family, see Ernest R. Groves, *The Family and Its Social Functions*, (Philadelphia: J. B. Lippincott Co., 1940), pp. 492-496.

were combined whether the religious or the political leaders exerted the more influence over the other depended chiefly upon the abilities of the leaders and the effectiveness of the institutions. At times the leaders of the two institutions were the same so that it cannot be said that one controlled the other. Since the political as well as the religious institutions depended upon the economic activities, both attempted to control and maintain the economic activities which were favorable to them regardless of the effects on other persons. Naturally if the results of the activities were favorable to other persons as well as to the institutions and their leaders, the more permanent and effective were the institutions. Moreover, the political institutions have always had sovereign power to control economic activities as desired.

With the separation of church and state the religious institutions no longer had direct control over political and economic activities. In both fields, therefore, the influence of religious institutions is now exerted only through their members who participate in economic and political activities. The extent and nature of this indirect influence of the religious are dependent upon at least two important conditions. In the first place, if the adherents of the religious institutions are loyal and obedient to their teachings, their behavior in political and economic activities will be more effectively controlled. In the second place, if the leaders of the religious institutions study the facts and conditions of political and economic institutions so that their own teachings can be more concrete in application the religious control will be more effective.

A practical application of religious teachings to specific political or economic conditions, if the unfair conditions give special benefits to those who have influence with religious leaders, may cause conflicts in the religious institutions. If, however, the religious leaders make a careful, intellectual analysis and application of religious principles to the economic or political conditions, in the long run the influence of the religious on other institutions will be effective.

Russia and Germany. Illustrations of the vital relation of religious activities to economic and political activities are presented by the recent experiences in Russia and Germany. In the earlier days of the Bolshevik regime in Russia the Orthodox Church was abolished clearly because the political authorities thought it would oppose the political and economic changes that were taking place. On the other hand, in recent years during the war, after the political and economic changes had generally been accepted by the population, the governmental authorities permitted, even perhaps encouraged, the restoration of the Church to stabilize the political and economic changes and to support the new nationalism that had taken form. The Nazi regime in Germany attempted to destroy Christianity generally, because of the opposition of its teachings to the Nazi political philosophy and practices. By 1953 in Germany, Italy, and France the political parties receiving the support of the chief religious groups became the dominant ones in developing political and economic rehabilitation.

Adjustment of Religious Institutions to Scientific Knowledge

In the development of scientific knowledge and techniques for control over the forces of the physical and social environments, it often appears that religious institutions are losing their influence in control of individual and social behavior. There are, however, many persons who are attempting to apply appropriate religious principles to their vocations, recreations, and other aspects of social behavior. Small clubs or classes have developed within local religious groups to study ways of applying principles of religion to everyday living. Many leaders of religious and economic groups are teaching practical methods of applying religious principles to various aspects of living. Sometimes special groups are formed and apply religious teachings to everyday living, just as the Young Men's and Young Women's Christian Associations provide living and recreational conditions in harmony with religious teachings.[13]

National organizations of various religious groups are attempting through committees or boards to bring their religious interpretations to bear upon various phases of social life. These committees not only study the practical applications that can be made, but also publish their recommendations so that their leaders and members in smaller groups may know, teach, and practice them in their various aspects of living, as in war and peace, economic activities, recreations, and family life. Finally, the National Council of the Churches of Christ in the United States has been developed for the cooperation of the various member denominations and their other national organizations in the study of such social problems as their religious practices, economic maladjustments, marriage and family life, international relations, and class and race conflicts, in order to find the necessary facts for valid conclusions in applying principles of religion to them for man's welfare. The World Council of Churches has similar purposes.

Summary

Religion is primarily concerned with the adjustment of men to their deities, and thus, directly and indirectly, to the environments in which

---

[13] For suggestions of general application to social control, see Charles A. Ellwood, *The Reconstruction of Religion* (New York: The Macmillan Co., 1922).

they live, both physical and social. During pre-scientific eras, religion resorted to explanations and methods now considered superstition. With the advance of science and practical knowledge, those religious organizations which have continued to exercise effective social control have had to accept factual knowledge and adapt their teachings to it. Leaders and members of religious groups are organizing to discover and apply practical methods of religious principles to life.

QUESTIONS

1. Define religion.
2. How is the unknown utilized for effective social control?
3. How is religious symbolism used in social control?
4. How does secular education affect social control by religions?
5. How can religious institutions influence political and economic institutions more or less effectively without a return to the union of church and state?
6. Upon what factor does social control through intellectual powers depend?
7. How does man's knowledge of the forces of nature effect social control by religion?
8. How do religious groups provide for a trained leadership, and what difficulties do modern religious groups have in this respect?
9. Why is institutionalization important to a religion?
10. Illustrate the problem religious groups have in applying religious teachings to the rapidly changing use of the forces of nature in the modern machine and electric age.
11. Correlate the elaborateness of religious ritual and the effectiveness of control exerted by the religion.
12. How do religious institutions provide training to their members for participation in religious groups, and why do they have more difficulty now than formerly?
13. Why do religious teachings include the overall picture of life?
14. What is the proper relationship between religious teaching and rational thinking?
15. How do religious groups come to use sovereign power, which is characteristic of political institutions?
16. How do modern religious institutions adjust their teachings to modern knowledge of health and disease?
17. Compare the older teachings of Christianity concerning sex and marriage with the newer teachings now being developed.
18. How can religious institutions influence political and economic institutions more or less effectively without a return to the union of church and state?

SUGGESTED TOPICS FOR TERM PAPERS AND FURTHER RESEARCH

1. What psychological hunger does religion satisfy?
2. Compare science, religion, and magic.
3. Compare religion and superstition.
4. Analyze carefully the changes and the effects of the changes that have occurred in social control through religious institutions after the development of the public schools in which formal religious instruction was prohibited.

5. Discuss the concept of separation of church and state.

6. Compare the effects of secularization in the United States with those in Europe.

7. Many advocates of change in economic life, such as Communists and other Marxian socialists, insist that religious institutions are an opiate to prevent laborers and the proletariat generally from demanding their economic rights. Analyze and criticize the reasons for this statement.

8. Develop and analyze the reasons for the organization and the functions of the National Council of Churches of Christ in the United States, and discover how it carries on its functions.

9. What is meant by the saying that religion is the conservative agency in society which tends to encourage orderly progress without destructive changes or static conditions? Show how and to what extent Christianity has served this purpose.

10. Give the reasons for the conflict of Christianity with a science, and show how that conflict is being resolved by religious leaders who approach religion from the point of view of social control of man's relations to the forces of the physical and social environments.

BIBLIOGRAPHY

Books

John Clark Archer, *Faiths Men Live By* (New York: Thomas Nelson and Sons, 1934). An analysis of twelve religious faiths that are found at present, giving their historical background and their relation to the cultural life of their adherents.

Ernest William Barnes, *Scientific Theory and Religion* (New York: The Macmillan Co., 1932). An exhaustive and critical discussion of the relation of science and religion, restricting the term religion largely to the relation of man to the supernatural.

L. L. Bernard, *Social Control* (New York: The Macmillan Co., 1939). A good description of the various methods of obtaining social control, many of which are used by religious institutions. Pages 471-475 specifically treat social control through religion but references to control through religion are made in many other places.

William Clayton Bower, ed., *The Church at Work in the Modern World* (Chicago: University of Chicago Press, 1935). A presentation in a general way of the work and influence of religious institutions in modern life from the point of view of the various churches and denominations. Presents chiefly the present activities for effective control of religious groups and the general methods to exert influence upon other groups.

Simon Doniger, ed., *Religion and Human Behavior* (New York: Association Press, 1954). Essays by authors eminent in psychology and religion on various aspects of the integration of scientific knowledge of human behavior with spiritual and religious behavior.

Charles A. Ellwood, *The Reconstruction of Religion* (New York: The Macmillan Co., 1922). A well-known sociologist presents his case on behalf of the teachings of Christianity.

—— *The World's Need of Christ* (Nashville, Tenn.: Abingdon-Cokesbury Press, 1940). An attempt to show that the Christian principles are being applied in successful families and can be applied to the relationships in economic, political, and other groups.

Frank Gaynor, ed., *Dictionary of Mysticism* (New York: Philosophical Library, 1953). Definitions of terms used in occultism, astrology, oriental religions, and other related topics.

E. O. James, *The Social Function of Religion* (Nashville, Tenn.: Abingdon-Cokesbury Press, 1940). A theological point of view of the sociological aspects of religion.

Rupert C. Koeninger, "Religious Education," Chapter 24, pp. 528-551, in Joseph S. Roucek, ed., *The Sociological Foundations of Education* (New York: Thomas Y. Crowell, 1942).

Halford E. Luccock, *Communicating the Gospel* (New Haven: Yale University Press, 1954). On the methods of dissemination.

J. W. Moody, *Church and Society* (New York: Arts, Inc., 1953). Catholic social and political thought and movements, 1789-1950.

Reinhold Niebuhr, *Moral Man and Immoral Society* (New York: Charles Scribner's Sons, 1936). A famed theologian applies sociological analyses to this (as well as his numerous other works) without knowing it.

Paul Radin, *Primitive Religion* (New York: Viking Press, 1937). Interesting theories on the nature of early religions.

Joseph S. Roucek, "Religious Institutions," Chapter XX, pp. 409-422, in James H. S. Bossard, Walter A. Lunden, Lloyd V. Ballard, and Laurence Foster, eds., *Introduction to Sociology* (Harrisburg, Pa.: The Stackpole Co., 1952). Surveys the recent sociological approaches to religion.

Rockwell C. Smith, *The Church in Our Town* (Nashville, Tenn.: Abingdon-Cokesbury Press, 1945). A sociological interpretation of the church's role in a rural community.

Edmund D. Soper, *The Religions of Mankind* (Nashville, Tenn.: Abingdon-Cokesbury Press, 1921). A description of the most important forms of religious institutions.

Joachim Wach, *Sociology of Religion* (Chicago: University of Chicago Press, 1944). A historical survey of the role of religion in social organization.

——— "Sociology of Religion," Chapter XIV, pp. 406-437, in Georges Gurvitch and Wilbert E. Moore, eds., *Twentieth Century Sociology* (New York: Philosophical Library, 1945). A systematic survey of the recent developments in the sociology of religion.

Wilson D. Wallis, *Religion in Primitive Society* (New York: F. S. Crofts, 1939). A valuable sociological analysis.

Periodicals

William C. Bower, "Religion on Released Time," *Christian Century*, LVIII (1941), pp. 980-981.

S. Brody, "Science and Social Wisdom," *Science Monthly*, LIX (September, 1944), pp. 203-214.

R. W. Brown, "An Observer Warns the Church," *Harper's*, CLXXVI (1937), pp. 18-25.

Jerome Davis, "The Social Action Pattern of the Protestant Religious Leader," *American Sociological Review*, I (1936), pp. 105-114.

M. D. Davis, "Weekday Classes in Religious Education Conducted on Released Time for Public School Pupils," *U.S. Office of Education Bulletin* (1941), No. 3, pp. 1-66.

M. A. Dawber, "Cooperative Movement and the Church," *Annals of The American Academy of Political and Social Science*, CXCI (1937), pp. 70-75.

J. H. Fichter, "Marginal Catholic: An Institutional Approach," *Social Forces*, XXXII (December, 1953), pp. 167-173.

George Fox, "An Old Issue in a New Guise," *Christian Century*, LVIII (1941), pp. 1027-1030.

Sidney I. Goldstein, "The Roles of an American Rabbi," *Sociology and Social Research*, XXXVIII (September–October, 1953), pp. 32-37.

E. Harms, "Development of Religious Experience in Children," *American Journal of Sociology*, L (September, 1944), pp. 112-122.

H. W. Holmes, "God in the Public Schools," *Atlantic Monthly*, CLXVI (1940), pp. 98-105.

Christen T. Jonassen, "The Protestant Ethics and the Spirit of Capitalism in Norway," *American Sociological Review*, XII (1947), pp. 676-686.

A. L. Kinsolving, "War and Our Religious Condition," *Virginia Quarterly Review*, XXI (July, 1945), pp. 355-367.

H. M. Philpott, "Conversion Techniques Used by the Newer Sects in the South," *Religious Education*, XXXVIII (May, 1943), pp. 174-179.

E. Schmiedeler, "Don Sturzo's Sociology of the Supernatural," *Catholic Educational Review*, XLI (June, 1943), pp. 342-346.

L. W. Southcott, "Religion and Education—Past, Present, and Future," *Teachers College Journal*, XV (January, 1944), pp. 68-69.

Pitirim A. Sorokin, "Rural-Urban Differences in Religious Culture, Beliefs and Behavior," *Publications of the American Sociological Society*, XXIII (1929), pp. 224-225.

Herbert A. Sturges, "Comparison of Orthodoxy and Piety," *American Sociological Review*, II (1937), pp. 372-379.

Howard Woolston, "Religious Consistency," *American Sociological Review*, II (1937), pp. 380-388.

Chapter VIII

Marriage, Home and Family

An adequate consideration of social control in relation to the family would appear to involve the treatment of at least three major aspects: (1) general societal controls over the family and marriage, such as, for example, the laws governing marriage and divorce; (2) familial controls over persons, such as the influence of the family in the formation of the child's early personality; and (3) inter-societal tensions in the family, such as are manifest in modern "individualism" through which extra-family values are brought to bear on family practices and values. The latter is illustrated by numerous women who marry but refrain from the majority practice of child bearing because they prefer "careers" to the traditional family role. Each of these three types of control will be treated in the present chapter.

Marriage and the Family

Considerable confusion centers around the distinction between the terms "marriage" and "family" especially among laymen. Briefly, a useful and basic distinction seems to be this. Family refers to a group of people. The family group usually includes, in our culture, husband and wife, their children by blood or adoption, and certain other persons related by blood or affinity all of whom share a common household. Sometimes the word "family" is used to include a larger circle of persons who trace lineage to a common ancestor or pair. In this sense we refer to "family reunions" at which a hundred or more persons may be in attendance. Perhaps it might be useful to distinguish *exclusive* and *inclusive* family in order to differentiate the group made up of the interacting married pair and their children who share a common domicile from the larger family "group" which is a group only in the sense of common lineage. Whereas, then, the family is a group of people, marriage refers to a set of rules and regulations (laws, mores, etc.) which are generally recognized as necessary or proper for persons in family relationship. These rules of conduct are manifest and multifarious. They begin at the cradle and continue to the grave. Never does one, even though he remains unmarried, entirely escape from their influence.

Societal Controls Over Marriage and the Family

The various societies and cultures of the world have, without exception, established ways in which the behavior of persons is regulated with respect to sex, marriage, and the family. In some societies these controls are so numerous and so intricate as to require volumes simply to explain them, and in our own merely the legal aspects of societal control require several volumes for careful discussion.[1]

It is an error, however, to think of societal controls over marriage and the family as being entirely or even mainly a matter of the law. As numerous and intricate as the laws of domestic relations are, they constitute but a part of the total structure of societal control. The mores and folkways, and "public opinion" with its taboos and compulsions, all control the behavior of persons by numerous extra-legal (and sometimes, as we shall see, illegal) devices. It thus appears desirable to separate the discussion of legal and extra-legal controls over marriage and the family.

Formal, Legal Controls. It is common knowledge that the laws of our society—federal, state, and local—regulate the behavior of persons in family relationship differently from the manner in which these persons are regulated in their other relationships and differently from nonmarried persons. Thus, for example, a wife may not be forced to testify against her husband in criminal proceedings; a husband is responsible for his wife's support and for the support of his children; and children who have attained their majority are legally responsible for the support of their indigent parents. In these and dozens of other ways the statutory laws and the "common law" regulate marriage and the family.

Statutory Legal Control over Marriage. It is not the purpose of this chapter to describe in any detail the laws of domestic relations in the United States. (For this the reader is referred to Vernier,[2] for a very extensive treatment and to Baber, *Marriage and The Family*,[3] for a shorter, but essentially accurate, account.) Rather it is our purpose to survey somewhat generally some of the main types of statutory control.

Is Marriage a Contract? Although commonly so referred to, marriage differs from a contract in at least two important respects: (1) An ordinary legal contract can be terminated at will by agreement of the parties thereto, provided no third party sustains damages thereby. In no American state can a marriage be dissolved by mutual consent. Instead, the

---

[1] Chester G. Vernier, *American Marriage Laws* (Palo Alto: Stanford University Press, 1931-1938) 5 vols. and supplement. A work probably without equal in this field.

[2] *Ibid.*

[3] Ray E. Baber, *Marriage and The Family* (New York: McGraw-Hill Book Co., 1939), chapters V, XIV.

law holds that the state (that is, society) has an interest in perpetuating the marriage and that only under certain designated and somewhat exceptional circumstances can it be terminated. South Carolina permits no divorce under *any* circumstances and New York only under one (adultery). (2) The second major way in which marriage differs from a contract is in the terms. In ordinary contracts the parties thereto make the terms. The main requirement imposed by the law in this connection is that, to be legally enforceable, a contract must not require anyone to do anything that is illegal at the time the contract is made. But in marriage the terms of the relationship are the same for everyone. In fact no persons married or contemplating marriage may make a legal contract which makes their marriage in any way different from anyone else's in the same state. A man and a woman might make a contractual agreement to the effect that if either wishes a divorce the other will cooperate in the creation of legal grounds for such action. But such a contract has no legal standing whatsoever and, in fact, in some states *may be* actually illegal. Certainly such a contract, if known to the court, is the basis for denying the divorce categorically. Likewise a man and woman may agree that after marriage the woman will work and support herself and her children by a deceased husband. But if after marriage she refuses to do so her husband is still legally responsible the same as all husbands are for the support of their families within the limit, of course, of their financia' ability. There are other ways in which the marriage relationship and the contractual relationship differ but these two are fundamental: (1) inability to terminate the relationship by mutual consent and (2) inability to make the terms of the relationship.

Marriage Prohibitions and Regulations. Marriage is prohibited in most states to certain categories of persons such as feebleminded, epileptics, syphiletics and insane. Likewise marriage is prohibited to persons in certain degrees of blood relationship, such as first cousins or closer in some states, and even sometimes to persons related through marriage (affinity) such as stepparents and stepchildren or between a man and his ex-daughter-in-law. Also on persons who are not specifically prohibited from marrying, numerous restrictions are imposed which, until they are complied with, do in fact prohibit marriage. In this category are laws requiring prospective marriage partners to have attained the legal age, to secure a license (increasingly often, a number of days in advance of the marriage date), to submit to a physical examination, to exchange marriage vows before some duly recognized marriage officiant and to record the signed license or certificate. Each state has its own laws on each of these points and others, and little uniformity, except for the general pattern, is apparent. The cynic will find ample encouragement as he reads the laws of the several states in regard, for example, to the minimum age for marriage, to inquire what evidence exists for considering children of fourteen years of age old enough to marry in one state while persons of seventeen are not considered to be mature enough in another state. Or perhaps one need not be a cynic to inquire why a person needs to be twenty-one years of age before he may cast a vote for village constable but is wise enough to choose a life partner at the age of sixteen! The sociologist, however, has become calloused to such considerations. He knows that it is futile to expect much logic or consistency in matters such as these because he has learned that these legal requirements are set up arbitrarily and are in the main only the codified mores of the persons who wrote or revised the laws supplemented by these persons' best guesses as to similar prejudices on the part of their "constituents." Our domestic relations laws, like Topsy, "jest growed." As time goes on, logic and rational criticism are having more and more influence, but the goal of uniformity and rationality in marriage laws is still far off. One writer recently referred to the "Medley of Marriage Laws" in the United States; perhaps "discord" would be a better figure of speech. In respect to divorce, parental responsibility, child labor, legitimacy, and other aspects of marriage relationships, the same facts are apparent: (1) variety in the number and types of legal control from state to state and (2) slow progress toward uniformity through the application of more rational methods of law revision.

"Common Law" Controls. A second type of legal control is found in the "common law," sometimes erroneously referred to as "unwritten law." The common law is in fact written but not written *as law.* Instead it is recorded in court decisions of the past which were based upon the application of general principles of justice to local and "common" ideas and practices as to what was regarded as right and wrong. The common law tradition is perhaps best known in respect to so-called "common law marriage"—a man and a woman living *as if* married and so regarded by their acquaintances but with no express legal sanction having been granted. In twenty-two states common law marriages are valid, although there are differences in the practical significance of such validity from state to state. In only four states are common law marriages declared by statute to be null and void.

Informal Controls. An often overlooked or underestimated manner in which sex, marriage, and family relationships are influenced by society is, in origin, very close to the common law tradition. In each society there will be observed widely held beliefs concerning what is proper, right, expedient, etc., in regard to the behavior of persons in family relationships. Some of these are codified and become laws, but many others

are influential by less formal—but no less effective—devices. Social ostracism, gossip, and ridicule have their influence upon forcing conformity
to group ideas and values. These devices have their force only because
there exists a widespread and more or less apparent consensus as to what
is to be regarded as right or wrong. Whenever this consensus is sufficiently weakened, the informal devices lose their potency or vanish
altogether. The "strong voice of Mrs. Grundy" may be a powerful force
in keeping the village blacksmith from calling on the constable's wife,
but it is quite unimportant in Greenwich Village. But even in large
urban centers it is well not to underestimate the controlling force of a
person's fear of gossip or other forms of informal control.

Informal controls may be either more or less exacting than the law.
There is, for example, no legal violation involved in a married woman
entertaining a male friend when her husband is away; but there is a violation of "propriety," "good taste," morality, etc., which in numerous cases
causes such behavior either to be avoided or kept "under cover." On the
other hand, there are states which have laws prohibiting the sale, possession for sale, or advertising, of contraceptive devices, but in these same
states widespread practice of "drugstore contraception" is actually in
evidence, and free (sometimes even quasi-tax supported) contraception
clinics are to be found. A well-trained and highly regarded judge recently told the writer that so far as the violation of the law on contraception in his state was concerned thousands of retailers, publishers,
teachers, druggists, and others could be prosecuted. Yet, year after
year, such wholesale violation of the law is openly tolerated because
many, if not most, of the people now accept birth control as legitimate.
It would be difficult for a court to secure conviction of a person who
pleaded "not guilty" to many of these laws, regardless of the evidence,
because public opinion would not support such action.

Conflicts Between Informal and Formal Controls

In the preceding paragraph two typical instances were cited in which
formal and informal controls over certain aspects of sex, marriage, and
family were at variance—sometimes the law and at others the mores being
the more restrictive. Many more such instances could be cited. In most
states a man has as much legal right to sue for damages sustained in breach
of promise as a woman has. And in some cases real financial damages
could be demonstrated even to the most exacting jurist. But since public
opinion will not support the law, it is in practice impossible for a man to
get such a judgment from the court. It is common knowledge, also, that
even though the laws regarding legal grounds for divorce are the same for
men as for women, it is much easier for a woman to secure a divorce

from a man than vice versa even though the evidence be identical. It is in our mores that "it is simply not sporting to let a woman down except in extreme circumstances." Again much of the pre-marital sex behavior is clearly illegal. Yet very rarely does a "case" emerge in the legal sense. And when it does conviction is very difficult, sometimes almost impossible, regardless of the evidence. Most cases fail to "come up" because the legally injured parties do not consider themselves to have been injured since their moral standards are very different from those which the law presumes. The cases are difficult to sustain if they actually do come to trial because it is widely recognized by judges and jurors alike that considerable change in standards of conduct has occurred recently and that to prosecute every case to the letter of the law would involve the court in an endless number of improvised "cases." Again, in two subdivisions of a state, counties and cities—regions which operate under the same law— very different "policies" often exist regarding the definition or meaning of the law and the type and amount of evidence required for prosecution. Laws regarding prostitution are an example. Then, too, laws are often so loosely written that, for instance, in one state an adult who quotes a vaudeville comedian *verbatim* in the presence of an eighteen year old could be prosecuted for "contributing to the delinquency of a minor" on two counts—obscenity and profanity! It should be borne in mind, however, that the officers of the law are quite conversant with all this and that a reasonably consistent policy of law interpretation and law enforcement exists with due respect for the local and provincial beliefs and practices of the people. Where the values of the society are in conflict or are inconsistent, verdicts will be issued which seem "too strict to be reasonable" or "too lax to be effective." But neither the law nor its administrators can be held responsible for the inability of a society to make up its mind, so to speak, on what is right and what is wrong in the area of sex, domestic relations, marriage, and divorce.

The Family as a Control Over The Person

The family may be conceived as "the Cradle of the Personality." Much research in recent years has demonstrated the great and profound effect of the early experiences of the child on his eventual adult personality.[4] For the purpose at hand, it is sufficient to point out that his own

---

[4] See H. Hartshorne and M. Mary, "Testing the Knowledge of Right and Wrong," *Religious Education*, XXI (October, 1926); Jesse Bernard, *American Family Behavior* (New York: Harper and Brothers, 1942), pp. 273 ff.; Lewis Terman, *Psychological Factors in Marital Happiness*, (New York: McGraw-Hill Book Co., 1938); G. Murphy, L. B. Murphy, and T. Newcomb, *Experimental Social Psychology* (1937), pp. 168-187; L. L. Bernard, *An Introduction to Social Psychology* (1926), pp. 307-309; Margaret A. Ribble, *The Rights of Infants* (New York: Columbia University Press,

family presents to the child the first, the most vivid and complete, and sometimes the only "object lesson" in adult living that he experiences. This is not to be taken to mean that childhood experience is wholly and solely determined by adult behavior patterns. Obviously, there are many other influences to which he is exposed, and these play upon the present-day child earlier in life, more often, and in more ways than they did in earlier generations. Reading, travel, and the movies are cases in point. But nevertheless, the child's own family constitutes a concrete reality of experience which develops in him as a complex pattern of overt and covert habits. These patterns he never entirely escapes in the sense that all new patterns are conditioned by those already existent. The evidence is clear that in spite of new experience childhood patterns tend to be resistant to basic change. And so the family conditions the child, first of all, to the family itself—to the idea that the type of family he experiences is the approved, in fact the only really conceivable, pattern for adult living. From time to time, the child learns to receive many different types of basic want satisfaction from the family and in the family *milieu*. This strengthens the belief and helps to root it deeper in emotional feeling. Thus the family, with some modifications to be sure, becomes in the child a "vested interest."

The Person as a Control Over The Family

The family does not entirely determine the pattern of attitudes, habits, and wishes of the adult personality. Other influences play their part and the element of "chance" is great (see Chapter III). It seems necessary to consider briefly the process of control over the family itself which results from the individuality of particular persons.

In an attempt to explain many of the fundamental changes in family norms during the last two generations many sociologists and social psychologists seem to have reached an approximate consensus to the effect that that pattern of values and related practices known vaguely as "individualism" constitutes the essence of the change. Folsom attempts to enumerate these newer values.[5] The individualistic ideology involves such ideas as these:

1943), analyzes the nature of the first personal relationship between the infant and his parents and the effect of this highly personal first adjustment on the child's future personality; James H. S. Bossard and E. S. Boll, *Family Situations* (Philadelphia: University of Pennsylvania Press, 1942); Ernest Watson Burgess and Harve J. Locke, *The Family, from Institution to Companionship* (New York: American Book Co., 1945); Manuel Conrad Elmer, *The Sociology of the Family* (Boston: Ginn and Co., 1945); Ray Hamilton Abrams, ed., "The American Family in World War II," *Annals of the American Academy of Political and Social Science*, CCXXIX (1943). These are but a few of the many studies of this field.

[5] Reprinted from J. K. Folsom, *The Family* (New York: John Wiley and Sons, 1934), pp. 224-225.

1. We live only once, hence why not make the most of it.
2. You can't give another person happiness; he has to find it for himself: hence look out for yourself. . . .
3. You can't make others happy unless you are a normal, happy, well-adjusted person yourself. . . .
4. The world needs many kinds of personalities. Be yourself.
5. Morality consists in being true to the code that fits your particular personality. . . . It may be wrong for you to do what is right for someone else, as well as the reverse.

With substantial numbers of persons basing their behavior upon these ideologies, numerous nonconformist or minority patterns of sex and family life have become prominent, as:

1. Women claiming marriage *and* a career simultaneously.
2. The practice of birth control, either to achieve "voluntary parenthood" or complete childlessness.
3. "Strange moralities"—premarital and extramarital sex freedom of various kinds and degrees.
4. Decline (almost absence of) arbitrary discipline of children by parents. It becomes almost the "duty" of the parent to refrain from thwarting the wishes of the child or superimposing his values on the child.
5. Each person in the family pursuing his own interests with a sharp reduction of the amount of time spent in the "family circle" and with little concern with the maintenance of common beliefs, values, or goals.

These are some of the overt manifestations of the philosophy of individualism.

The antecedent, and to a considerable extent antithetical, family pattern we may term "familism." Although undoubtedly there were in the past numerous persons and couples whose values were divergent, familism was in the United States up to World War I the prevailing pattern and in many areas still continues so to be, notably in the more remote rural areas, in the immigrant colonies in the larger cities, and among certain religious groups. The pivotal ideologies of familism are, like those of individualism, difficult to verbalize and to differentiate from one another, but the following may be of assistance:

1. The person attains most of his legitimate goals through the family; no conflict can exist between individual and familial goals because they are the same.
2. The predominant family values of familism are:
   a. Early marriage but with family approval.
   b. Disapproval of contraception when it is used to achieve either childlessness or very small families; often disapproval *per se*.

c. Woman's role is that of homemaker—no "careers."
d. Family care of aged, infirm, and other dependents; resultant household is relatively large.
e. The family as a strong economic unit; considerable, if not complete, pooling of financial and other economic resources of all who have them.
f. Considerable emphasis upon the family as a productive unit; "farming out" such functions as baking, laundry, canning, sewing, strongly disapproved.
g. Pride and status attend the family, as distinct from personal success and achievement; it is almost as satisfying to have some family member achieve a goal as to achieve it oneself.

A comparison of one's own personal values relating to marriage and the family with those of individualism and familism will reveal in most instances a combination of (and not improbable conflict between) familism and individualism. Most contemporaries of college age represent a dual acculturation, a sort of family value marginality (see Chapter IV), in which both the old and the new value systems are in evidence with either, or neither, clearly ascendant. Most of the family problems of our day have their genesis in this condition—contraception, careers for women, courtship problems, companionate marriage, divorce, marital adjustment, and so on. What we have come to call "social problems" (including, of course, problems in the realm of marriage and the family) are "problems" because different persons and groups in our society have different beliefs and definitions of social facts and varying opinions as to what, if anything, ought to be done about them. In other words a problem is a problem because no generally acceptable solution for or definition of the condition is in existence. Because of lack of space, the application of this important point of view will have to be confined to one illustration: careers for married women. Why is this a problem to many couples? Because outside employment of the wife presents at least two sets of difficulties. In the one group are such "practical" matters as the proper management of the household and especially the care of children. But why do couples under these circumstances need to have homes in the traditional sense? Why not live in the same manner as single persons? The answer is unescapable: because it is considered that a married pair *ought* to have a home of its own. So far as efficiency, economy, and convenience are concerned the home would not be indicated, but the familistic mores decree that a married couple *should* have a home. A second set of difficulties involves matters of social approval. One hears on every hand accusations and insinuations involving married pairs who "shirk their duty to provide a home" and women with careers who "are parasites on the race; who deny their birthright to children." And the accusers are not infrequently persons in the prolific one-child families! But moral judgments are rarely rational or consistent; they just are.[6]

Numerous husbands of career women are silently or audibly resentful of the fact that their wives are not, in fact, dependent upon them and in some cases actually receive a superior income. Likewise, numerous career wives manifest concern that the domestic virtues of which they are capable are not in evidence and feel that the implication of inability to maintain a home is unfair to them. Meanwhile they are constantly reminded that it is they who contribute to unemployment and relief costs because they are "taking men's jobs from them." It is not easy to develop and maintain a healthy attitude toward self and husband when one is conscious of such attitudes on the part of one's neighbors and friends. But at the same time individualistic values are in evidence both in self and in the group. Careers mean that a higher standard of living is possible both for the woman and for her husband and children. The same persons who assert vehemently that "a woman's place is in the home" are genuinely respectful of the higher standard of living made possible by her not being at home. The career woman may actually enjoy her work and be successful in rationalizing it as a genuine contribution, or may even be motivated by a service ideal of the most commendable sort. But the *problem* of the career persists. And so it is with other problems of marriage and the family. Both of the philosophies are present in contemporary American society and both exert significant controlling influences upon the overt and covert behavior of men and women. The conflicts between them contribute largely to the socio-genesis of our sex, marriage, and family problems.

Summary

In this chapter attention has been directed to three main streams of control: (1) societal control, both legal and extra-legal, over marriage, the family, and sex; (2) control of the family over the behavior of persons; and (3) control exerted over the family and marriage patterns by the person whose personality has been molded by extra-familial influences and values. Thus it appears that there are three interacting lines of influence, sometimes working in harmony with each other and at other times and in other ways at cross purposes as in the case of legal versus extra-legal influences and familism versus individualism. The thesis was advanced that family problems like other social problems have their socio-genesis in these societal conflicts and inconsistencies. But, if one is to be

---

[6] See John F. Cuber and Betty Pell, "Method for Studying Moral Judgments," *American Journal of Sociology*, XLVII (July, 1941), pp. 12-34.

realistic, these tensions must be considered as normal rather than necessarily pathological conditions in our present society.

QUESTIONS

1. Define marriage as distinct from family.
2. What types of control are exercised over the family and marriage?
3. In what ways does marriage differ from a contract?
4. Who sets the terms of a marriage?
5. How many parties may agree to the dissolution of a civil contract? To a marriage?
6. To what classes of persons may the privilege of marriage be refused?
7. In what ways other than outright prohibition may marriage be controlled?
8. What facts are apparent in respect to various aspects of marriage relationships?
9. What types of law contribute to control of marriage and family?
10. Define a common law marriage.
11. Is a common law marriage legal in the United States? Explain.
12. Discuss the effectiveness of informal means of marriage control as compared with formal means.
13. Is adult behavior the only determiner of childhood behavior?
14. How does a child condition new patterns with which he may come in contact?
15. What is the essence of the recent changes in family norms?
16. In the ideology of the individualist, what is morality?
17. How does the ideology of individualism affect child training and discipline?
18. What family pattern is antithetical to individualism?
19. According to the ideology of familism, what is the role of woman?
20. What are the economic implications involved in the taking of careers by women?

SUGGESTED TOPICS FOR TERM PAPERS AND FURTHER RESEARCH

1. The conflict of marriage laws.
2. The interest of the state in marriage and family relationships.
3. Religious interest in marriage and family relationships.
4. The contractual basis for marriage.
5. A national code of marriage and familial law.
6. A discussion of common law marriages.
7. The dispute over contraception.
8. Enforceability of current marriage laws.
9. The family as the "Cradle of the Personality."
10. The role of the family as a determiner of childhood personality.

BIBLIOGRAPHY

Books

Jessie Bernard, *American Family Behavior* (New York: Harper and Brothers, 1942). A thoroughly sociological and sociometric treatment of the family. Of particular interest in this connection are chapters I, V, VI, VII, XIX.

Ernest W. Burgess and L. S. Cottrell, Jr., *Predicting Success or Failure in Marriage* (New York: Prentice-Hall, 1939). A pioneer study.

A. W. Calhoun, *A Social History of the American Family* (Cleveland: Arthur H. Clark, 1917). An outstanding study of the colonial American family.

W. Goodsell, *A History of Marriage and the Family* (New York: The Macmillan Co., 1934). A valuable contribution to the history of the European-American family system.

E. R. Groves, *Family and Social Functions* (Philadelphia: J. B. Lippincott, 1940). Covers the social purpose of the family; a rigorous sociological treatment.

B. Malinowski, *The Sexual Life of Savages in Northwestern Melanesia* (New York: Liveright, 1929). A famed analysis of the family system of the preliterates.

"The Modern Family," *The Annals of the American Academy of Political and Social Science*, CLX (March, 1932). A symposium of valuable articles. Also valuable is the more recent symposium in the *American Sociological Review* (October, 1937), and *ibid.*, LIII (May, 1948).

Meyer F. Nimkoff, *The Family* (Boston: Houghton Mifflin Co., 1934). A systematic study of the family as a social institution.

Willard Waller, *The Family: A Dynamic Interpretation* (New York: The Dryden Press, 1938). Quite original in its sociological description of the family processes.

E. Westermack, *The History of Human Marriage* (New York: The Macmillan Co., 1921). A classic study of marriage among preliterates.

C. C. Zimmerman, *Family and Civilization* (New York: Harper and Brothers, 1947). A controversial book; purports to present a historical evaluation of the family in Western civilization; makes a strong case for familism.

Periodicals

E. Baber, "Marriage and the Family After the War," *Annals of The American Academy of Political and Social Science*, CCXXIX (September, 1943), pp. 164-175.

L. L. Bernard, "The Conflict Between Primary Group Attitudes and Derivative Group Ideals in Modern Society," *American Journal of Sociology*, XLI (March, 1936), pp. 611-623.

J. H. S. Bossard, "Family Situations and Child Behavior," *Journal of Educational Sociology*, XVII (February, 1944), pp. 323-337; "Law of Family Interaction," *American Journal of Sociology*, L (January, 1945), pp. 292-294.

G. Bryson, "College Courses and Marriages and the Family," *Sociology and Social Research*, XXVI (January, 1942), pp. 209-221.

E. W. Burgess, "The Family and the Person," *Publications of the American Sociological Society*, XX (1927), pp. 133-143.

Leonard S. Cottrell, Jr., "The Present Status and Future Orientation of Research on the Family," *American Sociological Review*, XIII (April, 1948), pp. 123-135.

John F. Cuber and Betty Pell, "Method for Studying Moral Judgments Relating to the Family," *American Journal of Sociology*, XLVII (July, 1941), pp. 12-34.

C. P. Dennison, "Parenthood Attitudes of College Men," *Journal of Heredity*, XXXI (December, 1940), pp. 528 ff.

Robert M. Dinkel, "Parent-Child Conflict in Minnesota Families," *ibid.*, VIII (1943), pp. 412-419.

"Family in Transition, A Symposium," *Religious Education*, XXXIX (May, 1944), pp. 131-168.

R. G. Foster, "Present Day Challenges in Education for Family Life," *Social Forces*, XX (December, 1941), pp. 244-256.

Paul C. Glick, "The Family Cycle," *ibid.*, XII (April, 1947), pp. 164-174.

Reuben Hill, "The American Family: Problem of Solution?" *American Journal of Sociology*, LIII (September, 1947), pp. 125-130.

E. R. Groves, "Education for Family Life and National Defense," *ibid.*, XIX (May, 1941), pp. 519-522.

H. Hartshorne and M. May, "Testing the Knowledge of Right and Wrong," *Religious Education*, XXI (October, 1926), pp. 539-554.

A. B. Hollingshead, "Class Differences in Family Stability," *The Annals of The American Academy of Political and Social Science*, CCLXXII (1950), pp. 39-46.

L. S. Hollingsworth, "Social Devices for Impelling Women to Bear and Rear Children," *American Journal of Sociology*, XXII (1916), pp. 19-29.

J. W. Macfarlane, "Inter-Personal Relationships within the Family," *Marriage and Family Living*, II (Spring, 1941).

Carson McGuire, "Family Life in Lower and Middle Class Homes," *ibid.*, XIV (1952), pp. 1-6.

T. C. McCormick and B. E. Macrory, "Group Values in Mate Selection in a Sample of College Girls," *Social Forces*, XXII (1944), pp. 315-317.

B. M. Moore and H. E. Moore, "Family, A Reservoir in Crisis," *Journal of Educational Sociology*, XV (January, 1942), pp. 279-286.

M. F. Nimkoff, "Occupational Factors and Marriage," *American Journal of Sociology*, XLIX (November, 1943), pp. 248-254.

P. Popenoe, "Marital Happiness in Two Generations," *Mental Hygiene*, XXI (April, 1937), pp. 218-231.

J. O. Reinemann, "Extra-Marital Relations with Fellow Employees in War Industry as a Factor in Disruption of Family Life," *ibid.*, X (1945), pp. 399-404.

H. H. Remmers and N. L. Gage, "Family Education and Child Adjustment," *Educational Research Bulletin*. XIII (February, 1943), pp. 21-28. Bibliography.

H. C. Schumacher, "War-Caused Problems of the Family," *ibid.*, XXI (December, 1942), pp. 260-268.

G. R. Younts, "Selected Bibliography on Marriage, the Family and Sex Education," *Religious Education*, XXXVII (July, 1942), pp. 232-240.

CHAPTER IX

Education

Education is an expansive term. It signifies a process as long as human history and as wide as experience. In the case of the individual it begins, possibly, in the mother's womb, and it continues until the neurons congeal. It is, as Brown and Roucek state, "the sum total of the experience which molds the attitudes and determines the conduct of both the child and the adult."[1] We may interpret this to include every influence, trifling or profound, which durably modifies thought, feeling, or action.

It is evident that education in its broad sense must appear in some form in all of the topics treated in this volume. Consequently it is necessary to establish limitations for the present chapter. We shall deal, therefore, only with education in its restricted sense in which there is assumed a body of learners and a body of instructors operating under formally recognized authority. This limitation obviously takes in the public school system; but quite as obviously it takes in much more. We are actually concerned here with all agencies which possess an institutional pattern and are definitely committed to instruction.

It serves the purpose of some people, now and then, to declare that the proper function of our schools is narrowly instructional. The schools should confine themselves, it is said, to teaching practically useful skills and knowledge. Such argument is sometimes convenient when educational costs are under consideration. Even those who take this extreme position, however, are very watchful to discover any defection of the schools as supervisors of youthful morals and loyalty to the *status quo*. It is indeed almost unthinkable that institutions such as the schools should, in any present-day community, be absolved as regards responsibility in the matter of social control. It is the deep-seated conviction of all public minded people that the schools, as agencies of the state, are primarily committed to the molding of citizens. And even where the legal relationship of school and state is nebulous or absent, the pedagogue is by common consent held more or less accountable for the ideals and attitudes of his pupils, and especially as to their conformity with socially approved patterns.

---

[1] F. J. Brown and J. S. Roucek, *Our Racial and National Minorities* (New York: Prentice-Hall, 1937), pp. xii-xiii.

Localization and Division of Educational Policies

Certain factors have prevented education from becoming a unified system that might be employed in a concerted fashion for purposes of social control. Our democratic predilections revolt against centralization in the federal government. The public schools are administered by the states, with large and varying degrees of autonomy in the hands of local boards. Furthermore, the public schools are not the only institutions for the education of youth. In 1940, forty-nine percent of American college students attended colleges not supported by public funds. Of the secondary school population, seven per cent attended private schools of one kind or another. On the elementary level, ten per cent attended non-public schools.[2] There were also, of course, great numbers in the many types of special private schools which abound in all parts of the country.

Private Institutions. State or political mandate does not extend over the privately operated schools and colleges in any appreciable degree, although it is within the power of the state to regulate these institutions. As social control agencies they are subject generally only to federal and state constitutions, to public opinion and custom, and to the discretion of the religious bodies or boards that control them.

Democratic Control of Education. In the United States education is the people's enterprise. In no other activity of government, with the exception of legislation, does the general population feel more free or competent to introject its ideas and to lay hands upon its operation. The public school belongs to one or several adjacent neighborhoods and the neighborhood children attend it. The local district originally paid the cost of the school, either by subscription or tax, and local support in whole or part prevails at the present time with few exceptions. The people whose children attend the schools are naturally concerned with what goes on there, and so likewise are the taxpayers and the various civic organizations of the community.

This localization of interest and responsibility is a tradition in American life. Our people have learned to regard the schools as objects of immediate concern in the democratic order, and they have resisted the trend toward removal of administrative control to larger political units. This trend has progressed because of the inescapable logic of advantages to be gained, but with it has gone no lessening of local censorship in the mind of the citizen.

Censorship. The censorship of the schools through the medium of public scrutiny must be attributed in most part to a desire that children be

---

[2] Data computed from *Americana Annual*, 1941, pp. 222-230.

taught properly. To be taught properly means, of course, to be taught in accordance with the wishes of the community. The community is most sensitive, in particular, to those aspects of teaching that have social and moral significance, and in watching these with jealous eye the community is exercising a prerogative of social control.

Certain aspects of local oversight merit special consideration. It is significant that while this plan satisfies the idea of democracy at first-hand grips with its own affairs, it may actually operate to the detriment of democracy. It may be the will of the community that teachers of certain religious faiths be debarred, that racial inequality be maintained, that the social studies be narrowly prejudiced, and that the school houses be refused as meeting places for unpopular groups. State laws bearing upon these matters are usually sufficiently general to permit local discretion.

Pressure Groups. It is further significant that the local community is under the immediate influence of special-interest groups and organizations. These may at times compete with one another in the political field, but certain of them commonly wield great power. They enjoy a friendly press, have the support of businessmen and property owners, and their men are in key positions. Thus they are able to control the make-up of school boards and consequently the local school policies. As to how the special interest groups will exercise their strategic position will of course depend upon the enlightenment of their leadership, and this may in fact be all that good democracy would desire. Too often it is baneful because it channelizes the schools, as social control agencies, along lines of socially restrictive attitudes.

Limits on Nation-Wide Control. Finally, it is obvious that local domination of school policies must stand in the way of any program of concerted social education conceived upon a wide geographical scale. Under the American system, no such program can be arbitrarily imposed from above. There is no constitutional authority for federal action of this sort, and state authority dissolves in general laws and administrative regulations.

This situation is aggravated by the cultural diversities and varying economic pressure areas of the nation. Striking contrasts can be drawn almost at random: rural New England and the deep South; Hollywood and Cedar Falls; Hyde Park and Las Vegas; an Idaho mining town and a fruit-growing section in California. Regional differences such as these comparisons suggest are numerous in the American scene. They portray the divergent attitudes and incongruous interests which inevitably reach the young through the medium of the schools.

It is clear that a uniform program of social education, centrally controlled, would be impracticable under American conditions. But this does not mean that we have to resign ourselves to the situation. What cannot be had by regulation may be secured by persuasion. Educators may be converted to a common program through the promulgation of "objectives." Many statements of objectives have appeared, especially in recent years, and some of these have exerted great influence upon educational thought.[3] Statements of objectives, however, commonly spread over the many purposes of education, giving but a share of space to the social. Thus it is with the famous *Cardinal Principles of Secondary Education*,[4] which still holds a high place among the formulations of objectives; and it is true of the recent excellent book of the Educational Policies Commission entitled *Purposes of Education in American Democracy*.[5]

Attempts to Formulate Educational Principles

In recent years national and state organizations have given increased attention to formulation of the principles and practices of democratic education for a good society. It is their hope to secure realization of these through reasonable appeal to school people and leaders in American life. Especially active have been the American Historical Association, the former Progressive Education Association, the National Education Association, and the American Association of School Administrators (the last two acting through their jointly appointed Educational Policies Commission).[6]

This campaign (or better, perhaps, these campaigns) to foster common social goals and a common effort is typically democratic in that it proceeds through leadership and persuasion. Attention of educators throughout the country has been concentrated upon the meaning of democracy and upon the problem of effective training. Most promising has been the influence upon teacher-training institutions where, generally speaking, educators are responsive to democratic ideals. Young teachers through-

---

[3] See Harold S. Tuttle, *Social Basis of Education* (New York: Thomas Y. Crowell, 1934), chapter I.

[4] Bureau of Education *Bulletin*, No. 35 (Washington: Government Printing Office, 1918).

[5] Published by the National Education Association (Washington, 1938).

[6] The American Historical Association, through its Commission on the Social Studies, has published several volumes of which the following should be consulted: *A Charter for the Social Sciences in the Schools* (1932), and *Conclusions and Recommendations of the Commission* (1934), (New York: Charles Scribner's Sons). The student should refer to the following reports of the Educational Policies Commission: *The Unique Function of Education in American Democracy* (1938), *Learning the Ways of Democracy* (1940), and *The Education of Free Men in American Democracy* (1941), (Washington: National Education Association); and see also footnote 5. A challenging statement is that of the Progressive Education Association, published as a supplement in their magazine, *Progressive Education*, XVIII (May, 1941).

out the country are going out from these institutions with at least a knowledge of our more refined social values; and in great numbers of instances they are imbued with an evangelistic zeal. Teacher training is perhaps the central strategy in the building of a better democracy. The most successful teachers, however, will be those who are able to deal tactfully with a world that is not all friendly to their ideals.

The principles and aims advocated by the various associations and commissions are necessarily general in character. It is the weakness of generalized ideals that people may subscribe to them widely but differ radically in their interpretations in specific instances. This is especially true of the formulations of the Educational Policies Commission which, in speaking for a nation-wide organization like the National Education Association, must find terms acceptable to divergent interests and culture areas. The door is open for the operations of local guardians in every community of the land. Thus the proclamation of the worthy sentiment that youth must be taught high ideals of human relationship, while piously accepted, may actually be interpreted without encroachment upon race prejudice or restrictions of civil justice.

Troubled Area of Agreement. Programs of education for democracy all agree that the schools must train the youth for effective thinking with respect to social and governmental affairs. This is a proposition that none can question. In its practical interpretation, however, it has led to widespread controversy, bitterness, and even violence.

Enlightened educational opinion holds for independent, objective thinking based upon all available information; but the effort to put theory into practice has stirred individuals, patriotic societies, special interest groups, and legislative bodies into action. "How history should be taught" has become a national issue. Teachers who have exposed the young to unpopular ideas have frequently found themselves in trouble. Spies have been planted in schools and colleges. National conventions of every description have passed resolutions. Verbal battles have been waged over the suitability of textbooks, and public burnings of textbooks have occurred.[7]

---

[7] The numerous issues and conflicts that have arisen over the question as to how the youth shall be taught to think about governmental affairs cannot be recounted here. For controversies over the teaching of history during and shortly after World War I, the student should consult Bessie L. Pierce, *Public Opinion and the Teaching of History in the United States* (New York: Alfred A. Knopf, 1926), chapters IV-VII. Another book by the same author, *Citizens' Organizations and the Civic Training of Youth* (New York: Charles Scribner's Sons, 1933), affords a wealth of material on the pressure activities of numerous organizations. For a comprehensive statement of methods used to make teachers conform, the student should read the chapter on "Extra-Scholastic Pressures" in the book by Howard K. Beale, *Are American Teachers Free?* (New York: Charles Scribner's Sons, 1936); and in the same book the index references under "Textbooks." *Readers' Guide* references under the same heading should be traced for more recent developments, including burnings.

Other Influences. While national and state organizations of educators
are promulgating programs, principles, and aims of social-civic education,
we find that noneducational organizations of many descriptions are taking a hand. The reference here is not to the political pressure activities
of these organizations, but to their fecundity in producing partial and
complete programs, depending upon the scope of their interests. They
turn out a flood of leaflets, brochures, books, and courses of training in
citizenship. Beale classifies these organizations as "ancestor worshipers,"
"military organizations with 'patriotic' purposes," and "the various organizations set up to further 'patriotism' of the one hundred per cent
variety." [8] Less picturesquely, Pierce presents eight classifications including several hundred groups.[9] Through the confusing situation we grope
toward a common goal. Clearly demoracy as a way of life for America
cannot be one thing in Maine and something else in Georgia, nor can it
be interpreted differently as we pass from one section of a metropolis to
another. It is not the charge of any special group, nor can it serve one
interest at the expense of another. Education as social control faces the
reality of these conflicts. How to find unity amid distraction, but without compulsion, is education's dilemma.

Control Through Selection and Discipline of Instructors

It is inevitable that school boards, acting upon their own judgment or
reflecting the dominant forces of the community, will exercise watchfulness over the selection and behavior of teachers. This solicitude is based
upon the reasonable assumption that desirable social control effects upon
the young can be secured only by teachers who believe in those effects
and exemplify them. It is frequently evident, however, that motives far
less academic guide the minds of board members. Especially in small
communities where the members actively engage in the selection, the
opportunity to regulate private lives is often piously indulged.

In actual practice, policies of teacher selection vary greatly. It is
fundamental, of course, that teachers possess both competence and moral
character. Approved practice permits that a superintendent may accept
testimony of these qualities from teacher training institutions and from
informed individuals, and that the board may act upon the superintendent's recommendations. At the opposite extreme we find fussy inquisi-
tiveness and surveillance.[10]

---

[8] Beale, *op. cit.*, p. 524.
[9] Bessie L. Pierce, *Citizens' Organizations and the Civic Training of Youth*, cited
above.
[10] See Kimball Young, *Social Psychology* (New York: Alfred A. Knopf, 1930),
pp. 347-352.

Desire for Conformity. The significant point is the disposition, where it exists, to regulate teachers as a means of assuring conformity of the children to local mores. By such means the schools, through the teachers, are made to reflect the attitudes of the community; they are prevented from assuming leadership in a program that would change attitudes. It remains that attitudes must be changed in many places if nation-wide hopes for democratic education are to be realized.

Inferior Prestige. An important factor in the situation centers in the prestige inferiority of the rank and file of teachers. There is a symptom of this in the effort among educators to have teaching recognized as a profession. The mere assumption of a label, however, will not offset certain things. One is the fact that prestige rarely accompanies a lowly economic status. Robert Littell, in a recent article, states that "For the school year 1944-45, about half of the nation's 850,000 teachers were paid less than $1800; 200,000 less than $1200; and 25,000 less than $600." [11] Littell compares teachers' average salaries with those of workers in private industry, showing for example that in 1943 the teachers received an average of $1599, while the average for workers was $2026.

Prestige is also affected by the relatively inferior education of teachers as compared with the higher professions. While teacher education is being greatly improved in various states and cities, it has been shown [12] that in the nation as a whole the average level of academic training for both elementary and high school teachers is too low for professional self-respect.

These conditions indicate a curtailed prestige which in many areas reaches the vanishing point. It would seem, nevertheless, that prestige of teachers is essential if they are to become a force in any program of social education. In this connection one must recognize that teachers' organizations are doing much to advance the dignity and self-respect of teachers. This is true of the National Education Association, the American Federation of Teachers, and, upon the college level, the American Association of University Professors. It is true, in varying degree, of the state and municipal organizations, depending upon the independence of their leadership.

Tenure. Low prestige is not only an objective social phenomenon, it is a matter of morale. It finds a reflection in the habitual attitudes of the teachers, making them more amenable to the numerous social pressures and operations of authority which impinge upon them. A major remedy for this impaired status is legalized security of position. The desirability

---

[11] Robert Littell, "Teachers' Pay—A National Disgrace," *Reader's Digest*, XLVII (October, 1945), pp. 89-92. Data from U. S. Office of Education sources.

[12] See Frederick E. Bolton and John E. Corbally, *Educational Sociology* (New York: The American Book Co., 1941), p. 111. Sufficiently recent data are lacking.

of tenure laws is generally recognized by leading educators, as is evidenced by the active interest of the National Education Association as well as many state and local organizations. "There are now 34 states that have tenure or continuing contract, providing tenure protection to about 45 per cent of the teachers of the nation and continuing contract to about 21 per cent." [13]

Practically all state tenure laws provide for a probationary period, usually three to five years, before the teacher is given permanent status. A strong disciplinary element inheres in this probationary provision, for teachers will be carefully scrutinized as to their acceptability. Teachers are not likely to obtain tenure without demonstrating that they are "safe" in whatever meaning the school board may attach to the word. Tenure law, in its operation and effect, does not entirely alter the situation which prevails in non-tenure areas, where teachers are employed on some form of contractual basis. In either case, for better or for worse, the employment situation embodies scrutiny and selection in the interest of the kind of social control acceptable to the community.

Licensing. Closely allied to tenure is the licensing of teachers. Until well into the present century most licenses to teach were issued locally and the obvious abuses were common. Limited licenses with frequent renewals gave authorities great power to control teachers, even to matters of private behavior. A fortunate development has been the gradual transference of the licensing power to state authority. At the same time, however, there has been a marked tendency to discontinue life diplomas and to require periodical renewals, thus keeping before teachers an obligation to satisfy recognized standards.[14]

Other considerations impinge likewise upon the consciousness of teachers, keeping them ever mindful of the wisdom of a reasonable conformity. Among these are the various systems of teacher rating and salary advancements. And where pensions are provided there is some potency in the thought that if you are good you will be provided for.

Punishments for Nonconformity. In the nation as a whole there is relatively little overt disciplining of teachers, one reason being that the teachers seldom do anything to warrant it. There is an astonishing number of instances, however, when the records are brought together as in the works of Pierce and Beale.[15] With extensive documentation, Beale recounts cases far too numerous to mention in which teachers and college professors have been disciplined for known or

---

[13] Frances Jelinek, "Tenure for Teachers," *Journal of the National Education Association,* XXXI (October, 1942), p. 217.

[14] For a discussion of trends in certification see Willard S. Elsbree, *The American Teacher* (New York: American Book Co., 1939), chapter XXIV.

[15] Pierce, *op. cit.;* and Beale, *op. cit.*

rumored beliefs, suspicions of radicalism, departures from local mores, sympathetic labor activities, use of proscribed reference material, and employment of liberal theories in teaching. Their disciplining has taken numerous forms including discharge, public reprimand, open persecution and defamation, search of premises, denial of legal rights, and even physical maltreatment. Occasional accounts of prejudicial discharge of college teachers appear in the press, and numerous instances are in the records of the American Association of University Professors and the American Civil Liberties Union.

The most famous case was the trial in 1925 of John T. Scopes, science teacher of Dayton, Tennessee, charged with violating the law of the state by teaching "certain . . . theories that deny the story of the Divine Creation as taught in the Bible," and for teaching "instead thereof that man has descended from a lower order of animals." [16] Much more recently other cases of zealous repression have attracted public attention. The national Congress, for example, in 1935 attached the famous "red rider" to an appropriation bill for support of the schools of the District of Columbia. By administrative interpretation this rider was construed to forbid even the mentioning of communism in the classrooms. After widespread ridicule and protest the particular act was repealed.[17] As late as 1940 the noted philosopher, Bertrand Russell, was forbidden by court action to accept an appointment to teach a course in the logic of mathematics at City College, New York, because of the "immorality" of his views on marriage.[18] And at about the same time, wide publicity was given to the action of Governor Talmadge of Georgia who, by "packing" the State Board of Regents, succeeded in ousting the dean of the School of Education and the vice-chancellor of the University of Georgia, and the president of the South Georgia Teachers College. The offense in each case was liberalism in respect to Negro education.[19]

Loyalty Oath. The disciplinary device which has stirred most resentment and controversy among educators is the loyalty oath. Laws requiring some form of this oath were loudly demanded during the 1930's, when the hunting down of people suspected of subversive taint was a major occupation. By 1935, twenty states had loyalty laws requiring oaths.[20] Such laws generally extend to college and university teachers when under the state system. Massachusetts even imposed an oath upon Harvard professors. The selecting of teachers as a class and making them

[16] Beale, *op. cit.*, pp. 232-234.
[17] "The Little Red Rider," *School and Society*, XLIII (April 11, 1936), p. 513.
[18] "Behind the Russell Case," *The Nation* CL (April 6, 1940), p. 436.
[19] "A Blow to Education in Georgia," *School and Society* LIV (August 2, 1941), pp. 71-72.
[20] "Loyalty Oath Laws for Teachers," *ibid.*, XLII (August 24, 1935), p. 267.

the object of this peculiar discipline has caused wide resentment, and has generally backfired by creating a smothered contempt for the procedure.

Problems of Control Through Instruction

We commonly assume that the outcomes of education depend upon the formal instruction of the classroom. We may be justified in this so far as measurable academic achievements are concerned; but in respect to social control the view is a very narrow one. If what we are interested in is the induction of children and youth into our ways of life, then we must realize that the school as a community experience means more than the school as a series of planned lessons. Altogether apart from the knowledges and skills that may be learned is the fund of social attitudes and habits that may be acquired through the intensified relationships of school life. These relationships are, of course, incidental even to the most formal lesson. In a much more important way, however, they occur through the natural give-and-take of individuals working and playing together throughout the day.

Theories. The importance of this fact has impressed many educators so strongly that they have sought to introduce natural and group activities as major functions of the classroom experience. This is a characteristic of what is called "progressive" education, and in respect to its effect upon the young as a means of social control, it comes into conflict with the "fundamentalist" view. According to the latter view, formal tutelage under authority must be used to implant basic attitudes, ideals, concepts, and habits. These opposing positions are but aspects of two theories of education with conflicting psychologies of learning and conflicting social philosophies.[21]

The theory which places stress upon social relationships and group activities is not neglectful of social control as a responsibility of education. It holds that if children and young people are to learn the ways of a good society, it must be through active experience. This experience, however, cannot be disorganized or haphazard. Oversight, wise direction, and good counsel are required; but at the same time initiative and informal activity must be preserved. The more conservative theory, upon the other hand, would prepare the youth for mature citizenship through controlled, albeit benign, discipline.

---

[21] Expositions of the two views are presented, respectively, by William H. Kilpatrick ("progressive"), in his book *Education for a Changing Civilization* (New York: The Macmillan Co., 1927); and William C. Bagley ("conservative"), in his book *Education, Crime, and Social Progress* (New York: The Macmillan Co., 1931). See also P. F. Valentine, ed., *Twentieth Century American Education* (New York: The Philosophical Library, 1946), pp. 395-402.

Freedom and Indoctrination. The view that education should provide training in independent thinking seems in many ways congenial to democracy. The basic principle is that of a free government in which the people participate. In such a government there is allowable a diversity of ideas which may be debated through the channels of discussion and resolved through due political process. A social order of this kind allows for readjustment and change following the will of the people, but its success must depend upon the ability of the people to think intelligently. Training in intelligent thinking is the central concern of John Dewey's great contribution to educational theory, and it has registered deeply in the ideas and practices of educators.[22]

Those who follow the Dewey influence, and they are many, hold that certain canons necessarily prevail in intelligent thinking and consequently in training for it. Among these canons is the pragmatic principle that problems (scientific, social, or philosophic) are truly solvable only through employment of the experimental method. This demands that judgments be derived from pertinent objective evidence and the testimony of experience. This is in line with the method of science.

Contrary to this method is the practice of indoctrination. This practice assumes that certain conclusions or presumed truths are undebatable, and these are to be implanted in the minds of the youth through education. It will be recognized at once that indoctrination must be favored by any party, creed, interest, or ideologic group which holds an exclusive position of power. Recent examples of thoroughgoing indoctrination were to be seen in the totalitarian governments.[23]

Educators do not disagree completely upon the issue of indoctrination. This is largely because a certain amount of indoctrination seems inevitable. For one thing, the culture in which one lives is a powerful indoctrinating influence. It has been pointed out, also, that we are indoctrinating when we inculcate a belief in the scientific method or in freedom. Many insist that we should indoctrinate in the basic principles of democracy. Practically speaking, the issue does not resolve to a matter of all-out acceptance or rejection; but if one accepts the principles of democracy it would seem that deliberate indoctrination is logically inconsistent.

Growing out of the foregoing problem is the question of controversial issues in the classroom. It is reasonably maintained that if young people

[22] Two books by Dewey which have probably most influenced the thinking of American educators in this connection are *Democracy and Education* (New York: The Macmillan Co., 1916), and *How We Think*, 2nd ed. (New York: D. C. Heath and Co., 1933).

[23] For an excellent discussion of indoctrination in its various implications, see John S. Brubacher, *Modern Philosophies of Education* (New York: McGraw-Hill Book Co., 1939), pp. 231-242.

are to learn to think intelligently they must form the habit of examining all sides of an issue. To promote the development of this habit, it is insisted, controversial issues must be admitted for class discussion.

Upon social and political grounds opposition is voiced by individuals and groups who can tolerate no intellectual compromise with unfavored doctrines. To admit these doctrines to fair discussion is to assume that there may be some good in them. An attitude of open-mindedness toward them is but a step removed from disloyalty. The very act of admitting them to fair discussion invests them with a cloak of respectability, and thus threatens the youthful mind with contamination. More than this, teachers who are capable of such tolerance of abhorred doctrines are suspect. Sinless patriots lend their protests, insisting that the young must be preserved in innocent faith that all things American are noble and pure.

The Rugg social science textbooks, which aroused a storm of protest a few years ago, were written with the purpose of presenting objective information bearing upon American history and social life from all angles. Without defending the Rugg textbooks, which have been considered controversial by public schools and civic organizations, they were intended to serve as a basis for unbiased study. Their inclusion of material unfavorable to conventional opinion antagonized various powerful interests with the result that they were driven out of several school systems.[24] Their author, endeavoring to implement an all-sided approach to social issues, was denounced as a propagandist and communist.

Education as Agent of Social Control. The potentialities for social control through education have suggested to some educators the possibility of formulating a "tenable theory of the good society and using education to influence individuals in favor of it." Counts declares: "If education is to grapple with a given social situation it must incorporate a social philosophy adequate to that situation. . . . Education, emptied of all social control and considered solely as method, points nowhere and can arrive nowhere. . . ."[25] This point of view finds strong expression in the volumes of the American Historical Association's report of its Commission on the Social Studies and in the 1933 report on social and economic problems of the Progressive Education Association.

---

[24] For a discussion of this *cause celebre*, see article by Alonzo F. Myers, "The Attacks on the Rugg Books," in *Frontiers of Democracy* VII (October 15, 1940), pp. 17-22.

[25] George S. Counts, *The Social Foundations of Education* (New York: Charles Scribner's Sons, 1934), pp. 534-535. This is one of the series of the Commission on the Social Studies of the American Historical Association. See also *Conclusions and Recommendations of the Commission,* cited above. For further discussion of the same point of view, see *Social Change and Education,* Thirteenth Yearbook, Department of Superintendence (Washington: National Education Association, 1935), chapters VIII and X.

The control advocated by these few frontier educators was in the direction of a more collectivized society, which they mistakenly anticipated from their reading of social trends in the middle '30's—an era of free thinking now gone and almost forgotten. It was an unpopular suggestion at best, as well as an impracticable one, and any remaining interest in it is merely as a contrast with today's climate of orthodoxy.

Events since World War II, and especially the growing menace of communism, have given strong reason for the flight of innovation from the field of educational thought. Education as an agent of social control presents a united ideological front. Despite the accusations of certain merchants of fear, the schools of America, as seldom before, are imbued with a conserving spirit and purpose as regards our economic and political institutions. In this respect our schools perform a function of social control that is more widespread and effective than that of any other institution. The social pressures of our day have profoundly affected the writing and adoption of textbooks, the methods of teaching, and the consciousness of school people, all in the direction of playing down controversial subjects, extolling the American way of life, and encouraging patriotism.

Despite the soundness of the public schools, they, together with the colleges, have passed through a trying period of search and criticism since the second World War. Special loyalty oaths have been widely imposed, and the process of investigation by committees and "fact-finders" has been initiated by both public and private bodies, national, state, and local. Educators concede that these investigations perform a public service in seeking out real Communists in the schools and colleges. But there is great concern and harassment when they threaten guilt by remote association or innocent involvement, punishment for mistaken judgments long repudiated, and blacklisting for unpopular views.

Educators have found especially provocative the numerous instances of direct attack and adverse publicity which purport to reveal subversion as distinguished from actual communism or the presence of Communists. Subversion in these cases consists in those policies or practices which the attackers choose to define as such. Wide publicity through books, magazines, pamphlets, and lectures has attempted to show that the schools are socialistic, that they create in students a distrust of American free enterprise, that they fail to impart moral standards, and that they undermine patriotism through, among other things, the use of UNESCO materials and favorable treatment of the United Nations.[26]

---

[26] There is an extensive literature dealing *pro* and *con* with this wave of criticism. The reader is referred to the bibliography presented by W. W. Brickman under the title "Attack and Counter-Attack in American Education," *School and Society*, LXXIV (October 27, 1951), pp. 262-269.

It is important to take notice of the fact that, generally speaking, the schools have greatly increased their interest in the cause of racial and religious equality. Social education has lately placed considerable emphasis upon this objective, especially with respect to the Negro in American life.

Other Educational Agencies of Social Control

Many educational agencies of social control operate outside the public school and college. Much that has been stated previously in this chapter applies in these cases. This is particularly true with respect to the private and parochial schools, although these offer a number of special problems.

Adult Education. Adult education, although administered largely by public school systems, may be considered as an enterprise carried on separately from the regular school functions. It is more and more recognized, nevertheless, as an exceedingly significant resonsibility in so far as it contributes to literacy, citizenship, and vocational competence. Its extension, however, into the fields of recreation and non-practical culture is often opposed upon grounds of economy. There is much concern over the fact that education is arrested, for most people, at an early age. There is an abrupt cessation of training in the processes of democratic government, and a release of the young to the tender mercies of pressure groups, quack reformers, and all the devices of propaganda.[27]

Religious Education. Religious education, generally speaking, strives to impart social ideals and to endow them with an emotional dynamic which will carry them into practice. It is usually handicapped, however, because of untrained teachers and the small amount of time at its disposal. School authorities have in many places permitted the holding of weekday church schools during school time, and this arrangement has itself raised important problems. There are doubts as to the wisdom of joining religion with public education; dangers of discrimination against unpopular creeds and sects; concern over the stressing of denominational differences. In too large a degree, probably, these schools are concerned with credal lessons and formal religious instruction.[28]

Youth Organizations. Bulking large in the picture are the various organizations for boys and girls—the Boy Scouts, the Y.M.C.A., the Girl Scouts, and similar groups. By employing the devices of recreation, symbolism, constructive activity, and social service, these organizations have made a

---

[27] See Hubert Phillips, "Adult Education," in P. F. Valentine, ed., *Twentieth Century Education* (New York: The Philosophical Library, 1946), pp. 584-604.

[28] For a thorough and critical study, see V. T. Thayer, "Religion and Morals in the Public Schools," *ibid*, pp. 558-583.

strong appeal among younger youth and are without doubt significant influences for good citizenship. The Boy Scouts draw 42 per cent of the eleven-year-old boy population. There are 47,801 Troop units and 10,249 Explorer units with a total boy membership of 1,316,508, exclusive of Cub units.[29] The Scout organization is largely confined to cities and is strongest in the smaller cities.

Educational agencies of social control operating beyond the regular schools could be enumerated at length, but we should find ourselves encroaching upon other chapters of this book. Such would be true with regard to the radio and television, the press, and motion pictures.

Summary

Education, as discussed in this chapter, is used in the more restricted sense of the term, applying to instructor-learner institutionalized patterns, which have teaching as a definite aim. Such patterns have an important place in our social control scheme, especially in view of our commonly accepted notion of the close relationship between education and the democratic process.

For the most part, education in this country is a state function, but there is also a strong tradition of local autonomy for the school, so that no specific and uniform set of goals is possible. Agreement among school systems and among educators on general ideals has been widely achieved, notably through the influence of the Educational Policies Commission as well as recent social pressures, but there is always an open field for disagreement in respect to methods and materials for attaining the ideals.

There is a persistent controversy between those who hold that preparation for democratic citizenship is best served through open and informed discussion of all issues, and those who believe that thought of the youth should be controlled.

An important aspect of education as an agency of control is the control of schools through the selection of teachers, which often goes so far as to invade their private lives as persons. Organizations within the profession are striving to raise teacher status and thereby give them some immunity from local, and often shortsighted, influences.

Aside from the schools themselves, there are many educational organizations and institutions that influence the young. These include adult education programs, Boy and Girl Scouts and similar organizations, church schools, etc. These are more limited in their scope and seldom raise the broad problems which confront the school systems.

---

[29] *Forty-third Annual Report of the Boy Scouts of America* (Washington: Government Printing Office, 1953).

QUESTIONS

1. Define education sociologically.
2. Can education be employed as a unified means of social control? Why?
3. To what controls are private educational institutions subject?
4. How is censorship of the public school system affected?
5. How do pressure groups exert control over the school system?
6. Why is it especially difficult to impose a concerted system of education on a large geographical area in the United States?
7. What extra-legal means may be used to impose such a program?
8. How are principles and practices of democratic society being formulated for educational purposes?
9. By what methods do the proponents of these compaigns operate?
10. What is considered to be the central strategy in the building of a better democracy?
11. Why are the principles voiced by the various education associations general in character?
12. What proposition of educational aims is a matter of general agreement?
13. How does the term "ancestor worshipers" apply to the discussion of education as a means of social control?
14. In respect to social control, is it correct to assume that the outcomes of education depend upon formal classroom instruction?
15. What fact do the proponents of progressive education feel they must recognize by their new methods?
16. How does the theory of the progressivists conflict with that of the fundamentalists?
17. What is the basic tenet of John Dewey's theories of education?
18. What is the antithesis of Dewey's theory?
19. Is it possible to eliminate completely the influence of indoctrination from education?
20. List several agencies of social control which are a part of our educational system.

SUGGESTED TOPICS FOR TERM PAPERS AND FURTHER RESEARCH

1. The effect of American liberalism on the educational system.
2. A study of the British educational system and the emergence of an administrative class.
3. Educational practices of a totalitarian state.
4. Advantages and disadvantages of local control of education.
5. Study the arguments surrounding the question of academic freedom.
6. Discuss the prevalent theories regarding the teaching of the social studies in the public schools.
7. Analyze the reports of the Educational Policies Commission with respect to their social control implications.
8. The nonformal aspects of education.
9. Contrast education and indoctrination.
10. Compare public education problems and religious education problems.

BIBLIOGRAPHY

Books

Robert M. Bear, *The Social Functions of Education* (New York: The Macmillan Co., 1937).

Arthur Bestor, *Educational Wastelands* (Urbana, Ill.: University of Illinois Press, 1953). A brilliant criticism of the existing educational philosophies and practices.

Theodore Braneld, *Ends and Means in Education* (New York: Harper and Brothers, 1950). A valuable effort aiming to define reasonable goals of education.

Francis J. Brown, *Educational Sociology* (New York: Prentice-Hall, 1947). One of the best-known textbooks covering this field.

Lloyd Allen Cook and Elaine Forsyth Cook, *A Sociological Approach to Education* (New York: McGraw-Hill Book Co., 1950). Well known for its stress on the community approach.

George S. Counts, *Education and the Promise of America* (New York: The Macmillan Co., 1945). A well-known educator re-evaluates his thinking in a sociological direction.

L. P. Eisenhart, *The Educational Process* (Princeton, N.J.: Princeton University Press, 1945). Has some pertinent sociological observations.

Ross L. Finney, *A Sociological Philosophy of Education* (New York: The Macmillan Co., 1928). Stresses more philosophy than sociology.

Wayland J. Hayes, *The Small Community Looks Ahead* (New York: Harcourt, Brace and Co., 1947).

Clarence King, *Organizing for Community Action* (New York: Harper and Brothers, 1948).

Clarence B. Loomis, *An Experience in Community Development and the Principles of Community Organization* (Clayton, Ga.: The Rabun Press, 1944).

Clyde B. Moore and William E. Cole, *Sociology in Educational Practice* (Boston: Houghton Mifflin Co., 1952). One of the latest attempts to develop the field of educational sociology.

W. F. Ogburn, *Social Education* (Stanford, Calif.: Stanford University, 1939). Ideas on education by a well-known sociologist.

Joseph S. Roucek, *The Sociological Foundations of Education* (New York: Thomas Y. Crowell Co., 1942). A symposium stressing that educational sociology is more of sociology than education.

—— "Some Contributions of Sociology to Education," Chapter 22, pp. 793-833; in Harry Elmer Barnes, Howard Becker, and Frances Bennett Becker, eds., *Contemporary Social Theory* (New York: Appleton-Century-Crofts, 1940). A systematic survey of the relation of sociology to education.

V. T. Thayer, *American Education Under Fire* (New York: Harper and Brothers, 1945). A vivid discussion of attacks upon the public schools.

Leslie D. Zeleny, "Sociology Applied to Education," Chapter IX, pp. 382-422, in Philip L. Harriman, Joseph S. Roucek, and George B. de Huszar, eds., *Contemporary Social Science*, Vol. I (Harrisburg, Pa.: The Stackpole Co., 1953). The latest survey of the trends in this field.

Periodicals

W. B. Brookover, "Sociology of Education: A Definition," *American Sociological Review*, XIV (June, 1949), pp. 407-415.

F. J. Brown and Thorsten Sellin, eds., "Higher Education Under Stress," *The Annals* of the American Academy of Political and Social Science, CCCI (September, 1955).

Francis J. Charters, "Four Convergent Trends in General Education," *Journal of Higher Education,* XV (June, 1944), pp. 307-314.

F. R. Clow, "The Rise of Educational Sociology," *Social Forces,* II (March, 1924), pp. 332-337.

Newton Edwards, "Education as a Social Instrument," *School Review,* LIX (October, 1951), pp. 394-402.

W. H. Hightower, "Some Issues in Education for Democracy," *Elementary School Journal,* LII (March, 1952), pp. 387-389.

Henry W. Littlefield, "The Selection and Preparation of the College Teachers," *Teacher Education Quarterly,* XI, 3 (Spring, 1954), 118-123.

S. A. Moorehead, "Dilemma of Democratic Education," *School and Society,* LXXVII (January 17, 1953), p. 39.

"Progressive Education: Its Philosophy and Challenge," *Progressive Education,* XVIII (May, 1941), supplement.

Joseph S. Roucek, "The Soviet Yoke of Education in Poland," *The Educational Forum,* XVIII, 3 (March, 1954), pp. 305-311.

Irwin T. Sanders, "The School Discovers the Community," *Journal of Educational Sociology,* XIII (March, 1940), pp. 397-402.

Dwight Sanderson, "The Relation of the School to the Sociological Status of the Rural Community," *ibid.,* XIV (March, 1941), pp. 401-410.

Fulton J. Sheen, "Education as the Guardian of the American Heritage," *Vital Speeches,* XVII (March 15, 1951), pp. 349-351.

James Lloyd Snell, "Social Attitudes of California School Board Members," *Frontiers of Democracy,* VI (February, 1940), pp. 141-142.

Leslie D. Zeleny, "New Directions in Educational Sociology and the Teaching of Sociology," *American Sociological Review,* XIII (June, 1948), pp. 336-341.

Harvey Zorbaugh, "Educational Sociology," *American Journal of Sociology,* XXXIII (November, 1927), pp. 444-454.

CHAPTER X

Social Classes

Social classes are one phase of the process of differentiation that characterizes nearly all human societies. It is true that among the most primitive peoples there is little distinction in occupations, mode of life or social standing, except those differences associated with sex and age. But all societies whose culture has developed beyond the most simple and crude show definite differentiation in function or occupation, in many of the folkways, in competitive interests, and in the ranking of different sections of the population.[1]

Definitions

Rank, Class. A section of a population whose members occupy a distinct rank is designated as a social class. By rank is meant the rights, privileges, and prestige which people enjoy. These rights and privileges have to do with the opportunities one has in his personal and cultural relations, the protection assured him by government, his opportunities for participation in the government, and his economic opportunities. By one's social prestige we mean the relative respect and esteem that is accorded a person by other members of the society. A social class is made up of both sexes and all ages, and all members of a family will belong to the same class except in cases where a child, on reaching adulthood, may pass into another class than that of his parents.[2]

Caste, Estate. There are two other terms that are used to designate similarly differentiated sections of a population—namely, caste and estate. A caste is a stratum of a population, the members of which occupy a definite position in a hierarchy of strata and who acquire their position by birth. The rights, privileges, and prestige—that is, the rank of the members of each caste—are definitely fixed for life in most cases. There may be also a repulsion or feeling of antipathy between the members of different

---

[1] For an account of the uniformity of the more simple societies and the beginnings of differentiation among the more advanced, see Gunnar Landtman, *The Origin of the Inequality of the Social Classes* (Chicago: The University of Chicago Press, 1938), chapters I-VII.

[2] For a more extended discussion of the nature of rank distinctions, see Cecil C. North, *Social Differentiation* (Chapel Hill: The University of North Carolina Press, 1926), chapter III.

castes which tends to keep them separated in their living arrangements, recreations and occupations. They are strictly endogamous, as to the caste, although exogamous as to families.

There is a group of occupations that is peculiar to the caste, and the individual may move from one to another of these occupations but is limited in his choice to those assigned to his caste. There are multitudinous taboos peculiar to each caste which not only limit the individual in his occupational choice, but which regulate the minutest detail of his life. A society completely organized on a caste basis presents a fixed and rigid scheme of life wth sharp and clear-cut lines separating the various elements of the population. Social position is clearly and permanently defined.

The population of India is the one best known to us in which the caste principle has been completely carried out so as to dominate all the social relations within the state. Many ancient societies, as those of Sparta, Rome, Egypt, and Japan during certain periods of history, maintained a caste organization for certain sections of the population. Many modern societies show rather definite caste tendencies with respect to certain elements of the populations, as is illustrated by the position of the Jews in certain European countries and that of the Negroes in the United States. Whether, however, in a given case any such population unit is actually to be designated a caste is largely a matter of definition, since there is no general agreement on the precise definition of the term.

Estate. The term estate has been used particularly with respect to the divisions of the population in the ancient world and under feudalism. The three most important estates under European feudalism were the nobility, the clergy, and the serfs. In some feudal societies another division was the freemen who differed from the serfs in that they owed no allegiance to the lord and had no protection from him. Frequently, however, a freeman voluntarily entered the status of the serf in order to secure the use of land or to gain the protection afforded by the lord. In some societies, in addition to the estates noted above, a body of slaves was also found.

Estate social organization differed from caste organization in a number of respects. There was no religious significance attached to the estates, as particularly is the case with respect to Indian castes. Membership in an estate was not so rigidly hereditary as in the case of castes. The clergy under feudalism was recruited from all classes. Freemen might become serfs, or serfs might be made freemen, and a freeman might, under extraordinary circumstances, be raised to the rank of the nobility. There was no mutual repulsion between estates as between castes, but a close cooperation and mutual dependence.

In some societies the serfs represented the body of laborers which had but recently emerged from slavery. In other cases serfdom was the status imposed by conquest when the conquerors did not desire a body of chattel slaves. In still other situations the serfs were those who had voluntarily offered themselves to a powerful military leader to secure the use of land or the protection which the government could not or would not provide. In any case, the serf under the completely developed system was bound to the soil, owed a definite amount of labor or of military service, or both to the lord, and received from him protection and the means of a livelihood.

Castes and estates are similar in that the law of the state provides for a differentiation of rights and privileges in both cases and in the degree of respect and dignity with which the members of the different classes are clothed. Function or occupation is also definitely defined by law. The whole social organization is built upon these premises. Economic and political rights are the more significant points of differentiation between the feudal estates, but among the estates as well as among the castes, civil and personal rights are also differentiated and the worth and prestige ascribed to the individual depend on the estate occupied.

Modern Changes. Modern social classes, while representing a somewhat similar differentiation, reflect the political and economic changes that have taken place since the breakdown of feudalism and the spread of political democracy. The distinctions in political, civil, and personal rights which characterized the feudal regime have disappeared. Mobility, both geographically and between occupations, is relatively free. The modern democratic state recognizes all individuals as standing on an equality before the law, and has brought into general acceptance the principle that every person is to be treated with the respect and consideration that his individual qualities merit, regardless of his class. Classes in such a regime rest essentially on an economic foundation, and the free movement into and out of classes has led students to designate such a system as one of open classes, in distinction from the more rigid and hereditarily fixed status of the caste or estate society.[3]

The two fundamental differences between open classes on the one hand and castes and estates on the other, apart from the different foundations on which they rest, are the hereditary principle and the fact that in a society of open classes the law no longer recognizes any distinction in rights and privileges and in the worth and dignity of the individual.

Social Class. In view of this fact, we must regard the differences between the different class systems to be largely a matter of degree. We shall,

---

[3] C. H. Cooley, *Social Organization* (New York, Charles Scribner's Sons, 1909), chapter XXI.

therefore, use the term social class as designating any section of the population occupying a distinctive place in the social order because of the rank, economic function, interests, folkways, mores, and ideology of its members. But at the same time we shall recognize that differences in the legal basis of the class distinctions and differences in the degree of mobility from one class to another justify the use of the different terms, caste, estate and open class. In some societies, as notably in southern United States, we find both caste and class tendencies operating at the same time.[4]

Class Control

Class functions as an instrument of control in two distinct ways. The first of these is seen in situations in which a social class which has acquired excessive power, in comparison with other elements of a population, uses that power to control the members of less fortunate classes. Ross has designated this situation as "Class Control." [5] He distinguishes it from true social control and defines it as "the exercise of power by a parasitic class in its own interest," whereas true social control is exercised for the common welfare. This situation has existed to some extent in most societies of which we have historical record.

Class Domination. Dominance of one class over another in the most elementary form is found in those societies which are constituted of a conquering and a conquered group. In such societies the class system is designed to perpetuate the mastery of the conquerors over the conquered. Whether the conquered are assigned a position as slaves, or serfs, or as an inferior caste, the arrangement constitutes an accommodation whereby the conflict is resolved and the relations of the conqueror and conquered are established on a peaceful basis. The inferior class position assigned to the conquered is in fact a control device to enable the conquerors to reap the benefits of their mastery under peaceful conditions.

The conquered group, on their part, at least have the advantage of not being annihilated and may even have the advantage of the military protection afforded by their conquerors. Moreover, by having their status established on a formal, legal basis, the conquered are protected from arbitrary behavior toward them by individual members of the conquering

See W. Lloyd Warner, "American Class and Caste," *American Journal of Sociology*, XLII (September, 1936), pp. 234-237; Earl Brown and George R. Leighton, *The Negro and the War* (New York: Public Affairs Committee, 1942); St. Clair Drake and H. R. Cayton, *Black Metropolis* (New York: Harcourt, Brace and Co., 1945). For additional references, see Julia Waxman, *Race Relations* (Chicago: Julius Rosenwald Fund, 1945), a selected bibliography.

[5] E. A. Ross, *Social Control* (New York: The Macmillan Co., 1901), chapter XXVIII.

group. They are given a definite status which involves some measure of protection, and whatever rights are due them under the terms fixed by the conquerors are guaranteed, often by law.

While the maintenance of the *status quo* depends on the use of force by the dominant class, at least in the initial stages of the arrangement, it becomes possible to relax more and more the use of this instrument of control as younger generations come on who have been conditioned to the situation from birth. Being born into an inferior social position and becoming habituated to the role of an inferior throughout all the years of mental and emotional development it is inevitable that by the time one reaches maturity he has come to accept the situation as natural, and the one to be expected. No exercise of force is necessary to keep such a person following peacefully along the path of submission for the remainder of his life.

Of course, if the subjected group in spite of persecution from above set up within their own circle a program of opposition to their masters and maintain an undying hope for release from the oppressors, they may defeat the conditioning of their younger generations to the inferior status. By keeping alive the thirst for freedom and equality they may in fact condition each new generation with the attitude of rebellion, which will require the ruling class constantly to maintain its position by force.

Means of Domination. There are, however, more subtle and less costly ways of keeping a conquered section of a population in subjection than by the use of a standing army. Ross points out [6] that, in addition to force, the means used by a ruling class to keep a subservient population under control are superstition, fraud, pomp, and prescription. One of the first steps is to clothe naked force in legal and institutional forms and relieve its harshness by measures of conciliation. Slavery is transmuted into serfdom, which is less irritating. Personal rights are gradually extended to members of the exploited classes while the fundamentals of control are retained through institutional organization. Freedom of mobility is eventually granted. The worker is permitted to retain a large share of his earnings and taxation is substituted for more brutal forms of extortion. A few members of the exploited classes who show outstanding ability are given posts of responsibility and honor among the rulers, and thus hope and ambition among the exploited are substituted for envy and hatred.

A cleverly led exploiting class has in its repertory a large variety of devices with which to subdue the minds and emotions of the masses. Religion may easily be distorted into superstition and, through the manipulation of belief in the supernatural and after-world, provide effective controls. Instead of being an incentive to brotherhood, social justice

---

[6] *Ibid.*, pp. 382-384.

and ethical idealism, religion may be used as a tool to make people content with their lot, obedient to their rulers, and defenders of the *status quo*. It is this kind of religion that later revolutionists label an "opiate of the people."

Another device to maintain control is the use of illusion to exaggerate such virtues as obedience, respect for authority, thrift, and hard work far beyond their real merit. Equally useful is the cultivation of reverence for the sanctity of custom and tradition. Whatever will make people devoted to the established order as it has been, and fix their attention on the glories of the past instead of on needed changes in the future, is useful to a ruling class.

Still another old means of capturing the imagination of the masses, and one that has been used for centuries, has recently been revived with great success by modern dictators. That is pomp, ceremony, and pageantry. While there is much to be said for the usefulness of such artistry as a means of control in a democratic society, its function in the hands of a ruling class or a dictator is quite different. It diverts attention from the suffering of the people, inspires awe toward the rulers, and arouses emotional support for the *status quo*.

Inter-class Etiquette as a Control Mechanism

A particular type of ceremony as an instrument of control by a ruling class is seen in the etiquette of personal relations which is developed between ruler and ruled. The class or caste structure as a device for maintaining a differential in opportunities and privileges is, as pointed out above, a part of the institutional structure of a society. It fixes such basic elements of the life of the individual as his rank, the group of occupations within which he finds his economic activity, his educational and other cultural opportunities. It resolves open conflict and makes for actual cooperation. But there remains the invisible wall of class distinction between members of the same society.

Forms of Etiquette. Individuals who must frequently have personal contacts, work together, even occupy the same households, are still in a way strangers to one another and aware of the fundamental differences which separate them. Some way must be found to make these personal relations tolerable and yet consistent with the fundamental realities of the class structure. This is found in the etiquette of class or caste relations. Forms of etiquette are essentially a ritual of personal intercourse and prescribe the forms of verbal expression and of other behavior that are accepted as the proper ones to use in personal relations. Professor B. W. Doyle [7] has shown

---

[7] Bertram W. Doyle, *The Etiquette of Race Relations in the South* (Chicago, University of Chicago Press, 1937). See also "Introduction," by Robert E. Park.

the significance of etiquette in regulating the personal relations of Negroes and whites in southern United States under slavery and under the caste-like system that, since emancipation, has supplanted it. The code covered forms of address and response, bodily posture and gestures, variations in behavior appropriate to different occasions and situations. The significance of every detail of the code was to indicate the inferior status of the slave and attest to his loyalty and respect for the white person. At the same time the code required that the white person, while conscious of his superior status, show his good will toward the Negro and frequently, in the case of a master and slave, intimacy, affection, and concern for the slave's well-being.

In the situation that developed after emancipation the crux of personal relations between whites and Negroes has been the maintenance of a code of etiquette that would give assurances of a continuance of a similar relative status of the two races to that which prevailed under slavery. Since the status had changed and many Negroes desired that the change be recognized, the period immediately following the Civil War was one of complete turmoil and disorganization. But, as the white Southerner eventually regained control of the situation and made it clear to the Negro that the whites would use force if necessary to maintain their supremacy, much of the old code of etiquette was restored. A few slight changes have been made in recognition of the fact that slavery no longer exists, such as the substitution of new terms like "Boss" or "Captain" in place of "Mars" or "Massa," and the choice of some more formal modes of address by a white person in place of the use of the first name in addressing a Negro of some education or prominence. But even now the code does not accept the terms "Mister" and "Mistress" for any Negro. Most of the essentials of the old code have been resumed. In the interest of peace and a *modus vivendi* the southern Negro has acquiesced in it, although on the part of the educated and more independent in spirit, the code is a hollow form without meaning, behind which the Negro may maintain a spirit of self-respect and personal dignity.

Many parallels in other societies could be made with the code of etiquette that has governed the personal relations of Negroes and whites in southern United States. In all societies where feudalism and the estate system or the caste system has prevailed, there grew up a code of etiquette that defined and controlled personal relations between members of separate classes. Whenever the society has been concerned with a clear definition of the differences of status of its members, and of seeing that every person "kept his place," it has made use of a very definite code of etiquette of personal relations across class lines. Most Asiatic societies still maintain such codes and most European societies still have **many** relics of ancient codes even where the democratic movement has done much toward leveling the legal distinctions between the classes.[8]

The writer recalls an incident that occurred in the barnyard of an English gentleman farmer one day in the first quarter of the twentieth century. A farm laborer approached the farmer, who was talking with the writer, to ask some directions concerning a piece of work in one of the fields. Before speaking to the farmer the laborer removed his hat, and in answer to directions from the farmer, replied, "Yes, Sir," "No, Sir," in the most deferential manner. Later, when the writer remarked to the farmer that to an American the attitude of the laborer appeared quite servile, the somewhat surprised reply was that such behavior on the part of the laborer was not servility but merely good manners. But the farmer had not removed his hat nor used the term "Sir" to the laborer.

Class Control Under Capitalism

While control exercised by a dominant class is seen in its most elementary form in estate and caste societies, it is by no means confined to societies with those types of class system. In modern open class societies where power is derived chiefly from the ownership and control of wealth we see many evidences of class control. It is true that the institutional organization of modern democratic societies has removed many of the cruder evidences of class dominance and has equalized personal and political rights to a very great degree. But it is obvious that the ownership and control of capital have given to certain sections of the population power that is used by them to maintain a disproportionate degree of control over other sections of the population.

The methods used by the capitalist class in modern society to maintain their control are necessarily different from those used by the dominant feudal estates and higher castes. Political democracy, universal public education, and a relative independence of the church make it much less easy for a dominant class to manipulate the minds and attitudes of the masses. Their control is exercised chiefly through the economic system and the manipulation of government.

Capital has come to play such a vital part in the production and distribution of the means of living that whoever controls capital not only holds considerable power over the wage earner, but over the whole productive and distributive system as it affects the welfare of all elements of the population. During the past seventy-five years in the United States the concentration in control of capital has been particularly marked,[9] and

[8] For other illustrations see Landtman, *op. cit.*, pp. 305-306.
[9] See A. A. Berle and G. C. Means, *The Modern Corporation and Private Property* (New York: The Macmillan Co., 1934), and Harry W. Laidler, *Concentration of Control in American Industry* (New York: Thomas Y. Crowell Co., 1931).

the dominant position in the economic order maintained by these large aggregates of wealth is a commonly recognized fact.

The ways in which government may be used to maintain special privileges for the few are numerous. Monopolies, grants of land to favorites, manipulation of taxation, grants of franchise, favoritism in awarding contracts for public services are a few of the most familiar.[10] Harold Laski has succinctly stated the relation between wealth and government: "Historically, we always find that any system of government is dominated by those who at the time wield economic power." [11]

Manipulation of Public Opinion. In a political democracy, however, this dominance cannot be maintained without some means of reaching the minds and attitudes of the masses who make decisions at the polls. Hence, in capitalist societies we find evidences of direct efforts of financial interests to shape public opinion and feeling in their favor. The chief channels through which the effort must be made are the press, the radio, the school, and the church which are treated in other chapters. The chief organ for the dissemination of news or information concerning the ongoing life of the world and of the nation in particular is the daily newspaper and there is no question but that the news that reaches the great mass of the population is refracted through the medium which transmits it, which is usually a capitalistic enterprise. The radio has become an important organ for the dissemination of information and opinion and is controlled by the same type of business interests as are the newspapers. The public school, being a public enterprise and being very close to popular sentiment, must be approached with greater indirection and caution than are the newspaper and the radio. A free church, severed from any connection with government, is a much more difficult institution for a dominant class to use than is a church which is an arm of the state. But a large proportion of the membership may consist of families of the owning-employing class and those on comfortable salaries. These have a direct interest in maintaining the economic *status quo* and consequently would object to the church taking any position in opposition to it.

Class and Personality

Personality Conditioning. The second major way in which class differentiation participates in social control is the function which the social class performs in shaping human personality. It is one of the elementary

---

[10] For a more detailed discussion of government as a device for creating and maintaining privileged classes, see Cecil C. North, *Social Differentiation* (Chapel Hill: University of North Carolina Press, 1926), chapter X.

[11] *Foundations of Sovereignty and Other Essays* (New York: Harcourt, Brace and Co., 1921).

teachings of sociology and of social psychology that the human personality is shaped by the reaction between the individual's inherited biological equipment and the culture which he finds about him. Out of this culture is drawn the materials and experiences which go into the making of the personality. Elsewhere in this volume it is shown how the folkways, the mores, the attitudes which govern the behavior of the individual are drawn from this social *milieu*.

A social class is a form of grouping that includes most of the peculiarities of culture that characterize the family, the occupational group, the neighborhood, the play and recreation group. That is, while each family has certain distinctive aspects of its behavior patterns that are unique for that family, the greater part of its behavior will be closely similar to that of other families in the same social class. The same is to be said of the neighborhood and of the occupational group. That is, a great many of the behavior patterns which the family impresses upon its children members are the patterns of the class to which the family belongs. The patterns induced by membership in an occupational group are distinctly class patterns. The neighborhood and play or recreation group of both children and adults are in nearly all cases constituted of people of the same social class. Hence the patterns of behavior which the individual derives from these groups reflect for the most part patterns of a particular class. We may, therefore, without regarding one's social class as the basic or exclusive influence in social control, recognize it as one exceedingly important factor in shaping personality.

The standard of living, that is, the level of consumption of economic goods and services to which an individual or family aspires, is one important determinant of behavior. Very much that one does and many of his ambitions have to do with his desire to maintain a particular standard of living. We hear much of the "American standard of living," but there is no such single standard. We have as many standards as there are social classes in America. A family which belongs to the higher financial group feels itself under obligation to maintain a certain number of servants and a summer home, to send its children to private schools, to provide a particular level of entertainment, wardrobe, etc., all showing "conspicuous consumption." A family of one of the middle classes feels under equal compulsion to keep up with the Joneses but at a different level from that of the Astorbilts. The family automobile must not be too old a model. The residence must be in the right location in the city, certainly not "across the tracks." The house furnishings must not be permitted to be behind the prevailing mode in use in other middle class families. The family of the farm-owning farmer and that of the skilled wage earner, while living at approximately the same level, will have different types of furnishings, will buy different types of luxuries, and will respond to different compulsions in their expenditures. Even the poorest native-born American family in the days of extensive immigration would feel a sense of shame if forced to live in the manner of some of the recently arrived immigrants.

Similarly, in ethical standards we find the different classes inclined to adhere to somewhat different codes. Thorstein Veblen was the first social scientist to point out [12] the differences between the mental processes and the ethical standards of the industrial wage earner and those of the financial and managerial class. The industrial worker is seen to be skeptical, matter of fact, materialistic, and undevout, while the pecuniary and managerial group has a high valuation of property rights, is conservative with respect to religion and family and political life and more conventional in its moral outlook. A similar analysis of the farmer, the professional worker, or the public official would reveal for each a somewhat unique type of attitude and ideals and folkways.[13]

Middle Class. The groups in present-day western society that are somewhat loosely designated as the middle classes are characterized by a set of mores sometimes contemptuously referred to by revolutionaries as "middle class or bourgeois virtues." These include high standards of cleanliness, abstention from personal combat, respectability, conventional sex behavior and family life, a strong devotion on the part of parents to their children and ambition for their children's getting ahead in the world, and a strong interest in education and so-called "cultural" pursuits. These mores, together with an intense interest in maintaining their status in a rank above the "laboring classes," are probably the most characteristic mark of the middle classes. A "good" middle-class family is one that observes these standards and impresses them on its children. And the play and recreation groups of middle-class neighborhoods add their influence to strengthening allegiance to them. The church and youth organizations in these middle-class neighborhoods are particularly concerned, not only in impressing them upon young people but in stimulating families to greater effort in their behalf.

Rank Status and Personality. Not only is the individual molded by the standards and mores of his class, but his personality also reflects the influence upon him of the status or rank imposed by his class. Rank affects personality through developing attitudes and through denying the individual or supplying him with the economic and spiritual goods of his

---

[12] Thorstein Veblen, *Theory of Business Enterprise* (New York: Charles Scribner's Sons, 1904). See also his *Theory of the Leisure Class* (New York: The Macmillan Co., 1899), for the classical description of the standards of consumption of the upper classes.

[13] For a more complete discussion of the relation of occupation and status to folkways and mores, see Cecil C. North, *op. cit.*, chapter XI.

society. Rank connotes a position in a scale or hierarchy. One's position is superior to those in the ranks lower than his and inferior to those in the ranks above him. The feeling of inferiority or superiority, or in most cases a combination of the two emotions induced by one's position, is an important factor in shaping attitudes that are significant for behavior.

Domination and Submission Attitudes. The haughty, domineering, arrogant, or condescending attitude which has characterized the members of the upper classes in practically all societies has been well portrayed in literature. Jane Austen's *Pride and Prejudice* and George Meredith's *Evan Harrington* are well-known examples. The modern version of this attitude is exemplified by the lady bountiful distributing charity from her limousine or the type of employer who declares that "the business belongs to me and I will not have any one telling me how to run it." These attitudes on the part of the dominant classes have frequently been matched by that of servility and meek obedience on the part of the underprivileged. The servant who comes to believe that, since each is born to his station in life, it is only proper that he should show respect for his betters, is the correlative of the master who is equally sure that he was born to rule.[14]

The attitude of humility and ready acceptance is not, however, always the effect which the lower rank status induces in the underprivileged. There may be bitterness, resentment and a permanent feeling of antagonism which expresses itself in oversensitiveness, a tendency to see slights and offenses where none were intended, the attitude of "carrying a chip on the shoulder." Professor Herbert Miller has referred to this characteristic attitude of oppressed peoples as the "oppression psychosis."[15] It undoubtedly explains much behavior on the part of suppressed peoples that otherwise is difficult of understanding.

The direct effect of rank in creating attitudes, however, is not the whole story of its influence on personality. There are indirect consequences arising from the access to or deprivation of the facilities for the satisfaction of human needs and opportunities for personal development. Physical health, intelligence, capacity for self-direction and for leadership, ability to participate usefully in the total life of the society are qualities of personality whose development depends upon the opportunities and facilities available to the individual. One's class rank determines these opportunities for the individual. The consequences of the differential in these opportunities are reflected in the differences that exist be-

---

[14] See, for example, *An Old Servant: Domestic Service* (Boston: Houghton, Mifflin Co., 1917); Adaptation of pp. 10-110 by R. E. Park and E. W. Burgess, *Introduction to the Science of Sociology*, 1st ed., pp. 692-695.

[15] Herbert A. Miller, *Nations, Races and Classes* (Philadelphia: J. B. Lippincott Co., 1942).

tween the health and mental and moral efficiency of the different classes. A failure to understand this fact has lent plausibility to the notion that the upper classes rule by the right of inborn superiority. The fact that a few members of the underprivileged classes by good fortune or unusual ability succeed in acquiring access to the opportunities for development and thus push their way up to higher levels does not alter the fact that the masses of the less privileged classes are denied opportunities for personality development equal to those of their class superiors.

The Negro. Concrete evidence of the effects of caste and class status on personality is provided in several recent studies of Negro youth in the United States. Frazier, Davis and Dollard, and Myrdal [16] by first-hand investigation have shown the effects upon the personality of American Negro youth of their inferior race position. The American Negro in the southern states and in the border states definitely occupies the position of a subordinate race. At the same time, within the Negro community, clear-cut class divisions exist. It is found that both of these forms of differentiation have significance for the Negro personality.

The race position creates barriers and limitations on participation in many of the activities of the community and keeps constantly before the Negro the fact of his inferiority. It also denies him equal opportunity for the satisfaction of his wants and needs and provides for him a lower level of income and other facilities for personal satisfactions and personal development. This inferior position is enforced by insult, ridicule, and physical violence, or the threat of these measures.

The direct effect upon attitudes of Negroes is resentment, bitterness, hatred, a feeling of discouragement and hopelessness. The resentment and antagonism are usually, however, not openly expressed except to other Negroes or to white people who are known not to share the southern white point of view. It is expressed, however, in disguised forms such as getting even by sabotage, slowness, lack of punctuality, clumsiness, and stealing. Also to get what he wants the Negro resorts to flattery, humor, secretiveness, acting "like a monkey," and lying. The feeling of discouragement and hopelessness results in poor work or non-attendance at school, misbehavior, and lack of incentive to do one's best work on a job. Why should one put forth his best efforts when there are few rewards to achieve, when it is known that insurmountable obstacles block the way to advancement?

[16] E. Franklin Frazier, *Negro Youth at the Crossways: Their Personality Development in the Middle States* (Washington, D.C.: American Council of Education, 1940); Allison Davis and John Dollard, *Children of Bondage: Personality Development of Negro Youth in the Rural South* (Washington, D.C.: American Council of Education, 1940); Gunnar Myrdal and others, *An American Dilemma: The Negro Problem and Modern Democracy* (New York: Harper and Brothers, 1944).

Important as the race distinction is, however, in shaping Negro personality, it is not as significant as is that of social class. Any observation of
Negro life will reveal that class position is the more significant factor
in creating the formative conditions of personality.

As in the case of the white population, class position creates the significant influences that shape Negro personality and determine the opportunities for, and limitations on, personality development.

As a matter of fact, the Negro class position determines very largely
the severity with which the racial factor bears on the individual. Lower-
class Negroes are found to accept their inferior position as inevitable and
to adjust their behavior to the situation. To them it seems something that
cannot be changed.

The middle-class Negroes, however, although outwardly accommo-
dating themselves to the situation, do not believe in the white man's
inherent superiority. They maintain inwardly a belief in their equality
with the whites and impress this attitude on their children.

The upper-class Negroes go further. They not only teach their children
that they are the equals of the whites, but seek to protect them from
discrimination. Ideologically they identify themselves with the white
upper class and maintain an attitude of equality with them.

These studies make it absolutely clear that so far as the American
Negro is concerned, race and class distinctions are extremely important
factors in shaping human personality; and there seems to be no reason
why the conclusion is not equally applicable to other sections of the
population.

Summary

The open class and caste distinctions that have come to prevail among
all modern societies provide effective controls over the behavior of
individuals. Control is shown in two ways: these distinctions create
patterns of behavior and limitations which govern each class in its relation
with other classes, and they provide the formative influence on personality
which is implied in class membership.

The patterns controlling the behavior of classes may be imbedded in
law or in the mores or etiquette of relations between members of different classes. Some classes may be limited to given occupational fields.
Force may be used and, in the early stages of any class system, may be
necessary. However, other and more subtle means are more economical
in enforcing such regulations. These other means include pomp, fraud
and prescription, and the manifestation of religion.

The effects of class membership on personality development are marked.
Feelings of superiority and inferiority or frustration arise from the

relative position occupied by one's social class. Many of the opportunities for self-development are denied to members of less fortunate classes and are made readily available to those of superior classes.

QUESTIONS

1. What is a social class?
2. Distinguish between caste, estate, and open class.
3. What is the purpose which a conquering group has in mind in setting up a class organization?
4. Does this have any advantage for the conquered group?
5. Briefly summarize the various substitutes for force which have been adopted by conquering classes to keep the lower classes under control.
6. How does a code of etiquette operate as a control device?
7. What means of control is used by the controlling class in our society?
8. How may government in modern democratic society be used by a class in its own interests?
9. How is the daily newspaper used as a means of class control?
10. Is the radio a neutral channel of communication? Explain.
11. How may the school serve class interests?
12. Is the Church a class controlled organization?
13. How is the concept of the social environment to be broken up into smaller homogeneous units?
14. Do we have an American standard of living? Explain.
15. Cite some distinctive personality traits of different occupational groups.
16. Briefly describe some of the more important mores of the American middle-class family.
17. What do you understand by class rank?
18. Point out some different direct effects of rank on personality.
19. How does rank indirectly effect personality through the opportunities it provides the individual?
20. Compare the importance of race position and class as influences affecting the American Negro.

SUGGESTED TOPICS FOR TERM PAPERS AND FURTHER RESEARCH

1. Make a study of the differences in the mores of different classes in your community.
2. Read Franklin Frazier, *Negro Youth at the Crossways*, and Allison Davis and John Dollard, *Children of Bondage*, and apply their methods of study to some members of some underprivileged group in your community.
3. Study the files of a daily newspaper for evidences of class bias in reporting the news.
4. Analyze the membership and official board of your church for percentage belonging to different classes, and find how far you think the policies and preaching of the church reflect the class position of the dominant class in the membership.
5. Read Thorstein Veblen's *Theory of the Leisure Class* and find how far you believe his ideas concerning upper-class standards of behavior prevail in a community with which you are familiar.
6. Read Jane Austen's *Pride and Prejudice* and George Meredith's *Evan Harring-ton* and describe the class attitudes portrayed.

7. Analyze your own aspirations, ideals, standards, prejudices, and preferences, and see if you can determine how many of them have a class origin.

8. Read Sinclair Lewis' *Babbitt* and draw up a characterization of Babbitt as a representative of the American businessman.

9. In a town of three thousand to ten thousand population, make a study of the membership of the school board and public officials over a period of several years. By interviews with various citizens, find what groups in the community give chief support to the election of these officials. On the basis of this information, determine whether there is any class domination in this community.

10. Read A. A. Berle's and G. C. Means' *The Modern Corporation and Private Property*, and Harry W. Laidler's *Concentration of Control in American Industry*, and summarize the evidence for class control of American economic life.

BIBLIOGRAPHY

Books

Louis Adamic, *Dynamite* (New York: The Viking Press, 1931). A popular presentation of a history of class conflict and violence in the United States, although the argument for the growth of class consciousness is not too convincing.

Edwin H. Cady, *The Gentleman in America* (Syracuse, N.Y.: Syracuse University Press, 1949). A literary study of American culture.

Richard Centers, *The Psychology of Social Classes* (Princeton, N.J.: Princeton University Press, 1950). An analysis of the origins of class consciousness in the United States today.

Charles H. Cooley, *Social Organization* (New York: Charles Scribner's Sons, 1909), Part IV. The earliest definite analysis of the distinction between the principle of caste and that of open classes. Also analyzes the conditions in a society making for social mobility and those retarding it. Still a fundamental contribution to the nature and significance of class in modern society.

Committee on Intergroup Education in Cooperating Schools, *Curriculum in Intergroup Relations: Secondary Schools* (Washington, D.C.: American Council on Education, 1949). Proposals as to how the school can help the democratic tendencies in our society.

Jerome Davis, *Capitalism and Its Culture* (New York: Farrar and Rinehart, 1935). An adversely critical study of the way in which the capitalist economy influences other aspects of American culture and creates a controlling class. The selection of specific cases results in a strong indictment of capitalism but interferes with a balanced, objective analysis.

W. Allison Davis, *Social Class Influence upon Learning* (Cambridge, Mass.: Harvard University Press, 1948).

W. Allison Davis and John Dollard, *Children of Bondage* (Washington, D.C.: American Council on Education, 1940). A good body of research material relating to the impact upon the personality of youth of membership in a minority race.

John Dollard, *Caste and Class in Southern Town* (New Haven: Yale University Press, 1937). An account of the manner in which caste and class distinctions permeate the life of a small Southern town, resulting in differential advantages and disadvantages to the various sections of the population. Psychoanalytic analysis not entirely convincing.

Bertram W. Doyle, *The Etiquette of Race Relations in The South* (Chicago: University of Chicago Press, 1937). An excellent and well-documented account of the rules of etiquette governing the contacts of Negroes and whites in Southern United States. It shows clearly the role of etiquette as a control device to maintain a superordinate-subordinate situation between the races.

E. Franklin Frazier, *Negro Youth at the Crossways* (Washington, D.C.: American Council on Education, 1940). An important piece of research which demonstrates the role of open class and caste as factors in shaping personality.

August B. Hollingshead, *Elmstown's Youth* (New York: John Wiley and Sons, 1949). An original study of the social class influences in a small town.

Floyd Hunter, *Community Power Structure* (Chapel Hill, N.C.: University of North Carolina Press, 1953). A unique analysis of the operation of power relations in a small town.

Gunnar Myrdal, *et al.*, *An American Dilemma* (New York: Harper and Brothers, 1944). An incisive study of the Negro situation in the United States, which propounds that it is due to the culture lag.

C. C. North, *Social Differentiation* (Chapel Hill, N.C.: University of North Carolina Press, 1926). A systematic description of the nature, bases, and effects of differences and distinctions among individuals in groups.

Pitirim R. Sorokin, *Social Mobility* (New York: Harper and Brothers, 1927). Contains a wealth of material on the various problems of social stratification.

Thorstein B. Veblen, *The Theory of the Leisure Class* (New York: New Library Association, 1954). A brilliant, and now classic, analysis of the standards and patterns of behavior of the upper classes.

W. Lloyed Warner and associates, *Democracy in Jonesville* (New York: Harper and Brothers, 1949). A noteworthy analysis of class and caste distinction in the United States, as all the other contributions of Warner and his associates, listed below.

———, *et al.*, *Social Class in America* (Chicago: Science Research Association, 1949).

———, and Paul S. Lunt, *The Social Life in a Modern Community* (New Haven: Yale University Press, 1949).

James West, *Plainville, U.S.A.* (New York: Columbia University Press, 1945). Follows the traditions of the pioneering work of Robert S. Lynd and Helen M. Lynd, *Middletown* (New York: Harcourt, Brace and Co., 1929), and *Middletown in Transition* (New York: Harcourt, Brace and Co., 1937).

Harvey W. Zorbaugh, *The Gold Coast and the Slum* (Chicago: University of Chicago Press, 1929). A very interesting analysis of the various social classes in Chicago.

Periodicals

W. B. Brookover, "The Implications of Social Class Analyses for a Social Theory of Education," *Educational Theory*, I (August, 1951), pp. 97-105.

Hadley Cantril, "Identification with Social and Economic Class," *Journal of Abnormal and Social Psychology*, XXXVIII (1943), pp. 74-80.

W. Allison Davis and Robert J. Havighurst, "Social Class and Color Differences in Child Rearing," *American Sociological Review*, XI (December, 1946), pp. 698-709.

Milton M. Gordon, "Social Class in American Sociology," *American Journal of Sociology*, LV (November, 1949), pp. 265-270.

Paul K. Hatt, "Stratification in the Mass Society," *American Sociological Review*, XV (April, 1950), pp. 216-222.

Alexander Inkeles, "Stratification and Mobility in the Soviet Union," *ibid.*, XV (August, 1950), pp. 465-479.

Seymour M. Lipset and Reinhard Bendix, "Social Status and Social Structure: A Re-Examination of Data and Interpretations: II," *The British Journal of Sociology*, XX (September, 1951), pp. 230-254.

Joel B. Montague, "Research Related to Social Class in England," *American Sociological Review*, XVII (April, 1952), pp. 192-196.

Harold W. Pfantz and Otis D. Duncan, "A Critical Evaluation of Warner's Work in Community Stratification," *ibid.*, XV (April, 1951), pp. 205-215.

Arnold M. Rose, "The Popular Meaning of Class Designation," *Sociology and Social Research*, XXXVIII (September-October, 1953), pp. 14-21.

Elbridge Sibley, "Some Demographic Clues to Stratification," *American Sociological Review*, VII (June, 1942), pp. 322-330.

Hugh H. Smythe and Shigemi Kono, "A Social Distance Test of the Eta Caste of Japan," *Sociology and Social Research*, XXXVIII (September-October, 1953), pp. 26-31.

W. Lloyd Warner, "American Caste and Class," *American Journal of Sociology*, XLII (September, 1936), pp. 234-238.

CHAPTER XI

How Science Modifies Institutions

Institutional Control. It is universally recognized that all institutions exercise some degree of control, and that the introduction or development of any form of culture manifests itself directly or indirectly in all of the institutions of the society concerned. Everyone is familiar with the commonly accepted notion that the introduction of Christianity into Europe resulted in fundamental changes in Western institutions; that the phenomenal changes in the culture of Japan during the past century have brought about revolutionary results in Japanese institutions; that the cultural upheavals of World War II are reflected in the institutions of all peoples, even those not directly involved in that struggle. It is hardly necessary to demonstrate that the institutions of a society are not all modified in the same degree nor in the same fashion by any given cultural change or series of changes. In illustration of this, we may cite the effects upon the governmental institutions of European peoples resulting from World War II. In many instances these were completely reconstituted. This can hardly be said in any other institutional field, although marked changes have resulted in economic, religious and other fields.

No attempt can be made here to consider all institutions. Their number is very great in modern, complex societies. Not all institutions are to be found in all societies, but some are so fundamental as to be found everywhere. Those that are universal must be regarded as of greater importance, at least to humanity as a whole. An examination of the culture of different peoples will show that their familial, religious, economic, educational and governmental institutions are of great relative importance.

What Determines Relative Institutional Importance

Since the purpose of an institution is to provide gratification of some human want, and since some wants are more urgent than others, the relative importance of an institution depends upon the urgency of the specific want concerned. This importance is in part attributed to the want by the people themselves. That this particular want may be regarded as unimportant by members of some other society is irrelevant.

However, all peoples take the attitude that the institutions above named are important elements of their culture. All peoples tend, also, to vest a large measure of social control in that institution or those institutions whose functions are to provide gratification of the wants they regard as most urgent. Therefore the institutions mentioned are important in all cultures and, for that reason, are selected here for specific treatment.

Meaning of Science

In discussing the effects of science upon the form and functions of institutions, it is necessary first to clarify the meaning of the term. Science is used here to refer to demonstrable knowledge of the facts of the universe, and methods of the application of this knowledge. All peoples, even the most primitive, have a considerable accumulation of knowledge which is essentially scientific, and make practical application of at least some parts of this knowledge.[1] Among primitives knowledge is so limited and, in its application, is so mixed with various concepts of the supernatural that little true science develops. Their institutions reflect this condition and center about other than scientific ideas to a marked degree. It must be kept in mind that modern man is subject to these same limitations in a lesser degree. All behavior has at its origin esthetic, ethical, traditional, customary and supernatural concepts which, in some measure, modify the acceptance and the application of scientific knowledge.

Relative Importance in Control. As suggested in the foregoing, the relative importance of science varies widely with different cultures. In part, this difference is due to variations in the development of scientific knowledge. These are fundamentally of two sorts; differences in the amount of scientific knowledge existing in the society, and differences in the particular fields of development. Both of these are modified by the prevailing attitudes toward scientific knowledge and its application. That Western institutions have been more affected by science than Oriental institutions is a commonplace, and few would demur from the opinion that this is due in considerable part to the more advanced state of science among European peoples. It is among them that scientific knowledge has accumulated most rapidly for eight or ten centuries. The nature of Western science, too, has made it an effective element in the development of Western institutions, and has influenced the direction of development. Western science, for many years, was paced by physics and chemistry.[2]

---

[1] For a good detailed treatment, see M. J. Herskovits, *The Economic Life of Primitive Peoples* (New York: Alfred A. Knopf, 1940).

[2] A series of informative essays on this point will be found in T. Veblen, *The Place of Science in Modern Civilization* (New York: B. W. Huebsch, 1919).

Material Progress. Since physics and chemistry are basic to the material universe, knowledge in these fields lends itself to material progress. This is precisely the field in which Western peoples have outstripped most Orientals. That this is accompanied by widely differing attitudes toward science on the part of the peoples concerned is obvious to those with even a superficial acquaintance with the ideologies of the two groups.

Changes in Institutional Control. Changes in cultural development are accompanied by changes in the relative importance of different institutions in the exercise of social control. In any society, each institution has for its motivation the discharge of certain functions. These functions are determined ultimately by the ideological complex of the people; and the attitudes taken by them toward the various institutions of their culture indicate, and in large measure determine, their relative importance. Among a people who, for whatever reasons, take the attitude that their spiritual welfare in the hereafter is of paramount importance, it is to be expected that those institutions, e.g., the religious, which provide gratification of this interest, will be predominant in the control of behavior. On the other hand, a people who regard material welfare as the most important phase of human existence will impute great relative importance to economic institutions. This is characteristic of modern Western societies. As a specific instance of change in relative importance as between religious and economic institutions, one may well consider the difference in attitudes shown by early Christians and by twentieth century Christian peoples, and the corresponding difference in the degree of control exercised by the early church and by modern Christian organizations.

The Influence of Science. Modern science reached its earliest and also its highest development in the physical realm. Hence, this development has most profoundly affected man's attitudes toward material things, and has modified institutions through their relations to material culture. The spread of science also has been accompanied by an acceptance of the scientific attitude toward things not in themselves primarily scientific. Since scientific knowledge is directly or indirectly dependent upon evidence which is conveyed to the mind through one or more of the senses, respect for science leads man to rely upon sensory evidence, and to reject the claims of those who appeal to authority not supported by the senses.

Because some institutions and the functions which they discharge are more closely related to the material universe, their relative importance increases with the growth of scientific knowledge at the same time that the influence of other institutions is being undermined by the acceptance of scientific authority. This shift in relative importance brings about conflict between the institutions concerned as one acquires control which the other attempts to retain. The so-called conflict between science and religion is an example. There is, of course, no such conflict. In so far as any conflict exists, it is among the institutions involved. Religious institutions discharge their functions in respect of aspects of life not amenable to scientific treatment. But these aspects were formerly regarded by large numbers of people as of paramount importance. Science has brought into greater prominence economic and other institutions dealing with mundane and material things. This change of relative importance is accompanied by a shift of social control to economic institutions.

Institutional Conflict

It is characteristic of social institutions that they struggle to retain and to exercise whatever control they have acquired and, usually, to extend it if possible. It follows that a shift of control from one institution to another is very likely to be accompanied by conflict, the one anxious to extend its power, the other to retain control already acquired and exercised. History is filled with accounts of these conflicts; indeed, it may be said to be characterized by them. Familiar to all are the struggles between church and state following the Middle Ages. There is the recent example of revolutionary Russia which undertook to destroy the church in order that a fuller measure of social control might be exercised by the state. In the United States we have a recent example in the activities of the Huey Long political machine, bringing the educational institutions of the State of Louisiana under complete domination for political purposes. Economic organizations of the class of "big business" have exercised a great deal of control, sometimes in defiance of the efforts of government. Labor organizations have more recently adopted a similar course.

Trends Toward Institutional Toleration. The modern trend has been toward toleration between institutions, particularly those of religion, economics and government. Still more recently, the doctrine of *laissez faire* has fallen into disrepute, and government has gone far toward domination of economic affairs. This is partly a reaction against the conditions of the last half of the nineteenth century, when government was frequently dominated by economic organizations. This domination was usually indirect, but came to be very effective. The past quarter century has seen the revival of governmental oppression of religion with the rise of totalitarianism. In accordance with the principle already presented, these inter-institutional changes in attitude and degree of dominance over each other are reflected in changes in their relative importance in social control.

In spite of these fluctuations, there seems to be some basis for the widely known assumption by Comte that knowledge passes through three stages beginning with the theological, followed by the philosophical and, finally, by the scientific.[3] Social control, being based upon the knowledge and the concepts existing within a society, varies accordingly.

Religious Institutions

Not only do all institutions exercise a degree of social control, but all are themselves subject to modification in conformity with changes in the culture of which they form a part.

Religious beliefs and their accompanying practices and ceremonies are found among all peoples, and everywhere they control or modify human behavior in ways and to a degree which cannot be disregarded by students of sociology. One of the elements of all religions is a recognition of the existence of the supernatural and of its influence over man and nature. The nature and extent of this recognition vary widely among cultures and from time to time. This variation is closely related to differences in the development of scientific knowledge. To understand this fully, one must have some definite grasp of the nature of the field of science and of that of religion.

Science and Religion. Science and religion are both—among other things—explanations of the nature of man and of the universe, their interrelationships and their origins. Religious explanations involve the recognition of some supernatural power controlling both man and nature, and are usually regarded as having originated both. These explanations involve ultimate powers, aims and purposes, and purport to be complete explanations of the phenomena observed. Science, being confined to the natural, does not offer answers of this ultimate sort.[4] It classifies knowledge gained by observation, drawing from these classifications conclusions, perhaps only tentative, which, because of the uniformity of behavior upon which they are based, are regarded as scientific laws. More and more, science tends to give attention to the "how" of behavior within the physical universe, and less and less to the "why." Religion furnishes an answer to "why."

Men everywhere seem to give some recognition to the existence of the knowable and of the unknowable. The first is the domain of science, the second that of religion. It must be remembered that a great body of knowledge possessed by modern peoples is inaccessible to peoples in a

---

[3] Comte uses the terms "Theological," "Metaphysical" and "Positive."
[4] Perhaps the most highly developed presentation of a purely scientific explanation of the universe is that offered by Herbert Spencer, *First Principles* (any edition).

more primitive stage of cultural development. This is to them a part of the unknown; therefore it is, in their minds, subject to explanations involving something of the supernatural—e.g., religious explanations. Since no people has attained a full understanding of the universe as it is known through the senses, this confusion of natural with supernatural persists in the minds of all. However, the narrow limits of scientific knowledge among uncivilized peoples leaves a wider range of phenomena to be explained by them in terms of the supernatural.[5]

The Growing Acceptance of Science. The foregoing implies a process which is obvious in the pages of history. As scientific knowledge increases, one phenomenon after another is found to conform to some established natural law or laws. As the realization of this penetrates the minds of the people, the scientific explanation tends to be adopted and the previously accepted supernatural explanation tends to be rejected. If the phenomenon is one which is important to human existence or human welfare, the people attempt either to control it or to adapt themselves to it. Where the explanation is a supernatural one, these attempts at control and adaptation will be of a religious nature. If the people are in a low stage of cultural advancement they resort to magic, or to some manner of appeasing or otherwise influencing the supernatural powers or beings assumed to be in control of the phenomenon in question. Where the scientific explanation is accepted, the means of control and adaptation will tend to become scientific also, and supernatural means will be abandoned. This change, like all other social and cultural changes, takes time. It is not unusual to hear persons who know the scientific explanation of rain making half-hearted appeals to Jehovah to send rain, but this becomes rarer with the passage of time. Ceremonials, such as the Hopi snake dance, designed to serve this particular purpose, mark the earlier stages of this process.[6] When a shift from religious to scientific explanation occurs in the minds of the people, a corresponding shift in social control takes place.

Decreased control by the church on the basis of strictly theological considerations has had the effect of widening its field of interests. In recent times practically all important religious organizations have extended their field of activities. Amusement, social contact, social betterment, sectarian education, and many other activities not strictly of a religious nature receive a large share of their attention. The charge is often made that the church has become "worldly"—meaning that it takes an active interest in the here as well as in the hereafter. It should be kept

[5] A reliable work treating this topic fully as a part of an admirable study of primitive religions is W. D. Wallis, *Religion in Primitive Society* (New York: Crofts, 1939).
[6] For description of the Hopi dance see G. P. Murdock, *Our Primitive Contemporaries* (New York: The Macmillan Co., 1934), chapter XII.

in mind that at least some part of the so-called decline in the power of control by the church is offset by increases of power resulting from these additional activities.

Special Interest Institutions and Groups

The Family. Anthropologists quite generally agree that kinship groups of various forms have been the basis of social organization during earlier stages of the development of advanced peoples. Throughout human history the family, whatever its form, has been the most important of the primary groups. It is still so regarded in those advanced societies in which other kinship groups have disappeared or lost their significance.

Specialization of Knowledge. The increased importance of the special-interest group in modern society as well as its increase in numbers is an accompaniment of the specialization characteristic of modern society. Specialized behavior such as that accompanying division of labor is characterized by and associated with specialized knowledge. Specialization of knowledge necessarily occurs wherever the accumulation of knowledge within a society reaches a point where it is difficult or impossible for each individual to acquire all of it. Specialization, on the other hand, tends to accelerate the process of the accumulation of knowledge. This is especially true in scientific fields, where each addition to knowledge further extends the horizons of research.

Special Interest Groups. One of the results of the process of specialization is the formation of groups based upon special interests possessed by some individuals but not common to the members of the society. Thus any increase in knowledge, after the most rudimentary forms of culture have been passed, tends to bring about the formation of groups based upon some special interest rather than upon kinship. The rapid increase of scientific knowledge in the past few centuries has created a vast number of these groups, many of which are so highly specialized that their special interests are hardly intelligible to members of other groups or to the general public. They are not necessarily intelligible to other members of the families of the interested persons. Nothing is more commonplace in modern society than men whose special interests are not participated in by their wives, and vice versa. An accompaniment of this is that their activities have no particular bearing upon the affairs of the family group except in the matter of income. It is the size of the income and not the way in which it is produced that principally affects the family group.

Specialization and Large-Scale Organization. Since highly developed specialists can exist only where their efforts are closely coordinated, specialization is conducive to large-scale organization. This, in turn, when it becomes characteristic of a society, tends greatly to reduce the relative importance of the primary group. The informal, face-to-face contacts through which the primary group exercises its controls are not effective in larger groups. As specialization develops with its tendency toward large groups, not only are the functions of society transferred to these groups but the method of discharge of these functions changes with the nature of the group. Hence we have centralization and delegation of power becoming increasingly important at the expense of the simpler processes of the primary group. The family, being a primary group, tends to decline in relative importance in accordance with this fundamental change. Much of the decline in control by the family is traceable to this trend rather than to the specific changes in family activity in the fields of religion, education and economics to which responsibility is commonly attributed. The latter are, in large measure, specific phases of a general change.[7]

Scientific development, therefore, provides both the immediate and the remote causes of many of the changes taking place in family organization in the present and the immediate past. It has made possible the specialization and commercialization of function, and also the shift of importance from the primary to the secondary group.

The Changing Form of the Family. Science contributes directly to modification of the family, also. One of the ways in which the application of scientific knowledge directly is working far-reaching changes in the family is in birth control. Contrary to popular belief, all peoples utilize some methods of birth control. But the degree of effectiveness of these methods has increased rapidly with more exact knowledge of the processes of reproduction which have been developed with modern biology. As pointed out earlier in this chapter, the acceptance of the findings of science tends strongly to break down traditional or religious attitudes which have often operated toward more rapid reproduction or, at least, have opposed any tendency to restrict births.

Economic Institutions. Within the past two centuries economic institutions have become increasingly important in social control. This is an accompaniment of the rapid economic development of the period and is, therefore, traceable in large part to scientific advancement.

As with other institutions economic organizations are affected both directly and indirectly by the development of science. The effects of the application of physical science in various economic fields are so well

---

[7] This point of view is well presented in R. D. Rood, *Matrimonial Shoals* (Detroit: Detroit Law Book Co., 1939).

known as to need no exhaustive discussion here.[8] The principal result has been a tremendous increase in productivity, both as to quantity and as to variety of products. In part this result has been achieved directly, but in part it has followed the liberalization of ideas resulting from an acceptance of the scientific attitude. Up to a late stage of human history many economic processes were dominated by traditional methods. Some of these were so firmly established as to constitute part of the mores. Others were rule-of-thumb methods long established by custom.

The general tendency toward specialization as a result of scientific development has taken important specific forms in economic fields. As elsewhere this specialization has been accompanied by centralization of authority and large-scale organization. In economic fields this fact has long been noted. Here, more than elsewhere, the advantages of large-scale organization are so great and operate so directly that the economic structure of all modern societies tends somewhat automatically to eliminate small-scale organizations.

One of the immediate effects of the application of science has been a tremendous increase in wealth. This is due to increased productivity. Capitalism, the prevailing form of economic organization in most modern countries, requires not only great accumulations of wealth, but is characterized by concentration of ownership. This is, of course, a phase of the general process of the concentration of power. Specifically, capitalism puts an extreme degree of social control in the hands of the wealthy—particularly the owners of capital goods. Social control tends to be in the hands of the wealthy wherever a wealthy class exists, but the nature of the control is modified by the form of wealth upon which it is based. It does not need to be demonstrated that the control exercised by an industrial wealthy class takes forms which differ widely from those prevailing under a wealthy land owning aristocracy. Changes in British society accompanying the rise of the manufacturing and commercial middle class are well known, and have been accompanied by the increased power of the House of Commons and the decreased power of the House of Lords.

Educational Institutions. The impact of science upon modern institutions is nowhere of greater import than in the field of education. The general effects of specialization and large-scale organization found in other fields have been manifested here also.

Specifically, the field of knowledge has been greatly extended and the emphasis placed upon the various fields has been shifted in important ways. Instruction in science has gone a long way toward replacing the

---

[8] For a good general treatment the reader is referred to D. W. Roberts, *An Outline of the Economic History of England* (New York: Longmans, Green, 1931).

older, classical material in all of the educational stages. This has now reached the point where many prominent authorities in the field propose a partial return to the older concepts of what constitutes education.

The great increase in accumulated wealth already discussed has lent itself to the establishment and maintenance of the most highly specialized schools in science. These schools, in turn, add rapidly to the store of scientific knowledge, and bring about its increased application. Accumulation and classification of factual knowledge are the basis of science, and the growing importance of research in educational institutions is well known.

The scientific method has come to be applied to the educational process itself. This has been in part through the application of psychology in the educational field, with statistics and mathematical concepts. Scientific devices, sometimes mechanical in nature, are more and more frequently employed. Here again the acceptance of the scientific method has brought about changes in the educational process involving subject matter not in itself scientific in nature.

Specialization in Education. One of the far-reaching results of the increased accumulation of knowledge in modern societies is the inability of the individual to master all of the knowledge accumulated. Among primitive peoples a major part of the store of knowledge possessed by the group is available to and in possession of all normal adults. As knowledge increases, the limits of human capacity as well as those of time make this impossible. No individual in modern Western society has mastery of all of our store of knowledge or of any major portion of it. One of the results of this situation is specialization in education. This, in turn, tends still further to expand the sum total of knowledge. Thus there arises the necessity of choosing from this constantly augmented stock of knowledge that which shall be regarded as essential to the normal individual. This, of course, is the principal problem of curricula. It is also the problem of the direction of the future development of culture. Where great relative importance is placed upon science and scientific achievement it is inevitable that the process of selection of curricular material shall be correspondingly affected, and that instruction shall be put into the hands of specialists in the various fields of science. Partly because of their specialization such instructors emphasize the importance of science and of specialization. In so far as the educational process is effective it propagates these characteristics of modern culture in each generation.

Social Transformation. Much of the rapid social change of recent times is traceable directly to applied science, and Western societies have become so accustomed to change that they regard it as normal. A great deal of what passes for a belief in progress is, in reality, only a vague recognition of this process of change. Since the concept of progress presupposes change for the better, modern education has come to be oriented, in part, toward bringing about changes believed to be desirable. Frequently this takes the form of attempts to guide changes already in progress in directions believed to be socially beneficial.

Atomic Energy Discoveries. An example is to be found in developments in the field of atomic energy attending the conduct of World War II. Stimulated by the necessity of defeating our enemies, earlier experiments were oriented toward destructive use. The original purpose having been accomplished, we are now engaged in attempts to develop socially desirable applications of the newly acquired knowledge. The history of the modern airplane is somewhat similar. Its scientific development was largely for military purposes and was adapted to civilian uses later. Schools of aerodynamics are now numerous and tend to be devoted to research and training in peacetime uses. Similar statements could be made concerning radar and television. Thus we have used recently acquired scientific knowledge in the destruction of totalitarian institutions in war, and now use it in the growth and readaptation of our own.

Education and Usefulness. The aims of science being largely utilitarian, the rise of science has been accompanied by a strong trend toward the "practical" in education. In fact, this is the concomitant of specialization and professionalization. In some part, it is a result of compulsory education. Since not everyone is capable of mastering the more abstract forms of learning, occupational education of a wide range is offered. But the nature of science directs men's minds to the material aspects of life and of the universe, and could not fail to manifest itself in a corresponding attitude toward educational procedure and concepts. Here we have something of the same conflict between scientific and traditional points of view that have already been indicated in our discussion of religious institutions.

The rise of the laboratory method of instruction is traceable directly to the development of science. This method is most readily available in the physical sciences, and it is here that its greatest development has taken place. The efficacy of the laboratory method, on the other hand, has had much to do with the rapid advancement of scientific learning. It has also predisposed scholars toward the point of view that truth is to be learned only by reference to evidence of the senses. The older fields of knowledge, not being amenable to laboratory methods of investigation, have suffered a relative decline, and the value of some of the more traditional fields has been seriously questioned. This unfavorable comparison has extended to the field of social science, so-called. Economists, sociologists and political scientists are constantly reminded both by each other and by the public that their findings lack the confirmation of experimental procedure under laboratory conditions. This lack of strictly scientific basis is probably the most serious handicap upon those persons and institutions attempting to exercise control through education in the social sciences.

The decline of the classics is another educational phenomenon traceable in part to the same causes. The materials of the classics not only do not lend themselves to scientific demonstration, they are often refuted by it.[9] Utilitarian things may be subjected to scientific demonstrations of their efficiency, or lack of it, but this is not possible in drama, music or religion. There are no scientific standards of excellence in these things. Science, from its nature, is specific and deals with material phenomena. It regards traditional explanations of these phenomena with suspicion or worse, and subjects all to the test of experimentation. Classical learning is largely traditional. To be sure, it is the product of human experience over long periods of time, but experience under uncontrolled conditions and subject to the most fanciful interpretations. There is no disposition here to belittle the value of classical learning. But the effect of classical learning is to encourage the play of fancy, to develop a philosophical attitude toward life, to uphold tradition and traditional behavior. These are precisely the things with which science does not deal and with which it is not in sympathy.[10]

Governmental Institutions

The modern interpretation of the functions of governmental institutions inclines to the point of view that they are the ultimate agencies of social control. Parallel to this is a recognition that all institutions participate in the processes of control. This makes it essential, if complete unity is to be attained, that government shall exercise control over other institutions. Complete unity, in fact, is never attained; but unification proceeds—at least geographically—in modern times.[11]

Elsewhere in this chapter it has been emphasized that science fosters specialization which, in turn, requires a high degree of integration. Government becomes progressively the principal integrating authority in modern society. This trend is an accompaniment of the loss or relinquishment of control by other institutions. Governmental conduct of the processes of education is a case in point. Another is the assumption on a

---

[9] See R. M. MacIver, *Society; A Textbook of Sociology*, (New York: Farrar and Rinehart, 1937), chapter XIV.

[10] A challenging discussion of the materials and methods of modern education is to be found in R. S. Lynd, *Knowledge for What* (Princeton: Princeton University Press, 1939).

[11] The classical, and perhaps the most extreme, presentation of the concept of government as the ultimate source of control is Hobbes, *Leviathan*. See any edition.

wide scale of care of dependents, child welfare, etc., functions formerly discharged by the family or by the church.

The Use of Science by Government. Specific instances of the direct application of science for governmental purposes are very numerous. Among them are: finger printing, identification by blood tests, and the manufacture of currency. Sanitation, quarantine, weather prediction, and intelligence testing are examples in different categories. The list is endless. It is interesting to note that democratic governments employ and foster true science in the interests of social welfare. This should not be regarded as an anomalous situation merely because social welfare is not essentially scientific. Modern man utilizes science to attain his ends of whatever sort. To most of us, science is not an end in itself. Extreme proponents of eugenics point to many instances in which science could be applied for ultimate social welfare, but the mores do not permit such application. Sterilization of the congenitally feebleminded is an example. These instances do not indicate a conflict between science and social welfare as has sometimes been said. Instead they show a lack of harmony between the traditional concepts of individual humanitarianism and that of group welfare.[12]

Noninstitutional Effects of Science

Throughout this chapter it is to be noted that many of the effects of scientific development upon social control are indirect. So far as social control is exercised by institutions, particularly by government, it is likely to be somewhat formal in nature. But informal processes of control are everywhere important to a high degree. Indeed, they frequently are more effective than the formal, as is shown by public opinion. Scientific progress, being mainly of a material sort, is so obvious as to receive the approval of most members of modern Western society. Therefore a liberal public opinion is likely to exist and social control by this means is modified accordingly. Much the same could be said regarding informal processes of education. Concepts, either traditional or liberal, are transmitted within the family and in various social contacts by informal and indirect means, and the nature of these concepts affects social control directly as well as through the medium of institutions.

Summary

Social control is directly and indirectly affected by the discoveries of science, as science, in turn affects the viewpoints, objectives, and tech-

---

[12] Attempts at scientific approaches to social problems are being made. One of the best is found in E. M. H. Baylor and E. D. Monachesi, *The Rehabilitation of Children,* (New York: Harper and Brothers, 1939).

niques of all institutions. The latter is especially notable in connection with religious institutions, which are mainly concerned with matters not amenable to scientific treatment. At first the church resisted advances in science as invasions of its own realm, but in later periods it accommodated inevitable advances in knowledge by accepting them. The change was not immediate nor complete, however, and in the practice of religion among advanced peoples many vestiges of older pre-scientific beliefs remain, even in the face of valid scientific explanations of phenomena.

Since economic institutions are concerned, in the main, with material things, science has brought widespread changes in this field with little resistance. Large-scale organization, greatly increased wealth, and concentration of economic power are among the most obvious.

In education, government, and familial institutions, in varying degrees and ways, the impact of scientific advance has been felt, as it has in less institutionalized channels of social control as, for instance, the realm of public opinion.

QUESTIONS

1. What is the effect on society of any new culture?
2. What determines the relative importance of an institution?
3. How is the acceptance of scientific knowledge modified?
4. What two facts are partly responsible for the variations in scientific knowledge?
5. In what fields have the Western scientists outstripped the Oriental scientists?
6. How does religion affect the progress of scientific development?
7. How has scientific progress affected man's dependence upon sensory knowledge?
8. How does the growth of scientific knowledge affect material institutions?
9. What is the real nature of the conflict between religion and science?
10. What are the three stages of knowledge as stated by Comte?
11. What is the usual accompaniment to a shift in control from one institution to another?
12. What element is common among all religions?
13. How is variation of this element related to scientific knowledge?
14. How does the religious explanation of the nature of man and the universe differ from that of the scientist?
15. With the decrease in control by the church on theological lines, what has happened to its field of interests?
16. What has the advancement of scientific knowledge meant to family organization?
17. When does specialization of knowledge occur?
18. What is the result of specialization of knowledge with regard to accumulation?
19. What effect has science had on the procedural and conceptual aspects of education?
20. In the society of high integration and specialization, what function is attributed to the government?

SUGGESTED TOPICS FOR TERM PAPERS AND FURTHER RESEARCH

1. The family as a means of social control.
2. The ruling class, what is it?
3. Make a study of the trend toward centralization of governmental power in the United States.
4. The exertion of social control by social welfare agencies.
5. Classical education versus specialization.
6. The Oriental acceptance of scientific knowledge as compared with that of the Western world.
7. Compare the methods of religion with those of science.
8. Discuss Comte's theory of the three stages of knowledge.
9. The effects of scientific advancement on the family.
10. Specialization in education and its social results.

BIBLIOGRAPHY

Books

J. D. Bernal, *The Social Function of Science* (London: Routledge, 1939). A scholarly survey of the functional aspects of science.

John Burchard, ed., *Mid-Century: The Social Implication of Scientific Progress* (New York: John Wiley and Sons, 1950). Surveys the current aspects of scientific developments.

H. Cantril, *Gauging Public Opinion* (Princeton, N.J.: Princeton University Press, 1944). How scientific measurements can be applied to the gauging of public opinion.

Stuart Chase, *The Proper Study of Mankind* (New York: Harper and Brothers, 1948). A popular summary of the "Science of Human Relations."

J. B. Conant, *Modern Science and Modern Man* (New York: Columbia University Press, 1952). A study of modern scientific achievement and its effects on modern man and his society.

D. Dietz, *Atomic Energy in the Coming Era* (New York: Dodd, Mead and Co., 1945). Social changes to be expected from developments in atomic energy.

Peter F. Drucker, *The New Society* (New York: Harper and Brothers, 1950). Problems and progress of society in the machine age.

Lawrence K. Frank, *Society as the Patient* (New Brunswick, N.J.: Rutgers University Press, 1948). The problems of society as well as of the individual personality can be treated only in relation to the contextual whole.

F. A. von Hayck, *Counter Revolution of Science* (London: W. H. Allen, 1952). The modern trend of scientific thinking.

J. Irving, *Science and Values* (New York: McGraw-Hill Book Co., 1952). The relation of science to society.

George Lundberg, *Can Science Save Us?* (New York: Longmans, Green and Co., 1947). A well-known essay pointing out the prospects and difficulties in using social science to help mankind to settle its most pressing problems.

R. S. Lynd, *Knowledge for What?* (Princeton, N.J.: Princeton University Press, 1939). A well-known essay on the relation between value-judgment and empiric knowledge.

Robert K. Merton, *Social Theory and Social Structure* (Glencoe, Ill.: Free Press, 1949). An effort to codify theory and research.

Talcott Parsons, *The Structure of Social Action* (New York: McGraw-Hill Book Co., 1937). The functional point of view of a well-known sociologist, also presented in the following work, as well as in other of his published papers.

―――― *Essays in Sociological Theory, Pure and Applied* (Glencoe, Ill.: Free Press, 1949).

L. Poole, *Today's Science and You* (New York: McGraw-Hill Book Co., 1952). A reliable study of modern scientific advances and its effect on the individual.

Bertrand Russell, *Dictionary of Modern Mind, Matter and Morals* (New York: Philosophical Library, 1952).

―――― *Impact of Science on Society* (New York: Columbia University Press, 1951). These and numerous works by this well-known British thinker are most provocative in their implications of the relation of science to society.

E. J. Saunders and E. R. Franklin, *Science and Ourselves* (London: John Murray, 1952).

Pitirim A. Sorokin, *Social and Cultural Dynamics* (New York: The American Book Co., 1937). A monumental survey, in three volumes, of the various developments in society in relation to science.

E. White, *Science and Religion in American Thought* (Stanford, Calif.: Stanford University Press, 1952). A study of the interaction of these two factors of society on each other and on American society.

Willard Waller, ed., *War in the Twentieth Century* (New York: The Dryden Press, 1940). Although the analysis is already outmoded by the developments of the consequences of World War II, the book is still important, as it deals with the sociology of war, a topic largely neglected by the American sociologists.

Periodicals

Read Bain, "Sociology as a Natural Science," *American Journal of Sociology*, LIII (July, 1947), pp. 9-16.

Rudolf Bierstedt, "Social Science and Social Values," *Bulletin of The American Association of University Professors*, XXXIV (Summer, 1948), pp. 312-319.

M. W. Bissell, "Has Science Failed Us?" *Saturday Review of Literature*, XXXIV (May 5, 1951), p. 22.

Herbert A. Bloch, "A Synthetic View of the Social Individual as a Primary Datum in Sociology," *American Sociological Review*, VIII (October, 1943), pp. 506-516.

Claud C. Bowman, "Evaluations and Values Consistent with the Scientific Study of Society," *American Sociological Review*, VIII (June, 1943), pp. 306-312.

L. Coch and J. R. P. French, "Overcoming Resistance to Change," *Human Relations*, I, pp. 512-532.

J. G. Jenkins, "Nominating Technique as a Method of Evaluating Air Group Morale," *Journal of Aviation Medicine*, XIX (1948), pp. 12-19.

D. Katz, "Polling Methods and the 1948 Polling Failure," *International Journal of Opinion and Attitude Research*, II (1949), pp. 469-480.

Martin H. Neumeyer, "Progress as Societal Self-Direction," *The Personalist*, XXVI (Winter, 1945), pp. 33-46; see other articles in the same issue devoted to the idea of progress.

Pauline Nicols Pepinsky, "The Meaning of 'Validity' and 'Reliability' As Applied to Sociometric Tests," *Educational and Psychological Measurement*, IX (1949), pp. 39-49.

Talcott Parsons, "Propaganda and Social Control," *Psychiatry*, V (November, 1942), pp. 551-572.

Leslie D. Zeleny, "Sociometry of Morale," *American Sociological Review*, IV (December, 1939), pp. 799-808.

PART III

Means and Techniques of Social Control

FOREWORD

The specific means and techniques of social control within the framework of the institutional structure are comparable to the thousand and one hidden conduits, pipe lines, shafts, pulleys, and cables which make possible the complicated life within the more readily visible walls, floors, and ceilings of a large apartment building. They are hidden, not in that they cannot, in part at least, be examined by the observant, but in that their complete functioning to sustain stability and renew flexibility in human relations is far from obvious. Here the engineer must come in with his carefully plotted blueprints to show the concealed details of operation.

Social control is usually such that its effectiveness is in direct ratio to the lack of awareness on the part of the controlled that they are being controlled. This brings the real difficulties of its study to the fore, and makes necessary the work of many experts to reveal all its devious ramifications.

In Part III an idea of the range of devices and methods is reflected in the chapters on Ideologies, Conceptual Means of Social Control, Language and Semantics, Art and Literature, Recreation, Leadership, Secret Societies, Nonviolent Means, The Sociology of Violence, Economic Control, and Economic and Social Planning.

Chapter XII

Ideologies

Much is being said these days—and properly so—concerning the war of ideologies.[1] It is true that the history of mankind is also the history of the wars of ideologies, exemplified, for instance, by the bloody struggle between Catholicism and Protestantism in the sixteenth century. But the present conflict differs from any in the past. Our modern era has produced a class of intellectuals well trained in the use of ideologies for social control purposes and capable of carrying on the warfare of ideas on a level never matched before. Furthermore, the amazing advances in science and technology of the past hundred years have challenged innumerable traditions, upset many fixed beliefs, and introduced a unique totalitarian character into the intellectual struggle so that today there is not a single system of thought which is not influenced by the present conflict of ideologies.[2]

Hence the knowledge of the utilization of ideologies as a means of social control, whether deliberate or not, becomes of utmost importance for the student of society. For ideologies are not only potent political creeds which set the armies of the world marching again in World War II; they are also the hidden forces which penetrate all aspects of social life and form a spiritual basis for the existence of every social struggle.[3] As powerful dynamic forces of contemporary social life, they give seemingly logical meaning to our politics and social efforts. They satisfy a need of all men to believe in a system of thought that is rigorous and reassuring. They are the most potent social forces, since men will die for their ideal of things as "they ought to be" rather than tarnish that ideal by practical compromise with things as they are. Ideologies, then, are quite essential to human lives, expressing the vital interests of social groups and satisfying their longing for a scheme of social betterment.

Yet the problem of ideologies as the supreme influence of purposive thinking in social life has been largely ignored by social scientists in

[1] Care should be taken to distinguish between ideologies and conceptual means of social control which will be treated in the following chapter.

[2] G. S. Pettee, "The Rise of New Ideologies and State Forms," in J. S. Roucek, ed., *Contemporary Europe* (New York: D. Van Nostrand Co., 1947).

[3] Joseph S. Roucek, "Political Behavior as a Struggle for Power," *Journal of Social Philosophy*, VI (July, 1941), pp. 341-351.

America. This is evidenced by the fact that we find no special article dealing with "ideology" in the *Encyclopaedia of the Social Sciences,* completed in 1935 under the most scholarly auspices. Most of the systematic work in this field has been done by European thinkers.[4] It has been only in recent years that the whole field of "irrational" behaviors as related to "ideologies" has received considerable and rather sudden attention from the American social scientists, particularly since the translation of the works of Karl Mannheim, Pareto, and Mosca.

The Role of Ideas

Ideologies are systems of evaluation that seek to explain our experiences in understandable and rational terms. As systems of evaluation they seek to stimulate and thus to precede action. They are indispensable to man in facing the reality around him; they provide him with a set of comprehensible values. As such, ideologies become motivators of social action by making life meaningful; for human beings, usually without being aware of it, are largely ruled by emotion, play-acting, and institutional mythology.

Doctrine and Behavior Relationships. It is commonly assumed that there is a direct relationship between doctrine and behavior—that those who talk as democrats are Democrats and those who denounce democracy are anti-Democrats. That this is an unwarranted assumption may be seen when we notice that men continue reciting the verbiage of doctrine long after their loyalties and behavior have taken new forms. The fact is that we all too frequently identify ideas by the noise they make in the world, rather than by their practical effects. Ideas have a real function in society, but the ways in which they work are conditioned by certain factors inherent in the ideological operation.

Relativity of Influence of Ideals. It should be noted that the influence of an ideal in social life is not dependent upon either its logic or its rationality, nor necessarily upon the value given to it by a majority of the society. There are ideals and ideologies which an influential section of society condemns as "bad," "immoral," or "injurious"; nevertheless, they influence social life. As an example we may cite the economic ideal of tariff protection or the ideology of chauvinistic nationalism and imperialism, universally condemned for two decades after World War I, and yet quite effective in their influence on the practical course of world affairs. On

---

[4] Jan Mertl, Karl Mannheim, H. O. Ziegler, G. Salomon, F. Meinecke, A. Dietrich, P. Barth, Sorel, Durkheim, Max Weber, Vilfredo Pareto, and Gaetano Mosca; for many of the recent specialists in this field, see: Robert K. Merton, "Karl Mannheim and the Sociology of Knowledge," *Journal of Liberal Religion,* II (Winter, 1941), No. 3.

the other hand, there exist a number of ideals formulated by the greatest thinkers of their times, recognized by a large part of society for their great value, and yet entirely ineffective and uninfluential in their results. We refer here directly to the ideals of "universal brotherhood," "tolerance," and the like.

True and False Ideologies. It is extremely difficult to deal objectively with the problem of ideologies as such. Ideologies may be—and this sounds paradoxical—either true or false. Some ideologies may be true, just as some propaganda may be true. Again, what is often regarded as "science" by one school may be called "ideology" by another.

Definitions

The term ideology has numerous definitions. It may be defined as a system of ideas or a confession of faith characterizing the way a particular group of persons views life, in terms of aspirations, morality, law, and philosophy. By some writers an ideology has been defined as a system of ideas which contemporaneously dominates a social behavior, as opposed to the ideas of other groups. For our discussion, ideology "is a theory of social life which approaches social realities and interprets them consciously or unconsciously from the point of view of ideals to prove the correctness of the analysis and to justify these ideals. . . . [It] is the projection of a certain ideal both into the future and into the past." [5]

The ideology of a class, caste, or other social group performs the same role in the functioning of a collective unit that the individual's conception of himself performs in the function of his personality. "As the individual's conception of himself projects his acts into the future and in that fashion serves to control and direct the course of his career, so in the case of a society its ideology may be said to direct, control, and give consistency, in the vicissitudes of a changing world, to its collective acts." [6]

Ideology, myth, and doctrine are terms which may be applied to the same thing with different though overlapping connotations. Those who hold to ideologies seldom question whether they are rationally coherent or incoherent, true or false, practical or impractical.

Myth. In contrast, "myth" is a functional term. The myth of a people may be partly expressed and partly implied in expression or action. It is a major determinant of human action, guiding the flow of energy of a

---

[5] Joseph S. Roucek, *op. cit.;* and J. S. Roucek and Charles Hodges, "Ideology as an Implement of Purposive Thinking in the Social Sciences," *Social Science,* XI (January, 1936), pp. 25-34.

[6] Robert E. Park, "Symbiosis and Socialization: A Frame of Reference for the Study of Society," *American Journal of Sociology,* XLV (July, 1939), p. 9.

people into the peaceful arts or the paths of conquest as the case may be. It is one of the major factors which shape and condition the institutions of a given society.

Doctrine. Doctrine is a somewhat more concrete term than myth. Where the myth includes the ethical and metaphysical source ideas, a doctrine is the aggregate of conscious and expressible rules of action based upon the myth. Confusion is apt to arise from the fact that any given body of ideas may include and merge an ideology, a myth, and a doctrine. It must be noted that conflicting doctrines, such as those of Democracy and Communism today, may rest upon largely identical myths in so far as they share such ideas as equality, and yet be wholly distinct as doctrines. Similarly, Communism and Fascism, although entirely antagonistic in expression, may lead to many common forms of action, such as the regimentation of thought.

Component Parts of Successful Ideologies

If an ideal is to become effective in social control, it must be presented to the masses in a convincing way. The success of any ideology depends on many factors—its completeness and internal coherence, its gorgeous vision of the future, its ability to hold men's imaginations, its pretense to provide a universal frame of reference of good and evil, its consistency, its convincing criticism of the present and picture of the future, and its ability to circumvent counter-criticisms. We shall turn now to the most important elements which make successful ideologies effective as directives and means of social control.[7]

The Answer to the Search for Rationality

Need for Comprehension. Man's task is to deal with the world, act in it, fight in it. That is why man is practically unable, for psychological reasons, to do without an all-round knowledge of the world, without an integral and integrated idea of the universe. Crude or refined, with our consent or without it, an ideological picture of the world settles in the mind of each of us, more effectively than scientific truth ever can, this terrific problem of "comprehending." Man, before doing anything, must decide for himself what he is going to do, a decision which is impossible unless he possesses certain convictions concerning the nature of things around him, the nature of other men and of himself. Only in the light of such convictions can man live. It follows that man must ever be

---

[7] For an analysis of the psychology of ideologies, see H. Lundholm, *The Psychology of Belief* (Durham: Duke University Press, 1936).

grounded in some ideology, and that the structure of his life will depend primarily on the beliefs on which it is established.

Simplicity of Rationality. Ideologies succeed by the impression of rationality and simplicity they are able to create, by being able to convince the follower that they tell the only and absolute "truth." They are ready-made "revelations," convincing the believers that *theirs* is the perfect system of right and wrong. By their very simplicity they attract the minds so anxious for simplicity and so abhorrent of the complexity and relativity of the scientific attitude. Social theories which are complex and which cannot be interpreted in simple terms cannot become the ideological foundations of mass movements. The "average mind" needs to have the causes and solutions simplified. "We derive a deep satisfaction from any doctrine which reduces irrational multiplicity to rational and comprehensive unity." [8] Nothing is more attractive to man's mind, burdened daily with a complexity of unexplainable problems attacking from all sides, than a sudden "revelation," the ability to "see the light," an extreme simplification which appears rational, logical, and which makes it easy to "understand" very complex phenomena. If this is lacking, man is subject to worries, fear, anxieties, and frustrations, and is susceptible to new leadership, conversion, or revolution.

Immutable Roots

Ideologies, while approaches to reality, are not so much intended to describe phenomena as to provide a "justification" of social aspirations, wishes, and desires. They aim to propound a series of "ought to be" social, political, and moral propositions and "justify" them with a variety of organic doctrines—Original Sin, Divine Law, Dialectic Materialism, Monarchism, Absolutism, Socialism, Communism, Individualism, Liberalism, Fascism, Nazism, and so on.[9] In other words, ideology is an entity which must have the appearance of rationality and be firmly grounded on fundamental principles. The human mind seems to need the certitude of acting "on principle," and therefore persistently generates the large, hazy, and often contradictory notions which make up ideologies.

Borders of Arguments. Ideologies automatically become the limits beyond which debate may not go. Arguments are permitted only within the framework of the ideology, and any attack on the ideology itself

---

[8] Aldous Huxley, *Ends and Means: An Inquiry into the Nature of Ideals and into Methods Employed for their Realization* (New York: Harper and Brothers, 1937), p. 13.

[9] For a survey of various theories of solidarity, cf. P. Sorokin, *Contemporary Sociological Theories* (New York: Harper and Brothers, 1928), pp. 210-211.

becomes a punishable heresy, since the faithful ones will tolerate no skepticism or criticism of the fundamentals.

The Use of Myths

All social movements require that men behave regularly and uniformly. Such behavior can be obtained only through the common direction of the wills of a multitude of individuals by the common directives of ideas—myths. Myths are the imaginative explanations of natural and human phenomena in the absence of more scientific data. Many of the myths about great leaders are expressions of man's playfulness of mind and his love of narrative, told in an attempt to entertain himself and those about him, as well as to raise his self-esteem by attributing superhuman, highly ethical and moral qualities to the figures representing his collectivity (race, nation, religion, group, tribe).

Glorification of Social Action. In a highly technical world the "social myth" is indispensable as a springboard for social action. Ideologies give rise to fictions which glorify the leaders [10] and the exploits of a group or some of its members. They enshroud happenings in sentiments and protective pathos, and offer dreams which give the group an escape from the hard facts of reality in the vision of a glorious future. The myths transmit values which are accepted uncritically as natural and right. The notions embodied in them seem to be axiomatic in their obvious truth, and give a concrete expression to the desire for a better order, offering both the criticism of the old and the picture of the new in ideological form.

Expressions of Vital Interests

Effective ideologies appeal to wide masses by expressing the vital interests of social groups, the grievances they profoundly feel, the ambitions which are most burning at the moment and for which many are ready to make the necessary sacrifices. Ideologies help bring emotional undercurrents to the surface and give expression to the wishful thinking of the masses, motivating mankind by providing successive ideals as social goals for humanity. They accomplish the submergence of differences by securing joint action for a common interest. The Democrat, the Republican, the Jesuit, the Nazi, each has vested interests in the points of view of his ideology. Out of the needs of groups there arise ethical demands which constitute part of the politico-economic ideology of those groups and of all other people upon whom they can impose their beliefs. This resulting

---

[10] Cf. Charles H. Cooley, *Social Process* (New York: Charles Scribner's Sons, 1918), chapter 11.

ideology is the base from which the sovereign powers, including law as the principal symbol of political force and power, are derived.[11] The broader the base and the more common the interests whose needs are expressed in the ideology, the less will be the friction, and correspondingly, the fewer will be the demands, the struggles, and the readjustments within the ideology. The ambitions, grievances, and vested interests expressed in an ideology must be common to many individuals, living preferably over wide areas, so that the ideology becomes a spiritual tie uniting a large number of people by their strong emotional reactions of unity and opposition to others. The more vital and vested the interests of the member sustained or enhanced in his ideology, the greater effectiveness it holds for him. The resulting ideological unity inspires self-sacrifice in a common interest, submerges personal conflicts, and thereby releases new energies for group loyalties to party, to nation, and to racial stock.

The Claim to Scientific Objectivity and Realism

Convictions of Liberating "Truth." If an ideology is to be influential in providing an impetus to social movements, it is necessary to have it presented as a scientific truth. Communism, for example, claims to be a social system built upon a "scientific" analysis of the social structure which permits its proponents to predict the future. Note, however, that it is precisely because Marxism has been an ideology and doctrine rather than a genuine science that it has exerted such a great power over the minds of a multitude of men.

Once the claim of an ideology to scientific validity is accepted by its followers, the ideology becomes a tremendously effective social force. A man will submit cheerfully to the rulers and the representatives of authority, have his head chopped off, wallow through the mud, and die of wounds in wars, as long as the "cause" is based on a doctrine claiming to be "the Truth." This "Truth" is always considered mightier and more truthful than all the previous truths, although history teaches that there is no absolute norm for what we call "the good" and "the bad," "the right" and "the wrong." These terms, rather, depend for their content upon the time, the place, and the social history of the groups using them.

The Granting of Elite Status

Angels and Devils. Since the ideologist "knows" the coming state of affairs, his doctrine divides mankind, in general, into two groups: (1) those who "know" the way to open the door to the "better world," and

---

[11] James Marshall, *Swords and Symbols* (New York: Oxford University Press, 1939), p. 143.

who are, therefore, willing to make the necessary sacrifices to bring about its realization; and (2) those who, in spite of all the chances to join the movement which is ready and eager to transform this "vale of tears" into the promised paradise, only retard the process by their obstinate obstructionism and opposition.

The world is thus divided into the "vanguards of progress," "the elite," "the believers," the "superior Aryan race," plagued by "the unbelievers," "the pagans," "the devils," "the democrats," "the capitalists," "the Jews," and the like. Those who follow the "true" ideology become the "moral" kind, the "superior" kind, because they represent the doctrine which is "moral" and "superior." Thus in Marxian ideology the proletariat is the only class which can create a "just" economic society. In Hitler's ideology the superior rank was granted to the pure Aryan, and the "devil" was symbolized in the Jew and the non-Aryan. The Jew in the Nazi revolution, in fact, played the same role as the bourgeoisie in the Russian revolution. Such classifications, however, are but variations of the old, old story of the struggle between the good and the evil, between the angels and the devil, between the forces of light and of darkness.

Since there is no room for disillusionment in an effective social platform, the creed is sweetened for the followers by what the realist is apt to call "hokum." Human frailties are assigned only to the opponents, the scapegoats. Everyone knows, Hitler kept telling us, that all Jews are parasites and that the plutocratic democracies are decadent. Even the well-known loyalty of Jew to Jew was a myth to Hitler. Such a sense of cohesion as the Jews possess, he held, is merely a primitive herd-instinct; they hold together only when threatened by a common danger or lured by a common spoil. When these ties are removed, they display selfishness, and in the twinkling of an eye become a pack of savage rats tearing each other to pieces.

Useful short cuts in the work for those who deliberately manipulate ideologies are their abilities to express an ideology in symbols and personalities. People seem to get more excited when they are reacting to symbols and personalities than when responding to abstract ideas. It is much easier for the Communist to despise the capitalist than the whole complex framework of capitalism, and the proponent of Democracy hated Hitler more than he hated the ramifications of the Nazi ideology. Specific objects or persons are much easier to conceptualize, to focus attention upon, than are more general and complex causes. They furnish a definite objective toward which verbal action can be directed. Christianity thus has its "devil," England of World Wars its "Hun" and "Jerry," and Nazi Germany its "plutocrat."

Pretensions to Universal Values

The problem of motivation is one of the most difficult questions confronting the psychologist.[12] It becomes, however, quite simplified for the ideologist, who not only "explains" that which drives men to join movements, but informs them in a true ideological way of their "needs." The ideology then becomes a tie which binds personal ambitions into group values so that the selfish character of individual and group demands gets lost, ideologically, in devotion to the cause which seems to rise above the group interest by pretending its loyalty to a universal value. Thus it is that each politician claims his ambition to secure office stems from his desire to serve his country, his people, and his God, and each party pretends that its motives are not to acquire power but only to "serve" or "save" the country.

Every ideology pretends that its primary loyalty is to a universal value, thus sanctifying its partial and particular interests. Because the ideological pretension to universality is necessary for successful social control by any aggressive group, its limited and selfish interests tend to become identified with as large a number of others as possible and its demands become integrated with the universal standards. The proponents of an aggressive ideology to be effective must be convinced that the values and meanings of their social group really represent absolute meaning and that their ideology is related to a larger source of meaning.

Operation Within the Framework of Conditioning

Human beings, as the result of the learning process, are "conditioned," i.e., habituated, to a definite sequence of facts as encountered in their environment. Within their cultural framework they learn to make the proper responses to sounds, objects, people, and other stimuli. Clever promoters of an ideology know this and seek acceptance of their doctrine by appealing to the established patterns, traditions, and sentiments. It is a device of "transfer" which the ideologist utilizes to carry over the authority, sanction, and prestige of something we are accustomed to respect and revere to something he would have us accept. The prestige of the authority of God was used to sanction the Nazi foreign policy. In America, both the Communists and the Nazis swore their allegiance to the American flag and professed their loyalty to the "true principles of Americanism." Both Hitler and Stalin, likewise, fought for the "true democracy."

---

[12] Hadley Cantril, *The Psychology of Social Movements* (New York: John Wiley and Sons, 1941), p. 30.

Extremes of Ethnocentricism

The Garrison State. A favorable and almost indispensable condition for the continued success of an ideology is the suppression of counter-ideologies which might attract the sentiments of the population. The necessity for this was demonstrated to the world in Nazi Germany and Fascist Italy by such acts as the dismissal and exile of all "politically unreliable" teachers and the muzzling of those who remained, the censorship of culture, the exclusion of everything "foreign" or "alien" or in any way divergent from the official culture as defined by the Propaganda Ministry. No ideology can tolerate a wavering of faith, and all must reject competing values. You either "believe" or are damned. "Either you are one of us, or you are against us," was Hitler's dictum. Or, as Mussolini stated, "We or they!"

Harmful Results. Unfortunately, when ideological ends are proclaimed to be absolutely good in themselves, when an ideologist proclaims that there is no meaning or value except in the ideological construction arbitrarily selected by him, grotesque and monstrous results follow. Remember the experiences of Galileo and the insane persecutions of the enemies of Communism, Fascism, and Nazism by maniacs claiming for themselves knowledge of the only "Truth." Theirs is the end so absolutely good in itself, so admirable, that those who pursue it need not bother about anything else. Communist, Fascist, Nazi, and all nationalist ideologies are alike in their affirmation that the end justifies the means, and that end is their triumph over the rest of the world. This, in their opinion, justifies the unlimited use of violence, terror, and cunning.

Glow Words

An ideology expresses its ideal in terms of "glow words"—terms that carry a strong and prevalent emotional tone, as for example: "nationalism," "socialism," "racial superiority," "liberty," "justice," "equality," "democratic methods," "dictatorship," and "fatherland." Since the chapter on semantics deals more fully with this problem, we need not go into it here. We should note, however, that endless confusion is promoted by labelling collections of things with words—"mankind," "Germany," "individualism," "Truth." While individual men or individual Germans certainly do exist, "mankind" and "Germany," in this sense, do not, except as fictions. Yet the ideologists are forever using such abstractions to prove certain points, failing to see that because no referents can be found for them, no two of them can possibly refer to the same thing. The *Tyranny of Words* is the result, and we soon reach the state where, as Humpty Dumpty said: "When *I* use a word, it means just what I choose it to mean—neither more nor less."

Sectarian and Factional Squabbles

Conservatives and Progressives. All ideologies, in spite of their claims to "simple " explanations of social reality, eventually become quite involved in their interpretations of fundamental principles. The real difficulty comes particularly when the ideas propounded by an ideology do not fit in with actual conditions (such as Marx's claim that the revolution would start in the most industrialized country in the world, whereas it actually started in Russia, then one of the least industrialized countries). All ideologies, sooner or later, degenerate into verbal or even physical struggles between the orthodox proponents of the ideology and the "liberals" or "progressives." The same ideological reasoning is bound to have different meanings to different converts, and internal misunderstandings and disputes grow up in the movement in spite of agreement on the "fundamentals" of the ideology. Hence every movement has its proponents of the Right and of the Left, those who insist on the literal interpretations of the ideology, and those who are trying to re-interpret the meaning of the ideology so as to fit in with the changing conditions of the ever-advancing reality. In short, all ideological movements become cursed with sectarian misunderstandings and disputes over the interpretations of the ideological principles, and with antagonistic factional movements which claim to adhere to the same theoretical teaching, but which quarrel about its interpretation. These ideological struggles rarely culminate in a positive result because the struggle is not for an objective explanation of the realities, but only an argumentation of subjective interpretations.

Interpreters of the Meaning of Meaning

Such disputes are promoted as a rule by two or more meanings of the ideologies themselves. To decide a struggle between the orthodox Marxists and the "revisionists" is impossible because the source of both is laid in the teachings of Marx and the arguments are woven about subjective interpretations of Marx's original doctrine. In the history of economic theory the teachings of Adam Smith provided the foundation not only for liberalism, but for the socialist theories of values as well.

Apostles. Every creed needs apostles who intensify, exalt, develop, refine, and work out the ideology so that it becomes a real political, religious, or philosophical system. The task of attempting to solve the interpretations of ideologies is given to a great personality or a body of learned men as the final authority. While Lenin lived, his writings or pronouncements gave the necessary authoritative re-interpretations of "unchangeable" and "scientific" Socialism; his function has been assumed by Stalin. The Pope performs the same service for the Catholic church. In the American political system the task is discharged by the Supreme Court. The masses leave this mediation to such specialists, who maintain and revitalize the doctrine, provide its re-interpretation, sometimes alter it, and at other times improve on it.

Perversions of Meanings. It is through this process of interpretation, of providing new meanings to old phrases, that the original ideology some- times becomes perverted. For instance, as a theoretical Marxist, Lenin treated the materialistic dialectic with due reverence, but as a practical revolutionist, according to Eastman,[13] he turned his back on it and ap- plied a science of revolution without benefit of Marxism. Like the prac- tical ideologist he was, Lenin professed the regular creed on the Marxist equivalent of the Sabbath and followed a secular practice during the rest of the week. As revolutionist, states Eastman, Lenin offered "as brilliant a political leadership as the world has seen"; [14] as dialectician, he was no better than other faithful Marxists.

Ideology versus Science

Although we like to think that we live in a "scientific age," the fact remains that the scientific habit of thought has not penetrated very deeply into our social thinking.[15] Ideological elements still force themselves into the whole field of natural and social sciences, particularly the latter. Even the social scientist who prides himself on being purely empirical is unable to cut himself away from ideological influences which take the form of philosophical and metaphysical postulates.

Without attempting to deal with the problem of social methodology, we may indicate here the fundamental difference in the methods and aims of the ideologist and the scientist.[16]

Scientific Method. The general method of science is to collect as much data as possible, then study the facts to see if they present uniformities—

---

[13] Max Eastman, *Marxism: Is it Science?* (New York: W. W. Norton, 1940).
[14] *Ibid.*
[15] G. A. Lundberg, *Social Research* (New York: Longmans, Green & Co., 2nd ed., 1941), p. 1.
[16] It is assumed, however, that social or other science cannot live in a kind of philosophical vacuum, completely ignoring all philosophical problems; scientific and philosophic problems are closely interdependent, although they are at the same time independent and can be treated in relative abstraction from each other. Cf. Talcott Parsons, *The Structure of Social Action* (New York: McGraw-Hill Book Co., 1937), pp. 20 ff.

scientific laws. A scientific law, the statement of uniformities found in the facts, means that the uniformity it expresses has been manifested up until the present. Tomorrow these new laws may have to be amended to square with newly discovered facts. The essence of scientific approach is not in the content of its specific conclusions so much as in the method whereby its conclusions are made and constantly corrected. The true scientist regards his best theories as hypotheses. He is constantly on the alert to analyze his own mental processes and to eliminate his own emotions from coloring his theories.

The Approach of the Ideologist. Pure science is always secular and horizontal in its reference, and cannot express the vertical tendencies in culture which refer to the ultimate meaning of life. This need is answered by the ideologist who holds his theories, his ideological principles, sacred and timeless and not to be contaminated by experiments since his creed claims to be a smooth and consistent flow of absolutes. If there are any tests at all of an ideology, they can be limited to those of internal consistency, authority, rationalistic thinking, and historical principles. The ideologist's creed is a set of articles of faith; he habitually confuses his thoughts and effects. That he uses the methods and the phraseology of science cannot conceal his true nature; his is the theological temperament applied to politics. His mythical descriptions of reality, although claiming to be "scientific," are inexact in describing detailed and historic facts, but have the virtue of giving men a sense of the depth in life. The ideologist makes it possible for man to believe in a meaningful existence which has its center and source beyond itself and enables him to preserve moral vitality because the world as it exists is regarded by him as imperfect, even though meaningful.

Trends in the War of Ideologies

Ours is not the first age which has produced new systems of ideas resulting in ideological conflicts. But no age, with the exception of the time of the religious wars of the sixteenth century, has seen such a variety of doctrines; without any exception no age has seen the struggle of ideologies run so deeply and in such complex patterns.

Certain major conditions make the present conflict, everchanging though it is, different from any in the past. Modern psychology and sociology have produced a class of intellectuals conscious of ideologies and of their nature, and able to wage the warfare of ideas with an awareness and on a level never matched before. We have ideologies as others have had them before us, but we alone build them and attack them on something resembling a professional level, which makes of them, more than ever before, instruments of social control.

Totalitarian Influences. One of the sharpest differences between the ideologies and conflicts of today and any previous ones lies in the totalitarian character of the intellectual struggle today. In all past doctrinal discord the conflict has been carried on against a background of agreed tradition. For instance, the French Revolution did change the calendar and weights and measures, but it did not attack the essential character of the sovereign state, or the gold standard, or capital punishment for crime. Today one cannot name a single premise of thought or behavior which is not at issue.[17]

Interpretation of Interpretations. Around the great doctrines which wage war literally, Communism, Fascism, and Democracy, is a morass of opinions more various than ever before in the world. The greater size of libraries, the plethora of books, and the more numerous detailed controversies make possible a greater number of permutations of doctrine than ever before. Also there is an altogether unparalleled use of the weapons of criticism.[18] Not merely the reasoned argument and its conclusions are threatened, but the whole rational character of each doctrine is under attack by its antagonists. Never before have so many intellectuals been talking and writing for whom it was a simple technique to attack not only conclusions but premises, not only political doctrines but their whole metaphysical underpinning. Today there is simply no area of life left without the influence of ideological struggles.

One of the most interesting aspects of the modern trend has been the rapidity with which the ideologies and their interpretations have been changing their meaning. Books written upon the ideologies rapidly become out of date. Notice, for instance, the number of books devoted during recent years to the interpretations and changing meanings of democracy.[19] Those which do not become completely obsolete in a few years retain a significance only as contributions to the slowly growing body of ideas about the ideologies which seem to have some stable validity. This could not be true if the ideologies we are concerned with were stable philosophies, clearly and permanently expressed in leading documents and speeches. It could not be true if Mussolini or Hitler or the leading protagonists of Democracy knew exactly what their principles were and to what they must lead.

---

[17] Pettee, *op. cit.*

[18] Karl Mannheim, *Ideology and Utopia* (New York: Harcourt, Brace and Co., 1936).

[19] For a survey of the most important ones during the 1940-1941 period, see J. S. Roucek, "World War II—A Survey of Recent Literature," *The Educational Forum*, V (May, 1941), pp. 461-484.

Secondary Ideologies. It would seem that there have been not only ideologies, but secondary ideologies about ideologies. What we have learned has not been simply what Fascism is, or what Communism is, but what a student or writer trained in certain methods of investigation is led to conclude about them. All along we have known many facts; but in addition we have included among our data certain judgments, such as "Fascism is a means of defending capitalism," which are not known facts but really preliminary conclusions reached at a certain date on the basis of the known facts at that time. It is necessary to distinguish such preliminary conclusions from the data proper. We must learn to study various ideologies not only as seen by the ideological opponents and proponents, but as they are.

Growth of Control of Ideologies. There is no question but that the use of ideologies as a means of social control will increase. The tremendous increase in communication facilities and the utilization of modern educational systems for ideological purposes, will more than ever before help the indoctrination of great masses of people with the ideologies propounded by the controlling groups. The impact of the policies of totalitarian regimes on democratic ways of life will increasingly lessen our faith in the efficacy of free thought and increase our need to rely on the use of all the devices that a successful ideologist can muster today. Men of action have always looked upon ideologies as their weapons, but it is only recently that men of thought have been driven to accept that position. After a period in which it was fashionable to regard them as mere adjuncts of material processes, ideas have returned to importance in our own time through their recognized influence on action in the mass of ideologies and propaganda flooding the modern world.

Hopes in Social Sciences. While it is true that many ideas today are mere illusions when we consider them from the point of view of their social basis, a warning is in place here. The stereotyped application of the concept of ideology to every pattern of thought is, in the last analysis, based on the notion that there is no philosophical truth, in fact no truth at all for humanity, and that all thought is conditional. We should not be led, however, by an acceptance of this point of view to discourage social science from its aim to point to the future. If anything, we need to adhere to the ideology of continued but hopeful struggle, lest mankind become completely disheartened by the frightful happenings of the present, lest men's belief in a worthy, peaceful, and happy direction of society perish from the earth.[20]

---

[20] F. S. C. Northrop, *The Meeting of East and West: Inquiry Concerning World Understanding* (New York: The Macmillan Co., 1946), propounds that the present forms of all Western cultures belong to the past because the assumptions behind

Summary

The history of man has been, in part, one of struggle among conflicting ideologies, but never before have they assumed the totalitarian penetration into all realms of life and thought as at present. This makes their understanding as a means of social control vital for those who would understand the problems and methods of social control.

As rigorous and reassuring approaches to very complex realities, ideologies meet a human need and thus gain their potency as social forces. The operations of ideas and doctrines are conditioned by their orientation to ideological patterns. These patterns are dependent upon neither their inherent logic nor the support by a majority in a society. Many ideals which have had universal acceptance and approval for long periods have been ineffective as social controls, while the ideologies professed by minorities may lead to significant action in keeping with their aims.

Successful ideologies have fairly uniform characteristics. Among them are completeness as apparent explanations of the facts of life, internal coherence, the promise of a glorious future, rejection of the imperfect present, and ability to withstand criticism. Their interest is chiefly, however, to justify doctrines and to provide for human minds the certitude of acting "on principle." Ideologies give rise to myths which embody notions seemingly axiomatic in their obvious truths. They gain wide support to the extent that they give expression to vital interests and grievances of many groups.

Claims to scientific objectivity and realism are necessary supports for effective ideologies today. They are made to appear the profound ultimate Truths, and divide mankind into those who "know" the way to a "better world" and those who are blind, and therefore obstructionists. The use of symbols and personalities are a short cut to gain response with definite advantage over difficult abstractions.

It is the fate of all ideologies, sooner or later, to give rise to factional disputes within the ranks of their adherents, resulting from varying interpretations of their component ideas. As a result there are set up authorities or tribunals whose function it is to pronounce the official interpretation.

---

then no longer square with scientific and hence philosophical truth. Since the discoveries of Galileo and Newton, Western societies have been based on a succession of scientific philosophies, each of which added its own mistakes in correcting its predecessors. Finally science itself took a turn, with the physics of Einstein, that knocked the props from under even the inadequate philosophies of Locke, Kant and Hegel. With no philosophical coherence at the top, faulty and contradictory Western ideologies have been at war, like the societies that cling to them. Northrop wants to find a worldwide philosophical formula that will synthesize the best of East and West.

An ideology is for the most part a rather strange mixture of scientific and everyday statements (some of them true, some of them false), of philosophical generalizations and principles, of orders, moral principles, expressions of decisions, and faith. But the ideologies cannot be regarded as scientific theories—false or otherwise. Scientists admit mistakes, change, and often refute their theories. But only a certain part of ideological sentences can best be compared to religious theories. A certain portion of religious theories can be checked and proved, and some can be refuted; dogmas, however, cannot be refuted. Science does not accept dogmas as facts, and the dogma-part of an ideology may be considered only as a symptom indicating the attitude of the group propounding the ideology.

On the international front, wars are not only battles of blood and steel, but also of ideologies. Men have been willing to die for their faiths, and faith is grounded in one's total view of life. These faiths inherent in the underlying and basic thought patterns of the cultures and civilizations of the various parts of the globe lend meaning to the present international drama, and will continue to exert their influence long after the present ideological wars will have ended. For instance, the relation of racial ideologies to the unrest among the colonial peoples can be easily traced to the battle for men's minds going on since the war between East and West, where the all-important goal is the mastery of men's beliefs and convictions. This is the sphere in which the Western democracies have most to offer; but it is here that they seem to have been least effective, due to the ability of Communist propaganda to distort, misinterpret, and misunderstand everything that the Western world stands for, hopes for, and and has been able to accomplish.

QUESTIONS

1. How does science aid the professional propagandist?
2. Where does one find most work done regarding ideologies?
3. Define an ideology.
4. What is the relationship between doctrine and behavior?
5. Is there a correlation between the logic and rationality of an ideology and its effectiveness?
6. Distinguish between an ideology and a myth.
7. Upon what factors does the success of an ideology depend?
8. Why must an individual have an all-around knowledge of the world and the universe?
9. What advantages does an ideology have over scientific explanations of the world?
10. What are the results of a lack of an adequately simple ideology?
11. How does an ideology differ from the findings of scientific research?
12. What must the ideology present in terms of the future?
13. Into what two groups does an ideology divide the population?
14. What short cuts are available to the proponents of an ideology?

15. What device is used to transfer authority from the ideology in acceptance to a new ideology?
16. What is meant by the term "glow words"?
17. What is the usual division of an ideology after the passing of its original authority?
18. What conditions make the current war of ideologies different from those in the past?

SUGGESTED TOPICS FOR TERM PAPERS AND FURTHER RESEARCH

1. The relationship between doctrine and behavior.
2. The "inevitability" of ideologies.
3. The use of the "future" by ideologies.
4. Man's need for a simple, rational ideology.
5. The justificatory attributes of an ideology.
6. The ideological methods of fascism.
7. The ideological weapons of the élites.
8. The use of glow words by an ideology.
9. The factional makeup of an ideology.
10. Modern trends in ideological warfare.

BIBLIOGRAPHY

Books

Franz Alexander, *Our Age of Unreason* (Philadelphia: J. B. Lippincott, 1942). A very readable analysis of the irrational forces in modern social life; see also his *The Medical Value of Psychoanalysis.*

R. N. Anshen, ed., *Moral Principles in Action* (New York: Harper and Brothers, 1952). A collection of essays by distinguished contemporary scholars (including M. C. D'Arcy, Werner Jaeger, Robert M. MacIver, Jacques Maritain, F. S. C. Northrop, etc.) on the problems of ethics and values and their relation to contemporary social and political problems.

Harold Baley, *The Lost Language of Symbolism* (New York: Barnes and Noble, 1952). An inquiry into the ideological origins of letters, words, names, fairy tales, folklore, and mythologies.

David Baumgardt, *Bentham and the Ethics of Today* (Princeton, N.J.: Princeton University Press, 1952). A scholarly analysis of the ideology of liberalism, with its various interpretations.

Howard Becker, *Through Values to Social Interpretation* (Durham, N.C.: Duke University Press, 1952). An excellent survey of the sources of persuasion.

David Bidney, *Theoretical Anthropology* (New York: Columbia University Press, 1953). See especially Chapter 15, "Ideology and power in the Strategy of World Peace," pp. 433-449. A very interesting effort to integrate the interdisciplinary field of cultural anthropology and social philosophy.

W. L. Bremmeck and W. S. Howell, *Persuasion, A Means of Social Control* (New York: Prentice-Hall, 1952). See especially Chapter IX, "The Language of Persuasion," pp. 141-162, and Part V, "Applying Persuasion to Speaking," pp. 241-392. A good introductory textbook; also valuable bibliographies.

C. M. Bristol, *The Magic of Believing* (New York: Prentice-Hall, 1948), Chapter IX, "Belief Makes Things Happen," and IV, "Suggestion is Power."

David Bryn-Jones, *The Dilemma of the Idealist* (New York: The Macmillan Co., 1950). Takes up the age-old problem of how to reconcile individual ethics—which are felt to be obsolete—with the necessity for compromise in the life of the individual and the group.

Hadley Cantril, *The Psychology of Social Movements* (New York: John Wiley and Sons, 1951). A good psychological introduction to the ideological aspects of social movements.

Ernest Cassierer, *Language and Myth* (New York: Harper and Brothers, 1946). The language is treated here in its myth-making rather than its discursive form; the common root of language and myth is their form of metaphorical thinking.

Richard Chase, *Quest for Myth* (Baton Rouge, La.: Louisiana State University Press, 1949).

Maurice Cornforth, *Science and Idealism* (New York: International Publishers, 1947). Marxist principles applied to the study of twentieth century "logical positivism."

Gerard L. Degré, *Society and Ideology* (New York: Columbia University Press, 1943). An inquiry into the sociology of knowledge.

M. J. Fisher, *Communist Doctrine and the Free World* (Syracuse, N.Y.: Syracuse University Press, 1952). The ideology of communism according to Marx, Engels, Lenin, and Stalin.

Alexander Herzberg, *The Psychology of Philosophers* (London: Kegan Paul, Trench, Trubner, 1929). An interesting effort to relate the "private life" of outstanding philosophers to their philosophies.

Edmund Husserl, *Ideas* (New York: The Macmillan Co., 1952). A general introduction to pure phenomenology.

Aldous Huxley, *Ends and Means* (New York: Harper and Brothers, 1937). Invaluable for a readable introduction to the whole field of rationality and irrationality.

Andrew Lang, *Myth, Ritual and Religion* (New York: Longmans, Green & Co., 1906).

Max Lerner, *Ideas are Weapons* (New York: The Viking Press, 1939). One of the most cogent expressions of the functional theory of ideas.

Bronislow Malinowski, *Magic, Science and Religion* (Boston: Beacon Press, 1948). Anthropolitica studies.

Gaetano Mosca, *The Ruling Class* (New York: McGraw-Hill Book Co., 1939). A classic study of the use of ideologies in politics.

Reinhold Neibuhr, *Moral Man and Immoral Society* (New York: Charles Scribner's Sons, 1936). One of the first influential American studies of the role of ideologies in social life.

F. S. Northrop, *The Logic of Sciences and the Humanities* (New York: The Macmillan Co., 1948). See especially Chapter XVI, "The Ideological Problems of Social Science," pp. 273-277.

—— ed., *Ideological Differences and World Order* (New Haven: Yale University Press, 1949). A symposium on the cultures and philosophies of many nations and political parties of the world.

D. W. Riddle, *The Martyrs, A Study of Social Control* (Chicago: University of Chicago Press, 1931). A dispassionate application of social history to the study of the New Testament; Riddle regards the persecution of early Christianity as group conflicts.

V. F. Sokoloff, *Science and the Purpose of Life* (New York: Creative Age Books, 1950). A scientist probes some of the apparent conflicts between science and religion and explains why he cannot accept a completely materialistic concept of man.

E. L. Tuveson, *Millennium and Utopia* (Berkeley: University of California Press, 1949). An eloquent cry favoring conservatism.

W. E. Vinacke, *The Psychology of Thinking* (New York: McGraw-Hill Book Co., 1952). A survey of the variety of normal human thought processes and the light which psychologists have been able to shed on them.

W. D. Wallis, *Messiahs: Their Role in Civilization* (Washington, D.C.: American Council on Public Affairs, 1943). Historic-analytic study, by an anthropologist.

Harold Walsby, *The Domain of Ideologies* (Glasgow: Maclellan, 1947). A study of the origin, development, and structure of ideologies stressing the psychological element and couched in somewhat metaphysical language.

W. L. Warner, *American Life: Dream and Reality* (Chicago: University of Chicago Press, 1953). A social anthropologist describes, analyzes, and interprets some of the important ideological aspects of the social life of America.

Hutton Webster, *Magic* (Stanford University Press, 1948). Covers the whole subject of magic, but only as found among so-called preliterate peoples.

A. W. Watts, *Myth and Ritual in Christianity* (New York: Vanguard Press, 1954). An interpretation of the meaning of Christian symbolism, presented "as the ritual reliving of the Christ-story through the seasonal cycle of the ecclesiastical year."

Florian Znaniecki, *Modern Nationalities* (Urbana, Ill.: University of Illinois Press, 1952). A brilliant sociological analysis of the ideologies of nationalism.

Periodicals

Theodore Abel, "The Pattern of a Successful Political Movement," *American Sociological Review*, II (June, 1937), pp. 347-352.

Gustav Bergmann, "Ideology," *Ethics*, LXI (April, 1951), pp. 205-218.

H. G. Brown, "The Appeal of Communist Ideology," *American Journal of Economics and Sociology*, II (January, 1943), pp. 161-174.

J. W. Buckham, "Idealism and Realism: A Suggested Synthesis," *Journal of Philosophy*, XXXIX (July 16, 1942), pp. 402-413.

L. C. Copeland, "Racial Ideologies and the War," *Sociology and Social Research*, XXVII (July–August, 1943), pp. 440-446.

Gerard Degré, "Ideology and Class Consciousness of the Middle Class," *Social Forces*, XXIX (December, 1950), pp. 173-179.

Rudolf Eckstein, "Ideologies in Psychological Warfare," *Journal of Abnormal and Social Psychology*, XXXVII (July, 1953), pp. 369-387.

C. J. Erasmus, "Changing Folk Beliefs and the Relativity of Empirical Knowledge," *Southwestern Journal of Anthropology*, VIII (Winter, 1952), pp. 411-428.

Rubin Gotesky, "The Nature of Myth and Society," *American Anthropologist*, LIV (October–December, 1952), pp. 523-531.

H. D. Lasswell, "The Religion of Ideological Intelligence to Public Policy," *Ethics*, LIII (October, 1942), pp. 25-34.

Hans J. Morgenthau, "Apositive Approach to a Democratic Ideology," *Proceedings of the Academy of Political Science*, XXIV (January, 1951), pp. 79-91.

R. Mukerjee, "Toward a Sociological Theory of Ethics," *Sociology and Social Research*, XXXIV (July–August, 1950), pp. 431-437.

Joseph S. Roucek, "Political Behavior as a Struggle for Power," *Journal of Social Philosophy*, VI (July, 1941), pp. 341-351; "Ideology as a Means of Social Control," *American Journal of Economics and Sociology*, III (October, 1943), pp. 35-45; III (January, 1944), pp. 179-192; III (April, 1944), pp. 357-370; "A History of the Concept of Ideology," *Journal of the History of Ideas*, V (October, 1944), pp. 479-488.

Bertrand Russell, "The Role of the Intellectuals in the Modern World," *American Journal of Sociology*, XLIV (January, 1939), pp. 491-498; "The Revolt Against Reason," *Political Quarterly*, VI (January–March, 1937), pp. 1-10.

H. L. Searless, "On the Ideological Front of Europe," *World Affairs Interpreter*, XII (July, 1941), pp. 198-208.

T. V. Smith, "Democratic Apologetics," *Ethics*, LXIII (January, 1953), pp. 100-106.

F. G. Wilson, "The Structure of Modern Ideology," *Review of Politics*, I (October, 1939), pp. 382-399.

CHAPTER XIII

Conceptual Means of Social Control

Inherent in every form of social control is the inculcation of a concept in the mind of the individual. The method of control may be violent or nonviolent, coercive or noncoercive, but in any case it implies the acceptance of some idea. People act not only in reference to their environment, but also in reference to what they know or believe. In this intimate relation between ideas and conduct, society, groups, and individuals find their most effective means of control. Because he derives most of his knowledge and beliefs from the groups to which he belongs, the individual is bound to conform in some degree to the standards of those groups. He interprets the reality about him in terms of ideas transmitted to him by others. He seeks the goals which others have taught him to hold as significant. To achieve these goals he uses means which others have instructed him to use. He displays his emotions in accordance with the commonly accepted justification for showing his feelings. There are, of course, deviations from group standards of conduct. Social control is seldom perfect in its operation, for in few instances is it the sole determinant of action. Moreover, the pressures of social control may force the individual in divergent or even opposing directions. Yet no person is entirely free from the influence of others. In any situation the individual's action is partly determined by his conceptual scheme, most of which he receives from the groups to which he belongs.[1]

Analysis of Conceptual Schemes

Although a knowledge of the processes through which the group transmits its ideas to the individual is essential to an understanding of the phenomena of social control, those processes lie outside the focus of this chapter. The main concern here is to discover the implications of different types of concepts used as means of control. For this purpose it is

---

[1] The preceding chapter dealt with the place of ideologies in the conceptual scheme of the individual. The discussion here will be confined to concepts from other than ideological sources.

imperative to have a clear and definite analysis of the various elements which comprise the content of the individual's conceptual scheme.[2]

Knowledge

An indispensable element which every group must implant in the minds of its members is a body of verifiable facts and the demonstrable relations among those facts. Although different groups vary profoundly in their interpretations of the concrete world and man's relation to it, none can long exist without some knowledge which is in essence scientific. Earlier anthropological theories maintained that primitive man was "pre-logical" and nonempirical in his adaptation to the environment, that he acted solely on the basis of tradition, ritual, and magic, and that none of these was realistic.[3] Recent research has quite disproved this view. On the other hand, the basic tendency in the sociological theories of the eighteenth and nineteenth centuries was to impute rationality to all human thought and action. Deviations from rationality were construed to be due entirely to ignorance and error and were expected eventually to disappear.[4] Neither of these extreme views is corroborated by observation. All societies and all groups within societies transmit from one generation to another some irrational, nonfactual ideas and some knowledge which is more or less adequate to the fulfillment of wants. This knowledge may range from the highly accurate and complex theories of modern science to the rough approximations to reality found in folklore. It may be interspersed with superstitions, magical formulas, and other forms of ignorance and error, but there is always a factual element which corresponds to reality. Moreover, the individual is usually aware of the distinction. A farmer may heed the superstition of planting potatoes with a certain phase of the moon but he will also take more realistic measures to insure a good crop.

Normative Beliefs

A second element in the conceptual scheme through which society achieves conformity from its members consists of normative beliefs. In simple terms normative beliefs are convictions that (a) it is right and

[2] The analysis which follows is based on objective standards of reference. For the distinction between objective and subjective standards of "truth," "knowledge," and "belief," see P. A. Sorokin, *Social and Cultural Dynamics* (New York: American Book Co., 1937), II, pp. 3-123.

[3] Cf. B. Malinowski's article on "Culture" in the *Encyclopedia of the Social Sciences.*

[4] This view has recently received support from modern social thinkers. For a comprehensive statement of the modern rationalistic position see H. E. Barnes, H. A. Becker, and F. Becker, *Contemporary Social Theory* (New York: D. Appleton-Century Co., 1940), pp. 854-856.

desirable to do or avoid doing certain things, and (b) it is right and desirable to do or avoid doing them in a prescribed manner. Ordinarily, normative beliefs are confused with knowledge, partly because the latter carries with it a compulsion that one ought to act in accordance with his knowledge, and partly because normative beliefs are erroneously considered verifiable facts. For our purposes it is important to make a clear distinction. Knowledge refers solely to verifiable facts and relationships. It does not state what ought to be. It merely describes things as they are. Normative beliefs are wholly concerned with things as they ought to be, even when belief is directly contradicted by fact. Normative beliefs are invariably relative to the groups which hold the beliefs. Knowledge is not relative in that sense. Knowledge is potentially universal but normative beliefs, being relative to the group, can never attain universality. Generally or specifically, normative beliefs cover man's conduct toward man, toward culture, toward nature, and toward the unknown aspects of the universe. They may be trivial, as the notion that one ought to extend and crook the little finger in holding a teacup, or they may be magnificent, as the conviction that one ought to sacrifice his life for his country.

Sentimental Beliefs

A third element in the ideational system which the individual derives from the group is a farrago of sentimental beliefs. These may be defined as an intellectual acceptance of nonnormative ideas and propositions which are wholly unverifiable by scientific means. In part this category consists of postulates which have no basis in the reality perceived by the senses. Such postulates are not abstractions from the concrete. They are sheer assumptions of the existence of things of which there is no perceptible evidence. A preponderance of religious ideas are of this type. Gods, devils, angels, heaven, hell, souls, and purgatory all lie outside the realm of perceptibility. The strong conviction that such intangibles exist, however, may stimulate human action with all the force of tangible reality.

Applying both to the spiritual and the mundane world are sentimental beliefs which impute undemonstrable powers and qualities to ideas and objects. Unlike scientific knowledge, such beliefs are not logical inferences from experiential data. They are unverifiable assertions. Consider, for example, the belief in the superiority of one's own group, nation, religion, political party, or race. Scientifically, the superiority of any of these can be demonstrated only by an objective standard of measurement. Almost invariably, however, the standard of measurement is the subjective one of the group's own values. That sort of standard insures a feeling of superiority but it does not meet the requirements of science.

Error and Ignorance

A fourth element in the system transmitted by society to its members is comprised of error and ignorance. Outstanding in the folklore of primitive and civilized man alike are false ideas of causal connections. A drought is related to an offense against the tribal god. The poverty of an individual is caused by his sinfulness. The prosperity or impoverishment of a nation is a consequence of the election of this or that person. Such causal interpretations are not sentimental beliefs for they are amenable to verification. The causes are ascertainable by scientific means. To the extent that false causal notions are held despite scientific means by which their falsity may be disclosed, they are errors. When scientific means are not available, they represent ignorance.

Quite apart from false ideas about causal relationships, error and ignorance also abound in the axioms, myths, legends, and superstitions current among all people. A widely diffused axiom in America asserts that crime does not pay. Actually, some criminals obtain not only high pecuniary but also other rewards from their profession.[5] Myths and legends are not limited to stories about nonexistent persons like Paul Bunyan. They extend also to the descriptions of groups, social classes, nations, and their activities. Popular ideas are likely to be highly inaccurate when they refer to other peoples, only slightly less so when they refer to one's own group. Superstitions, or groundless fears that a given phenomenon will be followed by an undesirable event, may be relatively insignificant. Such, for example, is the belief that misfortune will befall the person who breaks a mirror. Superstitious fears take on an added significance when they are related to the normative beliefs of the group. Many of the consequences envisaged by the person who contemplates breaking a rule have no basis in fact. The reaction to groundless fears, however, may be as strong as the reaction to factual conditions.

The Functions of Conceptual Elements

Applying the above analysis, we may now inquire into the relationship of these elements to human conduct as, and in so far as, conduct is determined by social control. Here again it should be noted that not all conduct is a product of social control. Nor is conduct solely a translation of ideas into overt behavior. All that can be demonstrated is that the various elements in a conceptual scheme are factors underlying behavior

---

[5] This statement is amply corroborated in a recent work by Harry Elmer Barnes, *Society in Transition* (New York: Prentice-Hall, 1939), pp. 675-719.

and that the latter tends to vary with those elements. It can further be shown that social control through conceptual means is effective to the degree in which each element is adapted to its function. Conversely, maladaption between an element and its function renders control ineffective.

The Role and Limitations of Knowledge

The role of knowledge in social control is limited to the devising and applying of means to immediate, clearly defined ends. Through the development and dissemination of scientific ideas society can increase the efficiency with which its purposes are achieved. It is not within the power of science, however, to prescribe the purposes. This is not to say that science can play no part in the creation of social purposes. In the first place, rational methods of persuasion, as attested by modern educational and propaganda techniques, are very effective. In the second place, science aids in the creation of social purposes by predicting the consequences of a given course of action and demonstrating that the pursuit of one goal hinders or facilitates the pursuit of another. Thus science can foster but it cannot prescribe social purposes. Human values, which are the justification of social purposes, are not derived from science. They are derived from the social fiat of the group.

When the group transmits knowledge without an accompanying normative limitation of its use, knowledge may be (and usually is) employed for antisocial ends. There is not, as some writers have recently stated, an inherent danger in the development of science.[6] True, the modern laboratory and factory have perfected equipment capable of more destruction than civilization has ever before known, but even the most deadly poison gas is subordinate to the purpose for which it is employed. Similarly, all knowledge is intrinsically neutral. It can be used as a means to approved or disapproved ends. Consequently, in order to maintain control over its members a group may select one of two courses. It may deny access to some areas of knowledge or it may prescribe limits and conditions within which the knowledge may be used.[7] Both policies involve the possibility that the benefits of knowledge will be sacrificed to the values of conformity. Too, the suppression of knowledge often leads to its surreptitious dissemination through informal and uncontrolled channels. For every group the acquirement and transmission of knowledge constitute a serious problem in social control.

---

[6] See the compilation by Jesse E. Thornton, *Science and Social Change* (Washington, D.C.: The Brookings Institution, 1939).

[7] An apt illustration of both types of control is provided by current practices concerning knowledge of birth-control techniques. One powerful religious group denies its members access to such knowledge. Another approves of the dissemination of techniques on condition of marriage.

Normative Beliefs Define Purposes

Normative beliefs serve several functions in the process of social control. Primary among these is the definition of purposes and interests for the individual in such terms that his actions will promote, or at least not hinder, the common aims of the group. A member of a group does not desire things at random. He wants what he has been induced to want by the valuation which the group places upon different objectives. How this valuation establishes consonance between individual interests and group aims is well illustrated by college football. The aims of the college in this connection may be to extend the basis for common interests among its undergraduates and alumni, to finance its sports program, to publicize itself, and to develop cordial intercollegiate relations. If the husky freshman has not already been indoctrinated with the desire to play football when he enters, that desire will soon be instilled in him by the high valuation the college places on football. In like manner every group develops in its members a pattern of wants and interests integrated with common group purposes. In the broader areas of society these purposes are essentially the maintenance of order in human relationships. Expressed chiefly in social institutions, there are ideals of order in economic, governmental, religious, educational, family, and other forms of relationships. In every realm of behavior, society attempts to mold individual desires and interests into designs compatible with these social ideals. Negatively, the individual is socially conditioned against wants which obstruct group aims. In a graduate school where the main objective is the development of science, the athletic student's desire to play football is quelled by the low valuation placed upon it by the school. To achieve its nationalistic aims the totalitarian government indoctrinates its youth against desires for individual freedom. Almost universally, incestuous desires are suppressed or eliminated from the individual's want pattern because their fulfillment would interfere with the aims of family life. Thus through conscious foresight or through unconscious adaptation, groups and societies exert their influence over the individual by fostering acceptable and destroying unacceptable desires, purposes, and interests.

Normative Beliefs Define Means

Another function of normative beliefs is to control the individual's choice of means so that the purposes of the group may be advanced and not thwarted by the actions of its members. The individual is seldom left to his own devices in the fulfillment of his wants. From the group he

learns that there is a right and a wrong way to do things.[8] Although the
distinction is often quite arbitrary, the "right" way can usually be shown
to serve a group function. Even the relatively insignificant action of
holding a teacup in the "correct" manner has its meaning in identifying
the individual as one who belongs to a definite social circle. In its more
significant aspects, the control over the individual's choice of means prevents activities which would jeopardize the highest values common to
the group. Without such control, and in spheres of behavior where the
question of efficiency is pertinent, the individual is likely to choose his
means solely on the basis of efficiency. In that case force and fraud will
predominate, for their effectiveness is readily apparent to everyone.
They are effective, however, only with reference to the individual's immediate purpose. Dishonest practices may lead to good grades in school,
but they are not conducive to attaining the ultimate values in education.
Too, when force and fraud become the predominant mode of action,
common values are destroyed. A college in which student trickery and
deceit prevail over honest work soon finds its diplomas worthless. The
value of graduating from that college, a value common to all its students,
is thus lost. To relate immediate to ultimate purposes and to protect its
common values, the group provides the individual with a range of choice
much broader than mere efficiency or inefficiency. The "right" means
integrate efficiency with other considerations. These may be esthetic,
religious, moral, legal, or any other group standard. Having set a broad
basis of choice, the group further exercises its influence by manipulating
the individual's selection. As in the case of interests and desires, the group
places a definite valuation on different possible means to a given end.
Accepting this valuation, the individual is constantly impelled toward the
"right" and away from the "wrong" means. This applies, as we have
noted, to action in which the question of efficiency is relevant. In some
forms of behavior, however, efficiency is irrelevant. The attainment of
objectives in religious worship, for example, is unverifiable to such extent
that the relative effectiveness of this or that means cannot be established.
In that case, the group exerts even greater control over the individual's
choice of means. Ritualistic behavior is characteristically precise, prescribed in absolute terms for every occasion. Individual deviations from
the prescribed ritual, if permitted, would soon destroy faith in the effectiveness of all ritual.[9] To protect itself against that eventuality, the group
rigidly dictates the forms of ritual.

---

[8] For treatment of institutional aspect of "right" and "wrong" ways of doing
things, see chapter IV, "The Fields of Behavior."
[9] This is not to say that ritualistic practices have no effect in society. They
may perform many functions, especially that of unifying the members of the
group. As an expression of unity, ritual is further forced to prohibit deviations
because they would contradict the purpose of unity. The connection between

Normative Beliefs Become Self-Regulative

A most vital function of normative beliefs is the transference of responsibility for enforcing group standards. Once the validity of a belief is accepted by the individual, he assumes an obligation for its enforcement in his own behavior. It is for this reason that the individual is in most instances quite unaware of the fact that he is being controlled by the group. Few people realize the extent to which the direction and force of their motivations are derived from others. The recalcitrant minority may be more or less constantly aware of the force of social control, but for the majority both the normative system and the responsibility for its enforcement are so internalized that their social genesis is seldom recognized. To a large degree this internalization is attributable to the most generalized "ought" in human behavior: the conviction that one ought to seek the approval of others. From childhood the individual is taught to value the approval of designated persons, or, more important, the approval of persons holding designated positions. He is also conditioned against seeking the approval of those whom the society holds in low esteem. Although approval and disapproval are external, their effect is determined by a process which operates wholly within the individual. This process is the universal one of self-approbation. Following the norms which are accepted as valid, seeking the approval of those whose opinions are valued, and integrating these with his evaluation of himself, the individual unconsciously acts in accordance with the standards of the group. Deviations from the "proper" aims and interests or from the "right" way of fulfilling them are undertaken at the risk of lowering self-respect. Conversely, conformity heightens self-respect. In the powerful drive for self-respect, social control has its most dynamic source.

Sentimental Beliefs Validate Norms

The role of sentimental beliefs in social control is chiefly that of establishing in the person to be controlled an acceptance of the validity of normative rules. Unlike scientific laws, whose validity can be demonstrated by experiment and verification, social rules possess no validity other than that expressed by belief. The physical law which states that at sea level water boils at 212° Fahrenheit obtains its validity from scientific demonstration. The validity of the social precept that one ought to

---

ends and means in ritual, however, is essentially arbitrary and not intrinsic. It can be shown that for the purpose of driving a nail into a board a hammer is more effective than a table fork. The relation between cause and effect is intrinsic. It cannot be demonstrated that for the purpose of producing rain prayer by means of a prayer wheel is more effective than prayer accompanied by the sacrifice of a pigeon. In both instances the relation between the prayer and rain is symbolic.

be truthful depends upon intellectual assent. The formation and maintenance of intellectual assent are the main functions of sentimental beliefs
in social control. In the fulfillment of this function few beliefs are so
prevalent as that which postulates the existence of deities and demons.
Whether it refers to the tribal gods of primitive man or to the God of
Jews and Christians, the belief in supernatural beings is invariably linked
with the basic norms of society. Posited as the highest authority of truth,
the gods are believed to approve the fundamental principles to which
human beings should conform. Imputed to have omnipotent powers,
they are believed to visit fearful punishment upon the disobedient and
to reward the obedient with temporary or eternal felicity. The omnis-
cience attributed to them is believed to bring all human conduct within
their purview for evaluation and judgment. Closely interwoven with
numerous assertions about the realm of the supernatural and man's relation
to it, illustrated by selected references to historical fact, religious propositions constitute a conceptual system within which social imperatives are
insulated against doubt or rational inquiry. Moreover, accepting one
element, the believer is logically impelled to embrace the entire system.
In Christianity, for example, the belief in life after death implies faith in
a vast concatenation of other beliefs, including the validity of a wide
range of social norms.

Similarly, although usually on a more limited scale, the validity of
normative beliefs is established through their linkage with tradition, moral
"science," metaphysical principles, and other ideologies which are unverifiable by scientific means. To illustrate, without aiming to attack honesty
as a virtue, let us consider some of the protective elaborations surrounding
the precept that one ought to be honest. Tradition presents it with
reference to the honest deeds of great men. Lincoln walked miles to
rectify an error involving a few pennies. Moral "science" asserts: "It is
not only unjust but also unkind not to be honest." [10] A well-known
metaphysical principle states that one ought to act in accordance with
maxims which one can will to become universal law.[11] These assertions
support the honesty precept. An analysis of their implications, however,
sometimes weakens the support and plants doubt in its stead. The Lincoln
story implies either that honesty is characteristic of important historical
figures or that honesty is a factor in the rise of such men. To these notions one might oppose the fact that Talleyrand was both an important
historical figure and a dishonest one. Thus from one point of view the
proof of the honesty precept does not lie in facts or in the logical relationships between facts. It is rooted in sentimental beliefs. In like

---

[10] J. H. Seelye, *A System of Moral Science* (New York, 1880), p. 74.
[11] It is a common characteristic of such principles to treat precepts in universal
terms. Actually morals are usually limited to an area smaller than the universe.

manner all other normative beliefs are based solely on sentiments. Consequently, the effectiveness of the former depends for support on the latter.

Sentimental Beliefs Also Unify Groups

The dominance of the normative element is also enhanced by sentimental beliefs relating to the unity of the group. The sense of belonging, "consciousness of kind," is in part immanent in the facts of group existence. Added to the facts, however, are non-factual considerations which serve to strengthen the bonds between group members. These considerations consist mainly of two correlative types: (a) beliefs which posit nonexistent similarities and ignore actual differences among group members; and (b) beliefs which posit nonexistent differences and ignore actual similarities between group members and people outside the group. Both types are well illustrated by the Nazi doctrine of Aryanism. This dogma asserted that Germans had a similar racial heritage which differed from that of all other people. Actually Germans are among the most mixed stocks of Europe and differ little from the people of neighboring nations.[12] The same forms of belief, although varying in content, are used by most groups to create a sense of unity far greater than that warranted by facts. Invariably integrated with these ideas are sentiments of superiority. Inverting the logical proposition that superiority is of necessity unique, claims to uniqueness are turned into assertions of superiority. Because the superiority is defined in terms of the group's own normative standards, the members are logically driven to accept the validity of the norms. To question them would be equivalent to questioning the superiority of their own group.

Error and Ignorance are the Basis of Some Norms

Error and ignorance, playing much the same role as sentimental beliefs, may be the sole basis for specific normative rules. Given a false conception of the causation of social phenomena there arise notions that one ought to pray to the gods, make sacrifices, consult the oracles, and keep taboos inviolate in order to direct the outcome of human action. Elaborately woven into ethical, moral, and religious doctrines, error and ignorance are the only support of some of the normative beliefs in every society. When knowledge removes the fallacies underlying them, such norms fade slowly out of the pattern of social beliefs. Not basic to the norms themselves, but often vital to their acceptance, are those fallacious

---

[12] Interestingly, the Aryan doctrine has been held by several European nations, notably by France. Cf. Frank H. Hankins' article, "Aryans" in the *Encyclopaedia of the Social Sciences*.

ideas which exaggerate the actual consequences of violating a rule. Thus there is a widely current belief that theft is sooner or later followed by the imprisonment of the thief.[13] Actually only a small fraction of those who commit theft are apprehended, a still smaller fraction are imprisoned. Despite the warnings of maxims, myths, legends, and other folk ideas that there are no exceptions, many of the violators of any norm suffer no consequence, simply because they are not caught.

Conceptual Means of Control May Be Used for Limited Purposes

Separately the various conceptual elements may be employed deliberately as means of social control by groups or individuals to gain dominance in some limited situation. For the purpose of increasing its sales, a business enterprise may exploit sentimental beliefs of morality, patriotism, or what not. Usually it creates new normative ideas about what one ought to want and how that want should be fulfilled. Through the use of ambiguously worded advertisements it may promote and utilize to its own ends various forms of error and ignorance. Similarly, politicians, reformers, educators, labor organizers, employers, and others exert their control over individuals through the means of scientific and nonscientific ideas.

Conceptual Means Relate Chiefly to Broader Aspects of Control

Considered as a whole, however, conceptual schemes serve to control individual action not merely for the limited purposes of individuals and groups but mainly for the more inclusive purposes of the entire society. Establishing some degree of conceptual uniformity, a society promotes and maintains predictability of behavior so that cooperation is possible. Obscuring by norms and sentiments the immediate and direct advantage of individuals and groups, it subordinates them to broader and more ultimate purposes. By the same means it minimizes conflicts which, without such considerations, would constantly threaten the social order. Furthermore, a society through its system of knowledge and belief provides continuity in social life. Though continually undergoing revision and occasionally deflected by wars, revolutions, and sudden social changes, such systems form the basis of action for one generation after another. In the performance of these functions it is the *system* of knowl-

---

[13] According to a recent survey, about 20% of the total number of thefts committed result in the apprehension of the criminal. Cf. Walter C. Reckless, *Criminal Behavior* (New York: McGraw-Hill Book Company, 1940), p. 24.

edge and beliefs, not its discrete parts, which assures the achievements of a society's aims. Contrary to the beliefs of the "rationalists" social needs cannot be met solely with the findings of science. "Truth," when it refers to the ultimate values in a society, is not discovered but decreed. In like manner every social belief quite independent of its validity or even its plausibility may have a function in the process of social control. Ignorance and error, although seldom designated by those terms, may be as essential to social order as the most accurate scientific theory. Not as a discrete unit but as an integrated part each conceptual element plays a role in the complex structure of human interaction.

Most Ideas are Interdependent

Because a society's ideas are to some degree integrated,[14] a major change in one element may involve corresponding changes in other elements. To the social philosophers imbued with the doctrines of evolution, the correlative changes in ideas appeared simply to be the displacement of error and ignorance by knowledge and understanding. Careful observation will show, however, that while knowledge increases cumulatively, sentiment and ignorance accompany it *pari passu*. The broader the extent of knowledge, the broader the area of sentiment and ignorance.[15] From the standpoint of social control the latter categories cannot be permitted to develop at random. They must be limited to sentimental and fallacious ideas which are conducive or at least neutral to the aims of society. An excellent illustration of this point is the introduction of the steel plow in certain rural areas. It was once believed that the steel plow "poisoned" the soil. To dispel this belief the plow manufacturers told farmers that the steel plow "strengthened" the soil. Both beliefs are quite false. Yet the one error obstructed the social aim of greater farm production while the other error was not obstructive. On a more significant scale, economic, political, religious, moral, and other types of ideas tend to integrate knowledge, sentiment, and ignorance with societal aims. Analyzed abstractively in scientific and philosophic disciplines, these ideas are constantly forced into a semblance of harmony in concrete life.

---

[14] The concept of culture integration involves many controversies. Some theorists maintain that all the traits comprising a culture are parts of an integral system, others hold that a given culture may have varying degrees of integration. Cf. Sorokin, *op. cit.*, I, pp. 3-53.

[15] Consider, for example, the development of the various sciences related to radio communication. In the laboratory, knowledge of these sciences has greatly increased. The average man, however, has merely added the mysteries of radio communication to his preexisting body of ignorance.

Why are Some Beliefs Rejected?

As a corollary to the hypothesis that the effectiveness of social control is in part dependent upon the acceptance of ideas, nonacceptance is one of the sources of deviation from social standards. Obviously, the rejection of an idea by the individual, like its acceptance, involves many factors lying outside the scope of the present chapter. Physical and mental defects in the individual or weakness or disorganization in the social structure, for example, are essential to an explanation of nonconformity in any given case. For our purposes, however, these are left out of consideration. Our concern here is the question: What conditions within the limits of the conceptual aspects of social control are related to the rejection of ideas? Although this question pertains to all conceptual elements, its relevance to normative beliefs is paramount. Unless normative beliefs are accepted, social control is meaningless.

Norms May Be Logically Incompatible

A condition which invariably involves the rejection of some normative beliefs in modern society is their logical incompatibility with other norms relating to the same action. Less prevalent in simple societies, this situation is common wherever the individual is a member of several groups. Differentiated in function and social position, each group tends to develop standards of behavior which are to some degree peculiar to itself. Participating in the activities of various groups, the individual is indoctrinated not only with conflicting but often with contradictory norms. Although he may compromise the conflicting standards to some extent, he is logically forced to reject those which are contradictory to the norms he chooses to accept. The process does not end, however, with the elimination of the logically contradictory norms. Inherent in the individual's conscious choice between norms is the realization that no norm is sacrosanct. Acting in accordance with this realistic attitude the individual will tend to evaluate all norms with reference to their effect upon his own interests. This is not to say that under such circumstances social control is rendered wholly ineffective, for in no instance are an individual's interests entirely self-generated. Some control remains operative but it is diminished in scope and intensity. Moreover, individual selection of norms results in the disintegration of normative systems. Consciously or unconsciously integrated through centuries of social experience, normative systems lose their unity when they are constantly submitted to the piecemeal selection and rejection of their component parts.

Norms May Lack Integration

Also contributory to the rejection of social norms are discrepancies between the means and ends prescribed by specific beliefs. In behavior which entails an intrinsic relationship between means and ends, such as economic activity, the goals may be so difficult to obtain in the socially approved manner that illegitimate action becomes for many the only available means of achieving them. The emphasis on acquisition of wealth as a respectable life-aim in contemporary society, for example, creates in large classes of individuals a desire they are unable to fulfill by the socially approved means they find accessible. In consequence some achieve the aim by the readily available but unapproved means of crime, vice, and graft. Conversely, approved means may not be directly related to socially desirable ends. This form of discrepancy is well illustrated by official adherence to laws which have outlived their original purpose. The enforcement of "blue" laws, for instance, may be a legal means to the advancement of a judge's personal interests but antagonistic to the broader interests of society. Thus maladjustment between normative means and ends gives rise to the acceptance of one and the rejection of the other.[16] Where the relationship between means and ends is symbolic, as in religious behavior, such maladjustment is less probable. Rejection of the norms in that case is more closely related to the nonacceptance of sentimental beliefs which support the validity of the entire system. The individual who lacks faith in the existence of a supernatural world is not likely to accept either the normative ends or means set forth in the dogma and ritual of a religious system. He may, of course, participate in the ritual for secular purposes but that would not constitute acceptance of the means in the normative sense.

Participation is Essential to the Acceptability of Norms

Not strictly within the limits of the conceptual aspects of social control but essential to their explanation is the relationship between social participation and the acceptance of social beliefs. When the individual takes part in the activities in which beliefs are grounded, he can appreciate the function of social imperatives and their supporting structures. He may not analyze precisely the role of any particular element in social control, but he can gain an intuitive conception of the purposes served by the system as a whole. If he attends religious services, he becomes aware of the unifying functions of religion. In educational institutions, he is led to

---

[16] The implications of this form of social maladjustment are clearly stated in an article by R. K. Merton: "Social Structure and Anomie," *American Sociological Review*, III (1938), pp. 672-682.

visualize the complexity and interdependence of human action. To the extent that he is active in political affairs, he recognizes the social necessity of balancing duties and rights. In brief, in whatever sphere of social organization the individual participates he is consciously or unconsciously impressed with the functions of various forms of social control. When the individual is excluded from participation, however, the conceptual elements of social control change their meaning. No longer internalized by the process of social approval and disapproval which forms the basis of self-appraisal, social beliefs become merely the external conditions of action. Far from being controlled by them, the individual employs them to his own interests. Conformity and nonconformity under these circumstances are a matter of individual convenience. Limited to a small proportion of the group or of the society, such individuals can be controlled by compulsory measures. Their predominance, however, renders even compulsion ineffective. Social control by conceptual means, therefore, is a function of social participation.

Summary

Since people act not only in reference to their environments, but also in relation to what they know and believe, the inculcation of concepts is inherent in all forms of social control whether such control is planned or a part of an unconscious striving for social order. Concepts include those abstracted from true knowledge and those which are normative beliefs with necessary factual foundation. There are also sentimental beliefs which are nonnormative, wholly unverifiable by scientific means, yet potent in the influencing of behavior. Error and ignorance, especially in supposed cause and effect relationships, also play an important part.

Knowledge, itself, may be employed either for socially desirable ends or for antisocial aims; and societies find it necessary both to limit the availability of certain kinds of knowledge and to limit its use to certain sets of conditions. Normative beliefs enter here to define purposes for individuals, and to limit means by which purposes may be attained. Normative beliefs, once accepted, are self-regulative in that they imply for the accepting individual the responsibility of regulating his own behavior accordingly. Norms, in turn, are validated by sentimental nonnormative beliefs. These sentimental beliefs held in common by members of a group serve to unify these groups.

In addition to their general societal utility, conceptual means of social control may be, and are, used by groups and individuals for their own ends and to gain dominance over other groups and individuals within a society.

There is always some inconsistency and conflict among beliefs of a group which lead to their logical incompatibility, and therefore rejection by some members. Norms of ends and means may also be so poorly integrated that legitimate means are rejected in favor of illegitimate in the attainment of socially approved goals.

Social participation leads to intuitive acceptance of the fitness of conceptual schemes of control. Conversely, exclusion from participation emphasizes such schemes as external controls, and to their use for individual ends rather than to conformity.

QUESTIONS

1. In what frame of reference do individuals act?
2. What elements comprise the content of the individual's conceptual scheme?
3. What form of knowledge is necessary to the survival of a group, and in what degree must it be present?
4. How do normative beliefs differ from knowledge?
5. What is the nature of sentimental beliefs?
6. What are some modern examples of causal interpretations based on error and ignorance?
7. Is all conduct a product of social control? Explain.
8. From where are human values derived?
9. What is the role of knowledge in social control?
10. What is the relationship between knowledge and normative beliefs?
11. What is the reply to the claim that there is an inherent danger in science?
12. What is the relationship between group valuation and individual interests?
13. How does society control the choice of means by an individual?
14. How do religious groups put this principle into use?
15. How do normative beliefs affect the placing of responsibility for enforcement of the social norms?
16. What is the purpose of sentimental beliefs?
17. How do sentimental beliefs succeed in unification?
18. By what means are conflicts minimized?
19. How is continuity provided in social life?
20. Describe the relationship between effective social control and the acceptance of normative beliefs.

SUGGESTED TOPICS FOR TERM PAPERS AND FURTHER RESEARCH

1. Analyze the major speeches from the recent elections in terms of knowledge, normative beliefs, and sentimental beliefs.
2. Analyze and compare the normative and sentimental aspects of a nationwide advertising campaign.
3. Compare the conceptual methods of control of democratic systems with those of totalitarian systems.
4. Discuss the role of participation as related to acceptance of group norms.
5. Discuss the relationship of lore and knowledge in a recent political or social theory.
6. Discuss the phrase, "The ends justify the means," from the point of view of social control.
7. The place of logic in a system of normative beliefs.

8. Theories of cultural interdependence of ideas.
9. Discuss scientific advancement in relation to man's body of ignorance.
10. Discuss rationalist theories of society and compare them with information relating to conceptual means of control.

BIBLIOGRAPHY

Books

Harold Bayley, *The Lost Language of Symbolism* (New York: Barnes and Noble, 1952). A study of the origin of letters, words, names, fairy tales, folklore, and mythologies.

David Bidney, *Theoretical Anthropology* (New York: Columbia University Press, 1953). See especially Chapter 2, "The Concept of Culture and Some Cultural Fallacies," pp. 23-53; Chapter 3, "Ethnology and Psychology," pp. 54-84; Chapter 10, "The Concept of Myth," pp. 286-326; Chapter 13, "Modes of Cultural Integration," pp. 366-399; and Chapter 14, "Normative Culture and the Categories of Value," pp. 400-432. Penetrating and scholarly essays.

Eliza Mariam Butler, *Ritual Magic* (New York: Cambridge University Press, 1949). A general discussion of the subject.

E. E. Cockerill and others, *A Conceptual Framework for Social Casework* (Pittsburgh: University of Pittsburgh Press, 1953). A pioneer work in this field.

McQuilkin DeGrande, *The Nature and Elements of Sociology* (New Haven: Yale University Press, 1953); see especially Part Five: "The Divisioning of the Societal Domain," pp. 281-602. A systematic theory concerning this area of sociological knowledge.

Dorothy B. Donnelly, *The Golden Well* (New York: Sheed and Ward, 1950). Attempts to discover a common ground of symbols.

Paul Hanly Furfey, *The Scope and Method of Sociology* (New York: Harper and Brothers, 1953); especially Chapter 9, "The Logical Structure of Science," pp. 199-216, and Chapter 10, "The Logical Structure of Sociology," pp. 217-233. A metasociological treatise.

Richard Hope, *How Man Thinks* (Pittsburgh: University of Pittsburgh Press, 1949). Covers man's traditional, symbolic, and experimental methods of logic.

Ernest Lehner, *Symbols, Signs and Signet* (Cleveland: World Publishing Company, 1953). Studies the relationship of symbols and social control.

Karl Mannheim, *Essays on the Sociology of Knowledge* (New York: Oxford University Press, 1952); especially Chapter II, "On the Interpretation of 'Weltanschauung,'" pp. 33-83, and Chapter IV, "The Problem of a Sociology of Knowledge," pp. 134-190. Brilliant essays by a well-known German sociologist.

Elton Mayo, *The Human Problems of an Industrial Civilization* (New York: The Macmillan Co., 1933). An inquiry into the problems of social control and industry.

William Norman Pittengen, *Sacraments, Signs and Symbols* (Chicago: Wilcox and Follett, 1949). The significance of Christian ceremony by an Anglican professor.

G. E. P. Sidaway, *Signs and Symbols* (Baltimore: Penguin Books, 1953). The meaning and use of symbols in history.

Charles L. Stevenson, *Ethics and Language* (New Haven: Yale University Press, 1945). A debate whether the so-called intrinsic goods (or final ends) are a necessary condition for all ethical agreement.

Ernest Weekley, *Words and Names* (New York: E. P. Dutton and Co., 1932). A study of the history of place names by a great English authority.

Periodicals

M. C. Albrecht, "The Relationship of Literature and Society," *American Journal of Sociology*, LIX (March, 1954), pp. 425-436.

R. E. Berberg, "Prestige Suggestion in Art as Communication," *Journal of Social Psychology*, XXXVIII (1953), pp. 23-30.

Gustav Bergmann, "Pure Semantics, Sentences, and Propositions," *Mind*, LIII (1944), pp. 238-257.

F. W. Bridgman, "The Prospect for Intelligence," *Yale Review*, XXXIV (March, 1945), pp. 444-461.

John Dewey, "Education and Our Present Social Problems," *School and Society*, XXXVII (April 15, 1933), pp. 473-476.

W. B. Cameron and T. C. McCormick, "Concepts of Security and Insecurity," *American Journal of Sociology*, LIX, 6 (March, 1954), pp. 556-564.

P. Kecskemeti, "Totalitarian Communications as a Means of Control," *Public Opinion Quarterly*, XIV (Summer, 1950).

Robert K. Merton, "The Unanticipated Consequences of Purposive Social Action," *American Sociological Review*, I (1936), pp. 894-904.

Ralph Pieris, "Speech and Society: A Sociological Approach to Language," *ibid.*, XVI (August, 1951), pp. 499-505.

Louis Wirth, "Consensus and Mass Communication," *American Sociological Review*, XIII (February, 1948), pp. 5-12.

CHAPTER XIV

Language and Semantics

Semantics in the World Today

In the ever-shifting arena of world conflict and attempts at world unity, deeds speak louder than words. Atom bombs, supersonic speed, guerilla warfare, radar, fifth column tactics, *anschluss*, isolationism, and global war are more than memories of words and phrases; they are also signs of the times. They are the lurid signals which point to the disastrous happenings of yesterday. Sweeping assaults which overtake and destroy men and their works have been the order of the day. A so-called "new world order" of steel and fire and ruin was marching against mankind. With mechanical power and scientific precision, this "order" has reached around the globe and struck cynical blows. Slowly, the nations yet asleep have come awake. But it took wholesale treachery and murder to rouse them. Words, apparently, had failed.

Overnight, we have grown sharply conscious of language and its many uses. Words of warning, of documented perils, of secret collusion are more readily detected and recognized for what they are in terms of what has taken place. Words of vengeance are brought to mind, words of diplomatic concealment are exposed, and words of power-mad dictators are even now recalled and denounced and publicized to the ends of the earth. The road to World War II has searchingly been delineated in a "river of ink" that has flowed not merely through the main arteries of news but also into the veins and capillaries of the entire political body.[1]

The Use of Words. Today, as we know, information flies with miraculous wings throughout the wide world. Words on wings carry news of rebellion, disaster, treason, victory, peace through the modern instrumentalities of press, screen, radio, and teletype. But with the news comes also propaganda, slanted in such devious ways that disbelief or false belief is the result, for words can be tricky weapons. Whether they are whispered by the lips of the unscrupulous or are mouthed over again by unsuspecting victims, words can, like poisoned arrows, be death-dealing in their flight. Nor can we even at this late date state with complacency

---

[1] See Joseph S. Roucek, ed., *Contemporary Europe* (New York: D. Van Nostrand, 1947); read chapters on "The Road to War" and "World War: Act Two."

that the evils of disingenuous propaganda, of totalitarian creeds, and of isolationist blindness are at an end. The war of words continues unchecked and with renewed vigor as national emergencies are transformed into states of distrust. Barely a year ago, huge propaganda machines on all fronts were humming to the lusty tunes of special pleadings and casuistical nonsense. Abstract concepts such as "race," "living space," "new order," "national destiny," *"Führer Princip,"* "co-prosperity sphere" and the like promoted a spurious faith in the masses. And, lest we forget, concrete symbols apart from words written and spoken were manipulated with such skill that swastika, fasces, rising sun, eagle, cross, crescent, lion became impregnated with a plethora of ineradicable sentiments. Thus word and object symbols are seen to exert immense and irrational sway over undisciplined crowds; they subtly prey upon even presumably intelligent minorities.

Origin of Semantics. Yet words can be also the tools of progress and of peace. Indeed, a retrospective glance at human culture persuades us that the unifying, conservative, and creative functions of language more than compensate for its lamentable misuse. Which brings us directly to the relevant subject matter of this chapter—the interpretation of language elements. And the question immediately arises: what is the meaning of meaning when applied to language as man's basic mental precision tool? This is where the science of semantics brings a fresh start and a more direct route to the common goal of understanding "self" and "world" by the analysis of the intellectual medium itself. Thus at the outset we stumble over a hint to the specific tasks imposed upon semantics in its very name. Derived from the Greek root "sema" which is the word for sign, "semantikos" bears the connotation significant, and the derivative "semasia" (i.e., significant) plus "logia" give us the earliest designation for this branch of knowledge—*semasiology.* As semasiology it continued to be known from approximately 1887, when Max Müller published his *The Science of Thought,* until 1897 which saw the appearance of Michel Bréal's *Essai de Semantique.*[2] From this period to the middle of the 1920's semantics has remained securely within the precincts of language study and has continued to the present day under the name supplied by Michel Bréal.

Functions of Semantics

Semantics developed into a series of half-old, half-new functions which by now seem well enough established and clearly recognized. It may be profitable to examine them briefly:

---

[2] Max Müller, *The Science of Thought* (New York: 1887); Michel Bréal, *Essai de Semantique* (Paris: 1897).

1. As a *tool of thought,* semantics discloses affinities with the theory of knowledge or epistemology, in that it shows the relationship between words and the entire structure of knowledge.

2. The general *idea of symbolism,* which underlies semantics, points to the fact that the arts are in their expressive features languages, the symbols of which can be learned and transmitted as a traditional source of learning.

3. In its *word analysis,* semantics specializes in tracking an idiom or term from a given period backwards and forwards in time in order to learn not merely its adopted clusters of meanings but, more importantly, if possible an inner core of significance maintained against time and circumstance.

4. The student of semantics is frequently more occupied with the philosopher's presumed task—the *exact definition of terms.* By training his light upon the denotative function of words, he clarifies the relatively limited and fixed meanings as they obtain in science and in professional and technical subjects.

5. Yet again, semantics may be profitably employed to lay out a fundamental method to *straight thinking* and to the exposure of crooked and illogical modes of thought.

6. Causes of *semantic illiteracy* may also be revealed through the resources of this mental discipline.[3]

7. *Clarification of professional terminologies* is another mighty task that awaits the would-be semantician of the future.

Man, the Speaking Animal

At this point it may well be asked what semantics and its many uses has to do with man, the animal that speaks. It would be even better to inquire in what sundry ways man and the linguistic processes and semantic discoveries are connected with the subject of social control. The answer to these queries will tend to show that a very intimate relationship exists between them.

Man's Endowment. To begin with, man's physical equipment proclaims him an animal that is singularly prepared for linguistic activity. The oral cavity, for example, has through evolutionary processes become a small resonating cavern. The free-hanging tongue is capable of wagging and curving and flattening itself, thus controlling the character and quality of the sound produced by the vocal chords vibrating under the impetus of air from the lungs. But capacity for speech is also tied up with the enlargement of the cranium, and in consequence with the more highly

---

[3] See later treatment under the sub-heading "Semantic Illiteracy."

developed frontal lobes of the cerebrum, the third convolution of which has, according to authorities, the regulative control of motor as well as linguistic performance.[4] Thus speech is construed as a motor activity. In the words of Dr. Goldberg, "language is a form of action." [5]

Furthermore, the erect posture of man accomplished a three-fold victory in this general direction. His chest was carried high and was free to expand and contract with every breath he took; the foot grew groundfast and secure in its feat of balancing and propelling the body through space over level or uneven terrain; the forepaw, at last liberated from four-footed ambling, and somewhat later freed from the swinging hold upon branches, could evolve into the manipulating hand—the master-tool of human civilization.[6]

As the hand progressed in dexterity, the tongue profited. By imperceptibly slow stages, it became a skilled imitator of the hand's digital nimbleness. And thus it ultimately was adapted into an even greater tool than the hand, becoming the instrument which modified and shaped the chromatic and guttural sounds emitted, thus translating them into meaningful elements of speech. Of the diverse causes which emphasize the intimate linkage between early man and his oral as well as written modes of expression, there emerge at least six cardinal instances of relationship. Numerous great scholars have, since the time of Plato (see particularly his dialogue Cratylus), labored with loving care over the language question in order to establish the central importance it occupies in human progress and, *a fortiori*, the tenacious hold it has upon the body and soul of its inventor. Let us consider these causes together:

1. *Organismic completeness* of participation in the act of speech is foundational. Few lay persons realize how thoroughly the whole body of man is active in this regard. Brain, tongue, throat, hand, lips, lungs, diaphragm, chest, glands, nerves, ganglia, blood stream, reflexes, musculature—all operate in a complex and harmonious manner, so that thought, sensation, and physical sound are blended and made one in clear and expressive speech.

2. *Ideo-motor responsiveness* is the old phrase for an ever-present tendency to imitate an object or a motion in nature by means of hand gesture or facial mimicry or bodily pantomime. In children's apishness and in savages' "monkey-shines" or again in students' parrot like responses (psittachism), one perceives definite proofs of this universal trait in man-

[4] See Louis H. Gray, *Foundations of Language* (New York: The Macmillan Co., 1939), chapter IV, pp. 88-93.
[5] Isaac Goldberg, *The Wonder of Words* (New York: D. Appleton-Century Co., 1938), p. 29.
[6] A thought provoking discussion of these and kindred problems is admirably presented in the well known monograph by Grace de Laguna, *Speech—Its Function and Development* (New Haven: Yale University Press, 1927), pp. 47-52.

kind. Even in "sophisticated" concert and theater goers one may witness minimal responses which mimic the song performed or the dialogue spoken. The power of cadenced sound and rhythmical motion is well nigh irresistible to young and old, innocent and worldly wise alike.

3. *Conditioning of reflex action* is certainly one of the central aspects of the power which language wields. It goes deeper into the neurological mechanism of the individual than the preceding influence. Depending upon the volume (loudness or softness), pitch (deep or high tones on the musical scale), quality (smooth, orotund, harsh, etc.), tempo (fast, slow, jerky), and their several combinations, various immediate reflexive actions are within the province of predictability. Thus the phrase "help . . . help!" screamed in ascending pitch and volume has an almost instantaneous effect on the listener.

4. The so-called *gregarious impulse* observed in animals and in human beings provides another cause for the magic attributes of speech. Since we are made alike and function in relatively similar behavior patterns, we come together for mutual protection and comfort, and the soul-satisfying warmth that springs from verbal intercourse. In the interest of life and livelihood, we throw out linguistic antennae when we inconsequentially talk of the weather or the crops, of the folks back home or the high price of butter and eggs. Idle palaver among neighbors, the witty banter among young sophisticates, or just spontaneous overflow of animal spirits in nonsensical prattle or *echolalia* in children and childish elders, all serve the same biological end of preservation.[7]

5. *The emphatic approach* is closely related to the gregarious and the imitative impulses. It means that any normal person tries both instinctively and with complete awareness to become like an object or happening which impresses him greatly. Great actors have a special gift in making their voices *pro*ject the sensation which has been *in*jected into them by the forceful impression of persons and events. Lionel Barrymore put this power into the one word "oil" (reference is here made to the early part-"talkie" film "The Lion and the Mouse"), by the soft spreading and closing of his lips and the soft throaty sound of the word.

6. *The wonder of frozen speech*, that is writing, draws into itself some portion of all the powers and influences of speech. What the written record loses in vital immediacy, it gains in fixity and finality. For the unsung inventors of writing before historic time were already accustomed to the magical potency of words, thanks to the intervention of sorcery and priest-craft. To this very day, the printed or linotyped

---

[7] This general phenomenon has been termed "phatic communion" by the late Dr. Isaac Goldberg; but consult particularly Bronislaw Malinowski, "The Problem of Meaning in Primitive Languages," in Ogden and Richards, *The Meaning of Meaning* (New York: Harcourt, Brace and Co., 1938), pp. 313-316.

message exerts a compelling influence over the bulk of mankind, which indicates one reason behind propaganda devices, especially in the way of posters, pamphlets, leaflets, and other public means of spreading manipulated news.

Frozen Speech

For the inquiring mind of primitive beings, speech was not enough. Group experience and group will were twisted to a sharp focus by what the old men of the tribe told, or what witch doctors and precentors chanted. But, oral tradition was not enough. It was too unstable and too momentary in its passage. The whirlwind of disaster could blow it all away.

From the time that prehistoric man invented crude symbols which he scratched on bark or papyrus (*ca.* 7000 years ago), or cut in stone or ivory (at least 25,000 years before Christ) [8] he was able to remember definitely what agreement he had drawn up with his fellows, for the record of lines or notches or tied knots showed up with "graphic" clarity. Thus the first writing was the symbolic sign on message or tally sticks, on Indian wampum belt, or Peruvian *quipu* (i.e. knotted rope), on Sumerian clay tablet. Together they form the *mnemonic systems* of writing in which the principle is that of sending a tangible and marked object as message. These were succeeded by the *pictographic systems*, as employed by the early Egyptians, the American Indians, and the Chinese. The principle was the still somewhat childlike one of sending a picture of a tangible object as message. A third step followed when the *ideographic systems* supplanted the older methods. As we look at the Chinese new character and at the Japanese and Cherokee syllabaries, we are confronted with stylized symbols of the pictures representing tangible objects. Finally (*ca.* 1500-1800 B.C.), the *phonetic systems* of the Proto-Semitic alphabet and Phoenician letters were adopted by the Greeks. Now, at last, after many trials and errors, man had devised a principle whereby the sound of the sign written down became the conveyed message. Writing was established for all the world to use as a dependable, quick, and time-conquering discovery.

Behind the huge crowds listening to radio broadcasts or watching the news reels, scrutinizing illuminated maps and scoreboards, or scanning the up to the minute teletyped "flash" stands mistily our prehistoric ancestor, the first talking animal. From the first phrase of warning in the primeval forest to the "extra" of the latest war bulletins, articulate pro-

---

[8] Standard works on the subject of writing are: Canon Isaac Taylor, *The Alphabet* (London: 1883); Edward Clodd, *The Story of the Alphabet* (New York: D. Appleton-Century Co., 1935); but consult also the recent study by Oscar Ogg, *An Alphabet Source Book* (New York: Harper and Brothers, 1940), pp. 51-77.

genitors have thrown between men the bridge of communication which spells the long story of civilizational advance, or—temporary debacle.

For the penalty of swift advance is severe. The abuse of language and the tragic errors attendant upon faulty and tricky word usage are legion. Hence, it is our duty to examine the dark as well as the bright aspects of language habits.

Life and Death of Words

While semantics deals strictly with the theory of meaning as applied to words, it has for long (*ca.* 1897—to the present) bent its efforts to the unraveling of the origin and development and decline of sense in words, following the tradition set by linguistics. As a matter of fact, some of the best semantic works are devoted to this phase exclusively.[9] The importance of such a procedure is that it inevitably illuminates the cultural life of mankind as well. Habits of mind, mores, customs of the country, occupations, inventions, pastimes, beliefs, fads, trends in trade and in government, and racial ethos are all reflected and indicated in the evolutions in words. For this reason, it will be admitted that the semanticist has forged a tool in word analysis which aids the historian and the social scientist materially in diagnosing the past and interpreting the present. Of special interest are the six major "laws," or working principles, which uncover the so-called life and death of words:

1. *Specialization* means over use of terms by a profession or trade with a consequent restriction of meaning. ("Meat"—AS. mete meant any kind of food, whereas now it has come to mean edible flesh). Words like "glass," "stone," "paper," liquor," "pipe," etc., retain the early general signification together with the one restricted by special trade use.

2. *Generalization* means expansion in the applicability of words. Lay persons find technical terms too difficult to manage, so they appropriate them for everyday use; hence, the original sharpness of designation is lost and the word is magnified in meaning. (For example, "disaster"—L. dis astrum, which signified the baleful aspect of a planet or star. By a circuitous route it has developed the sense of any sudden misfortune.) Other instances of extension in meaning are: "butcher," "broker," "salary," "fee," "picture," "virtue," to "throw," etc.

3. *Deterioration* implies a reluctance on the part of people to use a direct expression for an unpleasant object or situation. In this category belong names and idioms which stand for physical actions (*e.g.*, death is

---

[9] For reference to the history of linguistic science, see Otto Jespersen, *Language— Its Nature, Development, and Origin* (New York: Henry Holt and Co., 1922) pp. 19-99. For books on semantics consult the bibliography at the end of the chapter. Charles W. Morris, *Signs, Language and Behavior* (New York: Prentice-Hall, 1946), is an effort to work out a "theory of signs," which he calls a science of "semiotic."

refined into "demise," to eat becomes to "dine,"); pretty sayings or "euphemisms" are likewise applied to unattractive bodily traits, such as "pleasingly plump" for "fat" or "exquisitely svelte" for "hideously scrawny."

4. *Elevation* is occasioned by a contrary trend. It is engendered by a desire for vivid and compelling utterance. Concretely, this vivid use of language tends to adopt slang and colloquial speech into more cultivated usage. In consequence, the practice has led to an elevation or lifting of words in the strictly social sense, but with an inevitable weakening of the intrinsic intent of the words. In general, violent expressions and profanity and the lingo of the underworld belong here. (*E.g.* "gore," "guts," "sweat," "stink"; "damn," "Gawd," "nuts"; "broad," "big shot," "wolf," "wing ding," "hot seat."

5. *Analogy* or metaphor introduces the poetic use of words. Basically, this principle consists in the ability to see similarities in the attributes and relations of dissimilar objects or situations. There is above all the analogy with organismic parts, such as "head," "foot," "arm," "hand," "body," "heart," "knee," "eye," etc. The symbolical use of names for colors or for animals is almost inexhaustible.

6. *Folk etymology* points to the liberty which the masses take with words they little understand, but which they appropriate and recklessly change according to some vague linguistic notions of their own. Usually, folk etymology proceeds on the principle that words which sound alike must be alike in meaning and in origin; which does not necessarily follow. (*E.g.* pent house, Fr. appentis, means a roof over an out-of-door staircase.) It was changed by popular will into pent-house a "lean-to," and in modern times it designates a skyscraper apartment.

Language as an Implement of Social Pressure

Mechanization of the Means of Communication. A disturbing result arising from the mechanization of the means of communication is the mental effect on spectator and auditor alike. The unpleasant truth is that the greater portion of readers and listeners and beholders are suffering from semantic illiteracy.[10] Because of the immense and badly controlled power of machines over their creators, the multitudes have been reduced to a state of unquestioning and uncritical acceptance of whatever message is promulgated. An attitude of passivity has been engendered through

---

[10] The best book the writer has come across on this subject is Professor H. R. Huse's *The Illiteracy of the Literate* (New York: D. Appleton-Century Co., 1933); but consult a valuable chapter in Hugh Walpole's *Semantics* (New York: W. W. Norton, 1941), chapter 10, "Intensive Reading." Look up also the stimulating "Appendix" in Stuart Chase's *The Tyranny of Words* (New York: Harcourt, Brace and Co., 1938), pp. 363-384, in which he takes even himself to task for semantic illiteracy.

the multiple onslaught on the "public at large" by these mechanical con-trivances. Press, radio, cinema, loud speaker, teletype, and "look-see" magazines have ringed us around and bombarded us with slanted news "angles." Other publicity agencies like billboards, street car "ads," neon signs, posters, sky writing, illuminated maps, displays, "blurbs," world premiers serve us almost equally well. Millions of ears have been glued to receiving sets and millions of eyes riveted to the printed page, a phe-nomenon of which those in power are not unaware.

Small is the wonder, therefore, that the senses of modern men and women are flooded with "sound and fury signifying nothing"; or worse yet, with a concealed and sinister meaning. A mood of passive acquies-cence is instilled which by subtle degrees eventuates in an unreflective mentality. The volume and speed of disseminated news or entertainment or incidental propaganda have seen to that. But from uncritical reception there is but a hair's breadth to credulity and suggestibility. From sug-gestibility to the plane of predictable action the line of division is even finer.

The testimony of teachers, parents, technical experts, lawyers, scientists, and business executives would tend to prove that the arts of reading understandingly, writing effectively, and listening critically have all been seriously affected by the wholesale mechanization of education. The educator is not to be pilloried here as the culprit. He has striven valiantly to meet new social and industrial demands without sacrificing his educa-tional standards. He has of late gone further by going back to older "ideals" of teaching, as evidenced by the relatively recent movement back to the fundamentals of learning by drill and by rote and by sweat of the brow.[11]

Semantic Fallacies. Here it may be fitting to point out how semantics has come to the rescue. With its fine scalpel of discernment, it has cut away moribund tissue and laid open layers of mental fat which obstruct quick and adequate thought. For, while the semantic fallacies expose egre-gious blunders, they indicate by the same token remedial exercises. A fairly conventional list of fallacies would include the following:

1. *Identification,* which is the semantic fallacy of identifying word with thing; to believe that the word is the object. To call anyone a "moron" and to believe, without further analysis or investigation that this is so completely, is to be semantically in error.

2. *Abstraction* stands for the semantic fallacy of using abstract terms without full knowledge of the meaning or the level of abstraction in-volved. (Watch out for many words and phrases bandied about today;

---

[11] An authoritative exposition of educational trends is to be found in this volume in chapter IX, "Education."

e.g. "Aryan race," "European situation," "Pan-American solidarity," "principle of indeterminacy" and "integrated curriculum.")

3. *Confusion* is particularly one in which levels of reality are substituted for one another. Reality, or external nature, supposedly, is built up as a structure consisting of planes or levels of existence of increasing complexity. Now, Korzybski affirms that language must, in its structure, accommodate itself to the "structure of reality" as "described by the sciences."[12] But language is made by men who are mostly sentimentalists and dreamers, rapacious brigands, and biological creatures as well. The poetic and suggestive power of descriptive language—as in Milton, Dante, Goethe, Lucretius, Shakespeare, Cervantes—has not been considered, nor has man, himself, been sufficiently comprehended, I think.

4. *Nonreference* or vagueness of application means simply the absence or lack of the so-called *"what-when-where"* specification. In connection with nonreference, Dr. Bridgman of Harvard holds that we need "a far-reaching change in all our habits of thought, in that we shall no longer permit ourselves to use as tools in our thinking, concepts of which we cannot give an adequate account in terms of operations."[13]

5. *The two-valued orientation* signifies the fallacy of thinking in pairs of opposites from the basis of a single motive.[14] (*E.g.* "progressive—conservative," "Americanism—Fascism," "radical—liberal," "patriot—collaborator," etc. *ad infinitum*.)

6. *Suggestion and affective communication.* Of the two very similar fallacies, suggestion or "intentional orientation" includes the seven main tricks of propaganda technique. It works by indirection in that the intent behind the words used is concealed. It employs devices which exert a powerful influence by means of popular appeals. Strong feelings are aroused in favor or in disfavor of a subject presented.[15] Affective communication, or the use of emotionally keyed words, speaks for itself. By emotion-freighted *cliches* like "home," "mother," "native land," "soldier boy," "warmonger," "bloated capitalist," (the supply is endless), the unwary are trapped and ensnared by their all-too-human warmth. If the voice is raised in pitch and the volume increased and violent gestures are added, the effect will be proportionately enhanced. Speakers or, rather, shouters like Hitler and Goering were clear cut exemplars of affective communication at its perfidious worst.

---

[12] Alfred Korzybski, *Science and Sanity* (Lancaster, Pa.: Science Press, 1942), see Introduction, p. v.

[13] P. W. Bridgman, *The Logic of Modern Physics* (New York: The Macmillan Co., 1932), p. 31, and chapters I, II, and part of III.

[14] S. I. Hayakawa, *Language in Action* (New York: Harcourt, Brace and Co., 1941), pp. 125-141. A thorough and readable account.

[15] Refer to chapter XXIV on "Propaganda" for a full treatment of this important aspect of language control.

Semantics as Instrument of Cultural Advancement

At this stage one may ask: "In what positive ways may the revived study of semantics serve mankind today?" Up to very recently, the emphasis lay almost wholly on the analytical and critical sides. What creative as well as critical tasks can and are being undertaken?

First in radical and rudimentary service come the varied *semantic devices*, some of which were treated under "Semantic Fallacies." Here belong Ogden and Richard's *triangle of language symbolism* and Korzybski's *ladder* of the "structural differential." *Schematic notation*, another semantic device, follows the pattern set first by symbolic writing. Rudolph von Laban's and Vaslav Nijinsky's choreographic systems fit into this category. So also would Dr. Otto Neurath's *isotypic symbolism*. This latter invention is a new picture language which at a glance acquaints the reader with a world of facts. The method is simple. By printing small picture replicas of the object represented and having each copy stand for a certain number or trend or relationship, a mass of information can be "got across" in a short time. By the addition of color, statistical scales, dates, and outline maps, the author has blazed a trail of clear and accelerated reading which keeps step with the swift tempo of the twentieth century. The well-known series, *Headline Books,* has adopted this method founded upon the iso-type.[16]

Next in line is the *emendation of the alphabet*. Through the intermediary stage of international phonetic symbols, which is now pretty well established in all standard dictionaries, the alphabet must inevitably undergo further simplification. Whether it becomes known as the "phonobet" or something equivalent, makes little difference, so long as it approaches its ultimate goal of accurate reproduction of speech in the principle of *"sound-writing."* We shall read with greater facility and with less confusion if this accurate mode of writing is someday adopted all over the globe. Romanization (turning alien character into Roman type) has been going on in the Far East for decades. (The Japanese have the word "romajikai" to designate this phenomenon.)

But what of a *universal language* to simplify further the effort of coming to a mutual and accurate understanding? How much vexation of spirit and belligerency in action could be eliminated if people talked the same language and—with the same intent? To satisfy such a wish, artificial languages have been compounded, like Volapük, Esperanto, Novial, Occidental and many more; but with little success. Instead, living languages like Spanish and English have spread widely with the growth of commercial enterprises. Out of this situation has grown the attempt of

---

[16] Otto Neurath, *Modern Man in the Making* (New York: Alfred A. Knopf, 1939), pp. 7, 8, 13; 14-17; 24-33; 45-62.

Professor C. K. Ogden to simplify and clarify the King's English into *Basic English*. By stripping English down to 850 words, subdivided into three categories of *things* (600 nouns), *qualities* (150 adjectives), and *operations* (100 verbs), Professor Ogden hopes to obtain a twofold objective; "to serve as an international, auxiliary language . . . for use throughout the world in general communication, commerce, and science," and "to provide a rational introduction to English." [17] In other words, the emphasis is purely utilitarian. Still it is not proved that this diversified human race can be made to speak the same language.

Another series of benefits accruing can be subsumed under the general heading of *techniques of critical acumen*. Among these are well established disciplines which have gained a new lease on life, and several "brand" new ones:

1. *Thinking as critical discernment* is bound to become more orderly, accurate, and valid because of the imposition of objectivity and relevancy as new criteria of evaluation. These are the so-called "canons of symbolism" that have dictated a new strictness of interpretation which makes thinking, even scientific thought, more exact in its handling of verbal and technical symbols. Critical thinking will also involve a stiff course in detecting logical and semantic fallacies.

2. *Reading understandingly* as a sharpened technique will grow in a threefold manner. Intellectually, readers will search out and connect the meaning of the words read, besides pursuing the logic of paragraph structure; esthetically, they will sense the *depth* of emotion and imaginative meaning and values conveyed by the sound, the rhythm, the suggestive power of the words; intuitively, they will gain an *insight* into the purpose or motive or basic idea or essential quality of the reading as a whole.[18]

3. *The art of listening*, long neglected, cannot but reap the benefits of straight thinking and the general semantic scrutiny of words in their uttered context. The listening situation must be appraised as well as the kind of a person who is doing the talking and the specific occasion for the talk. Questions of a critical nature would interpose themselves in the listener's mind: "What is he talking about? Is his purpose legitimate and warranted by the facts submitted and by facts ascertainable? Does his emotion color his talk, or cause him to resort to logical tricks?"

4. *The art of talking*, whether conversationally or in formal address to an audience, should profit in general intelligibility and effectiveness. The speaker will learn to be ever mindful of the varied uses of words—

---

[17] C. K. Ogden, *Basic English* (New York: Harcourt, Brace and Co., 1934), pp. 3, 4.
[18] For an elaborate scheme of definition and interpretation, see Hugh Walpole's *Semantics* (New York: W. W. Norton and Co., 1941), pp. 128-136; consult also chapter V, "Contexts."

phatic communion, factual presentation, poetic suggestiveness, scientifi-cally valid abstraction, or legitimate affective communication. He will remember that words are phonetic symbols which point, or should be made to point, to a verifiable reality either of "fact or fancy."

5. *The art of writing,* will exhibit the same earmarks of communica-tiveness to an even higher degree. Obviously, the writer has both the time and the means (revision, conference, research, and the consulting of dictionaries, manuals and encyclopedias) to be even more exacting with himself than has the speaker who does not read his address.

6. *Propaganda immunity* is a consequence of enormous significance.[19] One wonders what opportunities the allied victory and a just and un-vindictive peace will provide for our language and idea experts? Perhaps, these six itemized gains may not be too much to expect:

   I. More adequate and less partial diffusion of information—from critically tested sources.

   II. The continuance of free speech; not unlicensed utterance.

   III. The further freeing of the press from economic or political pres-sure groups and the right to publish unpopular facts and ideas which are corrective and remedial in nature. (This applies to other agencies of communication, such as the radio, the movies, advertising, etc.) [20]

   IV. A widespread emphasis upon the education of children and adults in the methods of critical thought.

   V. Increased opportunity to study the devious ways of propaganda technique. A careful survey must be made to uncloak any ex-ample of propaganda analysis which itself is definitely slanted left or right.

7. The revived study of the so-called *"humanities"* [21] brings out the basic contention that the individual man has worth and dignity and ca-pacity for development, and that he is not a machine but an organism; that he dies under slavery but thrives under freedom. This tradition provides a perspective necessary in our troubled era.

World Peace and the International Use of Words

A last word about tomorrow's need for the clarity which semantics is able to insure. At the peace table, at the meetings of the UNO and of "The Big Three" specifically, language experts in full cooperation with

---

[19] Refer to chapter XXIV for a more detailed analysis.
[20] Consult chapters XXIII-XXVII.
[21] Patricia Beesley, *The Revival of the Humanities* (New York: Columbia Univer-sity Press, 1940). This is a standard work of reference. Reference must likewise be made to T. M. Greene, *The Meaning of the Humanities* (Princeton: Princeton Uni-versity Press, 1938).

able and carefully trained semanticists should continue to be present in order to break down diplomatic cant and political nomenclature into simple and understandable prose. The multi-lingual situation at future international conferences will require that accurate translation of terms from one idiom to another be assured. The difficulties are myriad. A record has, however, been made of some of the reasons for either success or failure.

Summary

In the final analysis, words can be made to mean what they are intended to mean. They can be made to refer to inanimate objects, to living persons, to actual happenings. They can be made to travel from speaking mouth to listening ear or from printed page to perceiving eye without distortion of meaning. Words, rightly used, can help the individual to become articulate and unafraid. They can serve the interests of the family, the neighborhood, the community, the nation, as well as the "brotherhood of nations," without hurt or malice toward anyone.

Some day, it may not be idle to speculate nor foolish to anticipate that the world's emissaries will meet and talk and understand each other and thus be aided toward world amity and enduring peace. If and when that miracle occurs, man will have at long last surrendered his animalistic heritage and entered into the full stature of his essential humanity. He shall some day think and speak better and more truly. This, too, can help to make him free and at peace with his neighbor and himself.

QUESTIONS

1. How is semantics related to the theory of knowledge?
2. Name the first system of writing.
3. Define semantics.
4. Why is the study of the history of words important from a social standpoint?
5. What is meant by specialization in terms of semantics?
6. Name the six principles used in the study of the history of words.
7. Define semantic illiteracy.
8. How have modern methods of communication affected the educational system?
9. What was the original field of concern of the science of semantics?
10. What attempts have been made to establish a universal language?
11. Show how the fallacy of suggestion includes the basic tricks of the propagandist.
12. By what means are words used as instruments of social pressure?
13. How is the gregarious expressed in human speech?
14. What is meant by the term "frozen speech"?
15. How is the term "deterioration" applied to the study of words?
16. What creative tasks are being undertaken by semanticists?
17. Show in what way phrases like "containment policy," "loyalty oath," "cold war," are signs of the times.

SUGGESTED TOPICS FOR TERM PAPERS AND FURTHER RESEARCH

1. Make a study of the semantic illiteracy of an advanced community.
2. Make a study of the connotation of certain words as compared with that of the same words twenty years ago.
3. Make a comparative study of the various theories of the origin of speech.
4. Make a study of the various suggestions for a universal language.
5. Compare the rise of the English language as the "diplomatic language" with the decline of the prevalence of French for the same purposes.
6. Follow the evolution of American slang with the definite intent of revealing certain intercultural traits and "homespun" social customs. (H. L. Mencken's classic treatise *The American Language* will prove invaluable.)
7. Study the theories relating to the importance of a universal language in preserving world peace.
8. Study the use of semantics by a recent totalitarian power.

BIBLIOGRAPHY

Books

Max Black, *Language and Philosophy* (Ithaca, N.Y.: Cornell University Press, 1949). Ideas on the philosophy of language from leading semanticists presented in a clear and coherent manner.

Frederick Bodmer, *The Loom of Language* (New York: W. W. Norton and Co., 1944). A good comparative study of language and languages.

Kenneth Burke, *The Grammar of Motives* (New York: Prentice-Hall, 1945). A recent study devoted to the semantic analysis of intentional meaning.

Stuart Chase, *The Tyranny of Words* (New York: Harcourt, Brace and Co., 1938). An unusually gifted layman's survey of the field. Vigorous, individual, and honest in handling; practical consequences of semantic illiteracy copiously exemplified.

Macdonald Critchley, *The Language of Gesture* (London: Edward Arnold and Co., 1937). An introduction to the study of language.

David Diringer, *The Alphabet, A Key to the History of Mankind* (New York: Philosophical Library, 1949). "A worthy successor to Isaac Taylor" in the vast field of symbolic writing systems, preceding and including the emergence of the Greco-Roman alphabets. Learned, stimulating treatment with excellent illustrations.

Isaac Goldberg, *The Wonder of Words* (New York: D. Appleton-Century Co., 1938). A wisely human and readable work on most phases of linguistics and semantics. Probably the best in the field.

J. C. Hixson and I. Colodny, *Word Ways* (New York: American Book Co., 1939). Perhaps the best book on the semantic aspect of word development. Excellent also for vocabulary building.

H. R. Huse, *The Illiteracy of the Literate* (New York: D. Appleton-Century Co., 1933). Professor Huse approaches semantic illiteracy from the linguistic and literary points of view. Humorous and sensible in treatment.

Paul Keczkemeti, *Meaning, Communication, and Value* (Chicago: University of Chicago Press, 1952). An attempt to show that problems of meaning, not reducible to formal logic and to empirical fact-finding, are nevertheless amenable to rational analysis, and that such an analysis is indispensable to a well-rounded philosophy.

Alfred Korzybski, *Science and Sanity* (Lancaster, Pa.: Science Press, 1951). Quite influential treatise on the scientific bearing of semantics.

Irving J. Lee, *How to Talk to People* (New York: Harper and Brothers, 1952). A simple and practical statement of causes for misunderstanding and the breakdown of communications as well as specific suggestions for improvement.

—— *Language Habits in Human Affairs* (New York: Harper and Brothers, 1941). Considerable experience with life situations has gone into the making of this little volume. Korzybski has written a well-deserved commendation of the book in the foreword.

C. K. Ogden and L. R. Richards, *The Meaning of Meaning* (New York: Harcourt, Brace and Co., 1938). One of the early and original books on semantics. Difficult; hence not recommended for beginners.

Oscar Ogg, *An Alphabet Source Book* (New York: Harper and Brothers, 1940). An up-to-date discussion of the historic developments of writing systems from the mnemonic to the alphabetical phase.

Sir Richard Paget, *Human Speech* (New York: Harcourt, Brace and Co., 1930). A great treatise, based on original experiments that have thrown new light on the orgin, nature, purpose, and possible improvement of human speech.

G. S. Pettee, "Politics and Semantics," Chapter XVI, pp. 337-353, in Joseph S. Roucek, ed., *20th Century Political Thought* (New York: Philosophical Library, 1946). An excellent survey of the relationship of semantics to politics.

Anatole Rapaport, *Science and the Goals of Man* (New York: Harper and Brothers, 1950). A book on "semantic orientation," dealing provocatively with scientists and values in the contemporary world.

J. Ruesch and G. Bateson, *Communication* (New York: W. W. Norton and Co., 1951). Contains a recent emphasis on the so-called "social matrix of psychiatry," and the conventions, values, and techniques of communication.

V. Selby, *What is Meaning?* (New York: The Macmillan Co., 1903). The first book in English to present the subjects of "signifies" or semantics in a very simple and straightforward manner.

Hugh Walpole, *Semantics* (New York: W. W. Norton and Co. 1941). A simplified account in the tradition of Ogden and Richards, with much new material and original analytical ability. Section on "definitions" is a real contribution.

Ernest Weekly, *Words and Names* (New York: E. P. Dutton and Co., 1932). An absorbing work on the history of place names by the greatest authority in English. Many other volumes.

Periodicals

Kenneth Burke, "Semantic and Poetic Meaning," *Southern Review* (1939).

E. Evans, "Notes on the Symbolic Process," *Mind*, LX (January, 1951), pp. 62-79.

L. Glicksberg, "Methodology in Semantics as Applied to English," *School Review*, LIII (November, 1945), pp. 546-553.

Jerom C. Hixson, "Our Living and Dead Languages," *Words*, III (October, 1937).

G. W. Kischer, "Linguistic and Semantic Factors in the Psychodynamics of War," *Journal of Social Psychology*, XVII (1943), pp. 69-73.

Alfred McClung Lee, "The Analysis of Propaganda: A Clinical Summary," *American Journal of Sociology*, LI (1945-1946), pp. 126-135; "The Press in the Control of Intergroup Tensions," *The Annals of The American Academy of Political and Social Science*, CXLIV (March, 1946), pp. 144-151.

G. A. Lundberg, "Semantics and the Value Problem," *Social Forces*, XXVII (October, 1948), pp. 114-117.

D. V. McGranaham, "The Psychology of Language," *Psychological Bulletin*, XXXIII (1936), pp. 178-216.

R. McKeon, "Semantics, Science, and Poetry," *Modern Philology*, XLIV (February, 1952), pp. 145-159.

O. H. P. Pepper, "Babel in Medicine," *American Philosophical Society Proceedings*, XCIV (1950), pp. 364-368.

M. Schlauch, "Words—Their Rise and Fall," *Scientific Digest,* XII (August, 1943), pp. 83-86.

C. K. Wright, "Import and Importance of Words," *19th Century,* CXXXVI (December, 1944), pp. 269-273.

CHAPTER XV

Art and Literature

To consider art in all its phases would be equivalent to studying the whole of civilization.[1] Even in the narrowly restricted way in which we here use the term, it must include sculpture, painting, drawing, architecture, certain phases of pottery, weaving, metal work, and even such things as horticulture and dress designing. Another expression of art is found in music and dance. The term literature is equally broad, but will be used in its commonly accepted meaning as comprising poetry, drama, and fiction—particularly those forms which make an appeal to the emotions.[2] We shall attempt to limit the field still more by ruling out the use of art and literature in advertisements, political speeches, and what we ordinarily term propaganda, although it is not always possible to keep from straying slightly within the borders of these fields.

Illusive Nature of Influence

Perhaps the most tenuous and illusive of all sociological data are those which deal with art and literature. Yet these two have ever been present at the scientist's elbow, not only receiving but in turn exercising a powerful but often unsuspected influence in many ways.

Social Sciences and the Arts. The social sciences in particular are closely tied up with the arts. This is true not only with respect to subject matter but in the types of mind or personality which are active in the two fields. In the pioneer days of sociology, Lester F. Ward noted that persons with artistic insight quite often turned their attention to social phenomena, especially social betterment or reform.[3] His explanation was that the true artist is fitted by training and disposition to observe defects and also conceive of ideals, and it is quite natural that he should exercise his gift in the field of social control. As examples he names Ruskin, William Morris, Edward Bellamy, Victor Hugo, Tolstoi, Wagner, Millet, Swinburne and George Eliot. He could have expanded this field widely. Such in-

---

[1] Irwin Edman, *Encyclopedia of Social Sciences*, II, p. 223.
[2] C. T. Winchester, *Some Principles of Literary Criticism* (New York: The Macmillan Co., 1908), chapter II.
[3] L. F. Ward, *Pure Sociology* (New York: The Macmillan Co., 1911), p. 83.

stances are not at all uncommon today and, as we shall see later, it is generally accepted that the artist is an exceptional agent of civilization. Edman accepts Shelley's statement that the poet is the "unacknowledged legislator of the world" and states that the fixed regimes of totalitarian countries have been wise in their way to exercise stringent control over the literary arts.[4] Others have pointed out that we must have poets, artists, and prophets to give us a sense of values, and some have even stated that the poet has a grasp of eternal truth which all can see after it has been shown them.[5]

While it is easy to see the close relationship between art and social control, it is frequently difficult or impossible to decide which is cause and which is effect. The predominance of religion in the Middle Ages was related to the magnificent churches and cathedrals, but to what extent each was cause and effect we cannot say. Similarly, the jitterbug music of today is all at one with much of our social life, but which is the deep-dyed villain and which is the suffering victim is quite a puzzle.

Techniques of Art and Literature

Changing Techniques of Art. The field of art is very broad and the techniques of the artist are multitudinous, changing through the ages with new discoveries and inventions. Even in the Paleolithic Age, quite a variety of media were employed. Hematite and other minerals were ground to powder and mixed with soot and animal fats to produce various colors, mostly limited to the reds, browns, and yellows. Hollow bones, still containing remnants of these paints show us how these early men carried their pigments. Lacking canvas or smoothed wood, the cave walls sufficed for their pictures, although they may have painted on skins. In addition to their painting, these Paleolithic artists carved life-like figures in stone, bone, and ivory, and possibly wood, using tools of obsidian and flint.

With the advent of the Neolithic, pottery became available, and this added a new medium which could be utilized in many ways. Its descendants in the form of china, porcelain, tile, and glass are a great domain of modern art. Preliterate tribes employed all the techniques of the Stone Age man and added many others. American Indians used many vegetable substances in obtaining colors for dyeing and painting. They also achieved artistic effects by mosaics of brilliantly colored feathers and by beads made of porcupine quills, shells, seeds, and other materials.

Modern artists use practically every known substance either for a surface on which to execute their work or for the material for their

[4] Irwin Edman, *Encyclopedia of the Social Sciences*, II, p. 224.
[5] Helen Everett, *Encyclopedia of Social Sciences*, IV, p. 348.

colors. The colors themselves are used as liquids, gums, and dry powders and are mixed with everything from water to heavy oils or egg albumin. Each material calls for special tools and techniques, each is peculiarly fitted for certain purposes, such as murals, portraits, or landscapes, and each in the hands of an artist produces a particular effect.[6]

Methods. In addition to the techniques of materials and tools, there are special methods by which the artist seeks to achieve the effects which he desires. Hue, tint, and saturation of color each has its own significance. The truly proficient artist must possess quite a knowledge of both physics and psychology. There are some principles which are probably universally accepted and employed by all artists and it is interesting to note that even the Paleolithic artists made use of them. One of these is to portray only a portion of what is represented and to suggest the remainder. Various feelings and attitudes may also be secured by the selection of colors, forms, and combinations. Orange, for example, is associated with warmth while blue and purple express quite the opposite.

Aside from these commonly accepted techniques of composition, balance, use of color, etc., there are many practices on which artists differ. Some insist that the most pleasing proportion of an object is found when the width bears the same relation to the length that the length does to the width and length combined. It is also contended that horizontal lines suggest repose, vertical lines, aspiration, and diagonal lines give the effect of strain or effort. Other artists deny these statements, and similar controversies rage around other such theories.

Literature and Music. The same uncertainties exist in the fields of literature and music. It is true that there has long existed a body of accepted principles by which poets and other writers have striven to secure effects. Sentences were balanced, repetition of the same sounds was avoided, the liquid consonants and open vowels were used to express ease and pleasure while the thinner and more closed letters expressed strain or distress. But all these practices are being discarded by the modernists. It is true that critics speak of "good" literature and "bad" but the same critic will acknowledge that the best authorities differ greatly in their evaluations.[7] About all the critic can say with any great degree of assurance is that some pieces of literature possess an indefinable quality which makes them live through the ages.

Music Techniques. The techniques in the production of music are as multitudinous as are those in painting and sculpture. There are the estab-

---

[6] Theodore M. Greene, *The Arts and the Art of Criticism* (Princeton: Princeton University Press, 1940), chapter V, *et passim;* A. P. McMahon, *The Art of Enjoying Art* (New York: Whittlesey House, 1938), chapter III.

[7] C. T. Winchester, *op. cit.,* p. 19.

lished techniques in the use of tone, combination, and rhythm. A few simple principles can be appreciated by the layman. Gradually expanding notes—i.e., notes which grow farther and farther apart—give an impression of power or majesty. A splendid example of this is heard in the old hymn, "A Mighty Fortress Is Our God." But we soon run into newly-born controversies. Even the generally accepted practice of using minors to express sadness or longing and majors to picture joy and exuberance has been shown in an unpublished psychological study to be questionable.

The Relation of Art to National or Tribal Life

The Degree of Civilization and Arts. Always there has been the closest relationship between the art of a period and the tribal or national life. W. M. F. Petrie says this relationship is so close that one may judge the degree of civilization of any specified time by an examination of its art.[8] He traced the civilization of Egypt back through the Neolithic Age and recorded several waves of high culture interspersed with deep troughs of barbarism or savagery. During the cruder periods, the art was simple, strong, and characterized by a certain dignity. As civilization progressed it became more ornate up to a certain stage at which the artists began to copy old forms instead of developing something new. Just here, says Petrie, the civilization began to deteriorate and the process was paralleled by the constantly more degraded copies until art became formless and meaningless.

Petrie's statements have been justly criticised. Sorokin, for one, raises objection to his use of evidence.[9] But these criticisms seemingly do not destroy his central theory and it is quite possible that it holds true in some way even for modern times. There is considerable evidence to support it. Could we fully comprehend any such relationship as may exist, we would possess a key to interpret world trends. Then we could speak with some authority about the bewildering condition of our times and know whether we are facing a collapse of civilization or whether such a catastrophe has already occurred and we are fighting our way back. Certainly, it would be fascinating to know just what significance might be attached to the appearance of surrealism in art and literature. Anthropologists have pointed out that all types of artistic expression have been present among different races at varying times. Surrealism was in vogue in Peru long before Columbus was born. Perhaps someday we may know just what all this means.

---

[8] W. M. F. Petrie, *Revolutions of Civilization* (New York: Harper and Brothers, 1912).

[9] Pitirim A. Sorokin, *Social and Cultural Dynamics* (New York: American Book Co., 1937), vol. I, pp. 199-206.

Art in Prehistoric Times

As far back as we can trace human records we find elements of art. Flint chipping in the Solutrean phase of the Paleolithic Age attained a perfection which must be put on a level with the sculpture of Classical Greece. Yet such an ornately chipped knife would perform no whit better than one crudely made. The elaborate workmanship was for beauty, not utility. However, it was not beauty alone that prompted this work but a belief that some supernatural relationship was involved. In fact the likenesses on the walls of the caves—which authorities tell us compare favorably with anything which has been produced since—were a type of prayer. The likenesses of wild cattle, cave-bears, and other animals which were feared are scarred as if speared and beaten. Evidently, they have been treated much as the Indians used to maltreat a painted "war-post" or the modern football player treats a tackling dummy which wears a letter of his coming opponent. The burning or hanging of someone in effigy is psychologically akin. In Solutrian art the figures of horses are never mutilated, but they have pictures of human hands on them. These caressing hands were apparently benedictions. The horses were harmless and constituted their main source of food, so all their prayers were for their preservation but for the destruction of cattle and other dangerous animals.[10]

Those caves must have been the scenes of wild parties in those old days as the warriors danced and shouted and hurled their spears at the pictured beasts. Such prehistoric "pep meetings" worked the participants into a frenzy and from cowering frightened fugitives they must often have become wildly confident aggressors who charged out of the caves en masse to fall upon the threatening beasts and slay them in triumph. Many of their handprints show fingers missing, and these were probably chopped off in their frenzy as votive offerings.

Art and Literature in Early Greece

Recited rituals and chanted music leave no records such as chipped stone and painted walls do, so we can say nothing concerning the "literature" of those prehistoric days. But early in the infancy of historic time the musical or literary influence was definitely present. Blind old Homer may be a mythical character, but if so he is a character very true to type. In the days when there were no books, newspapers, radios, or magazines,

---

[10] Norbert Casteret, "Discovering the Oldest Statues in the World," *National Geographic Magazine* XLVI (August, 1924), pp. 123-152; H. F. Osborn, *Men of the Old Stone Age*, 3rd ed. (New York: Charles Scribner's Sons, 1936), chapter V; William J. Sollas, *Ancient Hunters and Their Modern Representatives* (London: The Macmillan Co., 1924), chapters VIII and XI.

the wandering bard was a mixture of historian, public lecturer, news monger, poet, dramatic leader, and musician. The attention and interest given to his recitals are almost inconceivable in these blasé days. It has been said that the listeners would hear just one recital and go away to repeat it word for word. We do not experience such interest today.

These songs or chants were full of racial lore, celebrating victories, enlarging on the exploits of heroes, and magnifying the greatness of the leaders. They recounted in detail the assistance given by the various deities or the punishments and vengeances meted out. It would not be too much to say that often the wandering bard was the principal agent in controlling the lives of the people. Without him there would have been no racial nor regional solidarity, no information on what was going on and no incentive to religious or patriotic ardor.

We do not have to delve into ancient records to find the wandering bard. Within this century it has been not uncommon for just such singers to roam over parts of the Balkans, not far from Homer's native land, and sing their recitals even as he did. Such minstrels have not entirely disappeared today.

Art and Literature Among the Ancient Hebrews

Some of these early peoples were keenly aware of the influence of art and took steps to guard against it. One of the basic laws of the Hebrews —the second commandment—was a prohibition against making "any likeness of any thing that is in heaven above; or that is in earth beneath; or that is in the water under the earth." However, according to the interpretation of the Hebrew scholars, it was allowable to put together pieces of tile, shell, or other such materials. Hence, we call these works "mosaics" because they were not prohibited by the Mosaic code. Considerably later, the Mohammedan Koran also prohibited the representation of any living thing, lest it should lead to idolatry. This accounts for the typical checked and grilled decorations in Mohammedan buildings.

The Hebrew prohibition seemingly did not apply to the decoration of their temple. This imposing structure of white stone contained many pictures and many likenesses in bronze. Whether the original writer saw what the effect would be or not, the result of the commandment was to prevent any copies of the altar or temple from being erected. (This was not entirely true, but no law is entirely effective.) Had each community been allowed to make an altar of its own, the people quite generally would have neglected to go to the great temple and would have been content to make their sacrifices and prayers at home. As a result, all national or racial solidarity would have declined and disappeared. As it was, a strong feeling of compulsion about attending the yearly ceremonies at the temple developed and this resulted in such a unified people that they have maintained their social solidarity to the present day.

The Influence of Pilgrimages. The power which these yearly pilgrimages had over the people can be appreciated only if we think of them in connection with Hebrew literature or poetry. Hebrew poetry was characterized by highly figurative expressions and the repetition of the thought in different words, as: "What is man that thou takest knowledge of him? or the son of man, that thou makest account of him?"

The yearly pilgrimage to Jerusalem was a great undertaking. Families with their children, elderly people, and some not too strong would walk or ride on donkeys for weeks. Many would get sick on the way and some of them would die. Some would be attacked by thieves and robbers. Footsore and weary, they would cheer each other on by singing the familiar songs. Once having arrived, the spectacle would be overwhelming to the wilderness dweller. Altogether the magnificence of the temple, the grandeur of the ceremonies, the rolling music of the psalms, and the excitement of the crowd affected these people so deeply that apparently nothing could break them. Even the Romans, whose name is practically synonymous with power and authority, never succeeded in making them forsake their ways. What a great difference in the history of the world a few statues and decorated altars scattered around Palestine might have made!

Art and Literature in Greek Life

The situation in other countries was not greatly different from that among the Hebrews in so far as the influence of art and literature was concerned, although different expressions were apparent. In great contrast to the Hebrews, the Greeks glorified art and all but worshiped it. It was a part of their educational system and their scholars constantly tried to understand and explain it. Plato and Aristotle both had much to say in this field although as in all cases their treatments differed. As usual Plato was the philosopher and Aristotle was the scientist.

Plato's Concepts. Rather surprisingly, Plato's most elaborate excursion into this field is in his *Republic*. We would hardly expect to find so much careful attention given to music and literature in this elaborately worked out analysis of what a perfect government ought to be. Unfortunately, we do not have Aristotle's complete treatment preserved. His *Poetics* may have been mere lecture notes or a preliminary outline. The fragments are sufficient however to give us some insight into the way he felt about these subjects.

Plato evidently thought literature was highly important. His rulers had to be given an elaborate literary education, beginning in their infancy.

Furthermore, not all literary geniuses would be allowed in the ideal state, but only those who picture—or what he calls "imitate"—those things which are worth incorporating into one's character. What one imitates or sees imitated settles into a second nature with him, hence there must be discrimination and choice. Poets must first of all be servants of the community. They have the gift of representing life in such a vivid way that it stimulates the imagination. To Plato, the bad poet was the one who would throw himself into any and every character. This type of poet is quite popular with children and slaves, but should not be allowed to live in an ideal state. Music is treated in a somewhat similar manner, and only the simplest musical instruments are allowed, such as the lyre or the cithara. More complex stringed instruments and the flute are forbidden. Similarly, the simple rhythms are praised and the more complex rhythms are outlawed. Strangely enough, Plato had little to say about sculpture, although we think of the Greeks as being sculptors first and musicians afterward.

Aristotle's Concepts. What fragments of Aristotle's work remain consist primarily of a scientific analysis of poetry and literature, but it may be seen that he also was concerned about the types of such material to which one might be exposed. His best known statement is that literature, music, and especially the drama have a "cathartic" value, or allow the release of pent up emotions through a kind of vicarious participation.

Plato's Value. Plato's discussion in particular is most suggestive and interesting. It is evident that he was disturbed about certain events which were occurring right before his eyes. Apparently new and novel types of music were becoming popular and it frightened him. He much preferred the simpler instruments and the music with which he was familiar. Likewise, new types of literature were coming into use and their popularity with the *hoi polloi* was disturbing. (The fact that he rather neglected sculpture was probably due to the fact that no such innovations were appearing in this field.)

Although Plato's words were written more than two thousand years ago, they have a remarkably modern sound. If we just changed a few names and expressions, his treatment could be passed off for a current magazine article. A short time ago the writer was seated next to the dean of a school of music at a student program. When a number of selections had been played on a xylophone, the dean said, "Isn't it too bad to expend so much time learning to play on that when it is not a legitimate instrument?" This could easily have been Plato objecting to the flute. Modern "jazz orchestras" or "swing bands" have given us much more complicated rhythms and have introduced a multitude of new so-called musical instruments—muted trumpets, crack-toned trombones, moaning saxophones, and a bewildering array of gadgets which the drummer uses. If Plato were here today he would say just what he did more than two thousand years ago, as in truth is being said by a goodly number today.

It is not at all certain that Plato and our modern dean are not correct. If everyone could be satisfied with the dignified minuet, the Wagnerian operas, and the fine old hymns, there would be little danger of society "going to the dogs." On the other hand, we might become fossils. The situation always has been just what it is today, a struggle between the conservative and the erratic. Perhaps the most healthful situation is a proper balance between the two.

Another suggestion which we receive from Plato's somewhat labored discussion and from Aristotle's interest is that art, literature, and music must have played quite a prominent role in those days. The fact that they were so concerned indicates that these influences were plainly evident and pronounced. We know from other sources that their expressions were abundant. Aeschylus is said to have written from seventy to ninety plays; Sophocles, one hundred twenty-three; Euripides, ninety-two; Choerilus, one hundred sixty. There were well over a thousand plays available in Aristotle's day, and some of these were given hundreds of times. It seems, too, that these dramas had more influence on the Greeks than they would have on a modern audience. It is said that the sight of the Furies prancing across the stage in their fearsome masks would cause boys and women to faint. It is probable that the fun which Aristophanes, in his plays, poked at the dishonest leaders had more effect than anything else which could have been done. Altogether, the stage was a mighty force in Grecian society.

Music and dancing were as greatly emphasized as the drama and the great emphasis on gymnastics and athletics was largely esthetic in nature. In the plastic arts, the still existing masterpieces of Greek statuary and architecture speak for themselves. It has been said, "The Greeks never quite grew up; the Romans always were men." This means among other things that the Greeks were predominantly artists and dramatists, whereas the Romans were business men and law-givers. It is an open question whether or not the Greek method of control was preferable. Judged by their fruits, it would be easy to choose the Greeks.

The Roman Scene

It would not be fair to say that the Romans lacked the feeling for art. Especially in their earlier history, they spent much of their energy in production of the beautiful and dramatic. But in the latter age, their activities fell on evil days and the popular taste sank to a demand for the coarse and the bizarre. It was at such a time that Roman leaders realized they could control the populace only by giving them "bread and circuses." The spectacle was quite different from that of classic Greece, or even from the early days of Rome, but the principle of control was essentially the same.

Any attempt to picture the role of art and literature in the Roman and Mediæval days would necessitate a complete history of those times. The cathedrals, monuments, paintings, and the masterpieces of sculpture speak eloquently of their own significance. The folk arts were developed far beyond what would naturally be expected in a time so intellectually retarded. The tedious, time-killing work of the monks in their monasteries had its own peculiar niche. Just as the work of the monks tells a story of *ennui* and idleness, so the productive art of the period speaks of leisure and unhurried calmness. Many years went into the painting of some of these pictures—and it can be seen, too, just as the lightning speed of some modern hurried, nervous illustrator is shown in every line of his product. Altogether the work of the monks, the folk arts of the people, the calm and leisurely work of the masters, and the construction of the cathedrals and churches united to give expression to the life of the period. While these forms of art were true products of the time, they were also influences in themselves and must be conceived as important factors of control in the lives of the people.

Art and Literature Among Preliterate Peoples

Art and even literature of a kind play quite as important a role among unlettered peoples as they do among European and Asiatic races. In fact, the less civilized groups pay correspondingly far more attention to artistic decoration than our highly industrialized countries. The Navajo and other Southwest Indians center their entire lives around their art as it finds expression in basketry, sand painting, woven blankets, silver jewelry, feather and bead work. It would be impossible for these people to have any sort of a religious ceremony or any social activity whatever without artistic expression. The Navajo religion, as nearly as the white man can understand it, is worship of sheer impersonal beauty.

So full of symbolism is much of this art that it can almost be said to be a form of literature. In the arid Southwest, practically every design is a prayer for rain. The zig-zag lightning flash, the piled up clouds, the mountain peaks, and the raindrops are repeated over and over again in a rich multitude of modifications. Among the Plains Indians quite definite historical pictured records were kept. Their famous "Winter Count" [11]

[11] James Mooney, "Calendar History of the Kiowa Indians," *Seventeenth Annual Report of the Bureau of American Ethnology*, Part I, pp. 141-468.

was such a record, painted on a buffalo skin. We find that art is utilized in many ways by all races.

Stories and songs have an important role in the lives of most tribes. They range all the way from simple or humorous stories told to children to elaborate recitals which are so sacred in nature that only certain specially qualified persons—a type of high priest as it were—may recite them. These songs, stories, and legends have an influence over these people which is much stronger than even statutory law in many cases among ourselves. A survey of African natives, of Australians, Philippine headhunters, peoples of the Pacific Islands, and all the nooks and corners of the world would disclose that their lives are colored, guided, and to a surprising degree controlled through their art and literature.

Art and Literature in Modern Times—Unplanned Influence

In modern times art and literature have exercised their control in a number of ways. Until quite recently, this influence has been unplanned and largely unconscious. Some instances have been spectacular. It is said that Burne-Jones changed the type of English womanhood. The women attempted to resemble his characteristic painted figures and by dress, diet, and carriage succeeded to quite a degree. Milton's *Paradise Lost* has had greater and farther reaching influence than is commonly known. The generally accepted ideas of heaven and hell are taken directly or indirectly from his description. There is really nothing in the Bible which even remotely warrants such concepts. There is some uncertainty as to the extent of Rousseau's influence, but he did much to hasten the French Revolution even if he did not actually bring it about.[12] Much the same may be said of *Uncle Tom's Cabin* and the War Between the States.[13] Apparently Dickens changed the entire school system of Britain by writing *David Copperfield, Nicholas Nickleby,* and others of his books.[14]

There are multitudes of minor and less spectacular instances which *in toto* may have had more effect than the more dramatic and less frequent cases. The dress and behavior of American women were greatly affected by the "Gibson Girl" and the paintings of Christie and other popular artists. Currently, George Petty is said to be setting the type for modern women. The familiar passages from Longfellow, Shakespeare, Riley, Edgar Guest, and other poets and "rhymesters" have made deep but usually unrecognized marks upon our characters. Cooper and other such writers have made the American Indian an important idol for Americans,

---

[12] Havelock Ellis, *From Rousseau to Proust* (Boston: Houghton Mifflin Co., 1935), chapter V.

[13] Forest Wilson, "The Book that Brewed a War," *Reader's Digest* XXXVIII (May, 1941), pp. 103-107.

[14] J. L. Hughes, *Dickens as an Educator* (New York: D. Appleton Co., 1903).

and our national and individual lives have been cast in large measure in the Indian pattern. Sad to relate, also, certain types of crime and detective stories have had their effects as well.

Planned Use of Art and Literature

Not all the influences of art and literature can be said to be unplanned. Both have always been used in a deliberate way, but this practice has become more commonplace of late.

There is no sharp break between the planned and the unplanned and in many instances the material is on the border line. Elizabeth Barrett Browning's *Bitter Cry of the Children* probably belongs here, as does Dickens's work and *Uncle Tom's Cabin*. But often the planning is extensive and deliberate. In various phases of education, systematic programs are carried out in which both art and literature are made the center of attention.

Folk Arts and Crafts. A notable example is the revival of the folk arts and crafts and the rejuvenation of folk music in mountainous and other isolated areas. The folk of the Southern mountains have been encouraged to make candlewick spreads, hooked rugs, split baskets, pottery, hand-woven blankets and coverlets, and many other artifacts. This movement is having a profound effect, not only upon these people but upon the country at large. Thousands of formerly isolated people are now going to school, reading papers, practicing soil conservation and improved farming, living under more healthful conditions, and taking far more active part in national and community affairs than any one would have imagined a few years ago.[15] One phase of this work is to encourage home talent plays, social dances and concerts. This part of the program is not confined to the mountainous areas but is widely scattered among rural communities. When we realize that in the region of Wisconsin and the Dakotas farmers drive for more than a hundred miles through weather below zero to attend such programs, we begin to appreciate the influence they are having.[16]

Writers and Artists in Social Control

Individual writers, without entering any such definite group, use their talents to produce similar results. Familiar examples are Poole, Sinclair

[15] Allen H. Eaton, *Handicrafts of the Southern Highlands* (New York: Russell Sage Foundation, 1932); E. R. Hamilton, "Bedspreads Are Big Business," *Christian Science Monitor* (March 15, 1941), pp. 5 ff.
[16] Marjorie Patten, *The Arts Workshops of Rural America* (New York: Columbia University Press, 1937), p. 25.

Lewis, and Upton Sinclair. Probably Upton Sinclair's novel, *The Jungle*
aided greatly in changing the Chicago packing houses from centers of
filth and infection to models of cleanliness and sanitation. Certainly it
was a factor in precipitating a congressional investigation, a widespread
wave of magazine discussion, and national excitement, following which
the packing houses emerged quite changed in character. His *The Brass
Check* probably has had great effects on the newspapers of the country.

It is evident that Ward's observation of the artist's disposition to become a reformer or, at least, an active participant in public affairs applies
today quite as much as, or more than, it ever did. Some of our literary
men have even forsaken their original field entirely to devote all their
energies to what they hope may be more productive lines. The feelings
of these men are given typical expression by George Soule. In one of his
books which he presented to the Literary Club of his alma mater he
placed this inscription: "From one who began by writing poetry—and
found it necessary to deal in economics, in an attempt to make a world
in which poetry might have a chance." The number of those who feel
this way is legion.

Of course, it is not to be supposed that every artist who turns social
reformer or politician will act wisely and constructively. All types of
results may be expected. World War I brought out a multitude of such
persons, ranging from the poet D'Annunzio to musician Paderewski. It
should not be forgotten that Mussolini was a violinist of note and both
Hitler and Winston Churchill were painters.

Many literary men refrain from leaving their fields of poetry, drama,
or fiction, but use these as media for expressing their attempts to bring
about social changes. This is so common that it is assumed by many to be
the only normal course to follow. It creates something of a mild shock
when one refrains from doing so.

Archibald MacLeish. A notable case is that of Archibald MacLeish who
became the center of quite a literary storm some years ago. MacLeish insisted that a poet's or artist's real job was to stick to his art and not attempt to use it for reform.[17] He did much writing on political and
economic questions, but treated them in essays and editorials and attempted to keep them out of his literary productions. When he produced
his play, *Panic*, the reviewers and commentators quite generally up-
braided him for being neutral between the employer and employees. He
replied to his critics in a series of articles and editorials; his critics replied
in turn, and for a while the tempest was felt not only by the writer's clan

---

[17] A. MacLeish, "Poetry and the Public World," *Atlantic Monthly*, CLXIII (June,
1939), pp. 823 and 830; A. MacLeish, "The Poetry of Karl Marx," *Saturday Review
of Literature*, X (February 17, 1934), pp. 485-486.

but by thousands of lay citizens as well. It seems as if MacLeish may have changed his mind slightly later on, but the question will always be one for argument.[18]

Literature as a Social Force. The amount of attention to such questions shows how important the controlling force of literature is considered. Other indications of this attitude crop up all around. It is significant that Diego Rivera's picture of Lenin was removed from Rockefeller Center and destroyed.[19] A college professor reports that when he returned from a vacation in Mexico he was asked just one question at the border: "Do you have any socialistic literature?"

MacLeish's play referred to above is quite a contrast to a number of other plays produced at about the same time. Typical of these are Clifford Odet's *Till the Day I Die* and *Waiting for Lefty*. These are openly left-wing radical productions, strongly anti-Nazi and anti-capitalist. No doubt such plays have quite a significant effect, but the most interesting thing about them is their rarity. Even some plays and books which create quite a storm apparently have little lasting influence. Remarque's *All Quiet on the Western Front* gripped the world and to all appearances should have put a stop to war and preparation for war. It is plainly evident now that its effect was negligible, at least for that purpose. The history of this book illustrates one of the peculiar ways in which social phenomena occasionally take expression. Logically, the fundamental effect of Remarque's book should have been to destroy the militaristic spirit in Germany. Actually it probably did retard militaristic activity on the part of Germany's potential enemies. In this respect it is like many laws which have far different results from those intended.

The Influence of the Ordinary

We do much talking about the influence of these radical or unusual plays and books, but rarely think of the much greater effect of the thousands of others. Our children see again and again a picturization of privately owned stores and industries, individual control of banks and trading companies, a division of our population into employers and employees, monogamic life, Christian churches, three meals a day, baseball and football games, and typical American dances, clothes, foods, etc. The inevitable result is that these are accepted as natural, normal, and exclusively sensible. These constitute the great bulk of what they see, hear, and read in drama, poetry, and prose literature all their lives. If all

[18] Mason Wade, "The Anabasis of a MacLeish," *North American Review*, CCXLIII (June, 1937), pp. 330-343.

[19] Walter Pack, "Rockefeller, Rivera, and Art." *Harpers*, CLXVII (September, 1933), pp. 476-483.

such books and plays pictured something different, say five meals a day
or public ownership of banks, for just a few years, they would be
accepted just as readily. The youths of Germany, Italy, Japan, or any
other country accept just as completely what they continuously see and
hear. It is almost impossible for the people of a country to accept as
normal or desirable anything different from what they experience in this
way every day. Mussolini knew what he was about when he ordered
Italian artists to paint large matronly looking women in order to increase
the Italian birthrate.

As in the case of Mediaeval art, we cannot say to what degree these
modern expressions act as controls and to what degree they merely flow
from the existing conditions. The true situation is that there is a reciprocal relationship. Art and literature mirror the contemporary scene and
by doing so contribute to its continuance. So close is this relationship
that the reactions which develop over a period of time can be traced in
songs, cartoons, and illustrations.

Comic Strips. Comic strips quickly fall in line when a country goes to
war, enters a depression, or has any other marked period of unusual experiences. Sometimes they follow practices which are puzzling and challenging. During the decade of the thirties the comic strips all but
universally entered the field of the mystical, picturing witches, fairies,
enchanted forests, magic lamps, etc. Just why this bizarre material was
demanded is a puzzle. It would be interesting to know fully what was
behind it and what effect it had.

Songs. The trend of feeling during the depression can be followed in the
songs of the time. When the first evidences of a period of distress appeared, the songs were wistful and bravely tried to be hopeful. Typical
of these was, " 'Twill all come out all right if I keep painting the clouds
with sunshine." Later, their wide diversity mirrored the confused, uncertain conditions. Some of the songs attempted to make a joke out of the
depression, a fair sample being, "Brother can you spare a dime?" Others
boldly asserted, "Just around the corner, there's a rainbow in the sky."
The depth of hopelessness was probably reached in, "What to do about
it? Just put out the lights and go to sleep." All these were products of
the times, but they certainly exercised a great amount of control over
the thinking and acting of the people, just as such songs as "Keep the
Home Fires Burning" and "Smile, Smile, Smile" had their influence during World War I.

World War II and Songs. Interestingly enough and also puzzling is the
fact that World War II was not a singing war. Not a single war song
was produced which retained popularity for any considerable length of
time. There are several songs from World War I which are still more

popular than any song of World War II. Moreover, neither soldiers nor civilians sang as much as they did during the earlier war. At times the military authorities deliberately tried to develop singing habits among the soldiers but all such attempts failed.

The explanation is not simple. It has been suggested that the war was too grim for singing. But it was grimmer in China than any place else, and the Chinese took up group singing for the first time. Possibly the universality of radio music was the cause. We are still too close to World War II to see such things in perspective. Perhaps after the passage of a decade or two we may be able to understand why the second great war was so lacking in musical expression.

Complexity of Influence. Aside from the general effect of plays, poems, and songs, many of them have special features which exercise influence far beyond calculation. To illustrate this we may refer to a very popular play which in all probability was written without any attempt whatever to create an effect on society. "You Can't Take It With You" pictured Grandpa Vanderhof as an eccentric but unusually intelligent and very lovable old gentleman. In fact, he may be said to represent an ideal which verges closely on the perfect man. Yet he is pictured as scheming and lying in the successful attempt to avoid his income tax. The only possible deduction is that it is a highly commendable act to avoid paying this tax, so commendable, in fact, that any means to that end is fully justified. How much influence this must have had on the thinking and over the acts of American citizens! Yet it would never occur to more than a small fraction of one per cent of them that their behavior had been controlled in any degree whatever by seeing this show.

It is the complex of thousands of such little suggestions as this that really makes the life of any country what it is. Our customs follow closely the patterns which we are given. We cannot see this force working itself out very clearly, but it is there. It is merely a continuation of that important role played by art and literature throughout all history and there is every reason to believe that it will continue unabated so long as mankind inhabits the earth.

Summary

Art, in its many forms, has been used effectively for social control throughout the history of mankind, and among all peoples. Since the dawn of history literature has played a similar role. At the present time, it seems, more than ever before both art and literature are seen by many principally as means of bringing about social change, and much of modern criticism is based upon evaluation of such reform purposes.

The social control functions of art and literature may be either unconscious or planned. Probably among earlier peoples and contemporary pre-literate peoples, the unplanned control effects have predominated, but increasingly these tools are today used with deliberate intent to influence men and events. The effects are often quite different from those which would be predicted. Thus, a better understanding of these social forces is important for contemporary life.

What is seen daily by people in their surroundings, those images which are repeated constantly in their literature, become accepted as the normal and natural. Thus, in so far as art and literature depict the familiar they are potent supporters of things as they are. It is comparatively exceptional when artists and writers break away from accustomed ways of living and doing things and help to bring about revolutionary changes.

QUESTIONS

1. On what did Lester F. Ward base his observation on the relation between the social sciences and the artist?
2. What are some examples of Ward's statement other than those quoted?
3. What is the most difficult analysis to make regarding the relation between art and society?
4. In Petrie's analyses, what art phenomena accompanied eras of barbarism and savagery?
5. What was the basis of the Hebrew restrictions on art?
6. How did this affect the feeling of nationalism among the Hebrews?
7. What was Plato's concept of art?
8. Compare Aristotle's opinion of art and literature with prevalent theories concerning them.
9. Outline the Roman concept of art.
10. Give examples, other than those quoted, of planned influence of art and literature on society.
11. How did Remarque's book affect the course of international relations, if at all?
12. What was Dickens's influence on the British school system?
13. What is the derivation of the term *mosaic?*
14. What type of literature has the greatest affect on society?
15. In what form of art can the trend of the depression best be observed?
16. What artistic fact was noticeable during World War II?
17. What is meant by the term "complexity of interest"?
18. Explain the controversy surrounding Archibald MacLeish.
19. How did Mussolini attempt to secure an increase in the Italian birth rate?
20. What is the test of good literature, art, or music?

SUGGESTED TOPICS FOR TERM PAPERS AND FURTHER RESEARCH

1. Study the effect of artists directly upon the field of social work in the light of Ward's theory.
2. Discuss modern literature in its tension-releasing form.

3. By documentation, study the possibility of art and literature being used as a means of analyzing a society at a given moment.

4. Discuss the effect of art on recent events in foreign relations.

5. Study the attitude in the United States toward modern art.

6. Study the effect of music on a population under stress.

7. Study the list of the most popular songs in the United States in recent years and see if there is any comparison between the type of song and current social conditions.

8. Study the attitude of the Russian government toward art and literature since the Bolshevik revolution.

BIBLIOGRAPHY

Books

Warren Dwight Allen, *Our Marching Civilization* (Stanford, Calif.: Stanford University Press, 1943). Studies the relation of music to society, the influence of the march of civilization on music and vice versa.

Rose H. Alschuler and LaBerta Weiss Hattwick, *Painting and Personality* (Chicago: Chicago University Press, 1947). A study of the paintings of children reveals the effect of each child's specific and ever-changing experiences; biographical summaries and findings were interpreted as to the child's use of color, line and form, spacing, overlay, and preference for media.

LeRoy H. Appleton, *Indian Art in America* (New York: Charles Scribner's Sons, 1950). A survey of Indian craft technique; translations of Indian legends and lore.

Association for Supervision and Curriculum Development, N.E.A., *Fostering Mental Health in Our Schools* (Washington, D.C.: N.E.A., Year Book, 1950). Discusses the importance of maintaining and promoting the proper mental health in children through art as well as other areas.

Wheeler Becket, *Music in War Plants* (Washington, D.C.: War Production Board, 1943).

David Bidney, *Theoretical Anthropology* (New York: Columbia University Press, 1953), especially Chapter 7, "Evolutionary Ethnology and Natural History," pp. 183-214, and Chapter 10, "The Concept of Myth," pp. 286-326. A valuable anthropological approach. It should be checked against the "older" anthropological theories, such as Franz Boas, *Primitive Art* (Cambridge: Harvard University Press, 1927), and the theories of M. J. Herskovits, *Man and His Works: The Science of Cultural Anthropology* (New York: Alfred A. Knopf, 1947).

Faber Birren, *The Story of Color* (Westport, Conn: The Crimson Press, 1941). Color, its history and its application in the life of man.

C. G. Bradley, *Western World Costume* (Appleton-Century-Crofts, 1954). An outline of the development of dress in the West from primitive times to the present.

Clarence A. Brown, ed., *The Achievement of American Criticism* (New York: The Ronald Press, 1954). An anthology of three hundred years of American criticism.

Hugh Dalziel Duncan, *Language and Literature in Society* (Chicago: University of Chicago Press, 1953). A sociological study of the theory and methods in the interpretation of linguistic symbols, with a bibliographical guide to the sociology of literature.

Ruth Dunnett, *Art and Child Personality* (London: Methuen and Co., 1947). How an English art teacher utilized art for its recreational and therapeutic value.

Ray Faulkner, Edwin Ziegfeld, and Gerald Hill, *Art Today* (New York: Henry Holt and Co., 1949). Designed to heighten the enjoyment and understanding of art as an integral part of one's daily living.

Charles Feidelson, Jr., *Symbolism and American Literature* (Chicago: University of Chicago Press, 1953). Symbolism seen as an important force in the writings of prominent American writers (Poe, Emerson, etc.) from the seventeenth to the end of the nineteenth centuries.

Elsie Fogerty, *Rhythm* (New York: W. W. Norton and Co., 1942). A study of rhythm and its relation to sport, art, the dance, speech, poetry, drama, and other human activity.

Boris Goldovsky, *Accents on Opera* (New York: Farrar, Straus and Young, 1953). A series of essays stressing known and little-known facts and facets of opera, in relation to social trends.

Arnold Hause, *The Social History of Art* (New York: Alfred A. Knopf, 1953). A brilliant sociological analysis.

J. A. L. Jefferson, *Hymns in Christian Worship* (New York: The Macmillan Co., 1950). A history of the use and development of hymns and suggestions for their better use in public worship.

Joe Laurie, Jr., *Vaudeville* (New York: Henry Holt and Co., 1953). Entertaining descriptions of the old-time acts and actors, with some actual scripts.

Viktor Lowenfeld, *Creative and Mental Growth* (New York: The Macmillan Co., 1947). A textbook on art education with emphasis on integrating personality growth with creative development.

Frank Luther, *Americans and Their Songs* (New York: Harper and Brothers, 1942). America's growth traced in a chronological arrangement of its songs.

Wilfred Mellers, *Music and Society* (New York: Roy Publishers, 1951). An analysis of the growth of musical tradition and its relation to society.

Lloyd Morris, *Curtain Time* (New York: Random House, 1953). A study of the American theatre in relation to society.

Robert Cecil Pooley and others, *England in Literature* (Chicago: Scott, Foresman and Co., 1953).

Tom Prideux, *World Theatre in Pictures* (New York: Greenberg: Publisher, 1953). A collection of photographs that portray modern performances of drama that date from classic Greece and Rome to Broadway today; all periods of the theatre and many countries, Western, Oriental, African, are represented.

Herbert Read, *Art and Society* (New York: Pantheon Books, 1950). Explains the relationship of drawing, painting, and sculpture to magic, religion, and politics.

Robert Richman, ed., *The Arts at Mid-Century* (New York: Horizon Press, 1954). Articles by twenty-six critics who examine the contemporary status of literature, music, painting, sculpture, the drama, and the films and describe the activities of many of the most important creative arts of the twentieth century.

D. Schullian and Max Schoen, *Music and Medicine* (New York: Henry Schuman, 1948). Essays on a hisory of musical theory through the ages.

Roger Sessions, *The Musical Experience* (Princeton, N.J.: Princeton University Press, 1950). The meaning of music for the performer, composer, and the listener.

Upton Sinclair, ed., *The Cry for Justice* (Philadelphia: Winston, 1915). A collection of poems, essays, pictures, and other literary and artistic attacks on industrial and social inequalities. All of Mr. Sinclair's books should be evaluated as powerful influences in American social reform.

Piritim A. Sorokin, *Society, Culture, and Personality* (New York: Harper & Brothers, 1947); especially pp. 548-551, 646-649, 602-604. A continuation of this well-known sociologist's discussion of all forms of art in his original *Social and Cultural Dynamics* (New York: American Book Co., 1937-1943), and *Contemporary Sociological Theories* (New York: Harper & Brothers, 1928).

Adolph Sigfried Tomars, *Introduction to the Sociology of Art* (privately printed, 1940). An attempt at a serious scholarly description of the social significance of art.

Lev Nikolaevich Tolstoy, *What is Art?* (New York: Oxford University Press, 1930). Little sociology, but a powerful ideological appeal.

Periodicals

Stuart Anderson and others, *Annotated List of Technical Publications for Industrial Art Education* (Menomonie, Wis.: Stout Institute, Graduate Studies, 1950). Annotated bibliography in industrial arts and crafts.

Art Bibliography (New York: Teachers College, Columbia University, 1947). Complete lists of art books on all phases of art.

Art and Life in the School (New York: Arts Cooperative Service, 519 West 121 St.). This organization produces other pamphlets and useful material.

Association for Childhood Education International (Washington, D.C.: 1201 16 St., 1945), *The Arts and Children's Living.* A pamphlet stating a philosophy of art for children.

V. F. Calverton, "The Sociological Aesthetics of the Bolsheviki," *American Journal of Sociology,* XXXV (November, 1929), pp. 383-392.

Barbara Chartier, "The Social Role of the Literary Elite," *Social Forces,* XXIX (December, 1950), pp. 179-186.

Hans T. David, "The Cultural Function of Music," *Journal of the History of Ideas,* XII (June, 1951), pp. 423-439.

T. J. Davies, "Arts and the Crisis," *Educational Record,* XXIII (January, 1942), pp. 30-34.

James T. Farrell, "Literature and Ideology," *English Journal,* XXXI (April, 1942), pp. 261-273.

Z. C. Franklin, "Schools in a Wartime Recreation Program," *National Municipal Review,* XXXI (April, 1942), pp. 216-217.

Harry B. Lee, "Poetry Production as a Supplemental Emergency Defense Against Anxiety," *Psychoanalytical Quarterly,* VII (1938), pp. 232-242; "A Critique of the Theory of Sublimation," *Psychiatry,* II (1939), pp. 239-270; "A Theory Concerning Free Invention in the Creative Arts," *ibid.,* III (1940), pp. 229-293; "On the Esthetic States of the Mind," *ibid.,* X (1947), pp. 281-306.

Archibald MacLeish, "Poetry and the Public World," *Atlantic Monthly,* XLXIII (June, 1939), pp. 823-830; "The Poetry of Karl Marx," *Saturday Review of Literature,* X (February 17, 1934), pp. 485-486.

T. W. O. Motter, "Culture and the New Anarchy," *American Association of the University Professors Bulletin,* XXVII (June, 1941), pp. 295-304.

C. Ramsland, "Britons Never Will Be Slaves. A Study in Whig Political Propaganda in the Theatre, 1700-1742," *Quarterly Journal of Speech,* XXVIII (December, 1942), pp. 394-399.

A. K. Saran, "Art and Ritual as Methods of Social Control and Planning," *Ethics,* LXVI, Part I (April, 1953), pp. 171-179.

Mason Wade, "The Anabasis of a MacLeish," *North American Review,* CCXLIII (June, 1937), pp. 330-343.

J. Webb, "Art Helps to Prevent Delinquency," *School Arts,* XLVI (March, 1945), pp. 244-245.

Sidney Zink, "Moral Effect of Art," *Ethics,* LX (July, 1950), pp. 261-274.

CHAPTER XVI

Recreation and Social Control

In the general patterns of social change recreation assumes an ever-increasing position of importance in individual and social well being. Recreation takes its place with religion, education, health and work as the five essential factors molding individual personality and affording a community more abundant living. While these processes functioning in balance achieve growth and progress, the neglect of any process can create individual and social pathology.

The *need for* recreation, the *uses of* recreation, and the *benefits from* recreation are constantly increasing. Patterns of wholesome recreation shaped into effective programs of activity constitute a *must* as a living force in a modern democratic society. In scanning the social horizon of the present and peering into the potentialities and possibilities of social trends there is overpowering evidence to substantiate these statements.

The developments created from the emergency, new interpretations of national defense, concepts of morale, and the postwar effort itself with the chaotic yet intriguing procedures of reconstruction, reconversion and rehabilitation have created new demands. Add to these some of the many social forces of technology—labor-saving devices, monotony of machine work, elimination of children's chores, the demand for an economy of pleasure as opposed to an economy of drudgery—to offset high-powered specialization, the intricacies of urban dwelling, and the too often dull isolation of agrarianism, and we have an array of social forces testing our best thinking and leadership. And the future, with its gifts from the sciences, yet undreamed of inventions and discoveries, newer means of communication and transportation, conquest of the drudgeries of life, the social demands for better health, advancing techniques of education, and the overwhelming forces that will bring added joy to life's sojourn set before us salient goals for achievement and adventure. Recreation cannot fail to meet these social responsibilities.

The Uses of Recreation. The uses of recreation as positive and preventive forces in community organization are steadily receiving increased attention. A number of situations are current in the community at the present time offering specific illustrations. There is the place of recreation in the sum total picture of the proposals for physical fitness and universal military training. There is the national concern about the rise of crime and juvenile delinquency and the place of recreation as an aid in cure and prevention. The possibility of recreation in reducing absenteeism and increasing the production of the industrial worker is inviting. And the fascinating uses of recreation in physical and mental therapy indicate unlimited opportunities. All of the aspects of the day nursery, nursery school and kindergarten create new techniques. Recreation for elders, those folk over seventy years of age as a consciousness of kind group, whose numbers are constantly rising and will continue to grow, offers privileges of unique service. And the dynamic surge of Youth into Teen Towns, Teen Bars, and Teen Taverns, an avalanche of co-recreational interests and practices, demands constructive and positive approach and guidance. As we build a larger body of information and factual knowledge we will broaden the scope of the uses of Recreation.

Factors Conditioning Recreation. The factors conditioning recreation are receiving increased attention. The social changes that have affected community life in modern society have conditioned both the quantity and the uses of leisure, and they are largely responsible for the almost universal demand for recreation. The geographic setting and ecological factors are important. Natural resources, climatic conditions, topography, and geographic location are elements in the picture. The population situation must be considered as to its size and density; its physical and mental health; sex, age, race, and nationality; individuality, social mobility, population distribution, urbanization and ruralization. There are tremendous implications in the economic factors conditioning recreation. Inventions and discoveries bringing an expansion of material culture, technological development, machine-made leisure, occupational situations, wealth and income, and standards of living are basic to the community recreation program. Educational policy, political set-up, and community organization also condition the possibilities and trends.

Recreation and the Social Institutions

Recreation is closely allied with the fundamental social institutions—the family, the school, the church, the state and the community. Actions of these institutions toward recreation and the influence of recreation on the institutions are far-reaching in the control of individual personality growth and societal relationships. The objective of society and its institutions is the development and maintenance of an environment in which every individual may attain the maximum individual and social growth, may function normally in the midst of and through association with other

individuals, and may give promise of the perpetuation of the best qualities of the race. The individual does not exist in order to nourish institutional life, as has so often been assumed, but rather the institution and
social organization have evolved in order to meet the needs of the
individual in constantly changing social conditions.

The heart of social control lies in the social institutions which must act
as a buffer between the individual and social change and through which
society may marshal its forces. In simple terms, no institution may function completely and socially if its chief objective is the perfecting of its
own organization rather than the serving of its constituency and the
building of society.

Recreation and Family Life. Since it is impossible within the limitations
of the chapter to delve into the arts of recreation in relation to each institution emphasis is given to recreation and family life and certain aspects
of recreation in relation to the school and the church are presented. This
material will serve to illustrate institutional trends and possibilities.

Recreation in the families of the colonial period, during the expansion
of the frontier, in pre-Civil War days, and the reconstruction era, in the
"gay nineties" and the early years of the twentieth century all offer rich
opportunities for study and research.[1]

Out of the vast interplay of impersonally operating forces in modern
society a new type of family life is emerging. The confused and complex
interrelationship of social, economic, political, biological, psychological,
and philosophical forces all join together to create new attitudes, values,
and standards which are affecting all of the fundamental institutions.

New standards of family life have supplanted the older views. Old
norms and old controls have vanished. Too frequently changes have occurred so rapidly that no amended patterns have arisen. The time is
filled with trial and error methods in attempting proper adjustments.
Perplexed by the problems for which there can be no ready-made solutions, once the old formula is discarded, many families are bewildered
today and many are lost in the maze of rapid social change.

Recreation is deeply woven into these interrelations. Definite trends
indicate a severe loss of recreational leadership on the part of the family.
Along with the essential changes in all aspects of family life have come
new demands for recreation. At the same time recreation within itself
has made rapid advances.

Trends From the Home. In the light of facts and trends it is inevitable
that the emphasis of recreation will be away from the home and family

---

[1] A. W. Calhoun, *A Social History of the American Family* (3 vols., New York:
Barnes and Noble, 1945), offers much material on family recreation. See also Foster
Rhea Dulles, *America Learns to Play* (New York: D. Appleton-Century Co., 1940).

group toward larger aggregations based on public, private, and commercial recreation promotion. At the present time there appears no other way. All efforts to bring recreation back again into family life have had limited results. On the whole, however, the trends are toward the strengthening of community recreation, and family life will find its best values in definitely correlating its program with community activity.

Efforts to Promote Family Recreation. Throughout the nation numerous attempts are constantly being made to stimulate family recreation. The family is still the play center of the small child and the center of much informal social activity. A number of leaders have organized backyard playground campaigns with some success especially in the field of activities for small children. Homemade equipment plans have been furnished by recreation departments. There are numerous books and pamphlets describing games for home use. The field of hobbies has assumed large proportions within the past decade, and individual recreation is well cared for through many agencies catering to the hobby idea. While it is true that this has kept many individuals at home, there is little to indicate that the procedure has added much to family recreation as such. It is very difficult to obtain accurate information on family recreation. The National Congress of Parents and Teachers, the Child Welfare League of America, the Children's Bureau and the National Recreation Association along with other groups interested in family life are continually making surveys and offering suggestions to stimulate recreation in family life and to correlate family and community programs.

School. The whole process and program of education recognizes the newer tasks of interpreting human culture. Here is found a place in the curriculum not only for the traditional subjects but for the direction of the new leisure time which is of growing importance in the modern era. Training for the wise use of leisure is one of the seven cardinal objectives of education as enunciated by the National Education Association. The introduction of music, dramatics, arts and crafts, nature lore and camping, along with sports and active games, into the curriculum has a far-reaching significance for the recreation movement as it provides *now* for young people a wholesome environment and a rich program of activities that care for growing years and turn out a host of young people who, having acquired skills in recreation, will desire them as a carry-over into adult life.

Church. Recreation is an essential part of the church program. The church needs recreation and recreation needs the church. Joining with every other institution in modern society the church faces the question of how to provide for the constructive and wholesome use of recreation both by activities and facilities. The church cannot undertake the whole problem of leisure, nor can the church set about to solve it by itself. Other agencies must take their full share in enlarged responsibilities and possibilities. The church will find genuine satisfaction in participation. The church will experience revitalized social power as it moves forward with and into the field of recreation.

Administration and Organization

Growing Complexity. The field of administration and organization for recreation is constantly growing more complex. The general divisions of operation are under public, private and commercial direction. Problems of internal organization of a recreation department, financing community recreation, program planning and control, types of systems, maintenance and construction of areas and facilities, records, reports and filing systems, personnel problems, public relations, operations, legal aspects and publicity are involved in the proper functioning of community recreation. More and more we witness public tax support of the program of recreation on the part of the federal, state, county, and municipal governments. And well should it be this way. If education and health are essentials of government, then recreation should be. The trend is clear. In 1950 the amount spent for municipal parks and recreation totaled more than $269,000,000, and $87,000,000 was spent for land, buildings, and improvements.[2]

U.S. Support. The Federal Government is interested in recreation through some twenty departments. The chief among these are the National Park Service, the Department of Defense, the Veterans Administration, the National Public Housing Authority, and the Department of Agriculture, through its Extension Services.

Agencies. For many years the private and semipublic agencies have made substantial contributions to recreation. The National Recreation Association has led the field. National, state and local agencies for children, youth, and adults spread over the nation. The Boy Scouts, Camp Fire Girls, Y.M.C.A., Girl Scouts, Y.W.C.A., and a host of youth agencies are making powerful contributions to the recreation program. There is much work ahead for each and every agency, public or private. At times there has developed a very difficult fight with many undercurrents between some of the private agencies and public agencies. There is no need for quarrel between the two groups. If each will but dare to vitalize

---

[2] National Recreation Association, *Recreation,* the Yearbook, Mid-Century Edition, 1950.

the word "coordination" on the basis of efficient service real progress is assured in promoting community activities and interests for all.

Commercial Recreation. When a large number of people demand specific and special forms of recreation, and these forms can be standardized for quantity production and for a price within reach of the mass of people, there inevitably develops commercial recreation. This form of recreation has a large and legitimate place in the satisfying of the leisure time demands of the individual and the group.

As the demand for more enjoyable ways of spending leisure time becomes widespread, there is a need for the expansion of businesses engaged in providing recreation for financial profits. Theaters, vaudeville and burlesque shows, cabarets, concert halls, dance halls, pool and billiard rooms, bowling alleys and amusement parks are some of the older forms of amusement providing for a large part of the leisure time of many folks and long under the control of commercial interests. More recently the motion picture houses, radio broadcasting stations, and the automobile—all products of the twentieth century—have forged to the front as popular forms of commercial entertainment. Even with many of the activities now sponsored by public and private agencies there is a tendency to commercialize; especially is this true where there is assurance of profitable financial gain.[3] The professionalizing of many sports, as baseball and football, are examples of the commercialization of the public demand for recreation. Many tennis courts, swimming pools, summer camps, and golf courses are operated for financial gain.

From a sociological viewpoint commercial amusements are fundamentally important in two ways: (1) they stimulate and aid in determining the culture patterns for individuals and groups; and (2) they influence and modify moral standards. The appeal of interest must be pitched at a level to which the largest number can respond. Since the crowd obviously responds, then commercial amusements often become an index to tastes and senses of values of community life. When a people are willing to pay money for recreation, then the forms of recreation paid for become dynamic clues to existing culture. Before the advent of commercial amusements local communities were often distinguished by their forms of play and recreation. An analysis of these forms invariably showed certain values inherent in the current culture.[4] They are not in

---

[3] The radio and motion pictures are discussed in chapters XXVI and XXVII. They play an important role in recreation and are vitally related to the molding of individual and social patterns in the framework of folkways.

[4] Martin H. Neumeyer and Esther S. Neumeyer, "Commercial Amusements," chapter XIV, *Leisure and Recreation* (New York: A. S. Barnes and Co., 1936). Also, Robert S. Lynd and Helen M. Lynd, *Middletown in Transition* (New York: Harcourt, Brace and Co., 1937), pp. 242-243.

themselves vicious or harmful to the public good. It will be well to enumerate the points generally argued against these forms of recreation, then follow with the favorable factors and suggest methods and practices leading to a positive application for individual and community well-being.

The Case Against Commercial Amusements. There are four salient arguments constantly aimed to show the negative factors in commercial amusements. The first, and the one most commonly used, is the argument of "passivity"—the objection that commercial recreation emphasizes the place of the spectator and minimizes the place of the participant.

The second charge is that of substitution—the practice of *buying* something rather than *being* something, hence the art of self-expression is lost.

Demoralization is the third factor—that certain forms of commercial amusement lead to dishonesty, vice, gambling, crime, poverty, and sex delinquency.

The fourth point is exploitation—that under undesirable leadership, gate receipts become the only criterion and the emotions of children and adults are preyed upon for financial gain.

The Case for Commercial Amusement. Under the five headings of (1) Stimulation, (2) Facilities, (3) Enjoyment, (4) Accessibility, and (5) Inexpensiveness, the positive side of commercial recreation may be set forth.

A casual glance at the facts picturing the sources and agencies of leisure time activity will satisfy anyone as to the stimulating effect commercial amusements have had on the whole program.

In spite of all the efforts made to provide wholesome recreation by public and private means, there is an ever-increasing demand for commercial recreation. If all three (public, private, and commercial) combined their efforts, there would still be a shortage of activities to supply the demand. Further, commercial enterprises can provide facilities that would otherwise be long delayed where the progress of facilities depends upon taxation and public approval.

Commercial amusements, by their manifold opportunity to cater to a wide diversity of tastes and their power to produce the art of entertainment as an art in its highest and finest techniques, can lay claim as a direct producer of joy, pleasure and happiness.

The amusements provided on a commercial basis are usually conveniently located and available at all times of the year.

With the ever-increasing demand for amusements and the growing knowledge of their quantity production to meet the wide variety of tastes, the price has been brought within reach of the great masses of the people.

Meeting the Problem. The statements regarding both sides of commercial amusements contain elements of truth. The problems involved can be solved to the best interests of all concerned through the practice of *balance* and *control*.

Balance is simply another term for temperance, and temperance should be applied to all types of recreation. There can be no quarrel with commercial amusements indulged in with balance and control. The challenge is for individual and group judgment and sanity.

When all the citizenship has learned to practice balance then the ills of commercial amusements are at the minimum. Until this process of education has assumed larger force and effectiveness there is need for control. A number of ways to control commercial amusements are in practice: (1) Legislation, regulation, and enactments through police control, license, and supervision. (2) Interest of civic groups. Control may be exercised through the operation of public opinion. No amusement or institution which is repugnant to the standard of propriety held by most of the people can prosper long. (3) Trade control. A considerable part of the control may be automatic so far as the community is concerned. That is, it may be a control exercised within the trade. There is a definite and strong conviction that clean and wholesome amusement is ultimately the best business asset. (4) Censorship. The whole subject of censorship is admittedly a matter of taste, opinion, and judgment. (5) Elimination. Every city has its vigilance committees, anti-vice societies, leagues of decency or protective associations, promoted by those who serve as a sort of voice for morals and decency. Quite often these organizations seek to legislate certain types of amusements out of existence. There have been many "anti" movements. (6) Public provision. Many important needs would never be met if we depended exclusively on financial gain as the underlying principle of the service. The increasing number of municipal parks, playgrounds, athletic fields, golf courses and tennis courts, and the efforts of the more progressive school systems and churches provide, not merely facilities for active forms of recreation, but also leadership and training in the wise use of leisure are making it more and more difficult if not impossible for commercial interests completely to dominate the field of recreation.

Recreation and Pathology

The organized play movement resulted from the study of social pathologies, with a remedial and preventive emphasis. The sand garden stage, beginning in Boston; the Settlement House programs; the plans to check juvenile delinquency and crime; the place of recreation for the unemployed were all emphasized as selling points for community recreation programs.[5] Many recreation surveys have been undertaken with the hope of checking certain pathological aspects as one of the prime motives.[6] Numerous theses also offer evidence in this direction.[7] Program emphasis has centered around the eradication of negative forces and institutional leadership has fostered experimental procedure for clinical values. Recreational illiteracy is dangerous, and emphasis should be given to mend and patch the broken elements of the social order and to balance the recreational opportunities within unequal places. There is abundant evidence to indicate that wholesome recreation aids in ameliorating and actually eliminating individual and social pathology. There is also evidence to indicate that unsubstantiated claims have been made on behalf of recreation and its curative and preventive values. There is need for study, research, experimentation, and clinical activity.

The misuse or abuse of recreation is becoming a problem of paramount importance. Today, when modern civilization offers to every man the gifts of leisure, there is a real challenge to the ability of the individual or group. Today every man has the opportunity to enjoy a culture that in the yesteryears only a few enjoyed. And today, because of this gift of leisure, man possesses the hours for quick destruction. While it is true that recreation is not the sole cure nor cause for disorganization, it contributes a major share in the sum total of constructive living. In his book, *A Philosophy of Play*, Luther Gulick offers two conclusions:

"The individual is more completely revealed in play than in any one other way; and conversely, play has a greater shaping power over the character and nature of man than has any one other activity. A man shows what he really is when he is free to do what he chooses, and if a person can be influenced so that his highest aspirations—which are followed when he is free to pursue his ideals—are a gain, then character is being shaped profoundly.

"A people most truly reveals itself in the character of its pleasures. The pleasures of a people are not the sum of the pleasures of the individuals who compose that people, just as the psychology of the crowd is quite different from the psychology of the individuals composing the

---

[5] Clarence E. Rainwater, *The Play Movement in the United States* (The University of Chicago Press, 1922); Jane Addams, *The Spirit of Youth and the City Streets* (New York: The Macmillan Co., 1909); Miriam Van Waters, *Youth in Conflict* (New York: New Republic Inc., 1925); Cyril Burt, *The Young Delinquent* (New York: D. Appleton-Century Co., 1925); Walter C. Reckless, *Vice in Chicago* (Chicago: University of Chicago Press, 1933); Jesse F. Steiner, *Research Memorandum on Recreation in the Depression* (New York: Social Sciences Research Council, 1937).

[6] For example the Cleveland, Indianapolis, Buffalo, Chicago, and Maryland surveys.

[7] *Report of the Third College Conference on the Training of Recreation Leaders* (New York: New York University Book Store, 1941).

crowd. Conversely, the manner of its pleasures is the most character-determining force within a people." [8]

The delinquent, dependent, defective and degenerate masses of folk are all too numerous in the social order. The army of defectives can be classified under two divisions: (1) the physically handicapped and (2) the mentally defective and diseased. It has long been believed that recreation has an important contribution to make to the recuperation and rehabilitation of those physically and mentally ill. Evidence of the fact exists [9] and experimentation is going forward. Especially is this true in physical convalescence and in the treatment of mental illness. Meager attempts are being made to introduce programs promoting the thera-peutic values of recreation. Most institutions throughout the nation have not grasped the full potentialities in this respect. The time is not far distant when every modern institution for the physically and mentally defective will possess, as a part of its program, wholesome recreation leadership and facilities.

Modern psychiatry is using recreation as one of its chief mediums of cure and prevention. Again, much study and research is needed to bring forth added knowledge and techniques.

"Recreational therapy as a conditioning introductory medium through which other forms of treatment may more effectively function is stated by White in these words: 'The general scheme is to get the patient in as acceptable condition as possible to which end occupational therapy, amusements and athletic sports may contribute.' As a form of situational therapy in its capacity to assist the patient to form more acceptable per-sonal habits and more socialized intra- and extra-mural readjustments, recreational therapy will very probably develop its greatest possibilities in the modern treatment of the mentally ill." [10]

The Equalization Problems. Emphasis should be given to equalizing the recreational opportunities available to certain neglected groups, including people living in rural or sparsely settled areas, those in families of low income, certain Negro groups and other minority groups, dwellers in congested city neighborhoods, children just leaving school and not yet adjusted to outside life, with special emphasis on unemployed youth, and people with mental, emotional, or physical handicaps. For people living in rural or sparsely settled areas, there are bright spots such as the work of the 4-H Clubs, the Future Farmers of America, the consolidated school,

---

[8] Luther H. Gulick, *A Philosophy of Play* (New York: Charles Scribner's Sons, 1920), p. xiv.

[9] John Eisele Davis, *Play and Mental Health* (New York: A. S. Barnes and Co., 1938); same author, *Principles and Practice of Recreational Therapy* (New York: A. S. Barnes and Co., 1936).

[10] W. A. White, *Mechanisms of Character Formation*, (New York: The Mac-millan Co., 1920); John Eisele Davis, *op. cit.*, p. xviii.

paved and improved highways, church groups, and a few other similar forces. The problem of providing a wholesome program for the isolated area is a very difficult one, caused by problems of finance and leadership.

In considering recreation in the families of low income groups social responsibility is the key. The nation as a whole is just beginning to meet the situation. The federal government has assumed leadership. Surely there is no argument that individuals of these families should be deprived of recreational opportunities because of economic status. That question has been settled in public education, and it can be settled the same way in recreation. State departments of public welfare along with numerous civic agencies are now at work to equalize opportunities in this direction.

At the present time there are direct evidences to indicate a changing emphasis on recreation. Less and less is it thought of in terms of prevention and cure, but more and more in terms of values to the individual and the group.

Leadership and Training

Both professional and volunteer leaders are essential in the well functioning process. Adequately trained leadership, skill in the arts of leisure, loving life and folks, student of human nature, and a hard worker in the vineyard are general qualities required. It is a known fact that recreation is a profession, and as time goes on requirements and standards will steadily rise—elements within the profession and social forces from without the ranks will demand a better quality performance.

The training of recreation leaders is receiving added consideration. The three National College Conferences on the Training of Recreation Leaders have standing committees at work in the fields of Undergraduate and Graduate Curricula, Training Methods, Surveys, Studies and Research Projects, Field Work, and other related subjects. All the national groups interested in recreation stand firm on the need for *trained* leadership, both professional and volunteer.

In the past the community recreation field has been handicapped by the fact that training opportunities were inadequate and exceedingly limited, and it was necessary to draw its workers from individuals prepared for or experienced in related fields. It is still essential that the recreation movement seek outstanding individuals in all related fields and not limit its source of supply to any single field. Nevertheless, because of the increase in the number of colleges offering training for recreation work, more and more students are gaining knowledge of the field and are preparing for service in it. Furthermore, community recreation systems have afforded practical means for giving workers valuable experience and effective in-service and refresher training under competent supervision.

Research

As Jesse F. Steiner stated in his *Research Memorandum on Recreation in the Depression:* "Recreation as an important field for social research has only recently been given any serious considerations. The wide variety of social and economic problems, which engaged the chief attention of research students during the past two decades, rarely included recreation and leisure time activities." [11] The promotional and activity aspects of the field have been developed rather than scientific studies. Although some headway in research has been made, the field is wide open and sociology could assume leadership.

There is an abundance of material in bulletins and reports calling attention to the need for more programs and facilities, the challenges of leisure time, and community surveys of conditions and situations.

Much more abundant is the material in actual practice of games, sports, music, drama, arts, crafts, nature lore, social activities, and other major divisions of recreation. In fact, in two volumes by Mason and Mitchell [12] there are more than three thousand activities explained and illustrated. There are little factual data for quantitative, qualitative, and analytical study. In spite of the slow progress, authoritative studies of various aspects have been completed and are in progress.

The growth of the movement, national demands through the depression period and the crisis of defense, the expansion of regional planning, the demands of social pathology, recent expension of leisure time, community responsibility for recreation, the problems involved in administration with organization, finances, facilities, areas and centers, the interest of federal, state, and local government in recreation, the volunteer, leisure time habits and activities of individuals and groups, along with a host of other influences demand research for effective future growth.

Much of the material to date is tinged with factors that hinder effective research such as a lack of source material, scattered and fragmentary information, unreliable sources, inaccuracies, material that is too general, lack of agreement on different methods of tabulation, and lack of standardized forms and reporting systems.

The number and variety of federal government reports and publications, material from state planning boards and municipal recreation departments, annual reports and special surveys and studies from private agencies, college theses, and studies by faculty members and the special

---

[11] Jesse F. Steiner, *Research Memorandum on Recreation in the Depression* (New York: Social Science Research Council, *Bulletin 32,* 1937).

[12] B. S. Mason and E. D. Mitchell, *Social Games for Recreation,* and *Active Games and Contests* (New York: A. S. Barnes and Co., 1935).

committees from national, regional, and state groups offer a nucleus of good source materials.

Recreation Areas and Facilities

Facilities and areas of recreation have had a phenomenal growth in the last two decades. The W.P.A., P.W.A., N.Y.A., and C.C.C. spent more than two billion dollars on facilities and areas in the depression years of the early nineteen thirties. The Army, Navy, Federal Security Agency, Federal Works Agency, Federal Public Housing Authority along with the American Red Cross and United Service Organizations added further billions to the expansion of areas and facilities in the World War II period. Commercial recreation has had a tremendous surge forward and public and private forces of all types have expanded. Parks, playgrounds, athletic fields, stadiums, gymnasiums, community centers, sport areas, hiking trails, concert halls, theaters, radio stations, dance halls, camps and many other facilities can be listed as provided from one end of the nation to the other. Much gain has been made in the proper use, location, space, operation, appearance, maintenance, and construction of these facilities and areas.

National Morale

In examining the main currents in American life affecting recreation it is evident that a great amount of thought was directed during World War II in utilizing and holding a high level of unity and morale. The federal government through its several branches, the Army, the Navy, the Federal Security Administration, the Office of Civilian Defense, the Federal Public Housing Authority, and the Federal Works Agency offered extension activities and provided facilities and leadership.

Many conferences [13] were held to consider the emergency, notably the National Recreation Congress, the American Association of Health, Physical Education and Recreation, and the Third College Conference on the Training of Recreation Leaders. The United Service Organization, composed of six national private agencies, the Y.M.C.A., Y.W.C.A., the Salvation Army, the National Catholic Council, the Jewish Welfare Board, and Travelers' Aid, sponsored a recreation program in national defense areas. Numerous civic, patriotic, educational, fraternal, and religious organizations aided in civilian morale and through volunteer services enhanced the values of recreation to national life.

The national defense picture in respect to recreation assumed four

---

[13] American Association of Health, Physical Education, and Recreation, Washington, D.C.; College Conference on the Training of Recreation Leaders; National Recreation Association, 315 Fourth Avenue, New York City.

definite patterns for control as far as problem areas were concerned: (1) recreation in the Army and Navy military areas; (2) recreation in communities adjacent to military posts; (3) recreation in new and enlarged industrial centers; (4) recreation in all communities, urban and rural, large and small.

Army and Navy. The Army and Navy provided recreation within their respective areas. Both Army and Navy fully realized the value of recreation as a morale builder and are giving attention to the promotion of wholesome activities and the provision of adequate facilities.

The problem in the communities adjacent to the Army and Navy posts and the new and enlarged industrial areas where communities grew in mushroom fashion was serious. There were very few of them that could meet the emergency and they had to call for assistance. The federal government, along with the community, assumed responsibility through the coordinating leadership of the Federal Security Administration and the Federal Works Agency.

War Impacts. As war brought its total impact upon community life through the tension of conflict, reports of casualty lists of the dead and wounded, enlarged enlistments, economic stress and strain, along with patriotic fervor, the need for wholesome recreation grew increasingly more important. Also, to keep intact those social gains of the past years which had been the basis for such far-reaching social reconstruction and to endeavor to plan and build for the future demanded the full power of civilian strength. Appropriate types of programs and the utilization of available facilities call for spontaneity, initiative, and imagination of both professional and volunteer leadership. Morale is not totally dependent upon recreation. There is no doubt but that recreation aids in the generation of good morale, but morale does not rest upon any single facet of life.

"There can be no sturdy morale without a sense of dignity, and dignity derives from good organisms seeking a good life in a good society. Those who are specialists in recreation and do not at the same time aid us in bringing our democracy to greater fulfillment in all spheres of experience will fail in the end. The function of recreation in modern society is essential, but it should not become compensatory. He who furnishes recreation to the poor and does not also strive to eliminate poverty is already caught in a living confusion."[14]

---

[14] Eduard C. Lindeman, "Recreation and Morale," *The American Journal of Sociology*, XLVII (November, 1941), p. 405.

Summary

Recreation, both as a means and an agency of social control, is used universally, and with increasing understanding of its importance and complexities. It is an important means of training children for social membership in primitive and civilized groups; and among adults it is not only the satisfaction of basic human need, but also the deliberate instrument for influencing people.

The *need for* recreation and the *uses of* recreation and the *benefits from* recreation are constantly increasing. The factors conditioning recreation, such as social change, geographic setting, ecological factors, population situations, and many others, offer abundant illustrations.

Recreation is closely allied with the fundamental social institutions—the family, the school, the church, the state, and the community. The correlations of the institutions and recreation are far-reaching in the control of individual personality growth and societal relationships.

At present there are three principal types of recreation, classified according to the motivations and organizations which foster them. There are private recreation, public recreation, and commercial recreation, each having its place and peculiar advantages.

Attention in the past has been largely upon recreation in relation to social and pathological conditions, and as a therapy it has been widely used, even though there is much room for far greater use. The war situation placed emphasis upon recreation as a builder of morale, both for the armed forces themselves, and for the general populace. With the dislocations of war, however, there have arisen new and widespread problems, in the meeting of which greater coordination is an important development.

QUESTIONS

1. Name the five essential factors for molding the personality.
2. What factors condition recreation?
3. In relation to the family, in what direction do the latest trends in recreation lie?
4. How has recreation affected education in recent times?
5. How has religion met the new trend toward more recreation?
6. What societal factors are increasing the importance of recreation?
7. What are the fundamental fields of recreation and how are they related to social control?
8. How is the expenditure of tax money for recreation purposes justified?
9. What are the negative implications of commercial recreation?
10. How can recreation contribute to the pathologic forces of society?
11. Why is recreational illiteracy considered by many to be as dangerous as educational illiteracy?
12. What are the advantages of the new leisure of the individual?
13. What are the effects of World War II on recreational attitudes?
14. What is the place of the volunteer worker in the recreational system?

15. What solutions can be offered to the problem of equalization of recreational opportunities?
16. State the problem of commercial recreation.
17. What are the classifications of defectives?
18. State the need for recreation.
19. Indicate the influence of community customs, folkways, and mores upon community recreation programs.
20. What are the principal types of recreation?

SUGGESTED TOPICS FOR TERM PAPERS AND FURTHER RESEARCH

1. Study the results of the misuse of leisure time.
2. Study the theories of the relation between adequate recreational facilities and juvenile delinquency.
3. Study the results of the misapplication of recreational programs.
4. Study the differences in the play habits of the male and the female.
5. Study the problem of recreation for the aged.
6. Study the problem of recreation in relation to the needs and future of the nation.
7. Draw up a model recreation program for an average industrial city.
8. Study the effect of geography on recreation programs.
9. Discuss the impact of war on the recreational habits of the nation.
10. Make a comparison of American recreational habits with those of a selected European nation.

BIBLIOGRAPHY

Books

C. Delisle Burns, *Leisure in the Modern World* (New York: The Century Co., 1932). Philosophy, background, and contemporary trends of leisure in relation to technology.
H. Dan Corbin, *Recreational Leadership* (New York: Prentice-Hall, 1953). A useful description of the duties of leadership.
F. W. Cozens and A. Stumpf, *Sports in American Life* (Chicago: University of Chicago Press, 1953). Sociologically relevant discussion of the sports page, spectator sports, public images of American Presidents, their prowess, and sports as a cultural value.
H. G. Danford, *Recreation in the American Community* (New York: Harper and Brothers, 1953). A text in public recreation.
Foster Rhea Dulles, *America Learns to Play* (New York: D. Appleton-Century Co., 1940). The most comprehensive and effective history of recreation. A "must" for those interested in the field.
Encyclopaedia of the Social Sciences (New York: The Macmillan Co., 1934). Look for such topics as: "Recreation," "Leisure," "Play," and "Social Control."
Louise A. Fietz, *The Role of the States in Recreation* (Berkeley: University of California Press, 1947). A discussion of the duties and opportunities of the states in the field of recreation.
Elvin Oscar Harvin, *The Recreation Leader* (Nashville, Tenn.: Abingdon-Cokesbury Press, 1952). A statement of the requirements and duties of the recreation leader.
Lawrence P. Jacks, *Education Through Recreation* (New York: Harper and Brothers, 1932).

Anna May Jones, *Leisure Time Education* (New York: Harper and Brothers, 1946).
John A. Kinneman, *The Community in American Society* (New York: F. S. Crofts and Co., 1947). A textbook with good sections in recreation.
Eduard C. Lindeman, *Leisure—A National Issue* (New York: Association Press, 1939). An exposition of the meaning of leisure in a democracy and the responsibility of government for recreation, as an aspect of social planning.
Frank G. Menke, ed., *Encyclopaedia of Sports* (New York: A. S. Barnes and Co., 1944). Covers all references to sports, athletics, and games.
National Conference on Prevention and Control of Juvenile Delinquency, *Report on Recreation for Youth* (Washington, D.C.: Government Printing Office, 1948).
M. H. and E. S. Neumeyer, *Leisure and Recreation* (New York: A. S. Barnes & Co., 1949). A comprehensive, sociological approach to the entire subject of leisure time.
Arthur Newton Pack, *The Challenge of Leisure* (New York: The Macmillan Co., 1934). *Report of National Conference on Social Welfare Needs and the Workshop of Citizens Groups* (New York: National Social Welfare Assembly, Inc., 1948).
S. R. Slavson, *Recreation and the Total Personality* (New York: Association Press, 1946). An analysis of goals and methods for enriching recreation's contribution to wholesome living.
Jesse F. Steiner, *Research Memorandum on Recreation in the Depression* (New York: Social Science Research Council, 1937). The aspects and scope of recreational research, with special emphasis on the Depression period.
—— *Americans at Play* (New York: McGraw-Hill Book Co., 1938). A study of some of the more significant developments in recreation, especially in the fields of parks, playgrounds, competitive sports and games, commercial amusements, clubs, and travel.

Periodicals

Florence C. Bingham, "Community Life in a Democracy" (Chicago: National Conference of Parents and Teachers, 1942).
W. B. Bizzwell, "Learning and Leisure," *School and Society*, XXXIX (January 20, 1934), pp. 65-72.
M. M. Chambers, "America's Capacity for Culture," *ibid.*, V (April 16, 1938), pp. 489-494.
J. E. Davis, "Recreational Therapy, A New Field of Treatment in Mental Hospitals," *Hygeia*, V (August, 1941), pp. 605-607.
Merel Fainsod, "The Komsomols—A Study of Youth Under Dictatorship," *American Political Science Review* (March, 1951), pp. 18-40.
Z. C. Franklin, "Schools in a Wartime Recreation Program," *National Municipal Review*, XXXI (April, 1942), pp. 216-217.
J. S. Herron, "The School Community Versus Community Recreation," *American School Board Journal* (May, 1944), pp. 17-19.
John H. Herz, "Naziism," *Journal of Negro Education* (Yearbook issue, July, 1941), pp. 353-367.
R. R. Isaacs, "Educational, Cultural and Recreational Services to Increased Participation in Community Life," *Annals of The American Academy of Political and Social Science*, CV (November, 1945), pp. 129-138.
S. W. Morris, "Sports Heal War Neuroses," *Recreation*, V (October, 1945), pp. 343-344.
J. S. Plant, "Recreation and Social Integration of the Individual," *ibid.*, V (September, 1937), pp. 339-342.

Collis Stocking, "Gambling: General and Historical," *Encyclopaedia of the Social Sciences*, VI (1931), pp. 555-558, 561.
Youth Leaders Digest (Peekskill, N.Y.: Youth Service Inc.). Monthly—a guide to youth leaders.

CHAPTER XVII

The Leadership Process

Leadership is a process of interaction among the persons of a group, large or small, which moves it in the direction of a high degree of acceptance of: (1) shared values and goals, (2) the situation in which the members interact, (3) the leader, and (4) one another.[1] Thus, the leadership process may be considered as one of social control; and to the extent that the degrees of acceptance of the various factors mentioned can be measured, the degree of control attained by the process can be determined.

The Social Situation in Which Leadership Arises

Leadership is a process arising out of a social situation composed of at least four factors: a group, a need for group action, a leader, and followers. Each of these factors must first be considered briefly.

1. A group, consisting of two or more persons responding to one another, reciprocally, as values, may possess sociation (positive or negative inter-personal responses) ranging from a high degree of reciprocal positive responses to a high degree of reciprocal negative responses. Leadership, in part, would be considered as a movement toward higher and higher degrees of reciprocal positive responses. Thus, a teacher who increases the cordiality of classroom relations during a year is exerting one kind of leadership.

2. A need for group action. The situation must demand some form of action. For the leadership process to operate, the members of the group must begin to realize that the present situation fails to satisfy their needs adequately, they must perceive some discrepancy between their aspirations and their attainments in the present or in the future. For example, a group (a nation) attacked by an enemy may feel a need for more military protection. It is then ready for leadership, as was the case in the United States just after December 7, 1941. Again, as in the cases of a church, or an army, the needs of the group may be projected beyond the immediate present to the development of a leadership for the future.

---

[1] Compare Paul Pigors, *Leadership or Domination* (Boston: Houghton Mifflin Co., 1935).

3. A leader is a member of the group who participates in the leadership process more acceptably than any other member because he understands the nature of the role to be played by a person better than anyone else, and is able to assume that role. As a consequence of playing the superior role, the leader receives the greatest intensity of positive responses from his associates; that is, his status is high. An instance is that of a good football captain; this achieved position in the group gives the leader the opportunity to influence the actions and ideas of the others who then become followers.

4. Followers. Followers are the members of a group who play roles less adequate in the group than the leader and attain varying degrees of lower status. They follow the leader because of their confidence in him as a person and in his proposals for group action.[2] These, for example, are the players on the football team.

Leadership in a Democratic Society

Democracy and Autocracy Compared. The leadership process in a democratic society is different from that in an autocratic one. Democracy is a way of group life in which persons who live it share in making decisions concerning common problems. Autocracy, on the other hand, is a way of group life in which the decisions are made for the group by one person. Democracy, therefore, provides for a maximum of interaction and consequent flexibility of its associational life; but autocracy minimizes interaction and makes sociation relatively inflexible.

Leadership and Domination Compared. In a democracy group action is a result of the leadership process; but in an autocracy group action is a result of domination. Leadership, as has been pointed out, is the process by which a group takes action after interaction; this is a democratic process. Domination, on the other hand, is the process by which a person (dominator) limits interaction and forcibly controls the activities of the group in the direction of values or goals chosen by himself.[3]

This chapter is primarily a study of the leadership process in democratic situations.

The Function of a Democratic Leader. The leader in a democratic group fosters free interaction among the members of a group; and the group takes action in the direction of the goals set up in a particular

---

[2] Compare, A. J. Murphy, "A Study of the Leadership Process," *American Sociological Review*, VI (October, 1941), pp. 674-687; and William Foote Whyte, "Corner Boys: A Study of Clique Behavior," *American Journal of Sociology*, XLVI (March, 1941), pp. 647-664.

[3] Compare Pigors, *op. cit.*, chapter IV.

situation by the decisions made and accepted by leader and followers in the process of interaction.

No doubt one of the first functions of the democratic leader is to help make clear to all the members of the group the meaning of the free inter-action process and the fact that the standards of control of the group may be set up by the group itself—not imposed by any one person. The leader also helps the group to see clearly the goals toward which it may direct its positive or negative attitudes and actions; thus unified attitudes may be attained.

But the unified decision of a group to take an action or attitude is not easily obtained. First, the factors in the situation that limit or thwart normal interaction in the group (or the satisfaction of needs) must be understood; but the leader has more insight into the meaning of the factors and more acceptable suggestions to make as to goals to be set up than any other member. Thus, the leader is the one who becomes the center of the living of the group because of his usefulness as a group participant.

But the good leader does more than offer suggestions of merit; he stimulates the best possible creative thinking of all the members of the group—thinking directed toward the presentation of as many solutions as possible by all the members. Ideally, leader and members of the group will participate in a maximum degree of interaction—forming a truly dynamic group.[4]

More than this, all the while the leader must stimulate the development of a high degree of positive inter-personal attitudes and actions among the group members, for the differing suggestions of members are to con-tribute to the solution of common problems and *not* to create an op-portunity for persons to dominate others, even in a small way. The differences in status that do arise, as they will eventually, are to be based upon generally recognized merit alone. Finally, democratic action under democratic leadership will stimulate voluntary, not forceful, means of attaining the goals set up (except in the case of overcoming an enemy of the group). Since the decisions are based upon the participation of all, there is no valid reason why force should be used in attaining group goals within the democratic field. A voluntary restructuralization of the social field should be all that is necessary. Thus, democratic leadership stimulates the development of all members of the group in the search for solutions to common problems that may be settled by voluntary adjust-ments.

Experimental as well as theoretical evidence indicates that the *demo-*

---

[4] Jay C. Knode, "Democracy and Post-War Education," chapter XXI, pp. 433-456, in P. F. Valentine, ed., *Twentieth Century Education* (New York: Philosophical Library, 1946).

cratic organization of groups is a sound one. In this connection, the experiments of Lippitt and others are well known.[5] Boys in equated autocratic and democratic clubs of five members each worked on the making of papier-maché masks. In the autocratic group everything was done at the command of the "leader"; but in the democratic group the leader worked with the children and issues were decided upon by vote in view of the facts.

Responses of the children in autocratic groups were, in some cases, obedience, repression and apathy; in other cases submissiveness toward the leader but aggressiveness toward one another, rule breaking and a tendency to ignore the leader. Children in democratic groups responded by friendly behavior, cooperation, the showing of initiative and responsibility. They liked the democratic atmosphere best and were more willing to follow the leader in the democratic situation, not because the leader had so much purely personal power as because he was a central part of a process in which all members of the group were participating—in which all were sharing in making the decisions that directed them toward a common value. There was leadership, social control, and a high degree of morale!

Morale and Leadership

As the foregoing paragraphs have outlined, democratic leadership creates a high degree of morale in a group. If, however, morale is to be controlled scientifically, it must be defined in terms of measurable units. When this is done, it may become possible to determine the degree to which high morale is attained under certain kinds and conditions of leadership.

Morale Defined. Morale may be defined as the degree to which the members of a group express positive attitudes toward a cause, toward the immediate situation, toward one another and toward a leader (or leaders). Thus, a group may possess morale in varying degrees—ranging from high to low. Since in-groups wish a high degree of morale for themselves and a low degree of morale for out-groups, the question of morale and its control is generally considered one of great importance. Other factors being equal, the group with the highest degree of morale is the strongest.[6]

Measurement of Morale. Morale, as defined in the foregoing paragraph,

---

[5] Ronald Lippitt, "Field Theory and Experiment in Social Psychology: Autocratic and Democratic Atmospheres," *American Journal of Sociology*, XLV (July, 1939), pp. 26-49. An evaluation of the most pertinent literature in this field can be found in E. G. Olsen, "The Community and the School," chapter VI, pp. 56-70, in "Social Foundations of Education," *Review of Educational Research*, XVI (February, 1946).

[6] Cf. Gordon W. Allport, "Liabilities and Assets in Civilian Morale," *The Annals of the American Academy of Political and Social Science* (July, 1941), pp. 88-94.

can be measured. Such measurement is the first step toward a scientific control of morale and the intelligent application of leadership, for when efforts to control morale through leadership are made, the degree of control attained may be determined.

1. Measurement of the Degree of Acceptance of a Common Cause. One problem of morale measurement is to determine the degree to which a cause is accepted by the members of a group. This type of morale measurement is well illustrated by a recently devised *National Morale Scale* prepared by Miller.[7]

2. The Degree of Acceptance of the Immediate Situation. As important as is the acceptance of a common cause is the acceptance of the immediate situation in terms of its effect upon one's confidence in dealing with it in the future. These attitudes, too, can be measured with some degree of success; and the control of the leadership process is made more intelligent when the extent of this kind of morale is measured.

A good example of a measure of personal morale in the immediate situation is the *Minnesota Survey of Opinion* (short form).[8] This scale provides a measure of general adjustments and morale for the individual; and the morale of any group can be estimated from an average of the scores made by all the individuals. On this scale persons indicate the extent to which they agree or disagree with propositions like the following:

> "Times are getting better."
> "No one cares what happens to you."
> "The future looks very black."
> "Life is just one worry after another."

The hypothesis that individual morale *is* related to the immediate situation was demonstrated to be sound by Miller,[9] who applied the Rundquist-Sletto scale to 951 college trained adults. Then he compared the 100 who made the best and the 100 who made the poorest morale scores. He found certain relationships between institutional and socio-psychological life situations and morale. High morale was associated with a good

[7] For a copy of the scale and a statement of its reliability and validity, see Delbert C. Miller, "The Measurement of National Morale," *American Sociological Review*, VI (August, 1941), pp. 487-498. Additional unpublished statistical data are also available. For a critical evaluation of attitudes scales, see Ruth Strang, *Behavior and Background of Students in College and Secondary School* (New York: Harper and Brothers, 1937), pp. 254-263. Some attitude scales may be mere measures of opinion.

[8] E. A. Rundquist and R. F. Sletto, *Personality in the Depression* (Minneapolis: The University of Minnesota Press, 1936). This book gives a highly scientific account of the development of the *Minnesota Survey of Opinions*.

[9] D. C. Miller, "Economic Factors in the Morale of College Trained Adults," *The American Journal of Sociology*, XLVII (September, 1941), pp. 139-156.

income (over $2000 annual income), regularity of income, employment stability, a secure future, the fact of marriage, the status of one's job in the eyes of one's associates, opportunities for advancement, and other factors. Such studies make clear to leaders some of the factors in situations which contribute to a high degree of morale. Furthermore, the morale effects of changes may be measured; consequently, the leadership process can be more intelligently directed from the outset.

3. Measurement of Inter-personal Attitudes. There is a third important aspect of morale—the inter-personal attitudes of the members of a group. This fact was made strikingly clear by Roethlisberger and Dickson [10] who found that the most important factor in morale among groups of industrial workers was the inter-personal one. After trying every known scheme for improving working efficiency such as shorter hours, rest periods, special lunches, better lighting and so forth, these researchers found that the degree of cordiality among one's associates was the leading factor in group efficiency as measured by the hourly production of assembled relays.

It is now possible, under certain conditions, to measure the degree of sociation (positive or negative inter-personal responses) in a group by means of sociometric methods. Zeleny [11] has devised a *Group Membership Record* upon which the members of a community of groups (in industry, the army, the school and other groups) may indicate their inter-personal attitudes.

By the use of sociometric methods, supplemented by clinical and observational techniques, including the observation of spontaneous relationships among persons, valuable conclusions can be determined concerning the "associational morale" of a group. The matrix will also reveal possible new combinations of persons that would show increased sociation indexes. In this manner, the "morale" of working groups can be controlled as well as measured. The application of this knowledge to school classrooms, factories, army platoons, flight crews, and small navy units like a gun crew, with the aim of increasing the sociation indexes ("morale") of the sub-groups within these units, is possible. (The sociation index: the average of the units of intensity of all the inter-personal attitudes in a group—plus or minus the average or standard deviation. The sociation index—S—will determine the degree to which there is unity of interaction in the group. Thus, an S of $+ 1.00 \pm 0.00$ would indicate a high degree of group unity or morale, and an S of -1.00 ± 0.00 would

---

[10] F. J. Roethlisberger and W. J. Dickson, *Management and the Worker* (Cambridge, Mass.: Harvard University Press, 1940).

[11] Leslie Day Zeleny, "Measurement of Sociation," *American Sociological Review*, VI (April, 1941), pp. 173-188.

indicate a low degree of morale. For the mathematically inclined S may be expressed, thus:

$$(1) \qquad S = I \pm D = \frac{\Sigma I}{N(N-1)} \pm \frac{\Sigma(\bar{I} \sim I)}{N(N-1)} \text{ units,}$$

when I equals the intensity of an attitude, D equals the deviation, and N equals the number of persons in the group.)

4. Measurement of Attitudes toward Leaders. Within limits, the attitudes of members toward immediate leaders can be measured by means of a *social status index*,[12] which measures the degree of acceptability of a person in a group. If the social status of a person is defined as the average intensity of the attitudes of all the members of a group expressed toward a person in a particular situation, then this average intensity (with the deviations) may be called the *social status index*. This is valuable information for teachers, office and factory managers, military leaders and others, for with the sociometric information before them, sub-leaders can be identified, assigned to groups—and the membership of these sub-groups can be composed of persons who like to work with this leader and who like to work with one another. The degree of sociation in the new groups, as planned on paper, can be measured. Following this, the planned groups can be put into interaction and the results observed and measured. In this manner, the leadership process and morale can be controlled within defined and measurable limits.

Morale Problems. The leadership of a country or group is always faced with problems that may interfere with the attainment of the highest degree of morale. For example, despite the great unifying influence of the Pearl Harbor attack on December 7, 1941, the highest possible degree of morale was not attained. This was indicated precisely for Washington State College students a few days after war was declared by a marked increased agreement with the statement, "The future looks very black." With the facts before them, leaders know where to direct their efforts to improve morale.

As has been shown by measurement, low income and unemployment are associated with a low degree of morale; in other words, low income groups and the unemployed tend to have indifferent or negative attitudes toward any situation which seems to create their low estate. Such persons do not enjoy many of the benefits of democracy for they do not have enough of the opportunities of democracy to enable them to participate with any degree of success. One important step in attaining a

---

[12] For a complete statement of the methods of measuring inter-personal attitudes and determining a *social status index*, see Leslie Day Zeleny, "Status, Its Measurement and Control in Education," *Sociometry*, VI (May, 1941), pp. 193-204.

higher degree of morale is higher real wages for low income groups and the development of constructive plans for more and more secure employment in the future.

Another source of possible disunity is the existence of all kinds of groups or factions within a country. In the United States there are Negro-white groups, capital-labor groups, American-born Japanese-American-born white, country-city, rich-poor, Jews-Gentiles, favored racial groups-unfavored racial groups and many other antithetical pairings. Anything that would increase negative attitudes between such groups would lower national morale. Such would be the aim of enemy agents, to "divide and conquer." To increase morale a democratic leadership must develop a program that will enable members of diverse groups to identify or partially identify themselves with the attitudes of other groups, to learn quickly how to understand them and to share with them attitudes and actions directed toward the attainment of common goals.

Selfishness also hinders the development of a high degree of morale. There are individuals and groups who think of their own interest ahead of the general welfare. Examples are manufacturers of military supplies operating on a cost-plus basis who deliberately run up costs to make more profits, and labor groups who force the payment of excessively high wages for an exclusive membership. Such practices tend to undermine the confidence of the public in the immediate situation.

The foregoing are a few of the factors hindering the leaders from developing a high degree of morale. The Bill of Rights makes it possible for Americans to face the facts and releases the energies of the masses by providing opportunities for them to make decisions in view of the facts. Furthermore, Americans are used to cooperating in a "big way" and "putting things over." This is the program to which all Americans could pledge themselves and cooperate, under democratically selected leadership, to reduce or eliminate all factors, psychological as well as material, that interfere with the attainment of desired goals.[13]

The Selection of Leaders in a Democracy

The selection of leaders to guide the democratic process is a vital problem. Of first importance, perhaps, is knowledge—not book knowledge alone, but also the accurate, practical and precise knowledge that comes from experience in real situations. Second in importance is the acceptability of the leader to the followers. A leader is one whom others

[13] See Gordon W. Allport, "Liabilities and Assets in Civilian Morale," *Annals of the American Academy of Political and Social Science* (July, 1941), pp. 88-94, for a more complete discussion of the foregoing points.

follow and not merely a headman—certainly not a dictator. A leader in a democracy, then, is one who can become the "center of living" of the group of which he is a member. He knows the meaning of the group situation, he stimulates creative thinking, he fosters positive attitudes toward a common goal, toward the immediate situation, toward his associates and himself.

How can such leaders be selected wisely? If a society has a long term program for the selection of leaders there is little doubt that intelligence should be taken as an important basis for selection. This does not mean that intelligence in itself guarantees good leadership; it means simply that the intelligent can learn better and more quickly the form of behavior necessary for leadership.

Said Plato in this connection, "We must watch them from their youth upward, and make them perform actions in which they are most likely to forget or be deceived, and he who remembers and is not deceived is to be selected, and he who fails in the trial will be rejected. That will be the way."

Hollingworth [14] points out that modern scientific testing can identfy the intelligent; and she goes on to say that research has shown that the most intelligent (especially I.Q.'s near 160 or above) tend to be endowed to a superior degree with "integrity, independence, originality, creative imagination, vitality, forcefulness, warmth, poise and stability." Furthermore, Hollingworth points out that those of superior intellect can be identified as early as the age of seven years. The chances are more likely that these persons, *with proper training,* can become the center of democratic leadership processes in many different situations—social as well as scientific.

But selection upon the basis of intelligence alone is not enough. Not all of high intelligence develop desired social qualities. Actual functioning in real sociations is a necessary test of leadership. One way to determine the effectiveness of this functioning is by the observation of experts, who watch an individual's behavior in a situation and rate the performance. Parten [15] demonstrated the effectiveness of this method in the nursery school. The actual directing, following, both directing and following behavior of nursery school children was carefully observed, recorded and expressed in a numerical score. A high correlation ($r = .97$) between observed ascendency and leadership *ratings* made by the teachers based on their careful general observations was found. Thus,

[14] Leta S. Hollingworth, "What We Know About the Early Selection and Training of Leaders," *Teachers College Record,* IV (April, 1939), pp. 561-564. Quotation from Plato in the foregoing article.
[15] M. B. Parten, "Leadership Among Pre-School Children," *Journal of Abnormal Psychology,* XXVII (January, 1933), pp. 430-440.

rating by competent judges who have observed behavior in a situation in which they are competent to judge was shown to be a valid way of identifying leaders among nursery school children.

It was the method of careful observation and rating that the German Army used to select its officers. Despite the despised Nazi ideology, the German Army method of selecting officers was democratic. In selecting officer material the German psychologists and staff officers placed the candidate in many realistic situations and judged the success of his behavior. One of the many tests was to place the candidate before a group of soldiers and ask him to explain a task to them—how to make a coat hanger from a piece of wire, for example. He was judged by his performance and by the extent to which the soldiers learned what was taught.[16]

The basic principle underlying the whole scientific program for the selection of officers may be expressed in the following translated quotation from Simoneit:

"If a non-psychologist in daily life wants to get to know someone he looks into his eyes, listens to his way of speaking and his language, looks at his handwriting, reflects upon his thoughts and way of thinking, and observes him during his actions. The sensible professional psychologist will do the same."

The German program rules out the individual pencil and paper test and substitutes the ratings of several examiners following observation of performances. The German officer candidate must demonstrate to experts that he has the knowledge, experience and social ability to become the center of potential of a social situation, and is selected upon this basis.

Rating of Associates. Another important aspect of the identification and assignment of leaders is their acceptability to followers. This is touched upon by the German military psychologists; but it may be possible to do more with the use of sociometric techniques—especially in the selection of noncommissioned officers, discussion leaders, foremen or sub-foremen in factories and many other leaders. After a period of interaction in which persons in the group have had an opportunity to respond to other persons as values, the administration and scoring of the *Group Membership Record* followed by a calculation of a *social status index* for each person reveals the status of each; and those more than 1SD above the mean status would be the natural leaders in the group tested.

The reliability and validity of the foregoing procedures, which are

[16] See H. L. Ansbacher, "German Military Psychology," *Psychological Bulletin*, XXXVIII (June, 1941), pp. 370-392, and M. Simoneit, "Leitgedanken uber die psychologische Untersuchung des Offizier Nachwuches in der Wehrmacht," *Wehrpsychol. Arbeiten* (1938, No. 6) (Berlin: Bernard & Graefe (13:4838). As quoted by Ansbacher.

essentially rating methods, are high. The *Group Membership Record* itself has been shown to be reliable and valid.[17] More than this the studies of Soderquist, Swab and Peters and E. De A. Partridge have all shown the rating of behavior (by associates or by judges) in a particular situation to be exceptionally reliable and valid.[18]

The method to be used by democracy for the selection of leaders is very clear. In the beginning intelligent persons should be identified for special observation. Finally, those whom competent judges and associates, too, rate as most successful in adjusting to the leadership process may be selected.

A word may be said about the difference between these recommendations and some traditional practices. There has been much interest in the selection of leaders upon the basis of intelligence, aptitude, and personality tests. No doubt these methods are all valuable; but the serious oversight has been the lack of attention to the observation by experts of functioning in real situations. For this criterion in the identification of leaders there is no substitute.

"Traits" of Leaders. Much interest has been shown in the so-called "traits" of leaders. And many have believed, as has been pointed out in the foregoing paragraphs, that persons with certain "traits" would, therefore, become leaders. Such a belief is only partly sound. Says Murphy, "Leadership does not reside in a person. It is a function of the whole situation." [19] The work of Jennings [20] corroborates this conclusion. Her careful experimental studies lead her to conclude that ". . . the influence different individuals in different leader structures were able to exert was related to their being able to enter into and become convincing carriers of the social-cultural currents in the community, sometimes determining and directing their development."

As Murphy [21] points out, a discussion group situation demands stimulating participation, suggestions, criticisms and information. One who can become a center of interaction in such a group must be informal,

---

[17] See Leslie Day Zeleny, "Status, Its Measurement and Control in Education," *Sociometry*, IV (May, 1941), pp. 193-204, and "Measurement of Social Status," *American Journal of Sociology*, XLV (January, 1940), pp. 576-582.

[18] H. O. Soderquist, "Validity of the Measurement of Social Traits of High School Pupils by the Method of Rating by Associates," *Journal of Educational Research*, XXXI (1937), pp. 39-44; J. C. Swab and C. C. Peters, "The Reliability and Validity of Estimates (Ratings) as Measuring Tools," *ibid.*, VII (1933), pp. 224-232; E. de Alton Partridge, "Leadership Among Adolescent Boys," *Contribution to Education* (New York: Columbia University Press, 1934).

[19] Albert J. Murphy, "A Study of The Leadership Process," *American Sociological Review*, VI (October, 1941), pp. 674-687.

[20] Helen S. Jennings, "Structure of Leadership—Development and Sphere of Influence," *Sociometry* I (July, 1937), pp. 99-143.

[21] Murphy, *op. cit.*

talkative but not too talkative, critical and well informed. On the other hand, a scout leadership situation demands different "traits": "youth, general ability, athletic ability, size, strength, knowledge of games, sociability, high personal standards, scout rank and experience."

In different situations, the leaders are those who can respond most adequately to the needs of the situation. And situations change, especially in contemporary times; "traits" desirable in one period might not fit a little later in the social process. For example, a director of the OPA in a prewar period may not be able to rise to the occasion in a war period when extreme speed and administrative efficiency are necessary; and a leader like Chamberlain fitted the British situation only in peace; it was Churchill who rose to the demands of a wartime situation. Says Vaughan-Jones: [22] "The 'normal' leader is often the 'tail' of an unvocal, but none the less vital 'popular' movement. When circumstances order a 'right about turn,' the 'tail' becomes leader. For example, Hitler caught the turn of the tide from German Social Democratic advance." Without question the "traits" of Hitler were much different from the "traits" of the Social Democratic leaders. The "traits" of leaders are, therefore, in no small part selected by the needs of the situation. Such a statement does not deny the fact that leaders, who do arise, influence the situation according to their particular individual talents. Vaughan-Jones states further: "The 'traits' of leaders often determine the situation. For example, Juarez and the Mexican rebirth, Mustapha Kemal and the Turkish reforms, and Roosevelt and the New Deal. And the difference between German Nazism, Latin Fascism and Petain's neo-fascism was colored by the 'traits' of the leaders as well as by the situation—once the leader was in office." [23] The thesis of this discussion implies, however, that no "great man" can suddenly walk into a situation and mold it completely to his own choosing without force of arms. He must first adapt to the situation and become a center of influence—then, within limits, his own unique talents may be used in determining the "variations" on the central theme.

In view of the foregoing comments, it might seem a little inappropriate to consider the "traits" of leaders. Nevertheless, there are some "traits" that frequently appear among leaders and seem common to many situations. Research [24] has shown that one who arrives at the center of interaction in the leadership process is likely to be more *intelligent* than the followers. No doubt this is because it takes ability to understand the meaning of a situation and to play the role of leader in it. For this reason, too, *knowledge* is essential.

---

[22] J. Vaughan-Jones, Unpublished memorandum.

[23] Vaughan-Jones, *op. cit.*

[24] See Leslie Day Zeleny, "Leadership," in *Encyclopedia of Educational Research* (New York: The Macmillan Co., 1941), pp. 662-667.

The Development of Democratic Leaders

Research has shown that leadership ability can be developed.[25] The method now seems reasonably clear. Persons with latent talent must be given opportunities for special training. Perhaps the most important phase of the training (which should begin in the nursery school) is experience in followership and leadership in groups. Finally, as one reaches maturity, experience in leadership in the actual types of groups in which one may lead later is necessary. Obviously, this experience should be guided by experts at all stages—the main purpose of the guidance being to help the potential leaders to understand the full meaning of their experiences. To accomplish the foregoing results much of the training of leaders should be performed in dynamic groups or in realistic situations so that the success of each in playing roles in the group can be judged by experts and by one's associates.

Second, potential leaders should be carefully instructed in the meaning of democracy and democratic interaction. One who believes that leadership means domineering control and that all decisions are to be made by one for the others will not be respected except possibly in a military organization. Even in the military service, the best leaders are democratic in spirit and action in so far as the situation will allow.

Third comes knowledge. There are three kinds of knowledge—a general knowledge of the facts of science and social science which serves as a general foundation for wise decisions of everyone, the norms of the group in which the leader would function, and, finally, a knowledge of the "traits" of successful leaders. With respect to the last point, it may be said that some persons have knowledge, both general and particular, but fail to become leaders because they are not aware of the necessity for self-confidence, finality of decision, speed of decision, initiative, listening, respecting the group hierarchy, etc.[26] No doubt the guided experience in leadership would contribute to this goal.

Finally, a leader must acquire a keen sense of emotional control.[27] He must be a hard worker in order to acquire superior knowledge to perform more intelligently than others in a given situation; and hard work must become a habit followed throughout the years of one's life—or one's period of leadership.

Exceptionally hard work will give a good intellect superior knowledge;

---

[25] George A. Eichler, "Studies in Student Leadership," *Pennsylvania State Studies in Education* (State College, Pa., 1934).

[26] George C. Homans, *The Human Group*, Chapter 16.

[27] Hollingworth, *op. cit.* The remarks that follow are based on suggestions made by Dr. Hollingworth.

but herein lies a danger. A highly trained person may easily become impatient with the less competent persons in his group who have less knowledge, slower speed of decision, less initiative, and so forth. For example, a young teacher may make sarcastic remarks to dull children. The response to such remarks is negative—either in the form of conflict or withdrawal of cooperation. It is often at this point that otherwise successful leaders make a fatal mistake.

Another fault may be inability to work with superiors. A superior person may feel that he knows so much no one can tell him anything; and he resents being told what he doesn't know or even what he does know. Since, however, the social structure consists of a hierarchy of status relationships, nearly everyone is faced with the problem of adjusting to superiors as well as inferiors—and the adjustment must be in both directions. The person who has had years of directed participation in interaction as both follower and leader should develop the proper social adjustment.

Summary

Leadership is a situation-process allowing for the exercise of social control by an individual; and, as a process, leadership is an important consideration in the democratic way of life. It is necessary to distinguish between what is true democratic leadership and what is domination, sometimes called "leadership" in autocratic schemes. In the former the participating members of a group share in making its decision, while in the latter only the dominator makes decisions.

Modern studies have given us many insights into leadership, none of which is more important for predictive and selective purposes than the close correlation between leadership and intelligence. Not all intelligent persons have leadership qualities, but the best leaders are also among the most intelligent. This knowledge makes possible the selection of potential leaders at an early age and, by implication, their preparation for the tasks of leadership.

Students of leadership recognize that not only are there personal factors involved in leadership, but also situational factors. The leader is a function of the situation, and those who make excellent leaders in one type of situation may be unsuited in others.

In the development of leaders several considerations are important. Leaders develop from participating in situations where they are leaders, and in those where they are followers. Leaders must gain general and specific knowledge, and learn to act on that knowledge with decisions which have the element of finality. They must learn to understand and respect democratic processes. Finally, they must have emotional control, and learn to avoid that impatience which many people of intelligence and superior knowledge have for those less endowed or equipped.

One requisite for lasting leadership grows out of the fact that persons live in hierarchies of status, so that there are always adjustments to make to those above as well as to those of inferior status. The best leadership is able to function in this general framework of status gradation.

QUESTIONS

1. What elements obtain in the leadership process?
2. What factors give rise to leadership?
3. Describe the realization of a need for group action.
4. In a democratic situation, what is the relationship between the individual and the decisions to be made?
5. Differentiate between leadership and domination.
6. What is the function of a democratic leader?
7. Define morale.
8. How is morale measured?
9. How may one measure the acceptance by a group of a common goal?
10. What are the "traits" of a leader?
11. What is the method for democratic selection of leaders?
12. What factors in the United States make it difficult to have a unified following?
13. Explain the value of the social status index.
14. What is sociation?
15. Is individual morale related to the immediate situation?
16. What group factors limit the power of the leader?

SUGGESTED TOPICS FOR TERM PAPERS AND FURTHER RESEARCH

1. Leadership training and development in the United States armed forces.
2. Methods of leadership selection in the United States Civil Service.
3. Compare political leaders with military leaders in the United States.
4. Study the methods of developing leadership in the Prussian system.
5. Compare military leaders with political leaders in Germany previous to World War II.
6. Problems of leadership in industrial relations.
7. Morale building factors in the classroom.
8. Compare educational attempts at building leadership with the results after leaving the classroom situation.
9. Discuss the principles of democratic leadership.
10. The use of emotional control in leadership.

BIBLIOGRAPHY

Books

Herbert Agar, *The People's Choice* (Boston: Houghton Mifflin, 1938). On the working of leadership in our democracy.

Emory S. Bogardus, *Leaders and Leadership* (New York: D. Appleton-Century Co., 1934). A sociological survey.

Walter G. Bowerman, *Studies in Genius* (New York: Philosophical Library, 1947). Some novel and interesting observations.

Crane Brinton, *The Anatomy of Revolution* (New York: W. W. Norton and Co., 1938). A dissecting analysis of the various types of leaders during the troubled times.

Margaret Fisher, *Leadership and Intelligence* (New York: Columbia University Press, 1954). A study and criticism of Karl Mannheim's theory of the intellectual elite.

Robert Aaron Gordon, *Business Leadership in the Large Corporation* (Washington, D.C.: Brookings Institution, 1945). An investigation of the topic still largely neglected by the sociologists.

George C. Homans, *The Human Group* (New York: Harcourt, Brace and Co., 1950). Chapter 16 is excellent on leadership in small groups.

Sidney Hook, *The Hero in History* (New York: John Day Co., 1943). Cannot answer whether history makes heroes or heroes make history; concludes that the interplay is the causation.

Wilhelm Lange-Eichbaum, *The Problem of Genius* (New York: The Macmillan Co., 1932).

Ferdinand Lundberg, *America's Sixty Families* (New York: Vanguard Press, 1937). A study of the rich families.

Charles Allen Madison, *Critics and Crusaders* (New York: Henry Holt and Co., 1947).

Vilfredo Pareto, *The Mind and Society* (New York: Harcourt, Brace and Co., 1935). A classical study of how the ruling elites operate. Should be read in conjunction with Gaetano Mosca, *The Ruling Class* (New York: McGraw-Hill Book Co., 1939), another classic.

E. DeAlton Partridge, *Leadership Among Adolescent Boys* (New York: Columbia University Press, 1934). Uses the five-men-ten-men technique of identifying leaders. A scientific attempt.

Paul Pigors, *Leadership or Domination* (Boston: Houghton Mifflin, 1935). A classic in the field of leadership.

Psychology for the Fighting Man (New York: Penguin Books, 1944). Chapter XVI, "Leadership," pp. 302-317.

Dwight Sanderson, *Leadership for Rural Life* (New York: The Association Press, 1940). A very readable and practical work.

Pitirim A. Sorokin, *Social and Cultural Dynamics* (New York: American Book Co., 1937-41). See Vol. 3 of this famed work.

F. H. Soward, *Moulders of National Destinies* (New York: Oxford University Press, 1940). A collection of biographical sketches of contemporary political leaders.

L. M. Terman and others, *Genetic Studies of Genius* (Stanford, Calif.: Stanford University Press, 1925-32, 4 vols.). Well-known psychological studies.

Wilson D. Wallis, *Messiahs: Their Role in Civilization* (Washington, D.C.: American Council on Public Affairs, 1943). One of the few sociological studies of the "charismatic leadership" (developed by Max Weber).

Leslie Day Zeleny, "Leadership," pp. 662-668, in *The Encyclopedia of Educational Research* (New York: The Macmillan Co., 1950).

Periodicals

H. L. Ansbacher, "German Military Psychology," *Psychological Bulletin*, XXVIII (June, 1941), pp. 370-392.

T. E. Coffin, "A Three-Component Theory of Leadership," *Journal of Abnormal and Social Psychology*, XXXIX (January, 1944), pp. 63-83.

Robert E. L. Faris, "Sociological Causes of Genius," *American Sociological Review*, V (1940), pp. 689-697.

"How Soldiers Rate Officers," *Science Digest*, XIII (April, 1943), pp. 23-24.

Otto Klineberg, "Genius," *Encyclopaedia of the Social Sciences*, VI (1931), pp. 612-615.

Hans Kohn, "Messianism," *ibid.*, X (1933), pp. 356-364. This well-known historian has developed this theme in his *The Twentieth Century* (New York: The Macmillan Co., 1949), especially in Chapter V, "The Crisis of the Individual," pp. 61-74.

Harvey C. Lehman, "National Differences in Creativity," *American Journal of Sociology*, LII (1946-47), pp. 475-488.

Ronald Lippitt, "Field Theory and Experiment in Social Psychology: Autocratic and Democratic Atmospheres," *ibid.*, XLV (July, 1939), pp. 26-49; "An Experimental Study of the Effect of Democratic and Authoritarian Group Atmospheres," *Studies in Topological and Vector Psychology*, University of Iowa, Studies in Child Welfare, XVI, 3 (1940), pp. 43-195.

Paul Meadows, "Some Notes on the Social Psychology of the Hero," *Southwestern Social Science Quarterly*, XXVI (1945-46), pp. 239-247.

D. C. Miller, "Economic Factors in the Morale of College Trained Adults," *American Journal of Sociology*, XLVIII (September, 1941), pp. 139-156; "The Measurement of National Morale," *American Sociological Review*, VI (August, 1941), pp. 487-498.

M. C. Otto, "Fanaticism," *Encyclopaedia of the Social Sciences*, VI (1931), pp. 90-92.

Fritz Redl, "Group Emotion and Leadership," *Psychiatry* (1942), pp. 573-596.

Richard Schmidt, "Leadership," *Encyclopaedia of the Social Sciences*, IX (1933), pp. 282-287.

Joseph Schneider, "The Cultural Situation as a Condition for the Achievement of Fame," *American Sociological Review*, II (1937), pp. 480-481; "Social Origin and Fame: The United States and England," *ibid.*, X (1945), pp. 52-60.

Stephen S. Viser, "Environmental Backgrounds of Leading American Scientists," *ibid.*, XIII (1948), pp. 65-72.

Sanford Winston, "The Mobility of Eminent Americans," *American Journal of Sociology*, XLI (1935-36), pp. 624-634.

William F. Whyte, "Corner Boys: A Study in Clique Behavior," *ibid.*, XLVI (March, 1941), pp. 647-654.

Leslie D. Zeleny, "Characteristics of Group Leaders," *Sociology and Social Research*, XXIII (November-December, 1939), pp. 140-149; "Objective Selection of Group Leaders," *ibid.*, XXIV (March–April, 1940), pp. 327-36; "Measurement of Sociation," *American Sociological Review*, VI (April, 1941), pp. 173-188; "Sociometry of Morale," *ibid.*, IV (December, 1939), pp. 799-808; "Status, Its Measurement and Control in Education," *Sociometry* (May, 1941), pp. 193-204; "Selection of Compatible Flying Partners," *American Journal of Sociology*, LII (1947), pp. 424-431.

CHAPTER XVIII

Secret Societies

In the summer of 1941 Herr Goebbels produced for the edification of Nazi-controlled Europe what to him no doubt was a masterly sensation—a picture of Franklin D. Roosevelt in a Masonic apron. While the majority of Americans understand that Masonic affiliation is for the most part an innocuous badge of respectability, the Nazi propagandist was playing upon a deep-seated prejudice, not only against Masonry, but secret societies in general. What is secret is suspect. So, however much the Knights of This and That may protest that their activities are of no public concern, gossip and rumor will not down.

This chapter aims to discover how far secret societies are agencies of social control and in what ways. But first, since secrecy is a very human trait, we shall have need to decide what a secret society really is. Every human being possesses secrets, and no doubt organized groups keep certain matters secret for a while, but that does not make them secret societies. Communist party units in the United States have operated furtively, used aliases, and perhaps have a secret code. But if they are compared with an earlier conspiratorial association, the Carbonari, there is a difference. The Carbonari had a secret ritual, special regalia, various degrees of membership, each with formal initiations, all of which were permanent features of their group life. The working definition proposed for this chapter is then: a secret society is an association which possesses an institutionalized pattern of esoteric elements.

The Secret Society Pattern

The pattern of secret societies has certain common characteristics which, woven together, form a colorful combination of ritual, ceremony, and symbolism. Some combination of the following features is usually found: (1) a regular meeting ceremony; (2) an initiation ceremony; (3) an oath or pledge of secrecy; (4) elaborate ceremonies appropriate to special occasions—such as the anniversary of its founding or the burial of a member; (5) the wearing of special regalia; (6) the wearing of pins or emblems with special symbolic meaning to the initiated; (7) passwords or handclasps by which the initiated identify themselves to other members to whom they are not personally known; and (8) gradients of degrees within the society each of which has its set of secret ritual, etc.

The Interests Pursued by Secret Societies

The range of interests involved in the multifarious secret societies is indeed extremely wide as may be seen by listing the various categories in Gist's functional classification which are as follows: benevolent and philanthropic societies, insurance societies, revolutionary and reformist societies, professional and occupational societies, religious orders, mystical and occult societies, military societies, and orders of knighthood, college social and recreational societies, and criminal societies.[1] Since it thus can be seen that the secret society pattern has been adopted to implement the pursuit of nearly the entire range of human interests, it is clear that the student of social control will find some of little interest and others of much significance. Hence a classification of these various societies in social control terms is necessary.

Classification of Secret Societies in Social Control Terms

Such a scheme of classification follows:

A. Societies concerned with controlling their own members in the pursuit of interests of concern to themselves alone.
>   Examples: orgiastic societies; convivial societies; the more purely fellowship societies; benefit societies.

B. Societies primarily concerned with controlling their own members as above, but indirectly or secondarily concerned with controlling outsiders or the general social life.
>   Examples: Freemasonry, Knights of Columbus, college fraternities.

C. Societies primarily concerned with controlling others than the initiated, and secondarily interested in controlling their own members in the pursuit of the primary aims. This category is further subdivided into two categories.
>   1. Societies from the greater power groups, aimed at curbing the rise of groups with lesser power.
>   Examples: American Protestant Association, The Old and New Ku Klux Klans, Black Legion.

---

[1] Noel P. Gist, *Secret Societies* (Columbia, Mo.: University of Missouri Studies), XV, No. 4, p. 24.

2. Societies from the lesser power groups, directed at improving the status of the less privileged.

Examples: the Carbonari, Irish nationalist societies, the Knights of Labor.

D. Societies primarily interested in controlling others in their own interests through disorganizing and socially disruptive means.

Examples: criminal societies, such as the Cammorra, the Mafia, and the Triad (Chinese in United States.)

Societies will be referred to below as (A) self-interested associations, (B) intermediate associations, (C) societally active associations, and (D) criminal associations.

The History of Secret Societies

Secret societies or secret rituals do not appear in all primitive societies. Their principal centers are in Asia, West Africa, and North America.[2] Primitive secret societies have frequently developed out of pubertal initiation ceremonies. Webster[3] traces three stages of development. In the first stage, pubertal rites are performed upon all the males of the tribe. The ceremonies are exclusive to men and are integrated with the life of the tribe. When conditions conspire to break down the original custom-bound control, grades of secret rites develop where the advanced grades are more exclusive. To some of these advanced grades, functions of social control, such as vigilante and judicial functions, become attached. In the third stage, secret societies emerge as differentiated associations within the tribal community, performing different functions, sometimes purely sociable, sometimes magico-animistic, and occasionally they are supplementary adjuncts to a class structure.

Ancient Times. In ancient society secret associations developed around the so-called "Mysteries," such as the Egyptian mysteries of Isis, the Eleusinian mysteries of Greece, and Mithra worship which arose in the East and eventually spread to Rome. Lepper considers these ancient mysteries not so much as separate secret organizations but rather as integral parts of the society as a whole, performing functions connected with religion, statecraft, or both.[4]

Christianity. From the time of the triumph of Christianity over Mithra worship in Ancient Rome to the late Middle Ages, there was a lull in the

[2] Nathan Miller, *Encyclopaedia of the Social Sciences*, XIII, pp. 621-22.

[3] Hutton Webster, *Primitive Secret Societies* (New York: The Macmillan Co., 1931).

[4] John H. Lepper, *Famous Secret Societies*, (London: Sampson Lowe, Marston Co., 1932), p. 2.

development of secret societies. Christianity became not only the universal European religion, but also the main system of social control. Offering universal brotherhood, crushing all heresy with a militant fanaticism and efficient social organization, and providing an emotional release through its promise of eternal salvation and its rich proliferation of ritual, ceremony, and symbolism, the early church tolerated no rival associations.

Middle Ages. Toward the close of the Middle Ages there emerged certain secret associations which were prototypes of those to come later. The Templars and The Rosicrucians showed some resemblance to Masonry. The Vehmgericht presaged numerous "law and order" societies. The Steinmetzen, The French Compagnonnage, and the Charbonniers are precursors of secret labor organizations. Perhaps also might be added the Assassins, an heretical sect of Mohammedans arising around 1000 A.D. in Persia developing into a prototype of the modern racketeering associations.[5]

Modern Times. Secret societies in the eighteenth and nineteenth centuries in Europe were identified with two closely related movements—the attempt of the less privileged to democratize the social structure of their various nations, and the efforts of various nationalities to achieve nationhood. These two objectives were sometimes blended and sometimes distinct. The French Carbonari and the United Slavonians in Russia strove to democratize their own countries and Europe. The Hetairi in Greece, the Polish Templars, and the numerous Irish societies aimed more directly at national independence. The Italian Carbonari desired to free Italy but spread to other countries as an international revolutionary organization. In addition to the seemingly endless array of revolutionary societies, two other types of secret associations may be noted. Freemasonry, one of the most widespread and important of secret societies, the probable progenitor of many others, arose in England in the early eighteenth century. In the nineteenth century there arose several secret criminal societies of which the Italian Cammorra is a notorious example.

At the beginning of the twentieth century, secret societies in Europe seemed to decline. International Marxism and the later counter-revolutionary movements of Fascism and Nazism were underground, clandestine movements of necessity, but apparently with no institutionalized esoteric patterns. During World Wars I and II, old secret societies were revived and new ones formed to play prominent roles in the underground opposition to German control.

---

[5] See Lepper, *op. cit.*, for an account of this, and other earlier secret societies.

American Secret Societies

In the United States, in contrast with Europe, the latter part of the nineteenth century witnessed the rise of innumerable secret societies of many types. According to Mecklin, there were 568 fraternal orders in 1900, only 78 of which antedate 1880. He estimates that in 1923 perhaps seven per cent of our population belonged to fraternal orders.[6] Merz estimates 800 societies by 1927 with thirty million members.[7] It is probable that some of these groups do not conform to our definition of a secret society and that there is some overlapping of memberships in the above estimates. Still it is in any case clear that the United States is the scene *par excellence* for the study of secret societies. Since the depression of 1929 there has been an apparent decline both in the size of memberships and in the number of different societies.

The American secret societies which have exerted influence on the larger society of which they are a part are identified with the following general movements: "nativism," or the anti-Catholic, anti-Negro, and anti-alien movement, illustrated by the American Protective Association (1887), the Ku Klux Klan, and the Black Legion; the labor and agrarian movements, illustrated by the Knights of Labor and the Grange; and movements in this country identified with European nationalist aspirations, as in the case of the Ancient Order of Hibernians (Irish) and an American branch of the IMRO (Macedonian).

The Self-Interested Secret Societies

The larger number of secret societies, especially in the United States, concern themselves largely with intra-group interests. They enter the public arena only if they are opposed, and then only to protect their right to exist.

Sociability and mutual benefit societies, illustrated by the Benevolent and Protective Order of Elks, fall into this class. Many societies combine two or more interests, the more prevalent combination being the fraternal lodge with insurance benefit features. Since they do not attempt to influence society at large, they do not greatly concern the subject of this chapter.[8]

---

[6] J. M. Mecklin, *The Ku Klux Klan* (New York: Harcourt, Brace and Co., 1924), p. 217.

[7] Charles Merz, *The Great American Bandwagon* (New York: Literary Guild of America, 1928), p. 23.

[8] The reader is referred to Gist, *op. cit.*, for further discussion of these societies.

Intermediate Associations

Many secret societies are primarily interested in their own group life but in subtle indirect ways effect some control over the life of the community. Among such effects are the following: (1) membership in certain societies carries prestige in the community which gives the member an added influence in civic affairs; (2) secret societies discriminate in selection of membership among social types; that is, they take only the members of a certain religious or ethnic group, and bar certain types categorically; and tend, not always deliberately, to acquire a membership falling within a recognizable limit of socio-economic status, such as, middle class, workers, etc. As a consequence, the experience of membership tends to sharpen or reinforce a special group point of view on public problems as distinct from a broader social viewpoint.

College fraternities, for example, are mainly fellowship groups, but the fraternity system on a campus is an important mechanism of control. It plays a prominent role in controlling the extracurricular life of the campus and is an important mechanism through which the dean's office can influence standards of conduct and generally check up on the life of the students. Fraternities set the standards for proper collegiate behavior. The fraternity system is a status-defining institution since the various fraternities on a campus are thought of in terms of a hierarchy of most prominent, less prominent, etc. This sometimes keeps out of important offices in college organizations those who are not fraternity members, students of minority status origins, and "barbs" in general.

Freemasonry

Freemasonry arose in England near the beginning of the eighteenth century, spread rapidly throughout Europe, and later in the United States. This order possesses an elaborate pattern of ritualistic elements and the most elaborate organizational structure of all secret societies. There are thirty-three degrees and at least twenty-five auxiliary societies, women's, juvenile, collegiate, etc.[9] The membership of Masonry is drawn from the middle and upper classes. Catholics are forbidden to join by their church, although in recent years some Catholic laymen have become members. The official purposes of this order are fellowship and the cultivation of moral and spiritual character in the members. Any specific political or societal aims are disclaimed.

While Masonry is broadly one movement throughout the Caucasian world, any discussion of its influence upon society requires separate attention to Anglo-American Masonry as distinct from Continental

---

[9] Gist, *op. cit.*, p. 59.

Masonry. Although disclaiming any direct societal aims, Masonry does claim to cultivate a liberal, freedom loving, God worshiping, and internationally minded type of person in its members. If this aim is placed against the social background of English and Continental life, it is clear why Masonry had a less stormy career in England and Scandinavia than in the remainder of Europe. Since the northern countries were basically liberal in political and religious outlook, the vague societal aims of Masonry harmonized with those of the majority and controlling elements of these countries. Hence Masonry lived a relatively placid existence. When Parliament suppressed secret societies in 1798, it expressly exempted Masonry. By contrast, on the Continent, with less democratic political institutions and more Catholic-Protestant conflict, Masonry was periodically suppressed by either state or church influence. There is some evidence to indicate that French Masons played some role in the French Revolution.[10] The fact that many liberal reformist leaders in Europe were Masons furnishes some circumstantial evidence of Masonic political and anti-clerical activity. Continental Masonry was suspect to the Church because of its liberal theological ideas, to aristocratic rulers because it stressed liberal idealism, and to Marxist radicals because it cultivated a "bourgeois" social type. Revolutionary and counterrevolutionary totalitarian governments including Soviet Russia, Nazi Germany, Fascist Italy, Vichy France, Franco Spain, and all the "Quisling" governments outlawed Masonry.[11] Both British and French Masons passed resolutions condemning certain phases of the Versailles Treaty, indicating a spirit of international good will.

In the United States, Masonry has followed the English pattern. Whatever influence it may have exerted in controlling American society may be judged in part from the nature and intensity of the opposition to it. Masonry was opposed by Protestant clergy for its liberal religious ideas. Catholicism has opposed Masonry more effectively and persistently for the same reason and the added one that it presumes to develop spiritual qualities, a function which Catholicism claims to itself. There has been no noteworthy political opposition to the Masonic Order since the short-lived Anti-Masonic Party formed in 1827, following the Morgan incident.[12]

Since Masonry, in the United States, has not been accused by its opponents of playing any role in the larger national issues, whatever influence it has is to be seen in the influence of the individual lodge in the local

[10] F. H. Hankins, *Encyclopaedia of Social Sciences*, X, p. 182.

[11] G. Sven Lunden, "The Annihilation of Freemasonry," *American Mercury* (February, 1941), pp. 184-191.

[12] William Morgan was abducted and never seen again. It was alleged that Morgan was murdered by Masons because he threatened to publish a treatise exposing the secrets of Masonry. This the Masons stoutly denied.

community. Here again we have little concrete evidence, only the dubious circumstantial evidence of the "notions" entertained about the lodge by local non-Masons.

In appraising the local lodge as an agency of community control, the most significant fact is that Masonry is the aristocrat in the hierarchy of fraternal lodges. Membership in it is a badge of solid respectability and carries prestige. Thus the influence of a man may be increased because of his Masonic affiliation, and a Mason in distress may count upon more than ordinary attention from a fellow Mason or a lodge. Beyond this, there is insufficient evidence to establish any further controlling influence. The local Masonic lodge outwardly sponsors no political or social programs and its philanthropic activities are usually confined to other Masons, and their dependents. In this respect it differs strikingly from the more recent men's service-luncheon clubs which carry on much philanthropic work for the "underprivileged." [13] It is partly for this reason that some middle-class men belonging to both have found Rotary, *et al.*, more engrossing.[14]

Numerous other fraternal lodges in the United States, of which the Odd Fellows, Knights of Pythias, and the Red Men are among the better known, do not require separate treatment. In sociological character, these associations are similar to the Masons. In the local community, as lodges, they occupy ranks of lower prestige. They do not appear to have any broad national significance.

Conditions Favoring the Rise of the Self-Interested and Intermediate Societies. The search for the conditions which give rise to secret societies, as with all other groups, is complicated by chance factors, and by imitation and diffusion. There is little doubt that many of these groups, especially the fraternal ones, adopted the secret society pattern as a copy of already existing ones. The fact that the founders of a number of societies were, at the same time, members of one or more other secret societies suggests that the similarities are a product of imitation.[15]

The exuberant growth of secret societies in the United States from 1880 to 1910 is related to two conditions which favored the rise of myriads of associations of all sorts: a degree of economic superfluity, making possible the payment of dues; and the paucity of culture in our "business society" resulting in frantic efforts at diversion. The Beards attribute the revival of the Ku Klux Klan as much to the fun of going to conventions in strange places and wearing fancy uniforms, as to deep-

---

[13] C. F. Marden, *Rotary and Its Brothers* (Princeton: Princeton Univ. Press, 1935), chapters III and IV.

[14] *Ibid.*, p. 150.

[15] Gist, *op. cit.*, p. 45.

seated hatred of Jews or Catholics.[16] There is considerable evidence that the growth of many of these societies was overstimulated by high-pressure commercial salesmanship.

The Methods of Controlling Members. The types of societies examined thus far rely on the values of secrecy, and of ritual, ceremony, and symbolism to secure a sufficient solidarity for the pursuit of the group interests. While the oath to maintain the secrets of the order is frequently couched in threatening and self-threatening terms, it is not to be taken literally.

As MacIver writes,[17] "ritual invests an occasion with importance and solemnity" and "the rhythm of the procedure attunes the mind emotionally to the corresponding ideas." When ritual, ceremony, and symbolism are secret, as Simmel wrote,[18] they "heighten the value of the secret to the possessor and non-possessor beyond its real value. . . . The natural impulse to idealization and the natural timidity of men operate to one and the same end in the presence of secrecy, viz., to heighten it by phantasy and to distinguish it by a degree of attention that published reality could not command."

It appears that the spiritual climate of these fraternal orders does not cultivate attitudes or habit patterns of force or extra-legality, even though it may encourage a smug sense of superiority toward others.

The Societally Active Secret Associations

The secret societies of most interest to the student of social control are those whose main purpose is to effect some control of the larger society of which they are part. In general, societies of this sort arise in periods of social unrest when two sets of conditions are present: (1) when the power relationships between the various groups in the community are undergoing a change; and (2) when the basic societal institutions, especially the political or economic institutions, do not permit a resolution of this struggle for power to proceed in an open, public manner. Secret societies emerge among the lesser power groups attempting to wrest more privileges for themselves; and they arise within the greater power groups to maintain their present status. These two classes of secret organizations will be referred to as Radical and Reactionary societies.

The methods of control employed by both these classes of societies are

[16] Charles A. and Mary R. Beard, *The Rise of American Civilization* (New York: The Macmillan Co., 1927), p. 731.
[17] R. M. MacIver, *Society: A Textbook in Sociology* (New York: Farrar and Rinehart, 1937), pp. 338-339.
[18] George Simmel, "The Sociology of Secret Societies," *American Journal of Sociology*, XI (1906), pp. 464-465.

essentially the same and include these two phases: the conditioning in the members—through ritual, ceremony, and symbolism, and through the discipline of characteristically hierarchical social structures—of fanatical devotion, obedience to leaders, intolerance of others, and uncritical acceptance of stereotyped conceptions of others; and the use of extra-legal instruments to control others, ranging from intimidation through to the most violent physical coercion.

Reactionary Societies

The Ku Klux Klan. The original Ku Klux Klan arose in the South during the reconstruction period following the War Between the States. The situation in the white-Negro relationship was a sociological dilemma. The victorious Northerners had given the Negroes full legal equality with the whites. The illiterate freed slaves were not capable of assuming immediately the responsibilities of their new legal status. The failure of the Northern statesmen to perceive this dilemma and the readiness of "carpet baggers" to exploit the situation to their own advantage gave rise to the Ku Klux Klan.

The objective of this organization was to keep the Negroes in a subordinate social, economic, and political position. Its members were drawn from various elements of the white groups, including the aristocracy. Although the Klan was officially suppressed within a few years, it had essentially succeeded in its purpose. It left as its contribution to the social structure of the South a well integrated caste system which still functions effectively to "keep the Negro in his place."

Since the old Klan could not accomplish its aims legally, it became a secret society and adopted extra-legal methods. It relied chiefly upon intimidation which had great effect upon the superstitious, slave-conditioned Negroes. Threats and warnings delivered in the dead of night by hooded, white-gowned riders, and conclaves of these eerie figures assembled around burning crosses, terrified and intimidated the new freedmen. In more serious cases the Klan whipped and tarred and feathered the recalcitrants, or burned their homes. In extreme instances the Kluxers resorted to murder by lynching, as is admitted even by a sympathetic interpreter of the old Klan.[19] Frequently their exploits required breaking into jails, intimidating the prison keepers to get their victim; and intimidating, or even murdering, legally appointed prosecutors who attempted to convict Klansmen.

The New Ku Klux Klan. The new Klan was founded in Atlanta by William Joseph Simmons. The new order did not have clear continuity

---

[19] Stanely F. Horn, *KKK: Invisible Empire* (Boston: Houghton Mifflin Co., 1939), p. 70.

with the old. Simmons dreamed of founding a great "nativist" order and apparently borrowed the ritual, regalia, and nomenclature of the old Klan, capitalizing upon its tradition and prestige.[20] The new Klan grew very slowly until 1920, when it expanded rapidly throughout the country. Its purposes, more broadly nativist than the old order, were anti-Catholic, anti-alien, as well as anti-Negro, and eventually became anti-labor as well. According to Mecklin, its members were "descendants of the Old American stock, living in villages and small towns of sections least disturbed by immigration and industrialism." For the most part they "were ignorant, unthinking middle class persons." [21]

The new Klan also copied the methods of the old. Examples of clearly authenticated instances of violence include whippings and lynchings in four states; the whipping of a fourteen year old girl near Texarkana; the kidnaping of two brothers in Port Arthur in front of a police station while armed men prevented the chief of police from pursuing the kidnapers.

The new Klan had a seriously demoralizing effect upon the orderly civic life of many communities. Operating against elements more capable of resisting than were the Negroes, it provoked counterviolence. Loucks cites a number of riots when anti-Klan elements attempted to disperse the Klan parades.[22] Being secret, politicians, officials, store keepers, and editors were never quite sure who were members and how many members there were. This demoralized politics and intimidated those who sincerely wished to oppose it, and by thus dividing many communities, seriously impaired effective community spirit for the time being.

The Black Legion. In 1936, a thirty-two year old W.P.A. worker, named Poole, was murdered in Detroit. The hearings on the case indicated that he was killed by a gang of hooded hoodlums who were members of a secret society which came to be known as The Black Legion.[23] A police raid on the headquarters netted firearms, daggers, whips, hoods, robes, and literature indicating its presence in fifteen other states. In Jackson, Michigan, five alleged members were arrested on charges of whipping a man who refused to join. In the Poole murder prosecution it was brought out that many men were forced to take the Black Legion oath at the point of a gun. Further hearings in Detroit revealed plots to poison milk delivered to Jews; to throw bombs into public places; to jab people with poisoned needles.[24] The effective prosecution of these

---

[20] Emerson H. Loucks, *Ku-Klux-Klan in Pennsylvania* (Harrisburg: The Telegraph Press, 1936), pp. 16-18.
[21] Mecklin, *op. cit.*, pp. 99, 103.
[22] Loucks, *op. cit.*, pp. 52-57.
[23] *Literary Digest* (June 6, 1936).
[24] *Literary Digest* (September 5, 1936).

hooded killers—seven being given a life sentence—apparently destroyed The Black Legion. Always one must say, "apparently," since organizations of this sort, like the proverbial cat, seem merely to slumber between their many lives.[25]

Each of these three reactionary secret societies arose in a situation where an underprivileged group was seriously challenging their position. The old Klan was challenged by a sweeping shift in the legal position of the Negro. The new Klan and the Legion arose amid economic distress when frequently less nativist elements were better off than some nativists. In each case, the political institutions certainly in theory, and to a large degree in practice, protected the rights of the less privileged, leaving the extra-legal recourse of the secret society as the only way open to the nativist elements.

Radical Groups in the United States. In this country there have been some secret societies committed to improving the conditions of the less privileged elements by revolutionary techniques. Among them were the Molly Maguires, a terrorist labor society in the coal region of Pennsylvania, and the Fenian Brotherhood, established for fostering revolution in Ireland.

Less militant reformist associations in the United States adopted the secret society pattern in their earlier stages. The Knights of Labor (1869) was the largest of the early labor movements. Its object was to organize all labor into one big union against organized capital. It had a secret ritual, grip, and password. A peak membership of 700,000 was reached in 1886. This order lost prestige when it waged an unsuccessful strike against the Gould railway interests in which bombings and assassinations occurred. Following this it gradually faded away.[26] An important fact for our purpose is the abandonment by the Knights, in 1881, of the secret features. The secret pattern was adopted first because of the fear of employer spies. It was given up because its secrecy engendered strong public opposition which embarrassed rather than aided the movement. Subsequent labor organizations have not adopted the esoteric pattern.

The Grange, or Patrons of Husbandry, was organized in 1867 as a secret society for both men and women, spreading slowly at first in rural areas. Around 1870 it had a mushroom growth as farmers turned to it as a means of exerting political pressure to aid agriculture. The Grange has a rich pattern of ritual, ceremony, and symbolism which is by now only semi-secret. Apparently its vows, its initiation, and its inner control

---

[25] Another revival of the Ku Klux Klan occurred about 1936, this time with especial anti-Catholic and anti-labor animus. See Theodore Irwin, "The Klan Kicks Up Again," *American Mercury* (August, 1940), pp. 470-476.

[26] Gist, *op. cit.,* p. 35.

discipline take milder forms. With the enactment of Granger legislation, and the subsequent decline in the political interest of farmers, this society declined rapidly. It has, however, survived to this day, retained its ritualistic pattern, but functions largely as a social and cultural center in villages and small towns.[27]

The use of the secret society pattern and its methods of violence by radical or reformist elements in the United States has not been extensive. Where it has been tentatively adopted it has been given up as more detrimental than useful to the accomplishment of the radical aims. This interesting fact is accountable through the presence of relatively free political institutions which permitted those of lower social and economic status to advance their interests by open and public methods.

Radical Societies in Europe. Throughout the nineteenth century, as noted below in the historical survey, secret societies played a prominent part in revolutionary and nationalist movements. The Carbonari are a famous example.

The Cabonari. Arising in France in the days of Bonaparte, this society spread continentally and first became an active political force in Italy around 1814, aiming to free Italy from the Austrian yoke. The fundamental cell of the Carbonari was the "hut," where the members met with wooden stumps outside for sentinels and inside for officials. The axe was their emblem of authority. The ritual resembled that of Freemasonry, but according to Lepper, followed religious lines serio-comically. The real secrets were revealed only to members of the third degree.

The Carbonari attained great political influence in Italy, wresting control of Naples for a time, but was later suppressed. With the unification of Italy, it gradually subsided.

The Imro. In 1893 in western Macedonia was founded a society, modeled on the Carbonari and called the International Macedonian Revolutionary Organization, aiming to effect the acquisition of Macedonia by Bulgaria. Its symbol was a piece of black cloth, signifying serfdom, with "Liberty or Death" embroidered across it. Throughout Macedonia branches were developed with secret militia and hidden arms. It eventually became a state within a state. Its membership and activities are characterized by Roucek as follows:

"The use of naked force for the sake of a fanatical creed has been the outstanding technique of a superbandit organization, The Imro. . . . For nearly forty years, the chain of assassinations of enemies of Macedonian independence remained unbroken. The Imro was singularly effective in

---

[27] For an authoritative discussion of the Grange, see Solon J. Buck, *The Granger Movement* (Cambridge, Mass.: Harvard University Press, 1913).

disposing of its political opponents. Until very recently, it was safer to irritate the government than the Imro." [28]

Other examples of European conspiritive societies are cited by Rowan: [29] the Cagoulards in France, an anti-radical society playing into Nazi hands; the Ovra in Italy, formed by Mussolini, recruited from rogue elements; the Croat Utashi, more hard-hitting than the Imro, subsidized by Hungarians to fight against the Serbs; Otto Strasser's Black Front, formed within the Nazi movement to revenge the "Roehm murders."

Secret Police. The most interesting development of secret societies in the twentieth century is their integration in many instances with the state in the form of a secret police. Formerly governments had open police forces and secret police. The spies were primarily intriguers. But since World War I, many elements of the secret society, particularly the terrorist methods, have been conjoined with the police function of the state to form an unparalleled, ruthless instrument of oppression. This "transformation of a spy into a terrorist greatly increases the range and hitting power of combatant secret service." [30]

Underground. Under the desperate conditions existing in German occupied Europe during World War II, secret societies played an important role in the underground opposition to the Nazis. Roucek calls attention to "Les Gueux" (The Beggars), apparently a Dutch branch of the sixteenth century French society, who formed "the focus of stolid Dutch hatred of the Nazis, blamed by the Germans for recent widespread riots." [31]

In Poland, a reported daring attack, in which the Rudno town hall was burglarized and German funds stolen, was credited to a well organized secret Liberty Party, a band of Polish "Robin Hoods," who stole to help the oppressed Poles. This new sort of secret society, in contrast with the earlier ones, was more efficiently organized, more fanatically devoted to the cause, and steeled to the relentless use of all available techniques of violence without qualm. In Europe the days of ritualistic mummery, medieval titles, and plumed headdress are over. In place of high sounding, vaguely stated mottoes, the watchword is—strike first without mercy and now, or neither we nor our children shall ever have a chance.

---

[28] J. S. Roucek, *The Politics of the Balkans* (New York: McGraw-Hill Book Co., 1939), p. 19.

[29] R. W. Rowan, *Terror in Our Time* (New York: Longmans, Green and Co., 1941).

[30] *Ibid.*, p. 3.

[31] J. S. Roucek, "The Sociology of Secret Societies," *World Affairs Interpreter,* XII (Autumn, 1941), pp. 289-294.

The Secret Society as an Agency of Social Control

Since many other societies arise under the same conditions and employ similar methods to effect social control this section concludes by summarizing the advantages and disadvantages of secret societies as instruments of social control, in light of the foregoing material.

The Advantages. 1. Secrecy strengthens the solidarity of the group by heightening the emotional effect of ritual and symbolism and more positively merging the individual with the group.

2. Secrecy is indispensable when the purposes of the group are contrary to the governing authority of the state or when powerful opposition groups are present, especially when the opponents include the agents of the state.

3. In the situation above, secrecy makes it easier for the group to avoid responsibility for its acts.

The Disadvantages. 1. A secret society is often blamed for violence for which it is not responsible. This is the inevitable price paid for secrecy. Little sympathy need be wasted on the groups for this reason.

2. As a consequence of point one, public opinion and the state become aroused, and suppress the suspected society.

3. Secrecy presents special difficulties in the control of widely scattered local units by a central hierarchy. All the accounts of specific societies refer to branches getting out of hand. As few written records and membership lists as possible are kept and even these must frequently be destroyed.

4. Secret societies cannot develop into the magnitude of a mass movement. Secrecy is harder to maintain when the secrets are widely shared. And the appeal of a secret lies partly in the fact that only a few know it. The role of the secret organization is therefore limited to a coherent group of trusted associates or to being a cell within the larger movement.

5. The terrorist methods require the development of ruthless attitudes, thus promoting a degeneration of character which may defeat the "idealism" of the movement. While a Lenin may sanction the use of terrorist methods and still retain a measure of "idealism" concerning utopian ends, terrorism frequently becomes a fixed mode of action resorted to as an end in itself.

Criminal Societies

A theoretical distinction between criminal secret societies and the others is easier to draw than an actual one. Nativist and conspiritive groups, as we have seen, frequently break the law. There is, however, in both of these types of associations a conviction or a pretense of some great public good which their lawlessness serves. In theory the purely criminal society lacks either this conviction or this pretense. In practice, most of the well-known criminal societies claim to be rectifying some injustice. They may begin as phases of some social movement and ultimately degenerate into purely criminal aggregations.

On the whole, contemporary criminal organizations do not qualify as secret societies under our definition. In the United States, organized crime is a highly rationalized business proposition. While furtiveness is necessary and the "squealer" is dealt with summarily, there seems to be little ceremony or ritual.

Above have been mentioned the Vehmgericht and the Assassins. Other criminal societies include the French Gueux, or Beggars, founded about 1455; the Garduna of Spain, and later (1835) the Spanish Mano Negra; and the Whiteboys of Ireland (1761). All these groups possessed some ritualistic pattern and engaged in essentially predatory practices within the community. More famous than any of these were the Camorra and the Sicilian Mafia.

The Camorra. The authentic history of this Neapolitan underworld association dates from 1820. It arose in prisons and functioned to control the prison life itself. Branching out, it controlled the underworld society of Naples as well. Members of the underworld had the choice of joining the Camorra or being exploited by it. This society had a series of degrees in which the courage and zeal of the initiated were tested, sometimes for years, before they became full fledged Camorristas, entitled to the more lucrative rewards.

The Mafia. This Sicilian society had its origin in the armed bodyguards maintained by Sicilian landowners for the protection of their lives and property in turbulent times. Officially disbanded, it developed into a secret criminal organization. Later it acted as a sort of alternative system of government for the island in opposition to the official government. Since, as Vivian maintains, nearly all native Sicilians belonged to it, it was an institution of which the people were proud; and in spite of its high-handed methods, it seems to have been the main system of social control. Against the law, it *was* the law to most Sicilians.[32]

Characteristically the criminal societies exact illegal levies from persons and business enterprises, bribe justice, practice blackmail, and operate various tabooed sinful activities for those who can pay. They employ all the methods of terror, intimidation and force, including murder. Arising in periods of social disorganization, they exploit and further the process of disorganization for their own ends. On the other hand, they frequently maintain some rough and ready order where otherwise is chaos.

---

[32] Herbert Vivian, *Secret Societies* (London, 1934), p. 245.

They are also used by other groups with definite social aims to apply crude force at some strategic moment.

Recent Trends

In the United States in the post World War II period, secret societies appear to be declining in significance if not in total membership. The official records of such established fraternal orders as Masonry, the Knights of Columbus, and the Elks show small yearly increases in membership, but there is no report of the organization of any new such societies. Increased tension in Negro-white relations in the South, precipitated by the greatly accelerated move toward equality for all ethnic minorities in the nation, has affected the Ku Klux Klan adversely. Efforts to revive the influence of the Klan have met with strong public opposition in the South, as illustrated by the fact that by 1950, twenty-two cities in the South had outlawed masks in public gatherings.

In Western Europe likewise, since World War II the traditional fraternal orders show no marked resurgence. Aided by the American brethren, Masonic lodges have been reactivated with difficulty. The more positive interest shown by upper-class Europeans in the non-secret Oxford Movement may portend the decline in the traditional fraternal order. In the political area may be noted the sporadic revival of Nazi bunds in Germany, no doubt retaining some of the ritualistic appurtenances and secrecy characteristic of the earlier years of the Hitler movement.

Secret Societies and Societal Systems

Reflection upon the historical conditions out of which secret societies, as we have defined them, have arisen, suggests the hypothesis that they flourish best in a non-totalitarian society where there is a fair degree of open class differentiation. Since all types except some of the revolutionary societies are anti-equalitarian, the social structure must generate the desire for status superiority, which secret societies nourish, and at the same time the control system must permit limited expression of this desire. The whole pattern of secret societies—hierarchy of degrees, pseudo-militaristic discipline, attitudes of snobbish superiority and smug intolerance—are contrary to the essential spirit of democracy. In a democracy, the right of citizens to pursue the banal, esoteric ritual and practice of many American societies cannot properly be denied. But democracy need not tolerate the high-handed assumption of the state's prerogative of maintaining order. As Mecklin puts it, "in a country governed by enlightened public opinion, secrecy can only be tolerated when it is known to be in no way inimical to the public walfare." [33]

---

[33] Mecklin, *op. cit.*, p. 83.

In contrast, a totalitarian society requires the maximum cultural uniformity. Therefore the controlling regime bans any organized activity which sets any group apart and which indulges in secrecy. The rigid political control of a totalitarian society inevitably generates the desire for political rebellion, which can be given expression only through secret conspiracy. Such activity is known to exist behind the Iron Curtain.[34] However, we have no evidence that any such movements possess the ritualistic elements of secret societies as we have defined them.

Summary

Secret societies, from the viewpoint of social control, fall into several groups: those interested primarily in controlling their own members in the pursuit of the group interests only; those interested in controlling their own members, but also concerned with control over others and social life generally; those primarily concerned with controlling nonmembers; and those primarily concerned with controlling others by disorganizing and socially disruptive means.

For a number of reasons the United States has been unusually productive of secret orders. During the latter part of the nineteenth century these orders multiplied and flourished, associated with several such movements as nativism, labor and agrarian causes, and European nationalistic aspirations. Many fraternal orders arose to give expression to status distinctions. At midcentury, secret societies appear to be declining in significance in the Western world.

The societal system most congenial to the development of secret societies is a political democracy with some open class differentiation. Even though secret societies run counter to fundamental democratic processes, they must be tolerated in a democratic society so long as they do not usurp the state's functions. The totalitarian regime cannot tolerate secret societies of any sort.

QUESTIONS

1. What is a "secret society"? What are the characteristic elements in the society pattern?
2. What is the range of interests involved in secret societies?
3. How are the secret societies classified from the social control viewpoint? What criticism do you have of the classification presented in this chapter?
4. What reasons can you give for the scarcity of secret societies in the Middle Ages?
5. Compare the development of secret societies in Europe and the United States in the nineteenth century.
6. Trace the societal role of Freemasonry in the Western world.

---

[34] For example, the Kampfbund Gegen Unmenschlickett (Fighting League against Inhumanity) operating in East Germany.

7. What are the conditions favoring the rise of the "Self-Interested" and the "Intermediate" classes of secret societies?

8. Why did so many secret societies arise in the United States in the latter part of the nineteenth century?

9. What are the basic values of secrecy in controlling the members of a secret society?

10. What conditions favor the rise of "societally active" secret societies?

11. What are the methods of control characteristic of the "societally active" societies?

12. Compare and contrast the old and new Klans in as many significant sociological aspects as you can.

13. Compare the prevalence of radical secret societies in the United States and in Europe and account for any difference.

14. What are the values and limitations of secret societies as instruments of controlling society? Can you add any advantages or disadvantages to the proposition set forth in the chapter?

15. Why is it difficult to determine precisely which secret societies are criminal societies?

16. What activities do criminal societies pursue and what methods do they use to accomplish their purposes?

17. Discuss the author's hypothesis concerning the societal conditions under which secret societies flourish.

SUGGESTED TOPICS FOR TERM PAPERS AND FURTHER RESEARCH

1. The relation of secret societies to social control in tribal life.
2. The relation of secret societies to politics in tribal life.
3. The development of Freemasonry.
4. The influence of Freemasonry on politics in the United States.
5. The influence of Freemasonry during the French Revolution.
6. The patterns of underground movements in modern times.
7. The rise and fall of Ku Klux Klan.
8. The operation of the Mafia in the United States.
9. The patterns of Communist secret organizations.
10. The modern legal control of secret societies.

BIBLIOGRAPHY

Books

Paul M. Angle, *Bloody Williamson* (New York: Alfred A. Knopf, 1952). A documentary study of violence in a local area involving the Ku Klux Klan.

Ammon M. Aurand, Jr., *The Mollie Maguires* (Harrisburg, Pa.: Aurand Press, 1940). An account of a terrorist organization in the coal regions of Pennsylvania, 1861-1877.

Hoffman Birney, *Vigilantes* (New York: Grosset and Dunlap, 1941). The rise and fall of the Plummer gang of outlaws in and about Virginia City, Montana, in the early '60's.

Crane C. Brinton, *The Anatomy of Revolution* (New York: W. W. Norton and Co., 1938). On the operation of secret organizations in revolutionary movements.

Paul F. Brissenden, *The I.W.W.* (New York: Columbia University Press, 1919). A study of the syndicalist workers' organization in the United States.

Henrietta Buckmaster, *Let My People Go* (New York: Harper and Brothers, 1941). The story of the Underground Railroad and the growth of the abolition movement.

G. K. Chesterton, *The Man Who was Thursday* (New York: Dodd, Mead & Co., 1928). A fanciful account of conspiracy.

Maurice F. Egan and John B. Kennedy, *The Knights of Columbus in Peace and War* (New Haven: Knights of Columbus, 1920). Exhaustive account of impact of the Knights of Columbus upon public life in the United States.

Olga H. Gankin and Harold H. Fisher, *The Bolsheviks and the World War* (Stanford, Calif.: Stanford University Press, 1940). Documents on the origin of the Third International.

Noel P. Gist, *Secret Societies* (Columbia, Mo.: University of Missouri Studies, XV, No. 4, 1940).

Benjamin Gitlow, *I Confess* (New York: E. P. Dutton & Co., 1940). One of the leaders of the Communist Party reveals its history in the United States.

Charles W. Hechthorn, *Secret Societies in All Ages and Countries* (London, 1897). A comprehensive study of secret societies.

John H. Lepper, *Famous Secret Societies* (London: Sampson, Low, Marston Co., 1932). A good running account of the best known secret societies throughout history.

E. H. Loucks, *The Ku Klux Klan in Pennsylvania* (Harrisburg, Pa.: The Telegraph Press, 1936). A detailed account of the new Klan in the particular area.

John M. Mecklin, *The Ku Klux Klan* (New York: Harcourt, Brace and Co., 1924). The most penetrating sociological interpretation of the subject.

H. C. Pollard, *Secret Societies in Ireland* (London: R. Allen & Co., 1922). An account of the role of Irish societies in the Irish nationalist movement.

Arthur Preuss, *Dictionary of Secret and other Societies* (St. Louis: Herder Book Co., 1924). Written for the instruction of Catholic laymen, it furnishes brief material on many little known societies in the United States.

Herbert Vivian, *Secret Societies* (London: Thornton, Butterworth Co., 1927). An account of the better known societies with a conservative bias.

Hutton Webster, *Primitive Secret Societies* (New York: The Macmillan Co., 1931). An outstanding treatment of secret societies among primitive folk.

Periodicals

Theodore Abel, "The Pattern of a Successful Political Movement," *American Sociological Review*, II (June, 1937), pp. 34-35.

Clifford L. Constance, "Greeks on Campus," *School and Society* (1929), p. 409.

O. Crenshaw, "Knights of the Golden Circle," *American Historical Review*, XLVII (October, 1941), pp. 23-50.

K. F. Gerould, "Ritual and Regalia," *Atlantic Monthly*, CXXXII (1923), pp. 592-597.

R. H. Lowie, "Freemasons among North Dakota Indians," *American Mercury*, XXI (1930), pp. 192-195.

Wladyslaw R. Malinowski, "The Pattern of Underground Resistance," *The Annals of The American Academy of Political and Social Science* (March, 1944), pp. 126-133.

Jacques Maritain, "The End of Machiavellianism," *Review of Politics*, IV (January, 1942), pp. 1-33.

H. H. Martin, "Truth about the Klan Today," *Saturday Evening Post*, CCXXII (October 22, 1949).

Paul Meadows, "Revolution as a Field of Social Research," *Sociology and Social Research*, XXV (May–June, 1941), pp. 457-459.

Charles Mez, "Sweet Land of Secrecy," *Harper's*, CLIV (1927), pp. 329-334.

Joseph S. Roucek, "Sociology of Secret Societies," *World Affairs Interpreter*, XII (Autumn, 1941), pp. 289-294; "Methods of Meeting Domination: The Czechoslovaks," *American Sociological Review*, VI (October, 1941), pp. 670-673: "Sabotage and America's Minorities," *World Affairs Interpreter*, XIV (April, 1943), pp. 45-66.

Georg Simmel, "The Sociology of Secret Societies," *American Journal of Sociology*, XI (1906), pp. 441-498.

Eric Voegelin, "Extended Strategy," *Journal of Politics*, II (May, 1940), pp. 189-200.

CHAPTER XIX

Nonviolent Means of Social Control

Most of the chapters of this book deal with some phases of nonviolent means of social control [1] so it will be the aim of this one to treat systematically a few devices and techniques which do not fall under other topics and have sufficient in common to be discussed together. They may be found operating at several levels of social intercourse, ranging from such inter-group relationships as international affairs and world-wide religious programs, to the simpler intra-group processes on a person-to-person plane.

All nonviolent techniques are based upon the assumption that isolation for an individual or group is an intolerable situation, and human interdependence is inescapable. Whatever then tends to interfere with full participation in the affairs of human life gives rise to strong pressures which will bring about desired changes in attitudes and activities.

Nonviolent Techniques in International Affairs

The Failure of Economic Sanctions. A few years ago peace-loving peoples placed great store in economic sanctions as a panacea for a war-weary world, and the device as set down on paper seemed logical and convincing. Its principle was simply that, since every nation must depend upon other nations for raw materials and markets, an erring country might speedily be brought to conform to international standards of morality without resort to warfare if other nations would refuse economic cooperation with her. When the Italians marched into Ethiopia it appeared a simple matter, since Italy so much needed to engage in trade with others, to force her to change her ways by refusing to deal with her in trade and commerce. In this first major test, however, the program failed notably. When Japan decided to cast her lot with the Berlin-Rome axis, first threats of economic boycotts, and eventually the beginnings of application failed to deter her and actually hastened open war.[2]

---

[1] Especially those on state, government and law, religion, marriage and the family, education, class and caste, conceptual means of social control, ideologies, language and semantics, art and literature, recreation, leadership, economic control, and economic and social planning.

[2] For this and other aspects of some of the illusions in regard to the possibility of

Two kinds of reasons have been given for the failure of sanctions as social controls in the international field. The first is that they cannot work effectively in the absence of adequate international machinery to time and guide their application, so that efforts so far in this line have been "wishy-washy" and lacked the necessary whole-hearted support of participants. The other is best stated by Edwin Borchard: "Dictatorship is a concomitant of poverty and misery. How can it be cured by increasing poverty and misery?" [3] The implications can be broadened considerably for, regardless of the immediate problem of dictatorships, economic sanctions call for application of pressure at spots critical in a people's well-being and the reaction is very likely to be panic and explosion.

The Failure of Moral Sanctions. Equally unable to withstand the strains of crises has been the application of moral sanctions, as exemplified in the history of treaties which renounce war as an instrument of international policy. Here the weakness appears to have been in ignoring the fact that war may also be, and often is, an instrument of internal policy, and the very moral disapproval of other peoples may be welded into an instrument to unite more firmly one's own followers. No important nation in the modern world has kept its own moral skirts sufficiently clean to be very convincing when it points to the ethical derelictions of others.

Nonviolence in Religion and Philosophy

The Philosophy of Nonresistance. Cutting across international boundaries, many of the great religions of the world as well as quasi-religious philosophies of life have deeply impressed nonviolence into the thinking and behavior of hundreds of millions of people. Such systems of thought have come to be regarded as characteristically Oriental, but they are to be found in all parts of the world. Christianity is distinctly a religion of nonresistance as witness the Sermon on the Mount [4] with its unmistakable mandates: "But I say unto you, do not resist evil; whoever strikes you on one cheek, turn to him the other also. And if any man takes away your coat, let him have your cloak also." Most Christian denominations have come a long way from these early teachings and pride themselves in their "militancy." The psychology of passivity is far too subtle, and

stopping international war, see: Joseph S. Roucek, "Some Recent Illusions about Peace and War," *Social Education*, VIII (April, 1944), pp. 152-157, and "Illusions and Fictions in International Relations," *The Social Studies*, XXXVI (December, 1945), pp. 335-339 and ff.
[3] In Brown, Hodges and Roucek, *Contemporary World Politics* (New York: John Wiley and Sons, 1940), chapter XXIII, "Neutrality and Sanctions."
[4] Matthew V.

its application calls for too much patience to make it popular with Western peoples.

Probably the outstanding example of the successful application of a philosophy of nonresistance is found in the long story of Chinese history. Through many thousands of years the Chinese have been overwhelmed by waves of conquering barbarians only to quietly and peacefully absorb them while Chinese life has been little affected. Only of recent years, however, when the Chinese under Occidental influence departed from their time-honored ways and adopted militant methods have we begun to understand them. Whether their new philosophy will serve them as well as the old remains to be seen.

Mahatma Gandhi, in a notable message to the American people said: "When real peace and disarmament come, they will be initiated by a strong nation like America—*irrespective of the consent and cooperation of other nations*," [5] thus voicing the ultimate implication of all passive nonresistance policies. Few Americans believed they were listening to the counsel of wisdom.

Indeed, Gandhi had some claim to speak when and as he did, for he had demonstrated to an awed world that nonresistance can be turned into an effective instrument in dealing with the British who for more than a century and a half had refused to bend to the onslaughts of armed foes. He had sat, in his strange garb, at the council tables of the great and they had listened to him with respect, even though they did not comprehend. He had a loyal following of uncounted millions of Indians, unparalleled in modern times.

The General Strike and Industrial "Slow-Down"

In the conflicts between employers and employees, more or less effective techniques have been used essentially without violence even though in many cases they eventually led to violence. The scheme of the general strike, long cherished and occasionally used in Europe, and to a lesser extent in America, is the application of nonparticipation to bring pressure on governing or employing groups. The theory of the general strike is that, if a large number of workers in essential industries lay down their tools, the whole economy is disrupted, and those in control must yield to the workers in order to restore life to normal. Like economic sanctions in international affairs such programs rest on the assumption of interdependence among all people and all spheres of human activity. Like economic sanctions the general strike fails as an effective weapon largely

---

[5] Reproduced by Frederick B. Fisher in *That Strange Little Brown Man Gandhi* (New York: Richard Long and Richard R. Smith, 1932). (*Italics by author.*)

because it breeds fear and panic rather than reason, and is apt to lead to explosive reactions rather than compromise.

More restricted in scope and less radical in conception is the "industrial slow-down" as a technique. All the employees or those in key positions agree to curtail their energies and efforts sufficiently to bring about decreased production in a plant. In limited measure such tactics have been successful in exerting control by group over group, but the more severely they are applied the more resistance they create. Their logical termination in the "sit down" strike raised a furore of protest from employer and public, and frequent resort to violence.

Nonviolent Means in Intra-group Relations

Less spectacular, and therefore usually unnoticed, but far more revealing for those seeking to gain an understanding of the more subtle phases of social control, are the uses of nonviolence within groups to bring individuals into conformity with group standards. They include the more or less deliberate use of ridicule, gossip, scandal, argument, persuasion, and isolation. The reference is principally to situations, whether formal or informal, where the element of leadership is at a minimum but there is sufficient *rapport* among group members that they resort spontaneously to such techniques. Such techniques may be used in combination, or in graduated sequences if early efforts fail to bring about desired ends. There is always the element of trial-and-error since, even though these techniques are quite familiar to persons of any degree of social maturity, their psychological and social implications are but vaguely understood. In practice they are very effective when used against normal persons, but their total results may be quite unanticipated. They may be employed against fully participating members of a group, or against nonmembers who are temporarily and fortuitously under the influence of the group. In the beginning, in each case, their use is local, but on occasion they have spread through whole nations and populations as in undirected "whispering campaigns" against prominent persons in high places. Once started they may be seized upon by leaders or clever publicity men and artificially stimulated, in which cases their character changes and they become propaganda.

These nonviolent means of social control may be applied to bring erring individuals to change their ways, to prevent persons suspected of contemplating departures from group norms from actually so departing, to bring persons who remain aloof from group activities into fuller participation, to remove undesired persons from a group, to restrict the overambitious, and even to persecute innocent individuals for sadistic gratification. Examples of all such usages may be found in the unwritten

annals of every community in any part of the world, and their description bulks large in the "realistic" literature of town and village life.
Their operation and influence are often so obscure that only the most
discerning can see their cumulative importance in every-day social
control.

Socio-Psychological Considerations. Previous chapters in this book have
dealt at some length with the social psychological characteristics of
human beings which make them susceptible to social control, and in turn
stimulate them to seek to control the conduct and thought processes of
others. No effort will be made here to recount this material, but it is
well to recall a few fundamental characteristics especially pertinent to
the devices being considered. The individual has no life that could be
called human without associations in organized groups. Normal development of personality and enjoyment of life depend upon participation in
group activities, a degree of sympathy and understanding from others,
and a fairly definite identity and status. Any situation which tends, for
long, to cut an individual off from the satisfaction of such normal requirements becomes intolerable for him and sets up pressure for solutions.
Such solutions rarely include suicide, insanity or efforts at retaliation,
but usually result in changed conduct toward others as a means of rectifying the situation.

Malinowski [6] and other writers describe the use, among the most primitive peoples, of isolation and related devices to remove offending individuals from groups. There are many instances, both fictitious and
actual, of extreme reactions by persons when their affection for another
is not returned in full measure, or (as in the case of children) because of
lack of sympathetic response from parents. Actors become extremely
sensitive to the precise amount of applause they receive and have been
known to sulk if it fell one bit short of their expectations. All of us are
"sensitive" because it is human for us so to be, but, of course, degrees of
sensitivity vary greatly as the terms "thick-skinned" and "thin-skinned"
imply. The most "thick-skinned" persons, however, have their tender
Achilles' heels, which a persistent group can sooner or later find. None
of us can hold out indefinitely against nonviolent controls in person-to-
person relationships.

Extent of Use of Nonviolent Controls. The use of such nonviolent controls seldom becomes a matter of public record as do jail sentences and
hangings, so there are neither statistics nor documented observations to
give us definite information on how extensively they are used. Probably
some fictional treatments greatly exaggerate their importance in the

---

[6] B. Malinowski, *Crime and Custom in Savage Society* (New York: Harcourt,
Brace and Co., 1926), *passim.*

scheme of social control. More probably most serious studies in the field underestimate the significance of the part they play. The ideologies built around the conception of "nature red in tooth and claw" have tended to attract notice to the harsher and more violent phases of the struggle for existence, which at the human level is the struggle for social control. Such aspects are dramatic and colorful, and, by contrast, non-violent controls are usually drab and commonplace, concerned with a million trifles rather than with climactic episodes in the battles of giants. Yet it is quite probable that historically (even back to the days of the mythical cave-man ancestor), and at present, the unspectacular substratum of nonviolent controls at the intra-group level has more to do with the maintenance of social order than all violent means combined. An individual may quite well live his whole life through and encounter little actual physical coercion, but no one goes many days without feeling the sting of his associates' tongues.

Ridicule.[7] As a means for control over individuals on the parts of groups, ridicule may operate in one of two ways. It may be fairly institutionalized, as in some groups of "rough and ready" companions. A large part of their intercourse is the ostentatious making fun of each other on the slightest pretexts, and a qualification for membership in the group is the ability "to take it." Even when it serves, in such cases, as a test of individuals, usually it also has definite social control implications and may be quite effective in bringing about behavior and attitude changes. In occupational groups it is often a part of the discipline of apprentices, as when a youth aspiring to the printers' trade is made to look at "type lice" and search in vain for "striped ink." In so doing he becomes the laughing stock of other workers, and at the same time learns "his place." A large part of the public hazing in college fraternities and other secret organizations contains this same element. Even in training for service in the armed forces, the "rookie" is subjected to debasing situations and thereupon laughed at, to impress upon him his subordination to the group. It is notable and worthy of further socio-psychological investigation that groups of girls and women employ ridicule in this manner far less than men.

The other use of ridicule as a social control is that which is not a mark of inclusion within the group of the ridiculed person, but tends rather to single him out as definitely apart. It is less an expected part of organized activities, and is more apt to be somewhat sly and covert. Sensitive persons are very susceptible to such control, but apparently some who are less sensitive go their ways oblivious to the fact that people smile or

---

[7] For a discussion of ridicule as a means of social control, see Leslie Day Zeleny, *Practical Sociology* (New York: Prentice Hall, 1937), pp. 185 ff.

laugh at them quietly "behind their backs." Almost any conceivable departure in appearance or behavior from group norms is apt to call forth some degree of this type of ridicule, and on occasion the very fact that one conforms too well to his group standards may make him ridiculous to other members. The college professor who is so typical as to meet every expectation which goes with the stereotype of his calling may be laughed at for his typicality. The "Joe College" who looks and acts exactly as a college student is expected to act may thereby become the butt of many jokes. Such application of ridicule is aimed at making their subjects more "human" and therefore less perfect in their roles. But far more significant is the use of smiles and laughter to bring the misfit into closer alignment with the norms of his fellows. It may aim either at those who too far excel their associates in some activity and therefore have "swell heads," or at those who lag too far behind in some particulars and are therefore "dumb." It may, on occasion, be directed at those who go too far afield to acquire traits not ordinarily associated with activities of the group members, as the lady lion hunter, or the football player who sits up nights to study poetry.

Gossip.[8] In more serious vein, and often effective where ridicule fails, is gossip. Unfounded or exaggerated stories of the doings of mutual acquaintances make up a large part of the random conversation of members of all groups. The woman who is first to leave a bridge party lives in dread of what those remaining will say about her, even though her conscience is clear. Any informal gathering of men is apt to develop into an exchange of bits of pseudo-news reflecting upon absent mutual acquaintances. Children learn to gossip early in life. If there were a law of gossip it would probably be that, no matter how covertly, a bit of gossip kept circulating long enough will find its mark by reaching the ears of the person talked about. But even though it never does, the very knowledge we have of our associates and their tastes in gossip stands always as a warning to us to guard carefully against certain types of digressions from their standards.

Aside from individual differences in sensitivity, other factors enter to make some persons more vulnerable to the effects of gossip, and therefore more subject to its control, than others. Caesar's wife, by virtue of that distinction, must not become the subject for idle stories. Some professions are so much a matter of reputation that their practitioners must be especially wary. The banker, the minister, the school teacher, and

---

[8] For a discussion of gossip as social control, see George C. Atteberry, John L. Auble, and Elgin F. Hunt, *Introduction to Social Science* (New York: The Macmillan Co., 1941), p. 338. For many realistic illustrations, see Robert S. Lynd and Helen M. Lynd, *Middletown* (New York: Harcourt, Brace and Co., 1929), *passim.*

other selected occupational groups know this well.[9] One misstep, whether actually taken or merely suspected, has often been enough to ruin an otherwise promising career. Prevalence of gossip is a personnel problem of every large business or other type of functional staff. It may lead to misunderstandings and hostilities in domestic relations, or to the break-up of close friendships. The more a person is accepted on simple faith in any personal relationship, the less immune he is to gossip.

Scandal. Although some gossip may bring disastrous results to individuals, for the most part it is innocent enough in its intent and relatively slight, though persistent, in its coercive effects; it deals usually with the smaller infractions of folkways. When the real or fancied offense of an individual is considered very serious by the group, calling for immediate and stringent applications of informal social control, scandal is resorted to. Thus scandal is both less frequent and more purposeful, and often more immediately effective in bringing about sweeping changes in behavior and attitudes than is idle gossip. Where gossip tends to carry an air of uncertainty—"I don't really know this, but it is what people say . . ."—scandal has more certainty in its typical expression, "The fact is that . . ."

Types of infractions of mores which are *per se* scandalous are cultural variants, just as the mores themselves vary from time to time and group to group. Comparative studies reveal that among some peoples the most scandalous behavior is that which has to do with the secret practice of black magic or the infraction of mother-in-law taboos. In some countries recently the principal subject for scandal might have been a presumed statement against the prevailing ruler, or the amount of Jewish blood a person was supposed to possess. Characteristically, in our own culture, the principal scandals which arise from supposed breaches of the mores are those having to do with sex conduct or dishonesty in money matters, reflecting principal values of our group.[10] By contrast, in the urban France of a decade ago, irregular sex relations were a favorite subject for gossip, but for scandal only if tied up with international intrigue or murder. In some parts of the world dishonesty in money matters is considered so lightly that, while violations of the accepted code may be subject for much gossip, they rarely are taken seriously enough to constitute scandals (much to the consternation of many American travelers).

Scandals have to do with actions for which there is no adequate retribution in the thinking of the group, and the misdeeds are considered

---

[9] For the role of gossip in controlling extra-school conduct of teachers, see Willard Waller, *The Sociology of Teaching* (New York: John Wiley and Sons, 1932), especially chapter V, "The Teacher in the Community."

[10] Hornell B. Hart and Ella B. Hart discuss sex scandal in *Personality and the Family* (New York: D. C. Heath and Co., 1941), pp. 200 ff.

irrevocable. The woman who is believed to have offended against sexual morality, and the man who is believed to have stolen money entrusted to his care can never make sufficient amends for their conduct to still the voice of scandal. Thus, scandal differs from gossip in that its primary aim is not to change a mode of conduct. Its chief aim is to thoroughly and permanently isolate or remove the suspected individual, and to subject him or her to sufficient anguish to stand as a warning to others who might be inclined to follow in his ways. Scandal serves as a limiting factor, setting more or less inflexible boundaries to behavior, while gossip and ridicule serve as determiners of specific modes of conduct within those limits. The man who will not steal money for fear of scandal may, nevertheless, have very extravagant habits, and be subjected to gossip; or he may lack the necessary industry to maintain himself and family properly, and be ridiculed into effort.

Argument. Long into the night amid smoke from a dozen pipes a group of students may be engrossed in a "bull session" composed of endless argument, often seemingly heated in tone, and all probably meaningless to an outsider. Thus the group is exploring thought patterns and peculiarities of individuals and, by shouting them down, if necessary, attempting to bring those individuals into conformity. Such a relatively spontaneous use of argument as a social control must be distinguished from the formal and prepared arguments of the debating team or the campus political leader. The less formal "bull session" without institutional leadership is an example of a type of social control which is used in all group life. Such arguments, which may arise in almost any conversation that is more than a social ritual, serve to keep points of view on matters of joint concern fairly uniform throughout the group, and may sift out members who are persistently too "radical," i.e., too far from the general consensus of the group. Although there is much truth in the maxim that "who is convinced against his will, is of the same opinion still," it is also true that as a result of group arguments individuals come to "soften" the expression of their nonconforming opinions. While argument suggests a highly rational type of group control, at the informal level there are irrational elements inherent in its very spontaneity. The greatest impressions are apt to result from the forcefulness with which a statement is made, rather than from its soundness as fact or logic; the tone of voice or appearance of a member of the group may carry much more prestige than the content of the argument he makes. Such argument is more effective in controlling behavior on the verbal plane than in actually changing attitudes of individuals, but this still makes it important as a nonviolent means of control, since what people say and how they say it can be vital to group solidarity.

Persuasion.[11] As used by groups to control members, persuasion is usually much more effective than argument. It permits the use of a wide range of appeals to individual members, including those of sympathy, loyalty, affection, or courage without the pretense of either logic or reason. Where argument tends to emphasize the contrast of ideas and judgments of individuals, persuasion works by stressing common ideals and values, even to the point of making real differences of opinion appear to be basically the same ideas but clothed in slightly different terms. In all types of informal situations persuasion is used as a somewhat spontaneous means of directing the activities of group members. When argument fails, persuasion offers a surer technique. Although argument is limited largely to the modification of verbal behavior, persuasion lends itself, as well, to the changing of nonverbal behavior. It may be continuous through long periods of time and thus bring about lasting changes in the actual attitudes of an individual, or it may be a short-lived method of meeting an immediate situation. It is commonplace in the experience of every individual to have been persuaded at a particular time on a course of action, only to regret it later when removed from the immediate influence of those who were doing the persuading.

Isolation. One of the subtlest and most effective of spontaneous means of social control is that of the isolation of individual members partly or completely from participation in group activities. This may be accomplished in a number of ways. It may be done by simply ignoring the member to be disciplined, by a show of "coolness" toward him, or by singling him out for an obviously unwarranted amount of unwelcome attention, as in the case of excessive politeness on the part of a group whose ordinary relations are carried on at an informal level. The method may be used to drive a member from a group permanently, to bring him to conform to group ways in particular regards, or simply as punishment to act as a deterrent to other group members. Children appear to be the most sensitive to isolation [12] and many personalities have been warped for life by early experiences. As stated previously in the chapter, man the social being finds isolation intolerable, and lack of sympathy, understanding, and the affection of one's associates is a major tragedy.

Conditions in which Nonviolent Controls Operate. The general settings in which these types of controls are used have much to do with their relative influence. In rural settings, where groups are small and most people are personally acquainted with most others, their importance in

---

[11] For a discussion of persuasion in social control, see Zeleny, *op. cit.*, pp. 178-179.

[12] Ernest R. Groves, *Personality and Social Adjustment* (New York: Longmans, Green and Co., 1931), deals revealingly with the effects of isolation on children. See pp. 93-94.

the whole scheme of social control is relatively great.[13] Gossip and scandal in the small village is often the chief control over the behavior of residents. By contrast, in urban areas where associations are widely varied for any individual and where each may be anonymous in a large share of his activities, such controls are relatively ineffective. As would be expected, nonviolent controls of the types discussed are more dependable in primary group relations which are intimate and highly personal, and less to be relied upon in secondary relations. People who are highly mobile are less dependent upon particular locales and the same sets of associates than those who are not mobile, so that some occupational groups characterized by constant traveling are practically immune to gossip-scandal controls.

Where conditions are less favorable for the direct use of the controls which have been discussed in this chapter there is a tendency for groups to resort to vicarious substitutes such as the wholesale ridicule of large classes of people having certain qualities in common, or, as through the press, the wholesale application of threats of gossip and scandal.[14]

Dangers in Nonviolent Controls. As already noted, nonviolent controls in inter-group relations often arouse fears and antagonisms which defeat their purposes. This is true, and much more vividly, in personal and intra-group affairs. The very effectiveness of these controls operating on individuals lies in the fact that there is practically no defense against their operation, and individuals may only avoid their sting by preventive guards over their conduct. But even this gives no guarantee of immunity. The very nebulous nature of these controls, and the spontaneity which characterizes their application means that persons quite innocent of infractions may suffer quite as severely as the guilty, while many who are guilty may escape unscathed. The use of ridicule, gossip, scandal, and isolation techniques is not well planned in advance with a careful weighing of possible consequences. The informal group usually acts as a somewhat blind and irresponsible agent.

Although it goes without saying that many adult lives have been blighted or led into devious ways after single and impulsive infractions of mores, most attention has been given to effects in the formative years of childhood of subtle, and often cruel, group pressures.[15] Delinquent

---

[13] Kimball Young in *Social Psychology* (New York: F. S. Crofts and Co., 1931), pp. 571-572, describes the significant place of gossip in forming public opinion in rural life.

[14] Chapter XXV on "The Press" discusses this function of newspapers in community life.

[15] Groves, *op. cit.*, p. 269, discusses the fear of ridicule in children. The effects of isolation techniques in building lasting antagonisms of children toward parents is discussed by Hart and Hart, *op. cit.*, p. 434.

and criminal careers, behavior problems, and many forms of chronic social maladjustments have been traced to a single or few ill-advised uses of nonviolent techniques in the regulation of childhood conduct. Cases of suicide have been extreme reactions.

Summary

The application of nonviolent techniques to inter-group relations is little understood in the Western world, and in the hands of our European civilization these methods have proved to be very clumsy and ineffective instruments. Their application on the more intimate plane of person-to-person relations is universal and commonplace, however, and may be studied on every hand. Their effectiveness at this plane cannot be doubted, and may be much greater than their unspectacular nature would indicate. It is the effectiveness, however, of unguided, blind devices, and results may be more far-reaching and quite different from those contemplated. This is especially obvious where children are disciplined by groups. The danger in such controls arises from lack of general understanding of the nature of man as a social being, and his utter dependence upon the sympathetic regard of his fellows.

QUESTIONS

1. Upon what tenet are nonviolent means of control based?
2. Why did economic sanctions fail to avert aggression?
3. Why is the philosophy of nonresistance inadequate for Western peoples?
4. Is the philosophy of nonresistance a national philosophy?
5. What is the outstanding example of the success of the philosophy of nonresistance? Explain its success.
6. What is the general strike?
7. How does the industrial "slow-down" differ from the general strike?
8. Name some less spectacular means of nonviolent control.
9. How do modern theologians justify "militant" Christianity?
10. How effective is ridicule in bringing about control?
11. Illustrate the effects of a whispering campaign.
12. How do gossip and scandal differ from one another?
13. Why do refusals to join in group activities precipitate violence?
14. How does gossip promote social control?
15. Criticize gossip as a means of social control.
16. Under what conditions will nonviolent controls operate?
17. What is the effect of isolation as a means of social control?
18. What dangers are inherent in nonviolent means of control?

SUGGESTED TOPICS FOR TERM PAPERS AND FURTHER RESEARCH

1. The legal distinction between violence and nonviolence.
2. World government as a nonviolent weapon.

3. The techniques of the "sit-down" strike.
4. Study the techniques of Mahatma Ghandi.
5. Study communism's arsenal of nonviolent weapons.
6. The use of prestige in social control.
7. The use of pressures by religious groups for group allegiance.
8. The techniques of the rebels against social ostracism.
9. The techniques of the "underdog" to escape his social duties.
10. The use of "nonviolent" techniques in penal institutions.

BIBLIOGRAPHY

Books

Ethan P. Allen, "Non-Symbolic Instruments of Power," pp. 85-107, in Roy V. Peel and Joseph S. Roucek, eds., *Introduction to Politics* (New York: Thomas Y. Crowell Co., 1941). A survey of all methods of nonviolent coercion.

Eugene Anderson, *Process and Power Studies in Modern Culture* (Lincoln: University of Nebraska Press, 1952). The relation of power to social processes.

Thurman W. Arnold, *The Symbols of Government* (New Haven: Yale University Press, 1935). A pragmatic approach to the dynamics of symbolism in politics.

L. L. Bernard, *Social Control in its Sociological Aspects* (New York: The Macmillan Co., 1939). Especially Chapter XIV, "Social Control by Means of Non-Violent Coercion."

Emory S. Bogardus, *Leaders and Leadership* (New York: D. Appleton-Century Co., 1934). An interesting presentation of the problems of leadership based upon an investigation of the records of successful leaders.

Lyman Bryson, Louis Finkelstein, and Robert M. MacIver, eds., *Conflicts of Power in Modern Culture* (New York: Harper and Brothers, 1947). Conference on science, philosophy, and religion in their relation to the democratic way of life.

C. M. Case, *Non-Violent Coercion* (New York: D. Appleton-Century Co., 1923). One of the few comprehensive books in the field.

G. S. Counts and Mark Lodge, *The Country of the Blind: The Soviet System of Mind Control* (Boston: Houghton Mifflin Co., 1949). A current study of the U.S.S.R. and the effective methods of control.

Kingsley Davis, Harry Bredemier, and Marion J. Levy, Jr., *Modern American Society* (New York: Rinehart and Co., 1948). Some of the current problems of social control.

Richard B. Gregg, *The Power of Non-Coercion* (Philadelphia: J. B. Lippincott Co., 1934).

Aldous Huxley, *Ends and Means: An Inquiry into the Nature of Ideals and the Methods Employed for their Realization* (New York: Harper and Brothers, 1937). On the theoretical aspects.

Bertrand de Jouvenel, *On Power* (New York: Viking Press, 1949). The nature and history of power considered as the central government authority in states or communities.

Paul H. Landis, *Social Control: Social Organization and Disorganization in Process* (Philadelphia: J. B. Lippincott Co., 1939). Especially Chapter X, "Social Control and Social Problems in the Primary Group," and Chapter XIII, "Problems of the American Family as an Agency of Social Control."

Harold D. Lasswell, *Power and Personality* (New York: W. W. Norton and Co., 1948). A study of the psychological basis of political power.

Emil Lederer, *The Mind of the Masses* (New York: W. W. Norton and Co., 1940). A study of dictatorship and the "mass mind."

John Lewis, *The Case Against Pacifism* (London: Allen and Unwin, 1940).

F. E. Lumley, *Means of Social Control* (New York: D. Appleton-Century Co., 1925).

An outstanding study of such means of control as praise, flattery, persuasion, rewards, advertising, slogans, propaganda, gossip, satire, laughter, calling names, commands, threats, and punishment.

Robert M. MacIver, *The Web of Government* (New York: The Macmillan Co., 1947). Chapters V-VI give a sociological interpretation of various aspects of the problems of social and political power.

Roberto Michels, *First Lectures in Political Sociology* (Minneapolis: University of Minnesota Press, 1949). Includes stimulating discussions on the operation of the elites, leadership, and political parties.

Gaetano Mosca, *The Ruling Class* (New York: McGraw-Hill Book Co., 1939). Especially good on the "smoke-screens" used by elites to promote their rule.

Reinhold Niebuhr, *Moral Man and Immoral Society* (New York: Charles Scribners' Sons, 1932). Especially good is the consideration of coercion and persuasion in the two realms of individual and social conduct.

Theodore Paullin, *Introduction to Non-violence* (Philadelphia: The Pacific Research Bureau, 1944). Analyzes the various positions found within the pacifist movement in regard to the use of nonviolent techniques of bringing about social change.

E. A. Ross, *Social Control* (New York: Century Co., 1901). Remains the classic work on such subjects as public opinion, law, belief, social suggestion, education, custom, religion, personal ideals, ceremony, art, personality, enlightenment, illusion, and social valuations.

Bertrand Russell, *Power: A New Social Analysis* (New York: W. W. Norton and Co., 1938). A provocative discussion of many facets of the power problem.

N. S. Timasheff, *An Introduction to the Sociology of Law* (Cambridge, Mass.: Harvard University Press, 1939). Part III presents the sociological approach to the operation of power.

Count Leo N. Tolstoy, *The Kingdom of God is Within You* (Boston: Dana Estes and Co., 1905). The pacifistic ideology of the famed Russian thinker.

Max Weber, *Essays in Sociology* (translated and edited by H. H. Gerth and C. Wright Mills, New York: Oxford University Press, 1946). Part II is devoted to studies of class, status, party, bureaucracy, charismatic authority, and power structure.

Kimball Young, *Sociology* (New York: American Book Co., 1942). See especially Chapter 32, "The Nature and Function of Social Control," pp. 893-921.

Periodicals

American Sociological Society, "Social Control," in *Papers and Proceedings*, XII (Chicago, 1918).

Emile Benoit-Smullyan, "Status, Status-Types, and Status Interrelations," *American Sociological Review*, IX (April, 1944).

M. W. Beth, "Elite and the Elites," *American Journal of Sociology*, XLVII (March, 1942), pp. 746-755.

Edwin Borchard, "The Impracticability of 'Enforcing Peace,'" *Yale Law Journal*, LV (August, 1946).

H. C. Brearley, "The Nature of Social Control," *Sociology and Social Research*, XXVIII (November–December, 1943), pp. 351-381.

Esther Caukin Brunauer, "Power Politics and Democracy," *Annals of The American Academy of Political and Social Science*, CCXVI (July, 1941).

F. Stuart Chapin, "'Mass' versus 'Leadership' Opinion on Wartime Rationing," *Public Opinion Quarterly*, XI (Winter, 1947-1948).

Edward S. Corwin, "Constitution as Instrument and Symbol," *American Political Science Review*, XXX (December, 1936).

F. B. Davis and P. I. Rulon, "Gossip and the Introvert," *Journal of Abnormal and Social Psychology*, XXX, pp. 17-21.

Kingsley Davis, "Extreme Social Isolation of a Child," *American Journal of Sociology*, XLV, pp. 554-565.

J. Dickinson, "Social Order and Political Authority," *American Political Science Review*, XXIII (May–August, 1929).

J. Dollard, "Culture, Society, Impulse and Socialization," *American Journal of Sociology*, XLV (July, 1939), pp. 50-53.

Thomas D. Eliot, "Of the Shadow of Death," *Annals of the American Academy of Political and Social Science* (September, 1943), "A Step Toward the Social Psychology of Bereavement," *Journal of Abnormal and Social Psychology*, XXVI (January–March, 1933), pp. 380-390; "Human Controls as Situation Processes," *American Sociological Review*, VIII (August, 1943), pp. 380-388.

A. V. Hallowell, "The Nature and Function of Property as a Social Institution," *Journal of Legal and Political Sociology*, I (April, 1943), pp. 15-38.

Robert M. MacIver, "Some Reflections on Sociology during a Crisis," *American Sociological Review*, VI (February, 1941), p. 1-8.

James B. McKee, "Status and Power in the Industrial Community," *American Journal of Sociology*, LVIII (January, 1953), pp. 364-365.

Margaret Mead, "Customs and Mores: Changes 1930-1940," *ibid.*, XLVII (May, 1942), pp. 971-980.

Olive Melinkoff, "Occupational Attitudes of Interns," *Sociology and Social Research*, XXVI (May–June, 1942), pp. 448-459.

M. E. Opler, "Themes as Dynamic Forces in Culture," *American Journal of Sociology*, Vol. LI (1945), pp. 198-206.

F. Redl, "Zoot Suits: An Interpretation," *Survey*, LXXXIX (October, 1943), pp. 259-262.

K. Riezler, "Comment on the Social Psychology of Shame," *American Journal of Sociology*, XLVIII (January, 1943), pp. 457-465.

Joseph S. Roucek, "The Sociology of the Soldier in Peace Time," *Sociology and Social Research*, XIX (May–June, 1935), pp. 406-419; "Social Attitudes of the Soldier in War Time," *Journal of Abnormal and Social Psychology*, XXX (July–September, 1935), pp. 164-174; "The Sociology of the Prison Guard," Osborne Association, *News Bulletin*, VI (August, 1935), pp. 7-9, and *Sociology and Social Research*, XXX (November–December, 1935), pp. 145-151; "The Problem Facing Religion in Prison," *Social Progress*, XXVII (February, 1936), pp. 24-25; "Social Attitudes of the Prison Warden," *Sociology and Social Research*, XXI (November–December, 1936), pp. 170-174; "The Sociology of the Diplomat," *Social Science*, XIV (October, 1939), pp. 370-374; "The Sociology of the Nurse," *Sociology and Social Research*, XXIV (July–August, 1940), pp. 526-533.

Harold L. Sheppard, "The Negro Merchant: A Study of Negro Anti-Semitism," *American Journal of Sociology*, LIII (1947-48), pp. 96-99.

J. S. Slotkin, "Status of the Marginal Man," *Sociology and Social Research*, XXVIII (1943-1944), pp. 47-54.

Louis Wirth, "Segregation," *Encyclopaedia of the Social Sciences*, XIII (1934), pp. 643-647.

Philip Wittenberg, "Miscegenation," *ibid.*, X (1933), pp. 531-534.

James W. Woodard, "Some Implications from Our Present Knowledge Concerning Prejudice," *American Sociological Review*, XI (1946), pp. 344-356.

CHAPTER XX

Violence and Terror

The problem of violence is of utmost importance today—as it always has been. But no one can escape the realization that we are living through one of the greatest crises of civilization characterized by increasing vicarious violence and terror. War, the outstanding type of modern violence, is killing more people in an increasingly efficient manner, and terror has been increasing in intensity and frightfulness.[1]

Terrorist assassinations since 1900 have removed fully thirty heads of states and politicians. Victims of political murders have included Baron Tisza of Hungary, Dato of Spain, Granja of Portugal, Taalat Pasha of Turkey, Stambuliski of Bulgaria, Kej Hara and Inukaj of Japan, Emir of Afghanistan, President Naturowicz of Poland, Petrljura of Ukraine, Chan-so-lin of Manchuria, Obregon of Mexico, Vijanna of Brazil, Paul Doumer of France and Cerro of Peru. The year 1934 produced a veritable carnival of political murders including those of Dollfus, Roehm, Schleicher, Duca, Alexander, Louis Barthou, Pieracki, and Serge Kirov. In the Balkans secret revolutionary organizations have been particularly active. Thus, there occurred the killing of the archduke Ferdinand at Sarajevo in 1914, which was laid by Austria to a Serbian revolutionary society. The most obvious case of that kind was the murder of King Alexander of Yugoslavia at Marseilles in 1934. The Croatian and Macedonian terrorists, believing that they could break the Yugoslav state by removing King Alexander and thereby give "freedom" to Croatia and Macedonia, saw in the King's visit to France an opportunity to carry out their long-planned plot. Considering all the millions killed by the Nazis, particularly the Jews, Germany and the territory occupied by her during World War II has the contemporary record for assassinations, violence and terror.

Definitions

Force may be defined as physical or intangible power or influence to effect change in the material or immaterial world. Coercion is the use of either physical or intangible force to compel action contrary to the will

---

[1] Pitirim A. Sorokin, *Social and Cultural Dynamics* (New York: American Book Co., 1937), vol. III, p. 324.

or reasoned judgment of the individual or group subjected to such force. Violence is the willful application of force in such a way that it is physically or psychologically injurious to the person or group against whom it is applied.

Some writers have tried to distinguish between the legal and illegal aspects of violence. Thus Sidney Hook defines violence as "the illegal employment of methods of physical coercion for personal or group ends."[2] In its "legalized" form terror includes physical constraints, or less conspicuous, but very effective, social pressures (such as discriminatory economic, social, cultural, political and administrative measures.) Hence, when terror is utilized by duly constituted government the question of social ethics arises only as one of expediency, since the "right" to utilize violence is one of the most fundamental aspects of sovereignty.

Sociologically speaking, however, legalistic distinctions disappear when we realize that violence is but one aspect of the techniques of politics, and that all politics is a struggle for power. From time immemorial those who have struggled or sought power have used force, violence and terror to achieve their aims. Hence, in political struggles terror, although always condemned by the holders and executors of state sovereignty, becomes a very important factor when utilized by a politically subordinate group, whether minority or not, seeking to capture political power or aiming to impose specific ideas on the governing authorities. In this case violence is but one of the many forms of physical and mental conflict which, in its extreme form, becomes war. War is the ultimate extension of the use of terror for power purposes, and "lurks in the background of international politics just as revolution lurks in the background of domestic politics. There are few European countries where, at some time during the past 30 years, the possibility of revolution has not been an important factor in politics."[3] While, however, in international relations, "violence or threatened violence is customary"[4] within the framework of the state, the recourse to violence is more rare, and condemned in all illegal aspects, as an "unconstitutional," "illegal" form of revolution, since every national law prohibits the use of force as a political weapon.

Terror. Terrorism is one aspect of the whole field of violence, "the method or the theory behind the method whereby an organized group or party seeks to achieve its avowed aims chiefly through the systematic

---

[2] Sidney Hook, "Violence," *Encyclopedia of the Social Sciences*, VI, pp. 264-267. Theodore Paullin, *Introduction to Non-Violence* (Philadelphia: The Pacifist Research Bureau, 1944), is a valuable survey of various definitions and literature in this field.

[3] Edward Hallett Carr, *The Twenty Years' Crisis, 1919-1939* (London: The Macmillan Co., 1940), p. 140.

[4] F. L. Schuman, *International Politics* (New York: McGraw-Hill Book Co., 1941), p. 283.

use of violence." [5] The emphasis here is on "the systematic use of violence" directed, usually, against a group which needs to be subjected for
some definite purpose, by such methods as destruction of property, devas-
tation of land, killings of family members or the outstanding members of
the terrorized group. Terrorism differs from intimidation by its techniques; it is a mild form of violence. Intimidation is a preliminary step
to terrorism—threatening injury or mental harm in order to arouse fear
and the willingness to conform to the demands of the intimidator. Terror
differs, furthermore, from mob violence, by having a definitely limited
organization sustained by a well-worked out ideological program.

Fear and Terror. The backbone of all forms of violence and terrorism is
fear. The physiological effects of fear are increased glandular activity,
changes in circulation, neuro-muscular tension, and a temporary upset-
ting of the anabolic and catabolic balance. These are the actual responses
to the stimuli which cause emotional behavior. Fear is accompanied by
an increased degree of toxicity of the muscles, a rush of blood to the
brain and muscles, a decrease in flow to the digestive organs, and an
increased degree of secretion of the adrenal and other glands.

As the organism becomes more mature and its store of experience
grows, the fears become more complex and less apparent outwardly, but
they remain, nevertheless, as one of the primary factors influencing personality and behavior. In adult human life fear is still a conditioned
response, but is somewhat vague and generalized, responding to the
stimuli which tend to be abstract and symbolized. Terror techniques
play on the complexes of fear. The most elementary stimulus is physical
force, and the most extreme is torture or death, either on the block and
the firing squad or in a battle. Every effort is made to impress on the
people subject to such techniques that some such frightful results will
follow swiftly if the demands of the users of violence are not met. All
this produces the feeling of insecurity and strong emotional responses.

If a person is subjected to terror techniques it is logical that he is far
easier to influence or that he may be induced to adopt certain views, or
even to reverse his former beliefs, since he is eager, in most cases, to
seize upon anything which is offered as a solution. The effectiveness of
the threats is strengthened when violence and terror are identified with
a well propounded ideology impressing upon the attacked group that the
"old order" is losing ground, since it is unable to oppose terror by the old
established methods.

---

[5] J. B. S. Handman, "Terrorism," *Encyclopedia of the Social Sciences*, XIV, pp.
575-580.

Regulation of Violence and Terror

Force utilized by in-group members is regulated by folkways, mores, and ideologies; even such "outlaw groups" as gangsters have their own norms of behavior. "Culture patterns" limit physical violence used in the daily life of a people, such as the slapping of servants and children, or the beating of one's wife. But paradoxically enough, the most horrible forms of brutality have been sanctioned for the use of the legal authorities. "Restraint, the lash, torture in many forms, mutilation, humiliation, isolation, exile, and finally death are items in the thick catalogue of force. The rack, the boot, branding, the dungeon, the 'hell hole,' boiling water and molten metal, crucifixion, burnings, sawing and pulling asunder. These are only a few of the devices from time to time employed in the service of the state." [6]

Violence in International Relations. All efforts made so far to control violence in international relations have been glaring failures. International violence, in spite of all theoretical limits imposed by "international law," has never been limited in its ruthlessness. For international struggle for power is efficient and without conscience. No modern army, for example, would consider abolishing the use of poison gas or the atomic bomb only because these are classed "inhuman" by our social norms or by a group of philosophers. There are no methods too cruel to employ if any advantage is gained. The only limitations imposed are the exigencies of the moment and the ability to "get away with" such practices. But violence and terror, within the framework of statehood, are limited by the cultural standards which determine the extent and ways in which these tendencies are expressed, inhibited and sublimated. Children torture pets in ways that are considered inexcusable in adults. Males use violence at times when it would be deprecated in the female. The sticking of a dagger into the opponent's back is not considered moral in our culture pattern; we prefer the machine gun or the settlement of a minor argument by a fist fight.

The Geography of Brute Force

Violence is always evidence of periods of transition, a symptom of revolutionary moments. There are certain unsettled eras of history when brutality flourishes—and we are in such a period now. Violence is most characteristic of the countries seething with the desire to shake off foreign domination, whose citizens live under oppression and whose sons

---

[6] Charles E. Merriam, *Political Power* (New York: McGraw-Hill Book Co., 1934), p. 135.

are political refugees abroad, forced to become international adventurers, "men of no country"; the countries honeycombed with underground nationalistic, racial and patriotic movements. Suppressed nationalism, in particular, today gives rise to subversive activities, characterized by a guerrilla warfare and terrorism. The rise of the national states in the Balkans has been marked by violent revolutionary activities and violent opposition which have consequently long been accepted forces in the Balkan political life. In World War II, as in the days of old under the Turkish oppressor, the Balkans returned to those habits of turmoil which existed so long when robber-patriot bands wandered about the mountain forests slaughtering and raiding Ottoman Turks. Organized, armed Chetniks, living off the wilderness and the secret support of their compatriots, fought their own specialized Balkan type of warfare against the Italians, Hungarians, Bulgarians and their German masters. Mass murder once more had become a Balkan commonplace.[7] In subjugated Czechoslovakia mass executions went on—but the Czechs fought back with their own methods, again demonstrating that "power is not strongest when it uses violence, but weakest."[8] All over Europe, where modern conquerors were attempting to produce "The New Order," the modern serfs used various combinations of these three methods against the death-pangs designed for them by the "Herrenvolk": (1) passive resistance; (2) sabotage of all kinds including food hoarding, slow-down strikes, and bombing of railroads, and (3) individual assassinations and guerrilla warfare.[9]

Violence and brutality are frequently connected with imperialism. Generals Campos and Weyler learned this lesson in Cuba from the Cuban insurgents. The French had frequently to send their "foreign legion" to Algeria and Morocco. Usually subversive movements survive underground, breaking out over and again in open hostilities.

Violence and Totalitarianism. As recent events have shown, terrorism is most characteristic of the totalitarian states.[10] The intensity of the use of

---

[7] For the background of political violence in the Balkans, see Joseph S. Roucek, *The Politics of the Balkans* (New York: McGraw-Hill Book Co., 1939), chapters I, II.

[8] Charles E. Merriam, *Political Power* (New York: McGraw-Hill Book Co., 1934), p. 190. See Joseph S. Roucek, "Non-Political Methods in Politics," *World Affairs Interpreter*, X (October, 1939), pp. 290-303; Roucek, "Methods of Meeting Domination: The Czechoslovaks," *American Sociological Review*, VI (October, 1941), pp. 670-673; Roucek, "The Sociology of Secret Societies in World War II," *World Affairs Interpreter*, XII (October, 1941), pp. 289-294.

[9] Joseph S. Roucek, "The Strategy of Treachery and Espionage," chapter 19, pp. 387-416, in Thorsten V. Kalijarvi, ed., *Modern World Politics* (New York: Thomas Y. Crowell Co., 1945).

[10] Joseph S. Roucek, "War as a Symptom of our Social Crisis," chapter 29, pp. 661-672, in Thorsten V. Kalijarvi, *op. cit.*

violence increases in proportion as the democratic means of transferring power decreases and the arbitrary power increases. The resulting political struggles either crystallize in strife within the dominant party or the conflict between the dominant party and its opponents. Similar in origin are the multitudinous overturns which have given Latin America a reputation for petty revolutions. There, occasionally a dictator-president so grinds the faces of his subjects that all classes unite against him. This is what happened, for instance, to Machado in Cuba.

Praetorianism. The hierarchical organization of the military and its ability to use force is very conducive to its interference in politics. To draw a line determining when the use by the army of the brutal force in internal politics is for patriotic reasons, for the personal advancement of its particular interests, or the selfish ambitions of its leaders, is difficult. At any rate, these interferences bring about periodic outbreaks of violence in Latin America and Japan, in particular, or the Balkans. Praetorianism of military oligarchies appears usually in the countries characterized by protracted revolutions, warlike traditions, weak democratic systems, a powerful and self-conscious military class, and where the traditional forms of society are on the verge of dissolution (China, Japan, Latin America, and the Balkans). They are best exemplified by Japan's network of super-patriotic secret societies, headed by Mitsuru Toyama, which operated behind the scenes with a brutal fanaticism which the Ku Klux Klan never equaled. In the name of the emperor they rigged politics, liquidated moderates, broke ground for military adventures, served the army with intrigues, and kept the national fever burning.[11]

Gangs. A special brand of terrorism is provided by criminal bands, gangs and racketeers—when there is a lack or breakdown of stable agencies of social control, lack of settled community life and the inability of ordinary political processes to provide social adjustments. Besides in America we meet with such conditions in frontier societies where political and social life is unstable [12]—Russia, the Balkans, the Near East, Mexico and China. Aiming to share in the state's exclusive right to use force, such organizations develop their own governments. Al Capone, for instance, at one time was employing a private army of 2,000 men and managed an annual budget of many millions of dollars; he had a government with revenues and resources, law of his own, with collectors, killers,

---

[11] For a good account, see *Time*, January 6, 1941, p. 28.

[12] See, for instance, Hoffman Birney, *Vigilantes: A Chronicle of the Rise and Fall of the Plummer Gang of Outlaws in and about Virginia City, Montana, in the Early '60's* (New York: Grosset, 1941).

educators, agents and representatives, and both public and private police on his civil list.[13]

Techniques of Terrorism

The devices of violence and terrorism vary and depend on local conditions. The most dramatized of all such techniques is civil warfare. It is inseparably linked with destruction of property of opponents, shooting of police and of the representatives of the army, attacks on police barracks and ambushing of opponents with bombs, rifles and revolvers (as practiced in the revolt of Sinn Feiners against the British in Ireland between 1919 and 1921), guerilla warfare, assassination of the heads of the state (Tsar Alexander II and McKinley), and of the representatives of the system (the attempts to assassinate Lenin and President F. D. Roosevelt), murders calculated to create an international conflict embarrassing to the authorities (the assassination of the German ambassador to Russia in 1918). In the Balkans the traditions of feudal wars are even today integrated with the use of bullets and all kinds of forms of terrorism as the "standardized" political methods. On another plane, the cultivation of violence is known to us in this country in terms of the ordinary gangsterism, swaggering police officers, labor strikes and troubles, wardens of prisoners, and periodic lynching; in the use of physical force against persons in the execution of law, the infliction of death penalty upon the condemned man; the police give the "third degree" to prisoners, and the soldiers are called upon to "break" a strike. On the negative side there is refusal to give protection to the Negro just about to be lynched.

But while force and violence are a stock in trade of all organized government, force is, similarly, a weapon in the hands of the "illegal" opposition which may assassinate, kidnap, riot, seize government and private property, commit sabotage, smuggle, deal in contraband, boycott, carry on public demonstrations, or prevent the sale of mortagaged farms on foreclosure.

Although all techniques of terrorism are basically the same, there are slight variations in their furtiveness. The legal group may use the concentration camp, prison, execution, and some form of legalized torture, whereas the illegal group must confine itself to more "underhanded" methods—kidnaping, torture, murder, destruction of property by bombing or arson and sudden outbreaks. A good example here is the so-called "mental murder" of a former Russian secret police chief in Washington in February, 1941; in this case a group was forced to use illegal methods because its power did not legally extend beyond the borders of its own

---

[13] See, for instance, Craig Thompson and Allen Raymond, *Gang Rule in New York* (New York: The Dial Press, 1940).

country. A man may be hounded to death by constant threats to himself and his family, by shadowing, or by striking those close to him until in desperation, he commits suicide. Many "Trotskyites" were driven to this by constant persecutions.

The Techniques of Threats. Probably one of the most effective techniques of violence is that which can create the impression of its effectiveness by threats or minor acts giving promise of more violence, on the principle of "either or." This device has been known to every ruler since the beginning of history and has taken such forms as the "boiling in oil" of the critiques of the regime, military demonstrations, the screeching of the policemen's sirens, and the visits of battleships. One of the strongest arguments in the favor of this type of technique is the abhorrence of the average man, interested in his home, family, and job, of violent changes.

Back of such techniques there must be always the theoretical and public assumption that a movement is using violence, and will be able to use violence when and if necessary to do so. Any signs of the weaknesses or any indications of the renunciation of the use of violence on the part of any social movement is probably the most dangerous step it can take since it gives up its fighting power together with its negotiating power. A good example of such weakness is the famous statement of Chamberlain pertaining to Czechoslovakia: "How horrible, fantastic, incredible it is that we should be digging trenches and trying gas masks here because of a quarrel in a far away country between people of whom we know nothing." [14] Hitler proved to be the master technician of this kind of brutality. In using threats, so to speak, he economized, in some cases, on airplanes and army divisions by establishing a solid reputation for the qualities of unscrupulousness and ruthlessness. When the Nazis threatened they were likely to show their intended victims that they would not hesitate to machine gun civilians and to wipe out open cities, sometimes purely as a "demonstration."

The New Yorker (November 30, 1940, p. 11), developed this notion somewhat fatuously, in regard to our national defense during the opening plans of World War II:

"A first step in our defense program should be to develop a technique of menace. The United States is the most powerful country in the world, and the least alarming. Germany and Italy, far less strong, manage to exude the stuff of frightfulness. When Hitler meets his conspirators, he goes to a place called the Brenner Pass, and the name Brenner Pass, just in itself, has terrorized countless millions of radio listeners. It is impossible

---

[14] Neville Chamberlin, *The Struggle For Peace* (New York: G. Putnam, 1939), p. 275.

to conceive of anything trivial emanating from a meeting of two people in a pass. Surely the U. S. can dig up a Brenner Pass without any trouble. How about Death Valley? We think President Roosevelt should make frequent trips to Death Valley, there to confer momentously with Mackenzie King, and the report should be circulated that the two leaders are in perfect accord about their vital oil interests (the story is that they are discussing what is the best oil to boil dictators in . . .). So far the only preparedness gossip the Axis has picked up from America is that we have drafted a few rookies and that every training camp has hostesses. Japan is the most experienced and most talented exponent of menace. She is known as the Yellow Peril, to begin with. We are known as Uncle Sam. This uncle stuff is terrible today—too disarming. It would be better for this country to be known as Flash Gordon than as Uncle Sam. . . ."

Progressive steps leading from the threat of violence to actual violence have received considerable attention as "The Strategy of Terror." Hitler's technique, in summary, was to keep the nations divided, working on their mutual jealousies and feuds, concentrating his pressure on one country at a time, enforcing "moderate" demands which enabled him, when granted, to make further and less moderate demands infiltrating one country after another "peacefully" with "military instructors," "technicians" and "tourists," until the number and equipment were great enough to render further disguises unnecessary. In using diplomacy as an instrument of war, in driving a diplomatic wedge between countries to make a later military wedge unnecessary in some cases, in using threats, the "Strategy of Terror" was perfected. It is the strategy of treating diplomacy as a war weapon, as a way of economizing men and tanks and planes, making it a rule not to take by force what can be taken just as well by threats (Austria, Czechoslovakia, Denmark, Hungary, Roumania, and Bulgaria). Bloody victories were used as demonstrations of what happens to countries which choose to resist.

In the game of "The Strategy of Terror," the actual physical break through is the last stage of an attack, which is preceded by a preparatory stage consisting of lulling the enemy into a feeling of security and comfort through the judicious use of propaganda, weakening his existing ideology, creating internal dissension and lack of confidence in the leaders, and building up a myth of the invincibility of the attackers. Everything is aimed at the disorganization of morale of the opponent, who is then confronted with the "blitzkrieg" aiming to create a general breakdown by the careful application of harsh, unwavering cruelty.[15]

---

[15] It is important, however, to remember that terrorism may be used only on groups which, because of weakness, lack of unity, or an inability to retaliate as a result of some other internal fault, are unable to reverse the procedure and use those same methods on the attackers. Thus, it is also safe to say that preparedness does not insure peace, but helps to instill fear in other states.

This kind of war uses fundamental principles—doubt, distrust and enticement—which are as ancient and as well-worn as the principles of military combat. But its immediate tactics and strategy bear as little relation to the propaganda battles of the World War I period as the tactics and strategy of the dive bomber plus armored-column combination bears to the tactics and strategy of the 1916 trench warfare plus foot-soldier attacks. The strategy of terror in World War II was no longer, as it was in 1914-1917, a matter of defending one's own cause and trying to enlist good will or sympathy for it. It was an offensive operation, carefully correlated with diplomatic and military offenses, designed to destroy morale behind the enemy lines by whatever methods might seem most appropriate.[16] It manifested itself in the "extended strategy" that reaches out behind the enemy lines with parachute "suicide squads" on the one hand and a "fifth column" on the other.

Messianism of Violence and Terror. The techniques of violence and terrorism, when utilized in politics, depend on the fanaticism of the practitioners and the seriousness of the "cause." The "causes" represent the movements born of "new thought," political or religious grievances, the desire to shake off foreign domination, or simply criminal aims.[17] You find criminals among political agitators, rebels among serious thinkers, religious fanatics and self-seeking adventurers side by side. With the exception of the purely criminal organizations, such as the American type of "gangster," vague aims common to all are "the benefit of mankind," "liberty," the realization of "the new order," and other ideological slogans justifying the need to eliminate or punish the individuals or groups interfering with the achievement of desired goals. The practice of violence and terror needs a highly emotional and fanatical ideological framework, since there can be hardly any pecuniary rewards expected from violence, punishment, and death. The stakes are simply too high and the reward, at best, the promise of being noted by history; and at worst, death or torture. But this reward must stand high in the estimation of the violence practitioners, so that the "supreme sacrifice" can be taken for granted as far as the membership of such movements is concerned. In short, the psychology of terrorism is mostly that of romantic messianism, sustained by a rigorous creed;[18] courage, devotion, tenacity, and, above all, a blind

---

[16] Edmund Taylor, *The Strategy of Terror* (Boston: Houghton Mifflin Co., 1940); *The Axis Psychological Strategy Against the United States* (New York: New Europe, 1942); Ladislas Farago, *The Axis Grand Strategy* (New York: Farrar and Rinehart, 1942).

[17] Joseph S. Roucek, "The Sociology of Secret Societies in World War II," *World Affairs Interpreter* XII (October, 1941), pp. 289-294; and "Methods of Meeting Domination: The Czechoslovaks," *American Sociological Review* VI (October, 1941), pp. 670-673.

[18] R. R. Palmer, *Twelve Who Ruled* (Princeton: Princeton University Press, 1941),

trust in the idealism and the infallibility of the "cause." [19] They have a clear purpose, self-assurance and unscrupulousness to go ahead to attain their ends without regard for anything. Their advantage is gained from the fears and confused helplessness of the victim. Where the "others" watch the inexorable march of events, as muddled, helpless observers, these high-spirited fellows place themselves at the head of the column and proceed to make history with themselves cast in the roles of the "men of destiny." By identifying themselves with triumphant force and boldly disregarding all principle of "legality" and all that men consider "right" and "sacred," they are able to take risks incomprehensible to the average mind.

The dangers involved vary with the degree of "legality." A government practicing terror is always described as enforcing the law—but a successful revolution can surely bring terrible retribution on the unfortunate executioners of such practices. Thus "messianism" is necessary only for the "illegal" movements of violence since the ideological justifications for the use of physical force by the "legal" representatives is provided by their status as the executors of law. Since, when "messianism" is involved, the actual reward for the terrorist is high, the very execution of brutal acts advertises the success of such steps which are to lead to an ideological "heaven" propounded by the terrorist. Furthermore, these very steps advertise publicly the weaknesses of the opponent unable to stop terror. If the publicity values are not realized, however, then terrorism falls short of its own goal, since individual terrorist acts may be disposed of in the public news and mind as "just another murder."

The Utilization of Violence by "Peace-Lovers." Probably the most disconcerting fact confronting all opponents of violence is that nearly all social movements, in the acquisition of power and survival, have found it necessary, at some point of their existence, to use violence. Humanitarians eventually find it necessary to use force and thus are confronted with the necessity of providing the recurrent ideological justification for their practices: the end justifies the means.

The "illegal" practitioners of terror must also make pretenses at legality, although, properly speaking, their acts are open defiance of law. The

---

is a valuable study of the personnel of the Committee of Public Safety under the Convention driven on by their faith in Liberty, Equality and Fraternity to practice their fanatical terror. W. G. Krivitsky, *In Stalin's Secret Service* (New York: Harper and Brothers, 1939), is the study of a former Russian agent of plots, counterplots, intrigues and mysteries piled on mysteries; the work also contains an excellent chapter on the transformation of the Commintern from an agency of international revolution into an agency of nationalistic propaganda, and gives the inside story of the execution of Tukhavkhevsky.

[19] All these elements are well presented in Jan Valtin, *Out of the Night* (New York: Alliance, 1941).

usual reasoning is that the government's steps, based on the declaration of a state of emergency, is but another indication of the existing government's usurpation of powers not granted to it. The terrorist group represents itself as the representatives as such moral authority as the "people," "constitutional government," "proletariate" or "the oppressed nationality."

Assassination. There is a very close connection between criminality and revolution, and the role of assassin in cases of violent social transformations. The motives of the assassin are inseparably intertwined with the religious, political, national and social ideologies. Yet the following types of assassins representing certain dominant tendencies in the various struggles for power can be formed.[20]

1. Those who assassinate for personal motives, without any concrete political aim in the action, but whose act assumes a political character by the fact that it is directed against the head of the state or some other prominent persons connected with the state. Hatred, revenge, jealousy, and other passions are usually the cause of such acts, although they are sometimes hidden by a thin veil of ideological pretext (the assassination of President Garfield by the disappointed office-seeker, Guiteau).

2. The second type is assassination for power, for the gratification of power, for the advantages with which power is connected or for the elimination of dangerous or hated political opponents. It has always been alluring to ambitious and ruthless men to destroy the supreme possessor of power by revolts and assassinations. The Nazis of our generation gave a scientific base to such murders.

3. There are many cases of using diplomatic assassination in international relations for the elimination of dangerous opponents. During the times of the Crusades, one of the secret orders of the Ismailians, a Mohammedan sect, terrorized Christians and other enemies by skillfully executing political murders; driven by the fanaticism of a religious doctrine, they formed highly-organized military groups whose services were often used by both Western and Eastern princes, including Byzantine Emperors. Mussolini sent hired *bravi* (paid assassins) to Bagnoles in France to kill Carlo Rosselli who had too much influence among the Italian exiles opposed to Mussolini; the Nazis armed gang killed Theodor Lessing, a noted philosopher, on Czechoslovakian territory.

4. Murders committed for Reason of State are perhaps the most widely used in the history of political conflicts and the most dangerous, because the rationalization of a moral motive is always at hand. The *salus publica* knows no moral or religious considerations. Already Machiavelli extolled

---

[20] Oscar Jaszi, "The Stream of Political Murder," *American Journal of Economics and Sociology* III, (April, 1944), pp. 335-355.

many cases of assassination in the interest of the state and praised the ruthless methods of Cesare Borgia as applications of real statesmanship. The Nazi and Communist regimes of modern times have perfected this technique with refinement.

5. Religious assassinations are often connected with racial fanaticism and struggle for power. For many centuries the extermination of pagans, Mohammedans, Jews and heretics was regarded as highly commendable service and the Inquisition was a holy institution. The extreme cruelty of the Balkan politics can be partly explained as the result of centuries during which the killing of the Turks was widely practiced by the conquered Christian population.

6. In the sixth type of assassination the driving motive is national, often connected with struggles for constitutionalism, especially republicanism. In 1853 Victor Hugo urged the assassination of Napoleon *le Petit*. Felice Orsini, inspired by the theories of Mazzini, in the company of other conspirators, tried to assassinate the Emperor and the Empress in 1858. Jean Jaures, the great French humanitarian socialist, was assassinated in 1914 by a fanatic aroused by the nationalistic propaganda of the reactionary press. Serb history is rich in expulsions and murders of Princes and Kings; among eight Serbian rulers, between 1904 and 1934, four were murdered, three were exiled, and only one died while on the throne. In modern Japan, rival military groups often terrorized public opinion and the government by murders or the threat of murders—being seldom punished and often regarded as martyrs.

7. The oppression of the masses combined with a revolutionary dynamism produced an outburst of assassinations and counter-revolutionary repressions fostered by the socio-economic ideologies (Nihilism, Anarchism, Syndicalism and Bolshevism).

All these various currents of assassinations were accentuated and, in a certain way, intermingled in the period after World War I when the long suffering of the masses, the breakdown of orderly governments, the revival of tribal solidarity and national exclusiveness, the great number of neuropaths produced by the war, the acute class struggle between the proletariat, the landless peasantry and the former privileged classes caused a new wave of bloodshed and terrorism. If there are any indications for the future, they all point in the direction of the intensification of this process.

The State and Force

Violence and terror are the ultimate in devices for social control. Machiavelli's dictum is worth citing here:

"Love is maintained by a bond of obligation which, owing to the wickedness of human nature, is always broken if it clashes with private interests; but fear is maintained by a dread of punishment which never abandons you. Men love their own pleasure but fear at the pleasure of the prince who should, therefore, depend upon that which is his own and not upon that which is of others."

It is axiomatic, indeed, that the state, the most important of social institutions, and to greater or lesser degrees all social institutions, depend at some time on force or the threat of violence. The fundamental basis of the State is provided by political power and by its regular execution.[21] Power relationships must, therefore, involve the ability of the order-giving authority to create a belief in the subordinate that the command can be enforced. Hence the ability of a state to survive depends on its police force or the military—whether this applies to the internal or international situation. We have our police force to maintain obedience by means of force and fear. But the police, like the State in international relations, try to achieve the desired ends by negotiations, bribery, pacts, intimidation and all other available means of social control, since these devices are far cheaper and often as effective as violence and terrorism.

The Usefulness of Violence

Although numerous philosophers (as Kropotkin, Tolstoy and others) have maintained that fighting, violence and physical coercion are perversions from man's original pacific tendencies, the fact remains that the philosopher's opposition to violence is useful as a sort of "wishful thinking" which fails to confront reality. It is very intriguing to hear about the possibilities of eliminating violence by various forms of passive resistance and nonviolent coercion, as propounded by those claiming that force does not achieve permanent solutions. Efforts are made to transfer the conflict from one plane to another by appealing to humanitarian argument and admiration of brave, suffering martyrs. But in spite of the periodic condemnation of force, violence is a useful social instrument, especially if we acknowledge that law in the modern state is based upon force. This fact was known to the founders of this country and we may state here Alexander Hamilton's views in the *Federalist:*

"It is essential to the idea of a law, that it be attended with a sanction; or, in other words, a penalty or punishment for disobedience. If there be no penalty annexed to disobedience, the resolutions or commands which pretend to be laws will, in fact, amount to nothing more than advice or recommendation. This penalty, whatever it may be, can only be inflicted in two ways; by the agency of the courts and ministers of justice, or by military force; by the coercion of the magistracy or by the

---

[21] Joseph S. Roucek, "Political Behavior as a Struggle for Power," *Journal of Social Psychology*, VI (July, 1941), pp. 341-351.

coercion of arms. . . . It is evident that there is no process of a court by which the observants of the laws can, in the last resort, be enforced. Sentences may be denounced against them for a violation of their duty; but these sentences can only be carried into execution by the sword."

Weakness of Terrorism

Violence is weakest in its effectiveness when it cannot create moral sanctions for its practices. For all government, in the long run, rests on consent. If that statement seems academic, sentimental and unrealistic, it may be enlarged to read "rests on consent and habit." But habit has to be built up slowly and under conditions not too intolerable to the governed. Widespread and continued use of violence is suicidal. Violence is answered by violence, and the result is a physical struggle. A physical struggle inevitably arouses in the minds of those directly and even indirectly concerned in it, emotions of hatred, fear, rage and resentment. In the heat of conflict all scruples are thrown to the winds, all the habits of forebearance and humaness, slowly and laboriously formed during generations of civilized living, are forgotten. Nothing matters any more, after a while, except victory. And when at last victory comes to one or other of the parties, this final outcome of struggle bears no necessary relation to the rights and wrongs of the case; nor, in most cases, does it provide any lasting settlement to the dispute. In particular, the prophets of violence fail to understand that the average person—and therefore most of mankind—is averse to the continued terrorization and that eventually violence is always replaced by the comparative stability of social relations in which the prophets of violence and terror have no place.[22]

Summary

Violence and terror have reached alarming dimensions as instruments of social control in recent years. The appalling casualty lists of World War II, on the one hand, and frequent political assassinations, on the other, are outstanding evidence of this. Decimation of populations of occupied countries in Europe, and the concentration camps and underground terroristic movements bear further testimony.

Both the state, and groups acting illegally within states, find their ultimate resource in controlling others in some forms of violence and terror, and to foreswear the use of such extreme measures leads to ineffectiveness.

The principles underlying violence and terror are old, but many recent applications are new. Even in the brief period since World War I terror

---

[22] Jan Valtin, *Out of the Night*, is an excellent psychological study of the reactions of the terrorist underground worker to his vocation, as well as of his victims.

has changed from a defensive device to one of aggression in the relations among peoples, and is now accurately integrated with diplomatic and military strategy. The new uses of terror are to weaken an enemy and thus conquer, often, without the use of armies and pitched battles. Where such battles are fought they become demonstrations of the willingness of the conqueror to utterly crush opposition and apply unwaveringly the utmost violence against those who dare oppose them.

QUESTIONS

1. Define violence and terror.
2. What are the differences between the legal and sociological concepts of violence?
3. Define war.
4. How is fear related to the forms of social control?
5. Why is violence more or less regulated "at home" but not internationally?
6. What historical periods are characterized by violence?
7. What are the methods used by the subjugated people to fight "The New Order"?
8. Define praetorianism.
9. What regions of the world used violence in political processes?
10. Describe the techniques of menace.
11. What were Hitler's techniques of the "Strategy of Terror"?
12. What are the "messiah" elements involved in the proponents of violence?
13. What are the legal aspects of "violence" used by the legal authorities?
14. Why do the "peace-lovers" eventually have to resort to violence?
15. Outline the seven types of assassination.
16. Why does the state have to depend on force for its survival?
17. What are the useful aspects of the use of violence?
18. What are the weak aspects of terrorism?
19. Why is violence reaching such alarming proportions in modern times?
20. What is new about the practice of violence today?

SUGGESTED TOPICS FOR TERM PAPERS AND FURTHER RESEARCH

1. Compare the organization of the Fascist party with the two major American parties.
2. Typical careers of popular dictators and their lieutenants since the early nineteenth century.
3. The effects of nazism on the family in Germany.
4. The social situation in which (a) fascism and (b) nazism emerged.
5. Dominant Fascist and Nazi theories set forth in support of national imperialism.
6. Economic policies of Hitler, Mussolini, Napoleon I and III.
7. The function and control of occupational organizations in Nazi Germany and Fascist Italy.
8. Compare the dominant conceptions of the nation in Nazi Germany and in the United States.
9. Conscious and unconscious elements in fascism and nazism.
10. Compare fascism and nazism with the regimes of Perón, Cromwell, Napoleon I and III.

BIBLIOGRAPHY

Books

Ammon M. Aurand, Jr., *Historical Account of the Mollie Maguires and James Mc-Kenna McParlan* (Harrisburg, Pa.: The Aurand Press, 1940). The origin, depredations, and decay of a terrorist secret organization in the Pennsylvania coal fields during and after the Civil War.

Joseph Bornstein, *The Politics of Murder* (New York: William Sloane Associates, 1951). How assassins made history.

Paul F. Brissenden, *The I.W.W.* (New York: Columbia University Press, 1919). A study of the violent syndicalist movement.

D. W. Brogan, *The Price of Revolution* (New York: Harper and Brothers, 1952). How revolutions have been used to transform society in a good part of the world and how some revolutions have not run their course.

Hugh Byas, *Government by Assassination* (New York: Alfred A. Knopf, 1942). The terrorist techniques in Japanese politics.

Alan Bullock, *Hitler, A Study in Tyranny* (London: Odham's Press, 1952). Hitler's rise, operation, and fall.

Albert Carr, *Juggernaut: The Path of Dictatorship* (New York: Viking Press, 1939). Studies of twenty dictatorships from Richelieu to Hitler, but contains some errors of fact.

A. Cobban, *Dictatorship, Its History and Theory* (New York: Charles Scribner's Sons, 1939). A scholarly and readable analysis.

Guy S. Ford, *Dictatorship in the Modern World* (Minneapolis: University of Minnesota Press, 1939). A good general handbook.

Adolf Hitler, *Mein Kampf* (New York: The Stackpole Co., 1939).

D. C. Holton, *Modern Japan and Shinto Nationalism* (Chicago: University of Chicago Press, 1943), pp. 1-25. A concise description of the religious roots of Japanese nationalism.

Eugen Kogon, *The Theory and Practice of Hell: The German Concentration Camp and the System Behind Them* (New York: Farrar, Straus and Young, 1950). A detailed study of the Nazi extermination policy.

Kurt London, *Backgrounds of Conflict* (New York: The Macmillan Co., 1945), pp. 62-77; 142-152; 188-205. A description of the conflicting political systems in World War II, including fascism, nazism, and the Japanese Imperial Rule. Particular emphasis is placed on the intellectual antecedents of nazism and fascism.

Franz Neumann, *Behemoth: The Structure and Practice of National Socialism* (New York: Oxford University Press, 1942), pp. 83-129. A well-informed analysis.

Sigmund Neumann, *Permanent Revolution* (New York: Harper and Brothers, 1942), pp. 1-9; 36-72. One of the best accounts of nazism presented against a broad historical background.

Joseph S. Roucek, "Unorthodox and Non-Political Methods," Chapter 18, pp. 469-492, in Joseph S. Roucek and George B. de Huszar, eds., *Introduction to Political Science* (New York: Thomas Y. Crowell Co., 1950). Contains an extensive bibliography.

Gaetano Salvemini, *Under the Axe of Fascism* (New York: Viking Press, 1936). The techniques used by fascism.

George Sorel, *Reflections on Violence* (Glencoe, Ill.: Free Press, 1950). Some material included here has never been published in English—such as "In Defense of Lenin." The main work is the classic exposition of the author's 1906 doctrine of revolutionary progress, not through pacifistic means but by violence put into action by a small conspiratorial band.

Josef Stalin, *Foundations of Leninism* (New York: International Publishers, 1939).

A small but a significant treatment of the ideology and the techniques of violence which are to bring about the Communist heaven.

Edmond Taylor, *The Strategy of Terror* (Boston: Houghton Mifflin Co., 1940). How the "Strategy of Terror" operated under Hitlerism.

Curtis A. Wilgus, ed., *South American Dictators* (Washington, D.C.: George Washington University Press, 1937). Individual studies of dictators characteristic of certain Latin-American countries.

Periodicals

Theodore Abel, "Is a Psychiatric Interpretation of the German Enigma Necessary?" *American Sociological Review*, X (August, 1945), pp. 457-464.

Balticus, "The two G's: Gestapo and GPU," *Foreign Affairs*, XVII (April, 1939), pp. 489-507.

Richard M. Brickner, "Is Germany Incurable?" *Atlantic Monthly*, CLXXI (March, 1943), pp. 84-93, and (April, 1943), pp. 94-98.

C. E. Chapman, "List of Books Referring to Caudillos in Hispanic-America," *Hispanic-American Historical Review*, XIII (April, 1930), pp. 143-146.

Calderon F. Garcia, "Dictatorship and Democracy in Latin-America," *Foreign Affairs*, III (1924-1925), pp. 459-477.

Hans Gerth, "The Nazi Party: Its Leadership and Composition," *American Journal of Sociology*, XLV (January, 1940), pp. 517-541.

J. O. Hertzler, "Crises and Dictatorships," *American Sociological Review*, V (April, 1940), pp. 137-169.

Rudolf Hess, "Essay on a Fuehrer," *American Mercury*, LIII (July, 1941), pp. 95-96.

Ernst Kris, "Morale in Germany," *American Journal of Sociology*, XLVII (November, 1941), pp. 452-461.

Owen Lattimore, "Sacred Cow of Japan," *Atlantic Monthly*, CLXXV (January, 1945), pp. 45-51.

Eugene Lyons, "Dictators into Gods," *American Mercury*, XLVI (March, 1939), pp. 265-272.

Sigmund Neumann, "The Rule of the Demagogue," *American Sociological Review*, III (August, 1938), pp. 487-498.

K. Reizler, "The Social Psychology of Fear," *American Journal of Sociology*, XLIV (1944), pp. 489-498.

Joseph S. Roucek, "Methods of Meeting Domination: The Czechoslovaks," *American Sociological Review*, VI (October, 1941), pp. 670-673; "Non-Political Methods in Politics," *World Affairs Interpreter*, X (October, 1939), pp. 290-303; "The Sociology of Secret Societies in World War II," *ibid.*, XII (October, 1941), pp. 289-294; "Sabotage and America's Minorities," *ibid.*, XIV (April, 1943), pp. 45-66.

C. J. S. Sprigge, "Italian Fascism: A Retrospect," *Nineteenth Century and After*, CXXXII (October, 1942), pp. 163-169.

Eric Voegelin, "Extended Strategy," *Journal of Politics*, II (May, 1940), pp. 189-200.

Francis G. Wilson, "Political Suppression in the Modern State," *ibid.*, I (August, 1939), pp. 237-257.

CHAPTER XXI

Economic Control

In a Garden of Eden there was no economic control in the sense that we use the term today. If the resources of this world could be had for the asking, if they could be picked off the trees when needed or desired, then only man's energy and desire would be the limiting factors. Problems in the distribution of wealth and income, business organization and the state, private property and contracts would be irrelevant.

The Problem of Limited Resources. In the ordinary world of man the available resources are not abundant. For even the most elementary wants of man, goods must be produced or obtained and apportioned on some basis. Man cannot otherwise survive. Economic control is the inevitable outgrowth of man in society within the framework of limited resources. "Limited" is used here in the sense that every member of society does not have all that he desires or needs to the extent of being indifferent to the possession of more. Thus economic control is part and parcel of social control. It may be incrusted in custom, habit, or tradition and thus people may be unconscious of it; or it may be conscious and purposeful.

The Relation of Ideologies to Economic Facts. Production, distribution, and apportionment of goods and services are basic. But basic also are the culture and ideologies that cluster about those facts. For example, labor in itself is an essential economic fact, but whether the worker is a slave, a serf, or a wage earner depends upon the whole pattern of a social system. The same is true of the organization of agriculture, of business, or of government. Whether agriculture is scientific or not, whether peasants or free farmers till the soil reflect existing knowledge and the institutions of the time. In our time farmers do not usually combine religious ritual when they sow their crops to insure an abundant harvest as in a previous day, although our present-day farmer is just as interested in the harvest.

All this does not mean that because the apportionment of scarce economic goods is a problem in any society people are, or should be, indifferent to the institutional arrangements through which the goods are distributed. It did make a difference whether the arrangement was feudal or capitalistic and it does make a difference whether it is democratic or totalitarian. It may well be, one does not know, that someday people will be completely indifferent as to *how* goods are produced, *why* they are produced, *who* will get them, and *who* shall decide these questions. Whenever that time comes there will still be economic control.

The early economists were quite aware of the problem of economic control. In the eighteenth century it was considered the state's function to lead and direct in the exploitation of economic resources. This was the mercantilistic state. This was the state that granted monopolistic charters to eager merchant adventurers. This was the state that imported skilled artisans and established industries. This was the state that aided in the breakdown of the guilds with their localized trade and their confining monopolies. There came a time when the mercantilistic state no longer pushed adventurous businessmen into action, but then these adventurous men wanted the state to protect their East India Companies from competition. The expansion of English trade through her colonies, and the stories of great wealth to be had, led to a long series of claims that everyone had the right to go into business anywhere and that it was the duty of the state to keep its hands off and not grant favors, but merely to protect the gains attained through individual effort. Here we have the policy of *laissez faire*.

Laissez Faire and Economic Control

Adam Smith's Theories. Adam Smith, the "father of Economics," published his great work on the *Wealth of Nations* in 1776 to show just how wealth could be increased if the state would take a back seat and let men compete with each other for the fruits of this earth. In so doing, he argued, they would be led "as if by an invisible hand" to raise the general standard of living all over the world. Adam Smith certainly had no idea that such a system lacked control or direction. He disliked the conscious direction of the mercantilistic state, and his whole thesis was that under a competitive system a pattern of economic behavior would emerge. Men would be bound by the very forces of the market, by the necessities of the division of labor and the quest for profits. But, unlike mercantilism, men could operate with some freedom and discretion.

Theoretical Camps. Following Smith, economists generally divided into two great camps, although there was no unanimity of opinion in either. First there were those who envisioned an economic system as almost self-regulatory. The laws of demand, supply, and cost, operating in a free market, would set the prices, fix the wages, determine what should be produced, how much should be produced, who should manage the industry and work within the four walls of the factory, how much should be sent abroad and how much should stay at home. Then there were those who, far from denying the possibility of such a system, did deny that the common man would benefit. From early times to the present these economists pointed to long hours, child labor, inequality of income. Here was a mansion and there was a hovel. Not only that, but periodically the pattern of this so-called automatic type of control showed the stresses and strains of prosperity and depression.

The first group we call the classical economists; their spiritual successors we call the neo-classicists. The second group falls into no particular classification; they may be known as welfare, or historical, or institutionalists or socialist economists. They had this in common, however—they relied on the state to achieve the "good society." They generally talked in terms of "social control" to indicate a conscious, purposeful policy. In more narrow terms they thought of "economic control." The classical economists also thought in terms of a "good society," but their good society had a minimum of state control and a much greater reliance on the beneficent effects of competition. It should be clear that the problem was, and is, not one of a choice of terms like "control" or "self-regulating" or "automatic," but one of evaluating the kind of society one would like to have.[1] Both groups, irrespective of their differences, assume that the kind of society they would like is possible of achievement by man's efforts. Neither group would be interested in what either the state or man did within the limits of an economic system, if what was done was inevitable, predetermined, and thus not subject to change or modification. But where a system is established and thus, in a sense, operates through an elaborate pattern of traditional practices, customs and habits, there is the appearance of an unconscious, automatic order. Thus under capitalism the established practices of the market within a regime of private property presents economic control as a means of determining the behavior of men. The farmer grows his wheat, the miller produces his flour, the baker bakes the bread, the retailer sells it to the consumer. We expect each producer to receive something for his product. The progress from raw material to the finished product through the channels of markets and banks furnishes the habitual pattern and, as such, imposes an amazing network of economic controls. Not only is this true of the relations among producers, but within the economic association itself the controls seem even more obvious in corporations and labor unions. Each of these types of organization has its own pattern of rules and regulations.

Superficially society might appear to an isolated individual as one gi-

---

[1] Frederick Deibler, *Principles of Economics* (New York: McGraw-Hill Book Co., 1929), p. 29. See also Frederick Hayek, *The Road to Serfdom* (Chicago: University of Chicago Press, 1944); Barbara Wooton, *Freedom Under Planning* (Chapel Hill: University of North Carolina Press, 1944).

gantic strait jacket. In society liberty seems to have little meaning. Indeed, since the struggle against control or oppression appears to be against some organized group like the state or the church or the family, many are led to the conclusion that liberty increases in direct proportion as group control decreases. This is the basis of the doctrine of individualism. In economic affairs *laissez faire*, or more properly, "government hands off business," is its counterpart.

It so happened that in the eighteenth and nineteenth centuries economists like Adam Smith, David Ricardo, and John Stuart Mill were impressed by the ever-present control exercised by the state over the individual. To them, as to the more practical minded businessmen eager to avoid state regulation of their quest for profitable opportunities, *laissez faire* measured economic liberty by what the state *should not do*. The individual, they thought, must be left to his own fate or fortune. Proponents of *laissez faire* never dreamed of eliminating the state, because they had use for it. The state was to sanction and protect private property, and enforce contracts. This seemed a minor concession, but proved to be a most positive field of control. The ownership of a peanut stand, or pencil, or textbook might give one very little control over one's fellows. But suppose the property were a large corporation with thousands of workers? If the state, under the doctrine of *laissez faire*, were merely to protect this type of property, then it was another way of authorizing the owners to lay down the conditions upon which men may use such property. When it appeared that private owners could impose burdensome controls the agitation began for reforms such as shorter hours, minimum wages, prohibition of child labor, and protection of collective bargaining. These reforms required state action and were pressed in the name of liberty and "social control." At first this seemed like a reversal of the policy of *laissez faire*, for to increase the power of the state was considered a denial of liberty. Actually, the reforms were aimed at the power lodged in business organizations to rule the lives of others, as *laissez faire* was once aimed at the state when it ruled the conduct of business organizations.

Economic Interpretations of Control

So far we have assumed that economic control of some type could be taken for granted. Even so, there is much to explain. For example, how far do economic factors influence the thinking, beliefs, and actions of John Jones and Richard Roe? Could we state that their very lives are determined by economic factors? Could we say that one is not only "controlled" by the very way he produces his goods and services, but that the way he does these things determines how he lives and feels about his music, his religion, his politics, and his family?

The greatest difficulty found in accepting an economic interpretation is the notion that such an interpretation is selfish and sordid. It is objected that although man must have bread he does not live by bread alone. There are three reasons for this view.

1. Business enterprise made headway during the feudal period after much opposition. There was no disposition on the part of the nobility to accord petty traders the privileges of a high social status. In spite of the high position later achieved by businessmen, people suspected the economic motive when applied in other phases of community life.

2. There is persistent demand that great events or heroes be explained in a dramatic fashion. It is difficult to provide this need or demand by reference to an economic interpretation, since the economic appears to be prosaic and lacking in the uniqueness required of a great event or a hero. It is not quite satisfying to state that a particular hero is the "product of his time," just as is everybody else.

3. Many current economic interpretations are traced to Karl Marx. Consequently resistance to socialism in its real or imagined forms may become a resistance to the economic theory. Add to this the fact that some historians used an economic interpretation to "debunk" the community's sacred institutions and we can readily see how prejudice would act as a barrier.

"Perhaps the feeling of the ordinary man is best expressed by the witticism of a learned historian in an address before the American Historical Association to the effect that the members of this school (Economic) of interpretation were responsible for putting the "hiss" into history." [2]

It is difficult to determine how far this feeling was responsible for certain social scientists insisting that an economic interpretation was not necessarily socialism and that socialism as a movement was a distinct phenomenon.[3] Certainly such a view is accurate.

Socialism. In the Marxian ideology the development of society is conditioned by class conflict,[4] the present conflict being one between the capitalists and the workers. The conflict itself is a resultant of the property relationship in a capitalistic society wherein the employers own the property which the proletariat must use if they are going to make a living. To Marx this was an economic relationship out of which sprang

---

[2] Arthur Schlesinger, *New Viewpoints in American History* (New York: The Macmillan Co., 1922), p. 47.

[3] *Ibid.*, pp. 47-50. See also E. R. A. Seligman, *The Economic Interpretation of History* (New York: Columbia University Press, 1924).

[4] Karl Marx, *Capital* (London: Dent and Sons, 1933), chapters XII and XIII.

religion, ethics, and political forms. The state was an instrument and agency of the dominating class. Reforms or concessions made to the proletariat had a double function. First, they indicated class division; and, second, they temporarily kept the workers from overturning the basis of the class division, i.e., private property. But as Marx conceived it, capitalism contained the germ of its own defeat. As industrial integration should proceed, industry would have less use for workers at the same time that the number of workers would increase, their ranks swelled by the bankrupt farmers and middle class. Ultimately the proletariat would take over the mechanism of production and liquidate the capitalist class.

Certain questions may be raised here: (1) Is it necessary to assume economic motives as the active determinant of conduct? (2) Will a reference to specific economic interest explain conduct? (3) Is it necessary to assume, with Marx, the inevitable proletarian victory as a basis for an economic interpretation? (4) How far are noneconomic factors independent influences?

Many writers have both defended and criticized an economic interpretation but it is only necessary to discuss some typical examples.

Economic Motives and Vested Interests. A study of wide influence was written in 1913 by Charles A. Beard.[5] This was an economic interpretation of the Constitution, but devoid of any Marxist predictions. The object was to determine how far the economic interests of the Founders were represented in the Constitution. Beard disclosed that of the fifty-five delegates to the Constitutional Convention, forty-five had investments in public securities; fourteen held land for speculative purposes; twenty-four had money out at interest; eleven were interested in mercantile, manufacturing, and shipping enterprises; and fifteen owned slaves. Thus at least five-sixths of the members of the Convention "were immediately, directly, and personally interested in the outcome of their labors." [6] Although the Founders stood to gain by the adoption of the Constitution, Beard denied that the Constitution was made for their personal benefit, but rather that they represented that part of the community interested in the security of possessions and hence distrustful of the democracy of the states. For this view, Beard did not rely on Karl Marx but James Madison, for in the *Federalist* Madison wrote:

"From the protection of different and unequal faculties of acquiring property; the possession of different degrees and kinds of property immediately results; and from the influence of these on the sentiments and

---

[5] *An Economic Interpretation of the Constitution* (New York: The Macmillan Co., 1913).
[6] *Ibid.*, p. 149.

views of the respective proprietors, ensues a division of the society into different interests and parties." [7]

The type of economic theory propounded by Beard is one widely held in the newer school of historians.[8] But even if these historians steered clear of socialistic predictions and grounded their thesis on "proprietarian interest," they are met with the objection that economic interests and motives are "too simple an explanation." It is shown that on *both* the side of the Federalists and the anti-Federalists there were businessmen, moneyed men, farmers, debtors, creditors and workers. There was no class division. "The same class had different views in different parts of the country." [9] Thus reasoned Charles Warren, a critic of economic interpretation, when he refuted the views of Beard and his followers.

If there are no clear-cut class divisions and if merchants can be both for and against the Constitution, then how can there be any identity between economic interests and conduct? Warren raises the question and answers it in a way familiar to sociologists: the economic influence is only one of many; other factors like race, religion, and geography operate. Among these factors, the economic, according to Warren, played a minor part in the movement for the Constitution. The nature of his bias against weighing the economic factor is indicated by his statement that "To represent it as their [the Founders'] leading aim is to attribute a sordid and selfish purpose which neither their characters or their principles warrant." [10]

It is not necessary that there be a perfect identity between the economic interests and conduct. Certainly the backbone of the Federalist movement was found in those classes that feared the effect of democracy on their possessions. The restrictions placed upon the states in the Constitution indicate this. It does not mean that the anti-Federalists were propertyless. They were not; but to most of them, the Federal restrictions seemed inimical to *their* economic interests. If they had had greater representation at the Convention, the Constitution would not have been quite the same.

The spectacle of organized economic groups, holding tenaciously to an interest and determining the course of the law, is not satisfying to Warren. It is at this point that there is confusion. An economic inter-

[7] *The Federalist* (Hamilton's Edition, 1871), p. 106.
[8] H. E. Barnes, *History and Social Intelligence* (New York: Alfred Knopf, 1926); Fred Shannon, *Economic History of the People of the United States* (New York: The Macmillan Co., 1934). Also see Edward S. Corwin, *Twilight of the Supreme Court* (New Haven: Yale University Press, 1934): "The convention never for a moment relinquished the intention . . . of utilizing the new system for the purpose of throwing special safeguards about proprietarian interests" (p. 53).
[9] Charles Warren, *The Making of the Constitution* (Boston: Little Brown and Co., 1928), p. 73.
[10] *Ibid.*, p. 81.

pretation has to be broader than some specific economic motive or interest. An apparent defect of the economic explanation based on interests is the exclusion of psychological factors. Man is not completely rational, he does not always follow his own best interest. He is not solely an "economic man." Tradition, heroes, religion and the family enter as considerations in guiding his actions. How, precisely, should they be taken into account?

Scarcity and Abundance. One theory, disembodied from Marxian ultimates and wider in scope than the theory of economic interests, is that of the experimental school, led by John R. Commons and Selig Perlman.[11] In their theory economic groups and classes react to a consciousness of abundance or scarcity of economic opportunity. Where opportunities appear to be scarce, and this appearance is the direct result of experience, there will be a tendency to protect the opportunities by rules of apportionment. If the opportunities are abundant there will be a tendency to remove all obstacles and barriers.

If we refer back to the medieval guilds we get a picture of an economic system built upon an elaborate set of rules for the protection of the local market in favor of the guildsmen as against the non-guildsmen. Thus non-guildsmen could not "keep shops or sell merchandise by retail," nor, in certain towns, "buy corn on the market-day before three o'clock," and foreign fishmongers needed a license to sell, although this was not available "if any guildsman has fish to sell." The guildsmen themselves were to share purchases and thus eliminate any middleman. The number of apprentices was strictly controlled, as was the quality of the merchandise.[12]

The rules of labor unions can be explained on the same basis. A union is built on "job control." Rules as to apprentices, hours, wages, overtime, seniority, and jurisdictional divisions are to provide collective control of jobs. In this sense, jobs are scarce. Experience with depressions, hiring and firing and nonunion men reinforced this attitude toward the job. The union rules are equivalent to "rights," and the "rights" are looked upon as property.

On the other hand, during the expansion of markets and the development of machine technology, the employers or business class thought in terms of an abundance of opportunity. Union rules acted as a limitation on the use of property for gain.

"Because the labor movement in any form is a campaign against the absolute rights of private property, the extent to which the institution

---

[11] John R. Commons, *Institutional Economics* (New York: The Macmillan Co., 1934); Selig Perlman, *A Theory of the Labor Movement* (New York: The Macmillan Co., 1928).

[12] Charles Gross, *The Guild Merchant* (Oxford, 1890), pp. 45-50.

of private property is intrenched in the community in which a labor movement operates is of overwhelming importance to it." [13]

Hence to protect the "going concerns" of business was to free them from restrictions, but to protect unions as "going concerns" was to allow them to impose restrictions. It was no accident that collective bargaining was not legalized in England for years after parliament began removing feudal and mercantilistic obstacles from business enterprise. This does not mean that unions did not exist outside the pale of the law—they did —but as outlaws, and thus were limited in their claims for protection.[14] We must, then, distinguish between two groups of "going concerns," one developing under conditions of restricted opportunities, the other under conditions of economic expansion. In either case an elaborate system of rules is created, but for purposes entirely different. The rise of individualism under the impact of the expansion of opportunity did not mean the absence of rules, but only of those rules which blocked chance for gain. The middle-class revolutions in the eighteenth and nineteenth centuries did not destroy the law-making state, but they did succeed in imposing duties on the state that were contrary to the purpose of the submerged aristocracy.

A fundamental difference between the experimental theory and the Marxist or Beard formulations is that in the former noneconomic factors are taken into account. Under Marxism noneconomic factors are dependent upon an assumed economic thesis that makes the proletarian victory inevitable. With Beard noneconomic factors must enter as independent influences. In the experimental school noneconomic factors make the trend of history less predictable than it otherwise might be. For instance, the cultural values of the middle class have kept it from accepting a proletarian status even when driven by adversity to that income level. "Such forces as nationalism, religion, socialism, and even plain adventurism come vastly into play." [15] These psychological factors provide the motivation for action, but they are based on conditions of economic scarcity or abundance. Should economic opportunities decrease or fail to expand, forces would come into play to bring about collective controls of opportunities. It matters not that the group or class is actuated by considerations of religion, patriotism, or race—the result is the same; that is, the imposition of control. It is true that men are not actuated solely by economic interest, but they must react to those economic conditions that make their present conduct possible. They may not be conscious of desiring to protect private property for its own sake.

---

[13] Perlman, *op. cit.*, pp. 156-157.

[14] Herbert Heaton, *Economic History of Europe* (New York: Harper and Brothers, 1936), p. 708.

[15] Selig Perlman and Philip Taft, *History of Labor in the United States, 1896-1932* (New York: The Macmillan Co., 1935), p. 634.

They may actually believe that private property is sacred and noble, and join a crusade in its defense. In doing this they may even work counter to their own interests. Whether their activities are rational or irrational is not the point.

Human beings cannot avoid having economic interests whether such interests are individual, community, or national. It is a matter of sheer survival to claim interests of one kind or another. This is true now as it has been in the past.

Historical Roots of Economic Movements. Henri Pirenne has written of the influence of the Mediterranian Sea on medieval life. When it came under Mohammedan control it was closed to the West. The Roman Empire depended upon it. "Its [the Empire's] very existence depended upon sea mastery. Without that great trade route neither the government, nor the defense, nor the administration of the *orbis romanis* would have been possible." [16] Nor did the invasions of the barbarians stop commercial development. But with the closing of the Mediterranean, commerce languished, towns gave way to the manorial system. "The Mediterranean had been a Roman lake; it now became, for the most part, a Moslem lake." [17]

The crusades, the revival of commerce, the rise of the Italian cities of Venice and Genoa, and explorations—all this coupled with the Reformation, the Renaissance, and the rise of science led the way to a secularization of the mind and the development of a merchant class. These great movements of expansion made many individualists in fact, before they became so in theory.

Even mercantilism, looked upon by many economists as expressing a regulative state, cleared the internal economy of guild restrictions and put law-making on a national basis. Merchants and adventurers were not averse to using the state for gain. Adam Smith, the great critic of mercantilism, wrote:

"It cannot be very difficult to determine who have been the contrivers of this whole mercantile system; not the consumers, we may believe, whose interests have been entirely neglected; but the producers, whose interest has been so carefully attended to; and among this latter class our merchants and manufacturers have been by far the principal architects." [18]

Under mercantilism both the rise of business and the national state went hand in hand. The opposition to mercantilism came from those wishing to participate in the gains of expansion. They resented the governmental

---

[16] Henri Pirenne, *Medieval Cities* (Princeton: Princeton University Press, 1925), p. 1.
[17] *Ibid.*, p. 24.
[18] *The Wealth of Nations* (London: Dent and Sons, 1910), vol. II, p. 156.

privileges given certain merchants in the form of corporate charters. Corporations and monopoly were looked upon as one and the same thing. Hence the doctrine that if government did not interfere monopoly would be impossible. Competition, then, would regulate economic affairs. But we must emphasize that mercantilism, far from being inimical to the development of capitalism, was one phase in that development. The fact that it coincided with the rise of the national state tended to hide its economic function. By making local guild restrictions unnecessary, by aid in widening the market by its devotion to commerce and trade, the mercantilistic state was both a beneficiary and creator of economic expansion. But having been placed in this position its generous grants of monopolies kept newcomers from entering profitable fields.

Capitalism, then, was founded on expansion. Its ideology reflects that fact. Those who did not succeed protested against monopolies or the big interests. So all-embracing was the capitalistic ideology of opportunity that all remedies called for elimination of restrictions. We can understand, then, that little business, as well as big business, was suspicious of union rules. And it is largely the ideology of capitalism that keeps the lower middle class from being proletarianized. This class can attempt to hold both unions and big business in check.[19]

Where, during the mercantilistic era, the expansion was primarily in the field of commerce and exploration, under the factory system the industrial capitalist came to the front. A later development, at least in the United States, was the leadership of the financier. But whatever the phase of capitalism, the leadership was based on expanding opportunities and the ideology remained intact. Although the development of the corporation has changed the nature of property and ownership,[20] private property, in theory and in fact, is vigorously defended.

"Laissez Faire." The doctrine of *laissez faire* was a response to economic expansion. But we cannot understand *laissez faire* or nationalism unless we know what kind of a state a system of capitalism developed. One would suppose that *laissez faire*, the absence of governmental control, was the antithesis of nationalism. As a matter of fact the *logical* end of *laissez faire* was anarchism, a denial of the use of *any* government. William Godwin came to this conclusion.[21] Such speculations business interests never shared. Their state must protect property. Their state must not enter any *profitable* area or prevent others from entering. It so happened that to protect property was not putting the state in a minor

---

[19] Perlman and Taft, *op. cit.*, p. 632. See also Calvin Hoover, *Germany Enters the Third Reich* (New York: The Macmillan Co., 1933).

[20] A. A. Berle, Jr., and Gardner C. Means, *The Modern Corporation and Private Property* (New York: Commerce Clearing House, 1932).

[21] William Godwin, *An Inquiry Concerning Political Justice* (London, 1793).

position, because to protect property proved to be the regulation of *persons*. And the ownership of property meant the power to regulate *persons*. Property is not so much a thing as it is a "bundle of rights and duties." The state, then, regulated and controlled human relations. Can we not see this when protecting property may mean the control over taxation, strikes, union funds, and picketing? *Laissez faire* never was concerned with the *quantity* of state regulations, but with the *purpose* of such regulations. As a consequence the use of *laissez faire* did not hinder the development of a strong state, but a strong state could aid *laissez faire*. It is difficult for some to realize that the state, even under early capitalism, was a powerful instrument. Where the purpose is to aid and protect the acquisition of property we have political nationalism, as advocated by the Federalists. Where the purpose is to prevent privileged groups from controlling economic opportunities we have equalitarian nationalism, as advocated by the Jeffersonians, Jacksonians, and antimonopolists. Where the purpose is to establish administrative control or ownership of business enterprise, while leaving the ideology of private property intact, we have economic nationalism, as propounded by the New Deal. The first two types of nationalism developed under the prevalence of economic expansion; the last type is an outgrowth of economic scarcity, calling for the imposition of control to apportion available opportunities. In all three types the economic pulsations of scarcity and abundance have played a crucial part. We are not unmindful of the motives of love of country and the desire for unity, but as we stated above these motives must be implemented.

"The putting forth of nationalist doctrines was one of the mental exercises of the eighteenth century. Primarily it was the work of intellectuals and an expression of current intellectual interests and tendencies . . . [but] the modern age of large scale production and industrial economy has been prerequisite, in one country after another, and eventually in the world at large, to the ascendancy of nationalism." [22]

Growth of Economic Nationalism. Since capitalistic expansion was world-wide, one would suppose that an international state would have been a logical result. But economic interdependence is blocked by nationalism. Under the impact of a contracting economy since World War I, nationalism has intensified. "Buy British," "buy American," German "Autarkie" and the French "compartimentage economique" were familiar before the opening of World War II. Under conditions thus implied all the elements of race, religion, mysticism and national destiny come into play, so that the economic scarcity of opportunity is hidden

---

[22] Carlton Hayes, *The Historical Evolution of Modern Nationalism* (New York: Richard Smith, Inc., 1931), pp. 232, 233.

by other than economic motives. Indeed, the fact that large-scale industry is keyed to supply a market wider than the nation intensifies the
desire to avoid heavy losses in capital. From all classes come demands on
the state to underwrite losses. Such pressure leads to administrative control and planning. What is called "regimentation" is an expression of
apportioning opportunities through state administration. This is economic nationalism. This is economic and political integration.

In democratic countries this political and economic integration is likely
to be based on the actions of voluntary groups, so that economic nationalism reflects the demands of those groups participating in the creation of
new institutions. Under the dictatorships such as once existed in Italy
and Germany, the new associations and groups were state created and
served as agencies for purposes of the state as determined by a single
party. Consequently when conditions of scarcity continue, the alternatives available depend on whether democratic countries, such as England
and the United States, can develop an economic nationalism at the same
time that they avoid creating a state that can permit no interference with
those who are in control. They also depend upon whether most people
can rely upon the power and ability of economic organizations to carry
on the creation and use of wealth within the limits of markets and prices.
At the present time, the state, in every industrialized nation, has been
made the guarantor of economic stability and security. Unemployment
insurance, old age pensions, regulation of securities, and a host of other
controls bespeak the hazards of modern industrial life.

Economic Controls in War and Peace

Economic control seems more obvious during a period of war. The
noticeable scarcity of necessary and strategic materials such as zinc,
copper, aluminum or manganese makes immediate control essential. A
war economy is an administrative economy. Since it cannot by its very
nature endure long enough to reduce all of its controls to an institutional
or habitual pattern, we are continually aware of the controls and their
consequences. We look to *persons*, not *forces* to allocate goods and
services. The scarcities of materials and the urgency of the war effort
overcome most scruples concerning property titles or individual ability
to purchase. The economic controls seem so apparent, so pressing, and
so persistent that one is likely to feel that no controls existed during the
previous reign of peace. This we know to be an error.

Since the impact of modern war on an economy is far reaching and
compelling, so too are the necessities for economic controls as immediate
as military strategy and planning. Before the end of both the European
and Japanese phases of World War II the United States Government was

using approximately one half our annual national product. It is quite apparent that any agency or government that can command authority over such an enormous quantity of goods, services, and manpower can direct or influence the way of living. If an individual in New York City inherited $1,000,000, his added purchasing power could affect economic decisions by his choices for services and commodities, but his inheritance would hardly change the nature of economic society in New York or Maine or California. On the other hand, should this individual, like our national government in wartime, have the power to command half our national resources, then indeed could he affect the lives of all of us to some extent. His decisions could wipe out some industries in favor of others. Should he command all the aluminum for planes, pots and pans would disappear from the market. At the same time the price of pots and pans already produced would skyrocket unless our individual had also the authority to limit prices. With some justice our individual might ration what pots and pans remained so that those with higher incomes might not gain too great an advantage over those with lower incomes. This consideration is more pertinent where food is concerned.

The controls of war are part and parcel of the way we live in wartime. They differ from controls in peace in the values we place upon the end result of such controls. As war leaves its postwar problems, its casualties, its debts, its experience, so does it profoundly influence the economic system under which and for which the war was waged. Essentially, in war or peace, the basic economic problem is the production, distribution, and consumption of resources within a framework of economic and social rules whether written, unwritten, novel, conventional, or customary.

A defense economy lies somewhere between a war and peace economy. The urgency of the crisis or "cold war" determines the public reaction to economic controls. The administrative controls of World War II ended, for all practical purposes, in June, 1946. From then on, there was a steady rise in the price level, a large increase in both employment and production of those commodities desired by consumers who had built a large backlog of savings during the war period. It was not until the invasion of South Korea by the Communist armies of North Korea in June, 1950, that there was a strong enough public opinion for government price and wage controls, and then there was established an Office of Price Stabilization. But these economic controls could not be on the level of World War II. First, because the problem was not as pressing as in an all-out war; second, because public opinion did not back strong enforcement of economic controls; and third, because a rising price level was also accompanied by higher levels of living. In short, although prices rose faster than production, people in general were better off. With the stalemate in Korea and the leveling off of danger of a third world war, interest in government controls diminished rapidly. Administrative controls ended by early 1953.

It should be clear that economic control is ever-present. In peace, defense, or war, whatever the type of economic society or form of government, allocation of resources and labor must take place. In periods of peace, custom, habit, and institutions are the media through which economic controls operate. In times of emergency, crises, war, or defense, the need for new forms of control is more apparent. Where the whole community is involved in a crisis, as in a war or a period of defense mobilization, there is less disposition to rely on established practices. To profit by a scarcity of one's labor or commodities at such a time seems more reprehensible than to do so in times of peace.

The assembly line, the market place, the store, the office, the factory and the job constitute man's environment. By his intelligence man may devise more effective and higher standards of control, but he cannot escape them. Through a democratic process he may participate with his fellows in determining those controls he desires. Knowing that economic controls are more personal and complete in an economy with a high degree of scarcity, he may yet achieve the better life by producing and distributing in greater abundance, and thus relieve many of the stresses and strains of his existence. But when the stomach is empty, the spirit withers. One notion of a high economic civilization is where man's political, social, and cultural achievements are divorced from a high minimum of economic well-being. Where food and shelter are weapons or instruments of force, man is less free.

Summary

Because almost all the goods needed to satisfy man's human needs and desires are scarce, economic controls are a vital phase of social control. It is not necessary to hold notions that economic motives account for all human behavior and historical developments to recognize the pervasive and universal importance of economic considerations.

The history of the rise of capitalism through mercantilism, *laissez faire*, and more modern developments, such as the rise of organized labor, is also the history of the rise of nationalism in government. In democracies, political and economic integration in social control is likely to be based upon the actions of voluntary groups, which participate in creating new institutions. In dictatorial states, such new institutions for economic control are usually state-created. The problem of democracies is whether they can develop economic nationalism and at the same time avoid creating a state which can brook no interference with those who are in control.

QUESTIONS

1. What is the problem of limited resources?
2. Relate ideologies to economic facts.

3. What is the relation of the doctrine of *laissez faire* to economic controls?
4. What are the followers and opponents of Adam Smith?
5. What are the three objections to the statement that "man does not live by bread alone"?
6. Is it necessary to assume economic motives as the active determinant of conduct?
7. Will a reference to specific economic interest explain conduct?
8. Is it necessary to assume, with Marx, the inevitable proletarian victory as a basis for an economic interpretation?
9. How far are noneconomic factors independent influences?
10. What was Charles A. Beard's interpretation of the American Constitution?
11. What is the difference between Marx and Beard?
12. What was the influence of the Mediterranean Sea on medieval life?
13. What was the theory of mercantilism?
14. How did *laissez faire* develop into economic nationalism?
15. How is economic integration achieved in democratic countries?
16. How do the modern states guarantee economic stability and security?
17. What changes are brought into economic controls by war?
18. Why are economic controls most vital aspects of social control?
19. Is it necessary to hold notions that economic motives account for all human behavior?
20. What is the problem of democracies in relation to developing economic nationalism?

SUGGESTED TOPICS FOR TERM PAPERS AND FURTHER RESEARCH

1. What are the modern ideologies of economic controls?
2. The recent modifications of the theory of *laissez faire*.
3. Modern critics of state control of economics.
4. The role of organized groups in economic decisions of American government.
5. The idea of a corporate state.
6. The modern mercantilism.
7. The economics of war.
8. The economics of preparedness.
9. The economics of the "New Deal."
10. The influence of Keynes.

BIBLIOGRAPHY

Books

T. W. Arnold, *The Folklore of Capitalism* (New Haven: Yale University Press, 1937). Analysis of the capitalistic ideology.
A. A. Berle, Jr., and Gardner C. Means, *The Modern Corporation and Private Property* (New York: The Macmillan Co., 1933).
John M. Clark, *Alternative to Serfdom* (New York, Alfred A. Knopf, 1948). A balanced view of our mixed economy of free enterprise and government controls.
John R. Commons, *The Economics of Collective Action* (New York, The Macmillan Company, 1950). The last published book by a leader in the field of "Institutional Economics" and a member of the University of Wisconsin "Experimental School."
C. Day, *Economic Development of Modern Europe* (New York: The Macmillan Co., 1933). An objective and readable historical account.
E. A. J. Johnson, *Some Origins of the Modern Economic World* (New York: The Macmillan Co., 1936).
Alfred R. Oxenfeld, *Economic Systems in Action* (New York: Rinehart and Company, 1952). A valuable treatment of the economic systems of the United States, Soviet Russia and the United Kingdom.

Selig Perlman, *A Theory of the Labor Movement* (New York, Augustus Kelley, 1949). Originally published in 1928 and still a classic in the field. Along with Professor Commons, a pioneer in the "Experimental School."

A. C. Pigou, *The Political Economy of War* (New York: The Macmillan Co., 1940). A good survey of some of the chief problems of a wartime economy.

R. Tawney, *Religion and the Rise of Capitalism* (London: Murray, 1926). Economic interpretation applied to religion.

A. R. Upgren and E. Stahrl, *Economics for You and Me* (New York, The Macmillan Co., 1953). A brief and excellent discussion of the field of economics. Very readable.

Norman J. Ware, "Trade Unionism, United States and Canada," *Encyclopaedia of the Social Sciences*, XV, p. 4.

Periodicals

Charles A. Beard, "Idea of Let Us Alone," *Virginia Quarterly Review*, XV (1939), pp. 500-514.

M. J. Bonn, "The Structure of Society and Peace," *Annals of the American Academy of Political and Social Science*, CCX (June, 1940), pp. 1-15.

D. C. Coyle, "Social Control of Production," *ibid.*, CCVI (November, 1939), pp. 121-125.

Paul Fisher, "The National War Labor Board and Postwar Industrial Relations," *Quarterly Journal of Economics* (August, 1945), pp. 483-523.

Jerome Frank, "The New Sin," *The Saturday Review of Literature*, XXVIII (December 22, 1945), p. 3.

"Growth of Rigidity in Business," a Symposium, *American Economic Review*, XXX, supplement (March, 1940), pp. 281-316.

A. G. Gruchy, "John R. Commons' Concept of Twentieth Century Economics," *Journal of Political Economy*, XLVIII (December, 1940), pp. 823-849.

Walton Hamilton, "The Control of Strategic Materials," *The American Economic Review*, XXXIV (June, 1944), pp. 261-279.

A. L. Harris, "Pure Capitalism and the Disappearance of the Middle Class," *Journal of Political Economy*, XLVII (June, 1939), pp. 328-356.

Clark Kerr, "What Became of the Independent Spirit," *Fortune Magazine*, XLVIII (July, 1953), p. 110.

Frank H. Knight, "The Role of Principles in Economics and Politics," *American Economic Review*, XLI (March, 1951), p. 1.

———, "What Is Truth in Economics?" *Journal of Political Economy*, XLVIII (February, 1940), pp. 1-32.

M. E. Leeds, "Political Economy and the Industrialist," *Annals of the American Academy of Political and Social Science*, CCIV (July, 1939), pp. 72-79.

A. P. Lerner, "From Vulgar Political Economy to Vulgar Marxism," *Journal of Political Economy*, XLVII (August, 1939), pp. 557-567.

F. C. Mills, "Economics in a Time of Change," *American Economic Review*, XXXI (March, 1941), pp. 1-14.

"The New Competition," *Fortune Magazine*, XLV (June, 1952), p. 98.

"Price Control and Rationing in Foreign Countries During the War," *Monthly Labor Review*, LXI (November, 1945), pp. 882-899.

The Quest for Stability (Federal Reserve Bank of Philadelphia, 1950).

W. O. Scroggs, "What's the Matter with Economics?" *Saturday Review of Literature*, XXI (November 11, 1939), pp. 3 ff.

M. Thorpe, "Economic Fallacies," *Vital Speeches*, VI (May 1, 1940), pp. 436-439.

Ernest A. Tupper, "Guideposts to Industrial Mobilization," *Harvard Business Review*, XXVIII (November, 1950), p. 29.

J. Viner, "Short View and the Long in Economic Policy," *American Economic Review*, XXX (March, 1940), pp. 1-15.

Chapter XXII

Economic and Social Planning

If one were to plan an ideal English language, one in which each word had a definite and generally accepted meaning, the word "planning" would be thrown on the linguistic scrap heap. It is undoubtedly one of the most confusing, emotion arousing, heat engendering terms in our language today. For some it is the new panacea which will usher in the Age of Plenty; for others it describes something that is as old as human society; and for its severest critics it is merely "Communism in evening clothes."

The more the word is used, the less useful it becomes. A distinguished Princeton scholar reminds us that the word, as applied to economics, once had a definite meaning, to wit, socialism. But now the term is used by those whom he calls "wily capitalists" who have always wanted our government to "plan" our economy by raising duties on imports. The phrase "New Deal" indicates that the Democratic Party joined the planners in 1932, and since the Republican Party has always favored economic planning through the tariff device, we are now a united people. We all believe in planning—provided our plan is adopted.[1]

Because of the loose way in which the word is used, it is patently futile to marshall the arguments "on both sides," for as there are a thousand meanings, there are at least two thousand "sides." Any discussion of planning must begin with delimiting the subject and defining our terms. If planning means merely the application of intelligence to human affairs, it is obviously carried on by every individual, society, and business firm. We shall limit our discussion to the planning that is carried on by society through the agency of government.

The discussion will be further limited to such plans as government itself is to carry out, and will not include the planning services which government makes available for the use of others. Thus, the work of the Department of Agriculture in providing plans by which farmers may more profitably conduct their business, if they accept them, will be omitted. There are two phases of planning, *formulation* and *execution*.

---

[1] For a discussion of the degeneration of the word "planning," see James Gerald Smith, *Economic Planning and the Tariff* (Princeton: Princeton University Press, 1934), chapter I.

We shall deal only with such social plans as provide for the exercise of both functions by our government, whether federal, state or local.

Accepted Types of Planning

Social or governmental planning, in certain fields, is as old as society itself. With the exception of the Eskimos, and possibly the modern Danes, there have been no organized communities which have not made some provision for protection from external enemies. The people of modern Denmark made no plans for defense, not because they failed to recognize the problem, but because they decided, with some reason, that for them the problem was insoluble. Every society must also make some provision for the administration of justice and provide peaceful means for settling disputes between its citizens.

Modern states have found it necessary to plan many institutions and programs to meet modern needs. Monetary and banking systems must be established, schools must be provided, highways built, public lands must be developed or disposed of, protection provided for women and children, etc. These represent areas in which all admit the necessity for governmental action. With respect to every one of these matters, men will differ as to the course government should pursue, but they will all agree that the government must pursue some course, and they will want it to be as intelligent and as well planned as possible.

Controversial Types of Economic Planning

No plan can be executed or even prepared until society first accepts the goal which the plan is to achieve. If we are to plan, we must plan for something. This is a truism which is neglected by those who believe planning is a process which we can begin before we know where we want to go.[2] Planners and technicians cannot provide society with aims, for aims are in the realm of social values, above and beyond both engineering and logic.

It is the lack of agreement on aims which seriously handicaps many of the newer planning proposals. Agreement on aims can of course be had if the aims are stated in such general terms as "maintaining prosperity," "raising the standard of living," or the like, but division of opinion immediately develops if it is proposed to "reduce inequality" or provide "national self-sufficiency." In some localities a veritable furore is aroused if it is proposed to establish public birth-control clinics, or even to permit them to share in Community Chest funds. Proposals to require all chil-

---

[2] On the importance of aims see the Foreword by Lewis Mumford in Findlay Mackenzie, ed., *Planned Society* (New York: Prentice-Hall Inc., 1937).

dren to attend public rather than parochial schools are equally dynamite-laden. Plans of this type are as likely to lead to tumult and disorder as to the objectives which their proponents have in mind.

In strictly economic matters there is less divergence of aim, but there is at least one which is fundamental. Any government which is to have a comprehensive plan for the economic life of its people must first decide how hard its people must work, for that decision will determine the volume of goods and services which will be produced. Leisure, too, is one of the good things of life, and if one attaches more importance to an increase in leisure than to an increase of goods and services, no economist can ever prove him wrong.

Wartime Planning. One of the reasons why economic planning is more readily accepted in wartimes is because the question of goods versus leisure is, by common consent, put aside when the first shot is fired. A nation at war unites in applying a single test to every proposal, i.e., will it help defeat the enemy. We may sometimes differ as to how well a proposal meets that test, but as to the propriety of the test itself, there is no dissent. In the same way planning in the Soviet Union has been simplified because of the general agreement on the necessity for building up the capital equipment of the country. But if some one proposed that the aim of our planning should be to increase our industrial capacity, the objection would be raised that our economy has "matured" and that we are suffering from "excess capacity." [3] We would be divided over aims before we could even begin to plan.

Objections to Governmental Planning. Any proposal to increase governmental planning meets the further objection that the results of so many of our plans have proved disappointing. Every student of American history will recall the plans of the "canal building era," when several states literally bankrupted themselves by financing canal projects which proved to be almost if not quite worthless. All adults will recall the exultant screams of the Blue Eagle which announced the end of the depression, an announcement which, to say the least, was somewhat premature. And finally, they will recall the hopes attending the inauguration of The Noble Experiment (Prohibition). To recall these disappointments is not to prove that future plans must fail, but "once bitten, twice shy" is still an honored adage.[4]

One reason why the dispute over planning may prove to be endless is

---

[3] For a discussion of the possible aims of economic planning, both here and in the Soviet Union, see George Soule, *A Planned Society* (New York: The Macmillan Co., 1932), chapter VIII.

[4] For more detailed treatment of some of our past failures in planning see George B. Galloway and associates, *Planning For America* (New York: Henry Holt and Co., 1941), chapter X, and Smith, *op. cit.*

that it is difficult to determine the degree of success or failure of any plan aimed at a general improvement in economic conditions. It may be possible, in time, to demonstrate the desirability of a Boulder Dam or a Grand Coulee Dam, because these are instances of what is sometimes called "physical planning" to distinguish them from plans aimed to "restore prosperity." Prosperity, and its opposite, are the results of so many factors that it is logically impossible to prove that the adoption of any particular plan achieved the desired end. For instance, we adopted, early in our history, a plan to "protect" American industry by the imposition of duties on imports, but the argument over the wisdom of this plan goes on as merrily and as inconclusively as it did when the plan was first introduced.[5]

Although the professional economists as a rule have been lukewarm or even hostile to many of the more recent proposals for planning, it must not be assumed that they are opposed to social control in economic matters. To them, even more than to others, it is obvious that the government must plan and administer some kind of a monetary system, a banking system, provide for the regulation of public utilities, adopt a tax program and do other countless things which have a direct or indirect effect on our economic life. If our government were to perform adequately the limited number of tasks above named, it might require all the planning capacity we could muster for some time to come.

Visionary Planning. For the foregoing reasons, most of the more elaborate plans proposed for ending the depression and remodeling our present economic system have come from outside the circle of academic economists. Some of them have come from itinerant vendors of Utopias and a few from racketeers who exploited the hopes of the simple to make jobs for themselves in some organized crusade. The movement for economic planning in the United States has suffered severly because of its hearty endorsement by so many economic illiterates.[6]

Planning and Socialism. Many plans for the complete remodeling of our economic order call for a degree of governmental ownership and control that is indistinguishable from socialism. A recognition of this fact is, of course, no reflection on such plans, but it does suggest that we must be on our guard against the intellectual subtleties of those who refuse to

---

[5] It is disturbing to observe that this protectionist planning continues, no matter what party is in power, notwithstanding that it has been condemned in all its essentials by almost every professional economist in the country. For a modern statement of the economists' position, see Smith, *op. cit., passim.*

[6] It has been suggested that many of the more Utopian plans emanate from persons who are addicted to reading pseudo-scientific books on economics. Both these people, and the world, it is said, would be better off if they switched to such books as *Don Quixote* and *Alice in Wonderland.* See Smith, *op. cit.,* p. 17.

call things by their accepted names. The adoption of socialism is a proposal that merits the calm study of every adult, but it is unfortunate if a society, which had rejected such proposal when it was presented at the front door, must re-examine it at the back door under the more euphemistic name of "economic planning."

There can be no doubt that some of those who advocate economic planning have set socialism as their goal. For instance, George Soule, professional journalist (*The New Republic*), amateur economist, and prolific writer on economic planning, believes that the soft-coal mines and other "basic industries" should be publicly owned.[7] He admits that every step in the direction of economic planning is a step away from capitalism, "no matter how that word is defined." [8] He predicts that the more advanced stages of economic planning will bring us something "closely akin" to socialism.[9]

Collective Society. At this point it may be objected that planning, as a process, brings us neither to collectivism nor anywhere else. It is only after we have decided what aims we shall pursue that the planning process is employed to facilitate our arrival. In a sense, however, it is true that any governmental interference with private property, any substitution of political decisions for the decisions of private *entrepreneurs*, is a step in the destruction of a free enterprise (capitalistic) economy. This is true because there are roughly only two possible economic systems—one in which private controls are dominant, and one in which public controls are dominant. If the system of private controls is destroyed, we shall have, willy-nilly, a collectivist society.

Planning and International Relations

A serious difficulty arises from the fact that it is impossible to carry out national plans as though each nation were a world to itself. An isolationist policy for the United States was probably given its last trial during the period from the end of World War I to the opening of World War II. Nearly all of us are now convinced that the human race consists of a family of nations, albeit a very quarrelsome one, and no nation can live to itself alone. Any national economic plan must fit into some kind of world economy. We cannot plan production, exports or imports except in cooperation with the other nations concerned.

Visions of International Cooperation. Some planners assume that such

---

[7] George Soule, *A Planned Society, op. cit.,* p. 254.

[8] *Ibid.,* p. 277.

[9] *Ibid.,* p. 278. Other planners apparently believe that collectivism is the "wave of the future." See Galloway and associates, *op. cit.,* chapter XXXIII.

problems can be solved if the planning authorities in the several nations will consult and plan together. They underestimate the difficulties which arise when nations confront each other as buyers and sellers. There is then no impersonal process by which the terms of exchange can be agreed upon. In the past, apart from customs duties, quota restrictions etc., the low-cost producers, wherever located, have expanded their output, and individual traders bought in the cheapest market and sold in the dearest. In these commercial activities, the nations as such were not directly involved. When the Brazilian rubber producers lost their market to the rubber planters of Southeast Asia, no national prestige was involved and no reprisals were carried out by the Brazilian government. If, however, the shift in rubber production from Brazil to Asia could have taken place only after the planning authorities of Britain, Holland and Brazil had agreed on the change, it is unlikely that it would have ever taken place.

During a depression we become so critical of our unplanned or slightly planned economy that we lose sight of the merits of the free market system. Whatever its defects it does provide an impersonal, automatic method for determining the terms of trade between different countries. If we ever completely abandon this system and impose upon the national states the duty of negotiating the terms of exchange, we shall increase appreciably the opportunities for international strife. When one government trades with another, there are really no principles by which the terms of the trade can be established. We are faced with the old problem of the single buyer and the single seller, and price becomes a matter of bluff, pressure and the fear of reprisals.

A few planners are so conscious of this difficulty that they are sure that world planning will be necessary if any nation is to completely "solve" its economic problems.[10] One planner went so far as to suggest that when the war ended, the English-speaking peoples might embark on a career of "welfare imperialism" and apply the methods of the TVA and AAA to the "so-called backward countries." [11] The suggestion is reminiscent of the quip that we solved our unemployment problem by putting the Soviet Union and the British Empire on the W.P.A. Unfortunately, the world is made up of nations which thus far have not been able to cooperate sufficiently to maintain a durable peace, without which no international planning is even remotely possible.[12]

---

[10] See Soule, *op. cit.*, p. 259.

[11] See Galloway, *op. cit.*, p. 656.

[12] MacKenzie believes that peace is the prerequisite of a planned society, and he makes the interesting suggestion that an unplanned society can make more rapid and continuous adjustments to the exigencies of war than could a planned society. See MacKenzie, ed., *op. cit.*, p. XX.

The Plan of "Laissez Faire"

One economic plan of which planners seldom speak—and then only with disparagement—is the Plan-To-Have-No-Plan which was followed by Great Britain from about the middle of the nineteenth century. By that time Great Britain had practically scrapped the last vestiges of mercantilist planning and in their place had adopted the "obvious and simple system of natural liberty" for which Adam Smith had so cogently argued. Some will insist that a plan to have no plan is a contradition in terms, but this objection, on analysis, proves to be a mere verbal one. If a nation's representatives deliberately decide that production and trade will be best served if governmental interference is kept to a minimum, that nation has adopted a policy, and those who oppose such a policy do not advance the argument by denying it is a "plan." [13] The belief is general among economists that with this plan or policy Britain made greater economic progress than ever before in its history, and completely out-stripped the other European nations which were much slower in casting off the restrictions of the mercantilist and feudal systems.

Necessity for Governmental Planning. Although professional economists are critical of most of the proposals put forward by the more enthusiastic planners, they do recognize the necessity for governmental action. The whole field of money and banking, the planning and construction of public works, the formulation of a defensible tax program, the elimination or control of monopolies are but some of the areas in which governmental action is not only desirable, but indispensable. But for the general prosperity of the country, instead of governmental interference, the majority prefer to rely on the maintenance of a free market and the free enterprise system. The maintenance by the government of a free, competitive market is a kind of planning, of which even Smith, one of the ablest critics of planning, approves.[14]

Social Planning

Governmental planning extends to many fields other than economics. All governments, for instance, have taken measures to safeguard the quality and size of their populations. Qualitative controls have normally been limited to excluding certain types of immigrants, but some countries have made provision for the sterilization of the unfit, chiefly the feeble-minded. Eugenic programs suffer from the fact that Hitler adopted them

---

[13] For the nature of Britain's "Plan-To-Have-No-Plan" and its outstanding achievements see Smith, *op. cit.,* pp. 24-27, and for the gradual modification of that plan, see the contribution of Wesley C. Mitchell in MacKenzie, *op. cit.,* chapter V.

[14] Smith, *op. cit.,* p. 203.

in Germany but it must be recalled that several of our states had provided for the sterilization of the feeble-minded long before Hitler's rise to power. They will hardly abandon their programs because Hitler adopted them.

Population Problems. With respect to quantitative controls some states have intervened to increase their numbers, both by encouraging immigration and by offering economic inducements designed to increase the birth rate. For years France consistently tried to increase its birth rate by conferring various favors on the parents of large families, and by vigorously opposing the spread of contraceptive techniques. This policy was adopted by all the Fascist states. On the other hand, Great Britain and the United States have attempted to limit the growth of their populations. Britain has provided funds to encourage the migration of its citizens to its Dominions, and the United States, beginning with the passage of the first Quota Act in 1921, adopted the policy of restricting the number of immigrants, whatever their personal fitness might be. Prior to that time, our only controls had been designed to eliminate the personally unfit and the Orientals, but now they are not only qualitative, but quantitative as well.

It is apparent that the quantitative controls established by the various governments are all predicated on the theory that for every nation there is an optimum number. The population of some states is presumably too small and that of others is too large. The wisdom of these various policies cannot be discussed here, other than to point out that the optimum number from the point of view of the economists is sometimes quite different from the optimum number as seen by the generals and the clergy. Here again no plan can be adopted until the aims are first agreed upon, and agreement is not easy. French economists may show that the French people would live better if their number were reduced, but the French generals may reply that the nation may not live at all unless it maintains a population sufficiently large to resist aggression from the other side of the Rhine.[15]

Modern states are concerned not only with the number of their citizens but also with their health. Comprehensive state planning in this field is, however, of recent origin. The relation between sanitation and health was only dimly recognized in ancient times, and the streets of Athens served as sewers. Rome made some progress in the matter of paving and the introduction of pure water into her cities, but the problem of sewage disposal was largely untouched. It was late in the seventeenth

---

[15] For a discussion of the optimum, and comments on some of the literature on this subject, see Glenn E. Hoover, "The Quantitative Optimum of Population," *The Annals of the American Academy of Political and Social Science*, CLXII (July, 1932), pp. 198-204.

century before any cities were provided with sanitary sewers and as recently as 1877 there were still 82,000 cesspools in Philadelphia. The disposal of sewage and the collection of garbage and rubbish constitute one of the fields in which public planning and administration are generally accepted.

Health Problems. The extent to which the state should guard the health of its citizens is one of the most controversial questions of modern times. Most states require some showing of competency from those who practice the healing arts, but in the United Staes, at least, there are no universal standards. The licensing of healers, under our federal system, is a state function, and the state authorities are subject to pressure from groups of individuals who cannot qualify as practitioners of medicine. The result is that some states license persons to practice osteopathy, chiropractic, naturopathy, and perhaps even more esoteric arts. In addition, they permit the sale of herbs, allegedly curative and often allegedly Chinese, and everywhere permit persons to undertake, for pay, to treat the sick through the medium of prayer.

The federal government, however, recognizes only the healing arts which are taught in the recognized medical schools. In the Public Health Service, in the armed forces and in the veterans' hospitals only doctors of medicine are employed.

When provision is made for the licensing of scientific practitioners there remains the problem of how they are to be paid. In the main, medical service, like most other things, goes to those who can pay for it. With us, health is a "purchasable commodity"; those who can afford it are reasonably healthy and those who can't afford it are sickly. They are sick because they are poor and they are poor because they are sick. In the meantime young doctors must spend valuable time "getting acquainted" and making themselves known.[16]

Whenever political states become so "health conscious" that sickness and ignorance are considered to be calamities of somewhat the same magnitude, the demand arises for free medical service financed by public funds, just as free schools are available to all at public expense. The state provides for the education of its citizens and it ought also to plan and provide for their health. This is the logic of the advocates of socialized medicine, and it is not easily refuted. The medical doctors who are most opposed to socialized medicine can hardly claim that health is less important than education, but they insist that socialized medicine would lower the level of medical practice and transform doctors into prole-

---

[16] For the difference in morbidity rates among the various income classes, see the summary of recent studies in Harry Elmer Barnes, *Society in Transition* (New York: Prentice-Hall Inc., 1940), chapter XI.

tarians in the service of a bureaucratic and socialistic state. Dr. Terry M. Townsend, President of the Medical Society of the State of New York, who may be taken as a representative spokesman of the opponents of socialized medicine, maintains: that Americans abhor compulsion; that the scheme is no insurance at all, but is a sickness tax; that the workman will be further burdened with taxes which cannot be levied on the unemployed and the self-employed—and in this way the plan is discriminating and inequitable; that the administrative costs of compulsory health insurance, and the red tape connected with the bureaucratic machinery needed to administer the plan are time and money wasting; that the free choice of physicians and the traditional intimate relationship between doctor and patient will be destroyed; and that American private medical services recognize the present inadequacies in the distribution of medical care and will continue to extend free services wherever needed.

Whether or not medicine should be "socialized" as a part of a program of governmental planning is a question that leads into fields where lay opinion is not worth very much. The only instance of completely socialized medicine (other than for members of the armed forces) is found in the Soviet Union. The prejudice both for and against anything tried in that country makes it difficult to weigh the results of their experiment, but many observers who have a very low opinion of the Soviet "planned economy" are enthusiastic about the Soviet achievements in bringing the available medical services to those who need them. Such services are not always of the highest order, for the Soviet Union must operate within the limits of the possible. Nevertheless, some of our most distinguished scientists believe that the Soviet experiment in socialized medicine has been a successful one, and they conclude that a modern state can finance and administer a free health program as efficiently as it can operate a free education program.[17]

Socialized medicine is a more immediate possibility than socialized industry. Only a negligible part of our industrial equipment is publicly owned but more than seventy per cent of our hospital beds are already the property of the federal, state or local governments. An increasing percentage of our citizens are already enjoying free medical service at public clinics, dispensaries and hospitals. Those now in the military service will insist on an expansion of the services of the U. S. Veterans' Hospitals. Perhaps after having provided public medical service for the indigent, the veterans, the merchant seamen, the armed forces and some other groups besides, it will seem to be simpler and more efficient to go

---

[17] For a sympathetic account of the Soviet health program made by a distinguished scientist of John Hopkins University, see Henry E. Sigerist, *Socialized Medicine in the Soviet Union* (New York: W. W. Norton, 1937).

the whole way and make them available to all. If and when this is done, our planning capacities may be fully utilized for some time to come.

Housing. Governmental planners are already at work in the field of housing. Until recently residential construction has been left exclusively to private initiative, with results that many find shocking. As a nation we seem to have much poorer housing than we can afford, and although conservatives delight in reminding us that Lincoln was "ill-fed, ill-housed and ill-clothed," governmental intervention in this field will probably continue. It is impossible to summarize all the measures which our government has taken to remedy the housing situation. It is admitted even by those who have been connected with the programs that all of them have been experimental in character and that our policies have been timid and confused. The average citizen cannot understand why private housing received financial assistance through the Defense Homes Corporation, the Home Loan Bank, the Federal Housing Administration and the Reconstruction Finance Corporation; nor why public housing was constructed by the Navy, the Farm Security Administration, the U. S. Housing Authority and the Public Buildings Administration. This confusion can perhaps be explained by our war effort, but it can hardly be entirely justified. Apparently our planning agencies were badly planned.[18]

Constitutional and Political Implications

Most of the planners have given too little attention to the political and constitutional questions to which their programs would give rise. They seem to be in agreement that the planning staff will be manned by "scientists and technicians," but whether the planning board or commission is to have only advisory powers or will administer the plan as well is not clear. If a planning board is merely to make recommendations to the Congress, the mountain may well bring forth a mouse. Congress has shown a persistent hostility toward "brain-trusters," who "couldn't be elected dog-catcher" in their home districts. Certainly a board to advise the Congress on economic legislation could do no harm, but there is little in our national history to suggest that Congress would be very amenable to its advice.

If, however, a planning board is to be given administrative or legislative power, serious problems will arise. Will the board and Congress be given concurrent jurisdiction over economic legislation, or will the powers of the board supplant those of Congress? If the latter, the plan-

---

[18] For a clear and objective analysis of our housing problem and the efforts made to meet it, see Catharine Bauer, "Housing in the United States," *International Labour Review*, LII, No. 1 (July, 1945), pp. 1-28.

ners cannot get very far without an amendment to the Constitution and thus the Planning Age is pushed into the remote future. The American people are committed to the belief that governmental power should be exercised by the people's elected representatives. If we were to overcome this objection by providing for the election of the planners, we would have abandoned the core of the planning concept and be back where we started, with a new legislative body, under a different name, in which we should probably see many of the old congressional faces. When brought face to face with these constitutional difficulties, the majority of planners, rather reluctantly no doubt, admit that the function of any planning board must be to advise the regularly constituted authorities.[19]

Some planners insist that no government can be said to plan merely because it makes provision for some need, such as irrigation projects, higher prices for farm products, or shorter hours for workers. They consider these to be piecemeal and makeshift expedients unless they are coordinated into some sort of Master Plan, under which, as they say, problems will be attacked from the center rather than the circumference.

Critics of grand scale economic planning believe that, even if it were possible with a Master Plan to operate more efficiently, it would mean the abandonment of many of our personal freedoms. How, for example, can any central body plan the economic production of the American people, unless it can determine the tasks that are to be performed, where and when they shall be performed, who shall perform them, and the wage rates to be paid? In any event this seems to have been the result in the Soviet Union which is operating under the most comprehensive Master Plan ever attempted. This regimenting and "shoving around" of the workers might be congenial to those Americans who believe they may somehow remain outside of the proletariat, but even as consumers they would find their traditional freedom restricted. Stuart Chase reminds us that if the shoe industry were rationalized or planned so that about 80,000 workers, working steadily, could produce as many shoes as the present 200,000, the public would be compelled to buy only those shoes which had been planned. In the case of shoes this might make little difference if they were wide enough; but for all consumers' goods, the same rule would hold. Both as producers and consumers we should be compelled to adjust to the operation of the Master Plan.[20]

Planning is a process which requires a considerable concentration of governmental power. After the adoption of a few isolated plans it becomes apparent that some planning authority must coordinate the existing

---

[19] Soule, *op. cit.*, chapter IX.

[20] For the necessity of restricting or abandoning the right of consumers to choose their goods if general planning is to prevail, see Stuart Chase, "A Ten Year Plan For America," *Harper's Magazine*, CLXIII (June, 1931), pp. 1-10.

plans. For some years we have been planning to increase the price of farm products so that the earnings of farmers may more nearly equal the earnings of industrial workers. These increased farm prices raise the cost of living, and in accordance with plans to adjust wages to living costs, the wages of industrial workers are raised, which in turn gives rise to a demand for a further increase in farm prices. What is needed, evidently, if we are to continue with such plans, is an over-all authority which could formulate a single plan which would cover both farm prices and the wages of industrial workers. This would require a greater concentration of power than the American people have heretofore approved.

Post World War II Planning. With the enemy defeated, our government proceeded to abolish those restrictions which had most irritated the public. Rationing, price controls, and allocation of materials were soon discarded. However, the advocates of governmental planning had to be placated by the passage of the Employment Act of 1946. This act requires the President, assisted by a Council of Economic Advisers, to make periodic reports to the Congress, together with recommendations for the attainment of "maximum employment, production and purchasing power." Since the passage of the act, Congress had been dominated by a coalition of Republicans and conservative Democrats, and little attention has been given to recommendations of the President.

As the Korean crisis developed, many of the World War II controls were re-established, but after the Republican victory in 1952, most of them were abandoned. President Eisenhower and his advisers were apparently convinced that indirect financial controls which limited the expansion of bank loans and deposits were preferable to direct controls over prices, wages, and consumer credit. Most economists shared their opinion.

However, agriculture is one field in which governmental planning persists, no matter what party is in power. Our government, by making loans on such crops as grains and cotton, or by direct purchase of such perishable products as eggs, butter, dried milk, and cheese, plans for farm prices to be kept at a certain percentage of "parity." Farm prices are said to be at "parity" when they bear the same relation to the prices of industrial products as they did in the selected base period.

Whenever our government has fixed "political prices" for farm crops at a level above the world market prices, the results have been disillusioning. For example, our government bought potatoes which its own plans had made "surplus," and then dyed them to make them unfit for human consumption. It has had fresh eggs converted into egg powder, which is popularly considered to be almost inedible, and it has bought and stored both butter and cheese by the carload, without the faintest idea of how ultimately to dispose of its holdings. Governmental meddling with the prices of farm crops has done much to discredit governmental planning, both as a science and as an art.

Most foreign countries, Canada excepted, persisted in carrying on a large measure of planning for some years after the end of the war. In the first postwar election in Britain, the Labor Party (Socialist) came to power. The economies of both France and Italy were so shattered that the governments of those countries believed they had no choice but to socialize many of their bankrupt industries. Many industries which were not socialized were subject to a large measure of state control and direction, a policy known in France as "*dirigisme.*" This word deserves an equal place with "capitalism" and "socialism" because it describes the economies of more countries than the two older words combined.

Recent years have shown some decline in the popularity of overall planning. The Labor governments of Australia and New Zealand were defeated in 1949, the British government in 1951, and in 1952 the American people finally rejected the Democratic Party. The Republican leaders claimed to be the champions of a free-market economy—except perhaps for agriculture—and for the first time in years, planning is out of favor in Washington.

Summary

In conclusion it seems correct to state that the issue is not whether governments should plan, for they always have and they always will. The real issues arise with respect to the areas in which governmental planning is expedient and, more important, the wisdom of the various plans proposed. When the advocates of economic planning propose to substitute for our system of free enterprise and a free market some kind of a collectivist economy, owned and administered by the state, they encounter the opposition of those who seem to be best qualified in the science and the art of economics. Some increased measure of economic controls and public ownership are to be anticipated and perhaps welcomed, but planning in these fields should not be left to the demagogues and the dealers in nostrums.

As for social planning, increased governmental intervention is the order of the day, and we shall see more of it, particularly in the fields of health and housing. In time of war governmental planning must be concentrated on the attainment of victory, the formulation of peace aims and the immediate problems of postwar readjustment. Many of the plans that might have been adopted must be laid away in moth balls until a world order has been established in which nations may live without fear of aggression.

QUESTIONS

1. What are the phases of planning?
2. What must be done before any social plan may be executed?
3. What must government decide before it can determine an economic plan?
4. Why is economic planning easier to put into effect in wartime?
5. In what fields is there the greatest opposition to governmental planning?
6. Is there any agreement on the aims of economic planning?
7. What is the greatest opposition to governmental planning?
8. Why do most plans for economic planning come from outside the circle of academic economists?
9. Where do most social "plans" come from?
10. What must one be careful of when examining proposed social plans?
11. What is George Soule's feeling about economic planning?
12. What are the probable results on international relations of a planned economy?
13. How does MacKenzie feel about international economic planning?
14. What is the greatest problem regarding eugenics programs?
15. What political fact serves to delay the arrival of the planning age?
16. Is a policy of *laissez faire* the absence of planning? Explain.
17. What are the difficulties of a planned economy within the family of nations?
18. What are the advantages of socialized medicine? The disadvantages?
19. What is the real issue behind the controversy over planning?
20. Is it possible to demonstrate the success or failure of social planning? Explain.

SUGGESTED TOPICS FOR TERM PAPERS AND FURTHER RESEARCH

1. Economic planning in the Scandinavian countries.
2. Economic planning in Europe.
3. Study the health problems in the United States from the angle of socialized medicine.
4. The problems of a planned international order.
5. National economic planning and international trade and relations.
6. The view of the professional economist toward economic planning.
7. Population problems and totalitarian methods for their solution.
8. The constitutional aspects of economic planning.
9. The United States Supreme Court and the social planners.
10. The controversy over conservation in the United States.

BIBLIOGRAPHY

Books

Hollis P. Allen, *The Federal Government and Education* (New York: McGraw-Hill Book Co., 1950). How the United States plans in education.
Ingvar Anderson, *Introduction to Sweden* (Stockholm: Forum, 1949). Planning in Scandinavia.
J. Backman, *Adventures in Price Fixing* (New York: Farrar and Rinehart, 1938). A critical, historical survey of price controls.
Sir William Henry Beveridge, *Full Employment in a Free Society* (New York: W. W. Norton and Co., 1945). Well-known reports on the British planning. See also

his: *The Pillars of Security* (New York: The Macmillan Co., 1943); *The Beveridge Report: Social Insurance and Allied Services* (New York: The Macmillan Co., 1942).

Eveline Burns, The American Social Security System (Boston: Houghton Mifflin Co., 1949).

M. W. Childs, *Sweden: The Middle Way* (New York: Penguin Books, 1947). A popular glorification of Scandinavian planning; see also his: *This is Democracy* (New Haven: Yale University Press, 1938).

John M. Clark, *The Social Control of Business* (Chicago: University of Chicago Press, 1926). A stimulating book dealing with the general principles of control.

Emmeline W. Cohen, *English Social Services* (London: Allen and Unwin, 1949). Its growth and methods.

R. A. Dahl and Charles E. Lindbloom, *Politics, Economics, and Welfare* (New York: Harper and Brothers, 1953). A study of specialized social processes and planning.

Oscar R. Ewing, *The Nation's Health—A Ten-Year Program* (Washington, D.C.: Government Printing Office, 1948).

Friedrich A. Hayek, *Collectivist Economic Planning* (London: Routledge, 1938), and *The Road to Serfdom* (Chicago: University of Chicago Press, 1944). A critical and provocative treatment of planning.

John Jewkes, *Ordeal By Planning* (London: Macmillan, 1948). A critical examination of postwar British planning by an Oxford economist who participated in it.

Carl Landauer, *Theory of National Economic Planning* (Berkeley: University of California Press, 1944). A sympathetic treatment.

A. P. Lerner, *Economics of Control* (New York: The Macmillan Co., 1944). Planning in collectivist, capitalistic, and mixed economies.

Ben W. Lewis, *British Planning and Nationalization* (New York: The Twentieth Century Fund, 1952). An objective examination of planning by the Labour Government in Britain.

Harry S. Mustard, *Government in Public Health* (New York: Commonwealth Fund, 1945). President's Commission on Higher Education, *Higher Education for American Democracy* (Washington, D.C.: Government Printing Office, 1947, 5 vols.).

Lionel Robbins, *Economic Planning and International Order* (London: Macmillan and Co., Ltd., 1937). A cogent criticism by a distinguished British economist.

Bertrand Russell, *Freedom Versus Organization* (New York: W. W. Norton and Co., 1934). A brief but profound analysis by an eminent British philosopher.

James S. Simmonds, ed., *Public Health in the World Today* (Cambridge, Mass.: Harvard University Press, 1949). A valuable survey.

Henry C. Simons, *Economic Policy for a Free Society* (Chicago: University of Chicago Press, 1948). The case for freedom, by a brilliant American liberal.

Herman Stople, *Cogor Collaborator* (Stockholm: Kooperative Forbundat, 1946). Democracy in cooperative education.

Periodicals

Winthrop W. Aldrich, "The Incompatibility of Democracy and a Planned Economy," *Vital Speeches*, V (June 15, 1939), pp. 531-534.

Benjamin M. Anderson, "Governmental Economic Planning," *The American Economic Review*, XXX (March, 1940, Supplement), pp. 247-262.

Henry Clay, "Planning and Market Economy: Recent British Experience," *American Economic Review*, XI (May, 1950).

Kenneth Colegrove, "The New Order in East Asia," *The Far Eastern Quarterly* (November, 1941), pp. 5-24. Outlines Japanese planning.

Francis Coker, "American Traditions Concerning Property and Liberty," *American Political Science Review*, XXX (February, 1936), pp. 1-23.

George B. de Huszar, "Freedom Is Not Enough," *South Atlantic Quarterly*, XLIV

(July, 1945), pp. 272-279; "The Dangers of Authoritarianism," *South Atlantic Quarterly*, XLVI (April, 1947), pp. 182-191.

Feliks Gross, "Peace Planning for Central and Eastern Europe," *The Annals of The American Academy of Political and Social Science*, CCXXXII (March, 1944), pp. 169-176.

Carl Landauer, "Economic Planning and the Science of Economics," *The American Economic Review*, XXXI (December, 1941), pp. 825-831.

F. W. Reeves, "Education for Social and Economic Planning," *Educational Record*, XXII (October, 1941), pp. 479-490.

George H. Sabine, "The Historical Position of Liberalism," *The American Scholar* (Winter, 1940-1941).

H. C. Simons, "The Beveridge Program: An Unsympathetic Interpretation," *Journal of Political Economy*, LIII (September, 1945).

PART IV

Social Control and Public Opinion

FOREWORD

The increase in literacy and widespread education have made Public Opinion the outstanding phenomenon of our time from the viewpoint of social control. Side by side with the rise of large-scale effective public opinions, and functionally related to them, has been the development and growth of social organs which mold, and are molded by, collective tastes, desires, and decisions.

Part IV deals with such organs with their great potentialities for good and evil for the masses of mankind. It begins with the chapter on Public Opinion which sets the background and establishes the principles against which the following chapters on Propaganda, the Press, Radio, Motion Pictures, and Television are discussed in turn.

The discussion of these phases of the Public Opinion process is a necessary preliminary to the chapters in Part V dealing with the immediate and pressing problems which make an understanding of social control vital today.

Chapter XXIII

Public Opinion

Public Opinion: What It Is and How It Works

Definition of Public Opinion. The concept "public opinion" is much easier to understand if the terms "public" and "opinion" are defined more or less precisely. *Public* refers to groups of any size in which the members more or less consciously pursue common interests, although in popular usage it is applied to such larger groupings as the population of a town or city, state, or nation, or again to those who read newspapers, magazines, listen to radios, and the like. *Opinion* may be defined as a belief stronger than an impression, a notion or conviction founded on some kind of information or evidence.[1] Taken together, then, *public opinion* is a collective phenomenon; it is not a unanimous or even a majority opinion; it may even be held by no one person. It is best thought of, perhaps, as a composite opinion, a sort of synthetic average, formed from varying opinions held by the public. Since it is collective, however, it can be mobilized on some particular issue and directed toward some kind of decision.[2]

---

[1] For some understanding of the term *public* see Kingsley Davis, *Human Society* (New York: The Macmillan Co., 1949), especially chapter 13: Robert E. Park and Ernest W. Burgess, *Introduction to the Science of Sociology* (Chicago: University of Chicago Press, 1924), chapters 3, 12, 13; Otto Klineberg, *Social Psychology* (New York: Henry Holt and Co., 1940), chapter 12; Gardiner and Lois B. Murphy and T. M. Newcomb, *Experimental Social Psychology* (New York: Harper and Brothers, 1937), chapter 8; *Webster's New International Dictionary* (Springfield, Mass.: G. and C. Merriam Co., 1934), p. 2005; Herbert Blumer, in *An Outline of the Principles of Sociology*, edited by Robert E. Park (New York: Barnes and Noble, 1939), pp. 233-241. For an understanding of the term *opinion* consult *Webster's New International Dictionary*, 2nd ed. (Springfield, Mass.: G. and C. Merriam and Co., 1934), p. 1708; Walter Lippmann, *Public Opinion* (New York: Harcourt, Brace and Co., 1922); W. G. Sumner, *Folkways* (Boston: Ginn and Company, 1907).

[2] Ulrich Strauss, "Some Definitions of Public Opinion," in *Public Opinion and Propaganda*, edited by Daniel Katz, Dorwin Cortwright, Samuel Eldersveld, and Alfred McClung Lee (New York: The Dryden Press, 1954), pp. 50-51; Floyd H. Allport, "Toward a Science of Public Opinion," *Public Opinion Quarterly*, I (1937), pp. 7-23; James Bryce, *The American Commonwealth* (New York: The Macmillan Co., 1916), vol. II, pp. 251-266, and his *Modern Democracies*, vol. I, p. 153; Kimball Young, "Comments on the Nature of 'Public' and 'Public Opinion,'" *International Journal of Opinion and Attitude Research*, II (1948), pp. 385-392; Harold D. Lasswell, Ralph D. Casey, and Bruce L. Smith, *Propaganda, Communication and Public Opinion* (Princeton: Princeton University Press, 1946); William Albig, *Public Opinion* (New York: McGraw-Hill Book Co., 1939).

Formation of Public Opinion. Public opinion is concerned with at least three major phases: The rise of an issue, discussion and proposed solutions pro and con, and arrival at a consensus. When a public issue emerges, there is usually a preliminary phase of discussion, often consisting of little more than an attempt to define the issue and verbalize the hope for a solution. Later, as discussion continues, those concerned propose various and often divergent solutions. It is in this phase that the factors of agreement and disagreement become most evident. In time we pass into the third phase of the discussion, in which people begin to take sides; this marks the crystallization of opinion. Sometimes the divergences over possible solutions are sharpened; sometimes a merger or a compromise plan draws on two or more plans previously put forth. But in any case the discussion gives way to some evidence of a trend toward agreement or disagreement. The straw vote of public opinion polls is perhaps the most striking of the nonofficial measures of consensus. Often informal expressions of consensus are found in letters, petitions, and memorials to legislative bodies, executives, and others. Still others are in "Letters to the Editor" columns in newspapers. In political matters, of course, formal legalized voting is the acceptable measure of consensus.[3]

These phases of the process of opinion formation represent the barest essentials. There are many variations in terms of historically differentiated culture patterns. In the primary community of the colonial period and earlier rural United States public opinion centered largely around local issues. A consensus as to measures to be taken and officials to be elected to carry them out was reached through such institutions as the town meeting. This pattern has carried over today into our urbanized society, but the political party and the mass media of communication have taken over most of the functions of the simpler democratic public discussion. Moreover, today the citizen is expected to have opinions about complicated issues far beyond his local area or even his country.

Today the formation of attitudes on which public opinion rests depends upon a number of factors which help to shape the thinking which results

---

[3] Kimball Young, *op. cit.*; S. M. Lipset, "Opinion Formation in a Crisis Situation," *Public Opinion Quarterly*, XVII (1953), pp. 20-46; Harold Lasswell and Abraham Kaplan, "Publics, Public Opinion, and General Interests," in their *Power and Society* (New Haven: Yale University Press, 1950), pp. 31-33, 38-42; Margaret Mead, "Public Opinion Mechanisms Among Primitive Peoples," *Public Opinion Quarterly*, I (1937), pp. 5-16: Alfred McClung Lee, "Social Determinants of Public Opinion," *International Journal of Opinion and Attitude Research*, I (1947), pp. 12-29: Jerome S. Bruner and Sheldon J. Korchin, "The Boss and the Vote: A Case Study in City Politics," *Public Opinion Quarterly*, X (1946), pp. 1-23; G. D. Wiebe, "Responses to the Televised Kefauver Hearings: Some Social Psychological Implications," *Public Opinion Quarterly*, XVI (1952), pp. 179-200; D. B. Truman, "The Dynamics of Access in the Legislative Process," in his *The Governmental Process: Political Interests and Public Opinion* (New York: Alfred A. Knopf, 1951), pp. 221-251.

in an opinion on some issue. Playing a most important role in this process of developing attitudes and forming opinions are what are known as symbols.

Symbols and Attitude Formation

Symbols. Symbols are "combinations of words, personalities, music, drama, pageantry," and other such devices that make an impression upon the masses.[4] They may be slogans with which we are all familiar in the advertising of products: "Be happy, go Lucky!" "The instrument of the immortals," "The skin you love to touch," "Watch the Fords go by," "Ask the man who owns one!" Or they may be factors linked to popular sentiments which arouse the imagination and cause individuals to respond readily, as Americans do to such terms as Pearl Harbor, New Deal, Fair Deal, Democracy, Bataan, Capital, Liberty, Red, Yankee, Reactionary, Nazi, McCarthyism, CIO, AFL, NAM, Labor, Communism; while Russians no doubt react in much the same way to Marx, Lenin, Stalin, Monopoly, Capitalism, Imperialism, Fascist, Kulak, Stalingrad.

All of these are typical omnibus words or symbols carrying vague general meanings, but which have specific meanings for particular groups. They are appealing generalities, name-calling symbols, devices to reduce discussion through associating an idea with a good or evil subject and thus to get the individual to approve or reject a proposal without examining the evidence. It is through their use that people are stirred, moved, and led to take action. It is through them that those who would make and form public opinion are able to help shape attitudes behind the opinions which are made, shaped, and held.

Attitude Formation. Various studies have indicated that attitude formation is related to basic predispositions of individuals; that is, propaganda is more effective with people whose basic predispositions are already in line with the propaganda themes. That there is correlation between views on various issues is illustrated by a study of the loyalty oath at the University of California. An analysis of readership among the student body suggested that readers of more conservative papers tended to be more conservative on the policy of Communist employment than did the readers of liberal papers; as compared with professed Republicans, students who listed themselves as Democrats were disproportionately against the loyalty oath; as regards religious background Jews and Protestants were relatively liberal, while those of Catholic faith were more conservative; the children of professionals and farmers were more conservative than

[4] Alfred McClung Lee, *How to Understand Propaganda* (New York: Rinehart and Co., 1952), see chapter 3.

others on the issue; those students who relied upon themselves for support through school were found to be more liberal on the oath issue than those who relied upon parental support.[5]

Another study in a rural community by Richard L. Schanck[6] lends support to this explanation of attitude formation and injects another factor, the role of those interested in forming and shaping public opinion. Schanck found that the formation of public opinion is not necessarily a continuous development and that attitude formation leading to opinion moves by spurts. The process of development may be presumed to be more or less the same in other communities, differences depending, naturally, on variations in the areas being compared. First, biased individuals who are highly vocal may create an illusion regarding community attitudes that may not correspond with the real facts; at the same time, the continuous advocacy of a position by a minority leads the majority to believe that the stand may be fairly universal for the group. This is enhanced by a feeling of community loyalty, which causes many individuals to feel that if they must take a stand they should espouse the opinion held by the majority of their group. This leads those who formerly dismissed some solution as "Mr. X blowing his own horn," to see that "the community is solidly for this proposition," and the impression that a "great many" people are for it leads easily to the thought that "everybody" is for it.

Thus in the formation of attitudes that lead to the holding of an opinion, both perception and attitude formation are heavily affected by the nature of the connotations, the frame of reference, and the predispositions that individuals bring to a situation. The formation of opinion tends in large measure to be the result of the activation of these previous experiences and attitudes, and the opinions that are eventually taken up by the public as their own are first those in which a minority have an active interest. The latter then create the impression of universality which leads the majority to adopt the opinion as their own.

What are the instruments and techniques for creating this impression of universality which leads to the adoption of an opinion?

Opinion-influencing Instruments and Techniques

There are several ways in which people or groups, particularly legislatures, may be influenced to accept opinions: lobbying, petitions, letters, public opinion polls, pressure groups, individual leadership, and the mass

---

[5] S. M. Lipset, "Opinion Formation in a Crisis Situation," *Public Opinion Quarterly*, XVII (1935), pp. 20-46.
[6] Richard L. Schanck, "Test-Tube for Public Opinion: A Rural Community," *Public Opinion Quarterly*, II (1938), pp. 90-95.

media of newspapers, radio, magazines, television, and films. How do these instruments function, and how are these techniques put into operation?

Lobbying. Since legislation plays such a major function in American life and is basic to our form of government, some of these opinion-influencing instruments can be more clearly understood by analyzing how they operate in influencing legislation. Lobbying in American government is as natural as breathing is in the human individual, and is almost as complex in its operation and function. Part of this complexity springs from the innumerable groups and interests in American society which in one way or another tend to seek something from government. With so many conflicting voices clamoring to be heard, the only means of securing a hearing is to devise more effective applications of techniques by which views can be presented more effectively. Crude bribery or coercion, while still practiced, must now compete with subtler approaches.

1. The *Social Lobby* is a technique for creating a feeling of obligation and loyalty on the part of the legislator toward the lobbyist. It uses social entertainment to develop more or less close relations with legislators on the plausible assumption that it is harder to refuse someone who has been friendly to you than to turn away a more or less complete stranger. Sometimes the relationship extends indirectly to other legislators who are influenced by the appearance of friendship between the lobbyist and a fellow legislator.[7]

In general the social lobby technique works as follows, according to a former State legislator:[8]
"The legislator who remains aloof will find himself, if not quite ostracized, at least not 'one of the gang,' and will constantly be surprised at an unexpected solidarity on the part of a majority of his colleagues for or against a pending measure. His surprise will be dissipated when he learns that the night before the 'gang' were at an entertainment at a downtown hotel, where probably the subject of legislation was not even mentioned, but in some subtle way an understanding was reached as to what was expected of those present as all around 'good fellows.' "

This common technique received much attention during the Truman administration in connection with the investigation of what were called "Five Percenters."

2. *Pressure Group Lobbying.* Instead of attempting to influence legislation directly, the pressure group seeks to create an appearance of broad public support for its aims, support of which can be mobilized when the legislative situation demands it. This appearance may be genuine in the

---

[7] David B. Truman, *op. cit.*

[8] Henry Parkman, Jr., "Lobbies and Pressure Groups: A Legislator's Point of View," *The Annals*, CXCV (January, 1938), p. 97.

sense that views are expressed spontaneously and with conviction. Or, again, such expression may be artificial and contrived. The aim is to influence the determination of legislative policy.[9]

An example of indirect pressure group lobbying is found in the functioning of the Foundation for Economic Education. This organization has little direct contact with members of Congress, its major activities being the preparation and distribution of pamphlets, booklets, and articles presenting one side of public issues. The foundation distributed almost four million booklets and pamphlets between 1946-1950 and has records showing that 389 newspapers and magazines during that period in some way used its articles. Its president estimated that many times that number actually used the material. Its anti-rent control pamphlet, "Roofs or Ceilings," was deemed so effective that the National Association of Real Estate Boards bought and distributed half a million copies.[10]

Lobbying at the grass roots finds every group with a different tone, a different clientele, and a different technique of distributing materials. The Committee for Constitutional Government strives to saturate the thinking of the community. The Foundation for Economic Education is content with a carefully placed sprinkling. Some groups find secondary distribution simple. The NAREB has ready-made outlets for materials in many member boards and individual realtors throughout the nation. This is effective in that it means the advantage of central purchase with greater impact of local sponsorship.[11]

Pressure groups have long been aware of the power of the press and have sought to harness this power for their ends. One major means is to gain access to editorial news columns, which thus enables the group itself to remain anonymous. How this is done is illustrated in an exchange between a congressman and a representative of the Committee for Constitutional Government:[12]

Congressman: "I noticed, in many California papers what I would call standard editorials, of exactly the same text. In your processes, do you send out stereotyped editorials?"

C.C.G. Representative: "No; we do not send out canned editorials. We send out informative information which we hope the papers will print.

---

[9] *General Interim Report of the House Select Committee on Lobbying Activities* (The Buchanan Committee), House Report No. 3138, Union Calendar Resolution 298 (Washington, D.C.: U.S. Government Printing Office, 1950), pp. 23-43.

[10] U.S. Congress, House of Representatives, Hearings, pt. 8, Foundation for Economic Education.

[11] *General Interim Report of the House Select Committee on Lobbying Activities,* p. 40.

[12] U.S. Congress, House of Representatives, Hearings, pt. 5, Committee for Constitutional Government, p. 117.

In a fight like this one, we picked out about 20 editorials that told our side, and sent them to all newspapers in the United States."

Another method along this line is illustrated by a release of May 5, 1949, sent out by the public relations department of the National Association of Home Builders to local associations in its fight to defeat the government public housing program:[13]

"Congressmen read their home-town papers carefully. They follow trends as reported in the press. If your Congressman sees stories in his paper emphasizing the failure of public housing, he will be more inclined to vote against the pending measure . . .

"In many communities newspapers will use editorials if they are presented to them. Four suggested editorials are included. . . . If prepared editorials are not used by your newspapers, each of these can be used in another way. They can be addressed to the 'mail bag' column of your newspaper as a signed letter from one of your officers. If you would prefer to use them in this way, do so. Simply have them copied as a letter addressed to the editor of your paper and have one of your officers sign it.

"Because the pending housing legislation is so complex, a fact sheet is always helpful to newspaper editors, reporters, and radio commentators. One is enclosed. If you want additional copies, let us know. Distribute these to anyone who is in a position to influence public opinion."

An even bolder example of stereotyped materials to influence opinion is provided by the "Sylvester Says" series of the National Retail Lumber Dealers Association.[14] Quarter-column releases, many of which take stands on legislative issues, are distributed in mats to 1400 newspapers by the Western Newspaper Union, a nation-wide syndicated news service. The source is indicated on the mat, but not in the individual releases. In this way, the lumber dealers have presented their views to some four million readers who had no inkling of the source of the material.

3. *Literature and Letters.* Another much-used means of influencing opinion in regard to legislation is through the use of "literature" of varying kinds which is sent to members of Congress. Today more than 100,000 pieces of mail, on the average, are sent to Congress daily.[15] This use of the mails is one of the most, if not the most, practicable ways of maintaining a close relationship between Congress and the people; and with the great strides in education; the wide dissemination of news by radio, daily newspapers, magazines, and television; and the growth of huge organizations whose programs are affected by the federal govern-

---

[13] U.S. Congress, Hearings, pt. 2, Housing Lobby, exhibit H-260, p. 351.
[14] Hearings, pt. 2, Housing Lobby, pp. 484-501.
[15] Estes Kefauver and Jack Levin, "Letters that Really Count," in their *A Twentieth Century Congress* (New York: Duell, Sloan, and Pearce, 1947), pp. 170-184.

ment, has come a vast expansion in government itself. Add to this the typewriter, telephone, mimeograph, telegraph, and speedier printing, and one has the answer to the millions of letters that arrive annually at the Capitol in Washington.

The average Congressman now receives more than 100 letters a day. Letters are of all kinds: those asking personal favors and assistance with no direct bearing on legislation (constituent service mail); requests for information about pending bills, for copies of hearings or reports, for explanations of amendments or of a rule proposed by a bureau; petitions; chain telegrams; form letters and post cards; pamphlets; and brochures (most of these are ineffective, since no one reads them and they gather dust in Capitol files until carted away and destroyed); and individual letters all aimed directly at influencing votes. This is what is called "pressure mail." [16]

The letters that are most persuasive in affecting opinion are those which discuss factually how a particular proposal would affect the writer as a consumer, a farmer, a worker, an employer, a businessman, or in any other role. Letters that apply to the local situation are effective. Such organizations as the League of Women Voters, the American Association of University Women, the Federation of Women's Clubs, the National Planning Association and the American Bar Association devote much time to analyzing measures before Congress, and their communications are usually helpful to the Congressional representative.[17]

A word should be said about the "letters that don't come." Most constituents do not write, but expect their Representatives simply to "do the right thing," and it does not occur to them to lend him a helping hand. In 1946 during the fight over the Office of Price Administration, Congressional mail was running 80 per cent against the extension of O.P.A., yet a Gallup poll showed the public was more than 70 per cent in favor of extension.[18]

4. *Miscellaneous Techniques for Influencing Legislation.* Variations on the old practice of directly contacting legislators are endless. Some groups make their views known by letters, telegrams, and telephone calls. Others depend largely on personal contact with members of Congress, and still others organize delegations for marches on the Capitol. The Civil Rights Congress has often used this last approach and has on several occasions sponsored mass train trips to Washington for the purpose of what its officers call "speaking on" legislation.[19] This approach was also used by the followers of Senator Joseph McCarthy during the special session of the

---

[16] *Ibid.,* p. 172.
[17] *Ibid.,* p. 182.
[18] *Ibid.,* p. 183.
[19] U.S. Congress, Hearings, pt. 9, Civil Rights Congress, p. 12.

Senate in November, 1954, to investigate censure charges brought against the Senator.[20]

The various pressure groups using lobbying tactics base their arguments on what they call the "facts," which they have collected through research and informational activity. The pressure group is, naturally, inclined to exaggerate these activities. Facts are seldom presented for their own sake, or without having been carefully selected for maximum support of the objective. But where a full hearing is available to all interested groups, we can rely upon competitive watchfulness and public scrutiny as partial safeguards against misrepresentation of the facts by any one group.

Formal dinners for members of Congress and more casual and intimate gatherings remain an important part of the lobby group's stock in trade. Today resourceful pressure groups may seek to serve themselves as well as members of Congress by arranging remunerative speaking or writing engagements for the latter, or by such friendly activities as helping a new member to secure housing in Washington.[21]

A long-standing lobbying practice which has become increasingly prevalent during the past forty years is the use of the franking privilege of members of Congress for mass mailing of printed matter. Although it is unlawful for Congressmen or Government officials to lend the frank or permit its use by any committee, organization, or association, and fines are levied through the Criminal Code for such practices,[22] yet the practice continues, with the Committee for Constitutional Government serving as a prime example of getting mass distribution of various materials through the use of Congressional franks.[23]

Public Opinion Polls. Although public opinion polls are popularly considered as merely instruments to measure attitudes which people hold on some particular issue or item, in themselves their results are factors influencing behavior, tending to shape or shift opinion. This aspect of opinion polling was demonstrated concretely in the 1954 Congressional and local elections. When various public opinion polls showed that the trend was toward a landslide for the Democrats, the Republicans shifted their tactics and mapped new strategy in the waning phases of the campaign.[24] It is highly unlikely that this would have occurred if the polls

[20] "McCarthy Backers Rally in Capital," *The New York Times*, November 12, 1954); Max Lerner, "The Agitators," *New York Post*, November 18, 1954, p. 42.
[21] U.S. Congress, Hearings, pt. 2, Housing Lobby, pp. 54-55, 291-294.
[22] 39 U.S. Codes, Sec. 335, and 18 U.S. Codes, Sec. 1719.
[23] U.S. Congress, Hearings, pt. 5, Committee for Constitutional Government, pp. 99-101.
[24] "Surprising Vote," *The New York Times*, Sunday, November 7, 1954, section 4, P.E. See also issues daily of *The New York Times* for the week beginning October 24, 1954.

had not revealed such a pronounced shift from what Republicans had felt was strong support for the Eisenhower administration.

A serious defect in the average public opinion poll is that by posing "issues" to a person it is possible to get him to select among proposals about which he has little knowledge and little conviction. Under such circumstances, "overwhelming" support of a proposal, in the sense that a large number of people select it, does not necessarily mean that the public is firmly behind the proposal. In the area of international affairs, the desire for peace is so strong that specific proposals presented as contributing to the attainment of peace are likely to be approved if the pollster insists on an answer.[25] This phenomenon helps to explain the difficulty of drawing inferences from certain poll results. Americans who had been impressed by the "new era" of world cooperation as indicated by some poll results shortly after the war were rudely enlightened when the polls got around to the British loan. Although roughly two thirds of the population favored American participation in a world organization, only one third approved of the specific loan to Britain. The latter proposal called into play a different set of values.[26]

There are dangers in too great reliance upon public opinion polls. Questions may be phrased so as to induce the desired answers, as in the case of the poll which asks: "Would you prefer to pay your taxes in a lump sum as an income tax, or pay them a few cents at a time as a sales tax?" Again, the public may be asked to offer solutions to social problems of which they have no technical knowledge; the absence of new solutions may be interpreted as a desire for the status quo, disregarding the fact that unless some new solution to such problems has been widely publicized, people will tend to think only of techniques which are already familiar.[27]

The public does not have sufficient knowledge about most international governmental problems to pass intelligent judgment upon them. Modern government and international problems have become so numerous and so complicated that even experts must specialize on certain types of problems. The danger of applying public opinion polls to these areas lies

[25] Dorwin Cartwright, "Public Opinion Polls and Democratic Leadership," *Journal of Social Issues*, II (1946), pp. 23-32; Paul F. Lazarsfeld, Bernard Berelson, and Hazel Gaudet, *The People's Choice* (New York: Duell, Sloan and Pearce, 1944); Mildred Parten, *Surveys, Polls and Samples* (New York: Harper and Brothers, 1950), see pp. 23-36; Social Science Research Council, *Committee Report on Analysis of Pre-Election Polls and Forecasts*, 1948; George Gallup, "Testing Public Opinion," in *Public Opinion in a Democracy*, pp. 8-14, Supplement to *Public Opinion Quarterly*, II (1938); see symposium "The Public Opinion Polls; Dr. Jekyll or Mr. Hyde," *Public Opinion Quarterly*, IV (1940), pp. 212-284; Paul Studenski, "How Polls Can Mislead," *Harper's Magazine* (December, 1939), pp. 80-83; John C. Ranney, "Do the Polls Serve Democracy?" *Public Opinion Quarterly*, I (1946), pp. 349-360.

[26] Dorwin Cartwright, *op. cit.*, p. 29.

[27] *Ibid.*; George Gallup, "Testing Public Opinion," *Public Opinion in a Democracy*, pp. 8-14.

in the fact that people can be induced to express an opinion in a poll on matters about which they know little, especially since they may have no intention that their opinions should result in government action. Only when a problem has become subject to extensive public discussion and the issues are clearly drawn should one seriously consider polling results as a mandate.

We must remember that scientific polling of public opinion is a relatively recent technique and that, in the short period of its existence, public opinion has generally come to be looked upon as polling a form of human behavior. But there is as yet little agreement as to precisely *what* behavior the term "public opinion" refers. Some view public opinion as any expression on a controversial issue. Others say it is the rational judgment of a group, while there are those who see public opinion as the views and feelings current in a given population at a given time as it concentrates on any issue of interest to the population. Much of the controversy on this matter is centered about the interpretation of the phrase involving such factors as who is to be included in *the* public, the extent opinions must rest on information or on other more or less stable bases, how far can you ascertain the nature of public opinion from what members of the public do or say under varying conditions when questions are asked of them, its subject limitations, and is there one public opinion or opinions of differing publics and may the latter be combined into a single aggregate? [28]

The thing to keep in mind is that in the routine of day-to-day existence the individual's expression of opinions is considered a significant part of his behavior. We use this as well as other types of behavior as an indication of his attitudes, which it is. When expressions of opinion are made the subject of organized analysis in opinion polling, they remain significant indications. Yet simply because they represent a form of human behavior they are subject to error. Thus the best scientific work, whether predicting foreign policy, elections, or something else, should proceed with caution realizing that the results may vary within probable error limits and not lead the public to expect greater precision than the instruments— ranging from quasi-clinical devices such as thematic apperception tests to the routine interviews of the ordinary interviewer-respondent situation —can at present deliver.

[28] For more discussion on this subject see Frederick C. Irion, *Public Opinion and Propaganda* (New York: Thomas Y. Crowell Co., 1950); George A. Lundberg, C. C. Schrag, and O. N. Larsen, *Sociology* (New York: Harper and Brothers, 1954), chapter 13; Herbert Blumer, "The Mass, the Public and Public Opinion," in *New Outlines of the Principles of Sociology*, edited by Alfred M. Lee (New York: Barnes and Noble, 1946); Bernard Berelson and Morris Janowitz, *Reader in Public Opinion* (Glencoe, Illinois: The Free Press, 1953), pp. 3-13, 61-113, 555-570; Herbert Hyman, "Problems in the Collection of Opinion-Research Data," *American Journal of Sociology* (January, 1950), pp. 362-370.

Personalized Media of Communication. Personalized media of communication serve to influence opinion. Education, as a means of reproducing the culture, is a major medium, and its importance is shown by community concern that it remain in the "right" hands. Education is subject to unified control by public forces operating the government; but there are other personalized media not so subject to such control. These include the addresses of political candidates and other kinds of public speakers; professional politicians of the "boss," "heeler," and "district leader" types; agitators on various subjects; ministers; neighborhood gossips; and the like. These personalized media readily reflect many group interests which might not otherwise get their opinion across to the public.

Mass Media. Although people get information from many sources today, and all of these sources exert influence, it is mass media that operate as the major influence upon public opinion. Newspapers, books, magazines, and especially the radio, movies, television all reach a tremendous number of people. Most American adults read a newspaper every day. Although 50 per cent of the adult population report reading no books during the year, 82 per cent read one or more newspapers a day, with men and women reading them in about equal proportions, and about as often. Almost the same percentage, or 79 per cent, listen to a radio an hour or more each day; 69 per cent read one or more magazines regularly; 63 per cent attend one or more movies every month; and 21 per cent of the population hear one or more speeches in a year. Television is a rapidly growing newcomer to the field.[29]

About half the adults of America have read at least one government bulletin at some time, and the proportion is even larger among those who live in rural areas and small towns. Among men agricultural and reclamation bulletins lead the way, while among women bulletins on health, cooking and child care predominate. Government publications are rarely conceived of as a mass medium, but their wide distribution gives some indication of their potential for influencing public opinion and their effect upon it.[30]

Radio covers a wide range of activity, and today there are some 900

---

[29] Angus Campbell and Charles Metzner, "Books, Libraries, and Other Media of Communication," in their *Public Use of the Library* (Ann Arbor: University of Michigan Survey Research Center, 1953), pp. 1-14.

[30] *Ibid.*, Campbell and Metzner found that generally in the United States when people want information they seem to rely upon experts, especially when seeking an answer to a fairly practical question. These results turned up in their study: 56 per cent would consult a professional source or expert, 14 per cent would rely upon their own experience, 13 per cent would ask a friend, 9 per cent would look in a magazine for assistance, 6 per cent would consult a book, while 2 per cent would go to the library for help. But for information on foreign countries they would use institutional sources in the following proportions: 31 per cent would use a book, 13 per cent a service club of some kind, 11 per cent the library, 10 per cent would check a map, and a similar percentage would talk with friends, while 9 per cent would try to secure the information from some government agency.

standard broadcast stations on the air in the United States. Nearly 600 of these are affiliated with one or more national networks.[31]

Since television is a more recent medium for influencing public opinion, its full strength cannot yet be gauged accurately. But some research has been done on its influence in the Presidential campaign of 1952, the first in which television played a major part.[32] The public went out of its way to watch the campaign on television. Only about 40 per cent of the homes in America had television sets, but some 53 per cent of the population saw television programs on the campaign. On the other hand, the campaign news and material in newspapers and magazines and on the radio did not reach all of their respective audiences. More than 80 per cent of the population read daily newspapers and have radios and more than 60 per cent regularly read magazines; but in each case the number cited was smaller than the total audience reached.

The influence of each medium was difficult to assess; but when people were asked which medium had given them the most information about the campaign, the impact of television was striking. Although available to only a minority of the people, television led the other media in the number of persons in the nation who rated it most informative. Of those who actually watched the campaign on television (nearly all of whom were exposed to other media), 59 per cent considered television their most important source of information. In contrast, among the more than four fifths of the population who followed the campaign in newspapers, only 28 per cent rated newspapers as the medium from which they got most of their information. There were marked regional differences: the Northeast, where most television sets are located, relied most heavily on television; the South depended mainly on radio; and television led in both the Midwest and the West.

To what extent television influenced people to form an opinion on voting for candidates, there is no way of determining. Those who rated television their most important source of information voted for Eisenhower in about the same proportion as those who relied mainly on radio or newspapers. Magazine readers were considerably more Republican. Stevenson did better among television devotees than among those who preferred radio or newspapers, but geographical and other factors must be considered in evaluating this.

Psycho-Social Processes of Public Opinion

Some insight into the instruments which influence public opinion is necessary to understand more thoroughly the relationship between atti-

---

[31] Clifford Judkins Durr, "Freedom of Speech for Whom?" *Public Opinion Quarterly*, VII (1944), pp. 391-406.

[32] Angus Campbell, Gerald Gurin, and Warren E. Miller, "Television and the Election," *Scientific American*, vol. 199 (1953), pp. 46-48.

tude and opinion. The practices by which people are led to favor one alternative over another are almost limitless.[33] All of them involve either the control of fact or the control of interpretation. In reaching a conclusion about an issue, a person must have, on the one hand, what he thinks is an accurate account of the current state of affairs and its probable consequences and, on the other hand, a set of values by which he can judge the results. If those who make and shape public opinion falsify the facts for him, lead him to make a wrong prediction, emphasize certain values against others, or steer him toward a connection of facts with particular values that he would not normally consider relevant to the situation, they can influence his opinion. The use of all these practices to shape attitude and control opinion is what we call propaganda. Thus propaganda is the use of reasoning or facts in order to persuade another person to favor a particular kind of action that he might not otherwise favor. If the maker of opinion himself believes the reasoning or facts, the process is not propaganda but education.

It is difficult to make sharp distinctions between propaganda and education since they are both concepts of learning which require assessment in terms of specific or unspecified criteria, and in their functioning what almost always occurs is a combination of the two. However, in this chapter education is looked upon as an imparting of knowledge or skill considered to be scientific or to have survival value in a society at a particular time, while our definition of propaganda implies an attempt to affect the personalities and control the behavior of individuals toward ends considered unscientific or of doubtful value in a society at a given time.[34] It is realized that these are broad definitions of education and propaganda. Since fundamentally definite distinctions yet remain to be made between the propaganda and educational implications of most social processes, it is felt that, by focusing upon the science and values which they contain, some useful insight into their nature is provided that should help in comprehending the opinion forming process.

In the formation of opinion certain factors stand out. Individuals are acutely aware that others hold opinions on the same subject, and each tries to estimate the direction of these opinions. People who see and think or hold an opinion they hear others express as being very much like their own persist in estimating group opinion as close to their own. People with a narrow outlook either conform to changing group attitudes or distort their perception of where the group is. In general, people find some compromise between their private opinions and their conception of the group opinion when expressing an opinion publicly. Other factors that

---

[33] Herbert Blumer in R. E. Park's *An Outline of the Principles of Sociology*, pp. 248-249.

[34] Leonard Doob, *Public Opinion and Propaganda* (New York: Henry Holt and Co., 1948), pp. 237-241.

determine the relationship between individual and group or public opinion are: the degree of a person's identification with the group, his conception of the group's attitude toward nonconformity, his conception of his own role in relation to the group, and special personality traits.[35]

People tend to change their opinion on subjects more readily if the source of their ideas is considered reliable and less readily if the source is considered of little credibility. But it should be understood that people do not tend to retain information from reliable sources any more than they do that from what they look upon as unreliable sources.[36] Changes in opinions, when produced by direct interpretation, are more permanent than changes produced by rational means.

The strength of an opinion is generally closely associated with the level of information a person has about a subject. People with more frequent and adequate contact with the press, radio, and magazines seem to develop greater concern and more definite opinions about matters of public interest. A study of opinions and attitudes about Russia revealed that those who had little knowledge about the USSR held the most narrow and stereotyped views about Russia, and also showed a relative lack of concern about the Soviet.[37]

A person's attitudes are generally consistent with his characteristic modes of reaction. In this study of Russia it was found that those who had a tendency to blame others for failures and frustrations were inclined to blame Russia for U.S.-Soviet disagreements and to support a tough United States policy toward Russia. However, the more informed a person is, the less likely he is to let his feelings enter into his formation of attitudes.

Also, a person's attitude may be taken over more or less bodily from his associates or from what he looks upon as persons of prestige, using this as a means of identifying with them. But this is not the principal source of influence promoting relative uniformity of opinion within face-to-face groups. There is the fact that members of such groups are likely to have common information on a topic, because they share similar sources of knowledge and may be themselves the main source for one another. Conformity plays an important role in the determination of a

---

[35] Raymond L. Gordon, "Interaction Between Attitude and the Definition of the Situation in the Expression of Opinion," *American Sociological Review*, XVII (1952), pp. 50-58.

[36] Carl I. Hovland and Walter Weiss, "The Influence of Source Credibility on Communication Effectiveness," *Public Opinion Quarterly*, XV (1952), pp. 635-650.

[37] M. Brewster Smith, "The Personal Setting of Public Opinions: A Study of Attitudes Towards Russia," *Public Opinion Quarterly*, XI (1947), pp. 507-523; Irving Sarnoff, Daniel Katz, and Charles McClintock, "The Motivational Basis for Attitude Change," *Journal of Abnormal and Social Psychology*, vol. 49 (1954); S. E. Asch, "The Doctrine of Suggestion, Prestige, and Imitation in Social Psychology," *Psychological Review*, vol. 55 (1948), pp. 250-276. A number of Ph.D. dissertations on attitude change filed in 1953 by M. F. Barlow, E. R. Carlson, M. J. Rosenberg, M. Wagman, and M. S. White are available on inter-library loan from the Library, University of Michigan.

person's attitudes, and to the extent that the need for approval creates real pressure toward conformity, there must be conformity toward opinions of others as the person in question understands them.

Psychological Warfare

In the field of public opinion psychological warfare has come to play a most important role. During the past war much valuable understanding of the processes and function of public opinion developed through the use of propaganda. People learned that minds are vulnerable, just as bodies are. The method by which minds may be reached is known as psychological warfare or "sykewar." This is the use of propaganda against an enemy through the employment of modern media of mass communications, together with such other operational measures and devices of a military, economic, or political nature as may be required to supplement propaganda for the purpose of reaching mass audiences in order to persuade them to accept certain beliefs and ideas. On the one hand, it may involve the supplementing of normal military operations by the use of mass communications, and, on the other, the calculation and execution of both political and military strategy on studied psychological grounds. In wartime it is used to undermine the enemy's resistance, to dissuade neutrals from joining the other side, or to encourage friends and allies. It is inclusive in its sphere of operations and tends to place some confidence in modern sciences, especially psychology and cultural anthropology. It presupposes study and understanding of its "target," the audience toward which it is pointed.[38]

Two developments have given new impetus to this method, which historically is not a new instrument for influencing opinion since some semblance of it was used as early as the fifth century by the Chinese.[39] The first is the growth of mass media of communication to global scale, and the second is the kind of uneasy peace which characterizes the twentieth century.

In the two World Wars and especially since the early 1930's strategists

---

[38] Saul K. Padover, *Psychological Warfare* (New York: Foreign Policy Association) Headline Series No. 86, March–April, 1951; Paul M. A. Linebarger, *Psychological Warfare* (Washington, D.C.: Infantry Journal Press, 1948); Hans Speier, "The Future of Psychological Warfare," *Public Opinion Quarterly*, XII (1948), pp. 5-18; Daniel Lerner, *Sykewar* (New York: G. W. Stewart, Publisher, Inc., 1949); A. M. Lee, *How to Understand Propaganda*, pp. 211-212. The use of psychological warfare is understood in non-war times through the continued operation of such agencies as the United States Information Agency, the Voice of America, the British Information Service, and other similar agencies of various countries located in different nations.

[39] Sun Tzu, *The Book of War*, written in China in the Fifth Century, stressed the importance of destroying the enemy's will to fight through such means as noise, surprise, and other devices. P. M. A. Linebarger, *op. cit.*, has a good discussion on the history of psychological warfare in ancient times.

in western nations have made psychological warfare primary military business. They have come to realize the fundamental functions of social strategy, of popular acceptance, tolerance, and indifference, and of class and group divisions in forwarding the objectives of the whole armed forces and the peace conferences. In World War II every major belligerent systematically employed political propaganda and control of news as a weapon of warfare, and sykewar was recognized and accepted as a military instrument.[40]

American propagandists found that effective propaganda must take into account the hopes, demands, expectations, and background of an audience. They learned that ignoring audience expectation leads to situations where propaganda boomerangs. Thus during World War II American sykewar in the field made the initial mistake, in its leaflets asking German troops to surrender, of describing American treatment of prisoners of war in glowing terms. Actually the leaflets told the truth about how prisoners got cigarettes, candy, good food, chocolate, etc. But the Germans, used to Spartan rations and austerity, were convinced that the American leaflets were lying. Later when surrender leaflets were scaled down to German expectations, they became effective.[41]

Today, before and with and behind the actual military forces go the assessments of social organization, opinion, and common sentiments, the planning and the manipulating, and the "paper bullets" and radio barrages of those who are to influence common attitudes and actions. The general sequence for proceeding is about as follows: (1) the development of strategic intelligence, which deals with locating economic, political, and social strengths and weaknesses and finding sentiments among the enemy which can be capitalized upon; (2) the propaganda barrage aimed at selected groups within the enemy population; (3) the preparation for action through the development of open and undercover organizations; and (4) finally the desired types of movement, agitation, conquest, and other action are launched. This general system is applicable whether it is a "hot" or a "cold" war.[42]

Obtaining knowledge of the enemy is basic to sykewar. To meet this problem in time of war, the specialists interview enemy nationals in the United States, while simultaneously studying fictional, historical, economic, and political literature as well as folklore, for the insight these sources can provide. During the war with Japan there was considerable controversy over the kind of propaganda treatment the Emperor was to be accorded. One official opinion urged that the United States attack the imperial pattern as the prop of a fascist state. This group urged that

---

[40] Padover, *op. cit.*, p. 10.
[41] Padover, *op. cit.*, p. 48.
[42] A. M. Lee, *How to Understand Propaganda*, pp. 211-212.

there be no silence by the Allies which might be interpreted as tolerance of the monarchy after victory should be won. Another group opposed this policy and urged that "the solution of conflicts between the United States and other peoples can never rest on cultural imperialism that insists upon the substitution of our institutions for theirs." This group pointed out that the Emperor was the nucleus of the Japanese sentiment system and that to attack the Emperor institution would be to identify and prolong the resistance of the Japanese.[43]

The value of sykewar as a technique of control and a factor in molding opinion is as yet unknown. In a critical analysis of psychological warfare Sereno has pointed out that "this kind of warfare depends on the skill and ability of the syke warrior to understand the problems of the enemy or target people and their patterns of thought and action, and to affect them with all the means at his disposal. In other terms, it depends on detachment. . . . Other people's emotions become tools in their hands. . . ." So far no analysis has been made to estimate the overall success of psychological warfare, and Sereno feels that it helps political leaders to camouflage reality and to dodge responsibility: "Psychological warfare appears once more as the large-scale enterprise, the purpose of which is to reassure those who sponsor and practice it." [44]

Summary

Public opinion is a composite opinion formed from varying opinions held by the public which can be mobilized on some particular issue and directed toward some kind of decision. Today its formation depends heavily upon word symbols, emotionally loaded generalities used to make an impression upon the masses; these are used to maneuver the public into taking a stand on an issue without examining the facts surrounding it too closely. Those who attempt to mold opinion are wise to direct their appeal toward predispositions in people, since the formation of opinion tends in large measure to be the result of the activation of previous experiences and attitudes. The opinions that are eventually taken up by the public as their own are usually first those in which a minority have an active interest. To influence others to accept their opinion, the minority uses such techniques and instruments as lobbying, petitions, letters, public opinion polls, pressure groups, individual leadership, and the mass media of newspapers, radio, magazines, films, and television.

The practices by which people are led to favor one alternative over another are almost limitless. All of them involve either the control of

---

[43] D. Lerner, *op. cit.;* P. M. A. Linebarger, op. cit.; Clyde Kluckhohn, *Mirror for Man* (New York: Whittlesey House, 1949).

[44] Renzo Sereno, "Psychological Warfare, Intelligence, and Insight," *Psychiatry*, XIII (1950), pp. 266-273.

fact or the control of interpretation. In reaching a conclusion about an issue, a person needs what he considers an accurate account of the current conditions and their probable consequences, as well as a set of values by which he can judge the results. People who hold an opinion similar to those they hear others express persist in estimating the group opinion as close to their own. Generally people find some compromise between their private opinion and their conception of the group opinion when expressing an opinion publicly. Other factors that help determine the relationship between the individual's and the public's opinions are his identification with the group, his conception of the group's attitude toward nonconformity, his role in relation to the group, and special personality traits. The strength of an opinion is generally closely associated with the level of information the person in question has about a subject. People tend to change their opinion more readily if they consider the source of their ideas reliable, and changes produced by direct interpretation of materials are more permanent than changes produced by rational means.

An important development in the public opinion field is the use of psychological warfare to help influence people to form and adopt an opinion. This technique employs the modern media of communications for the purpose of reaching mass audiences in order to persuade them to accept certain beliefs and ideas. It is inclusive in its operations and relies upon modern sciences, especially psychology and cultural anthropology.

QUESTIONS

1. What is meant by the terms "public," "opinion," and "public opinion"?
2. What is the relationship between attitude and opinion?
3. How is public opinion formed?
4. What is the significance of symbols for understanding public opinion?
5. Is public opinion a continuous development?
6. Name and explain the use of major opinion-influencing instruments.
7. What factors stand out in the formation of opinion?
8. What is the relationship between the level of information one has and the strength of his opinion on a subject?
9. Does conformity play a significant role in forming an opinion?
10. What are some dangers in public opinion polling?
11. What is the difference between an individual and a group opinion?
12. How important is lobbying as a technique in forming public opinion?
13. What is psychological warfare?
14. What is necessary to take into account for psychological warfare to be effective?
15. Is the value of psychological warfare well understood at present?

SUGGESTED TOPICS FOR TERM PAPERS AND FURTHER RESEARCH

1. Select a topic of community interest and make an analysis of it to determine the status of "public opinion" about it.

2. Make a study of the characteristics of public opinion formation today and its formation prior to the development of mass media.

3. Choose a subject on international affairs; then analyze it from the standpoint of national and regional reaction to it.

4. Take ten well known symbols and show how they are effective in forming public opinion.

5. Make a study of American psychological warfare as it was used in particular parts of the world during World War II.

6. Analyze changes in technique in psychological warfare since the end of World War II.

7. Select six well known lobby groups and analyze their organization, purpose, and techniques, and measure their effectiveness in marshaling public opinion on matters in which they are interested.

8. Make an intensive study of pressure group tactics.

9. Make a study of opinion-influencing instruments and measure their effectiveness when used for different subjects.

10. Write a composition on "Mass Media and Public Opinion Today."

11. Analyze public opinion polls in various national elections.

12. Make a study of the relationship of attitudes and opinions.

BIBLIOGRAPHY

Books

William Albig, *Public Opinion* (New York: McGraw-Hill Book Co., 1939). A scholarly, comprehensive text used as a standard textbook in the field.

Gordon W. Allport, "Attitudes," chapter 17 in *A Handbook of Social Psychology*, edited by Carl Murchison (Worcester, Mass.: Clark University Press, 1935). Brief but excellent treatment of subject.

Wilhelm Bauer, "Public Opinion," *Encyclopedia of the Social Sciences*, edited by E. R. A. Seligman, XII, pp. 669-674. One of the best summaries available.

E. L. Bernays, *Public Relations* (Norman, Oklahoma: University of Oklahoma Press, 1952). A self-inquiry intensively done; contains a selected list of readings.

Emory S. Bogardus, *The Making of Public Opinion* (New York: Association Press, 1951). A summary of the author's own studies; has an extensive bibliography.

James Bryce, *The American Commonwealth* (New York: The Macmillan Co., 1916, first published in 1891). Part 2 of Vol. II, "Public Opinion," is an analytical study of American public opinion of that time as seen through the aristocratic lens of its author.

David Bulman, ed., *Molders of Opinion* (New York: Bruce Publishing Co., 1935). Presents the background of fourteen commentators and columnists.

Hadley F. Cantril, F. Mosteller, D. Rugg, J. Harding, F. Williams, D. Katz, J. S. Stock, *et al.*, *Gauging Public Opinion* (Princeton: Princeton University Press, 1940). Describes ways in which public opinion is sampled, analyzed, and interpreted.

Bernard Berelson, *Content Analysis in Communication Research* (Glencoe, Illinois: The Free Press).

A. B. Blankenship, *Consumer and Opinion Research* (New York: Harper and Brothers, 1943).

H. L. Childs and J. B. Whitton, *Propaganda By Shortwave* (Princeton: Princeton University Press, 1942). Techniques of persuasion.

C. H. Cooley, R. C. Angell, and L. J. Carr, *Introductory Sociology* (New York: Charles Scribner's Sons, 1933). Chapters 22-24 are concerned with public opinion.

Wallace Carroll, *Persuade or Perish* (Boston: Houghton Mifflin Co., 1948). Deals with persuasion and some consequences.

Leonard W. Doob, "The Psychology of Living People," in his *Propaganda: Its Psychology and Technique* (New York: Henry Holt and Co., 1935). The subject is a part of an outstanding monograph on propaganda.

C. I. Hovland, A. A. Lumsdaine, and F. D. Sheffield, *Experiments on Mass Communication* (Princeton: Princeton University Press, 1949).

Alex Inkeles, *Public Opinion in Soviet Russia* (Cambridge: Harvard University Press, 1950). An explanation of the function of the press, radio, and films in forming public opinion in the USSR.

Richard T. LaPiere, *Collective Behavior* (New York: McGraw-Hill Book Co., 1938). Presents characteristics of various kinds of crowds and publics.

H. D. Lasswell, R. D. Casey, and B. L. Smith, *Propaganda, Communication, and Public Opinion* (Princeton: Princeton University Press, 1946). A useful bibliography kept current in regular bibliographies published in *Public Opinion Quarterly* and *The Journalism Quarterly*.

Harold Lasswell and Abraham Kaplan, *Power and Society* (New Haven: Yale University Press, 1950). A study of the role and function of power.

Paul F. Lazarsfeld, Bernard Berelson, and Hazel Gaudet, *The People's Choice* (New York: Duell, Sloan, and Pearce, 1944). Study of American public during a presidential election campaign.

P. F. Lazarsfeld and F. N. Stanton, eds., *Radio Research: 1942-1943* (New York: Duell, Sloan, and Pearce, 1944). A good treatment of the same subject up to that time.

—— *Communications Research, 1948-49* (New York: Harper and Brothers, 1949). Studies in the field covering the period outlined.

Alfred McClung Lee, *The Daily Newspaper in America* (New York: The Macmillan Company, 1937). An evaluation up to that time.

Paul M. A. Linebarger, *Psychological Warfare* (Washington: Infantry Journal Press, 1948). An analysis of sykewar, including references to political warfare, and its use in World War II.

Walter Lippmann, *Public Opinion* (New York: The Macmillan Co., 1922). A classic in the field dealing with popular myths, stereotypes, and the ways they are enforced.

C. D. MacDougall, *Interpretative Reporting* (New York: The Macmillan Co., 1948). Handling and treatment of the news.

Robert K. Merton, *Mass Persuasion: The Social Psychology of a War Bond Drive* (New York: Harper and Brothers, 1946). A study of the techniques and conditions by which the radio star, Kate Smith, sold several million dollars worth of war bonds in one day.

Gardner Murphy and Rensis Likert, *Public Opinion and the Individual* (New York: Harper and Brothers, 1938). An extensive survey from the standpoint of measuring attitudes.

National Council for Social Studies, *Yearbook, 1950*, Vol. 21, pp. 11-34, contains an article by Herbert H. Hyman and Paul B. Sheatsley on "The Current Status of American Public Opinion."

Natural Resources Committee, *The Structure of the American Economy*. (Washington, D.C.: United States Government Printing Office, 1939). Pages 153-170 contain a section on "The Structure of Controls" which is a good treatment of factors and the operation of economic controls in American society.

Ulrich B. Phillips, "Popular Sovereignty," *Encyclopaedia of the Social Sciences*, XII, pp. 238-240.

T. R. Sills and Philip Lesly, *Public Relations: Principles and Procedures* (Chicago: Richard D. Irwin, 1945).

Bruce James Smith, Harold D. Lasswell, and Ralph D. Casey, *Propaganda Communication, and Public Opinion* (Princeton: Princeton University Press, 1946). Discusses the work of the public opinion analyst, the contents of communications and their effect, and contains an extensive bibliography on propaganda, communication, and public opinion.

David B. Truman, *The Governmental Process: Political Interest and Public Opinion* (New York: Alfred A. Knopf, 1951).

Julius Turner, *Party and Constituency: Pressures on Congress* (Baltimore: Johns Hopkins University Studies in Historical and Political Science, Series LXIX, 1951, Vol. I.)

Kimball Young, *Source Book for Sociology* (New York: American Book Co., 1935). See his "The Nature of Public Opinion," pp. 531-533.

Belle Zeller, "The States and the Lobby," statement in U.S. House Select Committee on Lobbying Activities, *The Role of Lobbying in Represent-Self-Government: Hearings* (Washington, D.C.: Government Printing Office, 1950), Part I, pp. 71-79.

D. Katz, D. Cartwright, S. Eldersveld, and A. M. Lee, *Public Opinion and Propaganda* (New York: The Dryden Press, 1954). An excellent collection of materials on public opinion and propaganda.

Periodicals

Wesley and Beverley Allinsmith, "Religious Affiliation and Politico-Economic Attitude: A Study of Eight Major U.S. Religious Groups," *Public Opinion Quarterly*, XII (1948), pp. 377-389.

Floyd H. Allport, "Toward a Science of Public Opinion," *ibid.*, I (1937), pp. 7-23.

Gordon W. Allport and Leo J. Postman, "The Basic Psychology of Rumor," *Transactions of the New York Academy of Science*, Series II (1945), VIII, pp. 61-81.

Herbert Blumer, "Public Opinion and Public Opinion Polling," *American Sociological Review*, XIII (1948), pp. 542-554.

Bernard Berelson, "Democratic Theory and Public Opinion," *Public Opinion Quarterly*, XVI (Fall, 1952), pp. 313-330.

Irving Brant, "The Press and Public Affairs," *The Quill*, XXV (1937), pp. 3-5, 18, 20.

——— "The Press and Public Leadership," *Social Education*, II (1938), pp. 3-10.

Dorwin Cartwright, "Some Principles of Mass Persuasion, Selected Findings of Research on the Sale of U.S. War Bonds," *Human Relations*, II (1949), pp. 253-267.

Richard Centers, "Attitude and Belief in Relation to Occupational Stratification," *Journal of Social Psychology*, XVII (1938), pp. 159-185.

Harwood L. Childs, "By Public Opinion I Mean," *Public Opinion Quarterly*, III (1939), pp. 327-336.

William O. Douglas, "The Black Silence of Fear," *New York Times Magazine* (January 23, 1952).

Roscoe Ellard, "Newspaper Analysis," *Propaganda Analysis*, I (1937-1938), pp. 16-18.

Fortune, "The Busy, Busy Citizen" (February, 1951).

A. L. George, "Communications Research and Public Policy," *World Politics*, III (January, 1951), pp. 251-268.

Herbert Goldhamer, "Public Opinion and Personality," *American Journal of Sociology*, LV (January, 1950), pp. 346-354.

Raymond L. Gordon, "Interaction Between Attitude and the Definition of the Situation in the Expression of Opinion," *American Sociological Review*, XVII (1952), pp. 50-58.

Learned Hand, "Is There a Common Will?" Michigan Law Review, XXVIII (1930), p. 50.

L. G. Hawkins, Jr., and G. S. Pettee, "OWI—Organization and Problems," *Public Opinion Quarterly*, VII (1943), pp. 15-33.

John Higham, "On Acquiring a Public Opinion," *Public Opinion Quarterly*, VIII (Winter, 1944-1945), pp. 488-489.

Institute for Propaganda Analysis, "American Common Sense," and "We Say *Au Revoir*," *Propaganda Analysis*, IV (June 24, 1941, and January 9, 1942).

Irving L. Janis, Arthur A. Lumsdaine, and Arthur I. Gladstone, "Effects of Preparatory Communications on Reactions to a Subsequent News Event," *Public Opinion Quarterly*, XV (1951), pp. 488-518.

Daniel Katz, "Psychological Barriers to Communication," *The Annals*, Vol. 250 (March, 1947), pp. 17-25.

—— "Do Interviewers Bias Poll Results?" *Public Opinion Quarterly*, VI (1942), pp. 248-268.

Joseph T. Klapper and Charles Y. Block, "Trial by Newspaper," *Scientific American*, Vol. 180 (1949), pp. 16-21.

Alexander Klein, "The Challenge of Mass Media," *Yale Review*, XXXIX (June, 1950).

Arthur Kornhauser, "Public Opinion and Social Class," *American Journal of Sociology*, LV (January, 1950), pp. 333-345.

Alfred McClung Lee, "Public Opinion in Relation to Culture," *Psychiatry*, VIII (1945), pp. 49-61.

Avery Leiserson, "Notes on the Theory of Public Opinion Formation," *American Political Science Review*, XLVII (March, 1953), pp. 171-177.

—— "Social Determinants of Public Opinions," *Internal Journal of Opinion and Attitude Research*, I (1947), pp. 12-29.

Martin Millspaugh, "Trial by Mass Media," *Public Opinion Quarterly*, XIII (1949), pp. 328-329.

Theodore M. Newcomb, "The Influence of Attitude Climate Upon Some Determinants of Information," *Journal of Abnormal and Social Psychology*, XLI (1946), pp. 291-302.

Peter H. Odegard, "Social Dynamics and Public Opinion," *Public Opinion Quarterly*, III (April, 1939), pp. 239-250.

G. Peel, "Science of Propaganda," *Contemporary Review*, CLXVI (November, 1944), pp. 268-274.

Ira DeA. Reid and Emily L. Ehle, "Leadership Selection in Urban Locality Areas," *Public Opinion Quarterly*, XIV (1950), pp. 262-284.

Kurt Riezler, "What is Public Opinion?" *Social Research*, XI (November, 1944), pp. 397-427.

J. S. Roucek, "Public Opinion in the Totalitarian States: Its Revolutionary and Ideological Character," *Social Science*, XIX (April, 1944), pp. 87-93.

C. F. Schmid, "The Measurement of Public Opinion," *Sociology and Social Research*, XXXIV (November-December, 1949), pp. 83-91.

Mapheus Smith, "Social Situation, Social Behavior, Social Group," *Psychological Review*, LII (July, 1945), pp. 224-229.

J. H. Springarm, *Radio Is Yours*, Public Affairs Pamphlet, No. 121 (New York: 1946).

Anselm Strauss, "The Concept of Attitude in Social Psychology," *Journal of Psychology*, XIX (April, 1945), pp. 329-339.

Francis G. Wilson, "James Bryce on Public Opinion: Fifty Years Later," *Public Opinion Quarterly*, III (July, 1939), pp. 420-435.

—— "Public Opinion in the Theory of Democracy," *Thought*, XX (June, 1945), pp. 235-252.

Elizabeth C. Winship and Gordon W. Allport, "Do Rosy Headlines Sell Newspapers?" *Public Opinion Quarterly*, VII (1943), pp. 205-209.

Kimball Young, "Comments on the Nature of 'Public' and 'Public Opinion,'" *International Journal of Opinion and Attitude Research*, II (1948), pp. 385-392.

CHAPTER XXIV

Propaganda

Propaganda is the deliberate effort to control the behavior and relationships of social groups through the use of methods which affect the feelings and attitudes of the individuals who make up the groups.[1] Since democratic societies designedly lay their citizens open to a variety of influences, and since these will inevitably include professional propagandists, it is important to begin our discussion with a clear-cut conception of the basic nature of the propagandistic process. In general use, "propaganda" has had such a diffuse meaning as to be worthless for purposes of discussion, inasmuch as most people simply define it as the purveying of lies by conscienceless writers and speakers. Such a definition at once makes one an easy mark for skilled propaganda and prevents one from understanding its methods and purposes.

We should underscore the consideration that propaganda operates according to plans instead of using its weapons in hit-or-miss fashion.[2] Its targets consist essentially of analyzed groups or types of persons whose probable reactions may be estimated in advance. The specific feelings and attitudes to be brought about are dealt with in terms of ultimate rather than merely immediate behavior responses. The true or false information, the manipulations of logic and the symbolic objects or ideas to be used are given careful analysis. The *media* or avenues to be utilized in reaching the target individuals are marshalled accordingly, and as far as possible the indirect as well as the direct effects of the appeal are predicted. It is in this sense of carefully planned activity that propaganda becomes a relatively new sort of social force, and that an understanding of the characteristics and objectives of propaganda becomes the chief defense of a democratic people against the assault of the false propagandist.

Such scientific propaganda is a comparatively recent development. We

---

[1] For other definitions see William W. Biddle, *Propaganda and Education* (New York: Bureau of Publications, Teachers College, Columbia University, 1932, p. 2; Leonard W. Doob, *Propaganda* (New York: Henry Holt and Co., 1935), pp. 74-76; Harold D. Lasswell, "Propaganda," in *Encyclopædia of the Social Sciences*, VI, pp. 521-526; Charles Bird, *Social Psychology* (New York: D. Appleton-Century Co., 1940), p. 310; Edward B. Reuter, *Handbook of Sociology* (New York: Dryden Press, 1941), p. 147.

[2] See Bird, *op. cit.*, p. 308; Harry S. Sullivan, "Psychiatric Aspects of Morale," *American Journal of Sociology*, XLVII (November, 1941), pp. 277-301.

shall see later how recent it is, but meanwhile we must establish thorough certainty of its sociological characteristics. During recent years the field of propaganda analysis, leading toward various more or less contrasting consequences, has revealed much in this connection. Such study, as Smith has shown,[3] has made propagandists more conscious of their own methods and techniques, and has besides revealed them to scholars.[4] But it has also stimulated the already live skepticism of Americans regarding all sources of information, and has alternatively led individuals to demand on one hand an absolute freedom of expression or, at the other extreme, a maximum of "desirable" censorship. Finally, perhaps, it has led toward counter-measures which may protect at least the informed American public against the inroads of anti-American propaganda. In a mature review of the sociological aspects of modern propaganda we must consider directly the motives which may underlie it, its relations to advertising, education and other organized approaches to social behavior, its primary targets, the basic weapons used, and the kinds of effects achieved by the use of those weapons.

The Motives of Propaganda

The motive of the propagandist is ultimately to influence the behavior of individuals and groups whose actions affect his own safety and welfare.[5] To define propaganda as the dishonest profession of conscious liars is, as we have said, to make a useless and even dangerous generalization, even though such propagandists as Viereck have accepted it. Accordingly one does not properly consider propaganda as necessarily the propagation of wrong views by questionable methods, or attempt to define it at all in terms of the rightness or wrongness of motives.

Some significance may be attached here to the kinds of groups or interests which may engage in the process of propaganda. It has been shown repeatedly that every pressure group within a national society may resort to its methods. Moreover, one cannot doubt that groups and organizations whose objectives must be considered socially constructive and even altruistic have used the whole range of the weapons in the arsenal of propaganda. The United States Public Health Service, for example, has been the central force in a campaign to establish a new

---

[3] B. L. Smith, "Propaganda Analysis and the Science of Democracy," *Public Opinion Quarterly*, V, No. 2, pp. 250 ff.

[4] See Clyde R. Miller, "Some Comments on Propaganda Analysis and the Science of Democracy," *Public Opinion Quarterly*, V, pp. 657-665.

[5] For an excellent statement, see Bird, *op. cit.*, pp. 306-308. George Creel, "Propaganda and Morale," *American Journal of Sociology*, XLVII (November, 1941), pp. 340-351, is very clear; for an opposed view, see George S. Viereck, *infra cit.*, p. 342. An earlier recognition of the contention of this section is in E. L. Bernays, "Manipulating Public Opinion," *American Journal of Sociology*, XXXIII (May, 1928), 958-971.

pattern of American attitudes toward venereal disease as a necessary preliminary to a campaign for its medical control. The American Red Cross does not hesitate to make an appeal to emotion through every variety of means possible. In these, as in, for example, the hardly comparable efforts of the Anti-Saloon League,[6] one sees at once the methods of propaganda and the motives of "men of good will." Nor can a long list of civic organizations, businessmen's groups, farmers' associations, even professional and educational interests, be accused successfully of having detructive aims or dishonest motives. Yet it would be easy to demonstrate that all these, and others like them, have used and continue to use the methods of propaganda.

We might even demonstrate that false propaganda, using fictitious information and exciting unjustified emotions, has been used for what most people would regard as socially constructive and desirable purposes, but we cannot fail to comment that this has been, even from a pragmatic point of view, unfortunate. The sober fact is that the most effective propaganda rests upon verifiable information, can readily justify itself in terms of the real interests of the target group, and summarily can show a genuine commonality of interest among the individuals who comprise that group.

George Creel has recently [7] demonstrated this contention in the record of Thomas Paine, master protagonist of the American Revolution. Like other leaders of causes which can justify themselves to the ordinary man by relying on frankness and truth, Paine was always in a position to prove his contentions. He maintained his influence because subsequent events and revelations served to make clear the honesty and insight with which he worked. However, the essential appeal to emotion is always dramatically present in his essays, and he does not hesitate to make his reader aware of it. Creel himself, with the help of Guy Stanton Ford and other scholars, carried on through the Committee on Public Information such a propaganda campaign at the time of the First World War. Despite criticism from various quarters the Committee refused to issue false atrocity stories or otherwise to depart from authentic appeals to the American people. Numerous unofficial rivals, of course, did not hesitate to do so, with the result that sooner or later their protestations lost the power to affect the general public.

It is, as a matter of fact, largely the activity of the irresponsible lay propagandists during the years between 1915 and 1918 which gave the term "propaganda" its unfortunate connotation to most of the American people. One need not doubt the positive intention of the over-zealous

---

[6] Peter H. Odegard, *Pressure Politics—The Story of the Anti-Saloon League* (New York: Columbia University Press, 1928) *passim.*

[7] *Loc. cit.,* pp. 343-346.

patriots of those years in their manufacture of information and their effort to create as much and as intense patriotic emotion as possible, but one does see that their ultimate accomplishment, after the passage of years, was in a measure to undermine confidence and unity among the people. It is the long-term result which proves their error and, at the same time, reveals the essential weakness of the false propagandist.

Education and Propaganda

It has not been easy to distinguish between education and propaganda. Nearly every writer on the subject of propaganda has addressed himself to the task of making such a distinction.[8] The scholars have concerned themselves so definitely with the matter, perhaps, because laymen have persisted in a series of plausible but generally useless contradistinctions. Woddy [9] has listed the popular distinctions, with a concise critique of each. Among other inadequate contrasts he points out: the view that education is the indoctrination of children, propaganda that of adults; the view that education is by definition what schools do, propaganda any other effort to mold thinking; the idea that education consists of teaching truth, propaganda of teaching lies; the notion that education is rational and propaganda necessarily irrational; the contention that education may be distinguished because its contents are desirable, while those of propaganda are undesirable; the calling of any effort to promote the general welfare "education," any support of special interests "propaganda"; the insistence that education supports while propaganda always attacks the moral values and standards of the society; the view that education is "open-minded," propaganda "narrow-minded"; and the argument that education is by definition a counter-argument against propaganda.

By way of contrast, Lasswell has suggested that although there are no hard and fast differences of method or of types of content, education as a process of indoctrination seeks to promulgate a skill, mental or physical, as its primary objective,[10] while propaganda regards its content ("subject matter") as always secondary, a means to the end of securing some immediately desired kind of behavior.[11] This obviously makes the differ-

---

[8] See, for instance, Frederick E. Lumley, *The Propaganda Menace* (New York: D. Appleton-Century Co., 1933), pp. 301-329; Doob, *op. cit.*, pp. 79-87; Biddle, *op. cit.*, especially pp. 10-19; Carroll H. Woddy, "Education and Propaganda," *The Annals of the American Academy of Political and Social Science*, CLXXIX (May, 1935), pp. 227-239; and Bird, *op. cit.*, p. 309. For the authorities who make no distinction between propaganda and education, see Harwood L. Childs, *An Introduction to Public Opinion* (New York: John Wiley and Sons, 1940), p. 88.

[9] *Loc. cit., passim.*

[10] This definition differs from those given in chapter IX, "Education," but there is no necessary conflict. The difference is rather one of emphasis and point of view.

[11] *Loc. cit.*

ences between the two processes matters of degree rather than of kind, but does provide a measure of such difference. Again, Bird [12] observes that propaganda proceeds primarily by the use of suggestion toward an emotional objective, while education uses, principally, the mental process of inquiry or investigation of detail.

Obviously enough, modern education seeks broad goals of improvement of the social attitudes and behavior of the maturing citizen, and in this sense verges on propaganda. Also, apparently, modern educators use pedagogic techniques other than pure memorization and drill, and therefore to a degree must use methods which might be described as propagandistic. However, it may be conceded that these are incidental to the major concern of education, which is as Lasswell describes it, and to the major methods as Bird suggests. We might agree then that a substantial working distinction between the two processes consists first of the contrast between the informative objective of the one, the emotionally directive aim of the other; and secondly in the relatively limited motive of education as compared to propaganda, the latter being consciously devised to bring about behavior which is not necessarily expressed in its content.

This whole question rests at last upon the hidden argument as to whether propaganda is inevitably invidious, and has its origin in the desire of educators to avoid charges that they practice "propaganda" in the popular sense of the term. One might suggest that even the most highly developed philosopher or scientist could not teach entirely without the use of emotional suggestion, that his viewpoint regarding society is very likely to permeate his teaching. It is fair to question again, though, the supposition that this implies that education is therefore inevitably meretricious. We may indeed suggest that, far from being sharply contrasted processes antithetical in every way, education and propaganda are processes of such a nature that any practical segregation of them is unlikely. This would leave the question of desirability or undesirability thus: if the teacher, the editor, the minister, the reporter or other professional man who deals in the molding of thoughts or feelings does so with social objectives which may be regarded as desirable, then his activity is also desirable. If, on the other hand, his objectives are not desirable, then his activities are equally to be deplored whether they are primarily educational or propagandistic. Dickens' character who taught small boys to pick pockets skilfully was not guilty of propaganda, but he was nevertheless guilty. Education, like propaganda, must be judged in terms of its aims and its products. Propaganda, like education, may be good or bad, but again like education it is not necessarily either.

---

[12] Bird, *op. cit.*, p. 309.

Advertising and Propaganda

More briefly we may consider another source of disturbance to many laymen and some scholars, the discrimination between advertising and propaganda. Primarily, of course, advertising has the purpose of creating a favorable attitude among prospective customers for a product or a commercial establishment, a purpose much more limited than that of propaganda. As Harold Brown [13] has suggested, this may be distinction enough, inasmuch as the skilled producer of advertising uses methods similar to those of the propagandist. Certainly works such as that of Link [14] suggest that modern advertisers study their methods and targets as thoroughly as any propaganda agency, and to much the same purpose of planning the appeal.

Commercial Propaganda. Doob points out that "commercial propaganda" goes farther than the step of advertising through purchased space or openly labeled advertisements. "Space-grabbing" and the work of the "public relations counsel" he puts into the same category.[15] The former is self-explanatory as being the achievement of getting free and unlabeled advertising from newspapers and periodicals. The latter, the representative who is not retained for direct advertising so much as for his ability to bring about indirect advances in the social status of the client, carries on a program evenly matched with broader forms of propaganda.

Advertising. It has been shown by Doob and others that advertising, defined in the narrow sense of a direct commercial appeal, may effectively be paired with propaganda, and may even improve its economic effectiveness as a result. This combination of commercial representations with efforts to affect the attitudes of hearers toward social policies has been demonstrated most skilfully in radio advertising. The Ford Sunday Evening Hour is one of many programs in which the combination is clear. A minimum of commercial reference is permitted, the body of the program is devoted to excellent music, and a brief commentary on current affairs is inserted. The result is likely to be that many hearers will associate the voice of the commentator with the prestige of the sponsor and both with the impressive music, so that an emotional transfer from one portion of the offering to another will strengthen all. A number of other examples could be cited, but it remains true nevertheless that as entities the projects fall into the category of advertising. During the war period there was a general tendency to emphasize patriotic themes in

---

[13] Harold Chapman Brown, "Advertising and Propaganda," *International Journal of Ethics*, XL, 39-55.

[14] Henry C. Link, *New Psychology of Selling and Advertising* (New York: The Macmillan Co., 1932).

[15] Doob, *op. cit.*, pp. 180-205.

commercial radio broadcasts. These tended to strengthen national morale and they had a propaganda value, but even so it may be admitted that the patriotic theme had at least in part a commercial intent.

Radio. Radio has re-emphasized that the most effective advertising is indirect, a by-product of entertainment or propaganda. The principle involved has long operated in the field of visual advertising, where advertising material which is esthetically pleasing has proved more effective than that which is merely informative. The appeal to the emotions and the senses created by photographs of children or lovely young women is a better argument for almost any product than a statement of specifications or technical characteristics. It is particularly significant that the automobile industry has for years advertised on this principle, and that even the great pharmaceutical concerns have done likewise. Again, some of the most effective "commercials" are the broadcasts of news commentators. It is of course impossible that all of these men should be able to exclude editorial comment from their renditions of the news, and some of them make a considerable point of interpretation and prediction. It becomes equally impossible that propaganda, in the sociological sense, should be excluded. Thus while advertising is presumed to aim merely at the public reception of a commercial interest, it may go considerably farther. But again, it is the nature or the objective of the implied propaganda contained in advertising which should govern any evaluation of it, not the mere fact that propaganda exists.

The Targets of Propaganda

We have said that propaganda seeks to affect the relationships of social groups by molding the feelings and attitudes of individuals, and that it is likely to be predicated on a careful analysis of the "target" group. While Lasswell among others [16] has emphasized this point, we should make a careful analysis of what it means. The target of propaganda is seldom anything so nebulous as "the masses" or "the public," but usually a carefully delimited and delineated type or kind of person. As an example the pro-fascist propaganda in the United States during prewar years was directed, first of all, at the minds of young men and women. It took into account the attitudes toward war bred into them by the postwar generation. It considered that, as the individuals whose sacrifices during a war are most poignant, they are likely to react against the prospect of another war. Accordingly, through numerous mouthpieces, they were encouraged to believe that the oncoming struggle represented the wilful destruc-

---

[16] Harold D. Lasswell, "The Person: Subject and Object of Propaganda": *Annals of the American Academy of Political and Social Science*, CLXXIX (May, 1935), pp. 187 ff.

tion of the young by the old, the destruction of young men to save old empires, the deliberate subordination of their lives and hopes to those of distant or disreputable economic interests.

Metropolitan Region. We cannot bespeak too strongly the sociological truism that a metropolitan society is a mosaic of differing interest-groups, and that the American people have long since moved into a metropolitan phase. Under the conditions of living in the metropolis individual problems of adjustment tend to merge with those of whole interest groups, and individual identity to disappear effectively in the development of central interests. Thus we find "organized labor" replacing the individual worker as a bargainer for industrial betterment, various associations and organizations of business and industrial interests replacing the separate entrepreneur or manufacturer in public affairs, and in general a growing consciousness among individuals of existing, in their relations to other interests, as parts or participants of specific groups whose general situation is the same. It is this characteristic which at once makes the propagandist necessary and inevitable, and highly effective in getting rapid results.

Measurements of Attitudes. Thus he is able to calculate, or to discover by field analysis with standardized attitude scales, the general reaction tendencies of his selected target-group. Through the pioneering efforts of men like L. L. Thurstone [17] and G. W. Allport the measurement of attitudes in individuals has begun to approach precision or at least a high degree of accuracy. However, even without recourse to such refined means the propagandist may assess the probable reactions of his target group and set up his appeal accordingly. That he may do so ineffectively is shown by the complete failure of the effort during 1941 to mobilize American women against the program of national defense, an effort admittedly financed in part by Axis agents. This followed from a complete misapprehension of the actual feelings of the target group, the mothers and wives of potential soldiers, rather than from failure to select the group and study methods of making a selective appeal.

War Propaganda. Fragmentary materials indicate that the German propaganda campaign which so seriously weakened French resistance in 1940 was a good example of selective propaganda. A long strategic campaign covering several years and utilizing the "kept" press, the radio, a sizable corps of "fifth columnists" in whispering campaigns, organized the assault

---

[17] See, for example: L. L. Thurstone, "Attitudes can be Measured," *American Journal of Sociology*, XXXIII (January, 1928), pp. 529-545, and "Theory of Attitude Measurement," *Psychological Review*, XXXVI, pp. 226-41; G. A. Allport, "A Test for Ascendance-Submission," *Journal of Abnormal and Social Psychology*, XXIII (Jan., 1928), pp. 118-136.

upon selected groups of the French people. It was dinned into youth that the last war had accomplished nothing but the wrecking of their parents' lives, and that this one could have no other effect. They were told with an infinite variation that they themselves had nothing to fight for, that the civilization around them was corrupt and decadent, that their leadership was completely incompetent and meretricious. The French peasant was reminded of the disaster of inflation, of the corruption of metropolitan politics, of the vast destruction of his resources which a long war meant. French women were influenced by a variety of appeals, and *le petit bourgeois*, the small business man, was infected with the conviction that the national government could represent only the extreme Left or the extreme Right, militant labor or militant capital. All together were submitted to a continuous pressure designed to reduce their confidence in one another and in the national society.

Consequently, when the appropriate time came, it was not difficult for the Reich Propaganda Ministry to bring about a social-psychological dissolution of French resistance. American correspondents report vividly the disorganization, bordering on sheer panic, that spread through the Republic on the heels of military defeats. In or out of uniform, Frenchmen were not prepared to maintain a stoical attitude toward reverses. The spectacle recorded by William L. Shirer [18] shows the *debacle* of France to be as much a sociological as a military defeat, in the sense that the German conquest was out of all proportion to German military achievements. Considerable credit must be given to the Propaganda Ministry for this accomplishment, and sober attention to the fact that there had never been any effective measures taken to forestall it.

One should observe that the selective pro-fascist propaganda continued in the United States through at least a part of the winter of 1941-1942. In it racial groups were appealed to, youth were told the old story of exploitation by wealth and their elders. A Boston source clarioned that Roosevelt and Churchill brought about the Japanese war for selfish personal reasons. A west-coast source described our military action as an aggression undertaken to protect British investments. A propaganda weekly sought to mobilize anti-Russian feeling wherever it existed, and to discredit the President and the War Administration as the *agents-provocateurs* of ultimate revolution.

In all this, if space were adequate, one could show the definition and delimitation of target groups. Labor becomes one, and even separate segments of organized labor. Youth as potential fighters make up another. The middle class is warned, directly and indirectly, against the machinations of labor on one hand and of "big business" on the other.

---

[18] William L. Shirer, *Berlin Diary* (New York: Alfred A. Knopf, 1941), especially pp. 394-419.

Wherever the skilled propagandist is at work, there are no undefined targets. Always are the situations and the consequent tendencies of specific groups aimed at in the campaign.

The Aims of Propaganda

Propaganda is always aggressive. By its very nature it seeks to supplant some feelings and attitudes with others or to create attitudes and feelings which did not previously exist. On the other hand, there are two diverse general aims of propaganda. One is that of "negative" propaganda, which looks toward the weakening or dissolution of social groups. The other is "positive" propaganda, which looks toward the building of morale, the strengthening of the unity of the target groups.

It is the first of these which is most generally recognized as *ipso facto* propaganda, and has had associated with it the use of false materials and the concealment of sources and motives. The creation of disunity can be attained as well through the achievement of confusion, contradiction and uncertainty as by any other means, so that false materials can be effective at least for a time. Even if the materials are later discredited, the disunity thus created is likely to persist.

There is no essential distinction of method between negative and positive propaganda. All of the same weapons may be employed, although their use must be attuned to the broad purpose of the appeal. What is important to repeat here is that propaganda aims always at *affecting subsequent group behavior by first affecting the feelings of individuals.* Any effect upon the individual is incidental, a means by which the aim of social control may be attained.

The Weapons of Propaganda

As for basic weapons, there are two in the arsenal of the propagandist. One is the force of the "folkways" and "mores," which is to say of the traditions and prejudices and beliefs generally accepted in the society. The other is the force of the psychological tendencies of individuals. In actual operation the two are scarcely separable, but they may be considered apart for purposes of convenience.

The Use of Traditional Background. Regarding the first, that of social tradition, it has often been observed that individuals tend to accept established ideas uncritically. However one may explain it the fact remains that ideas and attitudes tend to seem "normal" or "reasonable" almost in proportion to their familiarity. The apparent gap between the two basic weapons is bridged, indeed, largely by the simple fact that most individuals respond emotionally as well as uncritically to any suggestion based upon traditional attitudes. Habit, even mental habit, is an easy master whom one obeys without recognizing one's obedience.

It has often been asserted that the United States would make an easy target for "negative" propaganda because of the great diversity of racial and cultural groups particularly within her metropolitan populations. The background of cultural conflict involving such groups is certainly impressive, so much so indeed that the German propaganda minister once was quoted as believing national unity in America impossible. This appearance has apparently been deceptive, not only for the fascist propagandists but for others as well, since extremists of various stripes have failed signally to get any substantial results from appeals to American minority groups. It may be as Wirth implies, that[19] the members of such groups feel a unity in the common American aspirations toward security and freedom which overbalances the effects of traditional group antago-- nisms. The danger, if any exists, would appear to be that of the susceptibility of some segments of the native white population to inflammatory suggestions against the minorities.

The traditional status of any subordinate group can be used to advantage in negative propaganda against any social group or tendency with which they may be associated. Thus the Negro in the South and in northern cities, the immigrant in every region in which immigration from abroad has been important, women in the onslaught against various progressive movements, Catholics and Jews, all have been made to bear the brunt of attacks. In every case mentioned a traditional attitude has underlain an emotional appeal, and as often as not the group used has been, like the Jews in modern Germany, nothing more than a "whipping boy" for the propagandist.

Individual Psychological Tendencies. The second of the weapons we may consider to be existing knowledge of the general tendencies of the human mind regarded as an entity. Such knowledge leads to the use, according to Biddle, of suggestion, indirect and direct emotional appeals, and designed argumentation.[20] Each of these is a subordinate weapon usable for the purpose of controlling emotional reactions. The human tendency toward *transference* (the displacement of emotional reaction from one idea or object to another), the tendency to accept uncritically emotional appeals which are offered indirectly, the parallel tendency to respond favorably to an appeal based upon a familiar emotional association, the essential tendency to "suggestibility" which leads individuals to emulate crowd or group responses, and the tendency to respond emo-

[19] Louis Wirth, "Morale and Minority Groups," *American Journal of Sociology,* XLVII (November, 1941), pp. 415 ff.
[20] William W. Biddle, "A Psychological Definition of Propaganda," *Journal of Abnormal and Social Psychology,* XXVI (1931), pp. 283-295.

tionally to carefully stated argument, all are parts of the same pattern of mental behavior. This matter can scarcely be made simple or treated adequately in a paragraph, but it is the essence of the manipulation of individual behavior by the propagandist.

If we add to these the more familiar devices of the logical fallacy and the deliberate lie we shall have listed approximately the total of the sub-ordinate devices by means of which propaganda sets in motion its twin weapons of social attitude and individual emotion. These last named are of course not far apart, in that the one baldly states untruth while the other more or less emphatically implies it. In point of fact, the use of *transference* may be regarded as a form of logical fallacy, in that the feeling transferred, say, from a musical composition to the political philosophy identified with it does involve an elision at least analogous with illogic.

Manipulation of Symbols. Skilled propagandists, it should be noted, do not by any means limit themselves to the use of words. Rather, the tangible symbol is often an even more important instrument. Among the symbols used, for instance, in the Nazi propaganda within Germany one would have to include not only the swastika and the innumerable banners draped about the cities, the uniforms and the ubiquitous salute, the "Heil Hitler" and the badges and ribbons, but also the music of Richard Wagner and others, the lay figures of German mythology, the heroes of propagandistic drama, together with works produced by various Nazi sculptors and other artists. All of these together comprise the greatest onslaught against the suggestibility of a people ever attempted, and all together they must have led the individual German to suspect that, if he felt any sense of Nazi oppression or antagonism, he was very much alone.[21] By such means, and by his own participation in the carnival of symbols, even the non-Nazi individual was led to accept the inevitability of the movement by suggestion and to identify himself with it.

To all of this was added the steady stream of argument, logical or informational, which poured from the Nazi press and radio. Further, symbolic use was made of actions and of "stereotypes," those abstract notions whose origins and meanings are so difficult to define. One may recall the masterful use of symbolic acts by Mahatma Gandhi, who could appeal strongly to his people by refusing to eat, by weaving a bit of cloth or by evaporating a pan of sea water and eating the salty residuum. Hitler's use of "The" Jew as a stereotype of cupidity, cunning, degenerate lasciviousness, is probably the masterpiece of modern times, inasmuch as it made possible the use of evidence of the competitive efficiency of "The" Jew

---

[21] See Fritz Morstein Marx, "State Propaganda in Germany," especially pp. 16-21, in Harwood L. Childs, ed., *Propaganda and Dictatorship* (Princeton: Princeton University Press, 1936).

to prove his inferiority of character and motive. Such stereotypes must be regarded as symbols, even when they are not made visible. The modern cartoonist, however, has converted nearly all of them into tangible, conventionalized representations.

The Use of Logical Fallacies. The logical fallacies used in false propaganda can be recited briefly. Inasmuch as a correct or verifiable propaganda has no need of them, they are of course limited to the cause which cannot otherwise justify itself. In a brief but cogent volume Alfred and Elizabeth Briant Lee have described and exemplified the major fallacies.[22] Their list includes "name calling," "the glittering generality," "transfer," "the testimonial," "plain folks," "card stacking" and "the band wagon." Each of these techniques, with its self-explanatory name, is essentially an appeal to feelings rather than an argument which could withstand the cold test of logic. Alternatively they either lead the target individual to transfer feelings (transfer, the testimonial, plain folks) or to diffuse an existing attitude (the glittering generality, card stacking, the band wagon, name calling) so as to feel for or against the subject the propagandist has immediately in hand. In either case they rest upon the observation that emotion, or feeling, has certain strategic advantages over the appeal to reason.

In substance these advantages are that emotion is essentially uncritical, that relatively speaking one may "feel" instantaneously but "think" only more slowly, that there is a much greater variation in capacity to think through an argument than in the possible reactions to an emotional appeal, that rational thought tends to be defined and limited while emotion tends to be diffused and broad, and that in summary emotion is much more "contagious" than any other mental activity. All of these points are heavily documented in the field of social psychology, and together they mean that control of the emotionality of man is the surest way toward control of his behavior.

The Use of the Lie. A last item to be considered is the use of the lie as a technique of propaganda. As a two-edged sword which inevitably cuts both ways, the lie is studiously avoided by propagandists who can afford to use truthful information, but in other hands it does have, as we have suggested, a definite value. The Propaganda Ministry of the Third Reich used the lie successfully for several purposes, chief among them the creation of confusion. Thus, for example, it was possible to create such confusion in France by issuing an unending series of contradictory statements. In both the French campaign of 1940 and the Russian campaign of 1941 the Germans were able to gain at least part of the reward for

[22] Alfred McClung Lee and Elizabeth Briant Lee, *The Fine Art of Propaganda* (New York: Harcourt, Brace and Co., 1939).

military victories by merely claiming the destruction of enemy forces. Such claims actually totaled in 1941 as much as the official German estimates of Russian man- and machine-power.

The Soviet Refinements. After the defeat of nazism in 1945, Communist techniques of usurpation and expansion represented the culmination of a coordinated effort by the previous generations of skilled propagandists. Using propaganda as their basic technique, the Soviets have developed a "science of victory" which the Reds themselves consider to be their infallible secret of success.[23] The democratic forces of the world, headed by the United States, have been limping behind the persistent and aggressive Soviet propaganda campaigns.

American Morale and Propaganda

This brings us to the central point regarding propaganda and its motives. The widespread and carefully nurtured notion that all propaganda must be false is a first premise for the conclusion that any cause which uses propaganda must therefore be false also. The citizen who is convinced of this may very well reason that his own government and leadership cannot take any deliberate action to maintain morale without becoming suspect. This idea, a useful weapon of negative propaganda, appears to have been "sold" to the French people and leadership before 1940,[24] so that they were paralyzed in the face of a continuous German onslaught against French morale.

The essential reality is that positive propaganda, utilizing proved fact and honest logic as its base, may fairly use the emotional and symbolic devices which affect individual behavior. In modern times any right cause which is not defended by such a propaganda is virtually certain to be lost or crippled, and the American war effort might have been no exception. It is not the duty of a democratic society to make itself defenseless in the field of opinion, but rather to meet propaganda with propaganda, pitting the correct and justified against the false and negative.[25] For the citizen as a participant in the struggle, it is of the utmost importance to realize that morale-building propaganda is as much a weapon for his own defense as the *materiel* used by the army and navy, justified at once by the same practical considerations and the same ultimate reliance upon the values of democratic progress.

[23] Stefan T. Possony, *A Century of Conflict* (Chicago: Henry Regnery Co., 1953).
[24] See Pierre Cot, "Morale in France During the War," *American Journal of Sociology*, CLXXIX (November, 1941), pp. 439-451.
[25] For a good statement of this position see George E. G. Catlin, "The Role of Propaganda in a Democracy," *Annals of The American Academy of Political and Social Science*, CLXXIX (May, 1935), pp. 219-226.

Summary

The word "propaganda" has come to have an opprobrious connotation since the 1920's and 1930's as a result of revelations that the "atrocities" attributed to Germany during the invasion of Belgium in World War I were untrue, although proletarian critics defended the use of propaganda in fiction and poetry, claiming that all "good" literature has been propaganda. A striking and apparently successful use of propaganda was made during this period by fascism and nazism—and ever since by communism.

Although the use of propaganda on the international front has been looked upon as a sort of necessary evil, actually the use of propaganda by American business has been used to a remarkably successful degree. Commercial advertising, most types of political oratory, and most official releases to the newspapers and radio and television stations by governments and organizations are outstanding examples of current propaganda. The manipulation of public opinion, by appeal to the fears, emotions, and prejudices of groups of people in such a way as to persuade them to undertake, or stop, a desired action, or to inculcate in them a desired attitude, is one of the most striking characteristics of the modern means of social control. Urbanization and increased communication facilities have made the average man everywhere, and especially in the United States and in the totalitarian countries, a subject of persuasion in an ever-expanding and increasingly competitive marketplace of ideas. In fact, the basic difference between the totalitarian systems and the system of the democratic countries is that the dictatorships monopolize the "thought control," while the democratic regimes allow a comparatively free flow of competitive ideas not only in the area of economic life but also in politics.

The extensive—and the growing use of—propaganda must not blind us, however, to the fact that propaganda is neither bad nor good—scientifically speaking. The final stamp of approval or disapproval depends upon what cause the particular group propounds. From the American point of view, surely the American cause is "right"; but from the Soviet point of view, any pro-Soviet cause is also "right." The fact remains, however, that, in modern times, any right cause that is not defended by propaganda is virtually certain to be lost or crippled, as the American war and post-war efforts have shown. It is not the duty of a democratic society to make itself defenseless in the field of opinion, but rather to meet propaganda with propaganda, pitting the correct and justified against the false and negative.[26] For the citizen as a participant in the struggle, it is of

---

[26] For a good statement of this position see George E. G. Catlin, "The Role of Propaganda in a Democracy," *Annals of The American Academy of Political and Social Science*, CLXXIX (May, 1935), pp. 219-226.

utmost importance to realize that morale-building propaganda, and the propaganda on the international scale favoring the American cause, is as much a weapon for his own defense as the materiel used by the army, navy, and air forces, justified at once by the same practical considerations and the same ultimate reliance upon the values of democratic progress.

QUESTIONS

1. Why is the scientific study of propaganda of such a recent origin?
2. What was the original meaning of the word propaganda?
3. What are the motives of propaganda?
4. Why was Thomas Paine such a master propagandist?
5. What is the relation of education to propaganda?
6. What are the commercial uses of propaganda?
7. What are the numerous targets of propaganda?
8. How are the attitudes measured?
9. What were the main features of propaganda during World War I?
10. What were the main features of propaganda during World War II?
11. Why is propaganda always aggressive?
12. How does propaganda use the traditional background?
13. What are the psychological tendencies used by propaganda?
14. How are the symbols manipulated?
15. How are logical fallacies used?
16. How was German propaganda against Britain conducted?
17. Show the relation of American morale to propaganda.
18. What is the relation of propaganda to the aims of American democracy?

SUGGESTED TOPICS FOR TERM PAPERS AND FURTHER RESEARCH

1. Interest criteria in propaganda analysis.
2. How education is involved in propaganda.
3. How does propaganda influence educational work?
4. The propaganda for morale.
5. The use of propaganda by business.
6. The use of posters in propaganda.
7. The influence of propaganda among American minorities.
8. The pressures exerted by religious groups on radio.
9. The personal influence in propaganda.
10. The latest developments in scientific study of propaganda.

BIBLIOGRAPHY

Books

F. C. Bartlett, *Political Propaganda* (Cambridge, England: Cambridge University Press, 1940), a useful analysis of propaganda, its manner of political dissemination, and its effect upon its recipients.

H. M. Baus, *Public Relations at Work* (New York: Harper and Brothers, 1948). An over-all description of the elements, tools, practices, and techniques of public relations.

Edward L. Bernays, *Propaganda* (New York: Horace Liveright, 1928). Useful as one of the pioneer works in this field. Clearly and interestingly written, but very general in its treatment.

William W. Biddle, *Propaganda and Education* (New York: Bureau of Publications, Teachers College, Columbia University, 1932). The complex interrelation between the methods and objectives of education and propaganda is treated at length. The work is useful in supplying concrete demonstrations of the contrasts between its title processes.

Charles Bird, *Social Psychology* (New York: D. Appleton-Century Co., 1940). The chapters dealing with propaganda and public opinion are possibly the most explicit in print. The viewpoint of the psychologist regarding propaganda is made clear, especially in so far as it is supplementary to that of the sociologist.

G. L. Bird and F. E. Merwin, eds., *The Newspaper and Society* (New York: Prentice-Hall, 1942). A valuable collection of studies on the newspapers in the United States, which includes analyses of the nature of public opinion, propaganda, freedom of the press, the institutional impact of the press on the society, and the techniques of presentation.

Leonard Bloomfield, *Language* (New York: Henry Holt and Co., 1933), a penetrating study of the characteristics, nature, and meaning of language, dealing with the problem of meaning and the function of language as a propaganda weapon.

H. Cantril, *Gauging Public Opinion* (Princeton: Princeton University Press, 1943). An excellent exposition, not overly technical, of the methods followed in the analysis of public opinion. The student will find in it particularly clear demonstration of the safeguards against errors of research in public opinion.

Wallace Carroll, *Persuade or Perish* (Boston: Houghton Mifflin Co., 1948). A history of the psychological warfare waged by America against the Axis powers in Europe.

Zechariah Chafee, Jr., *Government and Mass Communications* (Chicago: University of Chicago Press, 1947). By and large this report by the Commission on Freedom of the Press comes out against government control.

Chicago University, Graduate Library School, *Print, Radio and Film in a Democracy* (Chicago: University of Chicago Press, 1942). Here is a well-organized statement of the ways in which public opinion is affected, inadvertently as well as purposefully, by materials presented through these channels. The student will find excellent illustrative and reference aids in this compilation.

Harwood L. Childs, *Propaganda and Dictatorship* (Princeton: Princeton University Press, 1936). A cogent study of the dependence of the totalitarian upon propaganda. The techniques of the European fascists as revealed here have more than historical interest.

—— *Propaganda By Short Wave* (Princeton: Princeton University Press, 1942). The role of radio in the building up of support for the embattled governments in World War II.

—— *Reference Guide to the Study of Public Opinion* (Princeton: Princeton University Press, 1934). A useful aid to the student who undertakes a research project in public opinion. Citations include standard works which are not likely to become out of date.

F. S. Cohen, *Combatting Totalitarian Propaganda* (Washington: Institute of Living Law, 1944). Significant for the insights offered into the distinctions between propaganda based very largely on falsehood and that which avoids it.

Leonard W. Doob, *Propaganda, Its Psychology and Technique* (New York: Henry Holt and Co., 1935). A very well organized, clearly stated interpretation of the psychological bases of standard propaganda techniques.

F. S. Dunn, *War and the Minds of Men* (New York: Harper and Brothers, 1950). There is no way in which immense social problems can be scientifically attacked at the level at which their urgency thrusts themselves upon social consciousness.

Luke Ebersole, *Church Lobbying in the Nation's Capital* (New York: The Macmillan Co., 1951). An analysis.

Elmer Ellis, *Education Against Propaganda* (Seventh Yearbook of the National Council for Social Studies) (New York: National Council for Social Studies, 1937). The surest protection of a democracy against propaganda, that of domestic special interests as well as that of international politics, lies in realistic education. A thoughtful presentation of the problems modern propaganda poses for American education.

G. H. Gallup, *Guide to Public Opinion Polls* (Princeton: Princeton University Press, 1944). To understand the status, functions and nature of public opinion analysis in the United States today, this guide is an absolute necessity. Contents are factual and delineative rather than generalized.

P. H. Gibbs, *America Speaks* (Garden City: Doubleday, 1942). A good source for illustrative materials on American public opinion.

Glenn Griswold and Denny Griswold, eds., *Your Public Relations* (New York: Funk and Wagnalls, 1948). Articles by thirty-two leaders in the field of public relations discussing the various techniques of organization, fund raising, and other aspects of publicity.

Feliks Gross, ed., *European Ideologies* (New York: Philosophical Library, 1948). The best systematic presentation of the propaganda claims of the dominant ideologies.

R. B. Holtman, *Napoleonic Propaganda* (Baton Rouge, La.: State University Press, 1950). Napoleon's use of propaganda as an important tool of politics and statesmanship.

Daniel Katz, Dorwin Cartwright, Samuel Eldersveld, and Alfred McClung Lee, eds., *Public Opinion and Propaganda* (New York: The Dryden Press, 1954). A collection of readings having a wide coverage of points of view, of types of studies, and of practical and theoretical problems.

Harold D. Lasswell, "Propaganda," *Encyclopaedia of the Social Sciences*, VI, pp. 521-528. The most cogent brief statement of the nature and purposes of propaganda in print. Although the direct references are limited to World War I and domestic American propaganda, every student should be required to read the essay. *Propaganda Techniques in the World War* (New York: Alfred A. Knopf, 1927). Included here because a large part of the modern literature stems from it, this study covers adequately every important phase of World War I propaganda. Lasswell and R. D. Casey and Bruce L. Smith, *Propaganda and Promotional Activities* (Minneapolis: University of Minnesota Press, 1935). Good for demonstrating the uses of propaganda in the affairs of ordinary life.

—— *Propaganda and Dictatorship* (Princeton: Princeton University Press, 1936). Analyzes the relationship between the use of propaganda and the assumption of power by the authoritarian states.

—— and Dorothy Blumenstock, *World Revolutionary Propaganda* (New York: Alfred A. Knopf, 1939). A study of propaganda promoted by the Communist revolutionary movement in Chicago.

—— and Nathan Leites and associates, *Language of Politics* (New York: G. W. Stewart, 1949). A valuable study of the relationship of language to the communication of political ideas.

——, R. D. Casey, and B. L. Smith, *Propaganda and Promotional Activities* (Minneapolis: University of Minnesota Press, 1935). An indispensable bibliography.

—— *Propaganda, Communication and Public Opinion* (Princeton: Princeton University Press, 1946). Good bibliography.

Harold Lavine and James Wechsler, *War Propaganda and the United States* (New Haven: Yale University Press, 1940). Covers not only the general aspects of propaganda, but also both domestic and foreign attempts to control American public opinion.

Paul F. Lazarsfeld, and F. N. Stanton, *Communications Research 1948-1949* (New York: Harper and Brothers, 1949). Studies American mass media in action.

Alfred Mc. Lee and Elizabeth B. Lee, *The Fine Art of Propaganda* (New York: Harcourt, Brace and Company, 1939). The liveliest treatment of propaganda techniques. Concerned entirely with labeling and exposing the devices of false propaganda, the book succeeds in dramatizing and identifying these devices so that they are apparent to any reader.

N. Lenin, *On Propaganda* (London: Lawrence and Wishart, 1942). This essay has excellent historical value for the mature student of propaganda, especially in demonstrating the place of propaganda in the Communist program.

R. E. McMurray and Muna Lee, *The Cultural Approach* (Chapel Hill: University of North Carolina Press, 1947). An informative survey of the means employed by the principal powers, and several of the smaller ones, to disseminate information abroad about their cultures.

G. B. Munson, ed., *Twelve Decisive Battles of the Mind* (New York: Greystone Press, 1942). An important demonstration of the impact upon society of great philosophical issues, and of their conversion into rallying points of social conflict.

H. C. Peterson, *Propaganda for War* (Norman, Okla.: University of Oklahoma Press, 1939). An examination of the influence of propaganda upon the attitudes of the newspaper-reading public.

O. W. Riegel, *Mobilizing for Chaos* (New Haven: Yale University Press, 1934). A study of influence of business, finance, and industrial interests on the news, and the effect of government censorship.

F. W. Riggs, *Pressures on Congress* (New York: King Crown's Press, 1950). A study of the repeal of Chinese exclusion.

Joseph S. Roucek, "The Nature of Public Opinion and Propaganda," Chapter XVII, pp. 354-382, in Roucek, ed., *Twentieth Century Political Thought* (New York: Philosophical Library, 1946). A survey of the literature up to 1946.

Wilbur Schramm, ed., *Communications in Modern Society* (Urbana, Ill.: University of Illinois Press, 1948). Fifteen studies of the mass media.

Boris Shub, *The Choice* (New York: Duell, Sloan and Pearce, 1950). The cold war and propaganda.

H. E. Snyder and M. S. Austin, *Cultural Relations with the Occupied Countries* (Washington: American Council on Education, 1950).

Georges Sorel, *Reflections on Violence* (London: Allen and Unwin, 1915). Sorel's theory of "social myth" is one of the most interesting concepts in analyzing recent social movements.

R. E. Summers, *America's Weapons of Psychological Warfare* (New York: The H. W. Wilson Co., 1951), The Reference Shelf, Vol. 23, No. 4. One of the most valuable collections of important studies.

C. A. H. Thomson, *Overseas Information Service of the United States Government* (Washington: Brookings Institution, 1948). A thoroughly well-informed and annotated summary of the wartime operations.

Hans Zeisel, *Say it with Figures* (New York: Harper and Brothers, 1947). The statistics involved in public opinion polling; their interpretation and classification; methods of examining the public mind and tabulating the results mathematically.

Periodicals

Winston Allard, "A Test of Propaganda Values in Public Opinion Surveys," *Social Forces,* XX (1941-42), pp. 206-213.

American Journal of Sociology, "National Morale," XLVII, 3 (Chicago: University of Chicago Press, November, 1941).

Read Bain, "Morale for War and Peace," *Social Forces,* XX (1942-1943), pp. 418-425.

William W. Biddle, "A Psychological Definition of Propaganda," *Journal of Abnormal and Social Psychology,* XXVI (1931-32), pp. 283-295.

Emory S. Bogardus, "Earmarks of Propaganda," *Sociology and Social Research,* XXVI (1941-1942), pp. 272-282.

Jerome S. Bruner, "Public Opinion and America's Foreign Policy," *American Sociological Review,* IX (1944), pp. 50-56.

E. H. Carr, "Propaganda and Power," *Yale Review,* XLII (September, 1952), pp. 1-9.

"Content Analysis for the Voice of America: A Symposium," *Public Opinion Quarterly*, XVI, 4 (Winter, 1952-53), pp. 605-641.

L. W. Doob, "Goebbels' Principles of Propaganda," *ibid.*, XIV, 3 (Fall, 1950), pp. 419-442.

K. E. Ettinger, "Foreign Propaganda in America," *ibid.*, X, 3 (Fall, 1946), pp. 329-342.

William Garber, "Propaganda Analysis . . . to What Ends?," *American Journal of Sociology*, XLVIII (1941-1942), pp. 240-245.

E. F. Goldman, "Poll of Polls," *American Mercury*, LXI (1945), pp. 104-108.

Edward Y. Hartshorne, "Reactions to the Nazi Threat," *Public Opinion Quarterly*, V, pp. 625-639.

Charles R. Hoffer, "A Sociological Analysis of Propaganda," *Social Forces*, XX (1941-1942), pp. 445-448.

Richard T. LaPiere, "Propaganda and Education: the Need for Qualitative Distinction," *Sociology and Social Research*, XX (1935), pp. 18-26.

Harold D. Lasswell, "The Function of the Propagandist," *International Journal of Ethics*, XXXVIII (1927-1928), pp. 258-268. "The Triple Appeal Principle: a Contribution of Psycho-analysis to Political and Social Science," *American Journal of Sociology*, XXXVII (1931), pp. 523-528.

Alfred M. Lee, "The Analysis of Propaganda: a Clinical Summary," *ibid.*, LI (1945-1946), pp. 126-135.

—— "Interest Criteria in Propaganda Analysis," *American Sociological Review*, X (1945), pp. 282-288.

George A. Lundberg, "Public Opinion from a Behavioristic Standpoint," *American Journal of Sociology*, XXXVI (1930), pp. 387-405.

Paul A. Palmer, "Ferdinand Tonnies' Theory of Public Opinion," *Public Opinion Quarterly*, V, pp. 584-595.

Joseph S. Roucek, "American Minorities," *World Affairs Interpreter*, XXII (July, 1951), pp. 194-201; "Communism Among the Americans of Foreign Birth," *Ukrainian Quarterly*, VII (Spring, 1951), pp. 116-126.

H. L. Searless, "On the Ideological Fronts of Europe," *World Affairs Interpreter*, XII (July, 1941), pp. 196-208.

R. F. Sterba, "Some Psychological Factors in Pictorial Advertising," *Public Opinion Quarterly*, XIV (Fall, 1950), pp. 475-483.

G. G. W., "Post-War International Broadcasting," *The World Today*, V (June, 1949), pp. 258-266.

J. L. Woodward, "Making Government Opinion Research Bear Upon Operations," *American Sociological Review*, X (1944), pp. 670-677.

CHAPTER XXV

The Press

Writings and other pronouncements on the role of the press in the scheme of social control fall, mostly, into one of two classes—that of the apologists or that of the critics. In the former there is a characteristic confusion of the ideals of what the press should be with the reality that it is, and in it are the works chiefly of those who are engaged in journalism or are teachers of journalism. In the latter is the work of a large group of social scientists and popular "debunkers," based upon the assumption that the press is chiefly significant because it readily lends itself to manipulation in the interest of persons whose operations are antagonistic to public welfare. There is very little published material that is neutral and objective.[1]

The Defenders of the Press. The defenders of the press make a convincing case that as an institution it is a bulwark of democratic processes, a sound mentor for public opinion, a fair and fearless exposer of wrong and defender of right. They point to the high ethical standards to which journalists claim to adhere, to the crusading campaigns in behalf of clean politics and public decency,[2] and to the martyrs among journalists who have braved death and persecution to stand by what they believed to be right.[3] If they acknowledge that the press in other countries may be corrupt and base, it is chiefly to throw into high relief, by contrast, the supposed virtues of the American type of journalism. It is their position, usually, that the press in a democracy should have a minimum of outside control over its activities and methods, and may safely be left to govern itself in the interest of the public. Lapses from social morality, as in the

---

[1] Examples of unbiased works are the scholarly books by Lucy Maynard Salmon, *The Newspaper and Authority*, and *The Newspaper and the Historian* (both London: Oxford University Press, 1923); and the articles of Robert E. Park in the *American Journal of Sociology:* "News as a Form of Knowledge," XLV (March, 1940), pp. 669-686; "News and the Power of the Press," XLVII (July, 1941), pp. 1-11; "Morale and the News," XLVII (November, 1941), pp. 360-377.

[2] Journalistic crusading reached its climax in America with the so-called "muckrakers," most active during the early 1900's. See C. C. Regier, *The Era of the Muckrakers* (Chapel Hill: University of North Carolina Press, 1932).

[3] Notable has been Don R. Mellett of Canton, Ohio, who achieved national fame for his fight against corruption. For a different type of "martyrdom" see *Time,* January 23, 1942, in section on the "Press."

case of "yellow journalism," are considered as exceptions to the general
rule that the press is a power for beneficent social control.[4]

The Critics. The critics attack the press from many angles, but, most
convincingly, they make two cases. One is that the press is owned by
capitalists, is a capitalistic and individualistic enterprise, draws its chief
financial support from the advertising of capitalistic firms, and is necessarily tied to a defense of the *status quo* in a capitalistic society. It is
charged that the public interest is quite often a secondary consideration
to profits in the minds of those who own and control the newspapers and
magazines. It is pointed out that the press is used on many occasions to
persecute advocates of reform and to uphold the cause of the privileged
few, whether in the local community or the national life. At the same
time, so it is contended, the press gives little or no attention to either
news or opinion which might be considered detrimental to the interests
from which it draws its substance.[5]

The second convincing case made by critics is that, in catering to the
masses, the American press has appealed to the lowest of tastes and passions, playing up the sensational and sexy side of life far beyond what
would constitute a true and fair picture of the national life. The press is
blamed, in part at least, for promoting criminality by the treatment of
crime news, for undermining morality by its treatment of divorce and
scandal, and generally for lowering the tastes of the American reading
public by careless and shoddy journalism.[6]

The Need for Objectivity. To reach a clear understanding of the place
of the press in the whole complex of social control devices and agencies,
it is well at the outset to recognize that neither the extreme apologist nor
the extreme critic is in a position to analyze objectively journalistic processes and forces. Their conclusions usually arise from their starting
assumptions rather than from the evidence they examine. The safest
approach is to realize that the press of the United States is neither wholly
good nor wholly bad; it is an involved mixture of both, with a generous

---

[4] Examples of this position may be found in all textbooks in journalism, and a
number of popular books, such as Silas Bent, *Newspaper Crusaders* (New York:
McGraw-Hill Book Co., 1939).

[5] Various expressions of this point of view may be found in Frederick E. Lumley,
The Propaganda Menace (New York: The Century Co., 1933), *passim.;* Carl M.
Rosenquist, *Social Problems* (New York: Prentice-Hall, 1940), pp. 44-45; L. L.
Bernard, *Social Control in its Sociological Aspects* (New York: The Macmillan Co.,
1939), p. 597 and p. 653.

[6] George Seldes in his *Freedom of the Press* (Indianapolis: Bobbs-Merrill Co.,
1931), Appendix A, quotes nineteen charges commonly made against the press, from
an address of Dean Ackerman of Columbia University; see also Paul H. Landis, *Social
Control* (Philadelphia: J. B. Lippincott Co., 1939), pp. 189 ff.; and Harold A. Phelps,
Contemporary Social Problems (New York: Prentice-Hall, 1938), pp. 278 ff., and
p. 543.

admixture of neutral qualities, from the standpoint of social control. Often it is impossible to judge on which side its greatest influence is wielded.

Complexity of the Press

Newspapers. The "press" is a very general term, and it takes on meaning only when the large number of different enterprises which make it up are brought to mind. There is the metropolitan daily newspaper, sufficiently uniform in its characteristics to be treated as a class. Yet, within this class, distinction must be made between two sub-classes, those newspapers which lean toward the serious side of news reporting and interpretation, and those which appeal to their readers mainly by the use of sensational devices, comic strips and attention-commanding pictures. Of course the difference is one of degree, and the metropolitan newspapers of the country would range between the two extremes, most being somewhat of a compromise in the middle ground.

Besides those of the great population centers there are the daily newspapers of smaller cities and towns and those which appeal to a single interest of city-dwellers, such as the sheets which deal in "tips" on horse races. The newspapers of smaller cities and towns are probably the most standardized of journalistic products, having in common their aping of larger metropolitan papers in appearance and content. Newspaper "chains" and syndicated "features" flourish in this field.

Most towns and cities also have a number of "shoppers guides," fairly uniform in type, but ranging from those which give space only to advertisers for "puffs" to support their advertised wares, to those which develop into true neighborhood newspapers carrying items of a more personal and local nature than is possible for the larger newspapers, and occasionally having strong editorial policy on local matters.

In rural communities the weekly and semi-weekly newspapers are numerous and play a significant role in the lives of the small groups to which they appeal. These papers frequently must compete for attention with larger town and city newspapers from nearby centers of population. Their main appeals are made through the printing of "gossipy" items about neighbors and acquaintances. Most weekly papers have very small circulations, running to a few hundred copies, and are unknown outside their own communities. A few have achieved "personalities" and have gained some regional or national fame. There are few states which do not have their "sages" who occupy the editorial chairs in village printing plants.

Other types of weekly newspapers include those with special interest appeals to particular occupational groups or types of producers, as poultry farmers, livestock growers, etc.; those which appeal to and promote particular organizations, as religious denominations, political pressure groups, racial or cultural minorities; [7] and those which spring up in a particular political campaign or reform movement to support a candidate, usually by ridiculing or attacking his opponents, or to appeal to prejudices which might bring support to some cause, as prohibition or old age pensions.[8]

Magazines and Journals. Important media of social control in our national life include also magazines and journals of various kinds. A few magazines have national circulations running into millions, and strong "newsstand appeal." Others have relatively small circulations which may follow socio-economic divisions of the population, occupational, religious, or educational groupings, or other special interests. There are many magazines with appeal to specific sex or age groups, and those appealing especially to the city, rural, or suburban dweller. Those with the largest following, and presumably the greatest forces in social control, cut across all segments and make general interest appeals. Their editorial opinions and pronouncements are subordinated to fiction or news digests, and they make liberal use of striking illustration and cover design. Magazines which, by contrast, stress editorial policy may have, with very limited circulations, a disproportionate influence on the public.[9]

Various professions and scientific or artistic fields have their own publications for current articles dealing with timely research, achievement, and thinking upon their particular problems. Such publications, with few exceptions, are subsidized mainly by dues-paying members of organizations, and, while considered indispensable to persons working within certain fields, have no appeal or influence outside those fields. Nevertheless, their influence within those fields may be so intensive as to somewhat offset the restricting factors.[10] Comparable are bulletins and monographs which are published at regular or irregular intervals by learned institutions and societies, fragmentary, restricted in interest to a few specialists, and having little discernible direct influence on large publics.

Government Publications. The term "press" should include, probably, the vast stream of publications issued by the United States government and various lesser governmental units. The federal government is probably the largest printing and publishing enterprise in the world, and its products, ranging from the *Congressional Directory* to Department of

[7] For a study of this latter type, see Robert E. Park, *The Immigrant Press and Its Control* (New York: Harper and Brothers, 1922).

[8] For an analysis of this use of journalism, see Peter Odegard, *Pressure Politics* (Columbia: University of Missouri Press, 1928).

[9] Examples are *The Nation*, *The New Republic*, and *Survey-Graphic*.

[10] An outstanding example of an influential journal of this type is the *Journal of the American Medical Association*.

Agriculture bulletins of advice on the canning of fruit for home consumption, have a combined audience which could probably not be duplicated.

Historical Development

Among social control agencies the press is a comparatively recent development, although not so new as the radio and motion pictures, which are dealt with in other chapters of this volume. Preconditions to the beginning of journalism were the adoption and perfection by Western Europeans of the Chinese inventions of the printing press and movable type. Previous to this a large part of what is now the field of the press was necessarily a function of other modes of communication, slower and restricted in range. For the most part, news and opinion were disseminated by word of mouth.

The real beginnings of what we now think of as the press, the mass use of printed materials issued at frequent intervals for wide consumption, came with fairly recent improvements in transportation. The steam railway, and later good highways and motor vehicles, together with cheap postal rates, greatly enhanced the appeal of, and increased the market for, periodical literature. It was with this mushroom growth in the last half of the nineteenth century that the possibilities of printed advertising became apparent to business and industrial enterprises, with a resultant change on the part of publications from a chief reliance on paid subscriptions to paid advertising for financial support. This shift involved journalism in a vicious circle, because with increasing advertising revenues following growing circulations there was great pressure for larger circulations. This, in turn, led to larger investments in machinery for efficient production of newspapers and magazines, and in features with greater appeal to more readers. Such investments could be made only if more advertising was to be had. The press became primarily a business venture, and some journalistic enterprises entered into the ranks of "big business." [11]

Most writers on the history of journalism point to the period of "personal journalism" in the United States as one in which a few gifted individuals had great influence over the public through their comments on and interpretations of current affairs. Notable is the evaluation usually placed upon Horace Greeley as an editor with a large following.[12]

---

[11] Notably the great newspaper and magazine "empire" of William Randolph Hearst prior to its partial breakdown.

[12] Cf. Willard G. Bleyer, *Main Currents in the History of American Journalism* (Boston: Houghton, Mifflin Co., 1927), chapter VIII, "Horace Greeley and the New York Tribune"; and Joseph S. Myers, "The Genius of Horace Greeley," *The Ohio State University Bulletin*, Journalism Series No. 6 (Columbus: Ohio State University Press, 1929).

While undoubtedly there have been great editors in journalistic history, their effectiveness in social control can easily be overestimated. Careful scrutiny shows that their failures to advance programs and candidacies mount up as impressively as their successes.

Recent Changes Affecting Press. In recent years an obvious change has come about in the general scheme in which the press must operate. The number of agencies and devices for social control with which it must compete or coordinate its efforts have multiplied rapidly—notably the radio and motion pictures. Less directly effective, but significant, have been the growth of billboard advertising, the great advance in book publication and the growth of libraries, and the increased range of orators and lecturers due to improved transportation facilities. Rare is the person now who must place his main reliance for current information, opinion, or entertainment on the press. The journalist must compete now, as never before, for his audience, and the attention he can command is ever less durable. Among the various enterprises included within the press itself competition has grown by leaps and bounds [13] so that the competitive factor has become the chief concern in newspaper, magazine, and journal publication.[14] To that concern all other considerations must be secondary if a particular enterprise is to survive.

The Press and Scheme of Social Control

It may be accepted as axiomatic that every agency of social control operates to bring group pressures to bear upon individual decisions, and also is subject to individual and group pressures in shaping its own ends and policies. This is true of the press as it is of the radio, the motion picture, legislative and police organizations, and individual leaders. No one of them ever operates in a vacuum in which there exists a simple relationship between a control agency and those whom it seeks to control. The analysis of control agencies must include an inquiry both into whom the agency attempts to control and to what ends, and to what influences the agency itself is subject.

Social Control by the Press. The press, by its very nature, attempts to control large numbers of people, either whole populations or large segments of them having common bonds and interests. The very nature of printing and mass distribution indicates, as the natural field of the press,

---

[13] For an almost continuous story of this competition it is well to follow the section on the "Press" in *Time.* There are few issues but contain an article on some phase of the perpetual internecine journalistic "wars."

[14] Even in the ranks of subsidized professional journals there are few which do not have rivals within their fields, and quite often within their own supporting organizations.

mass control. Common to all branches of the press is the aim of bringing great numbers of people, the more the better, to make like decisions in various important fields of thought and activity. In this the press falls into the same category as most other agencies of control. All agencies which have volume as a chief criterion of success are included. Excluded are a few simple agencies as the family and small exclusive clubs or other organizations which operate in terms of exclusion rather than expansion to the utmost limits of their possible influence.

Advertising. Common to most journalistic enterprises is the primary goal toward which their social control efforts are directed. This object is to bring about ever-increasing consumption of particular brands of advertised goods and services. A few of the journals of small circulation are exceptions to this rule, as are some of the publications of learned organizations and governmental units. Prosperous newspapers and magazines give more than half their space to paid advertising. This advertising represents the best that the printer's art can accomplish in commanding attention and persuading readers, and it usually stands out in contrast to the relatively drab appearance of the remainder of the periodical's content. For the average reader a well-prepared advertisement has a much stronger appeal than does an editorial comment or argument. The creator of advertisements is probably far superior as an applied psychologist to the writer of editorials or news articles, a superiority which is reflected in the differences in remuneration and freedom of expression which is, in most cases, allotted to the two types of workers. Further indication of the importance of advertising as a social control purpose of the press is that most large publications have developed, individually and collectively, elaborate "follow-up" devices for measuring as precisely as possible the effects of their advertising appeals in controlling the choices made by their readers. Such measuring devices are seldom employed to determine the effectiveness of the press through its other departments.

The Ideological Slant. The enterprises which make up the press, again with a few negligible exceptions, have as a second aim the reinforcement of the prevailing mores of the group. They present a many-sided picture of the world to their readers, almost always in terms which are compatible with relatively naive ideas of good and bad, fair play, sympathy for the "underdog," good sportsmanship, prosperity, and decency. One newspaper has a policy of blithely announcing at the end of every report of criminal activity that "Crime never pays," [15] and probably no periodical which took as its theme the more realistic notion that crime quite often pays well could long survive. Practically all journalistic enterprises join in condemning evil and praising good in those matters which pre-

---

[15] *The Denver Post.*

vailing morality insists must be interpreted by rule of thumb. Corruption, vice, "dope" peddling, and "white slavery" are, of course, bad. Patriotism, governmental economy (in general, not always in particulars), and rapid growth of one's community are good. On other matters where mores do not set a generally accepted stamp of approval or disapproval there is variety in the press' interpretations which often cancel each other as influences over the decisions of large numbers of people.

Public Exposure. A third function of the press as an agency of control is to enforce petty morality by threat of coercion in the form of public exposure. Most misdemeanants fear having their names unfavorably mentioned in the press as much as they fear jail sentences. In smaller communities where newspapers can give space to "personal" items the chief concern of most people who become involved in small difficulties is to keep their names out of the paper, as all newspaper editors know.[16] So powerful is this form of coercion that on occasion less scrupulous publishers have turned it into a principal source of revenue by more or less "polite" blackmail. It is a part of the experience of every newspaper executive to find that often his advertisers live under the impression that they are purchasing a partial immunity from the threat of petty exposures when they purchase advertising space, an impression which resides as well in many of the "old subscribers" of small town and village newspapers, usually without justification. The disillusionment of such people often brings painful experiences to journalists.[17]

The Venting of Frustrations. The press again operates as an agency of social control in affording to many people the opportunity to "blow off steam" by venting their stored up frustrations in printed words. Most newspapers cater directly to this need by having columns devoted to "letters to the editor" in which personal views may be expressed by everyone.[18] This device is usually inadequate to its purpose, which has given rise to the columnist of recent years, whose purpose is, largely, to express pent-up feelings for large numbers of readers by objecting violently and loudly to almost everything except those things most deeply rooted in group mores. The same newspaper may, and often does, carry several such columns, none of which need be in agreement with others or with the stated policy of the paper itself. Large circulation magazines have adopted identical or similar devices. Thus, by reading his own "pet" complaints against everything under the sun, forcefully stated, almost

[16] Another chapter in this volume (chapter XIX), deals with gossip and scandal as control devices.
[17] The writer of this chapter served ten years in various editorial capacities on small and large newspaper staffs.
[18] Most famous of such departments is, of course, that of the historic London *Times.*

everyone may derive satisfaction almost equal to that of having written the printed words himself. On the other hand, there are usually features in periodicals, which seek wide circulation, dealing entirely in "sweetness and light" for those readers who must frequently be and recurrently are reassured in convictions that all is well in this best of all possible worlds.

Comic Strips. Increasingly comic strips occupy an important place in the social control phases of newspapers and magazines.[19] They have crept into advertisements. They are an effective means of reaching an even wider group in the interest of the same social control aims as are pursued by the press generally. They can be made to create desires and demand for goods, both within paid advertising space and outside. They can be made to praise virtue and condemn evil day after day and week after week. They can be made to heap ridicule on petty infractions of the mores, serving the purpose of "gossip" by the similarity of their characters to "people we know who are just like that." They can vent widespread indignations vicariously, or carry on perpetual campaigns of sweetness and light.

The Effects of Various Information. Little has been said, so far, of the press as an organ for imparting timely information. Outmoded psychological theories posited the Rational Man, who, if properly informed, became automatically a good citizen, husband, father, and member of society. We have come so far from this simple notion of *homo socius* that many of the claims made for newspapers as controllers of people through simply giving them factual information may immediately be discounted. Nevertheless it is true that both day-by-day decisions of many people in particular fields of activity and long range policies are affected by information available through the press and radio. From the housewife who diligently scans the prices in bargain day advertisements to the captain of industry studying the stock market quotations, there is a highly rational process going on which would be different if it were not for the latest edition of the periodical that is being used. Forecasts are commonplace in business pages, sport sections, and society columns of newspapers, and people often make up their minds on their immediate courses of action in relation to such forecasts. Such decisions lie, usually, in what in a previous chapter has been described as the field of "doubtful behavior," or that in which no moral issue is involved.[20] Usually such informational controls represent no particular policy on the part of the publication, but arise, rather, from the folkways of newspaper making.

---

[19] ". . . Most magazines and newspapers are almost wholly recreational. Most people, although mildly interested in information, read mainly the 'funnies' . . ." Constantine Panunzio, *Major Social Institutions* (New York: The Macmillan Co., 1939), p. 270.

[20] Cf. Chapter IV, "The Fields of Behavior."

Their appeal is to specialists in particular fields of activity who have other informational sources upon which to draw, so that it is a combination of influences rather than a single one which enters into the decisions.

Controlling the Press. The press is not only an agency through which controls may be exercised, but is itself subject to social controls. Three types of forces limit its field of operations, help to determine the policies of particular publications, and indicate which aims they must pursue. They are the reading publics, external regulative agencies, and internal control machinery. The reading publics seldom exercise deliberate concerted control but unless the enterprise "plays the game" as the publics understand it, the publics may withhold their very necessary support and the enterprise languishes and dies. This has happened so often in newspaper and magazine publishing that all publishers realize the tragic implications for those who do not "know the game." Repeatedly newspapers and magazines have succeeded despite concerted boycotts by advertisers, their most direct financial supporters, by amassing great circulations which advertisers could not for long ignore. Thus "reader interest" would appear to take precedence over advertisers as controllers of the press, for the advertiser, sooner or later, must follow circulation. What publics want varies from group to group. Periodicals of general circulation must avoid extreme sophistication and adhere rather rigidly to a few well-tried patterns in news, fiction, and editorial presentations, keeping to the "common level." Those which appeal to limited special interest groups and segments of a population must follow patterns peculiar and familiar to their special fields. Thus appeal to rural readers differs from the appeal to urban readers, appeals to medical practitioners must differ from appeals to trade unionists, etc. It is quite true that many periodicals have been influential in changing the tastes of their readers to some extent, but such changes are not frequent and often involve costly trial-and-error experimentation.[21]

External Controls. External controls over the press include those embodied in laws of the nation and its subdivisions; boycotts and threats of boycotts by organizations and agencies, ranging from a routine source of official news, as a police department, to a large group of potential advertisers or readers; the leaders in political party organization in the case of newspapers having close affiliations with such parties; and the continuous unorganized flow of advice and criticisms of individual readers and advertisers.

Legal Control. National laws controlling the press include those which

---

[21] The difficulties and cost of changes in newspaper styles are illustrated and recounted by Bleyer, *op. cit., passim.*

govern the use of the mails, on which most periodicals are partly dependent for distribution of their products. These laws bar from the
mails indecent matter, advertisements of lotteries, and printed materials
advocating overthrow of the government or assassination of public officials. They also provide penalties for the use of the mails to defraud.
National laws enforce censorship in times of national emergencies.[22]
State laws place further restrictions upon journalism, with variations from
state to state both in what laws may be found on statute books and the
extent to which they are enforced. Libel laws, slander laws, laws against
extortion and fraud, laws controlling "truth in advertising," and those
which forbid publication of names of minors accused or convicted of
delinquencies are among the most common types of state regulations.
Libel and slander laws have, on occasion, constituted a major source of
worry for editors, especially in metropolitan areas where such laws have
been used to make the periodicals themselves victims of extortion. The
power of judges to bring about prosecution for contempt of court also
has been effective in controlling treatment of court news, and, on occasion, in silencing criticisms of judges and other court officials. Copyright
laws control the use by the press of materials from other printed or manu-
script sources. Laws that require frequent printed statements of ownership and control of publications are designed, in part, to protect the
public from being deceived as to possible motives underlying the policies
of newspapers and magazines.[23]

Boycotts. Open boycotts are relatively rare in the history of the press,
but stated or implicit threats of boycotts are a frequent occurrence.
Groups of advertisers may, in one way or another, make it clear that they
will advertise only if periodicals meet certain conditions, such as publishing news, and without charge, items which have as their purpose the
placing of advertised products in a favorable light. Motion picture
theaters and sports promoters are probably the principal examples, although not by any means the only ones. Groups of readers occasionally
unite, especially when they belong to the same organization or closely
related organizations, and threaten to discontinue, in mass, their subscriptions, unless a newspaper or magazine changes its policy. Such threats are
frequent in times and places of labor-capital disputes. Ardent prohibition-

[22] The constitutional provision forbidding Congress to abridge the freedom of the
press is not included here, since it is so vague and general that it has no direct influence as a control over the press.
[23] This treatment of a large and involved field of law is necessarily sketchy. For
more detailed and comprehensive discussions see W. R. Arthur and Ralph L. Crossman, *The Law of Newspapers* (McGraw-Hill Book Co., 1928); Stuart H. Perry and
Edward J. White, *Newspapers and the Courts* (Columbia: University of Missouri
Press, no date); and Gerald W. Johnson, "Freedom of the Newspaper Press," *Annals
of the American Academy of Political and Social Sciences*, CC (November, 1938),
pp. 60-75.

ists and anti-tobacco crusaders have resorted to such tacticts in efforts to control advertising accepted by periodicals.

Governmental agencies may arbitrarily limit the flow of news reports which they can control. Police departments, on occasion, will refuse to one or more newspapers access to their records, and similar practices are found in other agencies and governmental bodies. Usually such controls are over items of little interest to the newspapers, or are easily circumvented by skilled newspaper workers, to the embarrassment of the agencies.[24]

Political Influences. A tradition of the American press, and especially the newspaper, has been that each periodical should have an openly avowed affiliation with a political party, support its platform and candidates, and carry its side of every issue. This tradition has broken down, largely, with the rise of the "independent" newspaper, especially in the last twenty years. There remain, however, a few newspapers, some with national circulations, others smaller and local in influence, which maintain such a relationship and are known as Republican, Democratic, Socialistic, or other political advocate. Such newspapers, in varying degrees, are committed to follow the "party line," even though the practice is increasingly to reserve the right of the newspaper to criticize, or even oppose, the "party line" when it cannot agree.[25]

Individual Influences. The unorganized flow of advice and criticism from numerous individual sources exerts very little direct control over the practices and policies of journalism. The smaller the community and the more personal the appeal of the paper, the more weight each individual's opinion must be given, but even for the smallest of rural weekly newspapers to follow all such suggestions would be impossible. Often publications take criticism coming from opposed sources as proof of their own impartiality.

Internal Censorship. Each publication has its own internal rules and its own "style sheet," differing in some degree from those of other publications. Such instructions for workers in a particular enterprise may forbid publication of certain types of material, as say divorce news or certain types of crime news. They may deal with the mechanics of writing, as when they forbid that any news story shall begin with a "The." In some cases they specify that names of certain persons prominent in the community shall never appear in the news columns.[26]

[24] Nearly all biographical writings of journalists describe situations of this type, and means by which the boycotts on news are defeated.
[25] Bleyer, *op. cit., passim.*
[26] Willard G. Bleyer, *Handbook for Newspaper Workers* (New York: D. Appleton-Century Co., 1926) contains a sample style sheet.

Unwritten Codes. In many ways the most significant controls over the press reside in institutional values and the unwritten codes of journalism itself. In the traditional organization and functioning of the press certain "right" ways of going through routine activities have come to be generally accepted. A part of the training of every neophyte in the business is to ingrain thoroughly in him a recognition of such procedures, together with their rationalizations. For instance, the strict separation of business affairs, such as solicitation of advertising and subscriptions, from the editorial functions of gathering and writing news and interpretations of news prevails in nearly all newspapers and is strengthened by traditional running feuds between those workers engaged in the business side of publications and the editorial workers. The significance of this particular tradition for the press is great, since it places a strong guard against the influence upon the policies of the newspaper by those who contribute to its financial support. The standardized departmentalization of newspapers and magazines into those which deal with sports, or society items, or business news, serves as an internal control, for each such department has its own traditional values and guides which often could not apply in another department. To use the rules which govern the society page in presenting the sports news is unthinkable, and the rules for neither of these departments can be applied strictly to the treatment of general news. Those who write for the editorial page may express opinions freely, and are expected to do so; but such expression is rigidly forbidden those who write for the general news pages.[27]

Codes. In addition to these mores and folkways of journalism there are formal codes of various organizations of publishers and editors which establish high professional standards in idealistic terms. National, state, and regional bodies of this type have their own formal principles calling for strict honesty, impartiality, decency, and public morality. Such codes are usually a part of the teaching of schools of journalism which place great stress upon them, although it is probable that the great majority of practicing journalists have only the vaguest knowledge of what they contain. Their main service is to justify the press to outsiders.[28]

---

[27] Willard G. Bleyer, *Newspaper Writing and Editing* (Boston: Houghton, Mifflin Co., 1932), is a comprehensive description of the routine and folkways of newspaper workers. For the general setting of these practices, see Talcott Parsons, "The Professions and Social Structure," *Social Forces*, XVII (May, 1939), pp. 457-467.

[28] Joseph S. Myers, "The Journalistic Code of Ethics," *The Ohio State University Bulletin*, Journalism Series, I, No. 4 (February 18, 1922), contains a large number of such codes, as those of the state organizations of Oregon, Washington, and Kansas; those of particular enterprises as the Detroit *News*, the Hearst publications; and those propounded by prominent individuals, as Walter Williams, former dean of the School of Journalism of the University of Missouri, and the late President Warren G. Harding. George Seldes, *op. cit.*, gives the Code of Ethics of the American Newspaper Guild.

Summary

The press exerts controls over the publics to which it appeals, and in turn is controlled by them. Its chief interest, in general, is to bring about uniform favorable reactions to advertised goods and services. Other purposes, generally speaking, are to support the *status quo*, both in terms (in this country) of capitalistic society and of the prevailing mores and folkways of the group. The press like most, but not all, agencies of social control seeks to exert its influence over the largest possible group of people. An incidental function is in actually or vicariously permitting disgruntled people to object publicly to persons and practices they resent.

In turn, the press is subject to control by its reading publics who may, upon occasion, withhold their very necessary support. It is also subject to control by the government through postal laws and powers of courts to punish for contempt; and to internal controls, as are embedded in the folkways and mores of journalism and the publicized codes of ethics of the profession.

QUESTIONS

1. What extremes do writers about the field of the press usually take?
2. How do rural publications compete with city journals?
3. What type of magazines have the largest following and the greatest force in social control?
4. What developments influenced the market for periodical literature?
5. What is meant by the term "personal journalism"?
6. What recent changes have made the task of journalism more difficult?
7. What is the common aim of all branches of the press?
8. How does the advertising specialist compare in prestige and material advantage with the editorial writer?
9. In what terms do newspapers present their stories?
10. How do newspapers help people to vent their frustrations?
11. What effect have the comics on social control?
12. What is the theoretical relation between *homo socius* and the press?
13. What types of control limit the operations of the press?
14. What types of external controls may be applied to the press?
15. How does the federal government control the press?
16. Compare state and federal control of the press.
17. What methods may governmental agencies use to boycott the press?
18. What is the expected relationship between the press and political parties?
19. What is the relationship between size of area covered and the importance of individual influence?
20. How may courts control the press?

SUGGESTED TOPICS FOR TERM PAPERS AND FURTHER RESEARCH

1. A study of the laws of libel and slander in your state.
2. The human interest story and the modern press.

3. Study the influence of the press in a small community with only one small newspaper.
4. Study the effects of the comics on small children.
5. The use of the minorities press by foreign governments.
6. The use of cartoons in press.
7. The relation of the press to television.
8. The influence of the press in national elections.

BIBLIOGRAPHY

Books

American Newspaper Publishers' Association, Bureau of Advertising, *The Newspaper as an Advertising Medium* (New York, 1940), pp. 1-170. Extensive bibliography.

W. R. Arthur and Ralph L. Crossman, *The Law of Newspapers* (New York: McGraw-Hill Book Co., 1928). A handbook prepared for the newspaperman's point of view indicating the pitfalls for the unwary.

John Bakeless, *Magazine Making* (New York: Viking Press, 1931). A good exposition of the problems and techniques of editing, getting and holding circulation and advertising.

R. T. Baker, *A History of the Graduate School of Journalism, Columbia University* (New York: Columbia University Press, 1954). How the graduate school of journalism at Columbia University came into existence in 1912 after considerable conflict between the ideas of Joseph Pulitzer and Columbia University's President Nicholas Murray Butler, and the subsequent history of the school.

Thomas F. Barnhart, *The Weekly Newspaper: A Bibliography, 1925-1941* (Minneapolis: Burgess, 1941). Much material for reference.

Simon Michael Bessie, *Jazz Journalism: The Story of the Tabloid Newspaper* (New York: E. P. Dutton and Co., 1938).

George L. Bird and Frederic E. Merwin, *The Press and Society* (New York: Prentice-Hall, 1951). A revised edition of a study published in 1942 as *The Newspaper and Society*.

Clarence S. Brigham, *Journals and Journeymen: A Contribution to the History of Early American Newspapers* (Philadelphia: University of Pennsylvania Press, 1950).

Commission on Freedom of the Press, *A Free and Responsible Press* (Chicago: University of Chicago Press, 1947). A general report on mass communication and its influence on society.

Frederick G. Detweiler, *The Negro Press in the United States* (Chicago: University of Chicago Press, 1922). A good early study of the minority press influence. The more recent developments in the Negro and minority press are covered in: Joseph S. Roucek, "The Foreign-Language Press and Radio," Chapter 13, pp. 391-401, and Clifton R. Jones, "The Negro Press," Chapter 14, pp. 401-416, in Francis J. Brown and Joseph S. Roucek, eds., *One America* (New York: Prentice-Hall, 1952).

E. H. Ford and Edwin Emery, eds., *Highlights in the History of the American Press* (Minneapolis, Minn.: University of Minnesota Press, 1954). Twenty-seven articles trace American journalistic history from its antecedents in the English ballad singers to modern newspaper giants.

Jacques Kayser, *One Week's News* (New York: Columbia University Press, 1954). Comparative study of sixteen major dailies for a seven-day period.

Alfred McClung Lee, *The Daily Newspaper in America* (New York: The Macmillan Co., 1937). A substantial survey of the development of the press in the United States.

Frank Luther Mott, *American Journalism* (New York: The Macmillan Co., 1941). Especially good on magazine development.

George F. Mott, ed., *Survey of Journalism* (New York: Barnes and Noble, 1937). These various studies give an excellent insight into the complexity of the labors behind the newspaper or magazine.

Mary Noel, *Villains Galore* (New York: The Macmillan Co., 1954). An interesting and comprehensive history of the American story paper weeklies.

Frank North, *The News in America* (Cambridge, Mass.: Harvard University Press, 1952). How and why of press propaganda.

Lester Olsen, *Advertising Work Told with Pictures* (New York: Printer's Ink: Funk and Wagnalls, 1950). A behind-the-scenes story of advertising.

Robert E. Park, *The Immigrant Press and Its Control* (New York: Harper and Brothers, 1922). Although mostly outdated, this is a pioneer and valuable study of the minority press, dealing with backgrounds, content of periodicals, their history, and controlling factors.

Frederick Siebert, *The Rights and Privileges of the Press* (New York: Appleton-Century-Crofts, 1943). A good study of the censorship core of the press.

Bruce Lannes Smith, Harold D. Lasswell, and Ralph D. Casey, *Propaganda, Communication and Public Opinion* (Princeton: Princeton University Press, 1946). Indispensable as a reference guide and analysis.

UNESCO, *Press, Film, Radio, Television* (New York: Columbia University Press, 1951). An indispensable reference volume covering these media of communications in all countries of the world.

Llewellyn White and Robert D. Leigh, *Peoples Speaking to Peoples* (Chicago: University of Chicago Press, 1946). A report of the Commission on Freedom of the Press showing the importance of this freedom, methods to improve the quality of information and suggestions for maintaining world cooperation through communication.

Periodicals

Annals of The American Academy of Political and Social Science, CCXIX (January, 1942), "The Press in the Contemporary Scene," edited by Malcolm M. Willey and Ralph D. Casey. 26 articles, surveying the contemporary scene. Indispensable reading.

Graham Dukes, "The Beginnings of the English Newspaper," *History Today*, IV, 3 (March, 1954), pp. 197-204.

A. Harrigan, "Newspapers Without News," *American Mercury*, LXXV (November, 1952), pp. 84-89.

Gerald W. Johnson, "Freedom of the Newspaper Press," *Annals of The Academy of Political and Social Sciences*, CC (November, 1938), pp. 60-75.

Journalism Quarterly, Vol. XXIII in 1946, is an indispensable reference to the whole field of communications; contains classified bibliographies and reviews.

Alfred McClung Lee, "Recent Developments in the Newspaper Industry," *Public Opinion Quarterly*, II (January, 1938), pp. 126-133.

K. E. Miller, "Public Health Aspects of False Advertising," *American Journal of Public Health*, XXX (August 14, 1940), pp. 880-886.

Gerald Movius, "Comic Strip Propaganda," *Scribner's Commentator*, XI (November, 1941), pp. 17-20.

"NATO News Blackout," *Time*, LX (November 17, 1952), p. 88.

Robert E. Park, "News and the Power of the Press, *American Journal of Sociology* XLVII (July, 1941), pp. 1-11.

Joseph S. Roucek, "Foreign-Language Press in World War II," *Sociology and Social Research*, XXVII (July–August, 1943), pp. 462-471.

"Troubled Press: Washington News," *Fortune*, XLV (February, 1952), pp. 125 ff.

Paul H. Wagner, "The Evolution of Newspaper Interest in Radio," *Journalism Quarterly*, XXIII (June, 1936), pp. 182-188.

F. G. Wilson, "Public Opinion in the Theory of Democracy," *Thought*, XX (June, 1945), pp. 235-252.

CHAPTER XXVI

Radio

A social order is dependent upon communication among its members. From gestures to language marks the first big step forward in social organization and consequently in social control; the development of printing was the second step.

Four technological developments have come with startling rapidity during the past hundred years: the telegraph, the telephone, the motion picture and the radio. Although discoveries of great importance were made and utilized during the war, the last two mentioned are still in the developmental stage. However, they have reached the front rank as important influences on all phases of social life.

The fact that radio has made the human voice a means of instantaneous communication among millions of people has given it an advantage in communication not enjoyed by its predecessors. Its importance and potential influence are correspondingly greater. Education and religion have "taken to the air." Modern advertising has found it an unequaled medium. Sports events are conveyed instantaneously. The voice of our President can draw all the American people to his desk side.

On the other side of the picture is the memorable fact that the Nazis' first action in their initial attempt to seize Austria was the capture of the Vienna radio station RAVAG. Clearly it is evident that an instrument which can bring the human voice to so many people at one time, which can entertain and propagandize, which can describe and persuade, which can educate and coerce, must have tremendous potentialities for controlling individuals and groups within society.

The Radio and American Culture

Origin of Radio. The historical development of radio deserves a few words. A young Italian boy, Guglielmo Marconi, obtained the first patent for "wireless" in 1896. He is generally conceded to be the "father of radio," although, as is always the case with great inventions, his work was preceded by that of many scientists who had laid the foundations.[1] Marconi's Wireless Telegraph Company was formed in 1897 and was incorporated in this country two years later.

---

[1] A recent Supreme Court case challenged Marconi's claim to one or two technical inventions and patents, but did not question his right to the title "father of radio."

But it was not until nearly twenty years thereafter that the broadcasting of the human voice itself began in this country. Perhaps the first station in the United States was WHA which had been organized by the University of Wisconsin, first as an experiment in the Physics Department, and later to broadcast market reports, weather conditions and perform other public services for the people nearby.

Better known for its early broadcasting is station KDKA still functioning in Pittsburgh. This station began its regular operation in November, 1920. Its first studio was a garage near the home of one of the engineers. The only receiving sets were those of amateur telegraph operators. Most of KDKA's early broadcasting consisted of music, but they also broadcast the returns of the Harding election, an occasional church service, and a nearby prize fight.

Two years later more than 200,000 receiving sets were in operation and program development was proceeding at a phenomenal pace. Today nearly 1000 stations send their programs into more than 50 million receivers or over 30 million American homes. Radio has become a big business.

Today's Radio in the United States. The bigness of radio in America today cannot be understood adequately without resort to statistics. The following general statements may help to clarify the magnitude of this "the youngest of children" in the communications family: [2] (a) During the past twenty years some 80,000,000 radio sets have been built in this country; 55,000,000 sets are in use today. (During the war's early years there were 2,000,000 additional sets but these became too worn out to use and could not be replaced because no civilian radios were being manufactured.) (b) The listener's sets in use represent a total investment of $3,500,000,000. (c) Before the war, approximately 11 million new sets were being sold annually. (d) In 1945, 33 million homes were equipped with radios. However, only 31 million had radios in working order. This means that 87 per cent of all American homes were equipped with radio. (e) Approximately 83 per cent of these homes so equipped used their radios some time each day. (f) Over 90 per cent of all urban homes have radios. The overall figures for radios in rural homes is 73 per cent.

---

[2] These statistics are taken from the following several sources: Federal Communications Commission, *Statistics of the Communications Industry in the United States,* for year ended December 31, 1943. Federal Communications Commission, Accounting, Statistical, and Tariff Department, *Summary of Broadcast Revenues,* 1944; and other statistics. Advertising Age, *Leading Radio Advertisers in 1944,* March 5, 1945, p. 42, 43. Federal Communications Commission, *Employee and Compensation Data . . . By Standard Broadcast Stations, Major Networks and Regional Networks,* March, 1945. Radio Television Retailing, *Statistics of Radio as 1945 Opens,* Clement-Caldwell, January, 1945, p. 21. United States Department of Agriculture, Bureau of Agricultural Economics, *Attitudes of Rural People Toward Radio Service,* Study 123, November, 1945.

However, only 58 per cent of the rural homes in the South are equipped with radios. (g) Nine out of every ten Americans listen to the radio sometime during the day. The average American family listens almost five hours a day. This is more time than they spend at any other activity except working or sleeping. (h) In 1945, 20,000 people were employed by the standard broadcasting stations and networks, and another 25,000 worked as part-time artists, etc. The radio manufacturing industry gave employment to 530,000 people and had an annual payroll of $1,200,000,000. (i) The revenue from the sale of radio time has risen from $4,820,000 in 1927 to $246,339,532 at the end of 1944. (j) As of January 1, 1946, there were 950 standard broadcasting stations on the air and more than 400 additional applications for licenses pending. Forty-seven FM stations were on the air and more than 700 applications were either pending or had been conditionally granted. More than ½ million FM receiving sets were already in operation. (k) It is an interesting side-light to note that the number of American dwellings equipped with radio represents 213.0 radios for every 1000 in our population. California leads the United States with 279.2 radios per 1000. However, note the average number of radios per 1000 in some foreign countries: Sweden, 264.6; Denmark 255.4; and Iceland 207.9.

Such statistics might be elaborated indefinitely, but the ones cited are sufficient to indicate the important place that radio has achieved in the lives of the American people.

Trends in Radio Programs. From the earliest broadcasting of Harding's victory to President Roosevelt's war messages some twenty years later, the programs of radio have been constantly expanding and elaborating. Studies by the Federal Communications Commission, by research workers, and by the stations and networks give us a picture of some of the general trends: [3] (1) The proportion of music is decreasing, but the ratio of popular music to other kinds is increasing. (2) The amount of time devoted to newscasts and news analyses increased rapidly after Munich, still more after Pearl Harbor, and has fallen off only by a very small percentage since the end of the war. The total listening index for news programs in 1943-1944 was four times as large as that of 1940. (3) The percentage of drama and dramatic readings has practically doubled since 1932. However, this includes the familiar "soap opera" as well as programs of better dramatic content. For example, during the day-time

---

[3] The following information is largely taken from Kenneth G. Bartlett's "Trends in Radio Programs," *Annals of the American Academy of Political and Social Sciences,* CCXII (January, 1941), pp. 15-25, and brought up to date by further material from *Broadcasting—1945 and 1946 Yearbooks,* edited by Broadcast Advertising; and Harrison Summer's *Tomorrow's Radio Programs* (Washington, D.C.: Federal Radio Education Committee, 1944), pp. 10-12.

hours, serials now constitute nearly 60 per cent of the programs broadcast. (4) There is an overwhelming trend toward the use of network programs by local stations. Nearly 90 per cent of the average local station programs are either taken from a wire line, recordings or transcriptions. (5) There has been some increase in extemporized programs, public forums and discussions without script.

The Radio Listeners. With more than 50,000,000 sets in operation, and nine out of ten people listening, it is not too much to state that practically every American has become a radio listener.

Certain variations in types of listeners may be noted. In general, the larger the family income, the greater the chance that there will be a radio in the home.[4] However, studies indicate that there is a distinction in this connection between owners and users, with the latter being found in the greater proportion among the middle class, with the extremely wealthy using their radios even less than the poorer groups who do not own as many. Similarly, studies indicate that the greater the degree of education of members of the family, the less the radio is in use. In other words, the potential victim of the demagogue and propagandist uses his radio more often than the one better equipped to combat such influences.

When people listen has been the subject of much research. By far the lightest months in terms of listening are July and August. Listening in the winter months of November, December, January and February seems to be heaviest.[5] During the week Saturday afternoon has a comparatively lower listener's index, while Sunday evening has the highest listener's score. Evening listening between the hours of 6 and 9, particularly, is by far the greatest during the day. In the evening both sexes listen in about the same proportion. However, in terms of total time spent listening to the radio, women far outrank men.

What people prefer to listen to has been studied more than any other factor pertaining to radio [6] largely because of its interest to the commer-

---

[4] For an excellent summary of these and other points concerning the radio listener, see Hadley Cantril and Gordon W. Allport, *The Psychology of Radio* (New York: Harper and Brothers, 1935), chapter V. Although this is an older book, it is the most recent general book of its quality written on this subject. Also used for information in this section: Edgar A. Schuler's *A Survey of Radio Listeners* (Baton Rouge: Louisiana State University Press, 1943), a thorough study of the habits of Louisiana listeners from which a few general conclusions may be drawn; and Matthew N. Chappell and C. E. Hooper's *Radio Audience Measurement* (New York: Stephen Daye, 1944).

[5] *Broadcasting, 1945, Yearbook* (published annually by the Magazine Broadcast Advertising), p. 46.

[6] The Hooper and Crossley studies of what people listen to most are well known and used consistently by commercial advertisers. Gallup, Roper and other poll-takers in the public opinion field have also done occasional work. Paul F. Lazarsfeld of the Office of Radio Research at Columbia University and Frank Stanton of the Columbia Broadcasting System have developed what they call a "Program Analyzer" to test likes and dislikes in the content of a program.

cial sponsors of programs. Tastes among listeners vary widely according to sex, age, occupation, educational level and other factors. In general, variety and comedy programs recruit the largest number of listeners while serious talks, classical music, and general educational programs fall low on the scale. News programs are also popular.

The difference made by level of education is illustrated by the fact that studies have shown "heads of families" who have only a grade or high school education are least interested in serious programs. Compare this with the preferences expressed by Harvard graduates, now in middle age: Symphonic music received the highest preference rating; "Information Please" came second, and news programs and comments, third.[7] It is also interesting to note how time has changed things. In 1923 a radio station queried 25,000 listeners as to preferences. Eight per cent of those who answered desired symphony over any other kind of music.[8]

Rural Listeners. There are some rather discouraging facts about rural listening recently compiled by the Bureau of Agricultural Economics. Approximately 38.5 per cent of the country's inhabited territory is not reached by daytime radio service.[9] This is of course territory in which much of our rural population lives (in fact, 10,000,000 people). Radio could be of especial service to them because many have no phones and their newspapers arrive late.

According to the study just mentioned,[10] farm people spend less time than other members of our population listening to the radio. The women spend about 3.7 hours and 4 out of 10 of the men listen only 2 hours per day. Thirteen per cent of the farm people interviewed said that it would make no difference to them at all if their radios gave out. Another 13 per cent said it would make very little difference.

Farmers find programs giving news, weather conditions and market reports of tremendous value to them, if they are broadcast at times of the day when they can listen.

Children's Programs. Children comprise an important segment of the listening public. Mothers' clubs, educators, and others have objected for years to the type of program, supposedly for children, that fills the air with murder, horror and general blood and thunder.

The problem has assumed great enough proportions so that several groups and individuals have made careful studies. Under the auspices of

---

[7] C. J. Friedrich and Jeanette Sayre, *Radiobroadcasting and Higher Education* (Cambridge: Littauer Center, Harvard University, 1942), pp. 72-73.

[8] Quoted in Thomas Porter Robinson's *Radio Networks and the Federal Government*, (New York: Columbia University Press, 1943), p. 17.

[9] Statement made March 12, 1944, by FCC Chairman Paul Porter; quoted in testimony on Clear Channel Broadcasting before FCC, January, 1946, Docket 6741, p. 269.

[10] United States Department of Agriculture, Study 123, *op. cit.*

the Federal Radio Education Committee, a four-year study was made at Ohio State University. The study was divided into a survey of school programs and out-of-school listening. Children's psychological reactions were tested. Parents' reactions to children's listening habits were studied. The following are some of the conclusions in regard to criteria by which children's radio programs should be judged.[11]

Considerations Relating to the Ethical, Moral, or Social Ideals of American Life: (1) Children's radio programs should build faith in democracy. (2) Occupational skills which are essential to American life should be honestly and sincerely portrayed. (3) The role of minority groups of races and of nationalities which make up modern America should be portrayed sympathetically and realistically. (4) Children's radio programs should be authentic in broad historical or contemporary interpretation, factual detail, and artistic portrayal. (5) Children's radio programs should maintain standards of good taste. (6) Crime is not suitable as a dominant theme in a radio program directed to children. At least it is important to include in the story an indication of how the criminal "got that way." (7) The rich field of children's literature should provide the main part of the content of children's radio stories.

Considerations Relating to the Emotional, Intellectual and Social Development of the Child's Personality: (1) Radio programs should arouse in children a wide range of emotional responses, and avoid undue stress upon fear or aggression. (2) The child has a need for genuine characters of heroic proportions as imaginary playmates, and models to imitate, and with which to identify himself. (3) In fantasy and fairy-tale programs, the fantastic or purely imaginative elements should be clearly identifiable to child listeners as unreal. (4) The social problems of childhood involving friendship and respect for one's equals should be frequently and honestly portrayed. (5) Family relationships, mutual respect and understanding between parents and children, and family-problem situations should be portrayed honestly and realistically. (6) The suggestive power of radio should be utilized to lead the child into useful hobbies, activities, skills and knowledge. (7) Humor should be within the comprehension and appreciation of children. This also holds true for music, vocabulary, sound effects and other techniques.

The study makes this interesting comment: "educators and psychologists to a great extent, have failed to provide the professional showman with significant data or significant hypotheses which might serve as practical guides for the improvement of children's radio programs." [12]

There is also available a careful, scholarly compilation of most of the

---

[11] Howard Rowland, I. Keith Tyler, and Norman Woelfel, *Criteria for Children's Radio Programs*, (Washington, D.C.: Federal Radio Education Committee, 1942), pp. 11-21.   [12] *Ibid.*, p. 9.

studies that have been made of children's listening habits and reactions. Some of the findings are as follows: [13] (1) Children's average weekly listening runs from 5 hours and 15 minutes to 18 hours and 30 minutes. Peak listening occurs in the 12 to 15 year age group, and averages from 17 to 18 hours a week. (2) Girls seem to listen more than boys. There is some sex differentiation in types of programs liked, amount of recall and other points. (3) Children listen largely to what is available. Thus, they are highly influenced by the soap opera, the crime and mystery drama planned as entertainment for adults, not for children. (4) Children most often begin listening to a program because they wish to emulate a friend who does so, or because of the "inducements" offered such as prizes, badges, codes, books. (5) Two separate surveys established the fact that a majority of children prefer the movies to radio listening. (6) Parents seem to approve of more programs than they disapprove. One out of every 10 parents saw no beneficial effects of listening to the radio, but 1 out of every 6 saw nothing at all wrong with listening. (7) "Roughly speaking . . . approval of radio is based on educational grounds and the fact that it keeps children busy while disapproval is based on the emotional excitement stimulated. They [parents] were found to feel that the radio provides education in terms of actual information, help in school work and in terms of the development of interests, of critical powers, of a 'sense of the finer things in life.' On educational grounds they have been opposed to programs with corrupt English, coarse humor, to gangster programs and their emphasis on crime, to serial stories and their emphasis on 'love affairs and divorces,' and to programs with unreal or impossible adventures.

"The main bulk of parents' disapproval has been directed . . . against programs of the gangster, thriller and mystery type for the over-excitement created by them. . . . The disapproval was found to be stronger among parents with children under 12 years . . . and stronger among parents of children with poorer school grades. . . . The disapproval is particularly directed against such exciting programs coming at late hours. Parents in one survey were asked about interferences caused by radio. It was found that in 55 per cent [of the cases] radio was claimed to interfere with normal bedtime, in 36.8 per cent with household tasks, in 29.3 per cent with mealtimes and in 18.0 per cent with normal playtimes." [14] (8) There were many emotional effects of programs that could be noted in the child listeners. Particularly amongst 4th to 8th graders, 42 per cent of the children worried about the hero from one program to the next. (9) Of this same age group 26 per cent dreamed about programs,

---

[13] Herta Hertzog, *Survey of Research on Children's Radio Listening* (New York: Radio Council on Children's Programs, April, 1941).

[14] *Ibid.*, pp. 36-37.

especially the crime and mystery type. Of those who did dream 73 per cent had unpleasant dreams. (10) As a result of listening 12 per cent of the children had taken up a hobby. But, in an effort to ascertain what types of learning had resulted from radio listening, surveyors found that songs far outranked any other kind of new knowledge. (11) A special study was made in Michigan to ascertain the effects of radio listening on children's language and vocabulary. Of the parents questioned 41.8 per cent reported additions to their children's vocabularies, but they were such things as wolf howls, Donald Duck quacks, "Hi-ho! Silver," "Stick 'em up," and "T'ain't the way I heerd it."

There are a few occurrences that make the picture in children's programs more hopeful. Station WHCU in Ithaca, New York, has been making a real effort to select the best possible network programs and plan the local programs to supplement rather than duplicate them, and to suit material to different age levels.

Station WNEW in New York City "has arranged an interesting five point program schedule for children . . . with a special news program, narrated story series, series on dramatized books . . . and pre-school music programs.

"In Portland, Oregon, the combination of network programs and those on various local stations shows an interesting variety and balance . . .: the listings include two story book series . . .; a youth participation forum discussing books; a series on local industries; a Junior Town Meeting; a forum on teen-age problems; a nature quiz; a safety series; a series of original stories; a talent show; . . . the school music series from California" and many other valuable programs.[15] It is obvious, however, that over the nation, there must be improvement before most radio programs are suitable for young audiences.

Radio and Cultural Change. There is little doubt that the radio has made and will continue to make great changes in our culture patterns, but there is the ever-present danger of ascribing too much importance to this single invention. During the 1920's glowing accounts related how the radio was going to remake our way of life. Later on, in 1933, Ogburn pointed out some 150 important ways in which the radio had already changed American culture.[16] In 1937, one writer stated that "the party controlling the radio controls the nation; radio is the key to the minds of the people." [17] And from that time on until today we can read statements attributing to radio a vast power over our culture.

---

[15] Dorothy Lewis and Dorothy L. McFadden, *Program Patterns for Young Radio Listeners* (Washington, D.C.: National Association of Broadcasters, 1945).

[16] President's Research Committee on Recent Social Trends, *Recent Social Trends* (New York: McGraw-Hill Book Co., 1933), pp. 153-156.

[17] Ruth Brindze, *Not to be Broadcast* (New York: The Vanguard Press, 1937), p. 4.

As early as 1926, however, one observer was questioning the extent to which radio was to influence society.[18] By 1939 Albig was to point out that "the prophets of the early 1920's quite generally overestimated the immediate influence of the radio on political and ideational life, and underestimated its development as a purveyor of advertising and a new medium of mass entertainment." [19]

Today, it is increasingly recognized that radio's relationship to society is two-way; that the general type of culture pattern will influence radio's development and in turn will be affected by it. For example, in a totalitarian state, where all phases of culture were rigidly controlled by the government, the radio along with all other agencies of communications was so dominated, and its influence upon individual citizens was in the direction of the general aims of the state. The radio facilitated this domination, it assisted in the molding of public opinion more quickly and more thoroughly. But the radio itself did NOT bring Fascism or Nazism. Absolute rulers were known centuries before Hitler or Mussolini or before the coming of radio.

On the other hand, in a nation where there is considerable individual freedom and choice of action, the radio will still be of considerable influence in changing cultural trends. But that influence will be more indirect, and come about in the interplay of complex forces. Moreover, "in a country able to preserve its democratic institutions, radio will be politically less influential than in a dictatorship, the very existence of which depends upon the enforcing of propaganda upon the people." [20]

Furthermore, changes within a culture pattern, which depend little if any on radio, will in turn help to determine the extent to which radio will be related to change and control. Population trends, institutional changes and technological developments will affect the influence of all means of communication. Lazarsfeld has stated the situation very well: "The social consequences of the radio will come about via the influence on the attitudes and habits of people, but this role of radio will vary according to the different turns our social system takes. Should the population of our big cities slowly be decentralized, radio will be of greater importance for an increasingly suburban people. Should there be a trend toward even denser population centers, radio will not have such importance, because the movie downstairs in each skyscraper and the evening school at the corner of each block will do some of the work radio would otherwise do." [21]

---

[18] Marshall D. Beuick, "The Limited Social Effects of Radio Broadcasting," *American Journal of Sociology*, XXXII (January, 1927), pp. 615-622.

[19] William Albig, *Public Opinion* (New York: McGraw-Hill Book Co., 1939), p. 334.

[20] Paul F. Lazarsfeld, *Radio and the Printed Page* (New York: Duell, Sloan, and Pearce, 1940), p. 334.   [21] *Ibid.*, p. 330.

Radio and Social Control

Radio has become an important agent of social control in our democracy. It is of direct importance because it is an immediate agent in the formation of public opinion, and such opinion is one of the more important factors in social control. Indirectly it is also of considerable importance because it influences our language, our customs, and our institutions which in turn all relate to control patterns.

Radio and Public Opinion. The near monopoly over public opinion formerly exercised by the press has been broken forever. People's minds and emotions are increasingly being swayed by the spoken voice rather than by the printed page.

The writings of a Father Coughlin, of a Charles Kettering, or even of a Franklin D. Roosevelt might have made fairly dull reading; the same words thundered out over the airwaves convinced millions of people of a particular point of view in regard to "social justice," the philosophy of General Motors Corporation, or the New Deal.

Unfortunately we have not yet devised the techniques necessary to measure how much the radio influences public opinion: we are not able to break down public opinion into the respective parts played by the press, the newsreel, the radio, even the billboard. In spite of this lack of information, however we do know that the radio has become one of the most important of all such agencies.

Radio has certain advantages over the press which are noteworthy, in addition to the simple advantage of the spoken word over the printed one. Radio simultaneously reaches all elements of the population, and theoretically is thus a more democratic agent. It can dramatize and popularize events and ideas in ways which the press could hardly accomplish. Its speed of communication accelerates the focusing of public attention and tends to speed up change in popular opinion. The radio can give the opportunity for the discussion of controversial issues, and can therefore render a public service that the press cannot perform in the same way.

However, a word of caution should be given. Even as an agency in the formation of public opinion, it is possible to overestimate the influence of the radio. Father Coughlin had millions of listeners in 1936, but his particular candidate for President polled under a million votes. Roosevelt's overwhelming victories were ascribed to the triumph of radio over the press in view of the fact that most important newspapers bitterly opposed his candidacy. However a recent poll taken by *Editor and Publisher* showed that, of the newspapers that had taken sides in the elections, 208 had radio station affiliations. And of these, 56 or 27 per cent only

had been for Roosevelt. But 152, or 73 per cent had been for Dewey.[22]
The fact that Roosevelt's oratory quite outdistanced that of any of his
opponents is important but cannot be measured statistically.

Even the excitement caused by Orson Welles' famous program of the
invasion from Mars failed to excite more than a comparatively few neu-
rotics, and its importance has been stressed beyond all proportion.[23]

In spite of all the advantages that a persuasive voice over the ether
doubtless possesses, it is difficult to overcome traditions of race, nationality, class, religion, and politics; even Roosevelt probably changed few
old-line Republicans, and John L. Lewis failed to alter the convictions of
a majority of his own followers in 1940. The radio is an increasingly
important agent in forming public opinion, but fortunately, in a democracy, there are too many cross currents at work to permit it to become
the sole factor in making up people's minds.

Radio, Language and Mores. As a culture pattern becomes more democratic, language increases in its importance as a means of social control,
and force decreases. The development of radio has had several interesting effects upon language.

It has tended to increase the vocabulary and understanding of millions
of Americans. In some cases better use of language may have resulted
because of the unconscious tendency to conform to the faultless diction
which the announcer must use. Standardization of speech and the lessening of dialectical forms are still other probabilities.

Customs, habits and mores likewise are undergoing certain changes
because of the radio. The breaking down of isolation in many sections,
and the penetration into those areas, of urban ideas and standards is one
of the most important changes.

Regional variations, already on the decline in America, are becoming
still less important because of the radio. Such seemingly unimportant
customs as time of retiring and rising, morning exercises, fan letter
writing and numerous other habits have been affected by radio.

Although there is an unquestionable value in bringing regions of the
country and ethnic groups closer together, the radio can also serve to
perpetuate the cultural heritages of regions and nationality groups within
our country. This would serve to make an already varied culture in
America even richer and more colorful.

One of the Commissioners of FCC had this to say: ". . . networks
should not become one-way streets. A network can be merely a device

---

[22] Quoted in a speech by FCC Commissioner C. J. Durr, before the New York
Federation of Women's Clubs, October 27, 1944.

[23] For an interesting analysis of this particular program, and its implications for
social control, see Hadley Cantril, *The Invasion from Mars: A Study in the Psychology of Panic* (Princeton: Princeton University Press, 1940).

for taking programs from New York, Chicago and Hollywood and piping them into smaller communities. . . . But a network can also pick up outstanding talent from even the smallest hamlet and make it nationally available." [24]

Largely because of an interest stimulated by the research of the Library of Congress' Musical Archives, the radio today is serving to bring back to all groups in America a rich body of our folklore and folksongs. Such things give us an understanding of American development, in terms of the people who made our history.

Cleveland, Ohio, has made a famous experiment in which radio has been most important. Nearly 75 per cent of greater Cleveland's population is either first or second generation foreign-born. The city's leaders and educators decided some years ago to make a sincere effort to assimiliate and make secure Americans out of the new citizens. At the same time it seemed desirable, both for the people from other lands and for Americans who had been here a bit longer, to keep alive a pride in the various national cultural heritages and customs. Therefore, in Cleveland, the holidays of every nationality are celebrated and all are invited. Schools and churches plan various programs to honor national backgrounds. The city is constantly made colorful with national dances, parades, costumes and other symbols of cultures much older than ours. The radio has played a large and interesting part in the Cleveland experiment.

Radio and Religion. Although religion is probably less important as an agent of social control than it was a few centuries or even a few decades ago, it still possesses considerable significance, especially for certain segments of the population. Radio has never devoted much time to religious programs, and the number of religious broadcasts in proportion to other types of programs has decreased in the last decade. However, radio has performed some useful services in this area. Urban services have been broadcast to areas where ministers have been unable to go; better sermons are being made available to isolated communities. Invalids and others not able to attend church now are able to listen to broadcast services. To some individuals the excuse of listening to services by radio has doubtless been used to avoid attending regular church services.

Religious groups are most certainly aware of radio's importance to them. The Catholic Writer's Guild includes script writers. The Federal Council of the Churches of Christ in America maintains a Department of National Religious Radio. And the Congregational, Christian, Methodist and Presbyterian churches of the United States have a Joint Radio Committee which holds annual conferences.

---

[24] Clifford J. Durr, speech made at annual meeting of National Council of Chief State School Officers, Baltimore, Maryland, December 2, 1945, p. 8.

All of the major networks have adopted policies relative to the broadcasting of religious services, and while there is some difference, the basic elements are similar: emphasis is placed on nonsectarian and nondenominational messages; outstanding leaders and preachers are sought rather than the comparatively unknown ones; emphasis is given to the broad spiritual and social messages of religion rather than to narrow creed; educational aspects of religion are encouraged.

Religion in turn has had important effects upon radio; that of controlling, in some instances, the types of program through the organized pressure of religious groups. For example, the power of the Catholic Church has been used to prevent discussion of the topic of birth control over the air.

Since the days of Father Coughlin there has been an alarming tendency in this country for a quasi-Fascist type of preacher who has no pulpit other than the air to seek the radio as a means of disseminating his dangerous propaganda. Both the FCC and the radio stations have shown a great amount of courage in combating this trend. It is a difficult stand for any station or public body to take, for the broadcaster masquerading as a speaker of religious doctrine can and does level the charges of censorship of religion and the misinformed public becomes outraged.

Father Coughlin, who carried just such statements to his listeners, left the air when WMCA, the Detroit station over which he broadcast, asked to have the right to read and comment on his scripts before his broadcasts. Father Coughlin however, did not dare to give them this chance. He left the air at once.

Another famous case is that of the Philadelphia Gospel Broadcasters Association. Station WPEN dropped them because of the dangerous sentiments their speakers were voicing under the pretext of Christian teachings. The Association immediately set up a strong cry, hired lawyers and attempted to get the FCC to take action. The FCC, however, after study, refused to honor the Association's petition for a hearing.

Radio and Education

Education is supposedly one of our most important phases of social control. Its relationships with radio are becoming more numerous and complex. Educational broadcasts have been utilized in many schools as teaching techniques, especially in such fields of learning as music, dramatics, and the social sciences.

Adult education has also been stimulated by radio and thousands of individuals are now "studying courses" over the air. Talks to mothers on domestic science and child care; to farmers on pest control and soil conservation; to rural households on elementary aspects of health and hygiene; discussions of current political and economic questions: all are helping to bring education long sought by many adults. Colleges are both giving extension courses and publicizing their regular work by the radio.

The radio as an educative instrument has certain definite advantages: (1) Radio sharpens the perceptive mechanism. Through dramatization, through reaching the student in a novel and interesting way, material that might otherwise be presented coldly is portrayed vividly. Therefore learning is heightened. (2) It presents "history in the making"; brings to students a sense of participating as witnesses in the important events of their time. (3) It brings to the school program the voices and opinions of great men and women—scientists, statesmen and noted specialists in every field. (4) Great music can be brought into the school. The musical programs of the major networks have been utilized by many schools to the permanent advantage of students and teachers. (5) It sets the example for better use of the language, especially the spoken word, an area in which all teachers do not necessarily set the best example. (6) Radio can be used as an important supplemental teaching aid in nearly any traditional subject. (7) Continued use of radio in the classroom develops better habits of listening, provides wholesome recreational experience, gives esthetic satisfaction and helps to develop better standards of taste and judgment. (8) In a sense, radio compels or stimulates a teacher to be well-informed. Use of radio in the classroom should be followed by discussion and a teaching program. A teacher must have a thorough knowledge to keep up with radio's intangible and up-to-the-minute "personality."

Unless the school system operates a radio station of its own, the cooperation of existing commercial stations and networks must be relied upon. Educational institutions were among the earliest licensees of standard broadcast stations. University engineers pioneered in the construction of radio stations. By 1925, 171 licenses had been granted to educational groups. Between 1926 and 1934, the Federal Radio Commission licensed more than 100 standard broadcast stations to educational institutions. But, largely because of the increased competition from commercial radio, most of these educational stations were off the air by 1934.[25]

By 1945, only 31 standard broadcast stations were licensed to or operated by educational institutions. Twenty-two of these stations are completely noncommercial—that is, they sell no time to advertisers.[26]

Many local stations and networks have been cooperative in furnishing

---

[25] Federal Communications Commission, *Background Information on Educational Broadcasting in the United States*, March 7, 1945, p. 1.

[26] *Ibid.*, pp. 1-2.

time and talent for educational broadcasting. In doing so they are also fulfilling their public service responsibilities. Philadelphia is a noteworthy example of cooperation between the local stations and the Board of Education.

However, our American system of broadcasting is, after all, a business. We have accepted this and indicated the desire to keep it so with government supervision only. Therefore, broadcasters depend on the sponsored program for profit. As figures quoted earlier in this chapter show, educational programs unfortunately foot the list in popularity in many parts of the country. Broadcasters and sponsors are thus little tempted to aid this type of program. This partially accounts for the limited use of radio as an educative medium.

Radio Education's Second Chance. Frequency modulation has come to be called radio education's second chance. In 1940, following the allocation of FM channels to the public on a regular basis, FCC set aside certain of these channels for the exclusive use of noncommercial education stations. It is now very much up to the educator to avail himself of this opportunity.

Use of Radio by the School System. The public school systems of New York, Chicago, San Francisco, Cleveland and many other cities operate outstanding FM stations.

Perhaps the story of one of these stations would give valuable illustrations of the use of radio in the school both as a direct and a supplemental teaching device. The Chicago Board of Education holds the license to operate FM station WBEZ. The following is its stated basic policy: "Radio in the classroom must be a pleasurable listening experience; radio should supplement the work of the students and teacher within the classroom; radio should motivate some further action on the part of the listening students under the guidance of teachers." [27]

The Radio Council for the Chicago Public Schools formulates the policies for WBEZ and accepts the following basic responsibilities: (1) to the teacher and student in the classroom; (2) to the school administration as a public relations medium; (3) to the public to disseminate general information, education, news and entertainment.

In fulfilling its responsibility to the classroom, the Radio Council, which has a full staff of technicians, writes and produces programs for specific grade levels and definite subject areas. Literature, foreign languages, mathematics, safety, English, American history, news, art, and social studies are some of the subjects covered. A teacher's handbook is published with suggestions for her preparation, follow-up, word lists,

---

[27] George Jennings, "Radio in the Chicago Public Schools," *Education*, LXV (December, 1944), pp. 197-201.

supplemental reading and film lists. A program bulletin is published weekly. The station also leases a standard news service.

Three regular staff members of the Radio Council, who are also teachers, are assigned to various regions of the city. They are available to the principal and the appointed Radio Chairman, and teachers in each school for consultation on the use of the programs, and on other problems. Most of the talent for programs is supplied by students from high schools, junior colleges, and little theaters in the Chicago area. Thus, students receive broadcast acting and technical experience. The station also puts on many programs of interest to the general public. These have included: news, music, bond-buying programs and dramatized educational features.

Radio, Universities, and Adult Education. Several of our universities, particularly land grant colleges, are licensed operators of radio stations. These stations largely serve as a part of the state system. But they have a definite and important place in educational broadcasting. These stations are particularly valuable in the university's extension work. The courses usually lend themselves to radio—history, social sciences, literature, languages, psychology. However, the station operated by Michigan Agricultural College once had a course in poultry management with 500 listeners enrolled. Purdue experimented with radio courses in bookkeeping and typing.[28]

University radio stations also provide a valuable laboratory in all types of training for radio participation. Today more than 400 colleges offer some sort of a course in radio. The University of Alabama recently decided to set up radio courses in all seven departments of the College of Arts and Sciences in addition to a Department of Radio Arts. The radio workshop at the University of Syracuse successfully produces programs over local stations for civic organizations.[29]

Station WHA of the University of Wisconsin, one of the first stations to operate in this country, serves as a good illustration of the services performed by a university station to both college and state. It also tells the story of some of the typical problems and pitfalls of the university station.

WHA grew out of experiments in the Physics Department. A professor in the Extension Department saw its possibilities for his work and convinced others. The College of Agriculture also became interested, and funds were obtained from the University budget. In 1928, some seven or eight years after the station first began to operate, President Glenn Frank took a great interest in it and appointed a small group of men to study its possibilities further.

[28] C. J. Friedrich and Jeanette Sayre, *Radiobroadcasting and Higher Education* (Cambridge: Littauer Center, Harvard University, May, 1942), p. 18.
[29] *Ibid.*, p. 29.

During the depression, the State of Wisconsin was forced to cut funds for education and suddenly WHA found itself without a place in the university budget. Governor LaFollette, however, was approached and he became an enthusiastic supporter of the station. WHA was given emergency funds. During this same period new uses for the station were found. Pre-election broadcasts were held by both parties; sessions of the state legislature were broadcast; and the Board of Health and State Highway Commission found the station extremely useful.

In 1938 the station was transferred to the jurisdiction of the Board of Regents who authorized the appointment of a representative Radio Council including both university people and outside interests. Recently the station was returned to the direct control of the University with a separate budget of its own.

In 1939, WHA decided to expand so that it could serve every corner of the state. It applied to FCC for an increased power, clear channel license. Private broadcasters bitterly opposed this move. The bill to provide funds for this expansion was heartily endorsed by many civic groups. It passed the State Assembly, but was never acted upon in the Senate. The project had to be dropped.

Adult education is a field in which the commercial stations could do much more as well. The same problems that apply to all educational broadcasts arise here. Several years ago, in the interests of making better use of the radio as a medium for adult education, the National Advisory Council on Radio was formed. It is no longer in existence, but one of the results of its work is still seen in the education and public service counsellors who are now full-time employees of the networks. The NBC University of the Air and the CBS American School of the Air were also outgrowths of the work and conferences of the National Advisory Council. Forum programs in which both sides of current issues are discussed by experts are an important addition to adult education as well. Each of the networks has at least one outstanding program of this type.

The Government also takes a great interest in the use of radio in education. It began to do so when Herbert Hoover was Secretary of Commerce and had, under the Act of 1912, radio licensing powers. In 1935 the new FCC and the U. S. Office of Education sponsored, but did not finance, the Federal Radio Education Committee to bring the educators and the broadcasters together. The Office of Education also has a radio division which today is primarily engaged in stimulating and helping educational groups to take complete advantage of the FM channels reserved for their exclusive use. The Office of Education also maintains a script and transcription service to furnish such to all those who request them. A monthly list of educational radio programs is also published.

Radio's Full Educational Potential Is Not Used. In addition to the uneven race between the noncommercial stations and the advertiser financed broadcasters, there are many other problems to be considered before educational broadcasting can realize its full potential. Many schools do not have receiving equipment, although the installation cost would be comparatively low. Just as rural listeners in general are inadequately served by existing radio, so are rural schools. It is quite possible that the establishment of state-wide FM networks will go a long way toward solving this problem.

Two groups must be further educated to the use of radio in this area. The first is the public. Since educational radio is always faced with the grim problem of finances, it must often depend on state legislatures for grants. Recently the state auditor of West Virginia refused to approve an item in the budget of the State University to cover the cost of radio broadcasting. This auditor was unable to believe that radio broadcasting had anything to do with education. His comment was that some of the people concerned were merely trying to get publicity for themselves. The California State Legislature recently refused to approve an expenditure that would have enabled the addition of a radio expert to the State Department of Education. If the public understood educational radio's possibility better, they would be in a position to convince their recalcitrant state and local officials of the need for it.

Oddly enough the other group that needs educating is the educator. Radio has been difficult to sell to schools. It has been an unfamiliar medium. Very few teachers' colleges have courses to train teachers in its uses and potentialities. Also, many teachers seem to fear a form of technological unemployment that will result in their profession if radio is used.[30] Upon analysis, it does not seem possible that radio can ever become THE teacher. ". . . programs do not . . . supersede the teacher. Rather, the teacher can use such programs just as she uses textbooks, maps, and other classroom aids." [31]

Radio and Government. Radio is important to our democratic form of government in two different ways. It has become more and more of a "campaign instrument," part of the familiar argument, flag waving and speech making we go through in this country in the course of choosing our governmental representatives. The radio is also used by the group which is governing to perform an enormous number of extremely valuable public services.

As previously mentioned, radio is of comparatively less influence in

---

[30] Norman Woelfel and I. Keith Tyler, *Radio and the School* (Yonkers: World Book Co., 1945), pp. 6-7.

[31] Speech by Clifford J. Durr, at Conference on FM Education, Austin, Texas, September 27, 1945.

a democratic state than in a totalitarian one. However, the radio is becoming more and more important in American political life.

It has permitted candidates to reach all strata of the population without
resort to the press, and has consequently placed emphasis on the importance of fine speaking. Educational programs have given the people in
general the opportunity for greater political enlightenment on the issues
of the day. Nominating conventions have modified their practices since
every word becomes the instant property of millions of voters. Many
improvements will no doubt be made in the conduct of our elected representatives in the Senate and House chambers if the legislation which
proposes broadcasting Congressional sessions should pass. Many Congressmen also make good use of the transcription service in the Capitol. They make recordings of their views and speeches and send them
to home stations as a means of keeping in touch with their constituents.

The political party in power may tend to have more advantage in its
use of radio, not only because the President and other national officers
have somewhat freer access to the radio, but because the national networks have tended to be fearful of the Federal Communications Commission and its political possibilities.

Paul Lazarsfeld and his staff made an important study in the months
preceding and immediately following the 1940 elections. They made
careful and methodical surveys in a picked sample county (Erie County,
Ohio) to determine how the voter makes up his mind in a Presidential
campaign. This study revealed some interesting facts about the use of
radio.[32]

Voters were asked, in retrospect, to indicate the source which proved
most important to them. "Although the radio and newspaper ranked
about the same as general sources, the radio was mentioned half again
as frequently as the single most important source of influence. Half of
those who mentioned the radio at all considered it their most important
source of information, whereas only a third of those who initially mentioned the newspaper regarded it as most important." [33]

During the last two months of the campaign, when the amount of
political material on the radio was more nearly equal to that which had
been appearing in the papers, radio was mentioned more frequently as a
factor in influencing a change in the voter's decisions.

As a general summary of radio's importance, Lazarsfeld, Berelson and
Gaudet have this to say: "Differences in the way the campaign is waged
in print and on the air probably account for this [greater influence of
radio]. . . . a considerable amount of political material appears in the

---

[32] Paul F. Lazarsfeld, Bernard Berelson, and Hazel Gaudet, *The People's Choice:
How the Voter Makes Up His Mind in a Presidential Campaign* (New York: Duell,
Sloan and Pearce, 1944).　　　[33] *Ibid.*, pp. 126-127.

press from the beginning to the end of the campaign. . . . In time, the claims and counter-claims of the parties as they appear in cold print came to pall upon the reader who had been exposed to essentially the same stuff over an extended period. The campaign on the radio however, was much more cursory in its early phases and became vigorous and sustained only toward the close.

"Secondly, the radio campaign consists much more of 'events' of distinctive interest. A political convention is broadcast and the listener can virtually participate in the ceremonial occasion: he can respond to audience enthusiasm, he can directly experience the ebb and flow of tension. Similarly with a major speech by one of the candidates: it is more dramatic than the same speech in the newspapers next morning." [34]

Perhaps one of the most important services the radio can perform for our government is that of bringing the Chief Executive or other government officials directly to us with messages of importance, the latest explanations of administrative and legislative programs. During the war the radio was of tremendous importance in keeping the morale of the country high and in creating an understanding of the necessity for war measures. It is of interest to note that, by Hooper ratings, the President's radio message declaring war the day after Pearl Harbor was listened to by more people than any other program studied since such surveys began.

Many government departments have a particular interest in the radio as an aid in performing their services. The Federal Communications Commission's role is discussed in a later section. The use of radio in diplomatic and international relations has already been discussed.

The Department of Agriculture has used radio for more than twenty years. A whole section of the agency is devoted to preparing market news and reports which are used by over half the radio stations in the country. The study of rural listeners referred to earlier in this chapter showed that these market reports were the programs which the farmer felt were second most important to him of all broadcasts to which he listened. Eighty-three per cent of the farmers who listened spoke of the great help they received from these programs.

The Department of Agriculture keeps a staff of 187 federal market reporters who cover "the produce trade during the hours of active trading to obtain . . . a complete late accounting of trading, demand, supplies, quality, conditions, prices and marketing trends." [35]

The United States Department of the Interior maintains a modern broadcasting and recording studio to service the remainder of the government. Some of the transcriptions and other secret programs having to

---

[34] *Ibid.*, pp. 128-129.
[35] War Food Administration, *Marketing Activities* (December, 1944), p. 11.

do with the most important aspects of our psychological warfare were supervised and made in these studios.

Important training programs were made for the Army and Navy. Many other government agencies use these valuable facilities every day. Radio has become as important to the American Government as it has to the American people.

Radio and Economic Life. On all aspects of our economic life radio has made its impact felt. Some businesses have suffered, others have benefited by this new device. Advertising has been given a powerful new medium through which potential customers can better be reached and convinced. New commodities have been foisted upon the public more quickly because of the ease with which the populace can be reached by radio.

Hundreds of thousands of individuals have found employment in radio and allied industries; new occupations have risen to challenge the abilities of men and women. Hundreds of our young people have received special training in many of radio's newer developments in the Army and Navy.[36]

Farmers have profited greatly by the quicker receipt of weather information, by the dissemination of agricultural advice and by obtaining market reports.

Transportation, as well as production and consumption, has been affected. Radio beams have enabled a much wider development of commercial aviation; radio found one of its earliest uses in guiding ships at sea. Communication between planes, ships, and land stations has facilitated certain types of business transactions. The discovery and development of radar will revolutionize transportation and make all vehicles extremely safe means of travel.

Radio and Recreational and Artistic Life. Play and art are important phases of social control in all culture patterns. The radio has certainly had important effects upon these aspects of our life.

Millions of people can partake of entertainment that has never reached them before. National sporting events, great musical concerts, and fine dramatizations have enriched the lives of countless Americans. The revival of old songs has been encouraged; the interest in many types of sports and hobbies has been stimulated. Entertainment on trains, ships and in automobiles has been increased. Knowledge of the artistic and literary accomplishments of the past has been furthered.

Public recreation departments are more and more utilizing the radio

---

[36] Among the many excellent studies of occupational possibilities in radio is Kenneth Bartlett and Douglass Miller's *Occupations in Radio*, Monograph 12 Chicago Science Research Associates, occupational studies, 1945.

to bring good music to larger audiences, to stimulate home games, dramatics, and various rainy-day activities. Amateur theatricals are finding a fertile field on the air, and worth-while hobbies are being encouraged by recreational leaders through this same medium.

Like so many uses of radio other than the straight commercial, radio can do much more to enrich and add to recreational and artistic knowledge in this country. Apparently, more and more, many people are desiring such performance from their radios. Jascha Heifetz, the famous violinist, after completing his third trip for USO camp shows to service men abroad, returned more convinced than ever that thousands of Americans whom he met are hungry for good music and would become devotees of the classics if they could hear more of them.[37] Once more it is radio's responsibility to lead rather than to lag behind.

Radio and "One World." It is just such inventions as the radio that have made the world a small place, a place in which the cultures and activities of every nation are important to every other nation. The growth of understanding and the development of "one world" are of incalculable importance to our own country.

During the war, the Office of War Information and the Office of Inter-American Affairs operated 39 short-wave radio transmitters and broadcast a total of 168 hours daily in 41 languages. These programs served both as propaganda in the psychological warfare battles with our enemies, and as a means of creating solidarity and trust among the United Nations.

At the end of the war these functions were turned over to the Department of State and, at the writing of this book, this agency was making plans for a peacetime continuation of short-wave broadcasting to practically every part of the world. Studies were being made to determine whether the government should continue to operate, maintain and program the transmitters and frequencies it had used during the war, or whether such activities should be turned over to public and private corporations. The final decisions rest with Congress.

Various spokesmen for the State Department have expressed the importance of continuing such a program. Secretary of State Byrnes, in a letter to President Truman, stated: "There never was a time, even in the midst of war, when it was so necessary to replace prejudice with truth, distortion with balance, and suspicion with understanding." [38]

A State Department bulletin suggested: "Some areas of the world such as the Balkans, can be reached by news from America by no other means [except short-wave radio]. The Department feels radio is playing an

---

[37] Cited in speech by Congressman Emmanuel Celler, August 7, 1945.

[38] James F. Byrnes, Secretary of State, *Letter to President Truman*, December 31, 1945.

essential role in giving foreign peoples a better understanding of American aims, policies and institutions." [39]

Assistant Secretary of State, William Benton, in charge of Cultural Relations, said: Radio, and the other plans in the total picture of cultural exchange "add up . . . to a favorable beginning of a permanent, continuous two-way cultural and informational exchange which may eventually do more for world security than a fleet of battleships—and at a tiny fraction of the cost." [40]

Social Control of the Radio

In all modern countries the government has the ultimate control over all phases of communication. This control may be coercive and direct, or it may be more permissive and indirect. The totalitarian governments of Europe completely dominated the airlanes and utilized the radio directly for propaganda purposes.

In England, the radio has been regarded as means of public entertainment and information. Radio in Great Britain is supervised through the medium of a franchised corporation. In Canada there are competing public and private radio networks. The Canadian Broadcasting Company owns and operates certain stations, operates Canada's major network and regulates commercial broadcasting. But there are also privately owned and operated stations.

In the United States and most of the South American countries, radio has been developed primarily by private commercial interests for private profit, with governmental supervision being comparatively light.

The American System of Broadcasting. Private ownership and operation of radio have prevailed in this country, with a minimum of government regulation. This has meant comparative freedom from governmental propaganda, but comparative domination by private business propaganda. It has meant concentration of broadcasting power in the hands of large corporations, particularly the National Broadcasting Company and the Columbia Broadcasting System. There are three other smaller networks. These include the Mutual Broadcasting System, which, instead of owning stations, is cooperatively owned by a group of stations.

The American system of broadcasting has meant a remarkable quantity and quality of program and, at the same time, a limitation favoring pro-

---

[39] Department of State Bulletin, *Plans for International Information Service* (summary by Assistant Secretary Benton), December 30, 1945, p. 1046.

[40] William F. Benton. *"Can America Afford To Be Silent?"* speech before a meeting of the American Platform Guild, Washington, D.C., January 3, 1946. A thorough and interesting study of the potentialities in the whole field of international information is available from the State Department: Dr. Arthur W. MacMahon, *The Postwar International Information Program of the United States*, State Department Publication 2438 (Washington, D.C.: U. S. Government Printing Office).

grams in the interests of financial backers. If one were to attempt to chart the assets and liabilities of the American system of broadcasting he would have something like this:

Assets	*Liabilities*
1. Abundance and variety of programs exceeding those of any other nation.	1. Excessive advertising, tending to injure program appreciation.
2. Freedom from political and governmental censorship and domination.	2. Domination by private financial and business interests.
3. Competition, making for diversification of program content.	3. Censorship in interests of certain business and religious groups.
4. Large number of stations and consequently of programs.	4. Frequent duplication of programs in some areas, lack in others.
5. News reaching public quickly, and comparatively unbiased.	5. Certain types of news ignored or minimized.

Public Regulation of Radio. As the potential power of the new device, radio, became understood, as many unheard of developments became realized, some federal control and supervision of radio became increasingly necessary. Recognition that radio could affect every aspect of our welfare and culture came early. In 1910 Congress passed a law requiring all ships carrying fifty or more people to be equipped with "efficient apparatus for radio communication."

In 1912, eight years before station KDKA had begun broadcasting, Congress passed a rather comprehensive Radio Act. The bill was primarily concerned with wireless telegraphy, but it also contained provisions for licensing commercial broadcasting. The power to license was vested in the Secretaries of Commerce and Labor.

Patent Controls and Network Controls. The Government's efforts to exercise controls over broadcasting, in the public interest, fell into two main periods. While the two early measures mentioned were enacted into law, the government's efforts during radio's infancy were largely devoted to protecting the public from any monopoly or restrictions in the field of radio inventions and technical developments.

This activity reached its peak in 1932 when an anti-trust suit was launched against the Radio Corporation of America. RCA was charged with having a monopoly over virtually all aspects of radio manufacturing, and the case resulted in a consent decree aimed at breaking this "log jam" of patent and licensing agreements.

As radio became more and more of a force in America, the government began to concentrate more of its energy upon the regulation of the uses to which radio devices were being put. In 1926 two lower Federal Courts and the Attorney General decided that the Secretary of Commerce did not have the power to refuse to grant licenses or prohibit broadcasting on certain frequencies at certain times. Chaos resulted. Everyone fought for the most desirable frequencies. Many stations "wave jumped." The resulting program interference must have been very like the purposeful "jamming" used in wartime to make enemy radio broadcasts unintelligible to their own listeners. It was like rush-hour traffic without stop and go signals.

Congress provided a "traffic policeman" the following year in the form of the Radio Act of 1927. The power to regulate Interstate Commerce given Congress in the Constitution was used as a basis for this law.

The Communications Act of 1934. The best features of the Act of 1927 were kept in the sections covering broadcasting in the Communications Act of 1934. For the first time the phrase "for public convenience, interest or necessity" had been used in the Act of 1927. This concept was retained, and it had long since become familiar in public utility legislation.

The Act of 1934 was designated as an act "for the regulation of interstate and foreign communication by wire or radio." It is the law under which the Federal Government now regulates radio and other means of communication. The Federal Commuications Commission was established by this Act. The Commission is composed of seven members, only four of whom can be of the same political party. The members are appointed by the President subject to the advice and consent of the Senate.

The Act of 1934 gives the Commission some of the following general powers: ". . . The Commission from time to time, as public convenience, interest or necessity requires, shall . . ." classify radio stations, prescribe the nature of service to be rendered, assign bands of frequencies to the various stations, make special regulations designed to carry out the Act, study new uses for radio and generally encourage larger and more effective use, and have authority to make special regulations applicable to chain broadcasting.

Licensing Powers. The Commission is of course empowered to license all broadcasting stations and no station can legally operate without such a license. The Act instructs the Commission to grant or renew such licenses on the determination that "public interest, convenience or necessity will be served."

A license is granted for a period of three years only. Prior use of a particular frequency does not give the user any priority to or "ownership" of that frequency in any sense. In fact, the Act expressly reserves to the people of the United States the *title* to radio channels.

The Commission is also given the power to revoke licenses or refuse renewal. However, since its establishment in 1934, FCC has revoked fewer than half a dozen licenses and these usually on the grounds of false or perjured information filed with the application for a license.

The Commission is also furnished with the semi-judicial arm or administrative tribunal that has become a familiar device in certain executive agencies. The Commissioners, or employees designated by them, may call or subpoena witnesses, examine witnesses and documents, and do many of the other things that courts often do to obtain information necessary to the making of specific decisions. The Commissioners may also call investigations or hearings based on the complaints of private citizens. Recourse to the courts is available to any party who feels himself injured by an FCC decision.

The Act of 1934 also gave the President practically unlimited power over radio in case of "war or threat of war or a state of public peril or disaster or other national emergency." This provision is frequently attacked on the grounds that an unscrupulous chief exective could declare an emergency to suit his convenience and use this power for his own personal and selfish ends. Moreover, the President has been given the authority under the Act to reserve wave lengths deemed necessary for such governmental agencies as may need them.

It is interesting to note, then, that, although the President delegated his authority over radio during the recent war to a special Board of War Communications made up of members of many government departments, this Board never found it necessary to exercise the control provided.

The Federal Communications Commission did, however, perform several valuable wartime services. The Radio Intelligence Division investigated illicit and subversive broadcasting, helped planes in distress with radio signals, and engaged in many other activities. The Foreign Broadcast Intelligence Service monitored and edited programs from stations in fifty-five countries. News and intelligence obtained was translated and turned over to United Nations agencies and officials.

Chain Broadcasting Regulations. Chain broadcasting is defined in the Communications Act of 1934 as "simultaneous broadcasting of an identical program by two or more connected stations." Network broadcasting is more or less synonymous in that many stations are either wholly owned or affiliated with the major networks by contract. NBC or CBS, for example, agree in their contracts with individual stations to furnish them so many unit hours of programs, and the stations are paid for broadcasting these. Thus, all over the country we have programs of the major networks being broadcast simultaneously. This is possible in one of several ways. Programs may be transmitted by wire, usually through leased telephone lines. The transcribed—or specially recorded program—is also a familiar device.

The first network broadcasting took place in 1923. In January of that year a special circuit was set up between WEAF in New York City and WNAC in Boston.[41] In December, 1923, station WJZ, wholly owned by the Radio Corporation of America, and General Electric's WGY in Schenectady completed a wire hook-up.[42]

In a few years network or chain broadcasting had grown enormously. The major impetus was the growth of radio financing through commercial advertisers sponsoring programs. That is, parcels of time were sold to advertisers who then used the time both to entertain the public and to market their wares. Chain broadcasting provided a large circulation for these advertisers.

By 1938 three national networks: the National Broadcasting Company operating two networks, the Red and Blue; the Columbia Broadcasting System; and the Mutual Broadcasting System were responsible for almost half of the total business of all commercial broadcast stations in the United States.[43] These facts are significant because it was in 1938 that FCC began action which spelled its entrance into a new phase and interpretation of government control over broadcasting.

Prior to this time most of FCC's work had been of an engineering nature. The agency had assigned frequencies and operated on a technical level. However, in March, 1938, FCC issued its famous Order No. 37 authorizing an investigation "to determine what special regulations applicable to radio stations engaged in chain or other broadcasting are required in the public interest, convenience or necessity." Three of the Commissioners were appointed to hold hearings covering all aspects of chain broadcasting.

It is an interesting fact that the motivation for these investigations did not come from FCC but from Congress. In 1937, three resolutions had been introduced into the House of Representatives calling for an investigation of monopolistic controls over broadcasting. In the Senate, White of Maine had introduced a resolution calling for "a thorough and complete investigation of the broadcasting industry in the United States and of broadcasting, and the acts, rules, regulations and policies of the Federal Communications Commission with respect to broadcasting." [44]

Painstaking hearings continued until May, 1939. In June, 1940, the Commission issued its report including some draft regulations designed to curb practices indicated by evidence compiled in the hearings to be monopolistic, prohibitive to competition and against the public interest.

[41] Federal Communications Commission, *Report on Chain Broadcasting,* May, 1941, p. 5, footnote 1.
[42] Thomas Porter Robinson, *Radio Networks and the Federal Government* (New York: Columbia University Press, 1943), p. 12.
[43] Federal Communications Commission, Report on Chain Broadcasting, *op. cit.,* p. 3.
[44] Robinson, *op. cit.,* p. 65.

The regulations largely consisted of refusal to grant licenses to standard broadcast if any of the following conditions were present:

1. The station is prevented from or penalized for broadcasting the programs of other networks according to the provisions of its contract.

2. Other stations in the area are prevented from using network programs not used by the station in question, or if any station is hindered from broadcasting any program.

3. Contracts for network affiliations endure for more than a year.

4. A station is prevented from refusing any network program it considers contrary to the public interest.

5. The station is affiliated with a network organization which maintains control over more than one network (this was aimed directly at the break-up of NBC's Red and Blue networks).

6. The station contract prevents or penalizes it for altering its rates for sale of broadcast time other than that used for network programs.

As one might imagine, the issuance of these chain broadcasting regulations caused a flurry of protest and court action. NBC and CBS sought injunctions to prevent the Commission from putting the regulations into effect. Mutual sided with FCC. The case of NBC and CBS finally reached the Supreme Court which ruled that the networks were entitled to judicial review of the regulations before such were made effective.

In the meantime the Department of Justice had jumped into the fray. On December 31, 1941, anti-trust proceedings were brought against NBC and CBS. However, the case was drawn up with the proviso that proceedings would be dropped if the chain broadcasting regulations were upheld in the court battles then being fought over them.

FCC's chain broadcasting regulations were upheld by the courts in 1943. (NBC v. U. S. 319 U. S. Supreme Court, 190). Some of the results are familiar to all of us. In January, 1942, with the sanction of FCC, the National Broadcasting Company had already begun plans for the disposal of the Blue network. After the Supreme Court decision, this action was carried out and today we have the wholly independent American Broadcasting Company. A fifth network, the Associated Broadcasting System, which could not have been formed before the issuance of the chain broadcasting regulations, has recently come into being. And, undoubtedly many practices that stifled competition, affected the quality of programs, and kept newcomers from the radio field, have been brought to an end.

Statutory Authority. The controversies, legal and otherwise, which raged over FCC's chain broadcasting regulations, centered on two questions which the Commission itself phrased:

"First, has the Commission authority to deny a license or renewal on the ground that the applicants' contractual relations with a network either impair his ability to operate in the public interest or limit the maximum utilization of radio facilities by artificially restraining competition and restricting the growth and development of new networks?

"Secondly, in the event the first question is answered in the affirmative, could the Commission formulate into general rules and regulations the principles which it intends to apply in passing on individual applications." [45]

FCC relied on the Communications Act of 1934, itself, on testimony given at the time it and the Radio Act of 1927 were discussed in Congress, and on the language of certain Supreme Court decisions. The networks went to approximately the same sources for their arguments.

The Commission pointed particularly to the instruction given it to act "in the public interest," and to the provision that appeared both in the Act of 1927 and the Act of 1934 giving it power "to make special regulations applicable to stations engaged in chain broadcasting."

When the original Act of 1927, much of which was retained in 1934, was written, testimony and debate illustrated the intention of the drafters to provide the executive agency with the power to protect the public against broadcasting monopolies. Sections 311 and 313 of the Communications Act of 1934 empower the Commission to refuse licenses to any one adjudged guilty of breaking the anti-trust laws. However, the networks contended that these clauses left the decision as to what constituted a monopoly to the Department of Justice and only thereafter could FCC act.

In the Pottsville Broadcasting Case, January, 1940, Justice Frankfurter held that: "Congress in enacting that law [Communications Act of 1934] moved under the spirit of a wide-spread fear that in the absence of governmental control, the public interest might be subordinated to monopolistic domination in the broadcasting field. So, to avert this danger, Congress gave the Commission power to deal with chain broadcasting in clear-cut and unequivocal terms." [46]

The Supreme Court decision which upheld the regulations stated:

"The Commissions licensing function cannot be discharged, therefore, merely by finding that there are no technological objections to the granting of a license. If the criterion of 'public interest' were limited to such matters, how could the Commission choose between two applicants for the same facilities, each of whom is financially and technically qualified to operate a station? Since the very inception of federal regulation by radio, comparative considerations as to the service rendered have

---

[45] Federal Communications Commission, Report on Chain Broadcasting, *op. cit.*, p. 80.
[46] Quoted in Robinson, *op. cit.*, p. 92.

governed the application of the standard of 'public interest, convenience, or necessity.' " [47]

The Problem of Censorship. One of our most jealously guarded American rights is the guarantee of freedom of speech. Congress, in drafting the Communications Act of 1934, had this very much in mind. In strong language censorship or interference with freedom of speech was prohibited:

"Nothing in this Act shall be understood or construed to give the Commission the power of censorship over the radio communications or signals transmitted by any radio station, and no regulation or condition shall be promulgated or fixed by the Commission which shall interfere with the right of free speech by means of radio communication. No person within the jurisdiction of the United States may utter any obscene, indecent, or profane language by means of radio communication."

However, under the public interest clause, FCC has held certain types of programs to be "non-meritorious." Stations broadcasting these do so at the risk of having their licenses revoked, although, as pointed out earlier, such has seldom been the case. These frowned-upon programs include: advertisements for "quack" medical remedies, for nonscientific medical advice, for fraudulent business schemes, for gambling and astrological advice. Programs which tend to attack organized religious groups, which advocate extreme political and economic panaceas, and which are contrary to accepted moral standards are regarded as questionable and often refused by the stations themselves.

Some people may feel that censorship is implied or possible because of the limited number of new licenses that FCC can grant. This is unavoidable because there are just so many spaces available on the frequency band. This, then, places upon FCC not only the responsibility for giving licenses to those who will serve "public interest, convenience, or necessity," but the Commission must often choose from a number of applications the one who will serve the public interest BEST.

Thereafter, since, in a sense, an unavoidable natural monopoly exists, some agency representing the public must exercise constant vigilance to see that the stations in existence, those fortunate enough to have secured their "homesteads" on a parcel of the ether, operate in the interests of the general public, and not in the interests of a small group of advertisers or network owners. This would certainly explain the need for a changed and broadened interpretation of the functions of FCC much as any change in our society and economy accounts for new interpretations of the role of government in general.

New inventions in radio, such as frequency modulation, utilize a por-

---

[47] NBC v. U. S. 319. U. S. Supreme Court, 190, pp. 216-217.

tion of the radio spectrum not previously available and thus make many new stations possible. However, already 71.3 per cent of the applications made for FM station licenses have come from existing networks and stations.[48]

Advertiser Control versus Audience Control. Perhaps then, still a new period must come in the exercise of FCC authority. It is one that would be met with cries of censorship from some and would be received by others as a form of protecting the public's right to "free hearing."

It will be, at best, a difficult and controversial issue. People in the radio business point out that radio is already subject to many more controls than the press or the movies. This is most certainly true. On the other hand, studies have shown that the radio reaches by far the largest audience of any of the means of communication and that it has become more influential in opinion formation.

There are many who have written and discussed radio who feel that safeguards lie in "audience control." That is, audience likes and dislikes will ultimately control the content of a program because at least some of the audience represent potential markets to the advertisers who finance the programs. Thus, the audience must be favorably impressed. The advertiser is certainly conscious of these facts as evidenced by the amount of money spent on listener research. On the other hand, some feel that the advertiser has lost his sensitivity to audience likes and dislikes, for many of the polls show a marked distaste for the increasing commercialization of programs and the plethora of advertising.

Audience control reaches a point and then stops. It would extend with difficulty to the intangible realm of what is *not* heard, what is kept off the air. There are few instances in which audience control has penetrated the "opinion" program area. Recently one of the large networks notified a commercial sponsor that it would drop him from the air if he did not cease to use a certain radio commentator. This action was motivated by the receipt of hundreds of letters from listeners protesting against the warped views and extreme editorialization of the commentator in reporting the news. However, a week after the commentator was dropped by his sponsor, he was back on the air over another network and with a new advertiser backing him.

The problem of "advertiser control" is of much greater significance. Clifford Durr, one of FCC's Commissioners has phrased it as follows:

"Advertising pressures have crowded more and more meritorious sustaining programs from the air or relegated them to undesirable listening hours: and economic concentrations in the control of program sources have been built up which threaten that diversity in the sources of news

---

[48] Statistics, as of November, 1945, from FCC.

and opinion upon which we must rely for the safety of our democratic institutions." [49]

Even members of the industry have recognized and admitted the problem. Mr. Niles Trammel, President of NBC, stated before the Senate Committee on Interstate Commerce in December, 1943:

"The argument is now advanced that business control of broadcasting operations has nothing to do with program control. This is to forget that 'He who controls the pocketbook controls the man.' Business control means complete control and there is no use arguing to the contrary." [50]

As long ago as 1937, serious studies were made to determine the extent of this problem of advertiser control. Ruth Brindze and others pointed out many examples of radio control that had reached the point of class or group domination. Criticism of public utilities, of advertisers in general, of capitalism; espousal of such causes as birth control or unionism, and others have been kept off the air either by the networks or by the individual stations. The fact that the law holds the station equally responsible with the speaker for violation of the law may be blamed in part for this censorship, but hardly for all of it.[51]

Not only can the law be held guiltless as an excuse for such censorship, but the plea of "editorial selection" frequently advanced is a weak one. Miss Brindze has expressed the theory that "everyone in the radio world has one inviolate rule: nothing must be broadcast which will offend the bankers, the utilities, the industrialists, and the manufacturers, particularly those who advertise." [52]

Concern over this problem has continued. In 1941 and 1942, on the instruction of the Sanders Bill, FCC investigated a special aspect of the problem of advertiser control—that is: newspaper ownership of radio stations. The problem had become especially acute in 1941 when FM was opened for commercial operation. As of June 30 of that year, 43 of 99 applications for FM station licenses were from newspaper interests.[53] By November, 1945, 41.5 per cent of the applications for FM licenses had come from newspaper interests. If newspaper ownership of radio stations is carried too far, it will mean domination of our two main sources of news and opinion formation by a very small group of people.

---

[49] Clifford J. Durr, speech: *The Social Significance of Radio*, January 7, 1946, at a dinner of the Joint Radio Committee of Congregational, Christian, Methodist, and Presbyterian Churches of the USA, New York City.
[50] Quoted by C. J. Durr, Speech: *How Free Is Radio*, May, 1944, before the opening of the 15th Institute for Education by Radio, Columbus, Ohio.
[51] Numerous instances of censorship may be found in the excellent compilation of readings in H. B. Summers, *Radio Censorship* (New York: H. W. Wilson, 1939).
[52] Brindze, *op. cit.*, pp. 192-193.
[53] Federal Communications Commission, *Chain Broadcasting Regulations and Free Speech*, remarks by then-Chairman James Lawrence Fly before House Interstate Commerce Committee, June 30, 1942.

Congressman John Coffee of Washington touched upon this problem on the floor of the House of Representatives when he said:

"Twenty-six per cent of CBS's 1944 revenue came from four advertisers and 38% from four advertising agencies. . . . Another factor pointing towards increasing concentration is the fact that in 110 cities, in which there is only one newspaper published and only one radio station, these two vital ways of reaching the citizens are either owned jointly or are affiliated with each other." [54]

In 1945 the *first* test was made of whether or not public interest is adequately protected in view of advertiser control. The United Automobile Worker's Union, affiliated with the CIO, compiled a great deal of evidence to prove that labor had often been thwarted in its efforts to present its side of a question on the air, while the National Association of Manufacturers' and other employers' groups are often given free time to discuss the other side. The stations often refused time to labor on the grounds that the code of the National Association of Broadcasters ruled against the sale of time for the discussion of controversial issues.[55]

The UAW-CIO pointed to the fact that Senators Wagner and Hatfield had proposed an amendment to the Radio Act of 1927 that would insure a reasonable allocation of time to *all* nonprofit organizations, and a balanced discussion of controversial issues. The amendment was defeated but the Federal Radio Commission, and later the FCC, formally pledged themselves to assist all nonprofit organizations in obtaining the fullest opportunity for self-expression and to remedy any complaints filed by such organizations.

To test this pledge, UAW filed objections to the renewal of the license of a Columbus, Ohio, radio station which, they charged, had censored and deleted labor scripts or consistently refused time while giving it to the other side.

FCC granted the hearing on the grounds that the station might not have operated in the public interest, and thus set a precedent. The case was decided "out of court," however, when the station agreed to broaden its code of operation and to consider each applicant for time in a wholly unprejudiced manner.

Congress, too, has concerned itself with possible changes in the present laws. Almost since the passage of the Communications Act of 1934, there have been proposals for changes. These fall into three main categories:

1. Legislation backed by members of the radio industry has been introduced consistently. This legislation aims at reducing the jurisdiction of

---

[54] Remarks by Congressman John Coffee, *Congressional Record* (October 24, 1945), p. 10182.

[55] Ernest Goodman, "The Air Belongs to the People," *Federal Communications Bar Journal* (March, 1945), p. 5. Mr. Goodman was the lawyer for UAW-CIO in this case.

FCC, depriving it of any right to consider economic and social matters, and limiting it to engineering problems. Volumes of the testimony given at hearings on such proposed legislation have been published. But, as often as such bills have been introduced, they have never yet been reported from their Committees for consideration by the whole Congress.

2. In equal volume, legislation has been introduced that would expand the powers of the Commission and further interpret the original bill. Typical of such legislation is the Celler Bill of the 79th Congress which, among other things, proposes to add provisions to the Act of 1934 that would interpret public interest to mean listener interest. No finding of public interest could be made in any broadcast matter if FCC should find that the station had been used excessively for commercial advertising purposes. It is also provided that FCC should "Fix percentages of time to be allocated . . . without charge for particular types . . . of nonprofit radio programs" and that such percentages of time shall be set forth in the license. Legislation of this type has never passed, either.

3. There has also been a good deal of "perfecting" legislation. This might change details of the Communications Act, but not the philosophy.

Very gradually and cautiously the FCC itself, on the theory that new legislation is not necessary, is taking a few steps to broaden its interpretations of the Act under which it functions.

For example, 4 of 7 of the commissioners voted in early 1945 not to deny an application for a license made by one of the most powerful corporations in America for one of the country's most powerful stations. This application had been seriously challenged, yet the commissioners felt that to deny it would "create a chaotic situation in the broadcasting industry which . . . would cast doubt on the status of a great many licenses when next they come up for renewal." [56]

Contrast this with a tentative policy announced by FCC Chairman, Paul Porter, later in the same year. He indicated at that time that all applicants for renewal of licenses would face some analysis of their previous program content. When an applicant seeks his original license he must make certain definite promises as to the service he will perform. Thus, reasoned Mr. Porter, promises should be compared with performance as a partial basis for deciding license renewal.

It is inevitable that FCC should meet with criticism from individuals and groups. One side of the fence will accuse it of not having done enough, not having carried out the duties with which the law entrusted it. The other side will cry that the agency has overstepped the domain of the law. In general, it would seem that the general policies and practices of the Commission have been sound, and have reflected the current trends of thinking in this country. Commissions of this nature seldom

---

[56] Quoted in FCC Docket 6741, *op. cit.*, p. 338.

pioneer; they follow the general cultural trends, and the FCC has been
no exception.

Self-Regulation of Radio. There has been an insistent demand by the
industry itself for self-regulation. The companies have contended that
such internal control is the only truly democratic method, that it frees
radio from political domination, that it permits greater development
through the stimulation of competition, and that errors which may exist
now can be ironed out without governmental interference. Moreover,
members of the industry are aware that they must impose certain standards upon themselves or public demand will create the need for new
moves on the part of the government.

The National Association of Broadcasters has drawn up a list of
standards of practice and ethics for the industry. Essentially these are
as follows: [57] (1) *Public Questions*—Station licensees should allocate time
to the presentation of public questions with regard to the "value and
interest of the subject to the public." (2) *Political broadcasts* should be
presented by a "straightforward statement appealing to intelligence and
reason." (3) *News* is to be "presented with fairness and accuracy."
News "should not be selected for the purpose of furthering or hindering
either side of any public questions nor should it be colored by the opinions" of the station, sponsor, commentator or anyone else. (4) *Children's
programs* should be based upon "sound social concepts" should "reflect
respect for parents, adult authority, law and order, clean living, high
morals, fair play, and honorable behavior"; should be free from horror
and torture passages; should not contain advertising appeals that would
encourage dangerous social habits. NAB further proposed to engage in
continuous study with parent and child guidance groups, which it has
done. (5) *Educational broadcasting* is to be encouraged. NAB and its
broadcasters will cooperate with educators to "search for improving
applications of radio as a medium of education." (6) *Religious broadcasts* should promote spiritual harmony, and not "be used to convey
attacks upon another's race or religion." (7) *Commercial programs* must
be limited to those sponsoring legitimate goods, and must conform
with "legal requirements, fair trade practices, and accepted standards
of good taste." A chart is added giving suggested time limits for
the amount of advertising in proportion to a program's length. There
is no compulsion entailed in these suggestions.[58]

Unfortunately, these standards of practice are still more of an ideal

---

[57] National Association of Broadcasters, *Standards of Practice*, Washington, D.C.,
August, 1945.
[58] It is extremely interesting to contrast this with the following taken from the
NAB code of 1929: "Commercial announcements . . . shall not be broadcast between
7 and 11 P.M."

than an actuality. Children's programs, in spite of improvement, continue to be questionable in nature; educational broadcasting needs much more encouragement; the question of a balanced amount of time to both sides of controversial issues must be settled; and certainly many of the goods advertised on the air are open to question as are methods, language and the amount of time used in advertising them.

Radio and the Future

Radio has already developed with startling rapidity. It was a novelty in itself only thirty years ago, and yet today developments as refined as television are already a reality.

As a propaganda medium, radio helped Hitler's bloodless victories during his initial efforts to conquer Eurasia. It became also a powerful propaganda weapon for the democracies. In fact, the contacts between the Allies and their underground cells in the Nazi-conquered world could not have been carried on so efficiently without the help of radio. During World War II all major powers used radio jamming as a tactical weapon against enemy military communications; Germany, Italy, and Japan tried to block Allied broadcasts to the Axis peoples.

With the end of the war, peace did not return to the air waves. Everywhere in the dictatorial countries, and especially in the U.S.S.R., the control of all aspects of broadcasting became of special concern to the governments in order to control the minds of their citizens. In fact, some forms of control are now exerted in the more democratically minded countries.[59]

Radio has been playing a leading role in the gigantic war of ideas going on between the democracies and the Russian Colossus. Dwight D. Eisenhower and Harry S. Truman agreed on at least one thing, saying it in substantially the same words in 1952: "We cannot hope to win the cold war unless we win the minds of men." [60] And how effective this international weapon is can be seen from the experiences of the Voice of America. In early 1947, when the United States government found that the Kremlin was systematically misrepresenting America to the Soviet-controlled people, the Voice of America started daily broadcasts to the Soviet Union in Russian; in February, 1948, the disturbed Kremlin started to drown out the Voice's broadcasts—and has been doing its best to stop its effectiveness ever since.[61]

---

[59] How radio is controlled in each country is described in: UNESCO, *World Communications: Press, Radio, Film, Television* (New York: Columbia University Press, 1951).
[60] Edward W. Barrett, *Truth is Our Weapon* (New York: Funk and Wagnalls Co., 1953), p. ix.
[61] *Ibid.*, p. 116.

Although television is now a serious competition to radio (as pointed out in a subsequent chapter), all the excitement over television must not hide the fact of the steady production and sale of radio receivers. "Television set production has never equaled that of radio receivers in the number of units although, due to the price differential, the dollar volume of television has been three or four times that of radio." [62] In fact, the largest increases in radio set ownership have been in recent years in automobile sets and portables—that is, in the field of outdoor listening.

America stands, in fact, unique in the ownership of radio sets. More than 90 per cent of American homes had radio sets by 1942. In 1951, 187 million radio receivers (together with 224 million copies of newspapers and 15 million television sets) brought daily news and information to the world's peoples;[63] North America leads the world in radio with 447 receiving sets per thousand people. In the United States, there are 620 radio sets for every thousand people. The United States likewise owns half of the world's radio transmitters (and 90 per cent of the television sets); Europe 35 per cent; South America, Asia, and Africa together represent only 11 per cent.

It appears also that the market will be kept active for some years to come, at least, due to new designs and colors in table models, the clock-radio sets, and radio-phonographs. (It is estimated that 100 million radio sets have been produced since World War II.) While eleven stations went off the air in 1952, 101 new ones were inaugurated. Surveys show that the new owners of television desert their radios—at first; but after six months of looking, about 90 per cent go back to their radios. Furthermore, television cannot as yet supplant radio with its news broadcasting which can be gathered from numerous different sources.

Summary

Technically, radio has developed with startling rapidity; its social and economic implications are gradually beginning to appear clear. The problem of social control over the radio industry appears, at the present time, to be the paramount issue. Today our police, fire, forestry, and highway maintenance service, our commercial and military aircraft, railroads, taxicabs, ships at sea, coastal stations, to say nothing of commercial and educational stations, all utilize the airwaves in performing their functions and duties. Indeed, the public safety, land transportation, and industrial radio service are growing at least as rapidly as commercial and noncommercial

---

[62] G. C. Baxter Rowe, "Radio," p. 458, in *The New International Year Book* (New York: Funk and Wagnalls Co., 1953).

[63] UNESCO, *op. cit.*

television, FM, and standard (AM) radio.[64] All these radio services would be rendered ineffective were there no central authority to allocate channels to different services, or to assign specific frequencies to different applicants within the different services, or to maintain standards of good engineering practice. Technical interference, and the social services and industrial efficiency it threatens, were the primary concern of radio regulators before 1932; they have lurked behind the scene ever since. But the very nature of the Federal Radio Commission's job forced it beyond technical matters into consideration of program content and the institutional character of licenses. In the process of formulating standards by which to allocate bands of channels to different services and to license specific channels to specific applicants, the Federal Radio and Federal Communications Commissions gave content to the broad statutory concept "public interest, convenience and necessity." This is, indeed, a difficult problem. The radio industry just grew up—first as entertainment and a public service, then as an advertising medium, and finally as an important force in our entire culture pattern. As might be expected from American history, *laissez faire* predominated in radio until the American people began dimly to understand that this new force concerned us all, and that some regulation was needed to keep a few individuals from running away with the microphone. An increasing amount of regulatory legislation was enacted, and the government also entered into the question of monopoly control over broadcasting.

Democracy is predicated upon a high degree of individual liberty, but not upon an individualism which has no concern for the rights of other individuals or one uncontrolled by the common society or an interest in its welfare. Radio must never become a political monopoly such as it became in the totalitarian states, but neither can the American people afford to permit it to continue as a big business monopoly even over our thoughts and opinions, without proper control in the interests of national well-being. Private ownership will probably continue for generations to come; increasingly, too, however, must come intelligent social regulation. Increasingly must come greater public understanding of radio's potential influence, public education as to program content and improvement, and public enlightenment as to the necessity for keeping the airways open primarily for the interests of the entire American populace.

QUESTIONS

1. What is the trend in listening to news broadcasts?
2. What are the lightest months in regard to radio listening?

---

[64] Federal Communications Commission, *Annual Report 1950*, pp. 1-6; *Annual Report 1951*, pp. 1-10; *Annual Report 1952*, pp. 1-6.

3. What time during the day do most people listen to the radio?
4. What type of program attracts the largest audience?
5. How do statistics relating to the popularity of certain types of programs differ among urban dwellers and rural dwellers?
6. What were the results of the Ohio State University survey relating programs with crime as the dominant theme?
7. According to the Ohio State University survey, what precautions should be taken regarding broadcasting fairy tales?
8. What conclusion does the Ohio State University survey draw relating to past performances of educators and psychologists?
9. What types of programs do parents object to?
10. What is radio's relationship to society, generally speaking?
11. Is it possible to measure the effect of radio on public opinion?
12. What are some advantages of radio over the press?
13. What part did the radio play in Franklin Delano Roosevelt's victories?
14. Correlate the development of democracy with the increasing importance of words.
15. What effect does the radio have on the cultural heritages of regions and nationality groups?
16. What attempts have been made in Cleveland to assimilate various cultures?
17. What elements are considered by radio stations relative to the broadcasting of religious programs?
18. How do radio stations combat the possibilities of Fascist or other subversive individuals masquerading as preachers disseminating propaganda over the air under the guise of religion?
19. What are the advantages of radio as an educational media?
20. How did the development of frequency modulation affect the educational prospects of radio?

SUGGESTED TOPICS FOR TERM PAPERS AND FURTHER RESEARCH

1. Bring the figures of radio listening habits quoted in the chapter up to date and correlate the trend with the trend in international relations.
2. Compare the types of radio programs broadcast by a rural radio station with those of an urban station.
3. Study the programs of a radio station in relation to the Ohio State University survey.
4. Has the broadcasting of religious programs been harmed effectively by radio's experience with such men and groups as Father Coughlin and the Philadelphia Gospel Broadcasters Association? Use extensive documentation in proving your answer.
5. Study the methods of censorship imposed on radio broadcasting in the United States.
6. The rise of the Voice of America.
7. The "Radio Free Europe."
8. The use of radio in Asiatic propaganda by the U.S.S.R.
9. The present trends in the operation of radio stations in the United States.
10. International cooperation in radio.

BIBLIOGRAPHY

Books

Matthew N. Chappell and C. E. Hooper, *Radio Audience Measurement* (New York: Stephen Daye, 1944). Observations on the techniques of gauging audience reaction through the system devised by the authors.

Isabelle M. Cooper, *Bibliography on Educational Broadcasting* (Chicago: University of Chicago Press, 1942). A very complete bibliography.

Murray Edelman, *The Licensing of Radio Services in the United States, 1927-1947* (Urbana, Ill.: University of Illinois Press, 1950). A study in administrative formulation of policy.

Morris L. Ernst, *The First Freedom* (New York: The Macmillan Co., 1946). Chapter V deals with radio and is one of the best available statements about trends toward monopoly in this field.

Maurice Gorham, *Training for Radio* (New York: Columbia University Press, 1950). A UNESCO publication No. 587.

Nelson B. Henry, *Mass Media and Education* (Chicago: 53rd Yearbook of the National Society for the Study of Education, 1954), Pt. 2. The press, motion pictures, radio, TV, and other mass media seen with an eye to their in-school and out-of-school effect on the child or youth and on the normal experiences of the adult; but this book does not deal with educational films or radio or TV programs prepared directly for the schools.

Paul R. Lazarsfeld, *Radio and the Printed Page* (New York: Duell, Sloan and Pearce, 1941). A Survey of the educational aspects of radio, its relation to reading, and its potentialities.

—— and Frank Stanton, *Radio Research, 1942-43* (New York: Duell, Sloan and Pearce, 1944). Analysis of daytime radio serials, wartime radio, radio operations, other technical studies.

—— and P. L. Kendall, *Radio Listening in America* (New York: Prentice-Hall, 1948). Factual study of habits of radio listeners in this country.

Rogers Manvell, *On the Air* (New York: British Book Center, 1954). A British critic views the way in which radio and TV have developed in Great Britain, the United States, the British dominions and the U.S.S.R., the way the public has responded to it, and the powers of these modes of communication and their contributions to the arts.

Herbert L. Marx, Jr., *Television and Radio in American Life* (New York: H. W. Wilson Co., 1943, The Reference Shelf, Vol. 25, No. 2). An invaluable collection of numerous studies, with an extensive bibliography.

R. K. Merton and others, *Mass Persuasion* (New York: Harper and Brothers, 1947).

National Association of Radio and Television Broadcasters, *Experts Look at Radio and TV* (Washington, D.C.: The Association, 1771 N St. NW, 1952); and *Standards of Practice for American Broadcasters* (Washington, D.C.: The Association, 1948). A good case presented by the "practitioners."

O. J. Olsen, *Education on the Air* (Columbus, Ohio: Ohio State University Press, 1952), annual edition. Valuable on the usefulness of radio for education.

F. A. Rankin, *Who Gets the Air; U. S. Broadcasters in World Affairs* (Washington, D.C.: National Association of Radio and Television Broadcasters, 1949).

J. Howard Rowland, *Adolescent Personality and Radio: Some Exploratory Studies* (Columbus, Ohio: Ohio State University, 1943). A comprehensive psychological survey of the effect of leisure-time listening on adolescents.

—— and I. Keith Tyler, *Criteria for Children's Radio Programs* (U.S. Office of Education). Summary of the research findings and interpretations made by the staff of the project on the Evaluation of School Broadcasts, at Ohio State University.

Charles A. Siepmann, *Radio, Television and Society* (New York: Oxford University Press, 1950). A short but brilliant social evaluation of these media.

H. B. Summers, *Tomorrow's Radio Programs* (Washington, D.C.: Federal Radio Education Committee, U.S. Office of Education, 1944). Shows factors which account for the rise and fall of program popularity.

Llewellyn White, *America Radio* (Chicago: University of Chicago Press, 1947). A sensible survey.

E. E. Willis, *Foundations in Broadcasting* (New York: Oxford University Press, 1951). Covers radio and television; a good bibliography.

Periodicals

C. A. Barnett, "Role of the Press, Radio, and Motion Picture and Negro Morale," *Negro Education*, XII (July, 1943), pp. 474-489.
Lyman Bryson, "Broadcasting," *American Scholar*, XVII (Spring, 1948), pp. 221-224.
G. E. Carlson, "Radio and Social Control," *Association of Educational Radio Journal*, I (January 6, 1942), p. 2.
Doris Corwith, "Radio as an Educational Medium," *Educational Record*, XXXIII (January, 1952), pp. 24-29.
John Crosby, "Seven Deadly Sins of the Air," *Life*, XXIX (November 6, 1950), pp. 147 ff.
F. Eastman, "Hate, Radio and Morale," *ibid.*, II (February, 1943), p. 2.
M. and Lindley A. Ernst, "Freedom of the Air," *Saturday Review of Literature*, XXI (January 6, 1940), pp. 45-49.
Theodor Geiger, "A Radio Test of Musical Taste," *Public Opinion Quarterly*, XIV (Fall, 1950), pp. 453-460.
Harvey J. Levin, "Social Welfare Aspects of FCC Broadcast Licensing Standards," *American Journal of Economics and Sociology*, XIII, 1 (October, 1953), pp. 39-55.
F. Martin, "Radio Propaganda—New Style," *Theatre Arts*, XXVII (February, 1943), pp. 95-102.
Robert Lewis Shayon, "The World Floods Into Iowa," *Saturday Review of Literature*, XXXV (September 13, 1952), pp. 16 ff.
Paul A. Walker, "New Horizons for Educators" (Washington, D.C.: Federal Communications Commissions, 1952).
A. D. Willard, Jr., "Responding to the People's Will," *Listening* (1948), pp. 78-82.

CHAPTER XXVII

Motion Pictures

People throughout the world probably know the United States best by the picture of American life that they receive from Hollywood's movies. Not only is Hollywood America's foremost ambassador abroad, but it also exerts a telling influence upon the patterns of behavior of the American public itself. To understand the place of the motion picture in American culture, it is necessary to examine the movies first for the billion dollar industry that it is, and second for the powerful social and psychological force it exerts. The motion picture industry epitomizes big business as a taste-maker.

The Growth of the American Motion Picture Industry

The technical development of the motion picture may be traced back as far as the first psychological experiments on the projection of vision.[1] In 1870 Leland Stanford photographed a horse race by means of a series of still pictures. The late 1800's witnessed a series of international experiments in film projection carried on by Edison in the United States, by the Lumière brothers in France, and by Friese-Green and others in Britain. The beginning of the twentieth century marked the first commercial exhibition of a technically imperfect but curiosity-arousing "moving picture." Within the next forty years the motion picture industry was to rise to its peak of prominence as the foremost entertainment medium in the United States.[2]

Current Status. In 1946 the motion picture industry reached an all time

---

[1] N. Jackson-Wrigley and Eric Leyland, *The Cinema* (London: Grafton and Co., 1939), p. 186.
[2] Good descriptions of the early development of the motion picture may be secured from the following references: T. Ramsaye, *A Million and One Nights* (New York: Simon and Schuster, 1926); J. Mayer, *Sociology of Films: Studies and Documents* (London: Faber and Faber, 1946); B. Hampton, *A History of the Movies* (New York: Covici, Friede, 1931); L. Jacobs, *The Rise of the American Film* (New York: Harcourt, Brace and Co., 1939); M. Bardeche and R. Brasillach, *The History of Motion Pictures* (New York: W. W. Norton and the Museum of Modern Art, 1938); *The Film Daily Yearbook of Motion Pictures* (New York: The Film Daily, published annually).

high of $100,000,000 profit before taxes, secured from a public willing to pay $1,799,000,000 to see its product. In an industry as given as it is to the use of superlatives, it is difficult to appraise available statistics. However, there can be little skepticism concerning the 80 million average weekly movie attendance in 1946, or the 18,719 theaters in operation at that time.

The years 1946-1954, however, saw a steady decline in both the economic condition of the industry and its popularity with the public. Average weekly movie attendance fell to 34.4 million customers during the last three months of 1953. The number of craft workers in the studios dropped from 15,661 in 1946 to 9,313 in 1949. There could be little doubt that the motion picture industry was seeing black days. As described by Milestone, "Nobody goes to the movies. Business is bad. In all Hollywood only 370 actors are under studio long-term contracts, compared to a normal 1,200. Out of a total of some 1,800 writers who have worked on scripts during the last three years fewer than 250 are employed, and of these only about 50 are under long-term contract. One-third of all unemployment insurance applicants in the Hollywood area are studio workers. A long list of directors, a Hollywood *Who's Who*, are unemployed. RKO is dumping 150 finished screen plays on the writers' market for sale to other studios. A domestic gross of two and a half million dollars is a smashing success, compared with a wartime gross of seven or eight million. The average picture is lucky to bring back a million and a half. The foreign market is practically non-existent. This is the picture of Hollywood which confronts those who work in the industry. And there has not been a single suggestion for a cure that makes sense." [3]

In 1949, *Life* magazine sponsored a series of panel discussions of critics, scholars, exhibitors, producers, and consumers to discuss "What's With the Movies?" These experts offered six general criticisms to explain the steady decline in movie popularity. These were:

"1. Hollywood is trying to comply with thousands of prohibitions and its aim is thus becoming the barren and self-defeating aim of not displeasing anybody.

"2. In so doing Hollywood is neglecting its active audience and catering hardest to the habitual, passive audience which does it least good and will be the first to desert it for television.

"3. The search for the 'universal' picture will end in disaster, if sufficiently pursued.

---

[3] Lewis Milestone, "First Aid for a Sick Giant," *New Republic*, January 31, 1949, p. 15.

"4. The advertising and selling of movies to the public is elaborately and dishonestly bad.

"5. Hollywood deliberately confuses fantasy with reality, thereby providing neither the recreation of true fantasy nor the recognition of true experience.

"6. As a means to being more truthful and less standardized, Hollywood should spend less money on each picture and make more pictures of greater variety." [4]

Aggravating an already bad situation were such internal business factors as the forced separation of theater ownership from picture production, the jurisdictional labor troubles within the studios, increased competition from European films, charges of communist infiltration, and television.[5] The last factor of television has been seized upon by many analysts as the most important reason for the decline of the motion picture industry. The effect of TV upon the mass media is discussed in a separate chapter on television. Certainly the advent of television did result in a decrease in box office receipts, followed by a painstaking soul-searching on the part of the motion picture industry. However, the most recent evidence for 1954 and 1955 indicates that the worst effects of television have been felt and that the movie industry is making a strong comeback. Current statistics seem to indicate that movie attendance decreases until the television saturation of an area reaches about 68 per cent. At this point movie attendance appears to level off and shows no further decline.

The Future Outlook. Thus, there is every reason to believe that the motion pictures will continue to be one of the major media of mass communication. Attendance in the late summer months of 1954 jumped from an all time low average of 34.4 million customers a week during the last three months of 1953 to an average of 73.7 million customers. While the motion picture industry did come dangerously close to bankruptcy in the period following World War II, the downward trend has definitely been stopped and all future signs are positive for a rebirth of the industry. While Hollywood may be making fewer movies—in 1954 they made a total of only 264 features, about one-half the number turned out in the previous peak years—the gross from film entertainment income reached an all time high estimated at $650,000,000.

Probably the most important reason for this reversal has been the development of new methods of film projection. First on the scene was giant screen Cinerama in the fall of 1952, followed by the rapid development of 3-D films, cinemascope, stereoscopic sound, etc. These mechani-

---

[4] *Life*, May 16, 1949.

[5] Based on an analysis by Thomas M. Prior in *The New York Times*, February 6, 1955.

cal improvements, combined with the stabilization of the TV audience, appear to have given the movie industry a new lease on life. Foreign income has become more dependable as the world economy itself has become stabilized. This foreign market is extremely important since about one-third of a picture's gross earnings come from abroad.[6] New audiences provided by a new generation of movie-goers has resulted in an increase in the number of successful revivals. It would appear that a TV-bred generation is more and more beginning to discover the entertainment value of the motion picture. A new industrial development also holds promise for the future—the drive-in theater. Despite a decrease in the number of conventional theaters in the last decade, drive-in theaters have increased from about 300 in 1946 to 3,276 in 1954.[7] From all the current evidence it would appear that the motion picture industry is on its way toward meeting the challenge posed by the *Variety* headline, "Pix Baffled for B.O. Solution." The immediate future is sure to witness the continued resurgence of this industry as it fights to keep its pre-eminence in American culture and to fit itself into a changing world.

Control of the Motion Picture Industry

First and foremost for an understanding of the social control of the movies is the realization that the motion picture industry is big business. The main goal of the entire industry, from the producer down to the exhibitor, is to make money. Like any multi-million dollar business, the production and exhibition of motion pictures represents a tremendous capital investment which, above all else, must show a favorable percentage of return. As the producer in *What Makes Sammy Run?* puts it, "After all, pictures are shipped out in a can. We're in the canning business. Our job is to make sure that every shipment will make a profit." [8]

The basic structure of the industry, therefore, has followed the lines of the most profitable form of business organization. This has led the industry over the years into a series of conflicts with the anti-trust laws. Until recently the motion picture industry could be characterized as a "production-distribution-exhibition complex." The "Big Five"—Paramount, RKO, Loew's or MGM, 20th Century Fox, and Warner Brothers —dominated the entire industry for a long period of time. These five studios produced almost all Grade A pictures and a majority of all pictures regardless of quality. They owned large chains of theaters and controlled

[6] Eric Johnston, *The Motion Picture on the Threshold of a Decisive Decade* (New York: Motion Picture Association of America, Inc., 1946), p. 42.

[7] These figures and previous ones have been taken from the article, "Survey of the Movies," in *The New York Times*, February 6, 1955.

[8] Budd Schulberg, *What Makes Sammy Run?*, Modern Library.

the exhibition as well as the production of their product. At the time of the anti-trust suits from 1946 to 1948, these five firms owned approximately 3,137 theaters constituting over 50 per cent of the total box-office receipts in the country.[9] After long years of litigation, the government won its case and at the present time theater ownership has been divorced from motion picture production, block-booking which limited the choice of films which an exhibitor could show has been greatly modified, minimum admission prices for certain films has been banned, and exclusive showing rights have been greatly reduced. The net effect of this government intervention has been to limit effectively the monopolistic nature of the motion picture industry.

Self-Regulation of Motion Picture Content. The motion picture industry is the prime example among the mass media of self-regulation of content. Although the industry has periodically faced the threat of government supervision, it has successfully managed to avoid any official legislation. Following World War I the industry, in response to public indignation at the content of certain films and the subsequent threat of government regulation, set up the Motion Picture Producers and Distributors Association. The purpose of this agency was to monitor the content of motion pictures in order to forestall public criticism. Known for a long time as the "Hays Office" and more recently as the "Johnston Office" (Motion Picture Association of America), this organization is charged with the enforcement of the Motion Picture Production Code adopted in 1930.[10] Before and after a picture is produced, it is submitted to this organization for review. The Code is a powerful and effective control upon the content of America's motion pictures. The Code opens with the following provisions:

"1. No picture shall be produced which will lower the moral standards of those who see it. Hence the sympathy of the audience shall never be thrown to the side of crime, wrong-doing, evil or sin.

"2. Correct standards of life, subject only to the requirements of drama and entertainment, shall be presented.

"3. Law, natural or human, shall not be ridiculed, nor shall sympathy be created for its violation."

The subjects covered under "Particular Applications" include: "Crimes Against the Law," "Sex," "Vulgarity," "Obscenity," "Profanity," "Costume," "Dances," "Religion," "Locations" ("The treatment of bed-

---

[9] *Motion Picture Production Encyclopedia*, 1948; Ruth Inglis, *Freedom of the Movies* (Chicago: University of Chicago Press, 1947), pp. 43-44.

[10] *A Code to Govern the Making of Motion and Talking Pictures* by the Motion Picture Association of America, 1930-1949; *A Revised Advertising Code for the Film Industry* by the Motion Picture Association of America.

rooms must be governed by good taste and delicacy"), "National Feelings," "Titles" (which shall not be "salacious, indecent, or obscene"), and seven "Repellent Subjects"—ranging from "third degree methods" to "the sale of women"—which "must be treated within the careful limits of good taste." [11]

While this Code has permitted the motion picture industry successfully to avoid federal regulation, it has been widely criticized for its inhibiting effect upon the content matter of the movies. The net effect has been to make motion pictures less realistic and creative. In seeking material which would be harmless, the motion picture industry has quite often ended up with material that is only trite. This problem will be treated in more detail in the following section on the content of motion pictures.

Censorship Control. Of all the media of mass communication, the motion pictures are most subject to censorship of various forms. This probably reflects the greater concern which the movies, as compared with other media, have with moral issues. The movies are essentially dramatic presentations and as such deal with the mores and folkways of a society.

Motion picture censorship arises from three main sources. First, we find the self-regulation of the Motion Picture Production Code discussed previously. This Code is extremely detailed in the do's and don't's of movie production. Scripts are generally submitted for review before production begins and quite frequently changes are made to bring it into conformity with the requirements of the Code. Before the picture is released, it is reviewed once again for any possible violations of the Code.

A second form of censorship takes place on the legal level through local boards of review. These boards of review are official state or community organizations which must pass upon the exhibition of films within the state or community. New York State, for example, offers a civil service test for the position of Motion Picture Reviewer. Requirements for this position of film censor include a college degree, a knowledge of history, literature, a foreign language, a thorough knowledge of the New York State laws and regulations regarding motion pictures, high standards of morality, a good sense of justice, and mature judgment. Vision must be 20-30 with glasses, and hearing must be normal without a hearing aid. There were 200 applicants for this position in New York City alone.

A list of films which have failed to receive the seal of approval by local review boards is long and varied. In recent years it has included such films as *La Ronde*, prohibited in New York on grounds of immorality; *M*, banned in Ohio because it undermined "confidence in the enforcement of law and government"; *The French Line*, because of a

---

[11] An excellent discussion of this Code may be found in Leonard W. Doob, *Public Opinion and Propaganda* (New York: Henry Holt and Co., Inc., 1948).

suggestive dance; *Mom and Dad*, released after the cutting out of a Caesarian birth scene; *The Moon is Blue*, banned in Ohio, Kansas, Maryland, Memphis, Detroit, Kansas City (Mo.), Providence, Lawrence (Mass.), Elizabeth, and Jersey City.

In 1952 an historic decision of the United States Supreme Court ruled that motion pictures were entitled to the constitutional guarantees of free speech and free press. The case involved the Italian film, *The Miracle*, banned in New York as "sacrilegious." The Supreme Court found this term imprecise and stated that the censor trying to interpret it would be "set adrift upon a boundless sea . . . with more charts than those provided by the most vocal and powerful orthodoxies." New York could not vest "such unlimited restraining control of motion pictures in a censor." The Supreme Court concluded "that expression by means of motion pictures is included within the free speech and free press guarantees of the First and Fourteenth Amendments." This major victory against censorship finally overturned the Supreme Court's 1915 Mutual Film Edict that movies were "spectacles" and as a business "pure and simple" were not entitled to free speech. This action of the Supreme Court has opened the way for a reduction in legal censorship of the motion picture industry.

A final form of censorship springs from the self-interest of specific pressure groups. Various religious groups are concerned with either the effects of the film upon the morality of their adherents or with the unfavorable portrayal of their membership. Economic pressure groups object to many films which portray members of the different professions or trades in an unfavorable light. Various reform organizations bring pressure to bear upon Hollywood, opposing different practices such as smoking, drinking, gambling, etc.

One result of these various pressures is indicated by the following want-ad which appear in *The Screen Writer:* "Established writer would like a good up-to-date idea for a motion picture which avoids politics, sex, religion, divorce, double beds, drugs, disease, poverty, liquor, Senators, bankers, cigarettes, wealth, Congress, race, economics, art, death, crime, childbirth and accidents (whether by airplane or public carrier); also the villain must not be an American, European, South American, African, Asiatic, Australian, New Zealander, or Eskimo . . . No dogs allowed. Apply P.O. Box 13 . . ."

Perhaps the most influential of the pressure groups is the Legion of Decency, organized in 1934, which censors films for Catholics everywhere. This organization uses the following nomenclature in its appraisal of films: Class A, Section I means Morally Unobjectionable for General Patronage; Class A, Section II means Morally Unobjectionable for Adults, Class B means Morally Objectionable in Part for All. Class C means Condemned. A "C" rating for a motion picture is considered a death blow by the motion picture industry. The following statement from a round-table discussion on this problem presents the point of view of the opposition to this form of censorship:

"MODERATOR'S NOTE: The final comment on this problem by a member of the Table is deliberately left anonymous:

Mr. ———. The Legion of Decency is something that Hollywood should have fought and didn't. It is my personal opinion, not based on any disrespect, that they didn't fight it for the same reasons that they have never fought anything: they didn't want to stop the flow of film for one week. Now that fight is lost, presumably for good. I don't know what to do about it, but I think it should be recognized. Nobody questions the right of the Catholic Church, the Jewish church or any other group, to be heard and to voice its own opinion, even to urge its own flock to stay away from something disapproved. But with the Legion the process does not stop there. If an exhibitor has a film not approved, pressure is brought to bear on him not to show it in his community at all, and of course he caves in under the pressure. I think it is a serious situation for more than the picture industry; it is a form of control. I think it is evil for a minority to stop a majority from seeing a film, reading a book, or hearing an idea. I think any group has a right to protest a film, but not to put into effect a secret, forceful boycott." [12]

There can be little doubt that the net effect of censorship in the motion picture industry is to lower the quality of the motion picture. The attempt to please everyone and to offend no one hinders the presentation of a realistic and adult picture of life and its problems. The situation may perhaps be best summarized by the following report on censorship appearing in *The New Yorker* magazine: "William Wyler, who directed the Academy Award picture 'The Best Years of Our Lives,' told me he is convinced that he could not make that picture today and that Hollywood will produce no more films like 'The Grapes of Wrath' and 'Crossfire.' 'In a few months, we won't be able to have a heavy who is an American,' he said. The scarcity of roles for villains has become a serious problem, particularly at studios specializing in Western pictures, where writers are being harried for not thinking up any new ones. 'Can I help it if we're running out of villains?' a writer at one of these studios asked me. 'For years I've been writing scripts about a Boy Scout-type cowboy in love with a girl. Their fortune and happiness are threatened by a banker holding a mortgage over their heads, or by a big landowner, or by a crooked sheriff. Now they tell me that bankers are out. Anyone holding a mortgage is out. Crooked public officials are out. All I've got left is a cattle rustler. What the hell am I going to do with a cattle rustler?' " [13]

---

[12] *Life*, June 27, 1949.
[13] *The New Yorker*, February 21, 1948, p. 42.

Content of Films

Any evaluation of the content of motion pictures must face the conflict between movies as art or entertainment. A successful motion picture must make money. In general, the Hollywood executive feels that he must give the public what it wants and that what the public wants is escape and amusement. His general impression of public taste is rather low and he disclaims the responsibility for raising it. For many producers mass entertainment, it would seem, demands gaudy spectacles and the absence of substance. As Y. Frank Freeman, executive head of Paramount Studios, put it: "Let's get our sweat shirts back on and remember we built this business on mass entertainment." This is stated in a more dignified way by the British motion picture producer Carol Reed: "The function of the film is to entertain. If you can do more with a film, by all means do so, but you have to be very careful that the more doesn't make the total less." [14]

Opposing the professional movie-maker is an unorganized opposition from educators, artists, and serious critics of the mass media. They base their case mainly on the meaning of the term entertainment, maintaining that entertainment can also be instructive and meaningful. They point to the Academy Awards in motion pictures which indicate that films dealing with social problems and controversial questions quite often win awards and do make money. They maintain that too often a film is prejudged as over the heads of the public or as too controversial with no adequate basis for the judgment.

Stanley Kramer, a highly successful independent producer, disagreeing with most Hollywood producers, takes the position that "movie making is an art—call it a bastardized art form if you want . . . —but nevertheless it is an art. For too many years it has been assumed that movie entertainment had to be designed for the mentality of a 10-year-old congenital idiot. Once you can define something as narrowly as movie entertainment, then I have a small feeling that it isn't entertainment any more."

An examination of the actual content of the motion pictures reveals that they are overwhelmingly deficient as far as culture or education is concerned. An analysis of 500 feature films by the Ohio State University Bureau of Educational Research found that 29.6 per cent of the themes were devoted to love, 27.4 per cent to crime, and 15 per cent to sex. [15] A quantitative analysis of 100 motion pictures by Dorothy Jones discerned the following wants of the screen characters: 68.1 per cent wanted

---

[14] *The New York Times*, January 5, 1950.

[15] Edgar Dale, *The Content of Motion Pictures* (New York: The Macmillan Co., 1935), pp. 15-22, 224.

love, 26.1 per cent wanted fame, reputation or prestige, 15.9 per cent wanted safety, 13.8 per cent wanted a way of life, 9.6 per cent wanted money or material goods, and 9.0 per cent wanted rightness, to do their duty.[16] Various analyses have indicated the limited background from which the characters in the movies are drawn. The Jones study found that three out of five of the major characters were shown as economically established, free of parental influence, usually unmarried and with definitely limited social and economic responsibilities. Only 17 per cent were either poor or destitute, while almost one-half were either wealthy or well-to-do. An analysis by the Institute for Propaganda Analysis classified the different residences appearing in films and found that 69 per cent were wealthy or ultra wealthy while only 6 per cent represented the homes of people of low income.[17]

The general conclusion of these studies on the content of motion pictures reveals that for the most part the motion picture industry lives in a dream world of unreality and presents a stereotyped and over-simplified picture of characters and themes. As William Allen White claimed, the industry offers "little that is much better than the glittering toy for an imbecile giant." Wolcott Gibbs characterized the movies as "an astounding parody of life devoted to a society in which anything is physically and materially possible, including perfect happiness, to a race of people who operate intellectually on the level of the New York Daily News, morally on that of Dayton, Tennessee, and politically and economically in a total vacuum." [18] A survey in 1949, by the Common Council for American Unity of 1,702 foreign observers concerning European beliefs regarding the United States, found an overwhelming condemnation of Hollywood as misrepresenting life in the United States. As the editor of a European newspaper put it: "Too many Hollywood films paint such a totally unreal picture of America that it seems to foreign audiences a fantastic land which has no real connection with the grim realities of the world today." He is seconded by a European student who expresses his belief that "the deplorable trash emanating from Hollywood has already succeeded in convincing increasing numbers of Europeans that America consists of gangsters, sadists, pick-up girls, cowboys and skyscrapers." [19]

There can be little question that Hollywood's representation of the American scene is not calculated to induce serious thought on the part of the movie-goer. It would be wrong, however, to view this fact as a

[16] Dorothy Jones, "A Quantitative Analysis of Motion Picture Content," *Public Opinion Quarterly*, 6 (1942), pp. 411-428.
[17] "The Movies and Propaganda," *Propaganda Analysis*, March, 1938.
[18] *Saturday Review of Literature*, November 17, 1945.
[19] "European Beliefs Regarding the United States," *Common Council for American Unity* (1949), p. 23.

conspiracy on the part of the motion picture industry to lower American cultural tastes. The producers claim they are giving the public what it wants and that the fault lies with the audience which determines the box-office receipts rather than with the professional movie-makers. In order to evaluate this argument it is necessary to investigate the characteristics of the movie audience.

Movie Audience

The movie audience is a mass audience. While it may appeal to some groups more than others, i.e., young people attend more than old people, the millions of people who attend the movies weekly come from all segments of the population. A survey by *Fortune* magazine shows that 68 per cent of a cross-section of the nation report that they have been to the movies in the preceding three month period, 23 per cent had gone but not within the last three months, while 7 per cent had never gone. Thus, 7 out of 10 Americans may be labeled as regular movie-goers.[20] It is this majority which creates the problem of entertainment vs. art. It would seem that the larger the audience, the simpler the communication must be and the more it must seek a lowest common denominator. Entertainment must cut across special interest lines, while art and education can remain selective.

The motion pictures, like the other mass media, appear to be caught in a vicious cycle. As overhead and the cost of making films increase, the need to reach larger and larger audiences also increases. The need to reach larger audiences in turn leads to even more expensive films and higher costs. This search for the all-purpose film which will please everyone tends to produce a constant lowering of cultural standards. As stated by one motion picture director: "In Hollywood the business of making motion pictures is based on simple arithmetic. The more people who see a movie the more money that movie will make. Hence, the movie that will please the most people will make the most money. Therefore, the lowest common denominator of film entertainment equals the highest common multiple of film profits. That this sort of figuring leads eventually to artistic bankruptcy has often been pointed out by those certified public accountants of art, the critics."

An analysis of the age level of movie-goers has led to what has been called the "over 30" controversy. A survey by Gallup found that 65 per cent of the movie audience is under 30 years of age. This figure is interpreted by Gilbert Seldes as follows: "The inescapable fact about the motion picture audience is that 65 per cent of it is under the age of 30.

---

[20] *Fortune*, XXXIX (April, 1949).

The merciless tale of the statistics continues: beginning at the age of 19, people begin to fall out of the habit of going to the movies; they still go, but less often; they pick and choose more carefully, acting in fact as adults, and this process of going less and less to the movies is never reversed. Audience Research, Inc., has estimated that if all the people between the ages of 31 and 60 should go to the movies only once a week, the box office receipts after taxes would rise by 800 million dollars a year, and this does not count those between 19 and 30 who might be persuaded to go as frequently as they used to when they were younger. It has cost Hollywood a lot of money to kill off its own audience." [21]

A survey by *Fortune* magazine appears to substantiate the claim that Hollywood is losing its adult audience because it is underestimating the intelligence of this audience. Regular movie-goers were asked, "Are you going to the movies more often, less often, or about as often this fall as you were two or three years ago?" Three times as many stated they went less often as compared to those who stated that their attendance had increased. Among the college educated movie-goers the comparison was even more pronounced—11 per cent more often, 50 per cent less often, and 39 per cent the same. Asked why they were going less often, 1 out of 3 stated that they did not like the current selections. A full 50 per cent of these individuals felt that fewer good movies were being made. Asked why they did not like a movie they had seen recently, one-half mentioned the nature of the story as being "too silly"—14 per cent, "pointless—no plot"—10 per cent, "unrealistic"—10 per cent, "dull"—8 per cent, "too frightening"—4 per cent, "vulgar"—3 per cent. Asked, "Are there any particular kinds or types of moving picture you would rather not see," only 4 per cent mentioned "sad, depressing" pictures, while 63 per cent mentioned "horror, gangsters, and cowboy" pictures. The *Fortune* survey concluded: "Here is a definite indication that the movie makers are out of step with the audience." [22]

The current controversy over the movie audience thus involves a difference of opinion concerning the willingness of these movie-goers to attend a more serious type of motion picture. The advent of television, it is felt by many, makes it even more necessary for Hollywood to avoid the trite and meaningless picture. The need to recapture an adult audience and to hang on to the youthful audience once it reaches its 30th birthday also points toward the need for a more serious screen product. Finally, it is argued by many critics that better movies will raise the movie-goer's taste: "By a reversal of Gresham's law, the good movie tends in the long run to drive out the bad. The high school boy may not enjoy 'The

[21] *Atlantic Monthly*, November, 1948.
[22] *Fortune*, April, 1949, p. 40.

Grapes of Wrath' or 'How Green Was My Valley' as much as he had hoped, but if he is subjected to enough pictures above his intellectual or emotional level, that level will rise. He will find less satisfaction in the kind of melodrama he used to like. His taste can improve, and the screen can improve too—slowly but surely." [23]

The Effects of Motion Pictures

There can be little doubt about the influence which Hollywood has exerted and is exerting upon the folkways and mores of American society. Many of the styles and fads of today can be traced to examples set by Hollywood. Many of our stereotypes and symbols have been formed on the basis of the movie industry's casting departments. The absent-minded college professor with long hair, the gangster with a sneering, "foreign" look, the strong but silent "he"-man, all represent common characters of the silver screen.

The effectiveness of the movies in controlling the attitudes and behavior of millions of Americans has been attributed to three main causes:

"1. Movie-goers are typically relaxed and unaware that they are being affected by ideas and values.

"2. People put themselves in the part of the leading characters, accepting unconsciously the attitudes implicit in the role.

"3. Troubled individuals searching for solutions to their problems often consciously or unconsciously adopt the implicit movie answers to their own problems." [24]

Psychologically, the motion pictures constitute an excellent medium for propaganda. The audience is a captive one and cannot simply "turn the dial" to escape the propaganda. The payment of an admission fee also tends to commit the viewer toward feeling that he must pay attention. Watching the picture also requires one's full attention; there are no distractions from the family or the evening newspaper. The medium itself, consisting as it does of sound and pictures, is easily understandable and highly dramatic. Studies in the psychological laboratory indicate the superiority of the visual image both in gaining and holding attention.

Several studies have demonstrated the effects which motion pictures have on attitudes and behavior. Peterson and Thurstone, who tested a series of films on such subjects as race, nationality, capital punishment and war, did succeed in changing the attitudes of the viewers.[25] The famous

[23] Kenneth Macgowan, "And So Into The Sunset . . . ," *New Republic*, CXX (January 31, 1949), p. 24.
[24] *Ideas for Action*, Vol. 11, No. 1 (January, 1948).
[25] Ruth C. Peterson and L. L. Thurstone, *Motion Pictures and the Social Attitudes of Children* (New York: The Macmillan Co., 1938).

Payne Fund studies in the early 1930's concluded, "First, the motion picture, as such, is a potent medium of education. Children even of the early age of 8 see half the facts in a picture and remember them for a surprisingly long time. A single exposure to a picture may produce a measurable change in attitude. Emotions are measurably stirred . . . Second, for children the content of current pictures is not good. There is too much sex and crime and love for a balanced diet for children . . . Third, the motion picture situation is very complicated. It is one among many influences which mold the experience of children.[26] Blumer and Hauser found that "motion pictures were a factor of importance in the delinquent or criminal careers of about 10 per cent of the male and 25 per cent of the female offenders studied." But also, "movies may redirect the behavior of delinquents and criminals along socially acceptable lines and make them hesitant about, and sometimes deter them from the commission of offenses." [27]

More recent studies of American soldiers during World War II on the effectiveness of the *Why We Fight* film series also showed that the motion picture could affect attitudes and opinions in the desired direction. An important contribution of these elaborate studies was to point out the relatively greater effect of movies upon factual items and attitudinal items concerning specific subject matter as opposed to the relatively minor effect upon attitudes of a general nature.[28]

The 1947 investigation of Hollywood by the Congressional Committee on Un-American Activities pointed up the great concern with which some Congressmen viewed the possibility of communistic propaganda in the motion picture industry.[29] Hollywood's reaction to this investigation was to attempt to purge itself of all communistic employees, no matter what relationship they had to the production of the motion picture.

Findings of the Commission on the Freedom of the Press: In 1947, after three years of study, a commission composed of thirteen members, headed by Robert M. Hutchins and financed by a grant of $200,000 from Time, Inc., published its monumental findings on the movies, radio, and press. These findings, as they apply to the motion picture industry, included the

---

[26] W. W. Charters, *Motion Pictures and Youth* (New York: The Macmillan Co., 1935), pp. 49, 51.
[27] Herbert Blumer and Philip M. Hauser, *Movies, Delinquency, and Crime* (New York: The Macmillan Co., 1933), pp. 198-199.
[28] L. Hovland, A. Lumsdaine, and F. Sheffield, *Experiments on Mass Communication* (Studies in Social Psychology in World War II, Vol. III), (Princeton: Princeton University Press, 1949).
[29] *Hearings Regarding the Communist Infiltration of the Motion Picture Industry* (Washington, D.C.: Government Printing Office, 1947).

following criticisms: a failure on the part of the movies to furnish (1) honest and accurate reporting, (2) a forum for the exchange of conflicting ideas, (3) fair representation of various groups, and (4) a broad presentation of the goals and values of society.

Searching for the causes of these failures, the Commission divided the blame as follows: (1) pressure of the audience for low-grade films, (2) bias of the owners toward conservatism, (3) monopolistic tendencies and a lack of competition.

The main recommendations as they applied to the motion picture industry included the following:

A. What can be done through government:
   1. Recognition of the constitutional guarantees of the freedom of the press as applying to motion pictures.
   2. Encouragement of the development of new techniques and maintenance of competition.
   3. Informing the public of facts and policies of the government regarding the motion picture industry.
B. What can be done by the industry:
   1. Accept its responsibility as a carrier of information and discussion.
   2. Finance new experimental activities.
   3. Engage in vigorous mutual criticism with radio and the press.
   4. Increase the competence, independence, and effectiveness of its staff.
C. What can be done by the public:
   1. Non-profit institutions should help supply the variety, quantity and quality of motion pictures required by the American people.
   2. Academic-professional study centers for research and publication should be set up.
   3. A new and independent agency should be established to appraise and report annually upon the performance of the motion picture industry.[30]

The important role played by the motion picture on the American scene, both as a major industry and as a purveyor of entertainment, education, and art, is amply documented by the detailed findings of this Commission. The resurgence of the movie industry following its initial setback with the advent of television requires the continued appraisal of the job it is doing. Movies affect attitudes and behavior and their control poses a significant problem for the modern mass society of today.

---

[30] *A Free and Responsible Press*, By the Commission on the Freedom of the Press (Chicago: University of Chicago Press, 1947).

Summary

The motion picture industry in the United States is currently fighting a bitter battle to keep its pre-eminence as a mass media of communication in competition with television, radio, and the press. After leading the mass entertainment industry for close to 30 years, the movies are being seriously threatened by the new medium of television. At the present time a division of labor among the different media appears to be taking place and it is quite likely that the motion picture industry will continue as a major factor in mass communication.

The history of the motion picture industry is a history of "big business." Until recently, this industry could be characterized as a "production-distribution-exhibition" monopoly. It regulated its product through its own Motion Picture Association, subject to review by local censorship boards. It controlled the distribution and exhibition of this product through ownership of its own theaters and control over independent theaters. The sensitivity of the movies to various public pressures, and its desire to reach as large an audience as possible has resulted for the most part in the production of "safe" pictures with little reality or significance. As a consequence there has been a decrease in the adult audience "over 30" years of age and the desertion of regular movie-goers to the new medium of television.

The motion pictures have had a tremendous effect upon the leisure-time habits of the American public, and have constituted a major source of stereotypes, fads, styles, etc. While many experimental studies have shown the effectiveness of the motion picture medium in changing opinions, the motion picture industry itself has limited its function largely to entertainment rather than education. How the motion picture industry will change in the future as a result of increased competition from television remains to be seen.

QUESTIONS

1. What is meant by the "production-distribution-exhibition" complex of control in the motion picture industry?

2. In what sense would you call the movies "an instrument of propaganda"? Cite some examples of propaganda in current motion pictures.

3. Name three different sources of censorship of motion pictures. What effect would you say such censorship has had upon the content of motion pictures?

4. Discuss briefly the statement "The movies build mass values."

5. What were the six general criticisms offered by the *Life* panel on the motion picture industry?

6. How do the motion pictures affect the attitudes and behavior of the American people? Analyze the function of this media as a force in influencing public opinion.

7. Discuss the findings of the Commission on the Freedom of the Press in relation to the movies. Indicate why you agree or disagree with the specific recommendations.

8. What is meant by the "over 30" controversy concerning movie audiences? How can you explain it?

9. What are some of the explanations offered for the decline in motion picture prosperity in 1946?

10. What is the significance of the statement: "The movies are big business"? Trace briefly the development of the motion picture industry as a business enterprise.

11. List three of the conclusions of the Payne Fund studies of motion pictures.

12. Discuss briefly the work of the Legion of Decency.

13. Discuss the problem of monopoly as it applies to the motion picture industry. To what extent does a monopoly exist? What attempts are being made to control monopolistic tendencies? In your opinion are these monopolistic tendencies "good" or "bad"? Why?

14. List some of the provisions of the Motion Picture Production Code. What effect would you say this Code has had upon the quality of motion pictures?

15. How do special interests or pressure groups affect the content of motion pictures?

16. What have some of the studies on the content of motion pictures revealed concerning their themes, characters, etc.?

17. What are some of the factors which led to the resurgence of the motion picture industry after the invention of television?

18. In your opinion can entertainment and education be combined in the movies?

19. What is the significance of the statement: "The movie audience is a mass audience"?

20. What are some of the factors accounting for the effectiveness of the movies in influencing attitudes and behavior?

SUGGESTED TOPICS FOR TERM PAPERS AND FURTHER RESEARCH

1. Analyze three motion pictures that you have seen recently in terms of the possible effects they might have upon public attitudes or behavior.

2. Go through the local newspaper and classify the movies that have been shown in your neighborhood in the last year in terms of topic or content. Do the same for a newspaper of 20 years ago. Discuss the significance of the differences you find.

3. Interview the local movie theater owner to find out how he decides upon the pictures he is going to show. What are the local sources of censorship or public pressure in your community?

4. Look through the literature on juvenile delinquency and summarize those statements made which attribute juvenile delinquency to the effects of movies on teen-agers.

5. Critically appraise the study by Peterson and Thurstone on motion pictures and children in terms of current conditions. Would you say that their findings are still applicable today?

6. Make a list of motion pictures you have recently seen. Compare those that you liked with those that you did not like. How do you account for your different evaluation?

7. Carefully analyze the Motion Picture Production Code in terms of its up-to-dateness. What indications do you see of how the times have changed?

8. Describe some of the stereotypes that have appeared in recent motion pictures you have seen. Discuss these stereotypes from the point of view of realism and effect on public attitudes.

9. Can you think of any motion picture that has had a lasting effect upon you? Describe this effect and try to account for it.

10. Interview several of your friends to find out what kinds of movies they like and why. How do you account for these differences in taste?

11. Write a critical review of the findings of the Commission on the Freedom of the Press.

12. Make a study among your friends of those individuals who go to the movies regularly and those who go seldom. How can you explain the difference in their movie attendance habits?

BIBLIOGRAPHY

Books

M. Adler, *Art and Prudence* (New York: Longmans, Green and Co., 1937). A basic analysis of the cultural problems created by the motion pictures.

Annals of the American Academy of Political and Social Science, "The Motion Picture Industry," Volume CCLIV, November, 1947. A special issue devoted to the movies.

H. Blumer, *Movies and Conduct* (New York: The Macmillan Co., 1933). A scientific report on the effects of motion pictures upon attitudes and behavior.

H. Brucker, *Freedom of Information* (New York: The Macmillan Co., 1949). A scholarly analysis of censorship of the mass media of communication. Also contains interesting material on the growth and present functioning of the mass media.

W. Charters, *Motion Pictures and Youth* (New York: The Macmillan Co., 1933). One of the first studies made of the effect of motion pictures upon children and young people.

M. Ernst, *The First Freedom* (New York: The Macmillan Co., 1946). An account of censorship in the United States, including other media as well as the motion pictures.

M. D. Huettig, *Economic Control of the Motion Picture Industry* (University of Pennsylvania, 1944). An economist's analysis of the business basis for the motion picture industry.

Ruth Inglis, *Freedom of the Movies* (Chicago: University of Chicago Press, 1946). A report of the Commission on Freedom of the Press dealing with the motion picture industry. A sociological orientation.

Alex Inkeles, *Public Opinion in Soviet Russia* (Cambridge, Mass.: Harvard University Press, 1950). An interesting controversial analysis of the motion picture industry and the other mass media in Russia.

Lewis Jacobs, *The Rise of the American Film: A Critical History* (New York: Harcourt, Brace and Co., 1939). An early history of the development of the American motion picture.

Raymond Moley, *Are We Movie-Made?* (New York: Macy-Masius, 1938). A general evaluation of the motion picture industry and the effects that the movies are having upon public custom and taste.

——— *The Hays Office* (New York: Bobbs-Merrill Co., 1945). A detailed analysis of the formation and operation of the Motion Picture Producers and Distributors Association.

Elliott Paul and Luis Quintanilla, *With a Hays Nonny-Nonny* (New York: Random House, 1942). A lively account of censorship in the motion picture industry.

L. Rosten, *Hollywood: The Movie Colony; The Movie Makers* (New York: Harcourt, Brace and Co., 1941). A sociological analysis of the folkways and mores of people connected with the motion picture industry.

Temporary National Economic Committee, *The Motion Picture Industry—A Pattern of Control* (Monograph #43) (Washington, D.C.: Government Printing Office, 1941). A report on the government investigation of the monopolistic control of the motion picture industry.

The Film Daily Yearbook of Motion Pictures (New York: The Film Daily, published annually). A trade publication summarizing current statistics in the motion picture industry.

M. Thorp, *America at the Movies* (New Haven: Yale University Press, 1939). An analysis of the motion picture audience.

UNESCO, *World Communications* (Paris: UNESCO, 1951). A statistical summary of the motion pictures, radio, and press in different countries throughout the world.

D. Waples (Ed.), *Print, Radio, and Film in a Democracy* (Chicago: University of Chicago Press, 1942). A collection of articles dealing with the role of the motion picture industry in America, including its regulation and effects.

Martha Wolfenstein, *Movies: A Psychological Study* (Glencoe, Illinois: Free Press, 1950). A highly imaginative and original analysis of the content of motion pictures.

Periodicals

E. A. Bayne, "Film and Community," *Journal of Adult Education*, XIII (January, 1941), pp. 17-22.

Leo Handel, "The Social Obligation of Motion Pictures," *International Journal of Opinion and Attitude Research*, I (1947), p. 96.

Harry L. Hansen, "Hollywood and International Understanding," *Harvard Business Review*, XXV, No 1 (Autumn, 1946), pp. 28-45.

J. E. Hulett, Jr., "Estimating the Net Effect of a Commercial Motion Picture Upon the Trend of Local Public Opinion," *American Sociological Review*, XIV (1949), pp. 263-275.

R. Jester, "Hollywood and Pedagogy," *Journal of Educational Sociology*, XII (November, 1938), pp. 137-141.

Dorothy B. Jones, "Quantitative Analysis of Motion Picture Content," *Public Opinion Quarterly*, VI (1942), pp. 411-428.

Siegfried Kracauer, "National Types as Hollywood Presents Them," *Public Opinion Quarterly*, XIII, pp. 53-72.

Paul F. Lazarsfeld, "Audience Research in the Movie Field," *Annals of the American Academy of Political and Social Science*, CCLIV (1947), pp. 160-168.

Lewis Milestone, "First Aid for a Sick Giant," *New Republic*, January 31, 1949.

H. Miller, "Motion Pictures: A Social and Educational Force," *Journal of Educational Sociology*, XI (November, 1937), pp. 164-165.

"Movies: End of an Era?" *Fortune* (April, 1949), p. 150.

Martin Quigley, "Public Opinion and the Motion Picture," *Public Opinion Quarterly*, I (1937), p. 129.

Terry Ramsaye, "The Rise and Place of the Motion Picture," *Annals of the American Academy of Political and Social Science*, CCLIV (1947), p. 2.

W. Wagner, "Role of Movies in Morale," *American Journal of Sociology*, XLVII (November, 1941), pp. 378-383.

Mildred J. Wiese and Stewart G. Cole, "A Study of Children's Attitudes and the Influence of a Commercial Motion Picture," *Journal of Psychology*, XXI (1946), pp. 151-171.

Chapter XXVIII

Television

The world today is witnessing the birth of a new giant medium of communication—television. Within a period of only five short years, this new medium has made such tremendous progress that it appears to have already outdistanced radio and motion pictures. As recently as 1950 television could be discussed simply as an adjunct of radio. Today, however, this would be tantamount to describing the tail as wagging the dog. As pictured by Jack Gould, "Then came the panic: television in the fall of 1949. Almost overnight the fascinating laboratory toy of video emerged as the colossus of show business. And it struck at the vitals of the sound medium. . . . The radio audience swiftly grew smaller. . . . Thus, today, compared to what it once was, radio definitely has lost stature and importance. Its handicap is not only economic, but psychological. Television generates news and excitement in almost everything it does; radio is taken for granted." [1]

Statistics are difficult to cite for an invention that is changing so rapidly from day to day. Current figures are out of date before they are even published.[2] Plans for the future become even more and more grandiose. In 1948, what appeared then to be a fantastic prediction was that the year 1954 would see 16 million TV sets in use. This figure was actually reached in 1951, and today there are over 33 million TV sets in use.[3] Television national advertising revenue has already outdistanced that of the radio industry. A comparison of 1953 with 1954 shows television revenue for national advertising up 40.7 per cent for a total of $320,154,274, while network radio has dropped 14.3 per cent and non-network radio 44 per cent for a grand total of $264,242,169.[4] It seems entirely probable that the television industry will be among the top ten industries

---

[1] Jack Gould, "Radio *Has* a Future," *The New York Times*, April 17, 1955.
[2] Oscar Katz, CBS Director of Research, stated at the 1949 Annual Luncheon of The Pulse, Inc., "The simple but elusive fact is that it (TV) is neither stable nor mature. Television is young, fluid, and unpredictable."
[3] *The World Almanac*, 1955, p. 789.
[4] *Business Week*, April 9, 1955, p. 63.

of the United States and will do a business at least four times as large as that of radio.[5]

History of Television. Television will take its place as one of science's modern miracles. The technique for the broadcasting of sound and light simultaneously had its early history in the development of electronics. The first television scanning disk was invented by a German, Paul Nipkow, in 1884. Both Marconi and Edison contributed to the further development of television with their inventions of wireless and motion pictures. In 1906 Lee de Forest perfected the three-element vacuum tube which proved an important step in the development of both radio and television. Dr. Vladimir K. Zworykin in 1923 filed an original patent application for a small iconoscope, the "electronic eye" for television. From this year forward a rapid series of demonstrations and first performances marked the history of television as a commercial medium of communication. In 1927 the Bell Telephone Laboratories demonstrated wire-television between Washington and New York. The year 1928 saw the opening of W2XBS by NBC and in 1931 W2XAB by CBS for television tests. In 1936 the Federal Communications Commission held a hearing on the future of television. The first public showing of electronic television in the United States took place at the New York World's Fair in 1939. World War II interrupted the development of commercial television and although the Federal Communications Commission authorized commercial television effective July 1, 1941, it was not until 1947 that the FCC chose in favor of NBC's black and white television as opposed to CBS's color television. From that year until the present the television boom has been on.[6]

Since TV is so new, a brief account of its technical operation might be in order. Horton, in an interesting analysis of the standardization of television presents the following clear description: ". . . television, like the motion picture, depends on the physiological phenomenon of persistence of vision. The 'picture' is actually a running dot of light. . . . This dot traverses the surface of the viewing screen a specified number of times per second, just as the motion picture is presented at the rate of twenty-four frames per second. Below a certain threshold value of the repetition rate, the average viewer will perceive a disturbing flicker in the

---

[5] Predicted by NBC Vice-President Mullen and DuMont's Allen B. Dumont in *Time*, May 24, 1948, p. 72.

[6] See: "Historic Steps in Television," in Orrin E. Dunlap, Jr., *The Future of Television* (New York: Harper and Brothers, 1942), p. 180. Also, H. Beville, Jr., "The Challenge of the New Media: Television, FM, and Facsimile," *Journalism Quarterly*, XXV (March, 1948); and E. Engstrom, "Recent Developments in Television," *The Annals of the American Academy of Political and Social Science*, CCXIII (January, 1941), pp. 130-137; "Television! Boom!," *Fortune* (May, 1948).

image. This threshold varies with the brightness of the image and its size. The higher the repetition rate, generally speaking, the less flicker and the greater the permissible size and brightness of the image. But, on the other hand, if other conditions are equal, the higher the repetition rate, the smaller the number of lines. What is gained in some qualities is lost in another. The ideal system would have all these values maximized. But at any point short of the ideal goal, a technical compromise among these factors has to be worked out." [7]

Horton's analysis of this standardization is an interesting case study in social control. According to this author, television represents one of the few attempts of society to establish a new technology on an orderly and rational basis. Out of a basic conflict between engineers, enterpreneurs, and government representatives, each with different interests and aims, came the unprecedented standardization of a complete technological system at its very beginning.

The Control of Television

Television, while psychologically closer to the motion pictures in terms of perception, is by and large much more similar to radio in its ownership and regulatory features. An analysis of the growth of control over television presents an illuminating case study of the various interests involved in this area of public concern. On the one hand, the business interests were primarily composed of the radio manufacturers and the radio broadcasters but also included radio's competitors, the movies, and the press. On the other hand, the artists and educators were concerned with the cultural use of the new medium. The government was already involved in the regulation of radio and was obviously concerned with both the engineering and program standards of the new medium.

The radio industry took almost immediate control, even to the extent of going into the manufacturing as well as the broadcasting business. The major radio networks became the major television networks with only the addition of DuMont. Thus television, a potentially devastating competitor of radio, became in actuality part of the radio industry itself. The movie industry, on the other hand, attempted from the very beginning to fight television by withholding films, actors, directors, etc. However, this was a losing battle and today "television, which scared Hollywood initially, actually staved off disaster for production workers and the talent groups. TV filming is booming, with some $80,000,000 expected to be spent this year on the making of shows in Hollywood. This activity

---

[7] Donald Horton, "Television Standards and the Engineering Compromise," in Bernard Berelson and Morris Janowitz (eds.), *Reader in Public Opinion and Communication* (Glencoe, Ill.: The Free Press, 1950), pp. 224-225.

not only has kept open studios no longer in demand for theatrical picture purposes, but also has absorbed thousands of persons who otherwise would have been out of work." [8]

The Federal Communications Commission from the beginning was concerned with the regulation of television. First there was the problem of mechanical standardization. This was undertaken in 1940 and 1941 by a committee of engineers appointed by the industry at the request of the Federal Communications Commission.[9] The need for standardization can be understood from the following description by Horton: "The television signal consists of a complex of waves which have interdependent functions. . . . A television receiver works only if the receiver and the transmitter are designed to operate with the same number of scanning lines per second, the same plan of interlacing lines, the same synchronizing pulses, and so on. If competitive transmitters operated with different values of these variables, it would be impossible for television to become an effective medium of communication. It was obviously in the public interest to establish the entire television industry on the basis of a single set of technical standards such that any transmitter could be received by any receiving set put on the market by any manufacturer." [10]

In addition to the problem of engineering standards, the Federal Communications Commission had to face the problem of channel allocation. In order to meet this problem the FCC, in September, 1948, instituted a "freeze" on station building for a period of three and a half years.[11] The final FCC plan provided for a total of 2,051 TV stations in 1,275 communities serving a potential audience of some 44 million families. Under the proposed plan, there were to be two types of stations: 1,809 conventional commercial stations and 242 educational stations. The allocation of channel space to educational stations gave rise to a controversy which is still being hotly debated.

This debate brings us to the third group of individuals concerned with the control of TV, namely, the educators. From the beginning of television, educators were determined not to permit television to develop as radio had in complete disregard for educational functions. Jack Gould said, "The issue is whether responsible elements of the community are now sufficiently farsighted to avoid repeating in television the mistakes they made in radio. When radio first started some educators made a half-hearted attempt to use the air waves, but either through indifference or

---

[8] "Survey of the Movies," *The New York Times,* February 6, 1955.

[9] Donald G. Fink (ed.), *Television Standards and Practice:* Selected Papers from the Proceedings of the National Television System Committee and Its Panels (New York: McGraw-Hill Book Co., Inc., 1943).

[10] Horton, *op. cit.,* pp. 225-226.

[11] See "The Television Freeze," *Fortune,* November, 1949.

lack of public support, lost out to the commercial interests which quickly pre-empted most of the available channels. Twenty-five years later, when the impact of radio often was only too painfully apparent, the world of education was on the outside looking in." [12]

The commercial broadcasters are strongly opposing the allocation of channels to educational stations. According to Justin Miller, President of the National Association of Broadcasters at the time of the FCC hearings, educators were "shooting at the wrong target to ask channel reservation." He suggested that educators buy radio time. The commercial broadcasters further maintain that the educators are incompetent to use television and state that the colleges and schools lack the necessary funds. At the present time the FCC is reviewing applications from educational institutions for the operation of noncommercial television stations.

The birth of a new medium is bound to give rise to many controversies about its proper use. We have already discussed briefly the controversy over channel allocation. Another controversy that has arisen concerns the use of color on television. In 1950, after a bitter battle between the National Broadcasting Company and the Columbia Broadcasting System, the FCC approved the color transmission method of the Columbia Broadcasting System. This decision was bitterly criticized because the CBS color television was "incompatible" with existing black and white television reception and would require an adaptor or converter. The objection to this method was so strenuous that the system was never a commercial success. Finally, RCA developed a color system which was compatible and today color television is a reality. However, as was pointed out by Sir George Barnes, Director of Television for the British Broadcasting Corporation, the advent of color television might prove a mixed blessing. "Would there not be a temptation to rely on the splashy effect of color as a substitute for program quality?" [13]

To mention briefly one other controversy, television created the problem of legislative and judicial televising. The tremendous dramatic appeal of the television screen made court trials and legislative hearings attractive to a large audience. The proponents for the televising of hearings or trials argue: (1) The citizen has a right to attend public hearings or a case in court. Television makes this right a reality. (2) The chairman or judge is in a position to establish rules which would result in a sense of fairness or decorum and prevent any "hippodromes." (3) Television is a new medium and is entitled to the same rights of access to public events as any other medium. (4) Any injustices which occur are not the result

---

[12] *The New York Times*, November 26, 1950.
[13] *The New York Times*, April 27, 1955.

of television, but television merely focuses attention upon the legal problems of such forms of investigation.

The opponents of television argue: (1) Television is an entertainment medium and the audience listens to be amused rather than to be informed. (2) The strong lighting and equipment of television places the witness under an unnecessary nervous strain. (3) Fragmentary viewing of proceedings may lead the audience to catch only a small and disjointed fraction of the total testimony. (4) Televising of gangsters may unduly "romanticize" these individuals in the public mind. (5) Television may turn the courts and public hearings into platforms for propaganda.

The final decision concerning this controversy has yet to be made. Inherent in this decision will be the conception of television as entertainment or education and the evaluation of the public as competent or incompetent to make sound and fair judgments. A positive appraisal of the public, insofar as televising Congress is concerned, was made by Representative Jacob K. Javits of New York, who viewed television as "the best opportunity under modern conditions for bringing to the people knowledge of the basis for the far-reaching decisions made for the people. . . . In the last analysis, the good sense of the people is the ultimate protection of our democratic system against rabble-rousers. The more people who are directly exposed to demagogues in action—filtered through no eyes but their own—the more there will be who are practiced in reaching judgments with discrimination. I believe in bringing demagogues out into the open and taking our chances on the judgment of an informed electorate."[14] The public itself appears to be in favor of such broadcasts. The results of a public opinion survey indicate that 65 per cent are in favor of televising Congress for at least an hour a day with only 18 per cent opposed and 17 per cent doubtful. Congress itself appears to be more divided in its opinion. A magazine poll among 20 Senators found 9 in favor, 6 against, and 5 undecided. A confidential poll by Representative Javits of 188 members of the House of Representatives showed about an even split with 61 opposed out of 118 interviewed.

Content of Television Programs

The content of television programs, like that of radio broadcasting, is in the hands of the advertisers and broadcasters. In general, therefore, the previous evaluation of radio program content also applies to television content. For the most part, these programs are on a fairly low cultural level. They are designed to appeal to the lowest common denominator of a mass audience. Advertising rates, similar to radio, are based upon a

[14] Jacob Javits, "The Case for Televising Congress," *New York Times Magazine*, January 13, 1952, p. 12.

delivered audience of so many viewers. For the most part, therefore, television content deserves the appellation of "warmed-over" radio. Some individuals believe that television will have even a worse effect than radio and will be "the death of culture." [15]

A survey by the National Association of Educational Broadcasters of all television shows for an entire week in the New York City area revealed the following: "In the week of President Truman's State of the Union message, TV gave just 1 per cent of its time to public events. Religious programs got less than 1 per cent. News was on 5 per cent of the time, but almost a third of it featured typed news bulletins accompanied by unrelated music (e.g., a gay waltz was played during the report of Sinclair Lewis' death). Children's programs got 12 per cent of TV's time, but many of the shows seemed to bear little relation to youngsters' tastes or needs. . . . During the week, 2,723 commercial advertisements took up 55 hours (10 per cent) of program time. . . . On weekdays, commercials averaged up to 146 seconds, took up as much as 32.7 per cent of the day's telecast. No serious music was broadcast during the week. . . ." [16]

A more detailed analysis by Dallas W. Smythe revealed the following: "Whatever the motives, whatever the real gratifications from its use, three-fourths of television programs are ostensibly 'for fun.' Information-type programs amount to slightly less than one-fifth of total program time. And orientation-type programs constitute the remainder or slightly more than one-twentieth of total time . . . By all odds the largest program class is found in the entertainment-type group: drama. . . . The largest single subclass of drama is crime drama which alone provided just short of one minute out of six of all television programs in New York in 1953. . . . Variety is the second largest class of program on television. In New York in 1953 this class provided 12 per cent of total program time. . . . Four other classes of entertainment programs are important. These are quiz, stunt and contest programs (6 per cent in New York in 1953); sports events (6 per cent); music programs (4 per cent); and personalities programs (3 per cent). . . . The American television-using public receives its information-type programs within one-fifth of television program time. The largest single class of program in this group is news (8 per cent in New York in 1953). About half of this time is given to news reports and the remainder to special events (such as Garroway's and Murrow's programs) and sports news and interviews. . . . Information of a general sort for the whole audience (science, travel, etc.) is contained in about 2 per cent of program time, while similar pro-

[15] Jack Gould, "Television," *The New York Times,* April 24, 1949.
[16] *Time,* February 5, 1951.

grams aimed at the child audience amount to less than 1 per cent." [17]

Thus, there appears to be ample justification for the advice given by Norman Corwin to the individual who wished to work for radio and television: ". . . radiomen want 'the safe, routine, unspectacular, competent, journeyman script . . . with maybe a fresh twist no bigger than what you give to a lemon peel in a Martini.' In TV, the writer is even less important: he must step aside for Gorgeous George, Garrulous Godfrey . . . westerns, British films from the bottom of the vault, midget autos, roller-skating derbies . . . kitchen and fashion demonstrators, giveaways, and the upper slopes of Faye Emerson.' But if he is willing 'to curb his imagination' and to look on the medium as 'a trade outlet, not an art . . . it's a living.' " [18]

Censorship. Censorship of television programs is similar to that of radio programs and need not be discussed in special detail. The FCC evaluates the content of television programs according to the same standards of "public interest, necessity and convenience" as it applies to radio programs. The National Association of Radio and Television Broadcasters has developed a code similar to the one used by radio broadcasters. Of special significance for television are such admonitions as the avoidance of "such views of performers as emphasize anatomical details indecently" or a warning that "the use of locations closely associated with sexual life or with sexual sin must be governed by good taste and delicacy." Television, since the addition of sight to sound, even more than radio, has to face the problem of "indecency and morality." Television is always faced with the nightmare of the unintended strip tease. A standard precaution is to inspect all clothing and underwear rigorously before presenting any fight or rough and tumble.

The competitive aspects of a new industry like television have given rise to several instances of censorship. A panel discussion on "The Impact of Television" over the Mutual Broadcasting System was canceled. The Mutual System had no television network. A panel member issued the following statement: "Protests by some member stations of the M.B.S. network, as well as by network officials that discussion of television is contrary to the interests of radio broadcasts, caused officials of the 'Reviewing Stand' to withdraw the program." [19] In a similar manner CBS banned advertising for subscription television from one of its programs. According to the Zenith Radio Corporation the network refused to permit the program "Omnibus" to carry a commercial announcement relating to Phonevision. CBS explained: "Phonevision is not a product, it's a

[17] Dallas W. Smythe, "Reality As Presented by Television," *The Public Opinion Quarterly*, Vol. XVIII, No. 2 (Summer, 1954), pp. 149-150.
[18] *Writer* (mag.), article by Norman Corwin (February, 1951), pp. 35-37.
[19] *The New York Times,* August 6, 1950.

controversial issue. We don't allow any commercials to deal with controversial issues in the course of an entertainment, news or other program not specifically devoted to discussion of such issues." [20] Phonevision is a method which requires set owners to have a special device in order to receive special television broadcasts for which they must pay.

The Television Audience

When it first appeared on the American scene, television viewing was largely limited to public places—especially barrooms. There is even a case on record of the tavern owner who closed his bar from 2-3 P.M. so that children might come in to watch the television programs. The high price of the initial television sets limited the audience to that segment of the population which could afford it. However, within a short period of five years the price of television has been brought within the range of most American families, and at the present time television may be said to reach all economic groups and most geographical areas in the United States.

Perhaps the most important new feature of the television audience is its family nature. Several studies have indicated that the television audience is a family audience. One study asked a sample of television-set owners whether television had affected family life. "More than one-half of those with families said it had. The manner in which family life had been affected varied from, 'It's gotten us closer together in thoughts and ideas. Also keeps us together physically. There's a chumminess about it when you get together around a television set' to, 'The children refuse to go to sleep. We have trouble eating, they run in and out. Homework trouble too.'" Here are some of the ways in which television appears to have affected the family life of set owners:[21]

Per Cent

"Keeps family together more," "Stay at home more" 27
"Children stay up later," "Have trouble putting them to sleep" ... 17
"Have had to change the dinner hour," "Kid eats in front of set,"
    "Eats everything now" 8
Use television as a disciplinary measure, "If you're bad, you won't
    watch television" 6
Keeps children in, "Off the streets" 5
Interferes with work, "Children won't do homework" 3
"Keeps the kids quiet" 2
"Have to sit and watch westerns because kids like them," "Watch
    children's programs" 2

[20] *The New York Times*, April 7, 1955.
[21] M. A. Goldberg, *Politics and Television*, unpublished thesis on file at Columbia University Library.

The growth of a children's audience for television programs can probably be attributed not only to the greater attractiveness of sight and sound to children, but also to the imagination with which the television programs have approached the children's audience. "So far, television's 'Kiddie shows' have shown a marked departure from radio's juvenile programs. Adapting movie and vaudeville techniques, they have offered animated cartoons, puppet shows, children's parties, contests, and amateur hours with audience participation. . . . For the most part, these programs have been kept on a childish level, replete with slapstick, nonsense, and hubbub. Even the titles label them as designed for the kindergarten set: 'Howdy Doody,' 'Scrap Book,' 'Small Fry Club,' 'Junior Frolics,' etc." [22]

The almost irresistible attraction which television has for children has created a great deal of controversy about the negative or positive effects of such televiewing. Many surveys have shown that television's children audience has reached a tremendous size. This audience actually includes many three, four, and five year olds as well as teenagers. The daily listening among a sample of children averaged 3.86 hours. However, less than 10 per cent believe that watching television has made it more difficult for them to find time in which to do their own work. Perhaps the greatest effects concern movie attendance, with three out of four children stating that television has decreased their movie attendance.[23]

One indication of the growth of the television audience comes from a study on the use of television during the 1952 election campaign. Television outdistanced radio as a source of information about the campaign, with one-third of the population paying attention to the campaign by means of television. The conclusions stated by the authors of this study are extremely portentous when one realizes that the 1952 campaign was only the first in which television played a major part. "The first noteworthy fact is that the public went out of its way to watch the campaign on television. Only about 40 per cent of the homes in the U.S. have television sets, but some 53 per cent of the population saw TV programs on the campaign—a reflection of 'television visiting.' . . . When people were asked which medium had given them the most information about the campaign, the impact of television became even more striking. In the nation as a whole television, although available to only a minority of the people, led the other media in the number of persons who rated it most informative. . . ." [24]

---

[22] Josette Frank, *Comics, Radio, Movies—and Children*, Public Affairs Pamphlet No. 148, pp. 28-29.
[23] Survey reported in *The New York Times*, March 6, 1950.
[24] A. Campbell, G. Gurin, and W. E. Miller, "Television and the Election," *Public Opinion and Propaganda*, edited by Katz, *et al.* (New York: The Dryden Press, 1954), pp. 287-288.

By and large, the television audience is the same as the radio audience, with the addition of children. Both media appeal to mass audiences, representative of all segments of the population. To a certain extent, moreover, television may be said to have taken over the radio audience. Many studies have shown that evening listening or viewing in homes with both radio and television sets is limited almost completely to televiewing. A survey by Duane Jones Company of New York found 92.4 per cent of the public listening to radio less following the purchase of a television set. The Hooper ratings of program popularity indicate the shift of the radio audience to television most dramatically. In New York the 1948 rating for Jack Benny dropped from 26.5 to 4.8 in 1951. Radio Theatre dropped from 25.3 to 8.4, and Arthur Godfrey dropped from 20.3 to 5.9.[25] The meaning of these figures for the future of the radio industry will be explored in the next section.

The Effects of Television

Television appears to be living up to many of the predictions, often dire, of its effects upon the public and the other competing mass media. As described by *Time* magazine in 1948: "Television is all the talk—and all the talk is big. Its enthusiasts are sure that it will eventually (maybe sooner) make radio as obsolete as the horse—and empty all the nation's movie houses. Children will go to school in their own living rooms, presidential candidates will win elections from a television studio. Housewives will see on the screen the dresses and groceries they want, and shop by phone." [26] Now, not more than seven years later, many of these predictions appear well on their way to fulfillment.

Perhaps the greatest and most notable effect to date of television concerns its two main competitors—radio and motion pictures. There can be little doubt about the change in the radio listening and movie going habits of the American public as a result of television. Among 1,580 television owners interviewed by the Duane Jones Company in a survey in New York City, "92.4 per cent were listening to radio less than before they owned TV sets; 80.9 per cent were going to movies less frequently; 58.9 per cent were reading fewer books; 48.5 per cent read magazines less often; 23.9 per cent were even skimping on newspapers." [27] In the highly critical area of national advertising revenue, a comparison of 1953 with 1954 shows an increase in revenue taking place only for the television medium which rose 92.5 million dollars over the previous year, a gain of 40 per cent. Radio showed the greatest decrease, while magazines and

---

[25] *The New York Times,* June 27, 1951.

[26] *Time,* May 24, 1948.

[27] *Time,* February 1, 1949.

newspapers were barely able to hold their own. After a detailed comparison of the various advertising media, *Business Week* concluded: "The Winner—Television has become the nation's No. 1 mass-entertainment medium—an eventuality overlooked by the people who thought that TV's effect on other media would be no worse than that of radio. But radio's impact on people was never in a class with that of television. As an entertainment medium, TV in a few short years helped to change over the movie industry . . . Increasingly, advertisers are going to look on TV as their 'first-call medium,' . . ," [28]

Effect on Radio. Perhaps the greatest effect of television will be felt upon radio broadcasting. This is not to say that the radio industry will suffer, since, for the most part, the radio industry has converted itself to television. In 1949 a Gallup poll found that 25 per cent of the public believed that radio was doomed to extinction because of television—this at a time when less than one-half the population had even seen television. [29] A 1948 CBS-Rutgers survey found that children in homes with TV sets had virtually stopped listening to their radios. [30] The year 1950 showed a tremendous shift in the relative proportion of the total broadcast audience listening to radios or viewing television. In Baltimore the increase for television in a single year was from 18 per cent to 50 per cent, in New York from 15 per cent to 50 per cent, Boston from 10 per cent to 38 per cent, Chicago from 10 per cent to 40 per cent, etc. [31] The tremendous drop in advertising revenue and the constant loss of listeners to radio programs leave little doubt that radio, as it was known in the 1940's, is on its way out.

This is not to say that radio will disappear from the American scene. The high cost of television programs will continue to leave a radio market for low cost advertising. Although television has been installed in some automobiles, radio will continue to serve the 30 million radio sets on wheels. Radio will probably dominate during the daytime work hours of the average housewife, although a survey by CBS found 54 per cent of all daytime TV listeners listening to TV serials.

Effect on Motion Pictures. Whereas the radio industry was quick to join television rather than fight it, the motion picture industry from the beginning has attempted to win in competition with TV. It fought a losing fight, however, and at the present time the industry is taking steps to climb aboard the TV bandwagon. Hollywood is expected to spend some

---

[28] *Business Week*, April 9, 1955.

[29] *Variety*, June 15, 1949.

[30] John W. Riley, Frank V. Cantwell and Katherine Ruttiger, "Some Observations on the Social Effects of Television," *Public Opinion Quarterly*, XIII (1949), pp. 223-234.

[31] *Variety*, May 3, 1950.

$80,000,000 filming shows for television broadcasting.[32] More and more movie stars, producers, and writers are entering the new medium.

Many studies have shown a decrease in movie attendance since the advent of television. Research information from the Council of Motion Picture Organizations and the National Broadcasting Company shows a steady decrease in the average weekly movie attendance from about 85 million in 1946 to about 40 million in the year of 1954. During the same period the television audience rose from 0 in 1946 to close to 90 million at the end of 1954. A survey of the research organization, Sindlinger and Company, showed that movie attendance constantly decreased by 1 per cent for each 2 per cent increase in television-set ownership.[33] It would appear that the habitual movie-goer is the first to forsake the movies for the new invention of television.

The motion picture industry has attempted to meet the competition of television through technical improvements such as wider screens and through more careful selection in the type of film being made. "Today, Hollywood makes fewer pictures for the smaller audience. A lot of the Class B product is gone. In other words, the industry is making fewer, more expensive films." [34] Big screen movies, it is hoped, will make the television viewer more conscious of his small 21-inch screen. Phone-vision will enable the movie industry to bring motion pictures directly into the home on the TV screen for an additional charge to the viewer.

Social Effects of Television. It is impossible in the present fluid state of TV development to evaluate the final effects that television will have upon American society. That it will change the leisure time habits of the American public cannot be doubted. Radio listening, movie attendance, sports attendance, visiting, etc., are bound to be affected by this new medium. Whether television will influence "the social and economic habits of the nation to a degree unparalleled since the advent of the automobile" remains to be seen.[35] The "mutually compensatory character of the mass media" wherein "one medium benefits by the interest which another medium stimulates" in the past has enabled the press to meet the challenge of the motion picture, and the motion picture in turn to meet the inroads of radio.[36] It seems likely that the different media will in time stabilize their public use according to a division of labor.

Television's effect on other areas of life, such as family life, education,

---

[32] Estimate given in *The New York Times*, February 6, 1955.

[33] *The New York Times*, February 6, 1955.

[34] *Business Week*, April 9, 1955.

[35] *The New York Times*, June 24, 1951.

[36] H. M. Beville, Jr., "The Challenge of the New Media: Television, FM, and Facsimile," *Journalism Quarterly*, XXV (March 1948), pp. 3-11.

religion, political campaigning, etc., are already noticeable but far from settled. According to Robert Bendiner, "It has brought candidates and issues 'into the home,' greatly stimulated registration and altered traditional stumping techniques." [37] A study of the role of TV during the 1952 campaign demonstrated the importance of television for the future of political campaigning. Over 50 per cent of the population in the United States watched TV programs on the campaign.[38] Reinhold Niebuhr in *Christianity and Crisis* stated that the immediate effect of TV would be "a further vulgarization of our culture . . . Much of what is still wholesome in our life will perish under the impact of this new visual aid . . ." The *Christian Century* lamented that "the Roman Catholic Church, with its pageantry and color, will have an appeal in television which the Protestant churches lack." [39]

A study of television and family life concluded: "To sum up, the impact of television upon the family life appears to have been fairly great. Our respondents have indicated that they now tend to stay at home more than formerly. In addition, the trend seems to be toward more visitors in the home. The extra time spent at home leads to a corresponding decrease in outside activities. In many instances it also means an increase in household expenses which are spent in entertaining guests. The effect of television upon children has been even greater than upon adults. Half of them go to sleep later while the same is true of a fifth of the adults. Eating habits have changed in the case of 40 per cent of the children and 20 per cent of the adults. Many now eat in front of their television sets. The fact that the family is kept together by television means that children are kept off the streets. It also means that the children are neglecting their homework." [40] A research project, in 1954, by the University of Toronto, under a Ford grant, concluded that television was as effective in teaching as classroom lectures.[41] Arthur Daley described the effect of television upon attendance at roller-skating derbies: "Video has indubitably been of tremendous benefit to a few stray sports of normally limited drawing power. A visitor to our town a few months back was a form of mayhem called the roller derby. Advance agents tried to describe it and failed. It began as the flop of the ages. However, the show was televised and its rough-and-tumble charms thus were shown to those who never before had suspected its existence. By the time the marathon ended—a roller derby combined certain features of roller-skating, six-day

[37] *The New York Times Magazine*, November 2, 1952.
[38] Campbell, Gurin and Miller, *op. cit.*, p. 288.
[39] *Time*, February 1, 1949.
[40] M. A. Goldberg, *Politics and Television*, unpublished thesis on file at Columbia University Library.
[41] *World Almanac*, 1955, p. 790.

bike riding and football—the armory was packed with customers night after night. Extra matinees were added. The derby wound up averaging 5,166 spectators a performance for a hall which accommodates 5,200. The answer? Television." [42]

What the final effects of television will be must remain a question which only the future can answer. In the coming years it will be important to watch for the changes which this medium produces among its competing media of mass communication. In addition, the social consequences of this new medium will undoubtedly occupy the attention of social scientists for years to come. Perhaps the clearest picture that can be given at the present time still remains the conclusion of *Time* magazine which in 1948 remarked about the advent of TV: "Like the atom, television has in it tremendous possibilities of both good and evil. Educators are looking to the telescreen to solve the teaching shortage and improve the quality, if not the warmth, of the teaching process. They rhapsodize over the thought of an Einstein or a Toynbee lecturing to hundreds of classrooms at once. . . . But the best way to measure television's future is to look at the men who control it. And since radio and Hollywood are television's godfathers, the child will probably grow up in their image, with their considerable virtues—and their considerable vices." [43]

Summary

Television is the latest, and from all advance signs the greatest, of the mass media of communication. Combining as it does the psychological appeal of sight and sound with the comfort of home-viewing, television has found immediate, widespread acceptance among all segments of the American public. Each day witnesses new developments, technical, artistic and commercial.

For the most part television has adopted the model of radio for its regulation and control. From the beginning, the radio industry has assumed ownership and control of the new medium. Program production and regulation is similar to that of radio broadcasting. TV is supervised by the Federal Communications Commission, regulated by its own production code and sensitive to the pressures of various interest groups. Many of television's own special problems, such as educational televising, color television, the presentation of legislative hearings and court trials, the "sale" of special feature programs to the public, etc., have yet to be resolved.

Despite its youth, the effects of television are apparent everywhere. It

---

[42] Arthur Daley, *The New York Times Magazine*, March 27, 1949, p. 17.
[43] *Time*, May 24, 1948.

has surpassed the radio industry in advertising revenue. Wherever it has entered a community, movie attendance has fallen off sharply. Family leisure patterns have been greatly altered, while the tremendous popularity of children's programs have created a bitter controversy over the good or bad effects of television on children. Political campaign tactics have been radically revised. Attendance at sporting events, especially football, has been affected. Only the future can tell the full story, but all indications are that television will write a new chapter in the history of mass communication in the United States.

QUESTIONS

1. Discuss the effects of television upon both the communications industry and the public. In your opinion will television be a force for "good" or "evil"?

2. Television, like radio, is judged by the FCC in terms of "public interest, necessity and convenience." In your opinion how does television compare to radio in meeting these standards?

3. Discuss the controversy between TV broadcasters and educators on channel allocation. What are the main arguments of both sides? Which point of view do you favor and why?

4. Criticize the following statement made to justify the content of TV programs: "The public gets what it wants, nothing better nothing worse."

5. Is the constitutional guarantee of freedom of the press currently applicable to television? In your opinion should television have this guarantee?

6. How do you account for the rapid growth of television? Is television living up to advance predictions about its success?

7. What were the various interests or groups concerned with the development of television? How and why is each concerned?

8. Discuss the problem of televising legislative hearings or court trials. What arguments can be made in favor and against such programs?

9. Explain briefly what is meant by the following statement: "Television will grow up in radio's image."

10. In what ways is the television audience different from the radio audience?

11. Discuss censorship as it applies to television. Can you cite any instances of actual censorship?

12. Was radio or television more important as a source of information about the 1952 election campaign? How do you account for the greater superiority of one of the media?

13. Describe briefly the history of the development of television.

14. What are some of the factors which tend to make television a conservative force?

15. Did the movie industry attempt to help or hinder the growth of television? Why? How about the radio industry?

16. What is meant by the FCC "freeze" on the growth of television? How was this "freeze" finally resolved?

17. What is meant by the statement that television is simply "warmed over" radio?

18. How does television appear to be affecting the leisure time habits of the American public?

19. Discuss the growth of a children's audience to television programs. In your opinion will television have a positive or negative effect upon children?

20. What is the significance for television of George Bernard Shaw's statement concerning radio, "Get what you want or you will grow to like what you get"?

SUGGESTED TOPICS FOR TERM PAPERS AND FURTHER RESEARCH

1. Examine the television program listing in your local newspaper. Classify the various programs according to the type of program and the time of day. Discuss the significance of this tabulation.

2. Carefully review the findings of the Commission on the Freedom of the Press for the radio industry. How many of these results would you say apply to the television industry?

3. Interview the local theater owner, librarian, and radio station manager concerning the effect that they think television is having upon their business.

4. Look through the newspaper reports of the televising of the McCarthy-Army hearings. From these reports do you believe that the televising of these hearings was a good or bad idea?

5. Analyze the content of your favorite television programs. What are the main characters like? What do they want out of life? How realistic or true to life do you think these programs are?

6. Interview several individuals who have recently acquired a television set. Attempt to determine how this new set has changed their leisure time habits.

7. Write to the United Nations and ask them for information concerning the international status of television. What plans are currently being made for the international use of television?

8. Compare the commercial announcements made over the radio with those made by television. Which do you think are more effective and why?

9. Write the FCC for copies of the hearings concerning the allocation of television stations to educational institutions. Analyze the different arguments presented for and against the educational use of television.

10. Interview some mothers of young children to find out how they think television is affecting their children. How do they regulate the viewing habits of their children?

BIBLIOGRAPHY

Books

Axe and Co., *Television, 1948* (New York: 1948). An economic survey of the television industry.

Jennie Callahan, *Television in School, College and Community* (New York: McGraw-Hill Book Co., Inc., 1953). A comprehensive account of the use of television for educational purposes.

John Crosby, *Out of the Blue* (New York: Simon and Schuster, 1952). A selection of articles from the author's radio and television newspaper column.

Orrin E. Dunlap, Jr., *The Future of Television* (New York: Harper and Brothers, 1942). A detailed presentation of the early growth and problems of television. Interesting for its prognostications about the future.

W. C. Eddy, *Television: The Eyes of Tomorrow* (1945) (New York: Prentice-Hall, Inc., 1945). An account of the growth and current status of broadcasting.

C. Giraud and Garrison, G., *Radio and Television* (New York: Appleton-Century-Crofts, 1950). A comprehensive treatment of the two industries, including growth and control.

Richard W. Hubbell, *Television Programming and Production* (New York, Toronto: Murry Hill Books, Inc., 1945). An account of the technical and artistic elements in television program production.

Stanley Kempner (ed.), *Television Encyclopedia* (New York: Fairchild Publishing Co., 1948). A good source book for introductory material on television, including bibliographical references.

Herbert Marx, *Television and Radio in American Life* (New York: The H. W. Wilson Co., 1953). Development and control of the television and radio industries, the regulation of program content and the role played in American society.

Radio Corporation of America, *The Story of Television* (New York, 1951). A progress report on the development and current status of television.

Radio Daily and Television Daily, published annually. A current source of statistics on the television industry.

Oscar Rose (ed.), *Radio Broadcasting and Television* (New York: The H. W. Wilson Co., 1947). An annotated bibliography.

Gilbert V. Seldes, *The Great Audience* (New York: Viking Press, 1950). A critical analysis of the television and radio audience, including its composition and tastes.

Charles Siepmann, *Radio, Television and Society* (New York: Oxford University Press, 1950). A critical evaluation of the role of radio and television in America. It contains one of the most up-to-date chapters on television and its effects upon the public.

—— *Television and Education in the United States* (Paris: UNESCO, 1952). Part of the UNESCO series on press, film and radio in the world today. An analysis of the effects of television on education and an account of education vs. commercial fight for TV channels.

E. E. Willis, *Foundations in Broadcasting: Radio and Television* (1951). An early speculative account about the future of television (New York: Oxford Univ. Press, 1951).

Periodicals

H. Beville, Jr., "The Challenge of the New Media: Television, F.M. and Facsimile," *Journalism Quarterly*, XXV (March, 1948).

Emory Bogardus, "A Television Scale and Television Index," *American Sociological Review*, 17 (1952), pp. 220-223.

E. Engstrom, "Recent Developments in Television," *The Annals of the American Academy of Political and Social Science* (January, 1941), pp. 130-137.

Eleanor E. Maccoby, "Television: Its Impact on School Children," *Public Opinion Quarterly*, 15 (1951), pp. 421-444.

Edward McDonagh, *et al.*, "Television and the Family," *Sociology and Social Research*, 35 (1950), pp. 113-122.

Hurako Ohara, "Comparative Preferences of Radio and Television Programs," *Sociology and Social Research*, 37 (1953), pp. 305-311.

Fred L. Polak, "Television and Leisure," *Journal of Communication*, 2(2) (1952), pp. 15-25.

J. Riley, F. Cantwell, K. Ruttiger, "Some Observations on the Social Effects of Television," *Public Opinion Quarterly*, 13 (1949), pp. 223-234.

M. V. Seagoe, "Children's Television Habits and Preferences," *Quart. Film, Radio, Television*, 6(2), (1952), pp. 143-152.

Dallas W. Smythe, "An Analysis of Television Programs," *Scientific American*, 184(6) (1951), pp. 15-17.

—— "Reality as Presented by Television," *Public Opinion Quarterly* (Sumner 1954), pp. 149-150.

Charles E. Swanson, "Television Owning and Its Correlates," *Journal of Applied Psychology*, 35 (1951), pp. 352-357.

Part V

Contemporary Problems of Social Control

FOREWORD

The problems of social control, especially as they confront the American people today are not remote and academic, but immediate and real. They arise from new and startling regimentation and application of old devices and techniques which give them sinister possibilities. An understanding of them and their potentialities depends upon the grasp of the principles and facts which have been presented in the first four Parts of this book. It must be recalled here that social control is highly dynamic, and especially is this true in epochs of social change and expanding communications, so that even as we study what is going on about us the picture is changing in its specific details, if not in its broad outlines.

Part V presents some of the more significant phases of current social control phenomena, with emphasis upon those which are most vital to our own welfare and future as a people. Its chapters deal with "Totalitarian Ways of Life," and "Recent Types of Charismatic Leadership" and "Social Control and the Atomic Bomb."

CHAPTER XXIX

Totalitarian Ways of Life

A dictatorship is a governmental system in which "the principle of the separation and mutual control of the different agencies of government is replaced by a concentration of supreme power in the hands of one man or a group of men who are uncontrolled by a free and unrestricted public opinion, and who wield an absolute power over the executive, legislative, and usually the judicial branches of government.[1] To this might be added the fact that frequently the supreme power is held in an unorthodox, irregular, illegal, or extra-legal manner, by the *post facto* invention of some fiction of regularity or some straining of constitutional procedures. Not all dictators are treated in this chapter but 35 significant examples have been studied, selected from ancient Greece and Rome, from Europe since the Middle Ages and up to World War I, from Latin America in the nineteenth and twentieth centuries, and especially from postwar Europe and the Near East.[2] Each dictatorship was treated as a case. From these case data concepts of the ideal-typical characteristics or modal uniformities have been developed.

Concentration of Control

McIlwain states, "Disorder in the past has always been overcome by a concentration of power. It can be overcome by no other means now."[3] Since dictatorship grows out of disorder, it not only implies concentration of control; its success depends upon it. Such concentration was inherent in the old Roman constitutional dictatorships; it has unavoidably been the primary feature of all others, for dictatorship is in its very nature an assumption of extra-legal authority by the head of the state. Parliaments must be abolished, hamstrung, or converted into dummies,

---

[1] Karl Loewenstein, "Autocracy versus Democracy in Contemporary Europe," *American Political Science Review*, XXIX (August, 1935), pp. 571-572.

[2] Many of the names of these dictators will appear below in the summaries of more or less uniform traits.

[3] C. H. McIlwain, "Government by Law," *Foreign Affairs*, XIV (January, 1936), pp. 185-198. See especially J. O. Hertzler, "Crises and Dictatorships," *American Sociological Review*, V (April, 1940), pp. 157-169.

for no dictator can withstand the loss of power that would result from being held responsible to a body of legislators; government must be centralized as to authority, administration, decision, and the making of laws. You simply cannot have representative government and popularly seated power in a dictatorship. As Calderon has said, "Dictatorships are not societies of freemen, they give humanity uniformity and servility." [4] Hence all function through a small, cohesive, all-powerful inner circle, which acts with concentrated power and great dispatch.

All-Embracing Authority. Anything that stands in the way of a single-minded, one-willed state defeats the dictator's purpose, and is labeled "treacherous." The leader's authority thus, whether he be a Peisistratus, a Caesar, a Cromwell, a Napoleon, a Gomez, a Diaz, a Mussolini, a Kemal Atatürk, a Pilsudski, a Stalin, or a Hitler, is absolute and supreme, and his decisions are accepted as right; he has complete authority over all controlling, directing and informational agencies. Thus among modern dictators Kemal Atatürk wielded power comparable with that of the Sultans of the preceding half century; Stalin is perhaps as powerful as the Czars who ruled Russia before him; Mussolini at one time had more power than king and prime minister together had from the *risorgimento* to 1922; and Hitler's authority was probably more far-reaching than that of any Kaiser. On the other hand, whatever makes for local or class or factional autonomy and variation by diffusing power impairs dictatorship. It is no accident, therefore, that modern dictatorships suppress independent organizations of workers and employers, even religious organizations, in favor of State-controlled corporations, or by ruthlessly violent methods stamp out or "purge" recalcitrant factions in their own party.

Triumphant Claims. Furthermore, the dictatorial regimes must be "better" than any other form of governmental control. They *must* be more effective instruments for collective control than those in democracies; they *must* always be right and successful. There can be no equally good governors, no equally good party, and no competing philosophies of the state to serve as bases of comparison or criticism. Dictatorship must always be the triumphant and rightful dominance of one set of ideas, one particular party, and the one leader, and since these constitute the State, "Whatever the State does is good because the State does it." [5] To doubt this must be an offense against the State. To allow anything else would be to confess that the dictatorial form of government was not fulfilling

---

[4] F. Garcia Calderon, *Latin America, Its Rise and Progress* (London: Fisher and Unwin, 1914), p. 162.

[5] C. E. M. Joad, *Liberty Today* (London: Watts and Co., 1934), p. 142.

its purpose, and that would imply the necessity of establishing some other form of general control.[6]

Opposition to Democracy. Quite logically many of the dictatorships, particularly those of the post-World War I era, were decidedly anti-democratic and anti-liberal in their philosophy and anti-parliamentary in their action. When they do make democratic gestures these are a matter of hollow pretense. The indictment made by them is that the democratic state consists mostly of talk and parliamentary wrangling, and that in crucial emergencies it has produced paralysis or bungling rather than decisive action.[7] The people maintain, after considerable coaching by their dictators, that they would sooner have the rule of one man than of a mob or a debating society.

Modern dictatorships have united in ignoring, if not actually opposing, democracy and individual liberty. They have inverted the philosophy prevalent for a century and a half as voiced in the expressive formula of Kant, "Man is the end, and cannot be debased to the value of a means." According to Kant's idea one of the essential objects which a civilized state should pursue is to offer the widest possible scope to its individual citizens for free and diversified self-development.[8] However, discussion, toleration, criticism, personal freedom, self-determination, and the opportunities for free self-expression have been denied by the modern dictatorships; minorities, even majorities, have been ignored. The state, or the nation, or the "race," or the system, as determined and interpreted by the dictator and the single party or machine, have become the end. The "citizen" has disappeared, and the individual denizen has become not only the servant but the slave of the state. Terror and force have replaced persuasion and consent.

To insure effective control and a continuous application to the objectives of the regime, many institutions and activities must be regimented, especially those of finance, industry and agriculture, education, communication, religion and recreation.

Bureaucracy. Dictatorships are characterized by bureaucracies of huge proportions; in fact, bureaucracies are stronger under dictatorship than under any other regime. Cosimo de Medici and all of his family who

---

[6] Cf. E. G. Lee, "Dictatorships and Failure," *Hibbert Journal*, XXXIV (January, 1936), pp. 235-245. Mr. Joad makes this interesting comment: "A democratic government is legitimized by law and rests on popular consent. It can therefore afford to make mistakes, to concede that it is not infallible, to admit criticism. A dictator, not having the assurance of consent, cannot permit these liberties," *op. cit.*, p. 143.

[7] Cf. Max Lerner, in G. S. Ford, ed., *Dictatorship in the Modern World* (Minneapolis: University of Minnesota Press, 1939), pp. 8-9.

[8] Cf. C. G. Robinson, "Peace and the Dictators," *University of Toronto Quarterly*, IV (1934-1935), p. 158; J. O. Hertzler, *Social Progress* (New York: D. Appleton-Century Co., 1928), pp. 88-92.

followed him in control had a picked body of adherents in all government departments. Richelieu placed his own men in the army and every other branch of government as soon as he could. Napoleon developed one of the greatest bureaucracies the world has ever known, which interfered with every aspect of social and economic life. Francia, Diaz, and Gomez, among the Latin Americans, had armies of officials who created airtight regimes which accounted in no small measure for their long periods of autocratic control. The tremendously strong systems which have been built up in the contemporary dictatorships need only be mentioned. In all of these there was a vast increase of men to staff old and new government departments, always an inordinate increase of police and army, and of paid people in the single or dominant party.

There are substantial reasons for bureaucracies in dictatorships. In the first place, it is the only way in which a "totalitarian" regime may effect the essential centralization and maintain the meticulous regulation of industry and commerce, local and national politics, education, opinion, and recreation, and carry on its numerous projects in every department of social life. Secondly, any dictatorial regime which is to survive for more than a short time needs a numerous group of "safe" supporters. The inflation of the administrative personnel by thousands or even millions of employees dependent upon the regime for jobs and privileges is a continuous source of influence and strength in its behalf. New governing classes with a definite position in the *status quo* are thus developed. The desire for self-preservation on the part of this personnel may thus be counted upon to hold it together and give it omnipotence and longevity. Lyons pointed out that Stalin, Mussolini, and the rest stood at the apex of hierarchies of privilege, based upon hundreds of powerful sub-dictators, thousands of officials, and millions of small bureaucrats.[9] In the third place, a bureaucracy eliminates or suppresses all forms of local government, and all possibility of political apprenticeship or political education, save within the immaculate confines of the party or machine.

Emphasis Upon Leadership [10]

The concentration of power is vastly facilitated by resting it upon the *Fuehrer Prinzip*, or leadership principle, that is, capitalizing the human response to leadership and emphasizing the incompetence of the masses

---

[9] Eugene Lyons, "Europe's Number-Two Men," *American Mercury*, XXXVI (November, 1935), pp. 304-314.

[10] Leadership is treated in chapter XVII and XXIX. Here the discussion is confined entirely to certain more or less universal and long-standing features of *totalitarian* leadership. The ideologies of basic philosophy and rationalizations of totalitarian states are also integral traits. These will not be specifically treated in this chapter. For a more comprehensive discussion see chapter XII.

to rule themselves. According to this principle the supreme authority should be vested in the leader, and should be delegated by him to his subordinates who will exercise it upon the people. The dictator or the group promoting him crystallize this tendency in the titles assumed or given—titles which stimulate loyalty, focus allegiance, and make childlike submission a joy as well as a duty. Thus Caesar was made First Consul, dictator for life, and Pontifex Maximus; Octavius was made *princeps* and then "Augustus" (the revered); Cosimo de Medici was called "Pater Patriae" after his death—a reflection of the attitude toward him before his death; Cromwell was given the title "Lord Protector" for life; Paris, with ceremony, proclaimed Louis XIV *"Louis le Grand"*; the people called Francia *El Supremo*; Rosas was the "Illustrious Restorer of the Laws"; Guzman-Blanco had the title of "Illustrious American, Regenerator, Pacificator" bestowed upon him by his congress; Mussolini was *il Duce*; Hitler, *der Fuehrer*; Kemal Atatürk in 1922 was given the title *Ghazi* (the Victorious) and later *Atatürk* (Chief Turk); in 1929 Gomez was given the title *El Benemerito* (the Well-Deserving).

In the early and middle stages of a dictatorship the people invariably not only accept, but even welcome the "strong man," the "man on horseback," with his boldness, his self-confidence, his willingness and readiness to make decisions by his own fiat. Says Spencer, "The mass of people dote on one who, by a mystery of magnetism, inspires respect, makes them feel great through their kinship with him, their national symbol." [11] When dissension, strife, confusion, maladjustment, and hopelessness reign, people, in the words of Thomas Hobbes, are willing, even glad, to surrender their wills to an absolute sovereign in order to escape intolerable conditions. It may be added that their very hero-worship accentuates their feeling of dependence upon this leader.

This is due to the fact, as Sims points out,[12] that personalities are the most elemental forces that society knows. When policies, parties or programs fail, people are ready to fall back upon that ultimate factor, personality. "By the acts of one man society thus seeks to break the otherwise unbreakable impasse. Confused, multiple counsel is silenced by a single authoritative voice and conflicting programs are submerged by a single clearcut, audacious line of action." [13]

Especially has each dictator been able to impress the people with the fact that by following him they are enabled to risk themselves in his service, and become selfless parts of a great magnificent whole. As nota-

---

[11] H. R. Spencer, "Dictatorship," *Encyclopaedia of the Social Sciences,* (New York: The Macmillan Co., 1931), V, p. 135.

[12] N. L. Sims, "Swing of Social Change," *Social Forces,* XIV (May, 1936), p. 479.

[13] Loewenstein, on the basis of his study of postwar dictatorship, concludes that the "leadership principle" functions in time of national decadence or humiliation without regard to the special aptitudes of the leader himself. See especially *op. cit.,* p. 583.

ble modern instances we have Lenin, Stalin, Mussolini, Kemal Atatürk, and Hitler.

The Use of Symbolization. The dictator, in fact, frequently becomes an almost mystical symbol of authority, leadership, and national greatness. In various dictatorships there has been a tendency to look upon the dictator as a Messiah, to develop a ruler cult, and to deify the dictator. Mussolini, Kemal Atatürk, Pilsudski, Lenin and Hitler have been discussed among their people as Messiahs and accepted by some.[14] All this has a perfectly comprehensible psychology behind it. There is among the populace the impulse to see a human being who is strong, capable and absolutistic as an incarnation of beneficent power. Miss Spearman is impressed with the fact that the hero-myths which appear in so many parts of the world suggest that the fantasy of a beneficent all-powerful saviour is one which arises in the minds of many peoples in face of disaster. Modern scholars are of the belief that the deification of leaders has not been simply a form of flattery, but has arisen in part from a genuine psychological impulse. For example, Rostovzeff, the celebrated historian of Rome, is convinced that the cult of Augustus grew up spontaneously and was not imposed from above.[15] Joad points out that investing a political leader with divine attributes fulfills the double purpose of providing an object for the ordinary man to worship and enabling him to forego the "disagreeable" process of political thinking.

The official propaganda of many dictatorships suggests that there is a desire for a powerful and irrepressible ruler. Not only does it call attention to the overwhelming position of the dictator; its actually exaggerates his all-pervading influence, and asserts the joy, dignity and worth of obeying him. Thus do the distraught and humiliated individuals merge themselves with something which is assertive, powerful, and reputedly invincible.

The Use of Force

The Use of the Army. From the time of the Greek tyrants to the present day, the army has been not only a useful tool, but an indispensable part of every dictatorship. It is the agent through which the dictator exercises his force. Invariably he has a private army or, at least, a military group which renders him strong personal allegiance. The Greek tyrants had their bands of mercenaries; the semi-personal armies of Marius, Sulla, Caesar and Augustus rendered them invaluable services; the Medici and

---

[14] Diana Spearman, "The Psychological Background of Dictatorship," *Sociological Review*, XXVI (April, 1934), pp. 158-174.

[15] Article, "Augustus" in *University of Wisconsin Studies in Language and Literature*, No. 15, 1922.

Sforzas had their private military bands; Cromwell had his "Round-heads"; the early power of the "Little Corporal" rested upon the personal allegiance of his troops in the Italian and Egyptian campaigns; the Latin American dictators, without exception, gained and held office by means of semi-private armies; Kemal Atatürk's early control was achieved through the veterans who had served under him in fighting the English and defeating the Greeks; Lenin had the Cheka, and Stalin the O.G.P.U.; Mussolini ruled with the help of his Blackshirted squads; de Rivera functioned largely through the army; Pilsudski had his "Defensive"; and Hitler had the brown-shirted Storm Troopers, and his personal instrument, the Gestapo; Metaxas used the army as his personal tool. The police forces of our contemporary dictators have the power to seize, imprison, exile or sentence to death any suspect.

The dictator, to survive, dares not allow opposition to develop; it must be quelled immediately. Control must be centralized, immediate, unquestioned, and nation-wide; it often must be ruthless, and therefore the more impersonal and long-range it is the better. Local civil agencies cannot be depended upon to provide this. No better tool than a nation-wide private or semiprivate army or police force has ever been devised.

Dictators understand the fact that an army, especially if it is showy, flatters a people who have been humiliated, and gives them an exaggerated sense of strength and importance. At the same time, the dictator threatens international peace by his extra-legal methods, and creates a dangerous nationalism which may menace surrounding nations. In fact, the dictator *does not want a complete dissolution of those national hatreds and misunderstandings that tend to provoke war.* This international suspicion he capitalizes, and, by the fear engendered at home, consolidates his own power.[16] Finally, a foreign war may be fostered in time of waning influence as a means of maintaining a state of fear and crisis, of reviving enthusiasm and loyalty, and, through the necessary army, of providing employment, stimulating industry, and maintaining cohesion and loyalty. It appears that dictatorship can only prosper in an atmosphere of war.[17]

Espionage. Most dictators depend on a well-developed espionage system. Especially noted was the intelligence and spy system of Richelieu; that of Napoleon—a model for later dictators; and the large force of spies and informers of Gomez of Venezuela, a force upon which he spent two and one-half times as much money as he did on education. The spy systems of the dictators of Russia, Italy, and Germany, functioning both domestically and abroad, are known to all who read.

---

[16] See Count Carlo Sforza, *Europe and Europeans* (Indianapolis: Bobbs-Merrill, 1936), p. 7.
[17] See "War Most Effective Means of Perpetuating Dictatorships," *Science*, XXXVII (February 10, 1940), p. 92.

Terrorism and Ruthlessness. Systematic terrorism is a part both of the preparation for power and the maintenance of power, and produces almost universal cowardice. Terrorism and ruthlessness were used with great effect in maintaining power by Sulla; the Medici and Sforzas and by Cromwell, especially in Ireland; as well as by practically all of the Latin American dictators. In the postwar period the terroristic procedures of Lenin and Stalin in Russia, the People's party in Turkey, Pilsudski in Poland, Mussolini in Italy, Dolfuss in Austria, and Hitler in Germany, Austria and all of the other "protected" countries, were particularly conspicuous. It is possible that the terrorism of modern dictators is more severe than in any other period, since they are attempting to maintain absolute power over peoples habituated in some measure to govern themselves.

Several phenomena have become significant in modern terroristic tactics. A typical activity is "squadrism," the studied terrorization by bands roving over the countryside or by squads descending suddenly upon proscribed organizations, groups, or individuals, destroying property, brutally beating and killing people, kidnapping some too-troublesome member of the opposition and beating him into unconsciousness, or in some other manner intimidating individuals and groups. Another typical feature was the appearance in Italy, Russia and Germany of concentration camps, where members of the opposition, or even people vaguely suspected by some ignorant and inflated squadrist, were herded, often without trial, and when tried, were convicted by a court which was a travesty upon justice. In these camps the victims were subjected to systematic humiliation, physical and mental abuse, and other sadistic treatment. A further means of terrorization is summary execution or the threat thereof.

The One-Party System. Although the one-party system is, strictly speaking, characteristic only of the post-World-War I dictatorships, dictatorial parties with the power of dominating other parties to the extent of making them insignificant are rather frequent. Cosimo de Medici's party had almost complete control in Florence; when Cromwell had a Parliament, it was hand-picked; for several years the French Senate was practically Napoleon's personal party; the Latin American dictators, almost without exception, worked through subservient parties.

It has remained for the modern dictatorships to destroy all other parties and allow only one to be legally recognized and to rule without parliament or with a completely subservient parliament. Italy had only one party, the Fascist; Turkey only one, the People's; Russia has but one, the Bolshevik, or as it is now termed officially, the Communist; Germany had only the Nazi or National Socialist. In each of these instances, with the recent exception of Turkey where opposition parties have been encouraged, no rival party is recognized or permitted in the political arena. In all four, the single party not only monopolizes political power and runs the government by itself, but it is so inextricably interlocked with the government in mechanism and personnel that it is impossible to know where the party leaves off and government begins.[18] Hitler, in fact, succeeded in building up a situation in Germany in which he was not even responsible to the party, but the party was responsible to him. In Persia the *Medjliss* was composed of carefully selected members of only one party; in Poland Pilsudski recognized only the party of his followers; and in Portugal Salazar allows only his own party to be influential.

The reasons for the maintenance of the one party system and the suppression of opposition parties are obvious. When a coherent policy must be quickly and consistently carried out a government cannot afford to have its energies diverted and its attention distracted by the necessity of meeting factious opposition. Nor can it permit itself to be publicly embarrassed by such a challenging of its policies, or by revelations of mistakes or ineptitudes as would surely occur with opposition parties. The spell of unity and confidence must not be broken. Always the party is necessarily right; to doubt it in any way is an offense against the State.

A Manipulated Judiciary. Since the courts are the checks upon the executive and legislative power, no dictatorial regime is safe unless the bench is subordinated to the will of the executive. No dictator can be successful if checks upon him exist. Therefore, throughout history, dictators who have been successful for long have gained control of the courts and manipulated them in line with their own objectives. This has been done by weeding out the judiciary and markedly modifying or even abolishing a judicial system which stood in their way. Caesar reformed the judicial system and made it harmonious with his general scheme of control; Cosimo de Medici controlled the election of all magistrates; Cromwell controlled the courts and judges; Richelieu had extraordinary commissions—"fixed" courts—nominated by himself; Louis XIV functioned through his famous *Conseil d'État* which was a final judicial as well as legislative body. Napoleon controlled the courts everywhere throughout his realm from top to bottom. He ruled by decrees which were not reviewed by any courts. He abolished the immovability of the judges and carefully selected the new members of the court. He obliterated the last vestiges of separation of power, and all judges were selected from a list of "notables." Finally, the Senate could cancel judicial

---

[18] See also F. A. Ogg, *European Government and Politics* (New York: The Macmillan Co., 1935), p. 863; R. C. Brooks, "Democracies and Dictatorships: The Debit Side of Their Ledgers," *Proceedings of the Philosophical Society*, LXXV (1935), pp. 469-470.

decisions. Louis Napoleon had laws passed which enabled him to get rid of judges who refused to obey governmental orders. Among the Latin Americans, Francia abolished courts, and Diaz and Gomez manned the courts with men of their own selection. The post-World-War I dictators, almost without exception, dominated the courts completely, appointed their own men as judges, and allowed no variation from the objectives of the regime. They were not courts of justice, nor bodies of review, and were not intended to be, but were an effective arm of the administration in inspiring conformity and in punishing any who opposed it. A publication of the German Ministry of Justice several years ago stated, "A handful of force is better than a sackful of justice." [19]

Support by Plebiscites. In many cases dictators represent themselves as realizing the true will or the deepest interests of the people. They feel that a constituent power ought to have brought them into being. To give this an air of reality they see to it that the electorate always overwhelmingly supports their authority and their rules and procedures, internal and external. This they do by carefully arranged plebiscites in which opposition is made difficult, dangerous, or even impossible, and in which ratification is certain. It is quite possible also that elections and plebiscites deceive and flatter the people into thinking that they are being called into consultation on political issues of great importance, and thus mobilize the democratic ideal of the "will of the people."

There are innumerable cases, such as the plebiscites of Augustus, and the special control of elections by Cosimo de Medici. In 1653 Cromwell obtained the implied consent of the electorate for his regime. Napoleon, after the *coup d'état* of November, 1799, drafted a constitution which centered all power in the first consul and submitted it to a plebiscite. The consent was asked for and overwhelmingly given. The same thing happened again when he made himself consul for life and emperor. In theory these were free plebiscites, but actually the use of open registers facilitated a large measure of coercion, and the percentages of favorable votes were correspondingly high. There was also local fraud; for example, those who could not write were voted "yes"; and there was much actual intimidation by prefects and military officials. Louis Napoleon conducted two famous plebiscites—one following his *coup d'état* of December 2, 1851, and the other a year later, after his elevation to emperor. In both of these, those voting "yes" deposited a printed ballot, while those voting "no" had to write their ballot, and thus the "no's" could be readily singled out. Neither Napoleon Bonaparte nor Louis Napoleon allowed free

---

[19] For a brilliant discussion of the complete subordination of the entire present-day German legal system to the political authorities, based on a review of the recent legislative decrees and legal decisions, see Ernst Fraenkel, *The Dual State* (New York and London: Oxford University Press, 1941).

speech or free assembly prior to the plebiscites. Recurring dummy poll-
ings in Italy, Poland, Turkey and Germany have been conducted with
Napoleonic techniques as models. Hitler's plebiscites *after* the death of
Hindenburg in August, 1934; the one *after* the occupation of the Rhine-
land, and the one of April 11, 1938, on the accession of Austria, in each
case asking approval of his procedure *after the act*, are well known.[20]

It is significant that the Latin American and the Russian dictators have
not resorted to plebiscites. This can probably be explained on the grounds
that in these countries there were no democratic traditions prevailing
which would require a plebiscite.

Legalization. Some dictatorships have been established quietly and are
so legal in outward form that there has been no necessity for formal
recognition. Other dictators became such after having been legally
elected or appointed to some prominent public office; or by virtue of
having been born to office, as in the case of King Alexander of Yugoslavia. But no dictator, regardless of how he achieved his position, remains an illegal tyrant for very long. If he has not seized office with
the consent of established legal or constitutional bodies, he forces them
to approve him after he is in power, or he creates a body out of his own
supporters who will legalize him. In many cases he has supplemented
one or the other of these procedures with a "stacked" plebiscite that gave
him formal popular approval.

History is replete with examples of legalization of dictatorships. After
he was in complete control of Thessaly, Jason had himself elected *tagus*,
which was the title of the constitutional dictator selected to meet an
emergency. Marius had himself elected Consul by the Roman Senate;
Sulla was legalized as dictator by the Senate; and Caesar, at the peak of
his power, was legally made dictator for life by the Senate. Cromwell's
own "Barebones" Parliament created him "Lord Protector." Napoleon
Bonaparte had himself made First Consul by the remnants of the Council
of Five Hundred; at his asking the Senate gave him his life consulate and
later approved his desire to be emperor. These acts were also sanctioned
by popular plebiscite. Louis Napoleon developed a constitution of his
own which supported his position, and had himself approved by plebiscite. The Latin American dictators, in most cases, were officially elected
President after already being in power or on the verge of assuming
power.

Stalin has been careful to be a member of the strategic Central Committee and the Politbureau. Mussolini at first forced the king to make
him coalition prime minister, and two years later, premier without oppo-

---

[20] Cf. C. J. Friedrich, *Constitutional Government and Politics* (New York: Harper
and Brothers, 1937), pp. 113-117, 474-476.

sition; during most of his rule he held a large number of cabinet port-folios. His position was also confirmed, at least indirectly, by plebiscites. Kemal Atatürk was designated President in the constitution; Reza Shah Pahlevi was strong enough to force the *Medjless* to make him Shah; Primo de Rivera had himself made Prime Minister, a position which was later sanctioned in a plebiscite; Pilsudski made himself Minister of War and Chief of the Supreme Army Council and his chief acts were con-firmed by plebiscite; Hitler was declared Prime Minister by President Hindenburg, and at the latter's death the dictator had himself made Chan-cellor and President, and had his policies approved by plebiscites. No real dictator, it would seem, wishes or needs to be worried long about questions of the legality of his position.

Public Works and Entertainment

Most of the dictators have deliberately pursued a policy of carrying on great public works and providing frequent public entertainments —"stunts," festivals, ceremonies, parades. Peisistratus built roads and beau-tiful temples, improved fortifications, and increased the splendor of festi-vals; Caesar planned and started port construction, drainage and canal projects; Augustus constructed highways, theaters, temples, aqueducts and other great public structures, and provided games and other specta-cles in the theaters and stadia; Cosimo de Medici was responsible for many great public works and provided entertainments, festivals, spec-tacles, processions, balls and beast-shows; Louis XIV constructed roads, canals, palaces and parks; Napoleon repaired and constructed roads, bridges, canals and seaports, restored old historic buildings and built new ones; in the Latin American countries significant construction of public works was carried on by Francia of Paraguay, Rosas of Argentina, Guzman-Blanco of Venezuela, Castilla of Peru, Nuñez of Colombia, Gomez of Venezuela, and Diaz of Mexico; the great public works and public spectacles of the Russian dictators, of Mussolini, Kemal Atatürk, Salazar, Hitler, Metaxas, and others of the post-World-War I group need only be mentioned.

There are several more or less obvious reasons why there should be emphasis upon public works. In the first place, after a period of chaos and revolution, such as usually precedes dictatorship, the country is in a run-down condition and considerable reconstruction is necessary in order that the processes of production, distribution, communication, and military preparation may go on. But other reasons are probably more important. Great public works and public entertainments provide em-ployment for thousands, even millions, of discontented people, and thus add mightily to the numbers who feel under obligation to the dictatorial regime. Most important of all is the fact that these works flatter the people as a whole, give them things to be proud of, unite them around munificent material objects, distract their attention from their grievances, and block their possible opposition to the dictator by keeping their minds and enthusiasms on acts of the dictator which enhance his reputation and strength.

Fanatically Nationalistic Objectives

A considerable number of the dictators have emphasized militant idealistic objectives of a nationalistic or militaristic nature with fanatical passion. Some have been sincere in using these as a means of integrating their populations and advancing the national well-being, as they conceived it; all sought to use these as slogans and inciters to enthusiasm, as means of keeping group emotion at an evangelistic pitch. In many cases they have succeeded in converting their nationalistic objectives into a secular religion.

In the time of Augustus the "Empire" was the creed; Cosimo de Medici through all his works and his controls of opinion raised to sublime heights the "Glory of Florence"; Cromwell united his Roundheads with the ideal of the sober, God-fearing "Puritan Commonwealth"; Napoleon's compatriots marched and bled and died all across Europe and the Mediterranean area with a blind devotion and an overwhelming ecstasy for the "Grand Empire"; Louis Napoleon constantly repeated the slogan, "Empire means Peace"; the Latin American dictators, almost without exception, emphasized "national unity" as a slogan; with Lenin and Stalin, following Marx, the immediate goal has been the "Dictatorship of the Proletariat," the abolition of the bourgeois classes, and the achievement of the U.S.S.R.; Mussolini emphasized the emotion-charged concept of the "Restoration of the Roman Empire"; Kemal Atatürk satisfied and inspired his people with, first, "Turkey for the Turks," which included the expulsion of hated races and nationalities, and, later, the attractive "Modernization of Turkey." Finally, Hitler concentrated upon fanatical racial purity with his plea for an "Aryan Germany," and upon the inclusion of all Germans in the German Reich, and a "New Order" in Europe.

Such phenomena have their explanation in the fact that dictators, usually keen students of human nature and clever manipulators of human masses, know that if they can tap the deep feelings and strong emotions, and marshal them for their own use, they are secure for a while. The fears, hates, prejudices, sour memories, and long-standing beliefs are the best sources of such feelings among the defeated and disorganized rank and file. Thus frequently, as Sims points out,[21] the propaganda of blame is mobilized; ills are personified, and certain persons are made the scape-

---

[21] Sims, *op. cit.*, pp. 480-481.

goats for the evils of the nation. He speaks of "the scourge of 'anti-isms,' " the flood of negative, condemnatory and denunciatory appeals that are evident in contemporary European dictatorships.

Positive appeals are also made, however. All dictators provide objects that elicit adoration and love; all include in their programs ideals based on sublime national hopes; and many depend upon rabid historical fervor and past glory. Such patriotic and nationalistic appeals unify discordant elements, and lull possible critical minorities, or submerge them under waves of patriotic emotion.

Control of Public Opinion

Although dictators have always placed their primary reliance upon military force to hold the people in line, they have also utilized all available agencies for holding the people from within by selecting the thought materials at their disposal, by shaping their convictions, and by keeping a constant control over their emotions. They have suppressed all discussion and criticism, censored everything that might convey a contrary sentiment or an idea, and used every device at their disposal in propagandizing and indoctrinating the masses regarding their own philosophies and virtues.

Dictators have always withheld information from their subjects and used rumor and oratory as forms of persuasion. To this end, they have dominated the press. Richelieu established the first French newspaper as a means of influencing public opinion, and surrounded himself with a small army of scribes whose business it was to produce appropriate treatises. Cromwell also used the press; and Napoleon controlled news and the means of communication closely, issuing propaganda so lavishly that the saying, "False as a bulletin," appeared among his subjects. When public education developed, dictators appropriated it, and have used it ever since. Napoleon established schools and universities and supervised the curriculum at all levels. As the modern means of communication developed they have been taken over one by one and used to forge the chains of dictatorship upon the people. In fact, the dictator throughout history has not only been quick to utilize every new psychological and technological device, but has even, on occasion, invented new ones.

The modern dictatorship is founded not only upon a single highly disciplined party, but also upon the still broader mass created by highly centralized and carefully manipulated propaganda. Present Caesars, even more than those of the past, are interested in what Hitler called *Gleichschaltung*—that is, physical, emotional and intellectual coordination. Their processes of complete indoctrination rest upon numerous devices. Never before, in fact, have dictators had at their disposal for control purposes such an array of social agencies, devices, and situations. The new universal systems of education are marshalled for the purposes of the dictator from the kindergarten to the highest levels. Instructors are hand-picked and specially trained. The closest kind of supervision is exercised over every item of the curriculum, which is constructed according to the latest findings of educational psychology. Everything formally taught must, in fact, first of all contribute directly to form attitudes and habits that conform with and enhance the objectives of the dictatorial state.[22] Adult educational schemes supplement the other educational devices.

Journalism, radio and cinema are completely controlled from personnel to output, and stamp the same stereotypes on the millions of brains. All printed materials become instruments of government propaganda. Quite paradoxically, a greater literacy and more widespread reading habits than have ever before existed enable dictators, through a completely controlled and thoroughly propagandized nation-wide press, to influence everyone who reads. Modern linotype machines and high-speed presses vastly increase the volume of printed "dope" that is issued. The most advanced and clever advertising techniques and high-pressure salesmanship are also used with consummate skill. Rigid censorship and border inspection controls all reading matter, mail, and persons coming into the country. Demagogic orators, trained in the most psychologically proficient techniques of rabble-rousing, influence, through the controlled right to assemble and through the controlled radio, all who listen.

Every aspect of modern recreation is organized in the interests of the dictatorial regime. The writing and production of everything in the theater or cinema is controlled. For the first time in history sport has become a political weapon—a channel for propaganda and a device for military training. Young people, male and female, hasten to join sport clubs and other youth organizations to avoid the stigma of nonconformity and weakness. In these they are conditioned physically and psychologically for service to the regime.[23] The game is played to further the "game" of the dictators. Public demonstrations, national exhibitions and reviews, and mass assemblies, utilizing all the tricks of flattery, "crowd squeeze," patriotism, color, ceremony, bands and marching are employed to "goosestep" the emotions and feelings. Never have ready-made catch-

---

[22] See such studies as: Fritz Brennecke, *The Nazi Primer* (New York: Harper and Brothers, 1938); E. Y. Hartshorne, *The German Universities and National Socialism* (Cambridge: Harvard University Press, 1937); G. F. Kneller, *The Educational Philosophy of National Socialism* (New Haven: Yale University Press, 1941); G. A. Zimmer, *Education for Death* (New York: Oxford University Press, 1941); H. R. Marraro, *The New Education in Italy* (New York: Vanni, 1936); etc.

[23] See John R. Tunis. "The Dictators Discover Sport," *Foreign Affairs*, XIV (July, 1936), pp. 606-617.

penny phrases and slogans been used with so much success. All the liberties of the "Bill of Rights" variety, especially freedom of press, speech, and assemblage, are greatly restricted or completely denied.

In order to gag criticism all dictators seek to atrophy the thinking function in human beings. Objectivity, criticism and curiosity are forbidden; knowledge is disdained and free scientific inquiry is starved or forbidden. Instead of allowing the scientist to freely follow where reasoning and fact lead him, the dictator assigns him his conclusions in advance and forces him to invent supporting theories; the historian must emphasize the glories and achievements of the dictatorial regime and retail the standard hatreds and untruths; *Lehrfreiheit* and *Lernfreiheit* disappear, philosophy perishes, and the social sciences are reduced to practical techniques.[24]

Religion. Many dictators throughout history have concerned themselves with religion. If the prevailing religion could be used to support their regime they have supported it and strengthened its organization. If it interfered with the ideology which they sought to make universal they have attempted to destroy it. No competing philosophy or religion which gives peace, contentment, or escape, which encourages the worship of nonharmonious gods, can be condoned. All is stereotyped, camouflaged, sycophantic, debased and dull, despite the shrieking and the bustle. Goebbels wrote: "Propaganda has only one object, to conquer the masses. Every means that furthers this aim is good; every means that hinders it is bad."

In general it can be said that most of the dictators have had a master understanding of mass psychology and have used it unscrupulously to their own advantage. They have known how to use deception on a grand scale, how to arouse loyalties, how to flatter the populace, how to use material objectives and fear, and how to effectively mislead the masses and draw them into their own ways. They have been as clever as Machiavelli's Prince, and in most cases equally unashamed in utilizing any means to advance their own ends.[25]

Summary

Dictatorship, especially the totalitarianism of the decades of the twenties and thirties, controls almost every facet of life. Business, art, science, education, religion, recreation, morality are not merely influenced but

---

[24] J. R. Angell, "The Future of Intellectual Freedom," *American Scholar*, VIII (Autumn, 1939), pp. 468-478; Arthur Livingston, "Homemade Literature Under Fascism," *American Scholar*, VIII (Autumn, 1939), pp. 412-421; Waldemar Kaempffert, "Science in the Totalitarian State," *Foreign Affairs*, XIX (January, 1941), pp. 433-441.

[25] See Serge Chakotin, *The Rape of the Masses* (New York: Alliance Book Co., 1940).

are directly, arbitrarily, and completely subjected to the totalitarian regime. Modern technology, especially rapid communication and transportation, have made this control more universal and absolute than it has ever been before in similar types of authoritarian states. A knowledge of modern psychology has made it possible for bureaus of propaganda and indoctrination to shape the thoughts and direct the feelings of people. Terrorism and flattery, lies and lures, fear and pride, passion and prejudice, have been skillfully manipulated to produce the inevitable *Gleichschaltung* or "bringing to heel" of everyone.

Equality of rights and opportunities is scornfully rejected. The only persons who count as individuals are the charismatic leader and a few party bureaucrats at the peak of the elaborate social hierarchy. The individual citizen, in and for himself, is nothing. He is a mere cell among millions of others, existing solely for the state, or rather the party controlling the state. Liberty, in terms of the rights men have sought and won repeatedly through the millennia—freedom of person, of speech, of assemblage, of press, of contract, of movement, of occupation, of worship, of self-government, the right to free use of private property, the right to criticize, to petition, to bargain—are positively and exultingly rejected. Mussolini has boasted of the eagerness of Fascism to "trample upon the decomposed body of the Goddess of Liberty." Self-respecting, prideful, independent, expressive persons and groups have no place; those who dare to be such are proscribed, forced to flee, or "liquidated." Only the "yes-men," the regime-intoxicated ones, the insiders, the profiteers, the spineless, and the stupid can be content.

Totalitarianism denotes the single-party, dictatorial system of government, based on the "totality of the state," as opposed to the liberal conception of the state which allots to the state only certain portions of life while reserving others to the free decision of the individual. The "total state" extends the sphere of state influence over the whole of life, private as well as public, and exacts full submission of the individual to the demands of the state. Controlled by a few individuals, the modern dictatorships governing these totalitarian states represent absolute rules of a person or group without the necessity of the consent of the governed. The term dates from the old Roman republic; when the state was in emergency, a man could be appointed "dictator" by the senate for seven years, and held absolute power for this period. Then he had to retire, and constitutional rule was re-established. Modern dictatorship is either personal or that of a group or class (army, proletariat), but even in the latter case it is embodied in the person of a leader.

QUESTIONS

1. Define a dictatorship.
2. What is McIlwain's theory concerning the conditions conducive to the growth of a dictatorship?
3. What requirement of successful dictatorship restricts the dictatorship's control of foreign affairs, especially alliances?
4. What phenomenon of government is strengthened under dictatorships more than under democratic forms of government?
5. How do dictators facilitate the concentration of power?
6. How does hero-worship aid the "man on horseback"?
7. What is the most elemental force in society?
8. What is the object of deifying the dictator?
9. What purpose does the private army serve to the dictator personally?
10. How does the dictator use the national army to build up his power?
11. What is the dictator's attitude toward international tension?
12. Why is terrorism more severe today than in historical times?
13. Describe "squadrism."
14. What modern dictatorship has encouraged opposition parties?
15. Explain the phrase, "A handful of force is better than a sackful of justice."
16. What is the dual purpose of plebiscites and elections in a dictatorship?
17. Why is it that the Latin-American dictators do not resort to "fixed" plebiscites?
18. Name some methods whereby a dictator legalizes his position.
19. Give the most prominent reasons for a dictator's emphasis on public works.
20. What human emotions are being exploited by a dictator when he fosters nationalistic objectives?

SUGGESTED TOPICS FOR TERM PAPERS AND FURTHER RESEARCH

1. Methods of revolution peculiar to Latin America.
2. The social basis for revolution and dictatorships in Latin America.
3. Are Americans subject to the "man on horseback" complex?
4. Dictatorships and bureaucracy.
5. Methods of terrorism in Latin America.
6. Control of news reporting in a totalitarian state.
7. The religious aspects of a dictatorship.
8. The uses of the national army in a dictatorship.
9. Methods of legalization of a dictatorship.
10. Systems of youth control in a dictatorship.

BIBLIOGRAPHY

Books

Guiseppe A. Borgese, *Goliath: The March of Fascism* (New York: Viking Press, 1937). A penetrating analysis of Mussolini's dictatorship.
Albert Carr, *Juggernaut: The Path of Dictatorships* (New York: Viking Press, 1939). An analysis based on case histories of dictatorships of the last three centuries, pointing to common causal factors, broad relationships, and universal Juggernaut effects.
Alfred Cobban, *Dictatorship, Its History and Theory* (New York: Charles Scribner's Sons, 1939). The theory and practice of dictatorship studied historically.

William Ebenstein, *The Nazi State* (New York: Farrar and Rinehart, 1943). An excellent treatment of Nazi Germany, with special emphasis upon the universal goose-stepping practiced in every department of Nazi life.

Merle Fainsod, *How Russia is Ruled* (Cambridge, Mass.: Harvard University Press, 1935). One of the best of the many books dealing with contemporary Soviet regime.

Guy Stanton Ford, ed., *Dictatorship in the Modern World* (Minneapolis: University of Minnesota Press, 1939). A collection of valuable studies of the various dictatorships in the world.

John Gunther, *Inside Europe* (New York: Harper and Brothers, 1939). A journalistic but useful account of European political personalities and conditions.

Konrad Heiden, *Der Fuehrer* (Boston: Houghton Mifflin Co., 1944). The best study of Hitler.

E. E. Kellett, *The Story of Dictatorship* (New York: E. P. Dutton and Co., 1937). A concise treatment of selected dictatorships from ancient times to the present.

Hans Kohn, *Revolutions and Dictatorships* (Cambridge, Mass.: Harvard University Press, 1939). Presents an interesting comparison of Communist and Fascist philosophies.

Robert MacIver, *The Web of Government* (New York: The Macmillan Co., 1947). Chapter 7 gives an excellent survey of common features and specific forms of dictatorships.

Herbert W. Schneider and Shepard B. Clough, *Making Fascists* (Chicago: University of Chicago Press, 1929). An early but still useful study of indoctrination and civic training in Fascist Italy.

Diana Spearman, *Modern Dictatorship* (New York: Columbia University Press, 1939). Significant for its emphasis upon socio-psychological characteristics of modern dictatorships, and its psychological analysis of leadership and autocracy.

H. S. Spencer, "Dictatorship," *Encyclopaedia of the Social Sciences*, V (New York: The Macmillan Co., 1931), pp. 133-316.

A. Curtis Wilgus, ed., *South American Dictators* (Washington, D.C.: George Washington University Press, 1937).

Periodicals

J. R. Angell, "The Future of Intellectual Freedom," *American Scholar*, VIII (Autumn, 1939), pp. 468-487.

Robert C. Brooks, "Democracies and Dictatorships: The Debit Side of Their Ledgers," *Proceedings of the American Philosophical Society*, LXXV, No. 6 (1935), pp. 448-481.

P. E. Corbett, "The Casuistry of Dictatorship," *World Politics*, III (July, 1951), pp. 539-544.

R. V. Daniels, "The State and Revolution: A Case Study in the Genesis and Transformation of the Communist Ideology," *The American Slavic and East European Review*, XII (February, 1953), pp. 22-43.

G. M. Gilbert, *The Psychology of Dictatorship* (New York: Ronald Press, 1950). Based on an examination of the leaders of Nazi Germany.

J. O. Hertzler, "The Causal and Contributory Factors of Dictatorship." *Sociology and Social Research*, XXIV (September–October, 1939), pp. 3-21.

—— "The Effects of Dictatorship," *Sociology and Social Research*, XXIV (November–December, 1939), pp. 111-123.

—— "The Typical Life Cycle of Dictatorships," *Social Forces*, XVII (March, 1939), pp. 303-309.

—— "The Effects of Dictatorship," *Sociology and Social Research*, XXIV (November–December, 1939), pp. 111-123.

Waldemar Kaempffert, "Science in the Totalitarian State," *Foreign Affairs*, XIX (January, 1941), pp. 433-468.

H. D. Lasswell, "Garrison State," *American Journal of Sociology*, XLVI (January, 1941), pp. 455-468.

Karl Loewenstein, "Autocracy versus Democracy in Contemporary Europe," *American Political Science Review*, XXIX (August, 1935), pp. 571-593.

Fritz Morstein Marz, "Propaganda and Dictatorship," *Annals of the American Academy of Political and Social Science*, CLXXIX (May, 1935), pp. 211-218.

James H. Mersil, "Georges Sorel's Last Myth," *Journal of Politics*, XII, I (February, 1950), pp. 52-65.

Sigmund Neumann, "The Rule of the Demagogue," *American Sociological Review*, III (August, 1938), pp. 487-498.

Count Carlo Sforza, "Totalitarian War and the Fate of Democracy," *Annals of the American Academy of Political and Social Science*, CXVI (July, 1941), pp. 65-72.

Diana Spearman, "The Psychological Background of Dictatorship," (British) *Sociological Review*, XXIV (April, 1934), pp. 158-174.

L. S. Stavrianos, "Schooling Under the Dictators," *Current History*, XLIV (September, 1936), pp. 139-146.

John R. Tunis, "The Dictators Discover Sport," *Foreign Affairs*, XIV (July, 1936), pp. 606-617.

CHAPTER XXX

Recent Types of Charismatic Leadership

Definition. The term "charismatic leadership" has its origin in the Greek word *charisma,* meaning a special gift, an extraordinary power through which chosen persons are able to accomplish unusual feats or to work miracles. Thus, a charismatic person inspires awe, if not veneration, by dint of his unerring intuition or invincibility. The expression "charismatic leadership" owes its entry into sociological literature to Max Weber, the late German sociologist, and his theory of charismatic rule.[1] According to his definition, which is implicit in the following discussion, the charismatic leader derives his authority from the popular belief in his supernatural inspiration and guidance and the conviction that he cannot fail in his public undertakings.

History. Western and Oriental history abounds in longer or shorter periods of charismatic leadership. Political or religious authority concentrated in the hands of individuals whose pronouncements superseded law and custom was known in antiquity as well as in modern times. Julius Caesar, Mohammed, Cromwell, Napoleon, the Siberian Shamans, and Joseph Smith, the Mormon leader, wielded unprecedented personal authority among their followers. And yet, the recurrence of charismatic rule in the twentieth century found the world perplexed and confused about the current and future drift of history.

Germany and Italy

The Breeding Ground. Unique as the recent types of personal dictatorship have been, they bear out the historical experience that "exalted" leaders rise to power on the crest of a wave of collective frustration and what appears to be an insoluble social crisis.

The crisis of Germany after her defeat in 1918 may be used as a case in point. With the collapse of the imperial government at the end of World War I, long-nurtured hopes of German expansion in Europe and abroad came to naught. The downfall of the old regime broke the joint

---

[1] The theory was advanced by Max Weber in his *Wirtschaft und Gesellschaft,* now partly translated by H. H. Gerth and C. Mills Wright, *From Max Weber: Essays in Sociology* (New York: Oxford University Press, 1946), pp. 245-252 and 295 ff.

political control of the military hierarchy, the Prussian landed nobility, and the masters of German heavy industry, but it did not turn them into supporters of the Weimar Republic.

Defeat and national humiliation were only the first act in the drama of disillusionment. The persistence of unreconciled social antagonisms and political unrest weakened faith in the new state of affairs and prevented the growth of a generation of loyal republicans. An astronomical inflation which dispossessed a large part of the middle classes and the unparalleled depression of 1928-1933 produced a climactic panic.[2] All this proved to be too severe a test for the young Republic. It had become the battleground rather than the common platform of the surviving rival classes. The promise of stability and security without liberty began to ring more convincingly in the ears of the unemployed, the threatened middle classes, and members of the fallen Imperial Army than the principles upon which the Republic was founded. Political prophets of varied colors emerged and preached a radical departure from the existing order of things. "Germany, at that time, was full of messiahs," but, after their selective elimination one by one, only Hitler survived.[3] While it is true that Hitler and his party had the benefit of powerful patronage in the ranks of the imperial diehards, yet without the popular clamor for a great and strong man and without the genuine mass acclaim which Hitler found the Nazi revolution could not have descended upon Germany.

Similar conditions of domestic insecurity ushered in the rise of Italian Fascism. The disillusionment with the territorial rewards for Italy's entry into the war contributed to the growth of an overheated nationalism. Industrial strife, culminating in the temporary seizure of Northern Italian factories by workers, deepened existing social antagonisms. The breakdown of parliamentary government finally left the door open for the entry of the Blackshirts.

Totalitarian versus Charismatic

The recent governments of Italy, Germany, and Spain were both *totalitarian* and *charismatic*. These two principles of government need not, however, always coincide. *Totalitarian* governments monopolize all positions of political control, leaving none in the hands of private individuals. Such a rule may be exercised by a party, a class, or an individual.

Charismatic rule, however, always is the personal regime of a leader who is credited with supernatural inspiration, prophetic vision, a miraculous

---

[2] Wallace R. Deuel, *People Under Hitler* (New York: Harcourt, Brace and Co., 1942), pp. 44-54.

[3] Otto D. Tolischus, *They Wanted War* (New York: Reynal and Hitchcock, 1940), p. 7.

instinct, a divine calling, or any other form of charisma. It is this extraordinary ability of the leader which, in the eyes of his followers, justifies his personal rule and makes his authority binding. The Soviet System is totalitarian, whereas Hitler and Mussolini assumed charismatic authority and exercised it on a totalitarian scale.

Antitraditionalism. Most regimes which expect to endure claim legitimacy for their exercise of authority and their use of force. Rightful rule may be deduced from tradition, from the ballot, or from appointment, in accordance with the rules of accepted procedure. Charismatic leaders, however, do not take recourse to custom and precedent in vindicating their own rule. It is true that modern Caesars do make use of historical symbols. Mussolini frequently linked Fascism with the Roman Empire, with the Italian *Risorgimento*, with Dante and Garibaldi. Hitler, too, resorted to selected symbols of German history: to Potsdam, the seat of the Prussian military monarchy in the eighteenth century, and to Vidukind, the pagan rebel against the Western and Christian empire of Charlemagne. Such inspirational tributes to a distant past, however, are often made to serve and screen a radical departure from established and living tradition rather than to reaffirm it. For tradition and customary procedure are forces of restraint which limit the exercise of political power. No one can make unlimited use of coercive power without colliding with custom and usage.

The Primacy of Politics. Neither are such regimes anxious to commit themselves to articulate programs, economic plans, and clear-cut objectives. Caesars and Napoleons have as little respect for written programs as they have for the advocates of commercial soundness, the policy of playing safe, for the legal and moral scruples of the bureaucrat, and, in general, for the departmental point of view.[4] Oliver Cromwell's pointed confession, "I have as little skill in Arithmetic as in Law," is characteristic of leaders who insist on the fullest possible freedom of action. The primacy of politics over economics, morals, religion, law, family, or any other institution was clearly affirmed by Mussolini and Hitler and their historical antecedents. With characteristic bluntness, Mussolini declared:

"What do we propose? We answer without false modesty: to govern the nation. With what program? With the program necessary to insure the moral and material greatness of the Italian people. . . . We do not believe in dogmatic programs. . . . We allow ourselves the luxury of being aristocrats and revolutionaries; legitimists and illegitimists accord

---

[4] Hans Morgenthau, "National Socialist Doctrine of World Organization," *Proceedings of the Seventh Conference of Teachers of International Law and Related Subjects* (Washington, D.C., 1941), pp. 104-105; Sigmund Neumann, *Permanent Revolution* (New York and London: Harper and Brothers, 1942), p. 38.

ing to the conditions, time, place, and circumstance. . . . Fascism does not have a pretty program to be realized in the year 2000 for the simple reason that Fascism builds the structure of its will and passion from day to day." [5]

Naturally, modern Caesars were suspicious of thinkers and literati who continued to cling to the standards of traditional human conduct. Napoleon contemptuously dubbed them the "ideologists"; Mussolini and Hitler called them doctrinaries, or footloose intellectuals.

Imperialism. Recent charismatic rulers have risen to power not to carry out a program of domestic amelioration but to enter on a course of imperial expansion on a scale limited only by external resistance. It was for such aims that they organized the total resources of their countries. Fixed programs and rigid rules of procedure become impediments when only strategic opportunism, coupled with preparedness and good timing, offer a chance of success in a world political gamble. Says Hitler in *Mein Kampf:*

"Without paying attention to 'tradition' and prejudices it [the Nazi movement] must find the courage to unite our people and their strength to march forward on that road which will lead this people out of their narrow territorial sphere of life to new land and soil. . . ." [6]

To be sure, Napoleon, Mussolini, and Hitler carried out extensive road building and land reclamation projects. They abolished unemployment, and, in the course of their armament campaigns, they centralized to a great extent the economic and administrative machinery of their countries. Moreover, modern Caesars uniformly claim to replace inefficient and corrupt administrations by a streamlined and honest government of their own. Effective as such claims or accomplishments may be in propaganda campaigns, they are actually only by-products of extensive preparations for conquest—the ultimate objective of popular dictators in modern times.

Dogmatic Justifications of Absolute Power

The claim to absolute power and the legitimate use of force are based on three dogmatic assumptions.

The Mandate of Providence. First, the leader's rise to power is an act of Providence, or, in the words of Koellreuter, a Nazi jurist, an "act of grace," and is due neither to fortuitous circumstances nor to a majority vote. Goebbels announced in 1926: "The great leader will not be elected. He is there when he must be there." Goering decreed: "We love Adolf

---

[5] H. Arthur Steiner, *Government in Fascist Italy* (New York: McGraw-Hill Book Co., 1938), p. 13.

[6] Adolf Hitler, *Mein Kampf* (New York: Stackpole Sons, 1939), p. 27.

Hitler, because we believe deeply that God has sent him to us to save Germany." Hitler has hinted at the supernatural sources of his calling through such expressions as "Fate itself gave me my answer . . .," "Fate itself instructed me." [7]

Infallible Instinct. The second assumption is that Providence or some other transcendent power has endowed the leader with an infallible instinct in the affairs of his nation. "Mussolini is always right," was the standard phrase of the Fascist press. The same theme is expressed by Goering with reference to Hitler: "For us the Leader is, in all political and other matters concerning the national and social interests of the people, simply infallible. . . . It is something mystical, almost incomprehensible, which this unique man possesses." Says Wilhelm Kube, another of Hitler's subleaders: "Whoever heard the Fuehrer at Nuremberg . . . felt the same thing. There spoke in him the revelation of a Higher One." And Hans Frank: "Hitler is lonely, so is God. Hitler is like God." [8]

Mystical Identification. Third, the leader and the people are one. He has the people's mandate to carry out their unexpressed will. He and only he really knows what the people want, and he knows it better than the people themselves. In its Nazi application this doctrine assumes an air of mysticism. According to Hans Schmidt, a Nazi jurist, Hitler derived his authority from the law emanating from the "national soul." In the words of Hess, the former Deputy Leader, "Adolf Hitler is Germany, and Germany is Adolf Hitler." [9]

These assumptions formed binding articles of faith, and they were backed and instilled in the masses by the propaganda and coercive power of the regime. The practical conclusion from these tenets was that the leader does not need the consent of the people, nor is he responsible to them for his policies. The question of whether the Nazi government was established by a majority vote or by an armed coup does not bear on the legitimacy of Nazi rule. Since the leader is the spokesman of the people and the incarnation of their unconscious cravings, since he and the people are indivisible, a formal confirmation of his policies by the people is as unnecessary as their dissent would be impossible. Although no modern charismatic ruler could in the long run retain his authority without repeated (and organized) manifestations of loyalty, he does not need

---

[7] Otto Koellreuter, *Deutsches Verfassungsrecht* (Berlin, 1935), p. 142, quoted by Fritz Morstein Marx, *Government in the Third Reich* (New York: McGraw-Hill Book Co., 1936), p. 60; F. L. Schuman, *The Nazi Dictatorship* (New York: Alfred A. Knopf, 1935), p. 122; Hitler, *op. cit.*, pp. 74, 57.

[8] John Gunther, *Chicago Daily News*, November 2, 1933, quoted by Schuman, *op. cit.*, p. 365; *ibid.*, p. 122.

[9] Hans Schmidt-Leonhardt, *Deutsches Recht*, V (1935), p. 340, quoted by Fritz Morstein Marx, *op. cit.*, p. 68; Schuman, *op. cit.*, p. 309.

popular acclaim to justify his political conduct. The test of his charisma is not the ballot but prodigious and overwhelming accomplishments.

Fascism, Nazism and the Soviet System

It will have been noted that in the preceding discussion no detailed mention was made of the Soviet regime. This calls for an explanation in view of the unparalleled concentration of power in the hands of the Russian Communist party and its leaders, and particularly in view of the wide use of symbols exalting them. The Lenin corners in factories and clubs, the pilgrimage to Lenin's mausoleum, the popular use of the epithets "great" and "wise" in reference to Stalin, and the ubiquity of Lenin's and Stalin's portraits are cases in point.

Stalin. Charismatic leaders derive their authority from their personal magic, the popular belief in their personal inspiration, and their ability to resolve a national crisis into a series of spectacular accomplishments which exalt national glory and restore pride and confidence to the disturbed masses. A formulated and binding program of action plays no significant part in the justification of charismatic prerogatives. Although Stalin's personal role has visibly gathered weight in the shaping of Russia's politics since 1930, the socialistic program of action and the Communist creed still form the basis of the political order of things in Soviet Russia. Stalin's authority, while hardly limited in practice, rests on the belief that his leadership represents the most authentic adaptation of the party program to the strategic requirements of the present phase of the Revolution. The recent propagandistic exaltation of Stalin's leadership notwithstanding, supreme and lasting authority is vested in the doctrine of which the Soviet regime is believed to be the practical application.

Composition of Party Systems. A second important difference between the Soviet System and charismatic regimes concerns the composition of the governing party. The Communist party, ever since it developed into a mass organization, has been anxious to demonstrate its class character as a party of workers and peasants. Entrepreneurs and businessmen have not been admitted. By contrast, the Fascist and the Nazi parties did not intend to be class parties.[10] Their membership included the whole gamut of social variations, although the middle classes were somewhat overrepresented.

The objectives of social revolutions are primarily domestic, at least in their first phases, and their foreign policy is subordinate to the internal aims of the revolutionary party. This applies to Soviet Russia, particu-

---

[10] F. Borkenau, *The New German Empire* (New York: The Viking Press, 1939), p. 6.

larly since the liquidation of Trotsky and his internationalist followers, a group that put world revolution and its organ, the Communist International, before the program of economic reconstruction in Russia itself. Fascism and National Socialism, on the other hand, were essentially streamlined methods of preparing for conquest on an ambitious scale. The primacy of foreign policy over domestic affairs was a common premise of both systems. The Duce and the Fuehrer did not propose to change the social structure of their countries for the sake of change, but to mobilize for war. To be sure, the unparalleled scale of the economic, military, and psychological preparations profoundly changed life in Italy and Germany. A new political hierarchy was superimposed on the old. New industries were created, lockouts and strikes were prohibited, private organizations were suppressed, and a regimented economy took the place of the competitive system. As a by-product of the armament campaign, industrial concentration seemed to have gained momentum. Yet in essentials the Nazi and Fascist governments followed in the footsteps of Napoleon and stabilized the social equilibrium which prevailed before their rise to power. On the whole, the domestic program of modern charismatic governments is unity, class appeasement, and the total mobilization of the nation's military assets.[11]

Propaganda Strategy

An important innovation of the Nazi party was its extensive use of the meeting hall technique in preference to the printed word. The meeting hall provided the stage setting for the leader's personal appeal to the audience. There he could observe the effects of his speech and change his diction until he established rapport with his audience. From then on it was not the logic of his argument that won the battle, but the tone of his voice, his success in rousing an *esprit de corps* in the assembly, and a coordinated stage management.[12] The approach to the masses through

---

[11] For a different interpretation, asserting an overt or concealed affinity of Fascist and Nazi policies with the interests of the capitalistic and landed upper classes, compare Robert E. Brady, *The Spirit and Structure of German Fascism* (New York: The Viking Press, 1937), and John Strachy, *The Menace of Fascism* (New York: Gollancz, 1933). A somewhat similar position is held by A. R. L. Gurland, "Technological Trends under National Socialism," *Studies in Philosophy and Social Science*, IX, No. 2 (1941).

[12] Hitler, *op. cit.*, p. 463. For an exposition of the meeting hall situation and related types of collective behavior, see Robert E. Park and Ernest W. Burgess, *Introduction to the Science of Sociology* (Chicago: University of Chicago Press, 1924), chapter XIII; Richard T. LaPiere, *Collective Behavior* (New York: McGraw-Hill Book Co., 1938); E. B. Reuter and C. W. Hart, *Introduction to Sociology* (New York: McGraw-Hill Book Co., 1933), chapters XVIII and XIX; and the concise summary of Herbert Blumer, "Collective Behavior" in *An Outline of the Principles of Sociology* (Robert E. Park, ed.) (New York: Barnes and Noble, 1939), Part IV.

the meeting hall was paralleled by a secret society technique which was designed to catch the imagination of young men.[13] The appeal of such organizations was enhanced by an elaborate symbolism, colorful uniforms, and face-to-face contacts.

Institutional Charisma

The personal nature of such governments as Nazism and Fascism has often raised the question of whether an exclusively personal regime can survive its initiator and become a system. In the majority of known instances that has not been the case, for reasons stated below, but a large enough number of historical examples shows that belief in the supernatural mandate of one ruler can, after his death, become associated with his "office" and thus be transferred to his successors. The difference between personal and institutional charisma may be compared to the difference between shamanism and priesthood. The shaman is a spiritual mediator who assumes religious authority by virtue of some unusual faculty—for example, to precipitate a self-induced state of frenzy in which he is able to communicate with the spirit and convey its message to his followers. The priest, on the other hand, succeeds to an office already in existence, and it is in his official capacity that he becomes the repository of divine guidance. In other words, the shaman owes his spiritual authority to his "natural" qualifications, while the priest acquires the requisite faculties through his office.

Japan

The history of Japan since 1868 (the establishment of state Shintoism) offers a modern example of institutional charisma. The core of state Shintoism is the worship of the emperor as a deity whose worldly authority is neither limited nor circumscribed by the constitution. His exalted position has been attributed, according to Shinto doctrine, to four circumstances.

First, the Japanese emperors are lineal descendants of Amaterasu Omikami, the sun goddess, and are themselves divine.

Second, imperial rule was instituted by the same divine ancestress. Accession to the throne and the performance of the imperial ancestor

---

[13] Richard Behrendt, *Politischer Aktivismus* (Leipzig, 1932), chapter III; Ernest Manheim, "The Role of Small Groups in the Formation of Public Opinion," *The Southwestern Social Science Quarterly*, XX (December, 1939). For a more general discussion of the techniques of propaganda conducted through the medium of secret societies, compare E. Manheim, *Die Traeger der Oeffentlichen Meinung* (Bruenn, 1933), pp. 35-41 and 124-145, or the Spanish edition of the same publication, *La Opinion Publica* (Madrid, 1936), pp. 58-68 and 202-238.

worship confer divine guidance upon the ruler. Thus an imperial re-, script of 1870 (by Meiji, the founder of modern Japan) reads: "We solemnly announce: The Heavenly Deities and the Great Ancestress established the throne and made the succession secure. The line of Emperors in unbroken succession entered into possession thereof and handed it on. . . ."[14] Prince Ito, one of the authors of the recent Japanese constitution, declared: "The Sacred Throne was established at the time when the heavens and the earth became separated. The Emperor is Heaven descended, divine and sacred. . . ."[15] An official publication of the Japanese Department of Education of 1937 makes the unity of imperial rule and communication with the divine ancestors plain:

"The Emperor by means of religious ceremonies becomes one with the divine imperial ancestors. . . . In this way the spirit wherewith the Emperor rules the country is imparted. For this reason the worship of the gods on the part of the Emperor and His administration of government are in their fundamental aspects one and the same thing."[16]

Third, the Japanese people themselves are a chosen nation of divine origin and, as such, the bearers of a collective charisma. Thus there is a basic affinity between the people and their ruler.

"We are recipients from the 'kami' [national deities], by direct descent through the ancestors, of a specific endowment of tendencies and capacities, and if we permit this innate disposition to find normal expression, we achieve spontaneously filial piety, loyalty and love of fellow men. . . ."[17]

Fourth, the emperor is the embodiment and synthesis of the people. His thought and action express the essential aspirations of the nation so that no consultation of the people is necessary to achieve that identity of aims. "Subjects have no mind apart from the will of the Emperor. Their individual selves are merged with the Emperor. If they act according to the mind of the Emperor, they can realize their true nature. . . ."[18]

Emperor worship is not of recent origin. During the centuries of the Shogunate (the rule of military governors), the emperors were revered as incarnations of heaven, although they were kept in seclusion and divorced from the sources of power.[19] The combination of both authorities spiritual and political became the cornerstone of the unlimited imperial prerogatives and of the rapid rise of Japan to a first rate military power. At the same time, the ancient religious conception of *Hakkō Ichi-u*, according to which the peoples of the world should be brought under one "roof," was revived and reinterpreted. The principle of *Hakkō*

---

[14] Quoted by D. C. Holtom, *Modern Japan and Shinto Nationalism* (Chicago: University of Chicago Press, 1943), p. 6.

[15] *Ibid.*, p. 9.   [16] *Ibid.*, p. 7.   [17] *Ibid.*, p. 16.   [18] *Ibid.*, p. 10.

[19] E. Herbert Norman, *Japan's Emergence as a Modern State* (New York: Institute of Pacific Relations, 1940), p. 27.

Ichi-u can mean, and has meant in Japanese history, several things. At one time it expressed the desire to consolidate the Japanese clans under one imperial government. The term may also mean something akin to the Christian conception of the brotherhood of mankind. Since Meiji's rule *Hakkō Ichi-u* has been increasingly quoted to mean a world mission of the emperor to unite the peoples of the globe under his "roof." It is no mere coincidence that at the beginning of an era of absolute imperial rule the conception of a missionary imperialism begins to assume a religious significance. The reader will recognize the parallel between the Nazi concept of charisma and the Japanese system of divine rule. It appears that imperialism on a grand scale is an important factor in the modern exercise of political charisma, whether it is of the personal or institutional type.

Long Term Perspective of Charismatic Rule. Charismatic regimes rise mostly in periods of crisis, insecurity, and dissolution, and they usually retain these birthmarks until their end. Such systems have an amorphous structure in which the leader's personal initiative and improvisations take the place of the failing institutions. These the charismatic leader rarely restores to their "normal" functions. He substitutes spectacular accomplishments for working procedures and conventions which operate in a state of "normalcy." He fortifies his position by a personal bureaucracy which, given time, tends to grow to unusual proportions and to control increasing areas of life.

During the ascending phase of such a system, the bureaucracy serves as the personal tool of the leader, but charismatic bureaucracies face their crucial test when the question of succession to the supreme power arises. Few of these systems have survived their originators; most of them have ended in military defeat. A few, however, were able to endure by ending the initial period of improvisations and by adapting themselves to a stabilized state of affairs. In the course of this transformation the charisma of the originator usually changes from a personal attribute into an institutional authority of the successors, and with this change the prerogatives of their office become defined and restricted. Brahmanism, Mormonism, the Papacy, the Caliphate, and Lamaism are examples of the institutional survival of charismatic rule. In some historic instances the disciples, lieutenants, or descendants of the original leader constituted themselves as a charismatic caste which collectively assumed the supernatural qualifications of the founder.

Vulnerability of Divine Kingships. An unsuccessful ruler undermines the divine prestige of his office. The Shilluk of Africa are said to have ceremonially killed their divine kings at the first stage of their declining strength. It appears that the Shilluk saved the institution of divine kingship by periodically divorcing it from their kings as soon as they failed to justify public faith in their miraculous power. Similar customs prevailed among the Bunyore, the Dinka, and others.[20] The Emperors of China were said to have resigned after a serious drought or a national crop failure, for such calamities were interpreted as proof of their declining powers. Japan's defeat made the emperor's recent renunciation of his divine authority inevitable. Continued success seems to be the indispensable condition for the survival of charismatic rule.

Summary

Charismatic rule is an exceptional type of authority which rests on the popular acceptance of the claim to supernatural guidance. Faith in the infallibility of the leader in his public undertakings rarely survives defeat or changed circumstances which are no longer propitious to spectacular deeds. The end of World War II eclipsed two such personal regimes (Mussolini and Hitler) and an institutional form of divine rule (Japan).

QUESTIONS

1. How do charismatic regimes justify their existence?
2. What is State Shintoism?
3. Why are popular dictators suspicious of intellectuals?
4. What was the domestic program of the Fascist and Nazi parties?
5. What is the function of the plebiscite in a personal dictatorship?
6. What policies are expressed in the structure of the Nazi and Fascist dictatorships?
7. How was the Japanese Emperor's religious authority related to his political rule?
8. What is the difference between the Japanese Imperial Rule and the Nazi or Fascist dictatorships?
9. How were Nazi or Fascist subleaders selected and replaced?
10. Of which branches of government was Hitler in charge?
11. What is the attitude of charismatic leaders in general toward law and legislation, and what was the dominant Nazi philosophy of law?
12. What is the role of the expert and the trained administrator in popular dictatorships?
13. What means of propaganda were used most in Nazi Germany? How?
14. What means, other than propaganda, were employed in Nazi Germany to ensure the loyalty of the masses?
15. How can charismatic rule become permanent? What changes take place in such a process?

SUGGESTED TOPICS FOR TERM PAPERS AND FURTHER RESEARCH

1. Compare charismatic leadership to democratic leadership.
2. The myths built around charismatic leaders.

---

[20] James G. Frazer, *The Golden Bough* (New York: The Macmillan Co., 1940), pp. 264-282.

3. Compare the charismatic leaders of Europe to those of South America.
4. What are the special characteristics of charismatic leaders in Soviet Russia.
5. Trace the theories of charismatic leadership to Max Weber and his interpreters.
6. The religious elements in charismatic leadership.
7. The socio-psychological background of the nations with charismatic leaders.
8. The use of education by charismatic leaders.
9. The charismatic leadership of Franco.
10. The charismatic leadership developed in Asia.

BIBLIOGRAPHY

Books

Chester L. Bernard, "A Definition of Authority," pp. 180-185, in R. K. Merton, *Reader in Bureaucracy* (Glencoe, Ill.: Free Press, 1952). "The Functions of the Status System," pp. 242-255, *op. cit.;* also "Formal and Informal Status," by F. J. Rothlisberger, W. L. Dickason, and Carl Dreyfus, "Prestige Grading; A Mechanism of Control," pp. 258-265.

Albert Carr, *Juggernaut: The Path of Dictatorship* (New York: The Viking Press, 1939). Studies of twenty dictators from Richelieu to Hitler. Excellent on the whole, although it contains some errors of fact.

A. Cobban, *Dictatorship, Its History and Theory* (New York: Charles Scribner's Sons, 1939). A scholarly and very readable analysis.

Hans H. Gerth, "The Nazi Party: Its Leadership and Composition," in R. K. Merton, and others, *Reader in Bureaucracy* (Glencoe, Ill.: Free Press, 152), pp. 100-153.

Helmut Lehmann-Haupt, *Art Under a Dictatorship* (New York: Oxford University Press, 1954). What has happened to the fine arts (painting, sculpture, architecture, the arts and crafts) in Nazi Germany, Soviet-occupied Germany and Soviet Russia proper; how they have been used as an instrument of authoritarianism, what forms they have taken, what has happened to the artist, how the public has reacted.

Adolf Hitler, *Mein Kampf* (New York: Stackpole Sons, 1939).

D. C. Holtom, *Modern Japan and Shinto Nationalism* (Chicago: University of Chicago Press, 1943), pp. 1-25. An excellent and concise description of the religious roots of Japanese nationalism.

Erich Kahler, *Man the Measure* (New York: Pantheon Books, Inc., 1943), pp. 567-602. An informed description of the circumstances of the rise of Nazism.

Kurt London, *Backgrounds of Conflict* (New York: The Macmillan Co., 1945), pp. 62-77; 142-152; 188-205. A handy and very readable description of the conflicting political systems in the recent war, including Nazism, Fascism, and the Japanese Emperor system. Particular emphasis is placed on the intellectual antecedents of Nazism and Fascism.

Richard C. Meyers, "Myth and Status Systems in Industry," R. Merton, *op. cit.,* pp. 273-281.

William Miller, "Social Background of the Business Elite," pp. 303-312, in R. K. Merton, *op. cit.*

Franz Neumann, *Behemoth, The Structure and Practice of National Socialism* (New York: Oxford University Press, 1942), pp. 83-129. A good and well informed analysis.

Sigmund Neumann, *Permanent Revolution* (New York: Harper and Brothers, 1942), pp. 1-9; 36-72. One of the best accounts of Nazism presented against a broad historical background.

Robert Karl Reischauer, *Japan, Government and Politics* (New York: Thomas Nelson and Sons, 1939), pp. 24-33. A good brief introduction.

Periodicals

Theodore Abel, "Is a Psychiatric Interpretation of the German Enigma Necessary?" *American Sociological Review*, X (August, 1945), pp. 457-464.

Raymond Aron, "Social Structure and the Ruling Class," *British Journal of Sociology*, I, 2 (June, 1950), pp. 126-143.

M. J. Bonn, "New World Order," *Annals of the American Academy of Political and Social Science*, CCXVI (July, 1941), pp. 163-177.

Richard M. Brickner, "Is Germany Incurable?" *Atlantic Monthly*, CLXXI (March, 1943), pp. 84-93; and (April, 1943), pp. 94-98.

J. O. Hertzler, "Crises and Dictatorships," *American Sociological Review*, V (April, 1940), pp. 157-169.

—— "The Typical Life Cycle of Dictatorships," *Social Forces*, XVII (March, 1939), pp. 303-309.

Rudolf Hess, "Essay on a Fuehrer," *American Mercury*, LIII (July, 1941), pp. 95-96.

Gilbert Highet, "Axis Prose," *Virginia Quarterly Review*, XVIII (April, 1942), pp. 216-225.

Ernst Kris, "Morale in Germany," *American Journal of Sociology*, XLVII (November, 1941), pp. 452-461.

Owen Lattimore, "Sacred Cow of Japan," *Atlantic Monthly*, CLXXV (January, 1945), pp. 45-51.

Eugene Lyons, "Dictators into Gods," *American Mercury*, XLVI (March, 1939), pp. 265-272.

Sigmund Neumann, "Comrades in Error," *Virginia Quarterly Review*, XVIII (January, 1942), pp. 121-128.

—— "The Rule of the Demagogue," *American Sociological Review*, III (August, 1938), pp. 487-498.

James K. Pollock, "Areal Study of the German Electorate—1930-1933," *American Political Science Review*, XXXVIII (February, 1944), pp. 89-95.

C. J. S. Sprigge, "Italian Fascism: A Retrospect," *Nineteenth Century and After*, CXXXII (October, 1942), pp. 163-169.

Otto D. Tolischus, "God, Emperor, High Priest," *New York Times Magazine* (November 23, 1941), p. 10.

Chapter XXXI

Social Control and the Atomic Bomb

Social Control in the Atomic Age. The exploding of an atomic bomb over the Japanese city of Hiroshima, in 1945, has apparently revolutionized the nature of warfare and necessitated drastic modification of the entire system of control relationships heretofore existing between the nations of the world. In theory social control must be viewed as the scientific and disinterested employment of measures and techniques over the whole of a given society which aim at securing a maximum achievement of social well-being and satisfactions for that particular group. Historically, however, the devices and techniques of social control have been used primarily to facilitate the interests of ruling elites rather than those of society in general. History records utilization of every known device of force, mastery, domination, censorship, trickery, fraud, deceit, and appeals to superstition to gain and maintain for such elites the power and vested privileges to which they aspire.[1] As has been indicated in previous chapters these techniques have universally characterized control situations whether upon a level of individual relationships or of organized groups. On a national and international plane, the power-struggle for mastery of the world is intensified by the enormous underlying pressures to thermal temperatures.

In the contemporary state of affairs, elimination of the fascist states from the picture at the end of World War II seemed to offer the hope that the allied members of the United Nations, particularly Great Britain, the U.S.S.R., and the United States, the so-called "great powers," might work together to establish peace and create social controls which would eliminate future wars and promote world-wide well-being. This hope was doomed to disappointment, however, by the break-up of the alliance into the Anglo-American and Russian combinations which have been increasing their competition for domination of the globe. Postwar revival of the international power struggle between surviving national states posed once more the question of whether international society could be organized to secure the welfare of the peoples of the world as

---

[1] Cf. L. L. Bernard, *Social Control* (New York: The Macmillan Co., 1939), pp. 11-16; and E. A. Ross, *New Age Sociology* (New York: D. Appleton-Century, 1940), pp. 80-81.

a whole or whether the continuing struggles of the great powers to establish the supremacy of their way of life and of their ruling groups upon the rest of the world would continue.

By all indications of past history and of the existing political situation, it would only be possible to conclude that the power struggle between national groups would continue, breaking out at some later date in open warfare. The successful use of atomic power introduced into the postwar situation a new factor of such transcendent significance that it could be compared only with the discovery of gunpowder in the effect it would have upon existing power (and therefore control) relationships. Atomic power can be utilized both as a weapon of warfare and as a source of cheap energy for peaceful purposes. How it would be used and the extent of the emphasis placed upon its military or peaceful uses depended greatly upon the extent to which the great states of the world collaborated to control its use. But whether or not cooperation replaced competition, it was highly unlikely that the discovery and utilization of atomic power could have been prevented. The passing of the world into the Atomic Era was inevitable. The great question was how it could be controlled and used for the benefit of mankind. Splitting of the atom dramatized the tremendous advances of modern technology which had already started mechanical changes too complicated and varied in character for any single person to comprehend. Speeding up the pace of modern scientific invention was multiplying the stream of productive instruments flowing into the field of economic life. Faced with the startling changes demanded by these technical innovations in the economic, political, and social life of society and bewildered by the complexity both of the changes and of the machines and processes which produced them, the masses of the people groped blindly for leadership which they vaguely hoped would provide them with the sense of security which the ever-changing whirl of events failed to produce. Unfortunately, the democratic societies of the world, still imbued with outmoded ideologies and the antiquated machinery of nineteenth century democracy, were in no position to measure up to the needs of the times, while the fascist and communist dictatorships could only lead them into a way of life which denied the values of liberty and individuality and offering a cheap kind of security at the price of party dictatorship and regimentation of the masses. Neither the leaders of the democracies nor of the dictatorships seemed to possess the grasp of the fundamentals at stake in the Atomic Era or had the inclination to try to master and act upon them.[2]

---

[2] For a very significant article on this aspect of the situation, see Erich Kohler, "The Reality of Utopia," *American Scholar*, XV (Spring, 1946), pp. 167-179.

The Possibilities of Atomic Power

Peaceful Possibilities. Discovery of the means of release of atomic energy through the splitting of the atoms of uranium opened up tremendous possibilities of increased energy output per unit of manpower in the production of heat, light, and power for the operation of all types of machinery. The known amount of uranium ore in the world is limited.[3] However, other sources may be discovered. Other ores (such as thorium) also offer opportunities of utilization with additional experimentation and these are in much larger quantities. It is estimated that a given amount of uranium gives off three million times as much energy as the same amount of coal. Although the costs of production are much higher, it is obvious that, where it can be used advantageously, the production cost of energy released from uranium would be many times less than the cost of producing coal or water power. The dangerous rays generated from the splitting of uranium atoms would require heavy installations of insulated materials. Hence it is probable for some time to come that atomic energy could be used only in large enterprises where such installations are possible. Heating, lighting, and power plants using atomic energy could without doubt be established at once. Nevertheless, it is unlikely that they would be introduced rapidly owing to the dangerous destruction of values that would take place in plants operated by more expensive forms of energy and the large-scale unemployment and other unsettling social effects that would result.

Application of atomic energy to transportation in its various forms and to home uses (except utilities) would have to wait upon further scientific discoveries and inventions. Yet, the very contemplation of the possibilities already within the range of immediate accomplishment opened up enormously wide vistas of unparalleled increases in human comforts which would make possible advances to levels of welfare, culture, and civilization for all peoples of the world heretofore undreamed of. On the other hand, putting aside all questions of use of atomic bombs in warfare between the great powers and assuming the possibility of peaceful introduction of atom energy into the field of the technical and mechanical arts, the maladjustments occasioned by the extraordinary shift from existing sources of energy to the new form would of themselves raise problems of crucial importance.

Questions of ownership and control of the new plants and of the sale and distribution of atomic power, of the distribution of wealth and income produced by atomic energy, of what to do with the large numbers of unemployed thrown out of work by the new methods of production, and of the training of the masses of the people in the proper use of

---

[3] The estimated total is about 15 million tons.

leisure time would, no doubt, test the capacities of political leaders to the utmost. It seemed very clear that if control over the resources of atomic energy were transferred to private hands and the masses of the people compelled to secure income through work in atomic factories with which to purchase goods produced by atomic power, economic inequalities and consequent inter-group political pressures would become intolerable, and the inevitable result would be civil warfare so violent that it might destroy the existing basis of class cooperation and lead to generations of bloody struggle.

Fortunately the McMahon bill, in process of passage in the summer of 1946, provided for a government monopoly of the ownership and production of all fissionable materials in the United States and forbade private ownership and production. However, this bill was being passed at a time when little consideration was given to the commercial possibilities of atomic energy available for the future. Unquestionably when these become more clear, and opportunities for profit through the use of atomic energy in commercial outlets more apparent, huge pressures would be applied to government to license, lease, or sell energy to private producers. Moreover, the McMahon bill did not apply to foreign governments where atomic energy plants would also be constructed.[4] Business men had already taken the question of atomic energy into consideration but tended to take a conservative view of its potentialities for producing cheap goods, at least in the immediate future.[5]

In any case, even if the uses of atomic energy remained socialized, the problems of utilization of surplus labor power, distribution of income, and proper use of leisure time would require much thought on the part of social planners and controllers. The entire question of the peaceful use of atomic energy in productive enterprises threw into sharp relief past practices in social control and the necessity for a detached and scientific attitude became all the more a categorical imperative to those who would have the responsibility for charting the course of the peoples of the world in their hesitating and uncertain steps into the *terra incognita* of the Atomic Era.

Military Possibilities of Atomic Power. Skepticism aroused by current tendencies on the part of sentimentalists to exaggerate the possibilities of the atomic bomb should not be allowed to obscure its horrible potentialities for destruction and its effect upon the methods of warfare. Conservative students of the atomic bomb and its possibilities concede that from one to ten bombs accurately placed are sufficient to destroy

---

[4] See the "Atomic Energy Act of 1946," *Senate Report No. 1211,* 79th Congress, 2nd Session.

[5] *The Atomic Age Opens* (New York: Pocket Books, Inc., 1945), pp. 190-196.

any city in the world. Any nation possessing a sufficient quantity of bombs could destroy all of the cities of any consequence in any great nation in a single day. No adequate defense existed against the bomb and none seemed likely to be created in the near future. The tremendous power of the bomb concentrated in such a comparatively small object revolutionized the nature of bombing warfare. A half dozen bombers could carry as much destruction as was required of a thousand during World War II.

The fact that a plane need carry only one bomb lightens its load and thus vastly extends its range of action. It is estimated that the most modern of today's bombers can carry an atomic bomb four thousand miles, unload it, and return. This means that any great nation can attack the cities of its rival from its already existing bases. Thus the urban centers and teeming populations of a national competitor could be destroyed in a few hours and the attacker could then invade and occupy the victim's territory at leisure. The tremendous advantage of wealthy manufacturing nations over smaller nations resulting from their ability to build large numbers of expensive planes has disappeared. Superiority in the number of planes no longer guaranteed security since only a few bombers would be required to do the job. With the costs of war greatly reduced, the need for huge amounts of raw materials rendered obsolete, and no defense against the use of atomic bombs, small nations which were able to manufacture the bomb might use it successfully against a great power and make itself master of the situation. Such success, however, would be short-lived unless all other states were deprived of their ability to make bombs. Manufacture of a large number of bombs would not insure safety since a large quantity is not required to destroy the urban centers of a nation. Neither would secrecy regarding the techniques of the bomb's manufacture avail for very long since sufficient scientific knowledge about its manufacture was available to the scientists of all national states.

Experiments conducted by the United States at Bikini seemed to indicate that use of the bomb against navies would not be as effective as against cities and fixed military installations but possession of a fleet would be of little avail if the means of transportation and production of a nation were knocked out. Moreover, the ease with which the bomb can be transported puts a premium on military surprise, sabotage, fifth column activity, and treachery. Not only can bombs be transported by air; they can be brought within easy range on shipboard, shot into a country by rocket projectiles, or perhaps smuggled in and planted in places where they would explode at a time calculated to do the most harm. Owing to the ease with which the bomb can be manipulated and its horrible effectiveness, a great advantage immediately accrues to governments headed by dictators whose unilateral order might be sufficient to launch a storm of bombs upon an unsuspecting neighbor state.

It thus became absolutely certain that the old methods of international relations with their power struggles and occasional wars would no longer work. Uneasiness, fear, and national insecurity would render life almost intolerable. Reliance upon defense would no longer suffice. Attempts to prepare a defense against the bomb might mean driving the entire nation underground, a perpetual state of alarm, regimentation of the people under strict military controls, and imposition of rigid censorship. Elimination of the ease of movement and freedom of initiative which now makes life more tolerable would be severely curtailed.[6] The consequences of maintaining the luxury of independent nationalism and of refusal of leading national states to concert together to establish common, workable controls would be costly, indeed. Common sense and good judgment would dictate immediate action on the part of the "Big Three" nations toward abandoning selfish nationalistic and imperialistic policies and establishing world governmental agencies capable of successfully eliminating the use of the atomic bomb in warfare and concentration upon the solution of problems raised by its peacetime uses. Nevertheless, as will be seen, this is not the likeliest course of action.

Control Problems Raised by the Atomic Bomb

First reactions to the ghastly specters raised by release upon the world of the atomic bomb were in the direction of destroying it immediately and forgetting about it. Second thought, however, made it clear that this diabolical engine of destruction could not be destroyed permanently. Even if the factories which manufacture the bomb should be eradicated, the scientific knowledge of how to build it would remain and, without establishment of adequate international controls, could be utilized secretly for building other factories and manufacturing other bombs. Hence, the problem could not be disposed of that easily. Moreover, in view of the peacetime possibilities of atomic power, such a disposition of the matter would appear irrational in the extreme. Besides, any action which authorities in the United States might take to dispose of the problem in that way would have to be duplicated by like action on the part of all other nations. In result, it became obvious that destruction of atomic power would not work. Next, American leaders manifested a tendency to speed up production of the bomb so that the United States would have an ample store on hand before any other potentially hostile power could

---

[6] See the U. S. Strategic Bombing Survey, "How the U. S. Can Protect Itself," *United States News*, XXI (July 26, 1946), pp. 65-66; and L. A. Mander, "Civil Liberty After the War," *American Political Science Review*, XL (February, 1946), pp. 70-79.

begin to produce it in large quantity. While this would not prevent any nation possessed of bombs from attacking us, it would enable us to retaliate in such complete and thorough-going fashion that it might act as an effective deterrent to a hostile attack upon us with atomic weapons.

International Control or World Government

International Control. In view of the impossibility of eradicating the bomb once it had been exploded upon the world and of the very doubtful expedient of maintaining strict secrecy about the techniques of manufacture of the bomb while the United States hastened to construct as many bombs as possible, the Prime Ministers of Great Britain and Canada and the President of the United States met and promulgated the Agreed Declaration of November 15, 1945. The preamble to this statement recognized that the atomic bomb placed at the disposal of mankind an instrument of unparalleled destruction against which there was no adequate military defense, and which could not be monopolized by any one nation. Only the prevention of war, the Declaration went on to say, could give complete protection from the dangers raised by scientific invention. In order to deal with the problem, the Declaration proposed establishment of a commission of the UNO to make recommendations for creation of adequate controls over use of the weapon. When that had been done, the three leaders agreed to release the scientific information necessary to manufacture the bomb.[7]

In October, 1945, President Truman had called upon Congress to enact legislation creating an Atomic Energy Commission which would control all land, mines, and other sources of fissionable materials, the materials themselves, and all plants, processes, technical information, and patents used in the manufacture of atomic energy. Licenses to develop atomic energy might be extended to private users by the Commission and penalties were to be applied against any persons attempting to produce atomic energy independently. Two bills were introduced in Congress subsequently, the May-Johnson bill which provided that control of the commission would be in the hands of the military authorities and the McMahon bill which would establish a Commission of Civilians to administer the law. After considerable controversy, the McMahon bill became law. Provision was made in the new law for appointment of a member of the armed forces as "Director of the Division of Military Application." Otherwise the direction and administration of the law was

---

[7] For the text of the Declaration, see *United States News*, XIX:23 (November 23, 1945), pp. 12-13.

placed in the hands of civilians. Representing the government, the Commission retained ownership and control of all fissionable materials in the United States.

Instructions were issued by President Truman to the Secretary of State to set up a Committee to submit a plan for the international control of atomic energy to the UN Commission later to be established. With the aid of an advisory committee of experts, a committee headed by Dean Acheson and David Lilienthal intensively studied the problem and reported to the President in March, 1946. In essence, the report provided for creation of an international Atomic Development Authority (ADA) operating under the UN. This commission would have a monopoly over the conduct of all dangerous activities including mining of uranium and thorium, separation of fissionable isotopes, operation of power piles using denatured materials or running at a high power level, and manufacture, storage of, and research in, atomic weapons. It would license national agencies to conduct safe activities having to do with purely scientific research, medical applications, and production of atomic power with denatured materials. Composed of leaders in atomic science throughout the world, the commission would engage in scientific research to promote new developments in the field and supervise and check on any attempts on the part of any national state to evade control.

The United States would turn over its "know how" and its plants to the ADA by stages over a period of transition during which complete agreement would be reached among the nations and ADA would be created. The ADA would then take over plants and supplies of fissionable materials, and assume full control. All sources of uranium and thorium in all parts of the world would be owned and operated by the ADA. Thus the problem of inspection would be greatly simplified. Questions of intent would not have to be considered because the mere fact of ownership and operation of such mines or plants would be known to be an evasion.

Meanwhile, as a result of the Agreed Declaration, representatives of the western allies, in January, 1946, secured establishment of a UN Commission on Atomic Energy, and on June 14 Bernard Baruch, appointed as delegate from the United States, presented the Acheson-Lilienthal plan in a historic speech before the commission. He stated the alternatives as either acceptance of the plan of the United States which, in addition to the above proposals, called for the elimination of warfare between nations and removal from the charter of the UN of the veto power of the five major powers in so far as questions of the control of atomic energy was concerned; or an atomic armaments race between the great powers with possibility of outbreak of a terrible war which might destroy the human race or compel mankind to revert to the status of the ancient cave-dwellers.[8]

The proposal of the United States was warmly supported in principle by Canada and Great Britain but proved to be unacceptable to Russia which brought forward an alternative proposal. The Russian plan involved a solemn declaration by the nations of the world that they would forbid the production and use of atomic weapons and would destroy within a period of three months all stocks of atomic energy weapons. Within six months after coming into force of the agreement, the high contracting parties would pass legislation providing severe punishment for violation of the terms of the agreement by their nationals. The co-signers would declare in the treaty that any violation of the agreement would constitute a serious crime against humanity.[9] Two committees would be established under the Russian plan: one to facilitate exchange of information on atomic energy; the other to prepare plans for an international agreement to outlaw the atomic bomb and sanctions against its use. The demand of the United States that the veto power of the UN Council be removed as regards use of the atomic bomb was flatly opposed by Russia.

Apparently, the purpose of the Kremlin in presenting this plan was to leave it up to each state to enforce the treaty outlawing the bomb and by retaining the veto in the Council prevent UN action against a nation which violated the agreement. This would actually give the United States a temporary advantage because, while her present stock of bombs would have to be destroyed, she would still possess the plants to make more. Russia could violate the agreement with impunity, make bombs, and use them aggressively without the UN being able to prevent it. Thus, the Russian plan could not possibly create the kind of controls necessary to prevent outbreak of war in which atomic weapons could be used if the nation making war were one of the great powers. Rejection of this plan by the United States and reassertion of the American plan led finally on July 24, 1946, to an open refusal by Russia to accept it.[10]

Meanwhile the American plan had been submitted to searching analysis which revealed certain serious weaknesses casting doubt upon its efficacy to prevent war. The plan was largely the work of physical scientists who advised the Acheson Committee and the Committees of Congress to accept the idea of control and inspection by an Atomic Commission of the UN. Underlying this plan were two basic assump-

---

[8] See "A Report on the International Control of Atomic Energy," *Department of State Publication 2498* (March 16, 1946;) and H. C. Urey, "The Atom and Humanity," *International Conciliation,* No. 416 (December, 1945), pp. 790-800.

[9] See "Atom Control-Soviet Plan," *World Report,* I (July 4, 1946), pp. 44-46.

[10] Press release, July 24, 1946.

tions: (1) that all nations would permit Atomic Commission representatives free access to all parts of their territories, and (2) that the production and use of all fissionable materials in all countries would be a government monopoly such as was being set up in the United States, Canada, and Great Britain. This, of course, would greatly simplify the task of the UN inspectors. If these conditions were met the system of inspection might work. Some inspectors could be stationed at the mines. Others could engage in visual reconnaisance, circulate through the country, check on high grade machinery plants, exports and imports of fissionable materials, freight movements, new electrical installations or increased use of electrical power or radioactivity in the country. Establishment of low power atomic plants by each nation, if allowed, would greatly increase the problem of inspection, as would private operation of such plants.

In so far as the inspection system of the plan was concerned, it might be made to work, assuming acceptance of the basic principles of the plan by all of the nations of the world. But would this be enough? Only if (1) each nation was completely disarmed and (2) if after discovery that it was violating the agreement, the aggressor nation obeyed the orders of the Commission or of the Security Council if the latter was called upon to act. Neither of these points was properly taken care of in the American plan. Presumably, national states would retain their other armaments. If so, war could break out, using non-atomic weapons and the nations becoming involved in war might then proceed to violate the agreement and start making and using atomic weapons. The Security Council might then be called upon to enforce the peace against the aggressor nation but if it happened to be a member of the Security Council and particularly one of the great powers, the Council would be faced with the prospect of a major war. It might be thrown into confusion or indecision and prove unable to act under such circumstances or it might decide to use force against the aggressors. Even so by the time the secret had become known and the Council ready to act, the hostile states might have been able to make enough atomic bombs to enable them to launch a surprise attack upon the supporters of the UN and win the war.

Hence, even if Russia had been willing to accept the American plan and the United States had turned over to her all of the secrets of making atomic weapons, there could be no real guarantee that if the U.S.S.R. wanted to break the peace and use the atom bomb against the western allies in a desperate attempt to win domination over the entire world, she could not do so in spite of the plan. Essentially, the problem got back to the power conflict between the great national states of the world and the lawless system of international relations under which each state remained largely self-determining and no superior world authority existed to keep them under control." [11] Later developments revealed a widening gulf between the Russian and American positions. In the UN Committees created to work out a charter for the world atomic authority, the U.S.S.R. refused to consider erection of an independent atomic authority, insisting instead upon retention of atomic controls in the Security Council and the right to exercise the veto upon decisions in the Council relating to atomic matters. This, the United States, backed by a majority of the members, refused to concede. Meantime, the growing conflict between the two great powers over issues of foreign policy rendered the possibility of agreement ever less probable.

World Government as an Alternative

The terrific urgency to do something adequate regarding the atomic bomb led leaders of opinion, in 1946, to split into three groups. The first called for action on the part of governments of the world to destroy the atomic bomb, including knowledge of how to make it. The second sought to have erected a world authority composed of experts who would have a monopoly over the materials and their manufacture and use. The third could see no adequate solution to the problem save in creation of a world government. Those advocating the first solution would be satisfied neither with national ownership of atomic weapons nor the placing of such weapons in the hands of an international authority. To them it would be a source of constant uncertainty and fear that the bombs should exist in the hands of any agency which might use them against any of the peoples of world.[12] Yet, as has been pointed out, no way could be found to do away with the bombs without some form of international control or agreement and even then no certainty could exist that they would not be secretly made unless all knowledge of the manufacturing processes was destroyed along with the scientists themselves, who would naturally retain the basic essentials in their minds.

The proposal of the U.S.S.R. to destroy existing bombs would be of no permanent effect as long as nations possessed the means of manufacturing more, and its suggestion that a treaty be made to outlaw the manufacture and use of atomic weapons was patently defective because historical experience had indicated notorious lack of adherence of nations to their pledged word when their fundamental interests were at stake. The experience of the United States in regard to the Kellogg-Briand

---

[11] On this point, see J. M. Jones "Can Atomic Energy Be Controlled?" *Harpers*, 192 (May, 1946), pp. 425-431.

[12] H. C. Urey, "Atomic Energy in International Politics," *Foreign Policy Reports*, XXII (June 15, 1946), p. 88.

Pact to outlaw war was too recent to permit American leaders to accept this suggestion without implementation or some provision for means of enforcement. The Russian proposal for a committee to study and make suggestions regarding means of enforcement had possibilities but was too vague to give much assurance. American suspicions were also aroused by insistence of the Kremlin's representatives that the great power veto should be retained in the Executive Council of the UNO and that enforcement of infractions should be left to national states under domestic laws. Such regulations as these would leave the way wide open for an ambitious great power to defy the treaty and start manufacturing bombs with world conquest in mind.

On the other hand, Gromyko, Stalin's delegate to the UNO, expressed Russian suspicions of the motives of the United States in not releasing at once all scientific information pertinent to the making of atomic weapons. To refuse to do so, he said, was to impugn Soviet trustworthiness. This attitude hardly seemed consistent with the atmosphere of confidence and trust which should prevail in a situation calling for the utmost of international cooperation. Because of suspicions engendered by withholding the scientific information regarding manufacture of the bomb and the fact that other great powers would probably be able to discover the processes and develop atomic bombs of their own within a few years (estimates vary from five to twenty years depending on the amount of time and money spent), many scientists, educators, and writers contended for immediate release of information and removal of all censorship upon such matters by the United States.[13] Nevertheless, polls of American public opinion on this issue revealed majority opposition to such a move, and American leaders indicated their opposition to making public technical manufacturing secrets of the atomic bomb until adequate safeguards and controls had been established, meaning by this acceptance of the American plan. This, the Russians refused to do, characterizing, at the same time American experiments with the effects of the atomic bomb on naval vessels at Bikini as a "war of nerves" and an attempt to intimidate non-possessors of the bombs so as to increase American domination over the globe. In result, attempts of the great powers to reach an agreement on international control of atomic weapons failed, in 1946, due to mutual rivalries and suspicions of the great powers. In any case, even if the American plan had been accepted, it would not have guaranteed the world complete security at least in the form in which it was presented.

These considerations caused the third group to begin a broad campaign

---

[13] Cf. R. M. Hutchins, "The Atomic Bomb vs. Civilization," *Human Events Pamphlet, No. 1* (Chicago, 1945), p. 11; and O. S. Land, "Social Control of Atomic Energy," *The Antioch Review* (Winter, 1945-1946), pp. 511-512.

to bring about the creation of a world government. In the view of these men, unless a world government was created, the world would be faced within a few years with another war in which the belligerents would employ atomic and perhaps other, more terrible, weapons with results too devastating to contemplate. Every nation would have to begin at once to make preparations for atomic warfare. These, as has been indicated, would entail hardships of an almost intolerable character. No middle ground, they said, was possible. Atomic science was only in its infancy. New developments and inventions would within a short time make available to man still more powerful weapons of destruction. Rapid strides in communication and transportation and the growing interdependence of all parts of the world upon the others in trade, manufacturing, finance, and science were rapidly transforming the peoples of the world from a congeries of independent and isolated communities into an interconnected, mutually dependent, single world society. Every inducement of science, social well-being, and security existed, therefore, for leaders of the great states of the world to take the steps necessary to prepare the groundwork for this fateful movement of emergent evolution.

Principal obstacles in the path centered around the existence of independent, sovereign, national states supported by masses of people whose patriotic loyalty bound them together into a self-conscious community with a way of life separate and distinct from that of other national communities. It thus became clear to exponents of this view that the only lasting solution to the problem of the atomic bomb was the outlawry of war *in toto* and this could be accomplished only through establishment of a world state. Yet, the foundations of the political state lie in the existence of national communities with their conscious psychological differentiation from each other and the strong ties of loyalty and devotion of individual members of the body politic to the national group. Hence, this psychological relationship between the citizen and his nation must be converted into strong ties of affection for a world state.

How this could be done became a matter of speculation among proponents of this solution. One group emphasized the need for engineering public opinion toward the new world order. A number of physical scientists and others of high repute began to set up spontaneous organizations throughout the United States for the purpose of setting forth the facts to the public in the hopes that the people would become convinced of the necessity for creation of a world government. Included in the data made available to the public was the basic information relating to the atomic bomb, the facts regarding possible military uses of the bomb by the United States and other powers, the fact that the United States, although possessing a temporary monopoly of the bomb, would not use it against another nation without provocation, the necessity for giving up the national policy of isolationism, and the conditions of the organization and powers of a world government necessary to make it function effectively.

Other points that were submitted to the public were the desirability of avoidance of censorship legislation on scientific studies of atomic energy, knowledge of proposed legislation which might confer too much power upon the military authorities and hamper the work of scientists, and the necessity for freedom of research and unfettered exchange of scientific ideas between scientists of the world. In this regard, the physical scientists and their supporters attacked particularly the May-Johnson bill which would have established a Commission of nine members, all of whom could be military men, with power to control all exchange of scientific information, license private users, and stress the military phases of atomic energy. The McMahon bill was preferred but pressure was put upon Congress not to allow military men on the commission created under the McMahon bill.

To meet the need for immediate action, plans were laid to launch a campaign of education at once in support of world government. A three-fold plan of action was drawn up to cover the immediate future and inter-mediate period, and a long range period. Action in the immediate period was to attempt to relieve international tension and promote international understanding and good-will. Since nations would possess atomic weapons, the paramount consideration should be to prevent their use until more adequate control measures should be adopted. During the intermediate period, which would range over the next ten to fifteen years, the aim should be to use the machinery of the UNO to settle peacefully international disputes and push the Agreed Declaration and the Acheson-Lilienthal plan. The third period would contemplate establishment of a world government within the next twenty-five years.

The central point of the drive was to try to inculcate the international attitude and promote a shift of loyalties from the national to the world community. Supporters of the movement took heart from the success of the Nazis in Germany and the Communists in Russia in training the youth of those countries to a new ideology in a few years. Recognizing the tremendous proportions of the task, they planned to institute an internationalized program of study on all levels of education from the elementary schools to the colleges and universities. Special emphasis was to be placed upon this work in the high schools where thought patterns were to take on global proportions. Large culture areas such as the U.S.S.R. and its satellites, Latin America, and China and Eastern Asia, were to be presented in place of the narrower nationalistic or localistic studies now prevailing. The aim was to promote knowledge and understanding of other peoples and their ways of life in the form of general knowledge—not specialized training.

An adult program was also envisaged. The minority of the public devoted to reading was to be reached through newspapers and periodicals and the majority through avenues patronized by them such as movies, radio, comics, and popular magazines. Leading figures in the world of entertainment and publication were to be mobilized in support of the movement. A responsible board was to be named to select the types of information to be released and the channels through which it would be disseminated. Instructional aspects were to be avoided as far as possible and the information blended in with amusement patterns of one type or another.[14]

There is no question but that such a plan, if properly organized and executed, would go far in the direction of achieving the desired goal. Certain conditions, however, are necessary for success. These are (1) a large-scale effort either supported positively by the government or by a large proportion of the political, industrial, educational, entertainment, and journalistic leaders of the country, solidly organized behind the movement and backed by unlimited funds; and (2) time in which to carry out the program. Neither of these conditions were present in 1946. The success of the Nazis and Bolsheviks in indoctrinating the masses was due to the absolutely dictatorial powers wielded by one party, spearheaded by a selected few imbued with zeal and devotion for the party and its creed. No such conditions existed in the United States or seemed likely to be duplicated in the near future. Considering this handicap, it appeared unlikely that the educational program could gain sufficient momentum in twenty-five years to accomplish the desired result. Moreover, war might break out before the World Community backed by a loyal world citizenry could be brought into being.

Another approach to the problem contemplated working through the UNO, using it as a basis for further world organization by amending the charter and strengthening the powers of the organization until it would be able to enforce its rules, prohibit war, and monopolize control over atomic and other weapons of mass destruction. Focusing of attention on this approach revealed major problems of organization and adjustment. In order to strengthen the UNO, the great powers would have to be in agreement on essentials, but the split between the Anglo-American combination and the U.S.S.R. and its satellites seemed to place an effective bar to this. Atomic writers took this for granted and advocated at least a partial world government, using the UNO, and setting up world con-

---

[14] See *Atomic Energy—Friend or Foe* (University of Denver Press, 1946), chapter III.

trols in spite of Russia's opposition.[15] This would split the world into two competing coalitions each of which within a short time would be possessed of atomic weapons and in a position to use them.

Assuming that agreement with Russia could be obtained to remove the veto and expand the powers of the UNO, how much power should be given it? In order to enforce its rules, the UNO would have to possess preponderant military power over any other nation or combination of nations. This would involve transfer by the great powers of their atomic weapons to the UNO at the very minimum. The question was, would this be enough? It appeared unlikely that this would be a sufficient deterrent against outbreak of war by nations retaining all other war weapons. In consequence, the great powers would have to turn over their major armaments to the UNO. This would mean that the new world government would have to have sufficient space in which to act as an independent entity. Its agents, representatives, and military forces also would have to have freedom of movement within and between all countries of the world. It would have to have sufficient resources in men and materials to conduct its military and other operations. This would probably mean giving it the taxing power, since past experience with confederations compelled to levy requisitions upon member states indicated that anything short of that would fail.

Obviously, the present Executive Council of the UNO would have to be changed so as to make it less a body of foreign ministers of certain national states in council and more an executive body for the new global government. The veto power possessed by the five great powers would have to go. The Assembly of all the states would have to become more of a policy-forming body. In view of the tremendous problems of adjustment of various national viewpoints and conflicting pressures from national communities whose interests would be in violent opposition, it seemed probable that a global government would have to be equipped with adequate powers of coercion and to be adequate they should permit the world executive and judiciary to act upon individuals. On this point, a global government equipped with all necessary adequate powers seemed, yet, under existing conditions, impossible to achieve.[16]

Even extreme exponents of world government were compelled to concede that, if possible at all, the new creation would have to be federal in type, guaranteeing wide powers of autonomy to participating states, and equipped only with the powers considered strictly necessary to achieve its limted functions. If such a plan were undertaken, some optimists were convinced that it could be made to succeed almost at once.

---

[16] Cf. Hutchins, *op. cit.*, p. 116; C. E. Merriam "Physics and Politics," *American Political Science Review*, XL (June, cit.), p. 430.   [15] Urey, *op. cit.*, p. 91.

The policy of gradualism they condemned as failing to meet the exigencies of the problem.[17]

Critics of the world government plan saw certain major objections to it which appeared to be insurmountable and others which might render it highly objectionable. One great obstacle already in view was the division of the world into two great ideological systems and widely diverse ways of life. Historically, communism and capitalism had been deadly enemies and the peoples living under these systems had been heavily indoctrinated into attitudes hostile to each other. The desire of their ruling classes to retain and expand their power also militated against fusion or even compromise. Postwar international relations had emphasized all too clearly that the power struggle between these competing systems was being carried on all over the world in ever-increasing intensity. Experiments with the bomb were indicating that its effects, although terrific, were not cataclysmic, and the reactions of the Russians, while demonstrating respect for its powers, were not of a character to justify optimism that they would be willing to give up their nationalistic and imperialistic gains from World War II and submit themselves to a universal overlord. On the other hand, the United States by its refusal to divulge the scientific information on how to make the bomb, until international controls were created, and its attempts to dictate the terms of the plan it advocated, displayed its nationalistic temper and its reluctance to submit to world control.

The tremendous economic chasm separating the standards of living of different peoples of the world and of different classes of the same peoples was also a fundamental obstacle to the proposed change. Under a world system of government, nations in possession of the bulk of the world's wealth and income might be compelled to share it with other peoples thus lowering their own standards of living. Economic differences have always been basic causes of conflict and in the modern world they have emerged not only as serious causes of class conflict within nations but of struggles for higher standards of living by national groups. Both class struggles and struggles between national states for raw materials and markets have played their part in producing international rivalries and warfare. Organization of a world government might, to be sure, if given sufficient powers, be able to subordinate and control such strife just as national states have done in the case of contending groups within their borders. Yet, the existence of conflicts between nations and classes on an international plane constituted a major obstacle in the way of organizing such a government. Hence, the planners were confronted by a vicious circle.

---

[17] See T. K. Finletter, "Time Table for World Government," *Atlantic*, 177 (March, 1946), pp. 53-60.

Racial biases also stood in the way of complete cooperation. Many states maintained immigration barriers which barred admittance to their respective countries or imposed restrictions which reduced movements of certain races to those lands to a mere trickle. Differences of language, culture, and historical traditions of hate or hostility would also have to be overcome.

Even if these barriers could be overstepped, there would still remain questions of representation of the various peoples. Should representation in the proposed world legislature be in terms of population alone or should wealth and industrial power be included in the measure? Would the great powers dominate as they do now or would small states be given a voice? If large powers of government were conferred upon the global state, could they be exercised justly and fairly or would agents of the superstate representing the great powers tend to tyrannize over lesser peoples? In view of the great diversity in national cultures, systems of law, justice and policy, and stages of civilization of the nations of the world, how could a meaningful system of rights be established on a universal basis? These are the kinds of questions which would have to be answered before a world government would be possible.

Finally, even if the peoples of the Western nations should decide to merge into a world state, a highly doubtful contingency as shown by the difficulties of the NATO experiment, would the leaders of the U.S.S.R. be willing to agree? In view of Soviet expansionist tendencies, that seemed to be the real issue for the immediate future. Einstein favored entry of the Western states into a world union even if they had to accept all the terms laid down by the Kremlin. Abject surrender and the creation of a Soviet Union of the World, in view of recent revelations of life in Russia and her satellites, could mean only enslavement of the peoples of the world. Free government, as Sumner Welles put it, was the issue in World War II. It is also the issue now.[18]

Summary

The invention of the atomic bomb has placed the states of the world in a dilemma. If they continue the old system of power relationships, another war may ensue in which atomic and other weapons of unprecedented mass destruction will be used. Such a devastating result might mean the end of modern civilization.

So far, a compromise plan has been acceptable to neither side. Even if a compromise were accepted, the possibilities of evasion would be

---

[18] See Sumner Welles, "The Atomic Bomb and World Government," *Atlantic,* CLXXVII (January, 1946), pp. 39-42; and A. Einstein, "Einstein on the Atomic Bomb," *Atlantic,* CLXXVI (November, 1943), pp. 43-44.

great. Hence, no real security could be afforded short of a world government so powerful and all-pervasive that no national state could compete against it. Yet creation of a world state could not be successful without a tremendous shift in national loyalties and formation of a world community. Existing national, racial, economic, and cultural differences impose formidable barriers to such a drastic change. Even more formidable is the struggle for world power among the great states. In the face of these obstacles, there seems little chance to create a world state in the near future of the type needed. Thus the peoples of the world were faced with a decision so fateful that it might involve the extinction of the human race. If reasonable and just, yet adequately powerful, world political controls could be set up, the peoples of the world have offered them the promise of a material abundance resulting from the discoveries of science so great as to alter the entire economic basis of life on earth. If they cannot, the doom of mankind may already have been decreed.

QUESTIONS

1. Why is the atomic bomb such a terrible weapon?
2. What is meant by the Atomic Era?
3. Why do the democracies as well as the dictatorships seem to possess no grasp of the fundamentals at stake in the Atomic Era?
4. What have been the signs of the growing awareness of this problem by the democratic leaders?
5. What is the application of atomic energy to peaceful purposes?
6. What were the provisions of the McMahon bill?
7. What is the relation of atomic energy to social planning?
8. What is the relation of atomic bombs to aviation?
9. Why does the manufacture of a large number of atomic bombs fail to assure safety?
10. Show the relation of atomic bombs to the navy.
11. What are the control problems raised by the atomic bomb?
12. How is atomic energy controlled in the United States?
13. What are the plans of the United States to control the bomb?
14. What are the plans of Soviet Russia to control the bomb?
15. What basic principles are necessary for the control of the bomb?
16. What are the three groups of leaders regarding the atomic bomb?
17. Why is the sovereign state the principal obstacle to solving the problem of the bomb?
18. How is education related to the problem of the bomb?

SUGGESTED TOPICS FOR TERM PAPERS AND FURTHER RESEARCH

1. The relation of the discovery of the atomic bomb to Einstein's theories.
2. What were the steps leading to the discovery of the atomic bomb?
3. The role of President Roosevelt in the discovery of the bomb.
4. The military decision leading to the use of the bomb at the end of World War II.

5. The knowledge of the atomic principles by the Russians.
6. Atomic espionage.
7. The proposals of President Eisenhower to deal with the bomb.
8. The relation of the atomic bomb to social changes.
9. The pro and cons of the Soviet plan for the atomic bomb control.
10. The atomic bomb as an academic subject in American universities.

BIBLIOGRAPHY

Books

J. B. Conant, *Anglo-American Relations in the Atomic Age* (London: Oxford University Press, 1952). Considers points of friction between the two countries over the atomic bomb and ways of meeting them.

B. W. Leyson, *Man, Rockets and Space* (New York: E. P. Dutton and Co., 1954). A factual account of U.S. government experiments with rockets and the possibility of space travel.

J. J. O'Neal, *Almighty Atom, The Real Story of Atomic Energy* (New York: Ives Washburn, 1945). Presents the story of atomic energy and its implications in popular form.

J. K. Robertson, *Atomic Artillery and the Atomic Bomb* (New York: D. Van Nostrand Co., 1945). Shows the various ways in which atomic energy can be put to military use.

P. E. Sabine, *Atoms, Man, and God* (New York: Philosophical Library, 1953). A "must" in the literature on this subject.

H. DeWolf Smith, *A General Account of the Development of Methods of Using Atomic Energy for Military Purposes Under the Auspices of the United States Government, 1940-1945* (Washington, D.C., U.S. Government Printing Office, 1945). The famous Smyth Report giving the inside story of the development and military uses of the atomic bomb.

A. K. Soloman, *Why Smash Atoms?* (Cambridge: Harvard University Press, 1940). A nontechnical explanation of the purposes sought in atom-smashing as applied to physics and medicine.

J. C. Speakman, *Modern Atomic Theory* (New York: Longmans Green and Co., 1938). Describes in simple language the structure of the bomb.

H. S. Taylor, *et al., Molecular Films, The Cyclotron, and the New Biology* (New Brunswick, N.J.: Rutgers University Press, 1942). Describes the development of atom-splitting and its application to biology.

E. L. Woodward, *Some Political Consequences of the Atomic Bomb* (New York: Oxford University Press, 1946). Discusses the alternatives of atomic war or world government.

Periodicals

"A Report on the International Control of Atomic Energy," *Department of State Publication 2498* (March 16, 1948).

"Atom Control—Soviet Plan," *World Report* I (July 4, 1946), pp. 44-46.

"Atomic Energy Act of 1946," *Senate Report 1291,* 79th Congress, Second Session.

Bernard Brodie, "American Security and the Atomic Bomb," *Yale Review,* XXXV (March, 1946), pp. 399-414.

"Coming Struggle for Atomic Power," *New Republic,* CXXVIII (May 11, 1953), pp. 5-6.

Civil Defense and Atomic Warfare, A Selected Reading List (Washington, D.C.: Government Printing Office, 1953).

R. A. Dahl, ed., "The Impact of Atomic Energy," *The Annals of The American Academy of Political and Social Science,* CCXC (November, 1953).

Albert Einstein, "Einstein on the Atomic Bomb," *Atlantic,* CLXXVI (November, 1945), pp. 43-44.

T. K. Finletter, "Time Table for World Government," *Atlantic,* CLXXVI (March, 1946), pp. 53-60.

J. B. Gittler, "Social Trends and Atomic Energy," *Social Science,* XXVIII (April, 1953), pp. 67-71.

E. B. Haas, "The Impact of Modern Weapons on Diplomacy," *World Affairs Interpreter,* XXIII (Winter, 1953), pp. 404-414.

F. C. Ikle, "The Social Versus the Physical Effects from Nuclear Bombing," *The Scientific Monthly,* LXXVIII (March, 1954), pp. 182-187.

J. A. McCone, "A Basis for Survival in the Atomic Age," *World Affairs Interpreter,* XXIV, 4 (January, 1954), pp. 402-416.

L. Olds, "Grab for the Atom," *Nation,* CLXXVI (May 30–June 13, 1953), pp. 449-452, 466, 478-481, 496-499.

J. Robert Oppenheimer, "Atomic Weapons and American Policy," *Foreign Affairs* (July, 1953), 525-535.

L. L. Strauss, *A First Step Toward the Peaceful Use of Atomic Energy* (Washington, D.C.: Department of State, Public Service Division, 1954).

V. H. Whitney, *et al.,* "Exploding the Atom Myth," *U.N. World,* VII (January, 1953), pp. 49-63.

Index*

* Prepared by Harold Nevins, University of Bridgeport.

DATE DUE

GAYLORD			PRINTED IN U.S.A.